THE
LITERATURE
POLICE

For Andrew,

Many thanks for helping to
make this happen.

Warm good wishes,

Peter

February 2009
St Hugh's

THE
LITERATURE
POLICE

Apartheid Censorship and its Cultural Consequences

Peter D. McDonald

OXFORD
UNIVERSITY PRESS

OXFORD
UNIVERSITY PRESS

Great Clarendon Street, Oxford OX2 6DP

Oxford University Press is a department of the University of Oxford.
It furthers the University's objective of excellence in research, scholarship,
and education by publishing worldwide in

Oxford New York

Auckland Cape Town Dar es Salaam Hong Kong Karachi
Kuala Lumpur Madrid Melbourne Mexico City Nairobi
New Delhi Shanghai Taipei Toronto

With offices in

Argentina Austria Brazil Chile Czech Republic France Greece
Guatemala Hungary Italy Japan Poland Portugal Singapore
South Korea Switzerland Thailand Turkey Ukraine Vietnam

Oxford is a registered trade mark of Oxford University Press
in the UK and in certain other countries

Published in the United States
by Oxford University Press Inc., New York

© Peter D. McDonald 2009

British Library Cataloguing in Publication Data
Data available

Library of Congress Cataloging in Publication Data
Data available

Typeset by SPI Publisher Services, Pondicherry, India
Printed in Great Britain
on acid-free paper by
CPI Antony Rowe Ltd., Chippenham, Wiltshire

ISBN 978–0–19–928334–7

1 3 5 7 9 10 8 6 4 2

Who would dare decide today what is literature and what is not, given the irreducible diversity of all written works which, from infinitely different perspectives, tend to be regarded as literature?   Tzvetan Todorov

In a divided society, words cannot be expected to carry the same value.   Mafika Gwala

The lunacy of the apartheid system is nowhere better exhibited than in the field of culture.

Medu Art Ensemble

Contents

List of Illustrations

LIST OF ILLUSTRATIONS

In the case of illustrations, although every effort has been made to trace and contact copyright holder prior to publication this has not been possible in all cases. If notified, the publisher will be pleased to rectify any errors or omissions at the earliest opportunity.

Abbreviations

ANC	African National Congress
APB	Afrikaanse Pers-Boekhandel
ARM	African Resistance Movement
AWA	African Writers' Association
AWS	Heinemann African Writers Series
AZAPO	Azanian People's Organization
BBFC	British Board of Film Censors
BICA	Bantu Indian and Coloured Arts
BLAC	Black Literature and Arts Congress
BOSS	Bureau of State Security
BPC	Black People's Convention
CCF	Congress of Cultural Freedom
CNA	Central News Agency
COSATU	Congress of South African Trade Unions
COSAW	Congress of South African Writers
CYA	Creative Youth Association
FOSATU	Federation of South African Trade Unions
FPB	Film and Publication Board
FUBA	Federated Union of Black Artists
GDR	German Democratic Republic
H & R	Human & Rousseau
Mdali	Music, Drama, Arts, and Literature Institute
NAIL	New African Investments Limited
NALN	National Afrikaans Literature and Research Centre, Bloemfontein
NELM	National English Literary Museum, Grahamstown, South Africa
NGK	Nederduits Gereformeerde Kerk
OUP	Oxford University Press
PAB	Publications Appeal Board
PAC	Pan Africanist Congress of Azania
PCB	Publications Control Board
PEN SA	PEN (South Africa)
PEN (Jhb)	PEN (Johannesburg)
RPA	Ravan Press Archives, Macmillan SA, Johannesburg
RSA	Republic of South Africa
SABC	South African Broadcasting Corporation
SACP	South African Communist Party

SANNC	South African Native National Congress
SASO	South African Students' Organization
SBBFC	Students' British Board of Film Censors
Spro-Cas	Study Project on Christianity in Apartheid Society
SSRC	Soweto Students' Representative Council
UDF	United Democratic Front
WCPA	Western Cape Provincial Archives and Records, Cape Town

Note to the Reader

I use three styles of referencing throughout this book. To refer to most oral, printed, archival, or digital sources I use arabic numeral endnotes in the conventional way. For the censors' reports I cite I have adopted a parenthetical system based on the file numbers originally given by the censors themselves. Files for the period 1963–8 are identified as coming from the range coded BCS, which the Western Cape Provincial Archives in Cape Town added, followed by the year of submission and the report number, which the censors used (e.g. BCS 65/133). For files from the period 1975–90 I use the system established by the next generation of censors and followed by the archivists: 'P' for 'publication', followed by the year, then the month of submission and the report number (e.g. P77/9/133). In the relatively rare instances in which I refer to files that fall outside these two periods, I have given the details in endnotes. The main reason for this is that most reports from 1969 to 1974 appear not to have survived, and the few that have are in the National Archives in Pretoria, rather than in Cape Town. Finally, for any additional information I use web notes cued by lower-case letters, which refer you to the supplementary web site for this book. These notes are specifically identified on the site itself, which also includes a wide range of other documentary information as well as a database of around 450 censorship decisions. The site can be found at <http://www. theliteraturepolice.com>.

Writing about apartheid South Africa inevitably involves negotiating a complex and highly contested array of names for various collective identities, which, in the case the state's own official lexicon, were part of the apparatus of racist repression. The Population Registration Act, 1950, for instance, required each person to be classified as 'White', 'Coloured' (mixed race), or 'Bantu' (black African). The term 'Indian' (Asian origin) was added later. When I am citing this kind of legislation, or, more generally, referring to the government's own language, I use these terms in quotation marks. When I am discussing the way particular groups identified themselves, I follow the term they, or their chief proponents, commonly adopted. On this basis, for instance, I use the inclusive label 'Black' with the capital when describing the Black Consciousness movement of the 1970s, and the untranslated Afrikaans term *volk* to refer the white Afrikaans-speaking community, which, following the basic tenets of Afrikaner nationalism, was deemed to constitute a racialized, ethno-linguistic nation. For the rest, if I need to draw attention to the primary racial divide, I use the terms 'black' or 'white'. In most cases, however, I also consider the limitations of this as a way of understanding the social complexities of identity, which apartheid tended to pervert, ignore, or obscure.

As will be clear from the arguments outlined in the Introduction, this book focuses on the questions raised by the censorship of printed books identified as literature and written, for the most part, by South African-born writers of the apartheid era. For reasons of space and methodology, it does not consider the censorship of dramatic works, films, objects, or, indeed, printed matter in general. Those vast, and as yet largely unexplored, domains warrant investigation in their own right and detailed treatment in other books.

Unless otherwise indicated, all the translations in this book are my own.

Introduction

A Statement

Literature arrived in South Africa in 1824.

As its subtitle indicates, this book, which focuses on the final decades of white minority rule in South Africa from, roughly, 1948 to 1994, is about the cultural consequences of apartheid censorship. That it is also about the essential contestability of my opening statement calls for some prefatory comment.

At one level, the questions this apparently unexceptional proposition begs are fairly obvious and specifically historical. *Arrived*? Does this mean the many communities inhabiting the southern tip of Africa in the pre-colonial era had no literature? *1824*? Can it be that the Dutch traders who came ashore in 1652 at the behest of a private commercial concern, the Verenigde Oost-Indische Compagnie, and the settlers who followed brought no *literatuur* with them? At another level, the problems are conceptual, or historico-conceptual, and so perhaps less self-evident. *South Africa*? Was this in some sense a political state, as the capital letters imply, a cultural idea, or simply a geographical destination? *Literature*? Does this mean that the culture of letters arrived in 1824? Or are we talking about a specific subset of that culture, say, imaginative writing, or, indeed, something else altogether?

Questions of another, more linguistic kind might also be asked because this sentence, like the book you are reading, privileges the English language. Consider how different it would be, rendered in contemporary isiXhosa, for instance, one of eleven official languages in South Africa today: *Uncwadi lwafika eMzantsi Afrika ngo1824*, which translated literally means 'The book arrived in South Africa in 1824'. *Uncwadi* here serves as a metonym for 'literature' in the generic sense of 'imaginative writing'. Unlike the English sentence, the telling figural linkage between books and literature in the isiXhosa version opens up the tangled history of the incomplete conquest of indigenous oral traditions by an alien, script- and print-based colonial order. This process of cultural absorption, which was led by the various European missionaries who began to arrive in the course of the eighteenth century, accelerated in the second half of the nineteenth.

Some of these questions can be addressed in historical terms simply by saying something more about the abrupt and, as it turned out, inauspicious advent my opening statement purports to describe. Hence the first part of this Introduction, which makes a short historical excursus into the fraught cultural conditions of the British Cape Colony, or, to use its official colonial name in the early 1820s, the Cape of Good Hope. Any value this excursus has will be more than incidental if it also provides a larger historical context within which to make sense of one the strangest anomalies of apartheid censorship. Not all the statement's quandaries can be so easily resolved, however, and some might turn out to be, in principle, irresolvable. This is particularly true of 'literature', the most intractable of the four main terms. Hence the second part of this Introduction, which says something different about the predicament of literature in the twentieth century by making another short excursus, this time into a brief comparative history of censorship systems. Taking this two-part prefatory detour will help to sketch in a historical and methodological background to the period and questions with which I shall primarily be concerned. It will also go some way towards explaining the double emphasis of this book, which is as much a historical investigation into the relationship between literature and one of the most anachronistic, repressive, and racist states of the post-war era as it is an extended reflection on the states of literature in the second half of the twentieth century.

Questionable Categories

In March 1824 two enterprising Scottish settlers, the poet, journalist, and librarian Thomas Pringle (1789–1834) and his friend John Fairbairn (1794–1864), who was at the time forging a career as a journalist, entrepreneur, and politician, launched the *South African Journal*. It was, as their prospectus boldly announced, the '*first* Literary Journal in South Africa'.[1] Their venture was ambitious and, as they saw it, timely. For the previous century and a half the slave-owning, Dutch-controlled Colony had been little more than a 'disunited, wavering and temporary assemblage of adventurers' (vii). Since the British occupation, initially in 1795 and then more permanently in 1806, little had changed. Indeed, 'fluctuating between two Powers over whose movements the Colony could exert no influence' had only exacerbated its 'precarious state' (vii). During this protracted period of uncertainty 'few opportunities occurred for the adjustment of internal interests', the editors observed, 'nor were the times more favourable to the consolidation of native feelings sentiments, and views into a distinct and pervading character' (vii). Under the relative 'security' of 'British dominion', formalized in 1814 and helped by 'the growth of wealth, activity, and intelligence', the Colony now found itself at a turning point in its history (vii). 'With our ultimate views rooted beyond

2

the ATLANTIC', the prospectus claimed, 'we are fast acquiring, as a Community, self-respect, and home-importance' (vii).

As their title indicated, the new journal was intended to nurture this growing sense of autonomy and to overcome the divisions of the past by fashioning a more unified and distinctively 'South African' culture. In keeping with this aim, and going somewhat against the Anglicizing ambitions of the Tory colonial governor, Lord Charles Somerset, who made English the official language of the Colony in 1825, they conceived their venture as a joint English–Dutch publication, albeit with separate editions in each language appearing bi-monthly. This strategy made it possible, they claimed, to 'adapt it to the different wants and wishes of the two nations, as yet but imperfectly amalgamated'.[2] The Dutch edition was to be edited by the Reverend Abraham Faure, a minister in the Groote Kerk in Cape Town. Pringle and Fairbairn were aware that this hardly reflected the complex multilingual world around them. They acknow-ledged the existence of at least nineteen autochthonous African communities, including what they called the 'Koosas', the 'Bechuanas', the 'Namaquas', and the 'Barolongs', and hoped in future to be able 'to print our Journal in any or all of these learned tongues'.[3] That was some way off, however, because the devel-opment of written forms, not to mention stable orthographies, for these lan-guages was slow and, as they saw it, wholly dependent on colonial initiative. All they could do was ask 'Kosa' (i.e. isiXhosa) and other speakers, or readers, to 'wait with patience till Mr. SALT's Etymological Work on the Dialects of Eastern Africa, be entered on the shelves of the South African Public Library: and till our ingenious friend W. hath finished his erudite Dissertation on the Origin of the Amakosa language'.[4] In fact, the earliest known isiXhosa book, a short spelling guide, appeared in 1824, giving a further significance to that auspicious year. This inaugurated the mission-led tradition of African-language publishing, which continued in a number of relatively short-lived newspapers in the course of the nineteenth century, beginning with *Umshumayeli Wendaba* (The Pub-lisher of News) in 1837. The first secular newspaper, *Imvo Zabantsundu* (Native Opinion), which was published in isiXhosa and English and backed by white liberal patrons, appeared only in 1884, thirteen years before the first properly independent African newspaper *Izwi Labantu* (The Voice of the People).

Creating a public forum for literature was very much at the heart of Pringle and Fairbairn's project, though what they meant by this was not straightfor-ward. Their journal was 'Literary', firstly in the sense that it was dedicated to promoting the culture of letters. Following the editorial principles adopted by the 'standard Magazines and Reviews which have obtained so much celebrity in Europe', they proposed to publish writings on a wide range of topics including 'Commerce', 'General History', and the 'Sciences', as well as 'Literary and Philosophical Subjects'.[5] Among the specific models they had in mind were the Whig *Edinburgh Review* and the Tory *Blackwood's Edinburgh Magazine*, which formed part of the thriving periodical culture that carried the politically contested ideals of the eighteenth-century Scottish Enlightenment into the nineteenth. Prior to his arrival at the Cape in 1820, Pringle had extensive experience as an editor working within this tradition, to which Fairbairn also contributed as a journalist. Reflecting their ties to the various centres of this periodical culture, their journal was published not only by William Bridekirk, a bookseller, stationer, and bookbinder in Cape Town, but by established firms in London and Edinburgh.[6]

Their commitment to the idea of the 'Literary' as 'Letters-in-general' also underpinned one of their other key initiatives at the time. After publishing a series of articles by Fairbairn on the 'value of Literary and Scientific Societies' in the first two issues of their journal, they played a leading role in encouraging a group of other prominent 'gentlemen' of the Cape to establish the South African Literary Society in July 1824.[7] Like the journal, this voluntary association, or 'Institution', as they called it, which was to include a library and a museum, was designed 'to promote a taste for polite learning; to encourage the study and cultivation of science; and, to excite and cherish the love of research, and zeal for discovery in every department of liberal knowledge'.[8] Though such societies were 'numerous in most parts of the world, particularly in Britain, France, and America', they based their own constitution on the principles laid down by the Royal Society of London, formed in 1660, and the Asiatic Society, founded in what was then called Calcutta in 1784.[9] Fairbairn's second article promoting the idea also gave a detailed account of the formation in 1793 of the Newcastle Literary and Philosophical Society, to which he belonged.

Promoting the 'Literary' in this broad sense was not just a way of enhancing the quality of independent intellectual enquiry at the Cape. It had a specific moral purpose as well, which was, in their view, once again especially appropriate for the times. Noting that there had been a 'surprising improvement in the conversation, manners, and general aspect of society' in Cape Town and 'throughout the thriving and better settled portions of the Colony', they believed their own endeavours simply reflected the 'increasing popularity of solid and liberal Education', which would, they hoped, 'unite men together by means of their happiest feelings, and gradually transmute their coarse antipathies into a pure and wholesome emulation'.[10] This is where literature, in their second, narrower and more evaluative sense, came into its own. Though most literary societies focused on 'Natural Science', it had been 'found necessary', Fairbairn observed, 'in more limited communities' to take 'a wider range, and to admit into their plan polite literature, moral philosophy, metaphysics, and the principles of society'.[11] As their journal explained in a series of articles on William Wordsworth, 'polite literature', which constituted a particular class of imaginative writing, had an especially important role to play in all this because it possessed a special power over 'coarse antipathies'. Unlike Walter Scott's novels, which were not 'polite'—the 'whole surface of his composition is in violent agitation'—Wordsworth's less popular poems were, because they encouraged 'meditative pensiveness': 'his works are not given so much to quicken and beguile the temporal part of our nature, as to incite and support the eternal'.[12] As editors, Pringle and Fairbairn, following the general disdain in which nineteenth- (and eighteenth-) century 'men of letters' held the upstart genre of the novel, considered poetry the privileged medium of 'polite literature'. This preference was reflected in the contents of their journal's first issue, eleven pages of which were devoted to original poetry (just over 13 per cent). Their second issue included Pringle's quintessentially polite lyric reverie 'Afar in the Desert', which celebrates Romantic unworldliness, solitude, and exile. It does not follow, of course, that all poets or poems were necessarily 'polite'. As Fairbairn noted, the Newcastle Society, which excluded novels from its library until the end of the nineteenth century, refused to acquire Byron's *Don Juan* (1819–24). After one member rashly recommended this 'notorious' volume, it was, he reported, 'rejected at each successive appeal by an immense majority'.[13]

At this point it is possible to return to my opening statement and to address one of its more questionable implications. In saying 'Literature arrived in South Africa in 1824' I was referring to the advent of the culture of letters, as signalled by the publication of the *South African Journal*, and, more specifically, to the emergence into public debate at the Cape of the category 'polite literature'. By implication, this, of course, identifies literature as a colonial import, distinguishing it from the vast and complex traditions of indigenous orature, which pre-dated and, in some cases, survived the colonial encounter. Given the invidious historical legacy attached to this distinction, the merits of the label 'orature' are not immediately obvious or uncontentious. By excluding from the sphere of literature the diverse forms of indigenous cultural production in the 1820s, which encompassed the ritualistic songs of the small hunter–gatherer bands in the south and the courtly *izibongo*, or *tibongo* ('praise poems'), of the more firmly established kingdoms in the north, it risks invoking colonialist presumptions about the supposedly inherent superiority of literate cultures. These assumptions were particularly prevalent in the fields of anthropology and ethnology in the late nineteenth and early twentieth centuries, as Edward Tylor's *Primitive Cultures* (1871) and Lucien Lévy-Bruhl's *Les Fonctions mentales dans les sociétés inférieures* (1910) testify, though they were also given a new life within the emergent field of communication studies in the 1960s.

Tylor, 'the man considered to be the father of British anthropology', was among the first to give this hierarchical kind of thinking a special prestige. Yet, as Vail and White argue in *Power and the Praise Poem* (1991), Marshall McLuhan's influential analysis of the changing media environment in the post-war era did much to give it a renewed impetus.[14] Trapped by the 'utter inhibition and suppression of his mental and personal life which is unavoidable in a non-literate world', 'oral man' emerges in McLuhan's *Gutenberg Galaxy* (1962) as the benighted antithesis of the modern, Western, literate individual.[15] Setting up the distinction in such hierarchical, not to say moralistic and quasi-aestheticist, terms is not only invidious but intellectually unpersuasive. For one thing, as Vail and White demonstrate, it fails to acknowledge the historically variable and culturally specific poetics of orature. Within oral cultures, praise poets, for instance, are evaluated according to their virtuosity and verbal skills, which include 'wordplay', the 'gift for the elaboration of metaphor', and the 'manipulation of rhythm and of expressive sound'.[16] For another, arguments like McLuhan's founder because they overlook the fact that a 'convention of poetic licence that privileges poetry and song above all other forms of oral discourse' became over time an integral feature of various oral traditions, particularly in sub-Saharan Africa.[17]

Uncoupled from the hierarchical logic underlying this dubious legacy, the distinction between orature and literature acquires a new pertinence and po-tential. While avoiding awkward formulations like 'oral literature', it encourages a greater awareness of the long history of intercultural translation across these two traditions, which was at once creative and transformative, repressive and conflicted. As importantly, the distinction foregrounds the foreignness of litera-ture as a category, which, as we have seen, is still reflected in the contemporary isiXhosa lexicon. The use of *uncwadi* as a metonym for literature is, it should be said, complicated by the fact that most isiXhosa speakers today refer to their own oral traditions as *uncwadi lwemveli* (literally 'the book of origins'). In contexts where any ambiguity arises, literature in the sense of 'imaginative writing' is then specified more sharply as *uncwadi olubhaliweyo* (literally 'the written book').[18] By focusing on literature's foreignness in this way, the distinc-tion also has the advantage of drawing attention to its provenance as the artefact of a particular, concretely realized modernity.

That the emergence of the 'Literary' in their double sense was linked to an identifiable set of technological, economic, legal, and institutional conditions was not lost on Pringle and Fairbairn. As Fairbairn noted in his first article, 'On Literary and Scientific Societies', its origins could be traced firstly to the 'inven-tion of Printing' in the fifteenth century and, more particularly, to the expansion of the commercial book trade in the eighteenth; secondly, to 'that noble im-provement upon it, the Liberty of the Press', by which he no doubt meant the final lapsing of the repressive British Licensing Acts in 1695 and, again more specifically, the freedoms enshrined in the First Amendment to the Constitution of the United States in 1791; and thirdly, to the 'formation of Societies', to which 'the modern world has been so much indebted for many of its most valuable distinctions'.[19] The reference to America is not as oblique as it might seem. When Pringle first invited Fairbairn to join him at the Cape in 1822, he replied enthusiastically, asking 'what should hinder us from becoming the [Benjamin]

Franklins of the Kaap?'[20] It is difficult not to infer, moreover, that the American Declaration of Independence influenced their own desire to fashion an autonomous and unified 'South African' (or, in practice, Anglo-Dutch) culture. Taken together these historical developments had, in Fairbairn's view, opened up an unprecedented, peculiarly modern cultural space, which flourished outside the direct control of Church and State, 'undamped by patronage, and unrestrained by over legislation'.[21]

For Pringle and Fairbairn the political significance of this modern 'Republic of Letters', which Fairbairn called a 'mighty empire', was clear.[22] Echoing many of their liberal-minded contemporaries, they saw what the young Jürgen Habermas would later call the 'literary public sphere' as a precursor to the more fully developed 'political public sphere' out of which the democratic ideals of popular sovereignty and governmental accountability would emerge.[23] The proliferation of 'Literary and Scientific Societies' in the 'last half century' had, Fairbairn believed, led to an 'astonishing progress' in 'general knowledge, liberal sentiments, and sound political feelings'.[24] By fostering a spirit of critical debate, they encouraged 'competent witnesses accustomed to investigation' to subject any 'false reports' to careful scrutiny.[25] Such 'reports', he noted, gave rise not only to 'errors in science' but to 'superstitious opinions', which tended 'to pave the way for political despotism and every species of oppression'.[26] Like Pringle, he was at the time an outspoken champion of settler rights and good governance at the Cape. Reflecting their liberal ideals, and laying claim to their own form of democratic legitimacy, they insisted that they founded their own 'Literary Journal' to meet a need 'expressed by the well-informed of every rank in the Colony', and they, in turn, hoped it would 'meet the wishes of every class'.[27] In fact, given the cost of each number (2½ Rix-dollars), their readership was inevitably restricted and, as the rapid reduction in the size of their print run suggests—down from 1,000 for the first issue to 750 for the second—their new venture was not quite as popular as they had hoped. It is also likely that their readership, which probably had a social profile much like the membership of their local Society, was more homogeneous than they would have wished. All of the sixty-one founding members of the South African Literary Society were male and the overwhelming majority belonged to the learned professions, the Church, or the merchant class. They were among the elite few who would have been able to afford the annual membership fee of 15 Rix-dollars, which was only slightly less than the annual 20 Rix-dollar subscription for the English edition of the journal. Needless to say, though a number of nationalities were represented among the Society's founding members, including the British, Dutch, and Danish, all were colonists.

What Pringle and Fairbairn brought to the Cape in 1824, then, was not just a modern idea of literature but a broader vision of the institutional conditions that made it possible and, they believed, laid the foundations for its survival.

By establishing a liberal, bilingual, and perhaps eventually multilingual 'Republic of Letters' on the British, even peculiarly Scottish, model, they tied its fortunes to a future in which they envisaged a unified and properly autonomous 'South African' culture imbued with a civil and inclusive spirit of politeness. For all their utopian ambitions, they were pragmatic enough to foresee that their project was likely to encounter some opposition, especially from the colonial authorities at the Cape. Despite Governor Somerset's anxieties about the proposed journal—like many members of his class, who lived in fear of a new French-style revolution, he saw Pringle and Fairbairn as 'agents of Jacobinism and radicalism'—Pringle was given the go-ahead by London on condition that he published nothing 'detrimental to the peace and safety of the Colony'.[28] In a politic move designed to allay Somerset's fears, he and Fairbairn then ensured that it was produced not by a commercial printer but on the government press in Cape Town. In a similarly prudent spirit, when he came to draw up the general rules for their Literary Society, Pringle specified that 'any subject not involving the politics of the day, or controversial theology, shall be open to discussion'.[29] In his earlier announcement for the Society, Fairbairn had added the 'subject of Slavery' to the list of taboo topics as well.[30]

These self-imposed curbs were not driven just by political prudence. They also arose out of a particular understanding of the sociology of societies and the moral demands of liberal politeness, which imposed their own constraints on the emerging principle of free speech. Following one of the key tenets of liberalism, according to which the individual is the basic unit of social life and the embodiment of humanity in its fullest sense, Fairbairn suggested that their members 'should be considered merely as men of liberal minds, and not as Politicians, Theologians, Lawyers or Physicians'.[31] In other words, while their 'Republic of Letters' remained restricted to a male colonial elite, it was, in theory, meant to create a space in which all social identities, including those of profession and class, could be put aside. These discursive rules and constitutional arrangements would, Fairbairn believed, prevent 'a tendency to disunion and the formation of parties and cabals' and enable them to realize their larger ambitions as champions of a unified 'South African' culture by avoiding, 'as far as possible, the introduction of such topics as the history of mankind proves has never been discussed without a mixture of passion and heat'.[32] It is worth recalling that a decade after they proposed this idea various groups of Dutch settlers, aggrieved at British rule, particularly on the question of the abolition of slavery, decided to leave the colony, inaugurating the Great Trek north, which would become one of the founding episodes in the nationalist mythology of the Afrikaner people.

Despite these self-protective measures, their project to create a 'Republic of Letters' at the Cape failed before it was fully realized. In May 1824, after the second issue of the journal appeared, Somerset objected, via the Fiscal, the principal legal authority, to an article on the plight of the British settlers on the Colony's eastern frontier, which exposed the 'failure' of the 'scheme of emigration', ascribing it in part to the 'arbitrary system of Government'.[33] Threatened with the prospect of censorship, Pringle and Fairbairn announced that they would cease publication. The governor's autocratic intervention gave an added urgency to the debates about the formation of the Literary Society two months later and an obvious incentive for its chief advocates to seek Somerset's 'patronage and support' once again.[34] This Somerset refused, citing as his reason in a letter dated 16 August 1824 that 'he should greatly deviate from his duty, in giving countenance to an Establishment conducted by persons, who have *wilfully* paid so little regard to the Authorities and established Regulations of the colony'.[35] In a subsequent letter, he specified that he could not permit the formation of 'an association which might have a tendency to produce political discussion'.[36] Having arrived in March 1824, in other words, literature with all the significance Pringle and Fairbairn attached to it had by September effectively been closed down at the behest of the colonial state, embodied in the figure of the unelected governor.

All was not lost, however. The Dutch edition of the journal, which was, as anticipated, very different, survived for another eighteen years. Less concerned with 'polite literature', it contributed to the development of a local tradition of 'Letters' by publishing the diaries of Jan van Riebeeck, the founder of the Dutch settlement, though it was, under the Reverend Faure's editorship, mainly devoted to theological matters. Three years after Somerset's departure from the Cape in 1826, Fairbairn revived the idea of the Literary Society, although now without Pringle. Like Somerset, Pringle returned to Britain in 1826, where he took up the campaign for press freedom at the Cape. Given his awakening to the plight of slaves in the colony the previous year, which gave a wider humanitarian significance to his liberalism, he also went on to become a leading figure in the abolitionist movement. In 1828, six years before he put his name to the proclamation of the Act of Abolition, Pringle succeeded in winning the right to publish newspapers in the Cape without prior governmental approval, which was, given the various 'Taxes on Knowledge' and other legal constraints on newspapers in Britain at the time, a particularly significant local concession. This right passed into law under Cape Ordinance 60 of 1829. In this way the legacy of 1824 lived on not just in the statute book, or in the many local newspapers and journals that would emerge in the course of the nineteenth century, but within the broader political tradition of what would come to be known as Cape liberalism. Indeed, according to the historian Saul Dubow, the events of 1824 became one of the 'core foundational myths of South African liberalism'.[37] Seen in cultural terms, their impact was equally far-reaching, though it was less predictable and arguably more contested.

Questionable Parallels

It is tempting to see this episode in early nineteenth-century settler history simply as an inauspicious prefiguration of the fraught relationship between literature and the peculiarly repressive, racialized, and fragmented modern state that would eventually emerge in twentieth-century South Africa. Yet this reading belies the particular complexities of the moment and obscures one important aspect of its larger historical significance. While there can be no doubt about the passion with which Pringle and Fairbairn defended the emerging principles of press freedom, and, more generally, the liberal ideals of an autonomous 'Republic of Letters', it is equally clear that their commitment to a basic set of civil liberties was at every point circumscribed and complicated by their desire to promote a particular idea of culture. This is especially evident in the stipulations they made about which subjects might legitimately be discussed within their Literary Society, in the way they used the category 'polite literature' as a badge of cultural distinction, and in their preoccupation with Anglo-Dutch unity. If their 'Republic of Letters' was intended to open up a space relatively free from external interference, whether from Church or State, these various strictures meant that it also constituted a world of its own, which was governed by its own internal rules, tensions, and aspirations.

Understood in this way, the unpromising events of 1824 make sense less as an abstract drama played out between 'literature' and the 'modern state' than as a densely particular encounter between the censorious anxieties of the colonial governor, on the one hand, and the ideals of a self-regulating colonial elite, on the other. Given the looseness associated with the term 'censorship', the meaning of which often extends to any and every form of control, it is worth stressing that Somerset remained the only true censor in this scenario. He alone had the full backing of the British state and the authority to ban. By contrast, the powers Pringle and Fairbairn exercised as self-appointed arbiters of taste and guardians of the literary were not only more limited but fundamentally different in kind. As we shall see, this distinction between censorship proper and unofficial forms of cultural regulation has a particular relevance to the strange intricacies of the repressive system introduced in the apartheid era.

Seen in these more nuanced terms, the events of 1824, which could be said to constitute a founding episode in the South African liberal–literary tradition, had an unexpectedly complex cultural afterlife, which extended well into the twentieth century. As I show in the first part of this book, the kind of thinking that informed Pringle and Fairbairn's ambitious championship of the literary lived on in a number of the white-controlled literary magazines, publishing houses, voluntary writers' groups, and prize-giving bodies that attempted to defend a modernized 'Republic of Letters' throughout the dark days of apartheid. Despite their entanglements with this colonial legacy, not to mention the later complications that came with the cultural Cold War, and their compromised position within the dominant order, all the exponents of this tradition spoke out against censorship and prided themselves on their independence from the state. Some also actively opposed apartheid itself. Yet while the tradition had its honourable defenders—and, contrary to what is often thought, there were some on either side of the racial divide—it also had others who were not just compromised but complicit. This brought the tradition into disrepute, particularly among Africanist, Black Consciousness, and Marxist-Leninist groups who rejected its fundamental tenets and drew attention to the more questionable aspects of its mixed history. Of course, the cultural and political traditions of South African liberalism also came under attack both before and during the apartheid era from hardline Afrikaner nationalists who had their own reasons for decrying its influence. I consider the ramifications of these various tensions, as they played out in the field of culture, in greater detail in the chapters that follow.

At this point, however, I need to give some preliminary consideration to the implications of what is perhaps the least likely aspect of this troubled long history, partly to explain this book's double emphasis on censorship and literature, partly to say something about its title and organization. As the once secret inner workings of the apartheid censorship bureaucracy reveal—the details of which this book describes for the first time—some later versions of the liberal–literary tradition Pringle and Fairbairn initiated were not so much complicit as straightforwardly collaborationist.[38] Undoubtedly the most peculiar feature of the repressive system the Nationalist government set up in 1963 is that it put an inordinate, if not wholly unlimited, amount of power in the hands of a group of censors who saw themselves as the upholders of an uneasily hybridized liberal–nationalist version of the tradition Pringle and Fairbairn inaugurated in 1824, in effect, an Afrikaner 'Republic of Letters'. Inevitably this confounds the distinction I have just drawn between censorship and other forms of control, since it means that the censors, who were, first and foremost, the agents of the government's repressive anxieties about the medium of print (and film), and who were formally charged with the task of protecting the apartheid order from seditious, obscene, and blasphemous representations, were, at the same time, officially certified guardians of the literary, or, as I have called them, the apartheid regime's literature police. This book is centrally about the often unpredictable cultural consequences of *this* paradoxical situation, which, as I show in Chapter 1, was by no means historically inevitable.

Calling this anomalous group of censors, which included influential literary academics, educationalists, and some writers, the 'literature police' carries certain risks, particularly in so far as the phrase conjures up a fantastically nightmarish Orwellian world and behind that the actual terror of censorship under the Soviet Union. Yet, without in any way diminishing the pernicious effects of apartheid censorship, or, indeed, the broader terroristic operations of the state, it is important at the outset to make it clear that this particular association, and the implicit comparison it invites, is more misleading than illuminating. If any historical model is applicable to the South African case—and, as we shall see, none really is—then it is best to look to pre-revolutionary Russia, not to the Soviet Union, for a possible precedent. Like the system established by the nineteenth-century tsars, apartheid censorship operated under a semblance of legality, not through a series of secret strictures and directives; it was essentially prohibitive, rather than prescriptive; and, most importantly, it functioned post-publication.[39] Though South Africa had its own collaborationist publishing houses and writers' groups, it had no equivalent of Glavlit, the Main Administration for Affairs of Literature and Publishing Houses, created in 1922, and no professional body comparable to the USSR Union of Writers, founded twelve years later, both of which served to reinforce a system of total control over the medium of print and, especially during the infamous Zhdanovite era in the late 1940s, a strict aesthetic orthodoxy.[40] Historical parallels with East Germany (the GDR) are difficult to sustain for similar sorts of reasons.[41] Unlike these later censoring regimes, but like the earlier tsarist system, the apartheid bureaucracy was 'essentially pragmatic', as J. M. Coetzee put it, describing censorship in nineteenth-century Russia, in the sense that it required of the censors only 'a capacity to sniff out contagion wherever it occurred', not an elaborately articulated 'theory of the censorable' and, in particular, 'no aesthetic theory'.[42]

And yet it is precisely at this point that the analogy with tsarist Russia itself begins to break down. If the apartheid censors were there primarily to protect the state from 'contagion', like their Russian precursors, they were, as they saw it, also there to safeguard literature from the 'contagion' of the state, a complication that makes it difficult to see their role as 'essentially pragmatic'. Though the archival evidence shows that blinkeredness, the vagaries of taste, and crude arbitrariness often affected their decisions, particularly on the question of what warranted protection as literature, it reveals that 'aesthetic theory' of a sometimes fairly sophisticated sort played its part too. Yet, once again showing the limits of thinking comparatively, it does not follow that the apartheid censors were as obviously or systematically theoretical as their Soviet counterparts. At best their thinking was informed not by a fully articulated 'aesthetic theory' but by an implicit assortment of cultural doxa, all of which had a theoretical dimension and some of which the censors shared with other contemporary guardians of the literary both inside South Africa and elsewhere.

Part I of this book examines these highly contested guiding assumptions through a series of interconnected though differently structured narratives, each told from a specific point of view. After looking in detail at the shifting political contexts, legislative history, and practice of censorship from the perspective of the censors (Chapter 1), I consider the consequences of their collaborationist literary guardianship, firstly, for the publishers who were most directly affected by the system (Chapter 2) and, secondly, for the writers who, in various individual and collective ways, resisted censorship and, in most cases, the underlying political structure of apartheid itself (Chapter 3). Though these narratives make frequent reference to particular works—the writings of André Brink, for instance, feature prominently in Chapter 1—they intentionally avoid a detailed analysis of them, focusing instead on general debates about censorship, literature, responsibility, and the changing situation of the writer from the 1950s to the 1980s. I consider the details of selected works in Part II. Sometimes deliberately looking at the same event from a different angle, Part I also traces the previously obscured, on occasion strangely rivalrous, interplay among censors, publishers, and writers as they struggled over a series of questions to do with literature and its place in the national polity and in the wider resistance to apartheid itself. At various points in these longer narratives I also discuss the ways in which the larger dynamics of the Cold War, the rise of a transnational Black Consciousness, and the anti-colonial movement across Africa intersected with, and affected, these struggles.

Theory did not enter the system only via the cultural doxa, or specific beliefs about the status, nature, and function of literature, that guided the censors' thinking, however. Their guardianship itself rested on one key assumption that was, in the end, essentially, though not merely, theoretical. To make some initial sense of this we need to look not to the Soviet Union or tsarist Russia for the purposes of comparison, but to the problematic status literary experts were accorded under English law after the 1960s, and, more particularly, to the questions a later British government commission raised about the consequences of the Obscene Publications Act, 1959, which redefined the relationship between the British state and the field of culture in this one area of the law. Like the US Supreme Court decisions of the 1960s, this Act is rightly recalled as a landmark in the history of obscenity legislation because it afforded literature statutory protection as a 'public good', authorized courts to call upon literary experts to testify on its behalf, and led to the unbanning of D. H. Lawrence's *Lady Chatterley's Lover* in 1960.[43] Yet as the Commission, chaired by the philosopher Bernard Williams, commented in 1979, the well-meaning legislation was flawed because it presupposed an 'informed consensus' about literary merit that does not and, as a matter of principle, cannot exist.[44]

Bearing in mind the temporary banning under the Act of Hubert Selby's *Last Exit to Brooklyn* (1966), one of John Calder's less remarkable avant-garde publications, the Commission observed:

It is not surprising that [the Act] has been criticised as elitist in conception, and as saying in effect that corrupting books are to be permitted so long as they are admired by professors. This criticism is largely unjust, but it hits at a basic fault

13

in the Act, its absurd model of the role of expert opinion with regard to artistic or literary merit. The model is not so much elitist, as scholastic: it implies an informed consensus about merit which, for each work, already exists. In the real world, new works have to find their own way, and see whether they elicit appreciation or not. No one may know, for some time, what to think about them. It is not just a matter of the *avant-garde*: works in some despised medium or style may subsequently turn out to have had more meaning than most experts would have originally supposed.[45]

The underlying scholasticism of the 1959 Act was exacerbated by the fact that it required the experts to establish, *as a matter of evidential proof*, whether or not a particular work might warrant exemption on the grounds of merit. Given that such questions inevitably involve a long, uncertain process of cultural debate, the Commission argued that the 'public good' defence was 'misconceived' and recommended lifting all restrictions on the 'printed word'.[46] Books with illustrations were another matter. The only viable way of protecting the literary and safeguarding writers and publishers from prosecution was, it concluded, for the courts to play no part in the unavoidably contentious field of culture. Though apartheid lawmakers avoided these juridical difficulties by refusing to grant statutory exemption to literature, the Commission's remarks about the 'role of expert opinion' apply with particular force to the deeply scholastic assumptions on which the censors' literary guardianship rested. The difference, of course, was that they were called upon not to act as witnesses in open court but to serve as members of a government-appointed censorship board that deliberated in secret and had the power to ban works the censors deemed insufficiently meritorious.

The Williams Commission focused on the uncertainties of cultural value, particularly as they pertain to new works when they are first published. Yet, as the detailed records in the apartheid censorship archives reveal, the censors' scholasticism was not limited to the relatively narrow issue of value. Since they set out not just to determine what warranted exemption on grounds of merit but to police the boundaries of literature itself, their problematic expertise extended to the larger, even more intractable, problem of literariness per se. If they assumed that the label 'Literature', understood as an honorific, applied to an especially privileged public discourse located at the apex of a cultural hierarchy, above, say, orature, journalism, or mass-market fiction, they also made the less value-laden assumption that it constituted a clearly demarcatable object, which was distinguishable in some stable way from pornography or politically seditious writing. This meant they were scholastic in a double and, indeed, quasi-Platonic sense. They assumed, firstly, that the fundamental question 'What is literature?', whether framed in normative or descriptive terms, or both at once, could be answered definitively, and, secondly, that they were in a position to decide the answer by appealing to a set of essential characteristics all works identified as literary supposedly share. As we shall see, this kind of thinking also informed the way in which they used a host of secondary terms, including generic categories like 'poetry' or 'novel', evaluative tags like 'committed' or 'protest', and socio-political labels like 'Western' or 'South African'. Given their absurdly casuistical position, as shadowy guardians of the literary who possessed the power to ban, it is not surprising that these apparently high-minded problems had consequences that were more than theoretical. As the archival records show, the censors' scholastic self-assurance, which their own manifest lack of consensus belied at almost every turn, contributed to the unpredictability of their decisions and compounded the manifold injustices they perpetrated in the name of what they took to be literature.

A Perennial Question

As will be clear from my initial comments on the essential contestability of my opening statement, this book is written in a consciously anti-scholastic spirit. It is, to this extent, indebted to a well-established tradition of theoretical reflection on the perennial question of literature, which had its origins in post-war France and extended to the Anglophone world in the early 1970s. Writing in 1955 with Jean-Paul Sartre's influential, though much disputed, manifesto *Qu'est-ce que la littérature?* (1948) very much on his mind, the French writer and theorist Maurice Blanchot spoke for many later exponents of this tradition when he asked, echoing Sartre's title:

> 'What is art, and what can be said of literature?' Doubtless this kind of question is peculiarly ours, central to our times. However, since each time an answer is given, the question manages to be asked anew, as if it were indifferent to these answers, we can hardly avoid seeing in the 'anew' a particularly surprising insistence.[47]

Blanchot directed his mordant ironies primarily at Sartre's notoriously categorical pronouncements on the nature and function of literature. Yet his observations about the impossibility of ever closing the question down once and for all applied equally to the larger traditions of Western scholasticism that continued to dominate the field of literary theory at the time, and, indeed, to haunt Sartre's otherwise radically revisionist manifesto. Rejecting these traditions, Blanchot argued that the term 'literature' referred not to a determinate object with a definable essence, but to a disorientingly labile, even anarchic, space, the boundaries of which are constantly being drawn and redrawn. By shifting the focus of attention from the quasi-Platonic search for essences to the always unstable linguistic, conceptual, and institutional conditions that make the category of the literary possible, he effectively opened up a new line of theoretical enquiry to which, it should be said, other aspects of Sartre's own thinking also contributed.[48] In the decades that followed, other theorists took this alternative, anti-essentialist tradition forward in very different and, as I have argued elsewhere, sometimes conflicting ways.[49]

This new self-consciousness about literature's demanding capacity to evade definitive characterization derived in part, as Tzvetan Todorov noted in the early 1970s, from the recognition that in 'European languages the word *literature*, in its present usage, is quite recent: it barely dates back to the nineteenth century'.[50] The latest edition of the *Oxford English Dictionary* identifies 1812 as the year in which the English word was first used to refer 'to writing which has claim to consideration on the ground of beauty of form or emotional effect'. Given the inevitably questionable assumptions underlying this definition, and, indeed, all such lexicographical efforts, I would argue that the always volatile modern uses of the English word, the etymology of which can be traced back to the Latin *litteratura*, began to evolve after the advent of printing and to emerge more clearly in the course of the eighteenth century, and then only under a determinate set of conditions that were not solely linguistic. A number of other guarantors had to be in place as well—hence my emphasis in the first part of this Introduction on the circumstances surrounding Pringle and Fairbairn's abortive initiatives in 1824. As Todorov suggested, however, the sharper linguistic consciousness, which influenced the new historical turn within literary theory, also extended to the world beyond Europe as theorists became increasingly alert to the fact that 'many languages (those of Africa, for example) still have no generic term to designate literature as a whole' and that this 'absence' could no longer be explained by appealing to their 'so-called primitive nature' following the speculative prejudices of early ethnologists like Tylor and Lévy-Bruhl.[51]

These developments, at the level of theory, coincided with a growing interest critics and publishers around the world began to show in a new generation of writers in Africa who were embracing, reinventing, and contesting ideas of literature inherited from the European lettered tradition, making them as much a part of a modern African culture as the established traditions of orature to which they also remained aligned. As Es'kia Mphahlele has long argued and as others have recently confirmed, this process of intercultural translation was already well under way in southern Africa by the mid nineteenth century.[52] Yet the full implications of this shift, which formed part of the larger historical process of what Dipesh Chakrabarty has succinctly called the 'provincializing' of Europe, began to be registered in the wider world only in the 1930s following the rise of the Négritude movement in Francophone Africa and the Caribbean.[53] The emergence of two Nigerian writers, Amos Tutuola and Chinua Achebe, twenty years later, the first with *The Palm-Wine Drinkard* (1952), the second with *Things Fall Apart* (1958), effected a no less significant transformation in the English-speaking world. Following the poet Mafika Gwala, whom I quoted in an epigraph to this book, I would argue that this new self-reflexivity about the origins and mobility of literature as a category has a particular pertinence to a 'divided society' like apartheid South Africa in which 'words cannot be expected to carry the same value', and, we might add, in which ruling minority elites, whose points of reference remained chiefly European, could no longer claim exclusive ownership over the future of the literary (or, indeed, of modernity itself).[54]

For many of its advocates, this anti-scholastic mode of reflection arose out of and fostered a deep-seated scepticism, even suspicion of the very idea of literature. Adopting a broadly sociological approach, they drew attention to the mystificatory role various elites have played as protectors of the literary in the course of history, demonstrating that their guardianship has always been, at best, partial, contingent, and debatable, at worst, a mask for one or another kind of power. This book provides ample evidence to support such scepticism, though, as we shall see, the precise ways in which the censors served the interests of the apartheid regime as guardians of the literary, and, indeed, fitted into the broader structures of political and cultural domination, is not as straightforward as might be expected. At the same time, the evidence this book amasses, particularly from the archives of the many writers and publishers who resisted the regime's totalizing ambitions, also tells a different story in which literature figures not as an object of suspicion but as a powerful, if always unpredictable, mode of public intervention in its own right, which was sought out, and quarrelled over, by an extraordinary range of writers from almost three generations who laid claim to very different, though often intersecting, linguistic and cultural traditions. I touch on aspects of this other story at various points throughout this book, particularly in Chapter 3, where I examine the ways in which different writers theorized the space of the literary and, in so doing, put the censors' cultural assumptions in question.

This other, less disenchanted story emerges most explicitly, however, in the six essayistic chapters that comprise Part II, where I address its implications more directly. In these chapters, which examine the general debates outlined earlier in more focused ways, I look in greater detail at the censors' often copious reports, many of which read more like exercises in literary criticism than legalistic judgments, and at the specific, often singular, ways various interventionist writers responded to the threat (or spur) of censorship, the demands of political resistance, and the expectations of multiple readerships in their primary medium as writers, that is, the works themselves. This second section does not just provide a close-up perspective, or series of perspectives, on some further aspects of this vast, necessarily multifaceted subject, however. It extends and elaborates my overall argument by considering how specific works exposed the particular perversity of the censors' guardianship and tested the limits of scholastic thought more generally. In this way the book's

17

organization reflects a key aspect of its underlying anti-scholasticism. Dealing with the challenges of writing the unexpectedly tangled histories of literature and apartheid censorship involves having, as I argue throughout, to embrace irreconcilable inclinations towards trust and suspicion, or towards a 'pure' appreciation of the disruptive energies of specific works, which does not ignore their, or their guardian's, 'impure' situatedness within larger political, cultural, and institutional histories. The two-part structure of this book embodies this double demand.

PART I

Creating Spaces/
Guarding Borders

1
CENSORS

Governmental anxieties about the threat the medium of print seemed to pose to the established order in twentieth-century South Africa predated the Afrikaner Nationalists' rise to power in 1948. The first statutory Board of Censors in what was then the Union of South Africa, the racially segregated dominion of the British empire founded in 1910, was set up under the Entertainments (Censorship) Act, 1931. Rejecting the kind of thinking that led to the formation of the independent, industry-led British Board of Film Censors (BBFC) in 1912, the South African authorities chose to make this a governmental body, following the precedent set by the Irish Free State in 1930. The censors initially focused on the new medium of film and all forms of pictorial representation as well as theatrical performances. In 1934, however, their powers were extended to include imported books and periodicals. This change effectively strengthened the control the government, then led by the newly formed white supremacist United Party, already had over all printed matter produced abroad. The Minister of the Interior had always been the final arbiter of the earlier Customs Management Act (1913), which contained an all-encompassing clause prohibiting the importation of 'articles which are indecent, obscene, or objectionable', and, since the new censors' decisions only had the status of recommendations, this continued under the revised system.[1] This decision-making structure was subsequently confirmed under amended customs legislation in the 1940s and 1950s.

The prohibitions stipulated in the 1931 Act, which made no reference to questions of artistic merit, were extensive and detailed. Many were in fact derived from the extraordinary list of forty-three taboo topics T. P. O'Connor identified in 1916 in his capacity as the first president of the BBFC. This list was itself a consolidation of the annual reports the British Board produced in its first three years. Under a general statement covering sedition and public decency, the South African Act listed nineteen specific clauses banning 'offensive' depictions of anything from 'white slave traffic' to 'passionate love scenes', from 'drunkenness and brawling' to the 'rough-handling or ill-treatment of women and children'. Among these broadly moral clauses, however, were others covering 'the religious convictions or feelings of any section of the public', 'reference to controversial or international politics', and 'scenes representing antagonistic relations of capital and labour' or the 'intermingling of Europeans and non-Europeans'. The Act also specifically proscribed 'offensive' representations of the British monarch, who was then head of state.[2] Significantly the statement about 'intermingling' was the only key clause not based on O'Connor's list, though he had specified the need to censor references to what he apocalyptically termed 'race suicide'.[3]

Under this legislation the first Board of Censors, who worked in conjunction with customs, controlled the importation of books and periodicals throughout the 1940s and 1950s. Locally produced publications, at that point, fell under nineteenth-century provincial legislation and the common law. The foundations for what would, in effect, become the apartheid censorship system were laid only in 1954 when the newly elected Nationalist government, then still under D. F. Malan, launched a Commission of Inquiry into 'Undesirable Publications'. This inquiry was initiated in response to a court case the year before relating to an article on prostitution in two popular Afrikaans magazines, which provoked widespread moral panic in official circles, but it was also designed to address concerns various church groups had been raising about pornography throughout the 1930s and 1940s. As a former Nederduits Gereformeerde Kerk (NGK) cleric, Malan was particularly sympathetic to this campaign and, like his successors, he was happy to capitalize on it for political gain. For all leaders of the *volk* supremacist National Party, the quasi-established NGK and other Calvinist churches represented a vital link to the Afrikaner electorate throughout the apartheid era.

Seen in the context of other contemporary legislative developments, however, it is clear that the Publications Inquiry, which was tasked to review the regulation of locally produced as well as imported books, also suited the government's larger political ambitions at the time. It was just one among many new initiatives, the main aim of which was to use the powers of the state to seize control of the public sphere at a time when extra-parliamentary protest against the emergent apartheid order was still open and strong. The Publications Commission coincided, for instance, with an official inquiry into the press, which ran for an extraordinary thirteen years from 1950, and which was intended primarily to rein in the dominant white-owned liberal English-language newspapers; and it followed a raft of other legislation, the most notorious of which was the Suppression of Communism Act, 1950. Designed to outlaw the South African Communist Party, this Act was later used to silence most forms of political opposition to apartheid.[4] The appointment of Geoffrey Cronjé (1907–92) to chair the Publications Commission might also be taken as an index of the Malan government's wider ambitions.

Cronjé, a professor of sociology at the University of Pretoria, was a prominent apartheid ideologue of the 1940s. A member of the Broederbond (League of Brothers), the secretive organization committed to furthering Afrikaner interests founded in 1918, he was also, according to Giliomee, the 'nationalist academic with the most explicitly racist thesis'.[5] He was best known at the time for his extensive writings against miscegenation, which, as J. M. Coetzee noted, display a 'crazed' obsession with degeneration, contagion, and racial purity that put Cronjé's style of 'apartheid thinking' in a class of its own.[6] What is perhaps most relevant here is the force with which Cronjé articulated the moral repugnance—or, more accurately, racialized disgust—underlying some apartheid law-making. This was most evident in the legislation outlawing interracial sexual intimacy, initiated with the Prohibition of Mixed Marriages Act, 1949, and the Immorality Amendment Act, 1950, but it also figured conspicuously in the censorship legislation, which gave particular prominence to the need to protect public morals, and South Africa's racist political order, from the threat posed by supposedly repugnant representations of racial 'intermingling'.[7] Given this, it is not difficult to see why Cronjé might have been considered an appropriate figure to lead a commission which was, according to its official terms of reference, to make recommendations regarding the 'most effective means of combating, in view of the particular circumstances and the composition of the population of the Union of South Africa and the Territory of South-West Africa, the evil of indecent, offensive or harmful literature'.[8]

Compared to the press inquiry, the Cronjé Commission, as it came to be known, was conducted with brisk efficiency. It presented its findings in October 1956, having in the course of two years gathered a vast body of information from just under 400 individuals and groups, including librarians, publishers, literary experts, magazine editors, booksellers, lawyers, and clerics. It also instituted a series of special investigations of its own into the state of local (mainly Afrikaans) literature, into local magazines and newspapers, and into what it called 'Bantu' reading habits in Pretoria. Its key recommendations, which were formally published in September 1957, were draconian. It advocated a qualified system of pre-publication censorship; the creation for the first time of a national enforcement agency for the regulation of both local and imported books euphemistically called the Publications Control Board; and the formal licensing of all printers, publishers, booksellers, and periodicals. It also proposed that a further government-appointed Board be set up to hear appeals, thereby removing the need for any recourse to the courts. To justify these severe new measures, the Commissioners, who liked to present themselves not as moralizers but as scientific modernizers, relied heavily on US and Canadian government inquiries into pornography of the early 1950s, and vigorously championed the American psychologist Frederic Wertham's popular book *Seduction of the Innocent* (1954), a crudely mechanistic study of how comics 'caused' juvenile delinquency. It is worth noting that they conspicuously ignored the already large body of research critical of simple causal analyses of this kind.[9] What set the

Cronjé Commission apart from these studies, however, was its explicit politi-cization of what was ostensibly a social and moral debate.

The stricter, more centralized forms of statutory censorship it proposed were necessary in South Africa, the Commission argued, because the unchecked spread of pornography ultimately spelt political disaster. Its darkest fears, which neither its scientific pretensions nor its blandly bureaucratic prose man-aged successfully to mask, centred on the degeneration of the 'European'.

> As the torch-bearer in the vanguard of Western civilization in South Africa, the European *must be* and *remain* the leader, the guiding light, in the spiritual and cultural field, otherwise he will inevitably *go* under. The undesirable book can and must be drastically combated because it is obviously a spiritual poison. (41)

This was a rather wooden rendering of the more florid Afrikaans text, which referred to the *blanke* ('whites') as *die vuurtoring in die kultuur* ('the lighthouse or beacon of culture'). The original also made the Commission's idealist cultural assumptions, in particular its understanding of *kultuur* as the privileged ex-pression of a racialized *gees* ('spirit', or 'mind'), more obvious. Both versions employed the clichéd Victorian trope of the 'undesirable book' as a 'spiritual poison', however, which Nationalist MPs had already overused in heated par-liamentary debates about pornography in the early 1950s. On this logic the Commission represented pre-publication censorship as an indispensable cor-don sanitaire, which would keep 'Western' culture pure, thereby protecting 'European' guardianship and shoring up white political supremacy. This public health rhetoric of course presupposed that the pre-eminence of the whites as the bearers of light into South Africa's heart of darkness, which the Commission took to be 'an indisputable postulate and an inescapable truth', was not invul-nerable (53).

Preventing 'European' degeneration was one side of the Commission's racial-ized construction of the problem; the other centred on 'Bantu' perceptions of, and attitudes to, 'Western' culture. It said almost nothing about what it termed 'the Indians', and made only a few throwaway remarks about 'the Coloureds'; e.g. 'the Coloured is an artistically-inclined person' (264). Unsurprisingly, the only 'non-European' voice the Commission actually cited in its voluminous Report confirmed its racialist assumptions, adding a further gender dimension to its warnings. 'European woman' was 'placed on a pedestal by non-Europeans', this anonymous witness apparently reported, but this 'respect', and, by impli-cation, regard for white authority in general, was being undermined because 'undesirable' illustrations of white women were being allowed to circulate freely (53).[10] This claim perhaps encapsulates more succinctly than any other the paranoia underlying the Commission's thinking, not least if we recall that its investigations coincided with the signing of the Freedom Charter, the defining manifesto of the resistance, in June 1955, to which it made no reference.

What concerned the Commission most was the effect 'inferior things in the way of life and thought of the Europeans' were having on the 'semi-developed and culturally confused Bantu' themselves (263). Though its special study of the 'Bantu' in townships surrounding Pretoria concluded that magazines intended for a white readership contained much more 'undesirable' material than those for blacks, and that newly urbanized black readers preferred 'ecclesiastical books' and 'books for study', it insisted that 'certain magazines for the Bantu' were causing 'discontent and unrest' because they were estranging him from his 'own culture' (264). It did not name any specific titles, but the fact that it listed, bizarrely, 'jazz, jive, slang, etc.' among these inferior and alien 'European' influences suggests that it most likely had *Drum* in mind (264). This popular consumer magazine, launched in 1951, which became a key forum for a new generation of young black writers, had by the mid-1950s begun to articulate new ideas of a modern, urbanized African culture, explicitly rejecting the atavistic tribalist fantasies of apartheid. In its investigations the Commission consulted Jim Bailey, *Drum*'s owner, and cited *Drum: A Venture into the New Africa* (1956), a book about the magazine's early years by Anthony Sampson, one of its first chief editors.

If Western culture and the associated threats of white degeneration or black detribalization were the focus of the Commission's racialized rationale for stricter censorship, literature was at the centre of its narrower, nationalistic justification of its proposals. The 'undesirable book' also had to be 'drastically combated' in order to save Afrikaans literary culture, which, according to another of its special investigations, was in a rapid, seemingly irreversible, state of decline. This second rationale, which both reinforced and complicated the first, featured prominently in the Commission's main Report and became the focus of a public relations article Cronjé published under his own name in the leading Afrikaans cultural weekly *Huisgenoot* (Home Companion) on 7 October 1957.[11] Entitled 'Stop the Spread of Offensive Reading Matter', the article highlighted the results of the Commission's survey of books published in the Union between 1935 and 1954, a period which saw a rapid growth in the Afrikaans publishing industry, particularly in the area of mass-market fiction. The statistics purportedly showed that while the amount of 'undesirable' adult fiction in Afrikaans was increasing at an alarming rate, work 'of literary merit' had declined dramatically.[a] Picking up on the Commission's general hostility to all forms of mass culture, Cronjé suggested that this deterioration was being accelerated by the arrival of new foreign imports like the cheap American paperback and its associated popular genres (the Commission was especially worried about thrillers and crime fiction), which too many popular Afrikaans writers were enthusiastically emulating. In the 1960s Mickey Spillane, the popular American crime writer, would become one of the censors' more prominent targets.

To address the specific threat to Afrikaans literature the Commission suggested a dual approach: stricter censorship measures and a positive programme of uplift. It called for the creation of a state-subsidized 'South African Institute for Literature', which would coordinate a promotional programme to counterbalance the censoring role of the new Control Board; and it made numerous recommendations about how schools, universities, churches, and the book trade could educate the literary taste of the reading public. Such measures were vital, it argued, because the new forms of mass culture were corrupting Afrikaner values. In the face of this, a properly elevated Afrikaans literature needed to be affirmed because it was a repository of 'spiritual values', which were under threat in the modern age of 'mass communication and superficialization', especially among newly urbanized Afrikaners, who had 'completely lost their spiritual bearings' in 'cities with an English orientation' (211–12). These positive measures also reflected the Commission's belief that the 'literary artist' deserved the 'highest esteem' as not only the 'creator of literary art but also the mirror in which a community can see itself' (260). As we shall see, this idea of literature as a 'mirror' held up to the 'community', by which the Commission meant a racialized ethno-linguistic *volk* (i.e. white Afrikaners construed as a nation), had little to do with writers' freedoms and everything to do with their responsibilities as members of a *volk*.

When it came to literature, the Commission was not just eager to display its high-minded nationalist convictions. It also sought to demonstrate that it recognized the wider conceptual issues at stake by drawing attention to the fact that the censoring functions of the proposed new Board were defined in such a way as to afford literature some protection. While it did not go so far as to advocate granting it statutory exemption, as some more liberal Australian states had already done and as Britain and the United States were in the process of doing in relation to obscenity legislation, it did stress that 'account must be taken of the artistic merit of the literary material'. This was listed among five other factors, including the 'Christian outlook on life' and the 'racial composition' of the Union, which it felt should be given special consideration (148). It explicitly rejected full exemption on the grounds of its potential 'inflexibility' (143). The Commission also noted that it had made 'special provision for the manner of treatment of the subject', which meant that no 'content' was intrinsically 'undesirable' (30). It recognized, for instance, that while *Oedipus Rex*—a staple in such discussions—contained 'shocking' details, such as incest and eye-gouging, it did not follow that the 'immortal drama' would have to be banned. To justify this it appealed, in the first instance, to the familiar principle of functionality. The 'shocking' details were 'presented as truths connected with the characters and events, and *not for their own sake*' (30). It also invoked a grander, and as it pointedly noted 'most modern', theory of literariness, however (30).

Though the Report cited a number of theoretical works, including Roman Ingarden's *Das Literarische Kunstwerk* (1931) and Sartre's *Qu'est-ce que la littérature?* (1948), it was mostly indebted to Cleanth Brooks's *The Well-Wrought Urn* (1947) and, above all, to René Wellek and Austin Warren's *Theory of Literature* (1949). In this it was no doubt responding to suggestions made by the young Afrikaans poet and literary academic H. van der Merwe Scholtz, whose expert advice on literature it sought. Merwe Scholtz, who is often credited with introducing formalism to Afrikaans literary studies, would go on to become one of the key figures in the new censorship bureaucracy. Some of the Commission's formulations directly echoed Wellek and Warren's second chapter, on 'The Nature of Literature'. Following this lead, it defined all literature, including 'plays' and 'verse', as fiction, and as an 'entity, a closely-knit organisation which isolates itself from commonplace reality' and 'remains true to itself and its own legitimate rules' (30, 92). With these latest formalist tests, the Commission argued, it was possible to 'safeguard' genuine literary works (92). Such fashionable formalism, which surely makes the Cronjé Report one of the strangest documents in the troubled history of American New Criticism, was, of course, wholly consistent with the Commissioners' modernizing, scientific ambitions. Though their final position was, as we shall see, extremely equivocal, their apparent openness to the literary set them apart from the more zealous Nationalist politicians, who were happy to subject literature, and writing in general, to the laws governing all 'indecent behaviour in public' on the grounds of 'consistency', since writing was simply a public act like any other.[12]

'The Spiritual Life of a *Volk*'

The Commission had good reason to advertise its lofty literary preoccupations. It was well aware that its proposal to replace the old Board of Censors with a new Control Board, which would have additional powers over local publications, was going to be vigorously resisted not only by the government's political opponents but, perhaps more worryingly, by Afrikaner literary intellectuals. Concerns about the possible impact any new legislation might have on Afrikaans literature in particular had been raised in 1953 during the parliamentary debates which led to the Commission being proposed, and in December that year the foremost Afrikaans literary journal, *Standpunte* (Standpoints), published a survey in which leading Afrikaans and English writers, publishers, and critics spoke out emphatically against the proposals.[b] Yet, on this issue, it was one of *Standpunte*'s founding editors, N. P. van Wyk Louw (1906–70), the unofficial poet laureate and conscience of Afrikaner nationalism, who proved to be the government's most persistent and influential adversary. As Louw was also the single individual most directly responsible for putting literature at the centre of apartheid censorship, and the leading figure in the informal circle I shall call the *volk* avant-garde, it will be worth giving a brief account of some key aspects of his cultural and political thinking at this point before returning to the Cronjé Report and its consequences.[13]

More self-critical than ideologues like Cronjé, Louw nonetheless began his career as an uncompromising political nationalist. A long-standing member of the Broederbond, he defended the Afrikaner's political ambitions in the 1930s in robustly anti-colonial terms, siding with the hardline 'pure Nationalists' against the Anglophile United Party, while professing a fierce anti-communism and an unqualified admiration for the Nazis.[14] After the Second World War he became a more complex 'liberal–nationalist', advocating apartheid, which he attempted unsuccessfully to deracialize, as a political means of ensuring the Afrikaner's survival as a distinct *volk* in a 'multinational state'.[15] Typically, his defence of this separatist vision was at this stage haunted by ethical anxieties. In particular, he felt the Afrikaner's future would be in question when 'a large part of our volk comes to the dangerous belief that we do not have to live together *in justice* with our fellow-volke in South Africa—comes to suppose that *mere continued existence* is the main thing, not existence that is just'.[16] This influential observation, which first appeared in a *Huisgenoot* article in 1952, is telling as much for its ethical insights as for its political blindnesses. If, according to Giliomee, it reflects Louw's refusal 'to go down the route of ethnic survival at all costs', it also reveals the limits of his political imagination.[17] For Louw, it remained the case that the only way forward for the Afrikaner was as a *volk*, and that the only way of reading the politics of post-war South Africa was in Afrikaner nationalist terms (hence his reference to 'fellow-volke'). According to his biographer, he had little understanding of the realities of resistance politics, partly because of his strident anti-communism.[18]

Yet Louw was not just a political nationalist. He was also a cultural nationalist committed to a very particular idea of literature and of the writer as a critical intellectual. This made him something of a dissident insider, a testy and embattled minority position which he termed *lojale verset* ('loyal resistance', or 'opposition'). This phrase, which he coined in 1939, went on to became a byword in Afrikaner intellectual circles and a point of contention for some younger writers of the 1960s, above all, Breyten Breytenbach.[19] Yet for others, perhaps most notably the leading contemporary black Afrikaans poet Adam Small, Louw's sustained critique of the dominant forms of Afrikaner cultural thinking remained 'truly profound'.[20] Here it should be recalled that before the term 'apartheid' acquired its full political sense it was applied by more mainstream thinkers to Afrikaner cultural history, where it signified an achieved sense of distinction or separation, principally from Dutch and British colonial influence. This sense can be seen in the editorial comment included in the preface to the first cultural history of the Afrikaner, which was published in

1945: 'We have emerged from the stage of being a pioneer *volk* to a position where the Afrikaner today is urbanized and can consciously take account of his apartheid as a nation', with his 'own language' and his 'own outlook on life'.[21] Behind this lay the long history of the Afrikaner's struggle not just for self-determination but for language rights. The latter began in the late nineteenth century and was formally recognized in 1925 when Afrikaans replaced Dutch as the Union's second official language. For all his commitment to the language and its literature, Louw's own thinking was, as Small pointed out in a critically astute essay of 1972, consciously directed against the self-enclosed purism that permeated these more mainstream Afrikaner attitudes.

While recognizing that Louw's continued adherence to the idea of the *volk* remained a problem, Small focused on his theory of cultural interdependency, noting that, on Louw's analysis, Afrikaner culture had to be broadly humanistic, exploratory, and open to many influences, principally European but also African. According to Louw, as Small put it, '*my* culture *opens the way* for me to *the other*', providing the starting point for an always dynamic 'movement of and towards understanding' (216). For Small, Louw's emphatic rejection of a fetishistic Afrikaner insularity offered an object lesson in 'multicultural' coexistence, which had a particular contemporary relevance not just for young Afrikaners who were not familiar enough with Louw's minority views but for '*all* our youth' (201, 217). Writing as a sympathetic if wary commentator on the rise of Black Consciousness in the early 1970s, he noted that many 'young people in our universities' had chosen 'in frustration (for many reasons)' to 'isolate themselves from the larger community'. Yet 'by closing their ranks, by drawing a solid circle around them', they were, he felt, not only 'suffering from the deepest misconception about the meaning of identity'. They were making the same 'mistake' as 'that of many of those whom they oppose and decry' (217). In the fraught climate of the early 1970s, his provocative endorsement of Louw's alternative idea of Afrikaner culture was understandably not universally welcomed by the younger generation (see Chapter 3).

Yet if Small's untimely reflections drew attention to the subtlety of Louw's nuanced minority position, they also underplayed the extent to which his cultural thinking remained inseparable from his political commitment to apartheid. Paradoxically, this was not just because Louw was, for all his astringent criticisms of the Afrikaner, always loyal to the idea of the *volk*, but because culture was, in his view, deeply anti-political, not merely 'beyond politics' as Small put it (209). Taken as a whole, his writings as a cultural theorist constitute a specifically situated contribution to the history of thought linking literature both to nationalism and to the European high-cultural tradition of *Kulturkritik*, which privileged a particular style of what Francis Mulhern usefully terms 'metacultural discourse'. 'What speaks in metacultural discourse is the cultural principle itself', Mulhern observes, 'as it strives to dissolve the political as a locus of general arbitration in social relations.'[22] Louw's endorsement of this idea of the cultural as a rival, or, more strongly, a genuine alternative to an abstractly conceived notion of the political, goes some way towards explaining the paradoxical aspects of his anti-political thinking. In his view, the political future of the Afrikaner as a *volk* depended not just on apartheid but on the creation of an Afrikaner 'Republic of Letters', which he construed as an autonomous and contrary cultural space in which a new, modern Afrikaans literature and, indeed, Afrikaner identity could flourish. This was, in part, because he shared the Cronjé Commission's idealist, and essentially Romantic, view of literature as the privileged manifestation of the *volksgees* ('national spirit'). Yet, as a champion of the *volk* avant-garde, who rejected the idea that this spirit or identity constituted a stable essence, he insisted that avant-garde writers, not politicians, clerics, or merely patriotic writers, were its true guardians. This set him on a collision course with the leading Nationalist politician of his time, H. F. Verwoerd, and set him apart from the more unquestioningly loyal Afrikaner writers' group the Skrywerskring (Writers' Circle), founded in 1934. It also made him one of the most outspoken opponents of censorship, as he made clear in a polemic published some years before the Cronjé Commission launched its inquiry in the mid-1950s.

When a delegation of NGK and other clerics lobbied the United Party government in 1947, calling for the Minister of the Interior to curb the indecency of local, especially Afrikaans, publications, Louw condemned their initiative in emphatic terms. Writing in *Standpunte*, the principal platform of the *volk* avant-garde, he accepted that the state might have a minimal advisory role to play when it came to books for children, but, in keeping with his respect for some basic liberal tenets, he rejected any claims it might have over adult readers. Moreover, as he went on to point out, once a censorship system was in place it was 'not difficult to expand its terrain' by defining 'other things', besides pornography, as 'offensive'.[23] His main objections, however, were fuelled by his commitment to a specifically nationalist version of *Kulturkritik*. For one thing, he felt censorship should be opposed because it was in itself a sign of national weakness. 'We must learn from history that it is almost always new mass-revolutionary [he earlier referred critically to Nazi Germany and the Soviet Union] or antiquated and insecure cultures (that of France in the time of the kings and tsarist Russia) that trust the power of censorship; that stable and powerful cultures do not need it' (408).

Looking back at the fate of writers such as Flaubert, Zola, Hardy, and Joyce, he also argued that, since it was 'almost impossible' to keep the unstable categories of the literary and the pornographic clearly separated, censorship jeopardized what was 'central to the spiritual life of a *volk*' (404, 407). This did not mean he was defending a patriotic or, indeed, crudely expressivist conception of the literary. Partly because of the universalizing humanistic aspirations underpinning his conception of a Great Literature, reflected in part in his own interest in classical literary forms like poetic drama, he always insisted that a properly autonomous national literature was not a pure emanation of a pre-existent soul or essence but the locus of cultural experiment and renewal. For Louw, the avant-garde writer had to be free to be *both* the 'builder' *and* the 'critic' of the *volk*, or, more strongly, an exploratory 'pioneer on the border of that-which-was-never-before' (463, 399). Once again the reasons for this were ultimately political, since the 'destruction of the possibility of a great art developing is also the destruction of a *volk*'s highest right of existence' (408). It was, in other words, on specifically nationalist, as well as literary and liberal, grounds that he insisted on the need to protect avant-garde writers against interference from any external authority: Church, state, or 'mass opinion' (463).

If, as these comments suggest, Louw shared the Cronjé Commission's nationalistic cultural idealism and hostility to the mass, he was radically at odds with its idea of literature as the 'mirror' of the 'community'. The gulf between their respective positions can be seen most clearly in the Commission's more detailed exposition of its mirror analogy, which followed the more established Afrikaner thinking at the time. In its view, the formalist idea of the autotelic nature of the literary, which could be used to legitimize classics like *Oedipus Rex*, did 'not by any means connote that the artist may do whatever he likes as long as he does so artistically' (30). This was principally because 'every community has the "novelistic" characters and situations which are peculiar to it and which it offers the novelist as material for his creations; but what is deemed permissible in one community may be impermissible in another' (31). To illustrate the point, it noted that in the 'Afrikaans community illegitimacy is something which meets with social condemnation'; presumably it could have used interracial intimacy to make the same point. This imposed a particular burden on the Afrikaner writer, who had to be 'fully conversant' with the 'community's system of values', and meant that a work could be deemed 'artistically convincing' only if it handled such 'explosive material' in an acceptable manner (30). If a writer treated what was 'evil' as if it were 'conventional or even "good"', then 'his work is doomed in advance in so far as its "artistic" merit is concerned because he is really making use of material which he has falsified' (30). The tortuous logic underlying this anti-individualistic line of argument, which effectively turned the debate about writerly responsibility into one about realism, not only nullified the Commissioners' reassuringly sophisticated formalism, it put them at loggerheads with Louw and his allies, who immediately made their objections plain in a series of replies to Cronjé's *Huisgenoot* article, which were published on 21 October 1957 under the title 'Writers See Danger in the Cronjé Report'.[24] Louw himself responded in two articles published under the heading 'Sterilized Literature' in the liberally inclined Nationalist newspaper *Die Burger* early the following year.[25]

The Publications Act, 1963

It was only late in 1960, during the state of emergency precipitated by the police atrocities in the Sharpeville and Langa townships, that the newly elected Nationalist government of H. F. Verwoerd finally responded to the Cronjé Report. At that point it introduced an especially repressive bill, ignoring the Commission's positive suggestions for promoting literature but adopting its recommendations for a new centralized censorship apparatus with even stricter forms of pre-publication scrutiny. This draft legislation, which included censorship of the press, was widely condemned both inside and outside Parliament, with one of the most trenchant critiques coming from the South African PEN Centre, the oldest writer's group in the country. In a carefully argued, thirteen-page memorandum submitted to the relevant select committee, PEN SA denounced the bill as an 'undemocratic' violation of the rule of law and as a threat not just to the freedom of expression, literature, and the arts, but to political debate, the wider society, and the state itself.[26] On the last point it claimed, revealing another side to the mixed history of liberal thinking in South Africa, that 'censorship inhibits the dynamic development of the State by preventing free thought and expression among those of its servants who can produce ideas valuable to it; for example, the concept of Bantustans is itself only a few years old' (2). In keeping with its own internationally agreed principles, PEN SA was especially opposed to the idea of an expanded statutory Board of Censors, insisting that the courts alone could and should deal with pornography, the one area in which it felt state regulation was legitimate. Prefiguring some of the conclusions of the 1979 Williams Commission in Britain, to which I referred in my Introduction, it also insisted that 'literary and artistic merit cannot be assessed, certainly by non-specialists, except through free criticism and comparison with recognized works of art over a fair period'. 'A censorship system which claims to exempt works of art from banning or mutilation is in effect', the memorandum added, 'claiming to determine a work's literary or artistic value, and to do so before time and professional criticism have tested it.' This applied especially to 'serious new works' (3).

PEN SA's objections had little impact, though in 1962, after a further period of consultation, the government tabled a second, less obviously authoritarian bill that addressed some of its concerns, which the official opposition United Party shared, particularly regarding the press and the membership of the new Board. After some slight modifications, this finally entered the statute book in March 1963 as the Publications and Entertainments Act, the legislation that would serve as the cornerstone of the apartheid censorship bureaucracy for the next decade. The Act broke new ground by making the publication, printing, or distribution of 'undesirable' materials (excluding certain newspapers) produced both locally and abroad a statutory offence, punishable by severe fines and prison sentences. Since South Africa had severed its official ties to Britain and the Commonwealth two years earlier, fulfilling the National Party's long-held ambition to revive the traditions of nineteenth-century Boer republicanism, the new legislation was signed into law not by the Governor-General of the Union but by the State President of the new Republic.

As we shall see, the precise terms of the 1963 Act were a testament to the limited effectiveness of the white parliamentary process and liberal anti-censorship protests, which did not so much curb as obscure the government's will to power in this one area of legislation. In other areas there was little or no check on its determination to extend its powers of direct political censorship. In July 1962, for instance, it passed the General Law Amendment (or Sabotage) Act, thereby silencing 102 anti-apartheid activists, including the novelist Alex La Guma and the poets Dennis Brutus and Cosmo Pieterse, and forcing the closure of most of the leading oppositional periodicals of the time. Following the terms of the Suppression of Communism Act, this new 'gagging clause' banned various writers and journalists as persons, removing their rights of association, among other things, but it also made it illegal for them to be quoted in public. In the years ahead, the government would use this kind of legislation to silence most of the established black writers of the 1950s and 1960s and the leaders of the Black Consciousness movement in the 1970s.[27]

The system the 1963 Act inaugurated was indeed less repressive than that envisaged in the first draft bill and, to some extent, the Cronjé Report. It expressly ruled out pre-publication censorship; it excluded mainstream newspapers signed up to a new voluntary press code; and, most importantly for the opponents of the first bill, it made the Supreme Court, not a government-appointed board, the final arbiter in the event of an appeal. These concessions were, however, at best legalistic, at worst disingenuous. As it turned out, for all the euphemized references to post-publication 'control' rather than 'censorship', the publications that entered the new system came overwhelmingly from agents of the state, not from offended individuals or groups. Moreover, the respect the government was obliged to show for the independence of the (white) judiciary at this early stage proved largely empty, even though the courts in fact turned out to be more liberal than the new Board of Censors. Given the sovereignty of Parliament, and in the absence of a constitutionally guaranteed Bill of Rights, the courts were more or less impotent. Since they could not question the assumptions underlying the Act, they could comment only on its implementation, a duty they were asked to perform rarely, given the costs of appeal. In the decade between 1964 and 1974, when over ten thousand publications were banned, fewer than thirty appeals were heard (and many of these concerned *Scope*, a popular, mildly titillating local weekly).[28] In 1974, when the government brought in new censorship legislation, it went back to the Cronjé proposals, set up an extra-judicial Appeal Board, and all but abolished recourse to the courts.

If the powers of the new Board of Censors were, to some extent, less draconian than those the Commission had proposed, the detailed provisions of the Act were more so, not least because, as Louw and PEN SA anticipated, they included a sweeping definition of 'undesirability'. Though the Commission had included provisions relating to blasphemy, race relations, and communism in its own exhaustive definitions, it had, given its remit, focused on issues relating to obscenity and public morals, placing particular emphasis on miscegenation and interracial sociability. By contrast, the cornerstone of the new Act, at least as far as publications were concerned, comprised five main clauses, covering what could be deemed morally repugnant, blasphemous, socially subversive, or politically seditious. Since these key statutory provisions constituted the foundation of apartheid censorship (they were preserved in the 1974 Act), they are worth citing in full:

5 (2) A publication or object shall be deemed to be undesirable if it or any part of it—

(a) is indecent or obscene or is offensive or harmful to public morals;

(b) is blasphemous or is offensive to the religious convictions or feelings of any section of the inhabitants of the Republic;

(c) brings any section of the inhabitants of the Republic into ridicule or contempt;

(d) is harmful to the relations between any sections of the inhabitants of the Republic;

(e) is prejudicial to the safety of the State, the general welfare or the peace and good order.[29]

Bearing in mind the future direction of censorship legislation, this was, on the face of it, a relatively neutral set of formulations. Clause (b), for example, did not explicitly favour any particular religious faith. Though this wording remained unchanged in 1974, the new Act was prefaced by a further foundational principle, which recognized the 'constant endeavour of the population of the Republic of South Africa to uphold a Christian view of life'.[30] By that point, partly because the government was again under pressure from the NGK and other Afrikaner church groups, it dispensed with the veil of legislative neutrality and openly asserted its hegemonic claims, much to the dismay of the, by then, wholly ineffective parliamentary opposition.

The only explicitly political clause in the 1963 Act was 5 (2) (e), which dealt with sedition. Yet, as the Afrikaans text revealed more clearly, clauses (b), (c), and (d) were also intended to shore up apartheid policy; the same can be said for clause (a), a point to which I shall return. It rendered the vague and apparently neutral term 'section' as *bevolkingsdeel* ('population-part'). Unlike the English term, this had a particular resonance given the homonymic link between the Afrikaans for 'nation', 'people', and 'population', but its precise meaning was still far from self-evident. Indeed, it remained a more or less opaque code word until the mid-1970s, when the newly established Appeal Board, then chaired by the conservative judge J. H. Snyman, reviewed the case history and explained the lawmakers' intentions. By 'section' they meant '*any of the communities (or peoples) in the Republic considered as distinct from the rest*' and 'something more specific than groups, categories or ephemeral associations of people'.[31] Determining exactly which 'communities' constituted a 'section' even on this basis was tricky, Snyman accepted (he worried about political parties, trade unions, and regional identities, not about women or gays), but relevant factors to be considered included 'the physical or facial features of its members'; the 'racial or national make-up of the group'; 'communal traits, culture, practices, habits, behaviour patterns, emotions, beliefs, social outlook'; and whether or not membership could 'be terminated at will'. On this logic, he concluded, it was clear that while the term presented 'no difficulty in respect of racial, national or ethnic groups', a professional group, like the police, did not constitute a 'section' because 'its members are employees who may leave their employment or be discharged from it at any time'. This meant that the initial banning of Jack Cope's novel about the resistance *The Dawn Comes Twice* (1969)—the case the Appeal Board happened to be reviewing—had to be upheld in part because its damning portrayal of the South African police fell foul not of clause (c) but of (e). Clause (c), in other words, was, following the unstable but always restricted communitarian assumptions underlying apartheid, about the defamation of a racial, ethnic, or national group (i.e. a *volk*), and, unsurprisingly, it was regularly invoked to ban publications deemed to be anti-white or, more specifically, anti-Afrikaner.

Unlike the old Board of Censors, whose decisions had the status of recommendations, the new Board was technically an autonomous body, which meant that these vague formulations gave the apartheid censors extraordinary discretionary powers. This is particularly evident in the phrasing covering obscenity in clause 5 (2) (a), which section 6 of the Act explained more fully. Under the latter clause, the terms of which were, like most apartheid censorship legislation, derived from English law, the Act went on to stipulate what the already all-encompassing formulation in 5 (2) (a) meant in cases where there were 'any legal proceedings'. Section 6 (a) was a version of the landmark definition of obscenity under English law, generally known as the 'Hicklin test' of 1868: a publication would be 'indecent or obscene if . . . it has the tendency to deprave or to corrupt the minds of people who are likely to be exposed to the effect or influence thereof'. Unlike the original test, which was generally taken to refer to *any* readers, this formulation, it is worth noting, put the emphasis on *likely* readers. The next three stipulations shifted the focus from obscenity and the potentially harmful effects on the minds of individuals to public morals, emphasizing: 6 (b) the 'outrageous or disgustful' effect again on the likely reader; 6 (c) the 'improper' treatment of some forty-four topics, mostly derived from the 1931 Act and, behind that, T. P. O'Connor's 1916 list, including 'night life', 'gangsterism', 'tippling', 'lust', 'abortion', 'illegitimacy', 'scant or inadequate dress', 'homosexuality', 'sodomy', 'white slavery', 'adultery', 'human or social deviation or degeneracy', 'or any other similar or related phenomenon'; and 6 (d), to cover all bases, publications that were 'in any other manner subversive of morality'.[32] These catch-all formulations not only displayed the characteristic tendency of apartheid legislation towards ever greater euphemization—'human or social deviation and degeneracy', for instance, replaced the Cronjé Report's explicit reference to miscegenation and interracial sociability and the earlier references to 'intermingling'—they also created further difficulties of their own. In particular, the references to the 'likely reader', which contradicted the absolute criteria of section 5 (2), introduced a complication in the legislation's construction of the reading public that would be directly addressed only in the early 1980s.

The further stipulations under section 6 reflected the underlying conservatism of the Act and the importance it accorded to public morals, which always remained paramount in official justifications of censorship.[33] This emphasis was not, of course, peculiar to apartheid South Africa. It drew inspiration from the anti-liberal tradition articulated most notably by Patrick (later Lord) Devlin in his influential lecture *The Enforcement of Morals* (1959), where he argued that, far from being neutral with respect to the good life, the law had a responsibility to maintain social cohesion by protecting a putative common morality. In particular, Devlin claimed, it was necessary for the law to recognize the intense feelings of 'intolerance, indignation and disgust' held by any 'reasonable man'.[34] What the apartheid legislators did was to politicize and, of course, racialize this tradition by making government-appointed censors, who deliberated behind closed doors, the embodiment of the 'reasonable man'. Since the legislation imposed no obligation on the censors (or indeed the courts) to gauge actual opinion (Devlin, by contrast, defended the jury system precisely for this reason), it effectively turned the challenging empirical question 'What are public morals?' (or, more appropriately for a heterogeneous society like South Africa, 'Do they exist?') into a straightforwardly political one, 'Who decides?' Though the courts, over the years, tried to devise ways of making this process seem less capriciously prosecutorial—first via the legal fiction of the 'average man' and later via the more refined 'likely reader' test—these various protocols displaced, rather than addressed, the problem. They simply shifted the burden from the censors' (or judges') particular conception of public (i.e. largely *volk*) morals to their no less ideological understanding of South Africa and its communities, of readers and reading.

Given the emphasis on public morals, and, by extension, social cohesion, it is not surprising that the Act made no concessions to literature or to writers as a group—though, as we shall see, it did open up some possibilities when it came to the question of the Board's membership. It presupposed that determining and protecting any such norms was the preserve of the white Parliament, not a self-appointed cultural elite (nor, in the first instance, the courts). Not unexpectedly, van Wyk Louw saw this as a provocative affront, which he immediately turned into a crisis for the *volk*. The new Act was, he said in a letter to *Die Burger*, a 'moralistic' and 'anti-Afrikaans' law, which would encourage young writers to switch to English and publish abroad. Stepping up the invective, he added, 'I doubt even Milner himself could have thought of a more effective means to knee-halter Afrikaans and to give English free rein in South Africa.'[35] Sir Alfred Milner, the British High Commissioner who tried unsuccessfully to implement various Anglicization policies after the Boer War, had an especially infamous place in the history of the Afrikaner's anti-colonial struggle for language rights. In a radio broadcast some weeks later, Louw returned to the broader liberal themes of his 1947 essay and challenged the government's Cold War rhetoric. With this new Act, the politicians, he now argued, were betraying the ideals of the 'free world', and, more specifically, 'our Western literature', by falling into the trap of 'mimicking' the Soviet Union, their chief bogey.[36] Though this polemical move reflected the liberal–nationalist terms in which Louw championed the literary, it also revealed the more fixated side of his anti-censorship protests, which at times made it look as if safeguarding literature, in his modern sense, was not just a necessary but a sufficient condition for democracy. The more straightforwardly collaborationist Afrikaans Writers' Circle, by contrast, speaking through its chair, Abel Coetzee, sided with the government and saw no cause for alarm in the new legislation.[37,c] Later a number of its key figures, including C. F. Rudolph, F. C. Fensham, and Elize Botha, would go on to serve as academic advisers to the censors or as censors themselves.

With the support of other Afrikaans writers Louw continued his individual protests against the new legislation in the press, but towards the end of April 1963 his efforts took a new, more concerted turn. That month he put his name to a petition condemning the new system, which was signed by just under two hundred local writers and artists, including many liberal Afrikaners and members of PEN SA. Since I discuss the details of this petition in Chapter 3, I shall simply note here that the signatories included André Brink, Nadine Gordimer, Stuart Cloete, Jack Cope, Etienne Leroux, James Matthews, and Richard Rive, as well as W. J. du P. Erlank (the poet Eitemal), R. E. Lighton, Anna M. Louw, G. S. Nienaber, and S. V. Petersen. While all the former would be censored in the years ahead, all the latter went on, like some members of the Writers' Circle, to become censors themselves. As this suggests, relations between literature and apartheid censorship were about to become less predictable.

'A Fatal Compromise'

As the Act was already a fait accompli, the petition had little effect. Yet the timing was not uncalculated because in April 1963 the membership of the new Board had yet to be determined. Hence the petition's final plea that those appointed 'approach their serious task with all the responsibility and honesty of which they are capable'.[38] It was here, and here alone, that the Act made some safely non-committal concessions to the protests from writers by stipulating that the Board should have 'not less than nine members of whom not less than six shall be persons having special knowledge of art, language and literature or the administration of justice', one of whom would be designated chair.[39] When it was rumoured that Abel Coetzee or, worse still, the Nationalist MP Abraham Jonker, a primary mover behind the new legislation, were being touted for the chairmanship, Louw once again entered the fray. Having lost the battle at the legislative level, he now used all his influence, both in private and in public, to limit the damage by focusing on the lesser clash over appointments, a move which led him to make what the Afrikaans Marxist critic Ampie Coetzee later called 'a fatal compromise'.[40] With the support of *Die Burger*, which raised the spectre of a rift within the *volk*, Louw succeeded in persuading Gerrit Dekker (1897–1973) to become the first chair of the new Board, thereby ensuring that neither the politicians nor the Writers' Circle got control of the system. Given that the South African judiciary did not allow literary experts to testify in court in the 1960s, this was not a trivial concession on the government's part. Its consequences were far from straightforward, however.

A professor of Afrikaans and Dutch at the Potchefstroom University for Christian Higher Education (1932–63), and the author of the monumental *Afrikaanse Literatuurgeskiedenis* (Afrikaans Literary History, 1935–73), Dekker was at the time the most senior, and widely respected, critic in the Afrikaans literary world. For Louw, he was, for all his solidly Calvinist background, also a vital ally, who shared his conception of a *volk* avant-garde. As Louw put it in a talk on Dutch radio celebrating Dekker's sixtieth birthday in 1957, he was the most important champion of the Dertigers, the Afrikaner poets of the 1930s, of whom Louw was the most eminent, because he recognized their 'significance within the historical growth of our *volk*'.[41] At a time when they were, as young poets, regarded by the establishment as irreligious and unpatriotic upstarts, Dekker's endorsement, in other words, made it possible for them to be both nationalist and avant-garde. By reluctantly agreeing to become chief censor, Dekker put these cultural credentials at the service of the government, a decision which had lasting consequences for the system.

Most immediately, it transformed the role of the censor by making the Board, now the effective decision-making body, both the general arbiter of printed public discourse, responsible for deciding what was or was not 'undesirable', and the most powerful if least likely guardian of the literary. Louw saw this as a victory for literature in general and all South Africa's literatures (as he construed them) in particular. Once Dekker was appointed, he publicly commended the system, declaring in *Die Burger* that 'our English South African and our Afrikaans and our Bantu-literature can now continue unimpeded'.[42] Yet if it is true that the Verwoerd government, in accepting Dekker's appointment, could not be accused of suppressing the *volk* avant-garde, as Louw frequently noted Hitler had done, it was not exactly harnessing its energies in the style of Mussolini, nor was it creating space for literature as such. From its point of view, Louw's victory was a successful strategy of co-optation, designed to quell tensions within the *volk*, which had the added advantage of lending an air of legitimacy to the censorship apparatus itself, at least in the eyes of some literary intellectuals. The most significant conse-quence of this concession, which proved unworkable in the longer term, was that it put the question of literature—what is it and who decides?—at the centre of apartheid censorship.

With Louw's help, Dekker ensured that the Board was dominated by experts sympathetic to their cause. He appointed three Afrikaans literary professors, all former students of his, then in their early forties, as part-time members: T. T. Cloete, then at the University of Potchefstroom, A. P. Grové, and H. van der Merwe Scholtz, who were then both at the University of Pretoria.[43] To add a degree of language balance, Dekker also persuaded C. J. D. Harvey, a professor of English at the University of Stellenbosch, to join on the same terms. Harvey was well connected to the Afrikaans literary world not only because he taught at a white Afrikaner university but because he was, like Grové, on the editorial board of *Standpunte*. The two remaining part-time members were A. H. Murray, a professor of political philosophy at the University of Cape Town and the state's chief expert on communism; and T. M. H. Endemann, a professor of African languages at the new 'Bantu' University College of the North, who was recruited as a specialist on 'Bantu' publications. The core administrative business was handled by the four full-time members: two former magistrates (A. J. van Wyk, the deputy chair, and J. G. Sutton); and two former schoolteachers (N. J. Le Roux and Mrs J. P. Theron). Assisted by a panel of secondary readers and viewers, the full-time members were also in charge of handling film and most imported popular paperbacks. They were all based in Cape Town, then South Africa's principal port, which remained the centre of the censorship bureaucracy throughout the apartheid era. Though this meant that only five of the final eleven-member Board were literary experts, the balance of power was still considerably in their favour as only four members were required to constitute a quorum and the chair had a casting vote. Dekker immediately reinforced this by dividing the Board into a loose set of subcommittees, with one devoted to 'Literature' and another to 'Security'. This was intended to help deal with various practical problems—not the least of which was the fact that the members were dispersed around the country—but it also ensured that the Board's decision-making with regard to literature was dominated by a male, primarily Afrikaner, literary professoriate, an arrangement that remained in place throughout the 1960s and the early 1970s.

In a confidential speech given at the inaugural meeting of the Board in November 1963, Dekker confronted the awkwardness of his position. While acknowledging that the Act was 'harsh, even fiercely aggressive', he accepted the government's anti-liberal rationale for censorship and embraced his role as a guardian of the apartheid state.

> To begin with I recognize the right and even the duty of the State, which protects the population against dangers that are physically and morally undermining like immorality (*sedeloosheid*) and the misuse of drugs, *also* to protect the inhabitants of the Republic against the far subtler dangers of the undermining of moral (*sedelike*) and religious values, of state-order (*staatsorder*) and lawful authority.[44]

As a guardian of the *volk* avant-garde and ally of Louw, however, he recognized that other principles were also at stake.

> Secondly, it is my belief that censorship is a double-edged sword if it is not applied with regard for what in Western civilization is considered the most precious possession of the individual and the community: genuine spiritual–intellectual (*geestelike*) freedom. Seen in this way our task is a national calling in the broadest sense of the word. (2)

Carrying out this task was, he felt, achievable even within the draconian terms of the Act. Working from the premiss that their primary challenge was to negotiate the literature–pornography divide—always the main concern for the *volk* avant-garde—he noted that section 6 of the Act made a 'clear distinction' between the 'tendency and the (declared) aim of a publication' and stated that any assessment of the shock value of a work had to consider its effect on the 'likely reader' (2–3). This was a largely wishful interpretation, which went against both the letter and the spirit of the law by privileging questions of intentionality (and so, indirectly, literariness) and readership. Yet, Dekker insisted, interpretation was precisely their prerogative and the key to their 'national calling'. If 'we proceed calmly, conscientiously and with integrity', he suggested, 'we can be more than a merely negative factor in our national intellectual life (*nasionale geesteslewe*), we can be a positive, constructive force' (3). While this betrayed Dekker's clear priorities as a guardian of the *volk* avant-garde, it also reflected the extent to which he underestimated the pitfalls ahead. As it turned out, the Board's commitment to 'intellectual freedom' was as compromised and fragile as its consensus about what counted as 'literature'.

The Dekker Years

Dekker's five-year term of office from November 1963 to October 1968 was disappointing from the government's point of view, even though the new Board proved to be reasonably effective as a protector of its political vision and highly politicized idea of public morals. In 1965, to take a fairly typical year, around 44 per cent of the 702 publications banned were declared undesirable for broadly moral reasons, whereas 30 per cent were explicitly political; the reasoning behind the remaining 26 per cent, though unlikely to have been overtly political, was less obvious.[45] The trouble was that this grand total, which worked out as an average of just under sixty bannings a month, the highest the Dekker Board ever attained, represented a significant reduction on the rates achieved by the previous censorship regime, which covered imported publications only. The censorship of films remained more or less unchanged. From 1956 to 1963 the old Board banned over 8,500 publications, an average of ninety a month. This dramatic reduction, which fell to a low of 35 per month (total 426) in 1968, did not reflect any particular leniency on the new Board's part. As an internal memorandum reviewing its first three years explained, the problem lay primarily with the surveillance systems, which were proving far less effective than expected.

The overwhelming majority of publications came from customs, though even their submissions were down, and from reputable publishers and booksellers like Oxford University Press and the Central News Agency (CNA), South Africa's leading commercial bookseller at the time. More dubious firms like Petrinovic & Co. and Maurice Flax, who published 'offensive' paperbacks and who had previously submitted books on a regular basis, were now sending in little or nothing, the memorandum noted, and the police appeared to have 'neither the will nor the knowledge' to offer any assistance.[46] Even the general public, whose interests the Act was allegedly supposed to be serving, appeared unconcerned. After three years direct submissions from them had still not reached double figures. This trend was already evident to Dekker after a year in office, when, in an effort to improve the rate of submissions, he employed a full-time travelling 'publications inspector' to assist the Post Office and customs by checking on booksellers and newsagents around the country. This attempt to introduce more active forms of surveillance did little to help, however, not least because the inspector (J. J. Blom, a former assistant editor of *Huisgenoot*) had no real powers and rarely made any great discoveries. The position, the memorandum concluded, was 'in one word unsustainable and the consequences for our country and volk fatal' (2). Though the government tried to improve the Board's effectiveness over the years (after 1967 efforts were made to involve the police and customs more directly, including giving them formal powers of seizure on the Board's behalf), these various shortcomings eventually contributed to the radical overhaul of the legislation in 1974.

41

The Dekker Board soon ran into difficulties in its role as a guardian of literature as well. In theory, it was committed to an absolute principle: 'if it was literature', Merwe Scholtz said in an interview, 'it was through'.[47] In practice, the protection the censors offered was unsurprisingly neither consistent nor politically or culturally neutral. Their decisions were also very different depending on the language in which a particular book was written. Since no literary titles in any one of the nine African languages and only a handful in Afrikaans were submitted in this period, a pattern that remained broadly unchanged throughout the apartheid era, the overwhelming majority of those they scrutinized were in English. Of the Afrikaans works all were by the younger generation of writers of the 1960s, who went by the collective name of the Sestigers (literally 'Writers of the Sixties'). This was the group who, according to the blurb on Brink's first major English novel, *Looking on Darkness* (1974), 'deliberately challenged the local tradition of petty realism and helped break down the current taboos on sex, religion and related subjects, exploring the possibilities of fiction in a highly experimental way'.[48] Unlike the English titles, which came through customs, the Sestiger works were typically the subject of a formal complaint from conservative Afrikaner cultural groups, the NGK, or offended individuals acting under their influence. These complaints were often made months after publication and usually after heated debates among reviewers in the press. The exception was Breyten Breytenbach's debut collection of poems, *Die Ysterkoei moet sweet* (The Ironcow Must Sweat, 1964), a part of which was, rather unusually, submitted in typescript prior to publication by Bartho Smit, the Sestiger writer who was then also the beleaguered literary editor for Afrikaanse Pers-Boekhandel (APB), one of the major literary imprints of the period. Smit, no doubt under pressure from APB executives, was worried about the second line in the poem entitled 'breyten prays for himself'. After the first invocatory line, 'That Pain exists is unnecessary God', the typescript version adds parenthetically '(That God exists is also unnecessary)' (BCS 841/64).

In their correspondence with Smit, the censors pointed out that they had no powers over books before publication, but they offered to give him a provisional opinion on condition that he send them the complete proofs. This only added further complications. While Harvey and Murray thought the collection should be let through without cuts, on literary and liberal grounds, the majority had serious reservations not so much about the one line that concerned the publishers as about a series of other poems, including 'Holy Communion', 'Black Death 1348', and 'White Death 1960'. In the end, the impasse was resolved only when Smit retracted the proofs, which the publishers then expurgated themselves, following the Board's advice. They dropped the offending line Smit was initially most worried about, as well as 'Black Death', an irreligious poem about the medieval plague, and its companion, 'White Death', which, as Dekker put it, 'depicted the spiritual plague of our time in South Africa—tyranny and torture, once again with calls to God and thoughts about Holy Communion'. Though most of these poems resurfaced in subsequent editions of Breytenbach's work, it seems this one disappeared from the canon altogether, as did the second line from 'breyten prays for himself'. Much to Dekker's relief no one lodged any complaints about the expurgated version, which went on to win a major Afrikaans literary prize, adjudicated by, among others, van Wyk Louw and another leading poet of the *volk* avant-garde, D. J. Opperman.[d]

As this non-decision made clear, the censors did not always consider literary merit, or indeed literariness, to be a trumping value. By contrast, when formal complaints were made against other Sestiger works—three novels by André Brink, *Lobola vir die Lewe* (Lobola for Life, 1963), *Die Ambassadeur* (The Ambassador, 1964), and *Miskien Nooit* (Maybe Never, 1967); and two by the more established Etienne Leroux, *Sewe dae by die Silbersteins* (Seven Days at the Silbersteins, 1962) and *Die Derde Oog* (The Third Eye, 1966)—they generally followed the approach Dekker outlined in his inaugural speech, which presupposed that literariness could in fact be a sufficient defence. They passed all five novels, usually unanimously, not just because they were literature but because, in their view, they contributed to the evolving tradition of the *volk* avant-garde. Brink's *Lobola*, for instance, which signalled an experimental turn in Afrikaans fiction, was a 'sign of renewal in our prose-arts (*prosakuns*)', Dekker noted, echoing van Wyk Louw's influential assessment of the new generation of novelists in the early 1960s (BCS 377/64). In the case of the third novel in Leroux's Silberstein trilogy, *Die Derde Oog*, Dekker's cultural assumptions were even clearer. Banning it would, he argued, do great damage to 'our literature and the intellectual life of our volk' (BCS 130/66). This kind of thinking, coupled with an emphasis on the questions of readership, ran through all their deliberations in defence of the Sestigers, reflecting a degree of consensus about their status as an emergent *volk* avant-garde and, therefore, about the grounds on which they had to be protected in what the censors, not the clerics, took to be the interests of the *volk*. As the secretary of the NGK's Synodal Commission for Public Morals put it in his letter about Brink's *Lobola*, the Church sought to have these works banned because of their 'morally deleterious and polluting character'.

The exception was Brink's third major novel, *Miskien Nooit*, which, in Dekker's view, represented the 'most difficult case the Board has yet come up against' (BCS 52/68). Unlike Breytenbach's collection, which tested the censors' commitment to the literary defence per se, Brink's novel, which had already divided opinion in the Afrikaner literary world, threatened their consensus about what counted as a serious contribution to the *volk* avant-garde. The complaint, which was lodged on 2 February 1968 (almost a year after publication), once again by the NGK's Synodal Commission, centred on the novel's sexual explicitness, its profanity, and the promiscuity of its divorced male anti-hero, who, in keeping with its narrative experimentalism, is called André. The NGK was particularly exercised by the novel's self-consciously ironized use of sex to attract publicity and by the fact that it might be prescribed for schools and universities. After a three-month process of deliberation, which unusually involved the entire Board, the vote was evenly split: Merwe Scholtz, Murray, Endemann, van Wyk, and Le Roux were for banning; Grové, Cloete, Harvey, Theron, and Sutton were against. The latter were happy to follow the usual line in putting the positive case, but for Merwe Scholtz, who put the negative case most emphatically, this was precisely the problem. In his view, *Miskien Nooit*, unlike *Lobola*, could not be defended 'in the name of literature'. It was at best 'easy reading of doubtful quality', at worst 'fake merchandise'. Relegating the novel to the realms of the merely popular was his least credible line of attack. His principal objection was directed against Brink himself. Far from affirming the novel's artful literariness, all the postmodern game-playing—the ironized narration, the use of film scenarios to raise questions about the 'real', the autobiographical instability, etc.—only served to put Brink's own artistic cred-ibility in doubt. It showed that he was 'essentially indifferent to bona fide literature' and to the high seriousness of the *volk* avant-garde because he was willing to let it 'go to the wall' in such a 'flippant manner'. To protect 'a part of the reading public' and 'our literature', and indeed the future reputation of the Board, the novel 'had to be put in its place', Merwe Scholtz concluded. In taking this position, he questioned not only Brink's credibility, but, by implication, the integrity of his publisher, Human & Rousseau, and that of their literary editor D. J. Opperman, whose measured endorsement of the novel was included on the inside front flap of the first edition. Opperman is quoted as saying 'the affecting minor key (*mineur-klank*) of the book is especially compelling'.[49]

Faced with this impasse, it fell to Dekker, who, like Cloete, had taught Brink at the University of Potchefstroom in the 1950s, to cast the deciding vote and to sum up the Board's own position, which he did in a detailed ten-page report. Though he did not think the novel could be dismissed as populist 'easy reading', he accepted that the literary arguments in its favour were weak. In his view, it was not just that it lacked the 'unified conception' required of a genuine literary work. Torn between an 'amoral glorification of sexual freedom' and 'boundless sentimentalism' about 'the transience of things', it was caught in a 'destructive dualism'. Moreover, he agreed with Merwe Scholtz that its experimentalism, which he noted was borrowed from 'overseas writers', only served to underline its shallowness and put Brink's own standing at risk. 'We have before us the pathetic spectacle of an author squandering his unmistakable talent and styl-istic gifts on a playfully contrived, extremely sophisticated novel without the driving force and therefore also without the deeper synthesis of a serious life-study.' It was, at best, a 'thesis-novel' intended to assert the 'the right the artist has to describe passion'.

For Dekker, however, the moral case against it was equally feeble. Despite its thesis and lack of unity, its overall 'tendency' was not pornographic, and it would not have a 'damaging effect' on the 'sophisticated reader for whom it is intended'. Even André's recollections of his 'intimate relations with coloured (Asian, West Indian) women', which the Synodal Commission did not mention in its complaint, were acceptable, in Dekker's view, because they occurred abroad (the novel is set in Paris) and so did not amount to a 'direct argument for racial mixing in our country'. Finally, far from being blasphemous, the biblical references were a 'flippant demonstration' of the writer's 'right freely to incorporate well-known words' into his own text and to question the 'spirit of the Word'. It was, Dekker concluded, undoubtedly a test case, perhaps even a consciously contrived one, but for all his reservations he finally decided it did not warrant banning because it would not offend its likely readers. With this decision—his last relating to an Afrikaans work—Dekker managed by the finest of margins to preserve the Board's public record as a guardian of the *volk* avant-garde. It is worth noting, by way of contrast, that it regularly banned the new generation of controversial American authors including William Burroughs, Jack Kerouac, Norman Mailer, and Henry Miller.

Because of this, and because Dekker insisted that their deliberations had to be kept confidential, the internal tensions over the Sestigers remained hidden. When it came to works identified as belonging to the growing canon of South African literatures in English, however, they were more visible. Of the forty-one titles the censors appear to have examined in this category, it banned twenty-four (almost 60 per cent). Once again, their commitment to the literary defence per se was erratic. In some cases, particularly when it came to novels by black writers dealing with political themes and set in contemporary South Africa, they simply ignored the issue altogether. Grové's report recommending the banning of the exiled Peter Abrahams's *A Night on their Own* (1965), for instance, which the Board endorsed, made no mention of its literary qualities. Though Grové noted some problematic 'sex episodes', especially those involving 'mixing', he focused on the 'whole spirit' of the book, which was 'contemptuous of the government and its policy, [and] of the police' (BCS 59/65). By contrast, the censors recognized the literary merits of *Wild Conquest* (1950), Abrahams's historical novel about slavery in South Africa in the early nineteenth century, and *This Island Now* (1966), his critical account of post-colonial politics set on a fictional Caribbean island, and passed them in part because they had no direct bearing on contemporary South Africa.[50]

In other cases, notably Nadine Gordimer's *The Late Bourgeois World* (1966) and the 1960 reprint of Jack Cope's *The Fair House* (1955), they took the literary defence seriously, but were ultimately swayed by extra-literary anxieties. They considered both novels to be politically incendiary—the first has a contemporary South African setting, the second is historical—but they chose to

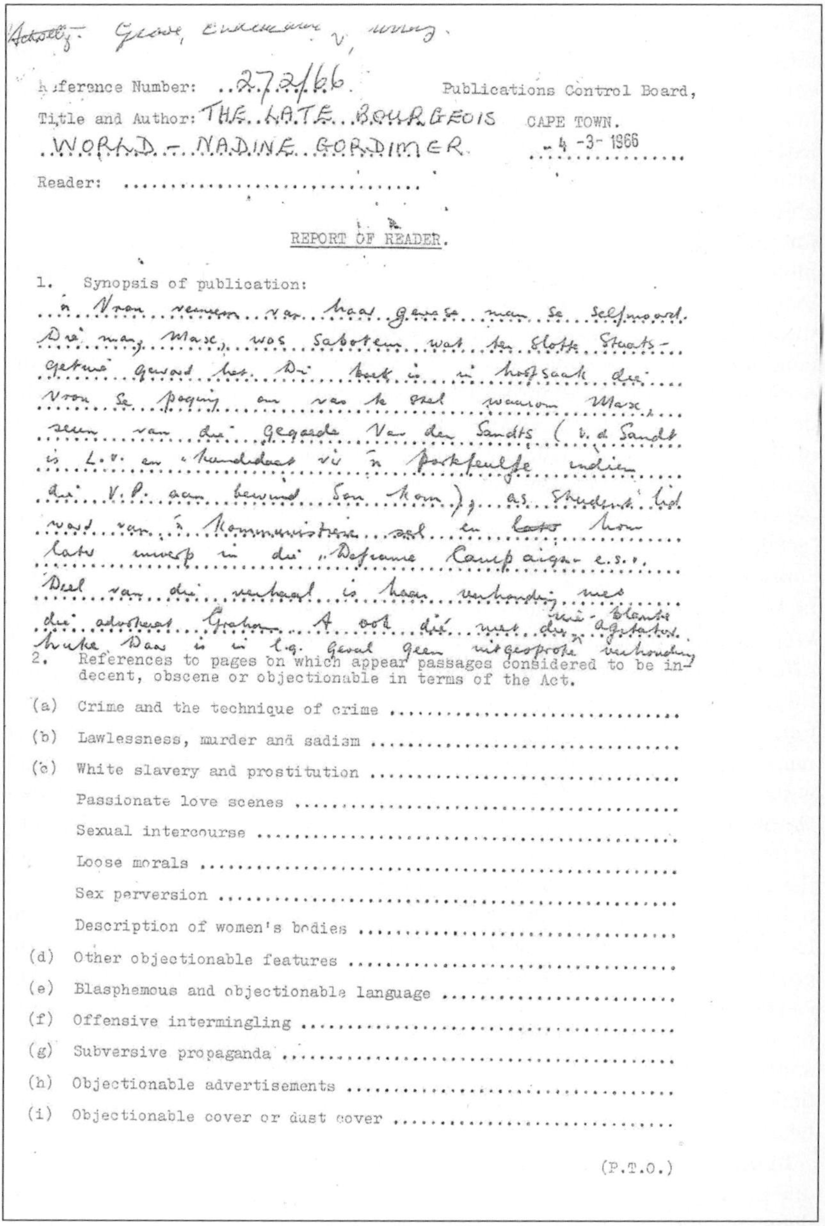

[Handwritten annotations and form text:]

Reference Number: 27.2/66. Publications Control Board,

Title and Author: THE LATE BOURGEOIS CAPE TOWN.

WORLD - NADINE GORDIMER - 4 -3- 1966

Reader: ....

REPORT OF READER.

1. Synopsis of publication:

[Handwritten synopsis in Afrikaans, largely illegible]

2. References to pages on which appear passages considered to be indecent, obscene or objectionable in terms of the Act.

(a) Crime and the technique of crime ....

(b) Lawlessness, murder and sadism ....

(c) White slavery and prostitution ....

Passionate love scenes ....

Sexual intercourse ....

Loose morals ....

Sex perversion ....

Description of women's bodies ....

(d) Other objectionable features ....

(e) Blasphemous and objectionable language ....

(f) Offensive intermingling ....

(g) Subversive propaganda ....

(h) Objectionable advertisements ....

(i) Objectionable cover or dust cover ....

(P.T.O.)

FIG. 1.1. An example of the report form the censors used in the 1960s and early 1970s. This one documents the Dekker Board's decision to ban Nadine Gordimer's *The Late Bourgeois World* (1966).

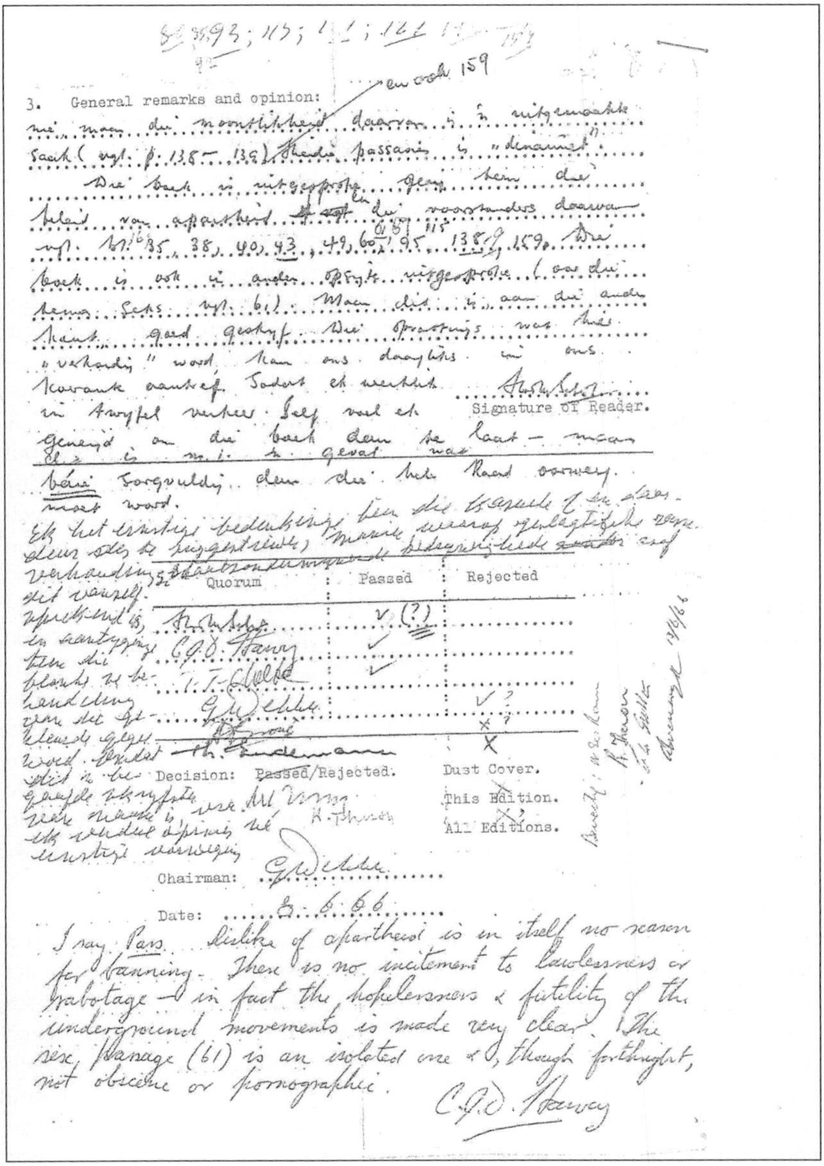
3. General remarks and opinion:

nie, maar die moontlikheid daarvan is 'n uitgemaakte saak (vgl. p. 138–139). Sulke passasies is "dinamiet".

Die boek is uitgesproke gekant teen die beleid van apartheid en die voorstanders daarvan vgl. bl. 16, 35, 38, 40, 43, 49, 60, 87, 95, 115, 138/9, 159. Die boek is ook in ander opsigte uitgesproke (oor die tema seks vgl. 61). Maar dit is aan die ander kant goed geskryf. Die opvattings wat hier "verkondig" word kan ons daagliks in ons koerant aantref. Sodat ek werklik in twyfel verkeer. Self voel ek geneig om die boek deur te laat — maar dit is m.i. 'n geval wat baie sorgvuldig deur die hele Raad oorweeg moet word.

Signature of Reader.

Quorum	Passed	Rejected
[illegible]	✓ (?)	
C.J.D. Harvey	✓	
[illegible]	✓	
[illegible]		✓ ?
[illegible]		× ?
[illegible]		×

Decision: ~~Passed~~/Rejected.

Dust Cover.

This Edition.

All Editions.

Chairman:

Date: 8.6.66

I say Pass. Dislike of apartheid is in itself no reason for banning. There is no incitement to lawlessness or sabotage — in fact the hopelessness & futility of the underground movements is made very clear. The sex passage (61) is an isolated one & though forthright, not obscene or pornographic. C.J.D. Harvey

FIG. 1.1. (*continued*)

exercise their power to limit their potential effects in opposite ways by banning the first and passing the second (see Chapter 4). They decided that to ban the paperback reprint of Cope's debut novel, twelve years after the hardback edition had appeared, would give it unwarranted publicity, increasing its likely reader-ship and potential for incitement, particularly among black readers. They claimed that the novel, which Dekker compared to Robert Ruark's *Uhuru* (1962), banned in 1966, gave a provocative and distorted account of the brutal suppression by the British of the 1906 poll tax ('Bambatha') rebellion in Natal, a key episode in the history of Zulu resistance to colonial rule.

The censors' inconsistent commitment to the literary defence was further complicated in the case of works in English by legal confusions surrounding their position on 'banned' or 'listed' writers. This had particularly serious implications when a host of writers, including Ronald Segal, Mazisi Kunene, Todd Matshikiza, Bloke Modisane, Es'kia Mphahlele, and Lewis Nkosi were 'listed' under the amended Suppression of Communism Act in April 1966, but the question had already been raised for the censors a year earlier. They initially decided, after taking legal advice, that they had no choice but to ban any such works, giving priority not only to the other censorship laws but to the question of authorship as such. Not surprisingly, this decision had disastrous conse-quences when it came to anthologies. It led directly to the suppression of Jacob Drachler's *African Heritage* (1963), Shore and Shore-Bos's *Come Back, Africa!* (1968), Lionel Abrahams and Gordimer's *South African Writing Today* (1967), and Richard Rive's *Quartet: New Voices from South Africa* (1963). As Alex La Guma (banned in 1962) was among the figures singled out in the last two collections, it is safe to assume that his second novel, *And a Threefold Cord* (1964), for which no report appears to have survived, was banned for the same reason. By contrast, the censors thought they did not need to make a decision about Ruth First's *One Hundred and Seventeen Days* (1965), her account of her own detention in 1963, because it was already covered by her banning order.[e]

The lack of clarity was a source of contention, however, and in some cases, particularly with Lewis Nkosi's collection of essays *Home and Exile* (1965) and Albie Sachs's *Jail Diary* (1966), the censors felt they were being forced to act against their own better judgement. About *The Jail Diary of Albie Sachs*, which had been secretly submitted by the police in March 1967, Murray commented anxiously and, it is hard not to say, presciently: 'in the future someone might make a study of books banned by the Board . . . and then accuse [it] of banning a work *merely on political grounds*' (BCS 25/67). After this a special meeting was convened to discuss the matter, and, in September 1967, a change of policy was introduced. From then on the Board would make its own ruling on a case-by-case basis, and if it decided not to ban a particular title by a listed person, it would simply inform the applicant and note that, despite this, they would still have to apply for permission from the Minister of Justice before distributing it.

Though this policy would change again in the years ahead, it had a direct bearing on the decision to pass Es'kia Mphahlele's first autobiography, *Down Second Avenue* (1959), which was submitted in July 1967, once again by the police (see Chapter 5).

These disputes over jurisdiction further complicated the censors' already erratic commitment to the literary defence, but, as we have seen in the case of the Sestigers, these were not the only quandaries they faced as supposed guardians of the literary. Indeed, when it came to works in English, their adherence to an awkward and variable admixture of assumptions about the nature and function of literature proved at least as influential as any other factor. Overtly political works, novels especially, were often banned not just because they violated the norms encoded in the Act, or condemned apartheid, but because they were deemed not to warrant the protective honorific 'Literature'. As the decision regarding Des Troye's *An Act of Immorality* (1963) suggests, this was not simply a matter of merit. Written by a 'Johannesburg Attorney' and billed as a 'startling exposé', this was the first locally produced literary work to be banned under the new legislation. It was sent in by the police acting on a tip-off from the wife of one of their detectives, who had bought a copy at her local bookseller.[51] Part psychological thriller, part fictionalized reportage, it tells the story of Johannes Burger, a catastrophically self-destructive 'public prosecutor' who, as the blurb puts it, 'prosecutes offenders under the Immorality Act' by day and 'under neurotic compulsion' breaks it by night. For Dekker, it was not only a 'highly undesirable publication' without any 'artistic value' (BCS 163/63). It could not be defended as literature because it violated the norms of fictionality and the humanistic ideals of disinterestedness. The writer was so 'outspoken' that he 'repeatedly tears off the mask of the novel form and inserts parliamentary debates and newspaper reports and sometimes appears himself with his "message" of a slashing attack on the Immorality Act and apartheid'.

In other cases, where the work's literary merits were more secure, the censors were simply capricious. Another novel sent in by the police, Richard Rive's *Emergency* (1964), a more carefully structured third-person political *Bildungsroman*, was an especially telling case. Like *An Act of Immorality*, it carried the self-protective disclaimer 'All the characters in this book are entirely fictitious', but it also included a series of prefaces testifying to its historical accuracy and explaining its precise setting in Cape Town during the immediate aftermath of the Sharpeville and Langa atrocities.[52] It belonged, as Dekker commented, to the genre of the 'topical novel' (*aktualiteitsroman*) (BCS 1084/64). Though Murray, the primary reader, thought it gave 'an exaggerated view of the "unrest"', he felt it satisfied the humanistic criteria because it did not 'go to extremes' or 'propagandize a doctrine'. Despite this, it had to be banned, he argued, because it portrayed 'promiscuous relations between the Coloured man [the central figure, Andrew Dreyer] and the white student [Ruth Talbot]'. Dekker agreed with

49

FIG. 1.2. The front cover of Des Troye's *An Act of Immorality* (1963), the first locally produced literary work to be banned under the new Publications Act.

Murray's literary judgement, but anxious about a possible appeal—he noted that the novel was dedicated to the leading Sestiger Jan Rabie and his wife, Marjorie Wallace—he questioned ('rhetorically', as he put it) the legal basis for Murray's recommendation because he could not see where the Act specifically outlawed interracial sex. In his reply, Murray insisted that the articles covering obscenity and public morals applied and, following the logic of Merwe Scholtz's dismissal of *Miskien Nooit*, now added that the novel was not worth protecting because it was just 'popular stuff'. In this case, Dekker and the Board concurred.

Specifically literary norms also informed the censors' hostility to mass-market genre fiction. In their view, neither Stuart Cloete, who came to prominence in the late 1930s, nor newcomers like Wilbur Smith and John Gordon Davis belonged to 'Literature'. This categorical judgement had a direct effect on their ruling against Smith's debut novel, *When the Lion Feeds* (1964), a decision which led to the first major court appeal under the new Act. Starting from the premiss that it was 'not strictly a work of literature'—'it is a historical novel which is really a thriller'—Harvey, the primary reader, felt free to ignore questions of aesthetic unity or overall tendency (BCS 649/64). In his view, which Dekker endorsed, the 'intention and effect' of individual scenes of sex and violence was sufficiently offensive to justify a ban on the grounds of obscenity and blasphemy. Heinemann, Smith's British publisher, then took the case to the Supreme Court, where the appeal was rejected for legal rather than literary reasons. After the trial, in a gesture characteristic of the tensions between the censors and the judiciary and within the judiciary itself, Justice F. H. L. Rumpff, the liberal judge who wrote a dissenting opinion in the case, ensured that all the supposedly obscene parts of the novel were quoted at length in an article about the trial published in South Africa's most popular Sunday newspaper, thereby giving them a far wider circulation than they would ever have had in book form.[53]

When Collins, Stuart Cloete's British publisher, submitted his best-selling debut, *Turning Wheels* (1937), for review in 1967 (the novel, which had caused outrage in the Afrikaner press when it first appeared, was first banned in 1937 under customs legislation), the censors were influenced less by their general hostility to the mass-market colonial adventure genre than by specific questions about its modes of characterization.[54] Though the novel, which was one of the first in English to depict the Great Trek, a founding episode in Afrikaner nationalist mythology, featured numerous rather mild sexual escapades, including adulterous miscegenation, the censors agreed that it was neither obscene nor harmful to public morals. It was, however, a blasphemous ridicule against Afrikaners (i.e. 5 (2) (b), (c), and (d) applied). For some, like Merwe Scholtz, the mere fact that it depicted the nineteenth-century Afrikaner trekkers as violent, pious, and promiscuous was enough; for others, including Dekker, its undesirability was a consequence of its shortcomings at the level of characterization. That it did not 'idealize' the Voortrekkers was not a problem per se,

Dekker noted (BCS 217/67). The more 'serious objection' was that it 'carica-tured' them and that this 'formed the essence, almost the whole content of the book'. It had to remain banned, in other words, not simply because it was an unflattering exercise in fictionalized history but because it lacked complexity and psychological depth. Significantly, as with *When the Lion Feeds*, the cen-sors' literary judgements proved more decisive in this case than any concerns they had about the effects the novel might have on a mass readership.

The Kruger Years I

Sometimes acting like a bad lower court, sometimes like an autonomous body, the Dekker Board introduced a permanent looseness into the system, which had a lasting impact on apartheid censorship. By adopting the literary defence at all, however erratically and inconsistently, it created a disjunction between the day-to-day practice of censorship and the actual legislation that was never fully eradicated. If this made Dekker and his colleagues seem oddly miscast for their role as censorious bureaucrats or hateful guardians of the law, it also undermined their own self-understanding as high-minded guardians of the literary, revealing the long-term consequences of van Wyk Louw's 'fatal com-promise'. Their actual role, which took shape almost unwittingly through the cumulative effect of their individual decisions, was to be the government's elite literature police, who served the regime by deciding what counted as literature, and warranted protection as such, and what did not. Despite various legislative and bureaucratic changes, this is what many of the more prominent censors remained throughout the apartheid era.

In most others respects, however, Dekker's period of office constituted a unique, rather than foundational, phase in the longer history of apartheid censorship. This was partly because relatively few publications were suppressed during his tenure. By contrast, during the controversial chairmanship of his successor, J. J. (Jannie) Kruger (1908–76), both the submission and suppression rates for books and periodicals of all kinds increased steadily. By this stage the government had also stepped up its surveillance operations and improved the coordination among the police, customs, and the censors. At its peak in 1973 the Kruger Board banned 889 (72 per cent) out of 1,230 publications submitted; whereas, in 1968, Dekker's final year, the censors banned 426 out of 798 (53 per cent).[55] This upward trend would continue throughout the 1970s under the new legislation. Seen in a longer time-frame, the Dekker era also stands out as the high point in the awkward rapprochement between the government and the *volk* avant-garde.

Since Kruger pointedly lacked Dekker's *volk* avant-garde credentials, his ap-pointment was itself a sign of things to come. Though he had made something of a name for himself as a literary reviewer in the 1930s, he was best known as a political journalist, especially as the former editor of the ultra-nationalist Afrikaans newspaper *Die Transvaler* (he took over as editor from H. F. Verwoerd in 1949) and as a cultural adviser to, and European representative of, the government broadcasting service (the SABC). He was also known as an especially crude defender of the self-enclosed cultural purism van Wyk Louw decried. In his 1972 article praising Louw's outward-looking and experimentalist idea of culture, Adam Small referred to Kruger as a representative of the dominant mode of thinking, citing his belief in the shibboleth of the 'true Afrikaner'.[56]

Yet Kruger's appointment did not bring about an abrupt change in the system. He inherited Dekker's Board in the first instance and continued to recruit key figures from the academic world who were sympathetic to the government. In 1969 J. M. Leighton, a professor of English at the Rand Afrikaans University, replaced Harvey; and then, during Kruger's first major reshuffle in early 1971, Merwe Scholtz, Cloete, and Grové, who stayed on as part-time members, were joined by G. S. Nienaber, professor of Afrikaans at the University of Natal. At the same time, R. E. Lighton, a minor novelist and retired professor of education at the University of Cape Town, joined as a full-time member. The rest of the initial Kruger Board comprised Murray, who became a full-time member, Mrs Theron, and the new vice-chairman, A. J. van Niekerk, a former civil servant. Another key part-time appointment at this time was J. P. Jansen, a professor of African politics at the University of Stellenbosch, who had a special interest in communism and Black Consciousness. Yet, if Kruger followed the pattern of appointments Dekker established, the contrast between their two periods of office could not have been greater. Some of this can be attributed to their very different personal styles and cultural assumptions. Kruger, who rapidly earned a reputation as an autocratic buffoon, was ridiculed in the Afrikaans and English press in a way Dekker had never been. It was also, however, an effect of broader historical developments that distinguished the 1960s from the 1970s, which saw a general hardening of attitudes on the part of the government and the emergence of new forms of cultural and political resistance.

Despite this, the censors' impact on works identified as belonging to South African literature appears, when seen in purely quantitative terms, to have been only slightly worse under Kruger. Though the archival record for the period 1969 to early 1975 is extremely patchy—almost no reports from these years seem to have survived—it is clear that the censors examined at least fifty-four literary titles during this time and banned around thirty-two of them (i.e. just under 60 per cent, a 10 per cent increase on the Dekker years). While they continued their largely moral campaign against mass-market writers like Stuart Cloete, Wilbur Smith, and John Gordon Davis, their principal targets remained politically challenging fictional works in English. Mary Benson, Myrna Blumberg, Jack Cope, C. J. Driver, Alex La Guma, Es'kia Mphahlele, and Tom Sharpe—all had novels or short-story collections banned, no doubt largely for political reasons, in the Kruger years. In this period, the censors also broke new ground by openly suppressing poetry for the first time. Though they passed a number of key works associated with the emergent Black Consciousness movement—notably Mongane Serote's debut, *Yakhal'inkomo* (The Cry of the Cattle, 1972), and its successor, *Tsetlo* (1974), as well as the anthology *To Whom It May Concern* (1974)—they banned James Matthews's seemingly more confrontational, and supposedly less literary, early collections *Cry Rage!* (1972) and *Black Voices Shout!* (1974) (see Chapter 7).

In 1974 the censors also finally broke the pact regarding Afrikaans literature by banning André Brink's fourth novel, *Kennis van die Aand* (1973), and his own English translation, *Looking on Darkness* (1974). Though the original censors' reports on the Afrikaans edition appear not to have survived, there is little doubt that this decision had at least as much to do with Brink's own change of direction as with the altered balance of power among the censors and, more particularly, with the new official hostility to 'committed literature', which the censor–poet T. T. Cloete did much to effect in the early 1970s. As an influential literary figure in the Broederbond, Cloete wrote a study for circulation among his fellow members entitled 'Protest Literature among the Writers of the Sixties and Seventies', in which he set out a political case against Brink and Breytenbach based on the high-minded aestheticist ideals of the *volk* avant-garde. As Galloway observes, this 'study-piece, which was so against the "politicisation of literature", was itself an ideological instrument confirming Afrikaner hegemony and part of a wider strategy intended to close down "dissidence" in the sixties and seventies'.[57] Cloete, who defended the censors' decision in the subsequent *Kennis* trial, also played a leading role in the suppression of Breytenbach's eighth volume of poetry, *Skryt* (1972), under the new system in 1975 (see Chapter 6). It is no doubt not a coincidence that he turned the phrase 'committed literature', which had a wide currency as a disparaging put-down in conservative Afrikaner literary circles at the time, into a tool for repressing the new, more radical forms of internal dissent soon after van Wyk Louw died in 1970. Despite his own aestheticist assumptions, it is unlikely that Louw would have supported such a move, particularly in so far as it served to strengthen the censors' powers. Tellingly, Louw's long-standing ally within the *volk* avant-garde the poet D. J. Opperman, who was always implacably opposed to censorship, was among Brink's defenders at the trial.

Though *Kennis* continued Brink's existentialist-inspired critique of puritanical *volk* values, it also reflected his post-1968 move towards his own experimentalist version of a Sartrean *littérature engagée*. For the first time, following the lead of the more established Sestiger Jan Rabie, whose innovative *Bolandia* series raised new questions about Afrikaner history and identity in the 1960s, he looked beyond the confines of the white, predominantly Afrikaner, world—Josef Malan, the first-person narrator, is 'Coloured'—and confronted the racism of apartheid

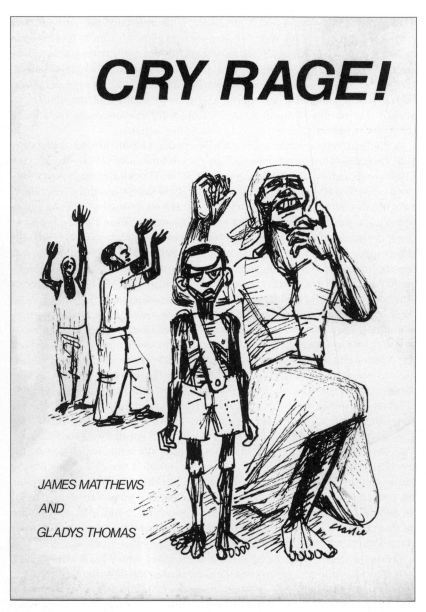

FIG. 1.3. The front cover of James Matthews and Gladys Thomas's *Cry Rage!* (1972), the first volume of poetry banned under the Publications Act, 1963. The cover illustrations were by Matthews's long-time collaborator the celebrated artist Peter Clarke.

head-on by addressing the violent history, beginning with the rape of slave women, endured by South Africa's mixed-race peoples.[58] It was, to this extent, a more 'committed' novel, along the lines Sartre set out in *Qu'est-ce que la littérature?*, though it did not conform to, or idealize, the associated Sartrean aesthetic. Josef Malan, who leads a theatre company dedicated to staging consciousness-raising protest plays that fall foul of the security police and the censors, is primarily an admirer of Antonin Artaud (1896–1948), the founder of the Theatre of Cruelty, not exactly Sartre's idea of a committed writer.

In the first Afrikaans edition, Brink also included a self-protective prefatory note emphasizing that his novel is not straightforwardly realist. Though the 'climate and history and circumstances out of which this story come might look like a recognizable reality, in the new context of the novel everything is fictional', he insisted. This applied to all the 'characters' as well, including 'officials, police etc.'. This did not mean that it was wholly disengaged from history, however, since, despite his indebtedness to the French *nouveau roman*, and his own self-conscious narrative experimentalism (the novel disrupts chronology, mixes 'literary' and 'non-literary' modes, and has Josef narrate his life story, and longer genealogy, from death row), Brink's idea of the literary, like Gordimer's, remained in the end fundamentally Aristotelian, albeit in a more historicist mode. 'The discernible surface of reality is never relevant as such,' his note continued, 'only the underlying patterns and relations.'[59] For Brink, in other words, the power of fiction lay not in its capacity to reveal universal truths about the human condition—as Aristotle claimed—but in the distinctively literary ways in which it represented the forces at work in history. Though he reiterated this point in the note for the English-language edition, which made no mention of officials or police, he began this abridged version with the following emphatic statement: 'Nothing in this novel has been invented, and the climate, history and circumstances from which it arises are those of South Africa today.'[60]

As the censors' reasoning indicates—at least in the version spelt out during the trial—they based their case against the novel as much on blasphemy, obscenity, and public morals as on sedition. On the last point, they claimed, the novel threatened the safety of the state and harmed race relations by dealing 'in an improper manner with the abuse of non-whites'.[61] In the Supreme Court hearing, which was held in August 1974—the censors' first literary case since *When the Lion Feeds*—the chief judge agreed that the novel was seditious, rejecting the defence offered by Brink and his allies, who were now permitted to testify. They emphasized the novel's likely readership and status as a work of experimental fiction. Echoing Brink's prefatory note, his principal supporter, the leading poet and senior figure in the *volk* avant-garde D. J. Opperman, argued: 'The function of the art work as mirror is no longer accepted; your likely reader sees a novel as a soap-bubble which offers a spherical vision, curved reflection of reality.'[62] Testifying on behalf of the censors, Cloete and

Grové rejected this argument. As Cloete put it, the 'novel is unusually strong, reality-directed and topical given the present South African situation'.[63] Recalling the terms of his Broederbond paper, he also noted that 'commitment', often with a 'neo-Marxist literary-sociological element', was a 'dominant tendency in contemporary literary theory'.[64] In Justice van Wyk's less high-minded view, Opperman's defence was just an 'excuse' designed to protect a potentially popular novel that attacked the police, whites, and Afrikaners in particular by 'deliberately' presenting a 'false picture of reality under the guise of fiction'. With only 'one or two exceptions', he noted, it depicted white South Africans as 'irresponsible, sadistic, debauched, lawless and unscrupulous'.[65] On the issue of sedition, however, van Wyk was outvoted (two to one) by his co-judges, partly because they defended Brink's right to political protest on liberal grounds. The court finally upheld the censors' decision only because all the judges agreed that the novel was obscene, harmful to public morals, and blasphemous. They were particularly concerned about the portrayal of Josef as a Christ figure, the parodies of the Bible and the Lord's Prayer, and the juxtaposition of sex and religion. When the novel was eventually released by the new Appeal Board in 1982, after an unsuccessful review under the revised legislation in 1976, the blasphemy charge proved to be the greatest obstacle.

The *Kennis* trial had far-reaching consequences not just for Brink, who became the focus of a campaign of harassment by the security police after the ban was imposed. While the British publishers used the controversy *Looking on Darkness* provoked in South Africa to make Brink's name internationally, the banning of *Kennis* divided opinion in the Afrikaner literary world and marked a turning point in the relations between Afrikaans writers and the government. Among other things, it led to the founding of the non-racial Afrikaans Skrywersgilde (Writers' Guild), which, unlike the collaborationist Writers' Circle, took a principled stand against all forms of censorship, and to the formation of the clandestine Afrikaans publishing imprint Taurus (see Chapters 2 and 3). For Brink, the ban also finally exposed the consequences of van Wyk Louw's compromise in the early 1960s and the censors' own collaborationist guardianship. In a sardonic open letter to Kruger, which he addressed with mock affection to 'Dear Uncle Jannie', he asked if 'uncle Merwe, uncle Theuns and uncle Apie'—Merwe Scholtz, Cloete, and Grové—were 'so broad' (i.e. wide-girthed and broad-minded) that they could straddle 'the stools of the literature they promote and the stools of the literature they "condemn"'.[66]

The Kruger Years II

By this stage the government already had its own reasons for wanting to step up its repressive powers. A changing political climate, marked by the rise of Black

Consciousness and black trade unions internally and the resurgence of the anti-colonial struggle in Angola and Mozambique, coincided with a renewed campaign by Afrikaner church groups to impose stricter censorship in the interests of protecting public morals and 'Christian culture in the West'.[67] Though these groups continued to be worried about the *volk* avant-garde, and the new generation of Afrikaans literary dissidents, they were mainly concerned about the fact that the more liberal courts kept on upholding appeals against the censors' decisions to ban popular magazines like *Scope*. The government, now under B. J. Vorster's more pragmatic but always security-conscious premiership, responded to these various pressures by initiating a process of review, beginning with an interdepartmental inquiry in March 1972, which led to a number of minor adjustments in the law. After 1973, for instance, the Minister of the Interior was empowered to ask the censors to review particular decisions. This was quickly superseded by a larger parliamentary inquiry, launched in May 1973, which developed into a full-blown commission. Chaired by J. T. Kruger, then deputy Minister of the Interior, this second censorship commission recommended that the old Act be scrapped, not revised, and proposed a wholly new bureaucratic and partly new legislative system designed to tighten the government's already firm hold on the vestigial public sphere.

The Kruger Commission, as it came to be known, which published its findings in early 1974, produced a very different report to the Cronjé Commission of the 1950s. At a mere seventy pages it was, for one thing, much shorter; for another, it was explicitly party-political. In fact, as the Commission fell out along party lines, it was obliged to produce two reports: the Report proper signed by Kruger and eight other Nationalist MPs (including F. W. de Klerk), and a shorter dissenting 'minority report' signed by the four Commissioners from the United Party, the all but defunct official opposition. Unlike the relatively short-lived multiracial Liberal Party (1953–68), led by the novelist Alan Paton, the white supremacist United Party (1934–77) was never a credible defender of liberal principles.[68] Nonetheless, adopting a broadly liberal position, the minority argued for the abolition of the Board—among other things they recommended the creation of a Publications Advisory Council—and strongly opposed the proposal to remove the right of appeal to the courts. Indeed, having noted the plethora of laws that included some element of censorship—they listed thirteen in all—they insisted that all such decisions should be left to the courts, which were at least subject to due process and open to public scrutiny.[f]

They also rejected the Commission's paranoid rhetoric. In contrast to the Cronjé Report, which had stressed the need to protect white guardianship and Afrikaans literature from the harmful effects of a permissive American mass culture, the Kruger Commission focused on the international communist conspiracy that was, it claimed, responsible for the nation's 'growing superficiality' and the 'weakening of its moral fibre'.[69] Citing *The Naked Communist* (1958) by the former FBI agent W. Cleon Skousen, it noted that breaking down 'cultural standards of morality by promoting pornography and obscenity' (Skousen's words) was part of 'an attempt by communism to subjugate the spirit of the nation' (4). There were also 'authoritative warnings'—here they referenced another American source, John A. Stormer's polemic *The Death of a Nation* (1968)—that the 'youth' were a particular target of this strategy (53). Significantly, this Cold War reformulation of the Cronjé Report's already highly politicized understanding of obscenity and public morals prefigured premier P. W. Botha's fiercely anti-communist 'total onslaught' vision by some five years.

The Commission's rationale for a stricter censorship regime was also unacceptable, according to the minority, because, like the Cronjé Commission, it relied on what were by then widely discredited assumptions about the specifically corrupting influence of pornography. Appealing to the latest US research, they suggested that 'erotic stimuli are not in themselves harmful and that even pornography (obscene erotic stimuli) may be less corruptive and depraving than is widely believed to be the case' (51). Following the new definition of obscenity proposed in the British Longford Report (1972), which was designed to address the flawed 1868 'Hicklin test', they recommended that the emphasis should now be placed on the extent to which a publication, 'taken as a whole', might 'outrage contemporary standards of decency' (52). (Far from supporting an increased liberalization of the law, Lord Longford's unofficial committee proposed this alternative, which echoed the US Supreme Court definitions of the 1960s, so the courts could prosecute pornographers more effectively. It shared Devlin's view that this had to be done to protect public morals.) This did not alter the minority's more principled opposition to government intervention per se, however. Even Longford's new definition raised problems because, they insisted, 'South Africa is a heterogeneous country of many races, creeds, cultures and customs and we cannot accept that the sectional outlook and values of any particular group, however strongly held its views or powerful its influence, should be arbitrarily imposed by law on others' (51).

The government ignored these appeals and endorsed the Commission's stridently anti-liberal and, indeed, anti-literary position. Though the Commissioners heard evidence in defence of literature from various writers' groups, including PEN SA and the Writers' Circle, as well as from Brink, who represented non-affiliated Afrikaans writers, it remained committed to the moralistic communitarian logic that dominated mainstream Afrikaner cultural thinking. 'Even if art should be judged by purely artistic norms,' they insisted 'care must be taken not to absolutise' it at the 'expense of true morality and decency' (5). In fact, seen against the background of the internal battles among Afrikaner elites, the new Act signalled a decisive shift on the government's part. It overturned Verwoerd's earlier concessions to the courts and the *volk* avant-garde and firmly entrenched Nationalist hegemony on the terms favoured by Afrikaner politicians and clerics. At the same time, it established a new censorship bureaucracy that was intended to look more representative and transparent but which had the additional advantage of ensuring that any members of the literary elite who remained within the system could not enjoy the powers they had as members of the old Board.

In the first place, the 1974 Act abolished the Board, replacing it with a Directorate of Publications, an administrative body that would be based in Cape Town. The Directorate's main function was to oversee the work of the more devolved and theoretically more representative censorship committees— the second tier in the new structure—that would make the actual decisions and that could, in principle, be constituted in various metropolitan centres around the country. While publications remained wholly in white hands under the new Act, 'Coloured' and 'Indian' representatives were now permitted to advise the committees on any questions relating to the exhibition of films to their communities. The 'Bantu' were still excluded. This limited inclusiveness, of course, presupposed that racialized communities remained the only bearers of norms worthy of official recognition. While the Act abolished the right of appeal to the courts, in response to pressure from both the Afrikaner churches and the judiciary itself, it attempted to ensure that the third body in the new system, the extra-judicial Publications Appeal Board (PAB), which would sit in Pretoria, appeared more accountable than the old censorship Board. The PAB still operated behind closed doors, but it was required to publish in full the reasons for its decisions and, in accordance with a qualified version of the *audi alterum partem* principle (literally, 'hear the other side'), it was obliged to allow appellants to make some limited representations. They could raise questions during the hearings but not 'give or adduce' their own evidence.[70] In a similarly technocratic spirit of openness, the Directorate was also required to specify, in the lists of banned titles published in the *Government Gazette*, the grounds on which its committees based their decisions.

This veil of transparency did little to disguise the obvious fact that the primary purpose of the new Act was to make the censorship system a more effective instrument of repression. As far as publications were concerned, it empowered the committees to ban the entire output of a particular publisher and publications on any specified subject. It also criminalized the possession, and not just the distribution or printing, of an 'undesirable' publication; gave the Directorate significant powers of seizure; and, following the bad press the censors attracted during the Kruger era, made it an offence to 'insult, disparage or belittle any member of the appeal board'.[71] In ideological terms, the Act was also designedly uncompromising, not least because it reflected the government's new willingness to placate Afrikaner church groups at the expense of the *volk* avant-garde. It included the introductory provision about upholding a 'Christian view of life' and, though it retained the five key absolutist definitions of undesirability in the old Act, it removed section 6, which contained awkward references to the outmoded 'Hicklin test' and to the relativistic likely reader. As the first chair of the new PAB, Judge J. H. Snyman, observed, the legislators had taken cognizance of Lord Longford's new definition of obscenity and extended its application, particularly with a view to excluding the literary elite. The censors were now required to determine what was 'undesirable' in relation to the '*median of standards* in the community' as 'represented by the average decent-minded, law-abiding, modern and enlightened citizen with Christian principles'.[72] The Act underscored this anti-elitist approach by once again granting no special exemption to literature—it was, as Snyman insisted, concerned only with '*reading matter*'—and by making no provision for literary experts per se, thereby closing off the one loophole in the earlier legislation.[73] It stipulated that the members of the committees would be appointed 'by reason of their educational qualifications', which, Snyman commented, meant that the 'approach must be that of the educationist, not of the literary scholar'.[74]

The Pretorius–Snyman Years

The new Publications Act, which was later adopted, almost verbatim, by a number of the pseudo-independent 'Bantustans', beginning with the 'Republic of the Transkei' in 1977, became law in October 1974 and the new bureaucracy was set up in April the following year.[75] This marked the beginning of the most repressive era in the history of the system. Between 1975 and 1980 the rate of submissions increased dramatically, up almost 50 per cent on the average achieved during the Kruger years. More direct intervention by the police played a major part in this. In 1978, the worst year in this initial period, they were responsible for over 50 per cent of the 2,520 submissions, with customs covering a further 32 per cent. By contrast, publishers submitted only 9 per cent of the total and members of the public as little as 5. All in all, in other words, the state and its agents were directly responsible for 86 per cent of the publications that entered the system. Unsurprisingly just over half of these (53 per cent) were deemed to pose a threat to security. Though the total number of banned publications also increased by almost 45 per cent during this period—from an annual average of 846 (1969–74) to 1,222 (1975–80)—the suppression rate remained more or less consistent at just under 60 per cent.[76] The most notable general trend was the steady increase in politically motivated bannings. Between 1975 and 1978 the proportion of publications suppressed under the political clauses in the new Act (47 (2) (c), (d), and (e)) rose from 25 to 44 per cent of the total. In addition, over 70 per cent of the publications banned for possession were political (the peak was 448 in 1978).[77] Though the political significance of these increases is obvious, it should be recalled that, from the government's point of view, censorship on moral or religious grounds was also intended to shore up apartheid.

The new Directorate included some members of the Kruger Board—Lighton, for instance, became deputy director and, until his death in 1976, Kruger served as an assistant director—but the directorship itself went to J. L. Pretorius, a former parliamentary legal officer who had helped draft the new legislation. Less powerful than the chair of the old Board, the director and his staff none-theless had a considerable influence over the censorship process. He selected which censors wrote the initial reports on particular works, which committees made the decisions, and, if he had any concerns about the outcome, he was empowered to ask the PAB to consider the case again. The chair of the new PAB was also a political appointment, even though the selection was technically handled by the State President, rather than the government. His responsibility was to hear appeals, which could be initiated by authors and publishers as well as the Directorate itself, and to convene the PAB, which was required to have at least three members, selected principally from a list approved by the State President. During this initial period, its key members included A. P. Grové and J. C. W. van Rooyen, a young professor of criminal law at the University of Pretoria who would succeed Snyman as chair and become a key reformer in the 1980s. As the 1976 appeal relating to Cope's *The Dawn Comes Twice* revealed, however, van Rooyen began his tenure on the PAB endorsing Snyman's firmly anti-literary interpretation of the new legislation.

Despite the considerable powers accorded to the Directorate and the PAB, which make it possible to call this initial phase the Pretorius–Snyman era, the day-to-day decisions under the new system were the responsibility of the ad hoc committees that were constituted from an approved list of between 100 and 250 censors. In theory, this larger, more dispersed decision-making structure was meant to overcome the over-centralized elitism of the old Board. In practice, it produced new kinds of concentration and, if anything, a greater looseness in the system. For one thing, given Cape Town's position as the seat of the Directorate and the country's main conduit for imported books, which at that point still arrived by ship, it remained the centre of decision-making as far as publications were concerned. Though Johannesburg became increasingly important, as book and especially film distributors began to make more use of air freight, the greatest proportion of censors came from the Cape Town area (41 per cent in 1975 rising to 48 per cent in 1984 and 1992). Their social distribution was even more restricted. Unsurprisingly, seen in the government's racialized terms, the censors were predominantly 'White': 95 per cent in 1975 falling to 83 per cent in 1984 and 66 per cent in 1992. This proportional shift reflected larger political developments. When the new tricameral Parliament was created in 1984, which allowed limited and always controversial political representation for 'Indians' and 'Coloureds', more applicants from these communities were selected (the

'Bantu' were still excluded). By 1992, when a democratic constitution was being negotiated, the pool of 110 censors included nine 'Coloureds', twenty-three 'Indians', and five 'Blacks' (according to the new official designation). Despite these changes, it should be recalled that publications remained a largely whites-only preserve, as 'non-Whites' were officially allowed to advise on films only. Moreover, it is worth noting that 95 per cent of the censors in the key Cape Town area were 'White' in 1984 and 85 per cent in 1992. In other words, while the new bureaucracy did bring in more women, particularly Afrikaans-speaking women, younger people, and more English speakers, it did not radically alter the demographic profile of the apartheid censor. In 1992 white Afrikaners, mostly men, still comprised the largest single ethnic group (46 per cent, 70 per cent men); academics the largest professional group (25 per cent); and members of the NGK the largest religious group (44 per cent).[78]

Since all the censors had to be approved by the government, in a selection process that took place annually until 1977 and every three years thereafter, their continued homogeneity is not particularly remarkable. As the application forms indicated, the government was not just interested in any prospective candidate's 'educational qualifications'. Applicants were required to specify not only language competence and professional experience, but also their race, religious, and cultural affiliations, and, if applicable, the name of the person or organization by which they were being proposed. That careful vetting was involved was obvious to most observers. As J. M. Coetzee remarked, most people he knew were, like him, 'convinced that "suitably qualified" was code for sharing the government's view of the world'. Nonetheless, in early 1976, when the government was on a drive to recruit more English speakers, he decided to test its bona fides by taking the radical step of applying himself. As a young bilingual literary academic at the University of Cape Town, who could also read three European languages, he was eminently well qualified, but, as he expected, he was 'turned down, without explanation'.[79] Not surprisingly, then, a considerable number of the successful early applicants were former members of the Kruger Board, many of whom were recommended by the Minister of the Interior himself: Cloete, Merwe Scholtz (now joined by his wife, Rita), Murray, and Jansen all served on, and often chaired, the new committees from the outset. This slow turnover of personnel would continue throughout the remaining years of the system. What was perhaps less predictable, given the anti-literary spirit of the new Act, was the significant number of Afrikaans writers and literary professors who applied and were accepted, some of whom, like Anna Louw and S. V. Petersen, were newcomers, while others, like the elderly poet W. J. du P. Erlank (Eitemal), had already served as readers under Kruger. Like Reginald Lighton, all three had signed the anti-censorship petition in the early 1960s. Another key appointment at this stage was Etienne Malan, a minor writer and former United Party MP who had attacked the censorship system on liberal grounds in the early 1970s. He would go on to become an influential deputy director responsible for publications in the 1980s.

The Pretorius–Snyman era was not only the most repressive in general terms. It proved to be the most damaging for works identified as belonging to South African literature as well. In all, the committees appear to have scrutinized around a hundred such literary titles in this five-year period, of which they banned just over 60 per cent. Given the bureaucratic complexities of the new system, these bald figures conceal more than they reveal, however. In the first place, while three-quarters of the titles suppressed were new submissions, the remainder were old bannings which the committees upheld on review. Under the new legislation any person willing to pay a fee of R25 (five times the cost of an initial submission) could resubmit a banned publication for review after a lapse of two years. This provision introduced one level of complexity into the new system. The separate appeal process, combined with a more or less firm distinction between 'Literary' and 'Security' committees, added another. Whereas the literary committees generally comprised writers, literary professors, and women graduates, like Rita Scholtz, the security committees were generally made up of retired policemen, military officers, politicians, or professors of politics.[80] Rita Scholtz, who played an increasingly central role in the 1980s as the chair of various literary committees, identified herself as a 'housewife' on her application form, though, as she also mentioned, she had degrees in English and Afrikaans literature. She wrote her master's thesis on the poet N. P. van Wyk Louw. Though Dekker had created a similar division among Board members in the 1960s, this seldom had much of an effect. By contrast, under the new system, where each committee was, in principle, responsible for its own decisions, the consequences were significant, not least because the division systematized the old Board's haphazard attitude to the literary defence. Predictably enough, the security committees were not overly concerned about literary matters. They focused on questions of authorship, and, more specifically, on the political affiliations and activities of writers.

Another change was that the literary committees were now under the scrutiny of the chief censor, who had a right of appeal. This had various often unexpected consequences. When a committee chaired by Cloete banned Wilbur Smith's *A Sparrow Falls* (1977) on the grounds of obscenity, for instance, Pretorius, who was not averse to keeping his more high-minded colleagues in check, appealed in part because he, unlike Cloete, recognized the novel's literary merits. On this occasion, however, the PAB sided with the committee and upheld the ban. The opposite happened when Cope's *The Dawn Comes Twice* came up for review. This time the committee, which comprised Merwe Scholtz as chair, with du P. Erlank and Anna Louw as additional readers, took a strong stance in defence of the novel's status as literature, only to have the PAB confirm the ban on appeal under the political clauses. The PAB also upheld the chief censor's appeal against the literary committee's decision to release *Lady Chatterley's Lover* in 1977.[81] The basis on which the chief censor made these judgements is far from clear. With other works, the contents of which were acknowledged to be politically controversial, even subversive, he let the committees' decisions stand. J. M. Coetzee's *In the Heart of the Country* (1977), Brink's *Oomblik in die Wind* (1976) and the translation, *Instant in the Wind*, Wilma Stockenström's debut novel, *Uitdraai* (literally, Turn Off, or Evade, 1976), Paton's *Too Late the Phalarope* (1953), as well as Gordimer's two collections of short stories *Livingstone's Companions* (1975) and *Some Monday for Sure* (1976)—all passed because the chief censor accepted the committees' reasoning, despite their explicitly literary motivations.

The unpredictability of the new system was perhaps most evident in the decisions relating to the Black Consciousness poets of the 1970s. Like most works by black writers, these were usually submitted by the police, read by security censors, and adjudicated by the security committee. While Mongane Serote's *No Baby Must Weep* (1975) and *Behold Mama, Flowers* (1978) appear not to have been submitted—unlike *The Night Keeps Winking* (1982), which was banned in 1983—the security committee did see and ban under the political clauses Sipho Sepamla's *The Soweto I Love* (1977), James Matthews's *pass me a meatball, Jones* (1977), and Ingoapele Madingoane's *Africa My Beginning* (1979). It also suppressed Barry Feinberg's anthology *Poets to the People* (1974), which included a number of Black Consciousness poets, and Steve Biko's foundational collection of essays *I Write What I Like* (1978). Both these collections were banned for distribution and possession. The situation was complicated by the fact that in the late 1970s the censors began, partly under van Rooyen's influence, to admit the possibility of a distinction between legitimate protest and sedition. In the case of Madingoane's collection, however, Jansen, as reader and chair, was in no doubt that it fell on the wrong side of this uncertain boundary. While he conceded that the 'pain-threshold' had to be higher because this was poetry and by a black writer, he was concerned about Madingoane's use of expressions such as 'Viva Frelimo' and 'Azania', the last being the 'name terrorists use for South Africa', and by his heroic portrayal of Hector Peterson and Steve Biko, as well as Robert Mugabe and Agostino Neto, both of whom were, he claimed, 'outspoken communists' (P79/4/78). Significantly, though the literary and security committees did occasionally confer, Jansen did not request an opinion from his literary colleagues in this case, and so *Africa My Beginning* was banned for sedition.

The reverse happened when Mafika Gwala's debut volume, *Jol'iinkomo* (literally, Bring in the Cattle, 1977), was submitted in August 1977, again by the police, and, more unusually, put before a literary committee. Merwe Scholtz, the primary reader, was impressed by Gwala's 'oratorical powers' and the collection's 'unmistakable' literary qualities, but felt it 'raised obvious problems'

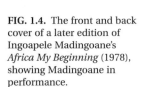

FIG. 1.4. The front and back cover of a later edition of Ingoapele Madingoane's *Africa My Beginning* (1978), showing Madingoane in performance.

Those conditions of life which every fair and honest human being can describe without a pause inspired me to write the epic **black trial**, and gave birth to the cry for Africa's exploited soul in the poem **africa my beginning.**

I did not know, but I had to know, that we in Africa are black men, born of women who loved oppressed men. This book is dedicated to the women who love us in bondage.

— Ingoapele Madingoane

66

No. 118 23 Januarie 1976	No. 118 23 January 1976
WET OP PUBLIKASIES, 1974	**PUBLICATIONS ACT, 1974**
VERBOD OP BESIT VAN PUBLIKASIES	PROHIBITION ON POSSESSION OF PUBLICATIONS
'n Komitee bedoel in artikel 4 van die Wet op Publikasies, 1974, wat kragtens artikel 11 (2) van genoemde Wet beslis het dat die ondergenoemde publikasies ongewens is binne die bedoeling van artikel 47 (2) van genoemde Wet, het kragtens artikel 9 (3) van genoemde Wet die besit van genoemde publikasies verbied. Genoemde verbod is kragtens artikel 9 (5) van genoemde Wet deur die Appèlraad oor Publikasies bekragtig.	A committee referred to in section 4 of the Publications Act, 1974, which decided under section 11 (2) of the said Act that the undermentioned publications are undesirable within the meaning of section 47 (2) of the said Act, has under section 9 (3) of the said Act, prohibited the possession of the said publications. The said prohibition was confirmed by the Publications Appeal Board under section 9 (5) of the said Act.

Inskrywings No. Entry No.	Publikasie Publication	Skrywer of voortbringer Author or producer
P75/8/101........	Tempo—Nr's: 221-22 de Dezembro de 1974; 229-16 de Fevereiro de 1974; 230-23 de Fevereiro de 1975; 250-20 de Julho de 1975; 251-27 de Julho de 1975	Albino Magaia.
P75/9/27........	Tempo—No 253, 10 de Agosto 1975.............	Albino Magaia.
P75/9/128........	Monópolios e miséria.............	Marta Harnecker and Gabriela Uribe.
P75/9/142........	Manual do Guerrilheiro Urbano e Outros Textos.......	Marighella.
P75/10/34........	Peking Review—No 32, August 8, 1975.............	Peking Review, Peking, China.
P75/10/35........	Pekin Information—No 36, 8 Septembre 1975.............	Pekin Information, Pékin, Chine.
P75/10/53........	Sex in Marriage—No 9: Photo illustrated.............	Michael Crissler.
P75/11/64........	Some Thoughts on Chairman Mao.............	Thuso Mofokeng.
P75/11/73........	O Que é o Marxismo?.............	Vladimir Ilitch Ulianov.
P75/11/100........	Forbidden Flowers.............	Nancy Friday.
P75/11/101........	Gay Love—No 8: Photo illustrated.............	Toni Books, England.
P75/11/111........	Sex in Marriage—No 8: Photo illustrated.............	Wendell M. Koble and Richard Warren.
P75/11/119........	Poets to the People—South African Freedom Poems.......	Edited by Barry Feinberg.
P75/11/128........	The Best from Playboy—No 8.............	Playboy Press, Chicago, Illinois.
P75/12/1........	A.N.C. Freedom Day Appeal—June 26: Grammofoonplaat/Gramophone record	Unknown.
P75/12/16........	Lessen in Liefde—Deel I.............	Unknown.

FIG. 1.5. All banned publications were officially listed in the *Government Gazette*. This shows the entry for Barry Feinberg's anthology *Poets to the People* (1974), confirming the ban for possession. It is listed alongside a host of other banned titles, including *The Best from Playboy* and *Some Thoughts on Chairman Mao*.

(P77/8/111). In his view, a sense of 'inevitable insurrection' characterized many of the 'best' poems. He was especially perturbed by the collection's underlying preoccupation with the reclamation of a genuinely African history, as evidenced in the final poem, also entitled 'Jol'iinkomo'. It was dedicated to 'the Children of Namibia' and it encouraged them to venerate their 'own national heroes'. He thought the poem inevitably recalled the volume's opening and reiterated one of its central themes. In a short prefatory poem, Gwala explained that the volume title, which referred to a traditional song about returning the cattle safely to the kraal, or pen, at night, also spoke to his obligation as a poet 'to bring some lines home | in the kraal of my Black experience'.[82] In his summing up, Merwe Scholtz drew attention to these interconnections, arguing that the volume therefore posed a 'dilemma', particularly in the wake of the student uprisings in June 1976. On the one hand, though it might be 'better to let people blow off steam', was this 'just steam', he asked. On the other, would banning not just 'add more wood to the fire which is already past smouldering point'? In 'our current explosive situation', he concluded that it probably had to be banned, but he was happy to be persuaded otherwise and to pass the final decision on to the security committee. At a joint meeting, chaired by Malan, during which Gwala's biography and political affiliations were scrutinized, he did indeed change his mind. As Malan put it, though some of the poems 'contained ways of thinking and points of view that would not always please whites', they displayed none of the 'venomous and revolutionary language' used by 'some leaders' of the Black People's Convention, one of the key Black Consciousness organizations, which was itself banned in October 1977. Moreover, he felt Gwala's 'poetic style' made the poems 'often incomprehensible on a first reading'. In this case, then, a joint committee decided that *Jol'iinkomo* warranted protection as literature, whereas the security committee alone decided that *Africa My Beginning* amounted to seditious propaganda.

During the Pretorius–Snyman era, the pact safeguarding Afrikaans literature, first broken by the Kruger Board, was all but defunct. In the six years from 1975 to 1980, most of the new Afrikaans literary titles scrutinized were banned (ten out of a total of at least fourteen). This had particularly damaging consequences for the new generation of writers who emerged in the 1970s and who began to raise more serious questions about apartheid and the future of the Afrikaner as a *volk*. The suppression of works by André Le Roux and Welma Odendaal in 1977, which anticipated subsequent rulings against Dan Roodt and the literary magazines with which they were closely associated, was particularly telling. While the magazines *Donga* (1976–8) and *Inspan* (1978) were banned principally for political reasons, all their individual works, like Roodt's magazine *Taaldoos* (1980), fell foul of the obscenity and blasphemy clauses. John Miles was the exception. A committee initially proposed that his comic postmodern satire *Donderdag of Woensdag* (Thursday or Wednesday, 1978), which describes

G.P.-S.32663—1974-75—3,000-3—P) SAP ref S.7/19/60/16(806)   DF I

DIREKTORAAT VAN PUBLIKASIES
PRIVAATSAK X9069
KAAPSTAD
1977 -8- 22
PRIVATE BAG X9069
CAPE TOWN
DIRECTORATE OF PUBLICATIONS

REPUBLIC OF SOUTH AFRICA

Serial No. *P.??|8|III* -
(For official use)

PUBLICATIONS ACT, 1974

PUBLICATION OR OBJECT

APPLICATION FOR A *DECISION/REVIEW

Director of Publications, Private Bag 9069, Cape Town, 8000.
    I hereby submit to you the publication or object described hereunder and—

        *accompanying this application
        *being forwarded to you by...

....

for examination and a decision whether the publication or object is within the opinion of a committee referred to in section 4 (1) of the Publications Act, 1974, undesirable or not.

Colonel Du Plooy	16-8-1977
Applicant	*Date*

* Delete whichever is not applicable.

A. APPLICANT

1. Name	2. Telephone No.
Col C J W du Plooy	29281 x 244

3. Occupation	4. Nature of business
S A Police	

5. Residential or business address	6. Postal address
	Private Bag X302 PRETORIA 0001

B. PUBLICATION OR OBJECT

7. Name and/or description	8. Subject
JOL 'IINKOMO	Publication - poets

FIG. 1.6. An example of the report form the censors used from the mid-1970s onwards. This one documents a literary committee's decision to pass Mafika Gwala's first collection of poems, *Jol'iinkomo* (1977).

9. Author or producer	10. Publisher and his address	11. Year and No of edition.
MAFIKA PASCAL GWALA	Craighall Mews Jan Smuts Avenue Craighall Park 2196 JOHANNESBURG,	1977

12. If it is not practicable to submit the publication or object (e.g. in the case of a statue), then specify hereunder the place where the publication or object may be examined by a committee.

C. PREVIOUS DECISION (complete only in case of an application for a *review*)

13. The above-mentioned publication or object was on a previous occasion found to be—

*undesirable by a committee in terms of the Publications Act, 1974;
*undesirable by the Publications Control Board in terms of the Publications and Entertainments Act, 1963;
*indecent or obscene or objectionable by the Publications Control Board in terms of section 113 (3) of the Customs and Excise Act, 1964.

Note: If known, specify hereunder the number and date of the *Government Gazette* in which the above decision was published.

*Delete whichever is not applicable.

D. AMOUNT ENCLOSED R.............................

Note: (a) The amount payable is—

	In respect of an application for a	
	decision	review
(i) in the case of a drawing, picture, illustration, painting, woodcut or similar representation, print, photograph, engraving or lithograph, figure, cast, carving, statue or model	R 1,00	R 5,00
(ii) in the case of any other publication or object, e.g. a book, magazine, etc..	5,00	25,00

(b) In the case of an application for a *decision* the amounts are payable only if the applicant is the producer or distributor of the publication or object.
(c) In the case of an application for a *review* the amounts are payable by each applicant

16. DECISION

The committee decided that the publication or object is—

*not undesirable;
*undesirable within the meaning of section 47 (2) the Publications Act, 1974.

....
Chairman of Committee

*Delete whichever is not applicable.

....of

21-9-77
Date

FIG. 1.6. (*continued*)

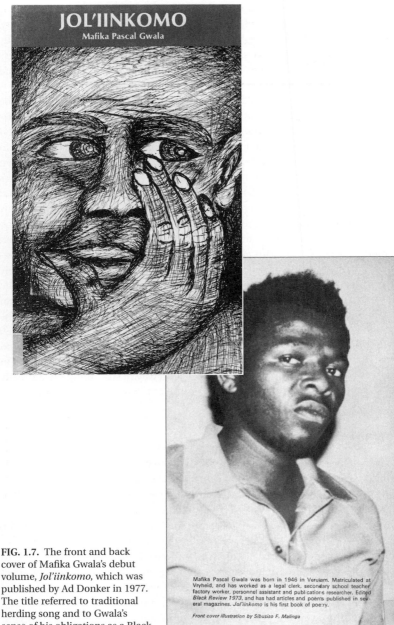

FIG. 1.7. The front and back cover of Mafika Gwala's debut volume, *Jol'iinkomo*, which was published by Ad Donker in 1977. The title referred to traditional herding song and to Gwala's sense of his obligations as a Black poet.

Mafika Pascal Gwala was born in 1946 in Verulam. Matriculated at Vryheid, and has worked as a legal clerk, secondary school teacher, factory worker, personnel assistant and publications researcher. Edited *Black Review 1973*, and has had articles and poems published in several magazines. *Jol'iinkomo* is his first book of poetry.

Front cover illustration by Sibusiso F. Malinga

71

the failed attempt by a group of artists to effect constitutional change by brainwashing the President, should be banned on the grounds of obscenity, blasphemy, and sedition, though, when the chief censor appealed, it was finally suppressed under the blasphemy clause only. By contrast, his children's story about boycotts at black schools *Stanley Bekker en die Boikot* (Stanley Bekker and the Boycott, 1980) was banned for sedition and for possession.

All these decisions attracted controversy and significant attention in the Afrikaans press, but it was only when the PAB overturned a literary committee's decision to pass Etienne Leroux's *Magersfontein, O Magersfontein!* (1976) that the system was, once again, put in crisis. The circumstances, which I consider in more detail in Chapter 6, were complicated because the committee had been willing to ban Breytenbach's *Skryt* (1972) a year earlier. When it came to Leroux's tenth novel, however, Merwe Scholtz, Anna Louw, and Etienne Malan mounted a determined defence on literary grounds. This was in part because they saw Leroux as still belonging to the *volk* avant-garde; whereas, Breytenbach, who was arrested on terrorism charges just after the *Skryt* decision, was by then deemed to have broken with all officially acceptable forms of Afrikaner dissidence. Initially the chief censor accepted the committee's decision. It was only when Afrikaner pressure groups, led by the NGK, lobbied the Minister of the Interior that it was reversed. Partly for his own political reasons—there was an election pending at the time—the Minister then appealed himself and, in the process, opened up the old divisions within the *volk*. In November 1977, when the PAB finally declared the novel obscene and blasphemous, Anna Louw and Merwe Scholtz both resigned as censors, not so much because they lost faith in their role but because they could no longer see a way of sustaining their already over-compromised guardianship of the *volk* avant-garde within the system.

Crisis and Reform

The crisis *Magersfontein* provoked went all the way to the Supreme Court after Leroux's Afrikaans publisher Human & Rousseau decided to contest the PAB ruling in early 1978. The court, which now (happily in its view) restricted itself to procedural matters (judges had long resisted the idea that they should be called upon to act as a super-censors), held that the PAB was wrong to privilege the average, as opposed to the likely, reader in the case of obscenity, but right to take the views of the average Christian into consideration when it came to deciding what was blasphemous. Though it rejected the appeal, and in effect lent legal sanction to the church groups' vociferous campaign, the outcome of the whole *Magersfontein* episode was not what the NGK expected. Partly as a consequence of various changes at the ministerial level, the government responded to the crisis by switching allegiance, once again, though this time in favour of the literary elite. In June 1978, under pressure from a delegation that included Merwe Scholtz, as well as members of the collaborationist Afrikaans Writers' Circle and the new dissident Writers' Guild, it introduced various amendments intended to protect literature without granting it full exemption. Most importantly, as far as publications were concerned, it empowered the chair of the PAB to appoint a committee of government-approved literary experts to act as special advisers and it made it possible for the PAB to release a book conditionally (with an age restriction or limited marketing rights).

These changes, which marked the beginning of the end of the Pretorius–Snyman era, had an immediate but localized effect. In November 1978 the chief censor decided to use Brink's *Gerugte van Reën* (1978), and his own translation *Rumours of Rain* (1978), as a test case for the new procedures after two committees—security for the Afrikaans version, literary for the English—decided to pass the novel. *Rumours*, which constitutes Brink's most sustained reflection on Afrikaner identity, details the gradual if partial disillusionment of its narrator, Martin Mynhardt, a loyal Afrikaner nationalist. Though both committees had concerns about its language, sexual content, and political implications, the literary committee was particularly anxious about an episode, related by Mynhardt's rebellious son, in which a black herd boy is brutally drowned by South African soldiers in Angola. On the advice of lawyers Brink had removed this incident, which could potentially have fallen foul not just of the Publications Act but of the Defence Act, from the Afrikaans edition. The chief censor appealed against the committees' decisions, arguing that the novel was both obscene and seditious. He singled out for special mention its 'sympathetic' portrayal of 'revolutionary activities', 'vilification of the police', and scenes of rape (P78/9/93). He also claimed that the committees had given too much weight to its status as literature and to the fact that, as a novel that would be read in private, its effects would be limited.

Following the new procedures, the PAB, still under Snyman, appointed an advisory committee of literary experts, chaired by Merwe Scholtz, who, like Anna Louw, was willing to participate once again, albeit in this new capacity under the amended legislation. Other members of the committee included W. E. G. Louw, van Wyk Louw's brother, and F. C. Fensham, a literary professor who was then chair of the Afrikaans Writers' Circle. They defended the novel principally on literary grounds, emphasizing its narrative experimentalism and its limited likely readership. In his chair's report, Scholtz mentioned that readers would need to be familiar with Roland Barthes to appreciate what Brink was doing. Given this, the committee recommended that the appeal be rejected unconditionally, a view the PAB reluctantly accepted. Though Snyman was less convinced than the experts that the novel's complex narrative strategies saved it from the charge of obscenity, he was willing to concede that its status as a work of fiction ensured that it could not be deemed seditious. The strongly worded anti-apartheid speech which Bernard Franken, Mynhardt's estranged friend, gives during his trial on sabotage charges would, he claimed, be undesirable if it appeared in a 'propagandistic pamphlet'. In a novel, where it reflected aspects of Bernard's character, which the reader comes to know 'through and through', it was acceptable.[83] Interestingly, at no point in the process did any of the censors comment on the fact that Brink based Franken's speech on the actual testimony of the celebrated Afrikaner communist Bram Fischer, given during the trial that led to his being sentenced to life imprisonment in 1966. They were alerted to this only in 1980, when Malan sent a letter to the new chair of the PAB, J. C. W. van Rooyen, with a press cutting in which Brink was quoted as saying that he had used this strategy to get Fischer's views into the public domain. The security committee, Malan noted, was 'worried' that novels like *Rumours of Rain* and Gordimer's *Burger's Daughter* (1979), another novel partly based on Fischer's life, were being 'deliberately' used to 'broadcast forbidden reading matter' (P78/9/93).

As it happens, *Burger's Daughter* was another high-profile case on which the 1978 amendments had a direct bearing. In October 1979 the chief censor was pressured into appealing against the security committee's decision to ban it under all five clauses, a decision Snyman's PAB again reluctantly reversed (see Chapter 4). Yet not all the appeals under the new amendments were successful. As we have seen with John Miles's *Donderdag of Woensdag* things could go the other way. On this occasion the PAB again grudgingly accepted the experts' lukewarm defence against the charges of obscenity and sedition. Though they did not consider the novel great literature, they thought its elaborate postmodern narrative displacements and 'strong element of defamiliarization' prevented it from causing offence. Nonetheless, the ban had to be upheld, according to Snyman, because the novel, which adopted a 'typically Marxist standpoint' on religion, would offend 'Christian feelings'.[84] It is worth noting that when Miles's novel was finally released with conditions after a further PAB ruling in 1983, the decision was based in part on evidence uncovered during a specially commissioned reader survey, the first and only study of the kind undertaken during the censorship era. The survey found that most members of the general public, not just the likely readers, would not consider the novel offensive.[85] Successful or not, these appeals were the exception rather than the rule. Most works, particularly by black writers, did not get a second consideration. The chief censor conspicuously showed no interest in testing the new procedures when it came, for instance, to Mtutuzeli Matshoba's *Call Me Not a Man* (1979) or Miriam Tlali's *Muriel at Metropolitan* (1979), both of which succumbed to the same initial fate as *Burger's Daughter*.

Characteristically, given the looseness of the system, it took another change of personnel before the legislative amendments had a more significant, if not necessarily more consistent, effect. As we have seen, van Rooyen, who formally took over as chair of the PAB in April 1980, began his tenure by following

Snyman's official line, a view he articulated more fully in his first full-length study of the censorship system published in 1978.[86] When his mentor was gently eased out of office early, however, he quickly signalled his reformist ambitions, sketching out his preliminary views when he took over as acting chair for the appeal hearing on Brink's *Dry White Season* (1979). Under his direction, he noted, the PAB would take the advice of literary experts more seriously, and so, by implication, attempt to rebuild the good relations with Afrikaner literary intellectuals that had characterized the Dekker era. It would also respect the primary tenets of the liberal tradition. He concluded his defence of *Dry White Season* by quoting Justice Rumpff's arguments in favour of free speech in his dissenting opinion in the 1965 Wilbur Smith trial. The PAB now 'endorsed' Rumpff's statement that 'a court should assume that Parliament, itself a product of political liberty, intends liberty to be repressed . . . only to such an extent as is *absolutely necessary*' (van Rooyen's emphasis).[87] Yet, for all his concerns about the literary, van Rooyen was neither a champion of the *volk* avant-garde, like Dekker, nor an especially committed defender of liberalism, like Rumpff. Though he liked to present himself, in general terms, as a 'moderate' adjudicating between communitarian and liberal traditions—at least by the early 1980s—he remained, as J. M. Coetzee argued, 'closer to Devlin than to [Herbert] Hart'; and, when it came to literature, in particular, he was motivated more by expediency than by principle.[88] Borrowing Woodrow Wilson's rhetoric, he argued in his second book on censorship that provocative literary works deserved protection because they were 'useful safety-valves for pent-up feelings in a milieu where they would be understood not as a call to political violence but as a literary experience'.[89]

Yet, if the ruling on *Dry White Season* looked forward, both in terms of the development of van Rooyen's thinking and PAB policy, it also looked back. When the novel was initially submitted by the British publisher's local distributors in August 1979 (the Afrikaans version was submitted by the police a month later), the security committee declared it seditious. Murray, one of the key readers, argued it should also be banned for possession. 'It should be remembered', he observed, 'that art and literature leaves their impressions subconsciously to a considerable degree and that the overall impression this book gives of RSA [the Republic of South Africa] is quite false' (P79/8/61). In the story, which is recounted at second hand, Ben du Toit, a decent, unremarkable Afrikaner schoolteacher, is initiated into the well-documented horrors of state violence when he is called on to help investigate the mysterious disappearance of the son of one of the school's black employees. In the end, the committee took a less hardline view, deciding it should be banned for distribution only because it 'denigrated' the security police by accusing them 'either directly or by implication of (a) dishonesty, (b) torture, (c) victimization, and (d) maltreatment'. They were especially concerned that the novel would encourage the 'average reader' to conclude that the security police were responsible for du Toit's own suspiciously convenient death. The chief censor, who, like most of his colleagues, recognized the novel's literary merits, appealed to allow the PAB's committee of experts to have its say.

In its report, the committee, which comprised Merwe Scholtz (chair), Fensham, Anna Louw, and Snyman, focused on the relationship between literature and history. There was no doubt that the novel made 'clearly recognizable and inferable references to South African actuality'. This was underscored, they argued, by the fact that Brink used court cases as source materials and by the novel's narrative mode. It is a 'sort of reconstructive report', and later a 'diary', in which the first-person narrator attempts to piece together du Toit's story out of fragmentary documents. For the experts, the problem, therefore, centred on the novel's status as 'literature', and, more specifically, borrowing the language of Brink's own preface to *Kennis*, on the 'degree and quality of the transposition of a specific piece of reality (primarily recent S. A. history) into the world of a novel'. According to their criteria, it failed in these terms and, unlike Leroux's *Magersfontein*, it did not represent a 'significant contribution to the art of the Afrikaans novel'. The characters were, on the whole, 'Brink stereotypes': Melanie, the 'little sex thing'; du Toit, the 'melancholy Brink lover'; the police, figures from a 'Nazi thriller'. Moreover, despite the narrative displacements, which, they felt, Brink was using to protect himself in the event of a court case, there was little doubt that this was his own 'commentary' on 'factual circumstances' and on the security police. Yet, if the novel could not be defended as literature, they did not believe it could be condemned as seditious propaganda. In the end, they argued against banning because, as the PAB had declared in the *Burger's Daughter* case, its 'approach to South African political affairs was so one-sided that the book was more counter-productive than propagandistic'. Van Rooyen, in his summary of the PAB's own final ruling, endorsed the experts' judgement, adding that the 'reasonable South African reader' would understand that 'he was dealing with a malicious writer who was using the art of the novel to launch a political attack'.[90]

'Repressive Tolerance'

The particular repressiveness of the Pretorius–Snyman era finally came to an end when van Rooyen's promotion in April 1980 was followed in July by the appointment of Abraham Coetzee as the new chief censor, or Director of Publications. Coetzee's appointment, which came fully into effect in January 1981, also marked the beginning of the final phase of apartheid censorship. From the government's point of view, particularly after the furore over *Magersfontein*, Coetzee was an ideal candidate for the job. Though he did not have Dekker's cultural credentials—he was a university administrator who began his academic career as a lecturer in medieval and early modern Dutch literature—he was widely respected among government-supporting literary intellectuals who, according Merwe Scholtz, saw him as 'part of the solution'.[91] In addition, as an ordained NGK minister, he was able to hold his own in discussions with Afrikaner church groups, as he was regularly required to do; and, as a former vice-principal of Fort Hare, South Africa's oldest and most important black university, he had first-hand experience of the realities of resistance politics. All these factors, combined with his skills at dealing with the media and the public, enhanced his credibility within government circles and, as a consequence, gave him some leverage when it came to dealing with the tense political climate of the 1980s.

Working at their different levels, Coetzee and van Rooyen inaugurated what the leading black publisher Jaki Seroke aptly called an era of 'repressive tolerance'.[92] This period was characterized by an awkward dissonance between the internal reforms of the censorship bureaucracy, which echoed P. W. Botha's wider strategies of political co-optation in the 1980s, and the government's aggressive suppression of political protest by more direct means, particularly during the states of emergency declared in the middle of the decade. Other contemporary developments, including the advent of video and the involvement of the censors in assessing television broadcasts from 1982, brought new pressures to bear on the system and gradually led to a shift in priorities. Most significantly, while the average number of 'films' (including video) scrutinized annually in the 1980s went up by 30 per cent, the number of publications entering the system decreased by the same amount (from an annual average of 2,137 in the Pretorius–Snyman period to 1,508 between 1981 and 1989). This was in part because from 1981 publishers were legally obliged to take on some of the responsibility for controlling imported publications. Whereas customs regularly submitted around a thousand publications a year in the 1970s, they now seldom put forward more than 400. The rate of submission from publishers, which was always low, also declined, however, and submissions from the police became more erratic. Though they usually sent in around a thousand publications annually at the beginning of the 1980s, a significant increase on the 1970s, they submitted just over 600 in the in the middle of the decade, no doubt partly because they had more direct powers under emergency legislation, and in 1989, when the first signs of significant change began to emerge, the figure went down to 537. Between them the police and customs nonetheless remained the principal conduit for publications, responsible for around 80 per cent of the total submissions throughout the Coetzee–van Rooyen era. By contrast, the general public seemed, if anything, to become steadily more indifferent to the whole process. Submissions from offended ordinary readers, or groups, dropped from 7 per cent of the total in 1981 to 3 per cent in 1989.

The censors themselves had little influence over the rate of submissions. What they controlled, of course, was the proportion of titles banned and here, too, the trend was downward, particularly after 1985. Whereas around 60 per cent of all publications scrutinized had been banned annually throughout much of the apartheid era, the figure dropped to 53 per cent in 1981 before falling unsteadily to 32 per cent in 1989. Though the chief censor, the committees, and the PAB all contributed to this shift, van Rooyen led the way with a series of key decisions in the early 1980s, followed, in 1982 and again in 1984, by a new statement of general principles. Driven by his belief in his role as a non-partisan arbiter between the liberal and communitarian legal traditions and among competing interest groups, and by his general conviction that 'publications control is a science and not merely a hit-or-miss game of darts', he set out to champion the arts, and, more specifically, to give a new legitimacy to 'protest literature', a move which did much to discredit the category among younger writers in the 1980s.[93] The foundations for this new approach were laid in a series of decisions, taken by the PAB in the early 1980s, which led to the release of the leading black literary magazine *Staffrider* as well as the related Ravan Press anthology *Forced Landing* (1981) and Sipho Sepamla's novel *A Ride on the Whirlwind* (1981). Van Rooyen also built up a series of key precedents by unbanning *Lady Chatterley's Lover*, *Magersfontein*, and *Donderdag of Woensdag*, as well as various issues of *Scope*, the popular weekly that had previously been the focus of numerous appeal trials.

When it came to obscenity and blasphemy, his new guidelines encouraged the censors to make the most of contextual information and the more nuanced likely reader test in the interests of opening up moral and religious debate. 'Vexations and even the shocking' had to be 'tolerated', particularly in the interests of art and literature, he argued, though the public still had to be protected from what might be deemed 'offensive' (39). When it came to the more obviously political clauses (47 (2) (c–e)), the guidelines were intended, on the one hand, to allow 'political debate, criticism and pleas for change' which did not amount to incitement—hence the PAB's decision to unban the Freedom Charter in 1984—and, on the other, to protect communities—as opposed to individuals—from 'ridicule or contempt' and the state from 'clear and present danger' (12). Significantly, van Rooyen now defined communities or 'sections' in less overtly racialized terms, citing, as examples, 'Blacks, Afrikaners, English-speaking South Africans, Jews, etc.' (11). Given the larger context in which the government was steadily increasing its own powers of direct censorship—not only through emergency legislation but with other statutory instruments like the Internal Security Act, 1982—the beneficial effects of van Rooyen's reforms were, at best, localized. They were also complicated by the ongoing uncertainties which affected the day-to-day operations of the system.

This was especially evident in the decisions affecting works identified as literary. While van Rooyen's guidelines considered 'literary merit' as a 'mitigating factor', and allied it to the question of likely readership, they kept to the terms of the 1974 Act by refusing to grant literature full exemption and by remaining equivocal about the criterion of aesthetic unity (7). 'Parts may not be judged in isolation,' van Rooyen insisted, while noting that 'a part or parts' could be 'so scandalous as to taint the whole' (31). This evasiveness at the level of principle was compounded by the ongoing tensions bred of the system's reliance on assorted experts to police the boundaries of the literary. While many books banned in the 1960s and 1970s—from Richard Rive's *Emergency* (1964) to Des Troye's *An Act of Immorality* (1963) and from Miriam Tlali's *Muriel at Metropolitan* (1975) to Madingoane's *Africa My Beginning* (1979)—were released for the first time in this period, some earlier works, like Alfred Hutchinson's *Road to Ghana* (1960), Ruth First's *One Hundred and Seventeen Days* (1965), and all of Alex La Guma's novels, remained banned on review. In addition, some new works, including Lauretta Ngcobo's novel *Cross of Gold* (1981), Mark Mathabane's best-selling autobiography *Kaffir Boy* (1986), and Peter Horn's collection of poems *The Civil War Cantos* (1987), were suppressed for the first time in the 1980s and remained so for the rest of the apartheid era.

The fate of Sepamla's *A Ride on the Whirlwind* (1981) offers a particularly clear illustration of the ongoing inconsistency of the system. When the police submitted the novel in June 1981, Coetzee initially sent it to Johan Heyns, a key supporter of his own internal reforms. Heyns, an eminent NGK theologian, went on to play a leading role in the Church's cautiously qualified critique of apartheid in the mid-1980s. In his view, the novel, which focuses on the psychological, social, and political tensions within the resistance during the 1976 Soweto uprisings, was 'not undesirable'. It contained nothing that was not already reflected 'daily' in the newspapers, he argued, and, anyway, its underlying message was not 'inflammatory' because it was too despairing about the possibilities for political change. His report then went to the security committee for a final decision. It disagreed with his conclusions and decided to ban the novel under the political clauses, principally because it cast the police in 'a very bad light', treated 'terrorists' as 'heroes', and was 'dedicated to the students of the Soweto uprisings' (P81/6/152). In this case Coetzee decided not to appeal, even though the Directorate was by then anxious about accusations of racial bias, as it had already shown by appealing against the decisions relating to *Staffrider* and *Forced Landing*.

Immediately after the ban was announced in September 1981, however, and before the case became a cause célèbre in the United States, Adriaan (or Ad) Donker, Sepamla's local publisher, took the initiative, obliging van Rooyen to appoint his own committee of literary experts. He brought Snyman back to act as chair, alongside Anna Louw and F. C. Fensham. They took a different view from both Heyns and the security committee. In keeping with their primary brief they argued that the novel, which they considered 'inflammatory', could not be defended as 'great literature'. It was too 'journalistic', too 'episodic', and it had 'little or no allegorical possibilities'. What they appeared to mean by this was that it read more like a piece of fictional reportage than a novel. Yet, considering its two likely readerships, they decided this was not necessarily damning. While its virtues as a work of psychological realism might usefully give 'white people, and even the police' an 'intimate insight' into the 'inner world of the local terrorist', its failure as literature 'thoroughly neutralized' its capacity to influence 'young blacks'.[94]

In reaching this conclusion, they also contradicted the view a slightly different group of literary experts—Fensham, Louw, with Merwe Scholtz as chair—took when they decided to uphold the ban on Wessel Ebersohn's *Store up the Anger* (1980), a fictionalized account of Steve Biko's murder. As in the case of *A Ride*, they argued it could not be defended as literature, but, in their view, this was precisely why the ban had to remain. Ebersohn's novel was, they insisted, dangerously seditious *because* it 'cold-bloodedly' used the 'criterion of fictionality' to disseminate 'propaganda'. Somewhat surprisingly, the PAB upheld both appeals, though its own attitude was far from consistent. It concluded that *A Ride* could be released because it was a tendentious 'historical novel', which, as a result of its one-sidedness', would not have an 'inciting effect'. Like *Burger's Daughter* and *Dry White Season*, its obvious political bias would somehow be 'counter-productive'. By contrast, *Store up the Anger*, which was equally critical of the state and especially the police who were responsible for Biko's death, was acceptable in part because its more limited likely readership would read it in a very particular way. Though most of the police had Afrikaner names—one is called van Rooyen—Ebersohn's readers would, the PAB concluded, see them neither allegorically as representatives of all Afrikaners, nor even literally as the police. They would recognize that they were just lawbreaking 'characters representing the criminal element'.[95]

Van Rooyen's supposedly more 'scientific' approach did little, in other words, to overcome the arbitrariness of the system. As Coetzee acknowledged, his own reforms as chief censor only complicated matters further, given the scope he had to 'manipulate things'. During the regular three-yearly recruitment drive in 1984, for instance, he caused some internal controversy by refusing to confirm A. H. Murray's reappointment on the grounds that he was 'biased', 'narrowminded', and did 'not fit into the machine any more'.[96] Though this did not dramatically change the outlook of the security committee—S. I. M. du Plessis, another professor of philosophy and one of Murray's protégé's, and Jansen remained on it—it did reduce the influence an older, increasingly hardline generation of censors had on the system. Coetzee's other efforts at reform—in particular, his increasingly careful selection of initial readers to 'get the best possible view' especially on literary and religious works—also proved far from straightforward. As we have seen in the case of *A Ride on the Whirlwind*, when the security committee overruled Heyns, this strategy did not always have the desired effect. Similar problems arose with Mbuyiseni Mtshali's second volume of poems, *Fireflames* (1980), which came up for consideration on three separate occasions in the course of the 1980s.

When the police initially submitted the volume in December 1980—that is, before Coetzee's appointment—the security committee, under Murray's chairmanship, banned it for sedition. The chief censor, however, decided to appeal on literary grounds, partly given the positive review Es'kia Mphahlele had recently given the collection. A week after the volume was submitted, Mphahlele, then the leading black critic in South Africa, had heralded it as a 'landmark of African literary history'. Though he had some reservations, particularly about its 'embarrassingly banal' translations of poems in isiZulu, he admired Mtshali's 'strident voice of self-assertion' and singled out for particular praise his original contributions to what he identified as a pan-African tradition of 'heroic verse'.[97] The PAB's committee of experts, chaired by the literary academic Rialette Wiehahn, saw things differently. It dismissed the volume, in a crudely argued report, as a 'pretentious' piece of 'propaganda' which, when it was not just 'laughable nonsense', represented a direct threat to the state. 'Mtshali's intention is to stimulate Black Power, to degrade everything white, to propagate the violent overthrow of the state.'[98] Though the PAB did not support this conclusion—it argued that the volume had to be banned only because it would harm race relations—it agreed that many of the poems were 'inflammatory' and anti-white. In his final report van Rooyen also attempted to justify the ban in the following extraordinary terms, which recalled the attitudes to African languages associated with colonial ethnographers: because 'many of the Black languages are particularly rich in imagery (*beeldspraak*)', he claimed, poetry had 'a special resonance with the black man' and fired 'him up more easily than prose'. When the volume came up for review during Coetzee's tenure—first in 1985, and again in 1988—the initial readers, both Afrikaner literary academics, emphasized its literary merits, sympathized with its political sentiments, and recommended it be released. On both occasions, however, their views were ignored. In 1985 the committee reiterated the PAB's earlier ruling and upheld the ban on the grounds of sedition as well, while, in 1988, another committee agreed to pass the volume but with strict conditions. Fearing that it might be picked up by 'agitators' (the worry that it could be prescribed at schools had also influenced the earlier decisions), the chair insisted that it could be held only in university and legal deposit libraries (P88/10/125), thereby limiting its readership to a small elite.

The repressive Publications Act, 1974, remained on the statute books throughout South Africa's transition to democracy in the early 1990s. After the ANC and other resistance organizations were unbanned in February 1990, however, Coetzee ensured that many of the publications suppressed under the old legislation were released. In the course of 1991 and 1992, the Directorate itself resubmitted over four thousand titles for review, almost all of which were passed. While Coetzee, who remained in post until 1997, was seen to be a safe pair of hands, the outgoing government of F. W. de Klerk clearly considered van Rooyen a liability. After two five-year periods of office, he was not reappointed as chair of the PAB in March 1990, largely because the government was anxious not to alienate its reactionary support base during the uncertain transitional period. His reputation as an overly liberal reformer, which had been growing throughout the 1980s, reached a peak in 1988, when the PAB released *Cry Freedom*, the film based on the relationship between Steve Biko and Donald Woods. The day after the decision was announced, the security police responded by seizing copies of the film under emergency legislation. At this point, too, van Rooyen himself became the target of a campaign of intimidation. As Coetzee put it, van Rooyen was the de Klerk government's 'sacrificial lamb', and, not unexpectedly, his two successors, Louis Pienaar, an advocate who served until 1992, and Dan Morkel, a professor of law who was in post until 1997, were more conservative.[99] Both Coetzee and van Rooyen were, however, to play a significant role during the transition to democracy, which also saw the end of the censorship era. In 1994, following the first democratic elections, they were both appointed to serve on a government working party tasked to draft new legislation in accordance with the Bill of Rights, the cornerstone of South Africa's new constitutional democracy. Indeed, in a move characteristic of the pragmatic and reconciliatory spirit of the Mandela presidency, van Rooyen was asked to act as the group's chair. This goes some way towards explaining why the ghosts of the past haunt the otherwise radically new legislation covering publications in post-apartheid South Africa, a point to which I return in the Postscript.

2
PUBLISHERS

For David Philip, one of the leading interventionist publishers of the apartheid era, South African book publishing in the second half of the twentieth century was 'in most respects much like book publishing elsewhere—school textbooks are seminal; technical books burgeon; cookbooks, bird books and escapist fiction lead the trade side'. The difference was that in South Africa 'the shadow of a divided society' lay over the book trade, 'most heavily over that in which I have been mainly involved—academic books and serious trade books for the thinking public'. That kind of publishing, which Philip called 'oppositional', was 'constantly affected by—and has sometimes even affected—the course of events under the Nationalist governments which have ruled South Africa since 1948'.[1]

Philip's comments serve as an important reminder that it was not only writers who took up the challenge of testing the limits of public discourse under apartheid, especially in the arts, literature, and politics. Internal publishers from Julian Rollnick, who launched the pioneering African Bookman imprint in the 1940s, to the Dinah Lefakane, who founded the black feminist press Seriti sa Sechaba (Spirit of the Nation) in the late 1980s, as well as a number of external, principally British publishers, had a significant impact as well. By determining for themselves, sometimes at considerable risk, what books were worth being produced 'for the thinking public', these publishers contested the attempts by the government and its allies to monopolize control of the public sphere and held open a space in which alternative visions of South Africa could be articulated and debated.

Unlike the principal British firms, most of the internal interventionist publishers (Philip identifies around fourteen in his brief survey) did not specialize in literature, but almost all included a range of literary authors on their lists and many had a strong literary bias. This complicated their position, partly because of the challenges peculiar to literary publishing per se, partly because of the specific ways in which South Africa's 'divided society' deformed the book trade. In any modern culture, literary publishing is never reducible to a simple commercial transaction. In the process of producing a particular kind of commodified public document, publishers working in this sector of the book trade also create, protect, and regulate the space of the literary. By associating a piece of writing with a particular imprint, by linking it to other works in a series or backlist, and by presenting it to various communities of readers and markets in certain ways, these indispensable brokers in the transmission process, who are too often written out of literary history, locate the work within the intricately structured, if never rigidly territorialized, field of contemporary culture and, in the process, label it as 'Literature', usually in a strongly normative sense. An ethical dimension enters into this process because this constitutive act of transmission is at the same time an uncertain wager on the future of literature as a category. While this is especially true for publishers who promote young, unknown avant-garde writers whose works might not at first be recognizable or acceptable as literary in any established sense, it applies, in some degree, to all publishers who champion new works, even those who specialize in mass-market genres.

At its most rarefied, in the case, for example, of a small, avant-garde press, the act of publication might be self-consciously minimalist, attesting to the work's status simply—though the process is never simple—as literature. More gener-ally, since publishers tend to ally themselves to larger socio-political as well as cultural projects, a wider range of norms and categories usually comes into play. In these cases, the publisher might present the work not just as literature, whether 'serious' or 'popular', 'mainstream' or 'marginal', 'mass-market' or 'avant-garde', but as, say, 'Afrikaner', 'protest', 'African', 'South African', 'Black', 'feminist', or 'gay', depending on the nature of their larger commitments and the categories available. Since all these terms are, in principle, debatable and, in fact, often disputed by reviewers, prize-judges, booksellers, and writers them-selves, literary publishing is a doubly hazardous enterprise. It is subject not only to the usual legal and financial risks of the book trade, but to the volatilities of the modern literary field, the origins of which can, as I noted in the Introduc-tion, be traced back to the emergence of the 'Republic of Letters' in eighteenth-century Europe and America. This is the small, fractious, relatively autonomous world in which literary norms, categories, and reputations are constantly made and unmade, and in which publishers play a central intermediary role as sponsors and guardians.

For literary publishers operating in apartheid South Africa these were not the only, or necessarily the most pressing, challenges. They had, in addition, to contend with the government's attempts to contain, if not close down, their activities via censorship legislation and other more direct repressive means. The perversities of the censorship bureaucracy itself—notably the fact that it operated post publication and that many of the censors were literary experts— put these publishers in a uniquely peculiar position. Unlike in the Soviet Union or East Germany, where the censorship bureaucracy and the state-run literary publishing apparatus were intimately linked, the Nationalist govern-ments in their guise as upholders of modern Western ideals were theoretically

committed to respecting the autonomy of the public sphere and private capitalist enterprises, and, as a consequence, the independence of literary publishers. In practice, as we have seen, they orchestrated a programme of
massive state intervention by listing particular writers, by intensively regulat-
ing the distribution of imported books, by refusing to grant literature unqualified legal protection, and by appointing a partisan group of literary guardians
as censors. As we shall see, when it came to internal interventionist publishers,
it used more direct means of harassment and coercion as well. One consequence of this elaborate exercise in bad faith was that literary publishers were
entangled in an absurdly high-minded, asymmetrical, and potentially devastating rivalry with the censors over the idea of literature itself, which brought
with it real risks of financial loss, imprisonment, or both, especially for internal
publishers.

Yet, as Philip's reference to South Africa's 'divided society' implied, it was not
only censorship, or explicit government policies, that deformed the book
trade. The internal and transnational publishing industry, which was almost
exclusively under white ownership and which was generally not interventionist, created its own distortions. Some publishers, including some multinationals, took a pragmatic, commercially minded approach and chose to act within
the constraints the government imposed; while others, notably the large-scale
Afrikaner-owned conglomerates that emerged in the 1970s, energetically embraced the publishing opportunities apartheid afforded, especially in the educational market. The dominance of white-owned publishers was, of course,
not a direct consequence of the Nationalists' political ascendancy after 1948.
It was one of the legacies of European colonialism and, more immediately, of
the rise of Afrikaner nationalism in the first half of the twentieth century. The
effects of these longer histories, which underpinned the racialized structures
of the book trade, persisted under apartheid, and, in some instances, became
more entrenched. In the case of English-language publishing, the colonial
legacy is evident in the fact that, until the early 1970s, many of the works
identified as belonging to the growing canon of South African literatures in
English arrived as imported books from London; while Afrikaans literary
publishing, which was from the outset dominated by major newspaper interests, remained highly politicized and nationalistic. The area most directly
affected by the advent of apartheid itself was literary publishing in the nine
African languages, which was from the 1950s increasingly taken over by
Afrikaner interests and refashioned along apartheid lines. It was in this area,
too, that the monopolizing ambitions of the Afrikaner-owned publishing industry had a greater impact than the government's own censorship bureaucracy. To make sense of this it will be necessary to give a brief history
of African-language literary publishing in South Africa, and so it is to this
that I turn first.

Censorship Versus Monopolistic Control

The link between printed forms of the four major African languages—isiXhosa, isiZulu, Setswana, and Sesotho—and questions of literary modernity was, as with Afrikaans, firmly established by the beginning of the twentieth century. Yet, whereas early Afrikaans writers were fostered, and occasionally frustrated, by a nascent nationalistically motivated publishing industry, writers in African languages had since the nineteenth century been heavily dependent on the patronage of colonial mission presses. Committed as they generally were to assimilationist policies of Christian Europeanization (Bunyan's *The Pilgrim's Progress* (1678) was invariably the first literary work they translated), these presses imposed their own strictures, ensuring that the first modern literary works in African languages conformed to their accepted standards. As R. H. W. Shepherd, the most energetic missionary champion of 'literature for the Bantu', remarked in 1945, 'the mass of the vernacular literature published in the past emanated, and still to-day emanates, from missionary presses, and naturally such literature has sought to fulfil the aims of missionary societies'.[2] As a consequence, literary modernity was, as Thomas Mofolo's (1876–1948) celebrated Sesotho novel *Chaka* (1925) testified, all but inseparable from Christian modernity. It was also generally understood within a nineteenth-century teleological narrative of cultural assimilation, to which both Shepherd and the first major historian of African literatures, D. D. T. Jabavu (1885–1959), subscribed. Oral-based African cultures, on this analysis, were consigned to a pre-modern limbo; and printed literatures, which were considered not simply European in origin but European in essence, figured as key signs of modernity to which African writers could and should aspire, albeit on terms acceptable to the mission presses.

By the turn of the century, however, other, more secular and sometimes more independent cultural spaces were opening up both within and outside the mission presses. The most significant were the black-controlled newspapers aligned to the anti-tribalist New African Movement, and later to the South African National Native Congress (the precursor to the ANC), founded in 1912, notably John Dube's (1871–1946) *Ilanga lase Natal* (The Natal Sun, 1903) and Sol T. Plaatje's (1878–1932) *Tsala ea Batho* (The People's Friend, 1910). These papers, which survived in a state of precarious independence until the early 1930s, when they were absorbed by a white-owned newspaper group, took forward the tradition M. W. B. Rubusana's *Izwi Labantu* (The Voice of the People) inaugurated in 1897. Unlike its older rival, J. T. Jabavu's *Imvo Zabantsundu* (Native Opinion), which was launched in 1884 and backed by white liberal patrons in the Cape, *Izwi* was a more genuinely independent African paper. The new generation of editors created a platform for the emergent African nationalist movement and contributed to what Ntongela Masilela has called the 'secularisation of the New African intellectual and literary imagination'.[3] Book publishing, by contrast, remained under white ownership, though some publishers, like the University of Witwatersrand Press, followed the example of some mission presses by making a point of employing black editors. Together with the liberal-minded segregationist J. D. Rheinallt Jones (1884–1953) and Clement Doke (1893–1980), the University Press launched the scholarly journal *Bantu* (later *African*) *Studies* in 1921 and the long-running Bantu Treasury Series in 1935. By publishing many of the major contemporary African-language poets—notably S. E. K. Mqhayi (1875–1945), J. J. R Jolobe (1902–76), and B. W. Vilakazi (1906–47)—Doke established himself as the most eminent guardian of modern African literature of his time. By the 1930s, some mission presses and some new, white-owned commercial publishers began actively, if sometimes anxiously, to encourage the new, secular trends, not least by publishing the first novels by African writers. Shuter & Shooter, an educational firm founded in 1925, brought out John Dube's *Insila ka Shaka* (The Bodyservant of King Shaka, 1930), which is generally considered the first novel in isiZulu, as well as R. R. R. Dhlomo's (1901–71) early fictions; while Shepherd's Lovedale Press published Plaatje's English novel *Mhudi* (written in 1920, published in 1930) and the novel credited with being the first in isiXhosa, A. C. Jordan's (1906–68) *Ingqumbo Yeminyanya* (The Wrath of the Ancestors, 1940).

Though it cannot be claimed that these publishing initiatives created a wholly alternative cultural space unburdened by the assimilationist assumptions of the mission presses (in founding his Treasury Series, Doke, for instance, was, Attwell suggests, probably informed by the 'kind of thinking' associated with Shepherd and Jabavu), they did help put the debates about African literary modernities on a new footing.[4] While Mofolo, Dube, Plaatje, Dhlomo, and Jordan all came to very different thematic and narrative conclusions about the encounter between tradition and modernity, their decision to adopt and adapt the novel form itself reflected the contemporary struggle to articulate new solidarities and a new, secular sense of self and history, which disturbed the simple cultural boundaries and genealogies of assimilationist thinking. These ambiguities and creative tensions, which were as much about the past as about the future, were expressed with particular clarity in a fractious public exchange of the late 1930s between Vilakazi and the critic and playwright H. I. E. Dhlomo (1903–56). Though ostensibly about technical questions in isiZulu poetics (Dhlomo was critical of Vilakazi's attempts to introduce European writerly rhymes into traditionally oral verse forms), the tensions underlying the dispute in fact went to the heart of the contemporary debates about the status of a multifarious pre-colonial African heritage within a modern cultural formation. For Vilakazi, who wrote in isiZulu, the way forward was to modernize Africa; for Dhlomo, who wrote in English, the more urgent need was to Africanize modernity.[5]

At first the new Afrikaner publishing houses had little or no interest in African-language literatures. Though some of the major firms, notably J. L. van Schaik (founded in 1914), Nasionale Pers (1915), and Afrikaanse Pers (1932), published a few titles in the 1930s and 1940s, particularly in languages like Sepedi which were less well served by the mission presses, they began to develop a more serious interest in the field only after 1948, and, more particularly, after the 'Bantu Education' and 'Bantustan' policies were put in place in the 1950s. From then on, and, indeed, throughout the apartheid era, they endeavoured to reshape the market by creating a series of *national* canons of African literature, which reinforced, or at least did not unsettle, apartheid thinking. This involved promoting works that could be seen to legitimize the determinedly anachronistic idea that South Africa's historically diverse indigenous ethnic polities, now reconceived as narrowly territorialized 'Bantu *volke*', had to be saved from the depredations of Western modernity and detribalization. Though never concerted or systematic—there were too many publishers chasing too many markets—the priorities of Afrikaner-owned firms were evident early on. In 1953 Afrikaanse Pers, now renamed Afrikaanse Pers-Boekhandel (APB), brought out E. M. Ramaila's (1855–1946) frequently reprinted *Seriti sa Thabantsho* (The Spirit of Thabantsho, 1953), an anthology of Sepedi praise poems and historical narratives, and awarded it first prize in its own 'Bantu Literary Competition'. This ethnographic interest in oral traditions, praise poetry, animal tales, myths, and histories, which Afrikaner-owned publishers developed throughout the apartheid era, was, of course, nothing new. Mission presses had been doing the same thing since the nineteenth century and, for some champions of African literature, like Doke, such initiatives could happily be developed alongside modernizing projects like the Bantu Treasury Series. Even New African modernizers, like Plaatje, had been actively involved in creating a printed archive of the past. Indeed, as he noted in his preface to *Mhudi*, he hoped to use the proceeds from the sale of his novel to 'collect and print (for Bantu Schools) Sechuana folk-tales, which, with the spread of European ideas, are fast being forgotten'.[6] In the hands of the Afrikaner-owned publishers, however, Plaatje's anti-assimilationist aims, which again coexisted with his own modernizing ambitions, were redirected in the interests of apartheid, which turned orality into a fetishized cultural essence and ethnic self-awareness into racialized *volk* pride.

African writers working with European-derived literary forms posed a problem for apartheid cultural planners, who self-consciously rejected the missions' assimilationist ideals and set out to suppress the unifying ambitions of the New African movement. The solution was 'separate development' in the cultural sphere. A modern, printed literature, which apartheid thinking continued to associate exclusively with Europe (or the West), was now something African writers had to be left to achieve in their own time as members of distinct ethno-linguistic *volke*—much as the Afrikaners had done, albeit more gradually. In the early 1970s these attitudes were clearly articulated in the *Standard Encyclopaedia of Southern Africa* (1970–6), a quasi-official reference work published by Nasou, the educational division of Nasionale Pers. The brief entry entitled 'Bantu Literature', which began by noting that 'all Bantu peoples have a traditional literature (unwritten) and also a modern literature', quickly emphasized that modern 'Bantu writers' had still not come to terms with the formal demands and autonomy of 'Western' literature: the 'Bantu writer simply writes down a story as it unfolds in his mind' and remains wedded to the 'didacticism of the traditional stories'.[7] It followed that modern 'Bantu literature' merited praise only on thematic grounds. What counted, above all, was the way it handled 'social problems'. Unsurprisingly, then, the novels, short stories, and poems from the period 1950 to 1970 which the entry singled out for special commendation apparently focused on the 'uprooting of traditional society as a result of pressure from Western civilisation', or the 'confusion of the Bantu mind', or, a favourite topos in the apartheid canon, recounted tales of a child who 'leaves the home in the reserves to go to the great city, there to be lost to his own people'.[8] Alluding to this kind of thinking, Es'kia Mphahlele remarked that, in the stories APB was 'consciously boosting for publication' in the 1950s, the 'hero must return to the rural areas'. 'No other perspective will be published by this press,' he added.[9] Many of the writers recognized for their supposedly acceptable treatment of such themes, some of whom won literary prizes awarded by the Department of Bantu Education, were published by APB and other leading Afrikaner-owned imprints of the 1950s and 1960s. By the 1980s, though Shuter & Shooter retained a share of the isiZulu market, and though Lovedale, multinationals like Oxford University Press, and local university presses remained active on the margins, the field was dominated by van Schaik, Via Afrika, and Educum. The last two were the educational African-language subsidiaries of the giant Afrikaner conglomerates that emerged in the 1970s, Nasionale Pers and Perskor.[10]

The fact that Afrikaner publishers, some of whom included Cabinet ministers among their directors, came more or less to monopolize African literary publishing in the apartheid era goes some way towards explaining why censorship had little or no direct impact on it. Though a white 'Bantu language' specialist, T. M. H. Endemann, was included on the first censorship board, he was not replaced when he stepped down in 1968 because, as the chief censor, J. J. Kruger, noted in 1973, no books in these languages had ever been submitted.[11] In the late 1970s and 1980s, when the language of each submission was officially recorded for the first time, a more accurate picture emerged, which nonetheless confirmed Kruger's assessment. While the total number of English titles submitted annually could be measured by the thousand (1,802 in 1979, for instance), Afrikaans submissions seldom went above the low twenties (twenty-one in 1979) and those in African languages remained in single figures (three in 1979).[12] In the rare cases when the censors commented on African-language literatures—generally in translation—their responses were, for the most part, approving. While observing that the innovatively inclusive *Penguin Book of South African Verse* (1968), edited by the noted liberal guardians of the literary Uys Krige and Jack Cope, covered 'poets from all language and racial groups', and that it contained some overtly political poems by white writers as well as some by Vilakazi which 'inevitably' dealt with the 'race problem', Merwe Scholtz argued that the collection could be passed because it was a 'bona fide literary selection', which did not make the 'race-problematic' its 'starting point'. 'Considering the likely readership,' Harvey added, 'the idea of banning is quite absurd' (BCS 5/69).

A more revealing case was Credo Mutwa's popular ethnographic collection of tribal lore and custom *Indaba, My Children* (1964), which a small local firm submitted prior to publication. Though anxious about its fiercely anti-Christian sentiments, the publishers, Blue Crane Books, hoped the censors would recognize its value. The author, they claimed, 'is a fanatical supporter of our general apartheid-policy and he gives all our enemies much to think over' (BCS 385/64). In response the censors expressed some concerns about the section on religion, which the publishers agreed to tone down, but they were unanimously in favour of passing it. Its 'strong plea that the Bantu be left to build on his own spiritual foundations', combined with its emphasis on the 'bad influence of certain imperialistic political policies', made it, in Murray's view, a serious contribution to 'religious and political' debate. Though numerous factors probably affected the low submission rate for African-language publications—not least the fact that the system had no credibility among black readers, and that the police probably lacked sufficient linguistic expertise—there is little doubt that the dominant stake Afrikaner-owned publishers had in the market after 1960 played a central part. In exchange for considerable economic rewards, they worked closely with the official African-language literature police, the white inspectors who controlled the 'Bantu' school syllabus, ensuring that governmental censorship in this area was all but superfluous. Faced with this, some writers, most notably the leading isiZulu poet Mazisi Kunene, whose second major epic, *Anthem for the Decades*, was in fact banned, felt they had no option but to translate their works and seek publication abroad. *Anthem* was published in English as part of the Heinemann African Writers Series in 1981.

Afrikaans publishing

Standpunte *and the compromises of the* volk *avant-garde*

When the poet N. P. van Wyk Louw began his project to create a modern Afrikaner 'Republic of Letters' in the 1930s, he was not concerned about the threat of government censorship. The focus of his initial anxieties was the emergent Afrikaner publishing industry. In 1935 he formed a subscription publishing venture called the Coalition for the Free Book with a small group of like-minded writers in an effort to bypass firms like Nasionale Pers and van Schaik who then dominated Afrikaans literary publishing, which, in Louw's view, was too preoccupied with the school-book market, and to create space for the younger generation's avant-garde ideals. This initiative, as the Afrikaans literary historian J. C. Kannemeyer has observed, was 'more important for the development of Afrikaans literature' than the formation of the Afrikaans Writers' Circle a year earlier.[13] Though Louw's group was united in its opposition to the publishing industry's narrow moralism and commercialism, and to the parochial conception of the *volk* which the publishers shared with the Circle, it was predictably riven by internal disagreements, impeded by financial difficulties, and short-lived. It lasted two years, during which it published only four titles, including a translation of Flaubert's Sadean tale of parricide *The Legend of Saint Julian Hospitator* (1877) and Louw's second volume of poems, *Die Halwe Kring* (The Half Circle, 1937). For his next volume, Louw reverted to Nasionale Pers, who remained his principal publisher until his death in 1970.

With characteristic persistence, however, Louw revived the Coalition's ideals after the war, co-founding the literary magazine *Standpunte* (Standpoints) in 1945. Initially set up as a private limited company, largely underwritten by Louw and his brother, the magazine, which was pointedly subtitled 'An Independent Quarterly for Literature and the Arts', soon earned a reputation as the principal forum for the *volk* avant-garde with Louw typically leading from the front. In April 1947, just as he was poised to enter his most experimentalist phase as a poet, he published a series of notes under the combatively disdainful title 'Tourist Art', in which he denounced those who believed there was a 'recipe for a national style', or, indeed, that there were any stable 'national characteristics'. Prefiguring the terms of his first polemic against censorship, which appeared six months later, he also argued that the 'whole idea' that the 'critic (or statesman or cultural philosopher or even the journalist) can say to the poet in advance how his art must be or should be is absurd'. To build a genuinely 'modern' literary culture he insisted the writer had to be allowed to 'hold himself open' to future possibilities, and, if necessary, 'stand against his time'.[14] Though the magazine was mainly devoted to Afrikaans literature, its outlook was always internationalist, albeit with a primary orientation towards Europe. 'With *Standpunte*', Dekker commented revealingly, 'we have a magazine on the European level—for the first time.'[15] Reflecting Louw's emphasis on cultural interdependency, it was also multilingual, although, once again, only within strict limits. It carried contributions in English, Dutch, and Afrikaans, and the all-male editorial board, which Louw and his brother at first dominated, included a Dutch co-editor from the outset and from 1952 a local English

FIG. 2.1. The cover of the first number of *Standpunte*, dating from 1945. The magazine became the principal platform of the *volk* avant-garde.

literary figure as well. The writers Anthony Delius and Guy Butler, who served in this capacity in the 1950s, were followed by the censor C. J. D. Harvey (1961–83) and finally by J. M. Coetzee (1983–6).

The magazine, like Louw's contestatory literary republicanism, soon become entangled in the murky realpolitik of cultural life under apartheid. After a decade in which it managed to survive on a precarious, undercapitalized footing, it became increasingly dependent on large subsidies from Nasionale Pers. This particular compromise, which caused immediate difficulties, would have serious consequences in the long term, leading to its eventual closure on political grounds in 1986. By the mid-1960s, following the disputes over the membership of the new censorship Board, its close association with the system (three long-serving members of the editorial board, Cloete, Harvey, and Grové, who was chief editor throughout the 1960s, were censors as well) made its much-vaunted independence look emptier still. While these various compromises tainted Louw's ideals, other contemporary developments threatened the magazine's status as the voice of the *volk* avant-garde. The younger generation of Sestigers, literally the 'writers of the Sixties', who rapidly achieved notoriety in conservative Afrikaner circles as the new upstarts, launched their own 'little magazines', making *Standpunte*, which was already beginning to be considered overly academic, seem just an important part of the history of Afrikaans literary modernity. Though Louw, in keeping with his principles, strongly supported the loosely affiliated Sestigers group (he wrote a series of thoughtful essays in the early 1960s on the 'renewal' of prose fiction, for instance, championing, among others, Jan Rabie, Etienne Leroux, and André Brink), almost none of the younger writers appeared in *Standpunte* itself.[16]

The exception was the prolific, prodigiously energetic André Brink (b. 1935). Despite being one of the principal theorists of the younger generation, and co-editor with Bartho Smit of their short-lived flagship magazine simply entitled *Sestiger* from 1963 to 1965, Brink became a regular contributor to *Standpunte* and joined the editorial board in 1964. It was an awkward alliance from the start. The tensions, which initially centred on Brink's libertarian attitudes to religion and sexuality, at first made sense in relatively predictable terms as a generational conflict over literary and other norms within the *volk* avant-garde. In these disputes Grové, who did not share Louw's carefully discriminating appreciation of the younger generation, became the voice of the establishment, while Brink figured as the iconoclastic newcomer. Though Grové published Brink's provocative article 'On Religion and Sex', which caused a sensation in early 1965, he persuaded him to withdraw a piece defending homosexuality two years later on the grounds that it would give *Standpunte* 'improper publicity'.[17] It was only after 1968, when Brink began openly to question the politics, not just the aesthetics and social attitudes, of the *volk* avant-garde, that his association with the magazine began to rupture.

Significantly, the older generation was not Brink's only target by this stage. In the epochal year of 1968 he joined forces with Breyten Breytenbach, Adam Small, and others to challenge those of his fellow Sestigers who were happy to continue seeing themselves as an emergent *volk* avant-garde. Concluding a series of heated exchanges about Afrikaner identity and the situation of the Afrikaans writer in the November 1968 issue of the Sestiger magazine *Kol*, he commented:

> If I speak of *my people*, then I mean: every person, black, coloured [*bruin*, or mixed race] and white, who shares my country and my loyalty towards my country. This is the essence of my argument that our *whole* country must be opened up for writing [*oopgeskryf*, literally 'written open'] and that we writers should start taking account of what 'our whole country' really is.[18]

This was in an open letter addressed to Bartho Smit (1924–86), the most senior Sestiger and the most inventive, controversial, and, as a consequence, unstaged playwright of the period. As we have seen, Smit, who remained a loyal nationalist, was also the embattled literary editor for the publisher APB. I return to the details of Brink's letter and the *Kol* debate as a whole in Chapter 6.

In keeping with the liberal principles on which Louw originally founded it, *Standpunte* was not initially against Brink's new political turn. Though he and Grové clashed on various issues, including censorship, the magazine published Brink's acerbically satirical poem 'We Shall Overcome', which refers to

> my great *volk*,
> Rescuers and Protectors of the West
> since the sad burial of, blessed memory, God.[19]

The poem focuses on American atrocities in Vietnam and is spoken in the voice of the unnamed President Lyndon Johnson, but it also opens up other, more local readings by parodying the Lord's Prayer, exploiting referential equivocation (it begins 'I sit here in my White House'), and by using its title as a subtly unstable, ironized refrain. When it appeared in the issue for June 1968, it produced what seems to have been the only formal complaint to the censors against *Standpunte*, which put Grové in the absurd position of having to defend his editorial decisions, though now as a censor. The Afrikaner church group that lodged the ultimately unsuccessful complaint was not concerned about the poem's possible subtexts. That it seemed overtly atheistic and pro-communist was sufficient. Grové himself did not think much of the poem, but he defended it in part because it was, in his view, all about America (BCS 722/68). Four years later, in April 1972, *Standpunte* sparked a more widespread furore in Afrikaner circles by publishing the opening chapter of *Kennis van die Aand* (Looking on Darkness), Brink's first attempt to open up the 'whole country' to writing.

For all this, however, the internal tensions among the editors remained, and eventually reached breaking point. Brink was alone among his co-editors in having at least three pieces rejected in the late 1960s and early 1970s—an article advocating universal franchise, a poem denouncing the government more directly, and a sex episode dropped from the final version of *Kennis van die Aand*—and in 1976, after he made a series of statements in the international press condemning the government and praising the Afrikaner communist Bram Fischer, his colleagues forced him to resign. As Harvey put it, he had 'alienated himself from our editorial climate and tradition'.[20] When Brink was reinstated in 1983, at the same time as J. M. Coetzee was appointed English editor, Nasionale Pers immediately threatened to withdraw its subsidy if the magazine came to be seen as 'the organ of a clique or faction or particular agenda', a threat it finally carried out three years later when Brink, who was then briefly chief editor, attempted to publish an article of his own challenging the emergency regulations that were then in force.[21]

Human & Rousseau, APB, and the Sestigers

Standpunte's position within the Afrikaans cultural field after 1960 was, in some respects, uniquely compromised, but its fatal entanglements with the censorship bureaucracy and government-supporting publishing houses were by no means unusual. Indeed, as the early publishing history of the Sestigers suggests, their own position, as an emergent *volk* avant-garde, was no less fraught, although it was, if anything, more precarious and volatile. They had to deal not only with the guardians of *volk* morality, with the nationalistic publishing industry, and with the censorship system, which put the whole idea of a secure dividing line between literary insiders and outsiders in question, but with their own increasingly fractious internal divisions. This put additional stresses on their often testy and strained relations with the institutions of the *volk* avant-garde, notably their two main publishers in the early 1960s, APB and Human & Rousseau (H & R). Like the Sestigers themselves, both firms were caught up in what Koos Human, one of the founders of H & R, later called the 'climate of megalomania, banality, repression and lies within which writers and publishers had to work' during the apartheid era.[22] The precise nature, and consequences, of their entanglements were, however, significantly different.

On the face of it, there was little to distinguish the two firms as publishers of the Sestigers. H & R, who appointed the senior *volk* avant-garde poet, veteran anti-censorship campaigner, and editor of *Standpunte* D. J. Opperman (1914–85) as their literary adviser, included Brink, Leroux, Rabie, Smit, and Breytenbach on their list; and they published the Sestiger literary magazine *Kriterium* (1963–6). After taking on Bartho Smit in 1962, APB developed an equally strong Sestiger list, including Chris Barnard, Breytenbach, Ingrid Jonker, Rabie, Small, and Smit himself. Viewed historically, however, the two publishers occupied very different cultural positions within the Afrikaans literary world; and, viewed from the inside, as it were, their attitudes to the younger generation were radically opposed. For APB, the association, which developed largely because of Smit's energetic championship of the Sestigers, was a tense and brief diversion. The firm, which had made its reputation as a publisher of popular Afrikaans fiction in the 1940s and 1950s, was a well-established part of the nationalist publishing industry. With Prime Minister H. F. Verwoerd as chair of its Board of Directors, it was also closely allied to the political elite and, as a northern concern, it was located on the conservative side of the north–south regional split between Transvaal and Cape Afrikaners. After various mergers it became part of the northern Perskor conglomerate in 1971.

It is perhaps not surprising, then, that no complaints were made against APB books to the censors in the 1960s. Instead senior executives, who were 'bitterly' opposed to Smit's avant-garde enthusiasms, orchestrated a campaign of their own.[23] They began by effectively shutting down the first Sestiger 'little magazine', simply called *60*, a short-lived attempt by the younger generation to hijack *Tydskrif vir Letterkunde* (Magazine for Literature), the periodical of the collaborationist Afrikaner Writers' Circle. The APB management threatened to cut the magazine's government subsidy and forced Smit to resign as editor in 1962. It was as a consequence of this that the group launched *Sestiger* the following year. As we have seen, Smit, no doubt under pressure from senior executives, was also obliged to expurgate Breytenbach's inaugural volume, *Die Ysterkoei Moet Sweet* (The Ironcow Must Sweat, 1964) after consulting the censors. When the collection then won the APB literary prize in 1964, which was judged by, among others, van Wyk Louw and Opperman, the executives sidelined Smit and drove their few remaining younger writers away, leaving the field open to H & R and even Nasionale Boekhandel, their main rival, who began cautiously to include some Sestigers on its own list. Though Smit would continue to publish some controversial literary works by younger writers in the years ahead as part of Perskor, including Welma Odendaal's collection of politically themed short stories *Keerkring* (Tropic, 1977), which was banned ostensibly on the grounds of blasphemy and obscenity, and an expurgated version of Breytenbach's pseudonymous 'travel-diary' *'n Seisoen in die Paradys* (A Season in Paradise, 1976), which the censors passed, he never again had the limited leeway he briefly enjoyed in the early 1960s.

APB's fraught liaison with the Sestigers testified to the strength of the opposition the younger generation of writers met from established Afrikaner publishers. In this context H & R provided an invitingly hospitable alternative. For one thing, it was based in the more liberal Cape; and, for another, the two young entrepreneurs who founded it in 1959 and gave it its name were not committed supporters of the Nationalists. Despite this, for some younger writers, notably the poet Antjie Krog, its position became increasingly problematic once it was absorbed into the large Cape conglomerate Nasionale Pers in 1977. As its decisions regarding *Standpunte* indicate, Nasionale Pers, the main rival to Perskor was firmly behind the government. Yet, for all its precarious political independence, H & R still championed the Sestigers as an emergent *volk* avant-garde from the start. As Koos Human remarked, 'we thought in the same way and spoke the same language'.[24] This 'elective affinity' shaped the new firm's growing list, quickly earning it a reputation as one of the most controversial and important Afrikaans literary imprints of the period. The fact that it also became the target of a moral campaign led by the NGK and other Afrikaner church groups both reflected and boosted its cultural prestige. H & R published all six novels against which complaints were made to the censors in the 1960s: Brink's *Lobola vir die Lewe* (Lobola for Life, 1963), *Die Ambassadeur* (The Ambassador, 1964), and *Miskien Nooit* (Maybe Never, 1967); as well as Leroux's *Sewe dae by die Silbersteins* (Seven Days at the Silbersteins, 1962), *Die Derde Oog* (The Third Eye, 1966), and *Isis, Isis, Isis* (1969). What the church groups hoped was that the censors would use the new legislation, which they had long been pressing the government to introduce, to curb the avant-garde publisher's secularist, modernizing ambitions. As it happened, the campaign backfired. By passing all six novels, albeit sometimes only by the narrowest of margins, the censors kept their pact as guardians of the *volk* avant-garde and declared their own allegiances within in a long-standing internal struggle over the idea of literature among Afrikaner literary, political, and clerical elites. If all six novels threatened *volk* morality in the eyes of the Church, they confirmed and extended the viability of the *volk* avant-garde—or so H & R and the censors believed.

By the time the censors began to suppress Afrikaans as well as English literary works, beginning with Brink's *Kennis van die Aand* (1973) in 1974 and Breytenbach's *Skryt* (1972) a year later, the fragile consensus underlying the *volk* avant-garde had already broken down. While Leroux remained an H & R author, and, as the *Magersfontein* (1976) episode revealed, continued to receive the full backing of the censors allied to the *volk* avant-garde, Brink and Breytenbach, like a number of writers from the younger generation, began to distance themselves, to varying degrees, from the movement and its associated cultural institutions. Though Adam Small, another key figure in the 1968 *Kol* debate in which, as we have seen, Brink raised questions about the future of the Sestiger movement, was never an H & R author (he was first published in Afrikaans by HAUM and then by APB), he contributed to the fallout by establishing closer ties to the emergent Black Consciousness movement and by beginning to publish in English as well as Afrikaans. In 1975 he brought out a collection of quatrain poems entitled *Black, Bronze, Beautiful* with the new local English-language publisher Adriaan (or Ad) Donker.

The tensions were, however, most evident in the very different ways in which Breytenbach and Brink's publishing careers unfolded. Having left South Africa in 1962, Breytenbach had always been at one remove from the local literary scene. In 1968, however, he made a decisive break with the *volk* avant-garde after an acrimonious public dispute that centred on political questions.

Following this, he dramatically and permanently ended his brief alliance with H & R, a rift that revealed the depth of the publisher's *volk* loyalty. After switching from APB to H & R with *Huis van die Dowe* (House of the Deaf, 1967), his third volume of poems, Breytenbach moved to Buren, a small independent firm founded in 1968, who published some of Athol Fugard's early plays and had an interest in politically engaged literature and books on Cape wines. It published one by the censor Merwe Scholtz. Buren went on to produce five Breytenbach titles in the late 1960s and early 1970s, sometimes in private editions, including *Oorblyfsels* (Remnants, 1970), a small collection of political poems rejected by APB and H & R, and *Om te Vlieg* (To Fly, 1971), his surrealistic and quasi-autobiographical attack on white complacency. Though Opperman advised H & R against publishing the latter, in part because he found the 'excremental obsession tedious', they went ahead, only to abandon their plans when they could not find a printer willing to take it on.[25] Tellingly, the only title Buren did not publish in this period was *Skryt*, which appeared under the imprint of Breytenbach's Dutch publisher, the prestigious literary imprint Meulenhoff, ensuring that the controversial collection had a more than usually limited circulation in South Africa.

Despite siding with Breytenbach and Small in the *Kol* debate, Brink continued to have an awkwardly conflicted relationship with H & R throughout the apartheid era. Indeed, it could be argued that while Breytenbach simply turned his back on the *volk* avant-garde, Brink tried to undo it from within, following the same strategy he adopted in relation to *Standpunte*. Yet he, too, moved briefly to Buren, after H & R rejected *Kennis van die Aand* in 1971. On this occasion the publishers acted on Opperman's advice, as they had done a few years earlier when Brink submitted 'Die Saboteurs', his first overtly political novel. Opperman felt this earlier story, which had already been refused by two publishers on political grounds and was, in the end, never published, was 'undistinguished' and 'unexciting from a literary point of view'.[26] As Opperman's subsequent report on *Kennis* appears not to have survived, it is not clear what reservations he had about it, though it is likely he rejected it on similar grounds. Given the way things would develop, it is worth noting that Buren took *Kennis* on the recommendation of Ampie Coetzee, the leading Marxist critic and one of Brink's allies in the internal disputes among the Sestigers. As Coetzee argued in his reader's report, in which he acknowledged the risk of censorship, the novel was worth publishing because 'this is a document of oppression, exploitation, mistreatment, murder; this is a document of the story of the coloured in South Africa'. 'The time has now come', he continued, echoing Brink's own arguments in the *Kol* debate, 'for the Afrikaans novelist to represent what is really happening to a part of his people.'[27] The fact that Opperman later went on to defend the novel against Cloete and Grové in court suggests that there was, in his view, a clear difference between government censorship and self-regulation by publishers. It should be said that H & R itself had second thoughts about *Kennis*. Having initially refused to take it in the early 1970s, when the official hostility to 'committed literature' was at its height, they campaigned to have the ban overturned later in the decade, and when it was finally released in 1982 they brought out their own edition.

In the early 1970s, however, there was little doubt about where H & R stood when it came to politically controversial works. When they published the teenage prodigy Antjie Krog's (1952–) debut volume in 1970, for instance, they did not include her most politically incendiary early poem, the sexually charged, wistfully utopian, and resolutely anti-racist 'My Beautiful Land', which had caused a local media sensation when it first appeared in her school magazine. A year later it resurfaced in *Sechaba* (Nation), the ANC's banned in-house journal, where it was presented as a welcome sign that 'where there is so much hatred a germ of love yet grows'.[28] As Breytenbach argued in an essay of 1971, such editorial compromises, which were a testament to the 'rot to which the Afrikaner intellectuals (and their publishers and teachers) have succumbed', helped to explain why 'no Afrikaans book has yet been prosecuted'.[29] Censorship was not necessary in this field, he suggested, because the 'Establishment' had other, more 'discreet' methods of dealing with its own 'dissenters' before publication.

> Senior intellectuals when consulted in their capacity as guardians of the Culture will advise against unnecessary and disruptive controversy: 'high instances' will pick up the phone to enquire, to threaten or even to bargain; a member of the Publications Board (who may also be a respected *literatus* or a writer) will intervene (beforehand) to confirm in private.... If all else fails the printers will simply refuse to print the objectionable work.

All this was done because the 'Poet–Thinker', who had 'always played a very important role' in 'the "fight for survival" of the tribe', was expected to be 'an exponent of its tribal values, not a dissenter'.

As the evidence from the censorship archives suggests, this description applies particularly well to a publisher like APB, who represented the dominant forces within the contemporary Afrikaans literary world. With H & R, however, the situation was more complex. In this case, the cleavage was not so much between the loyal tribal bard and the upstart dissident as between two forms of cultural resistance, one that could be accepted within the terms of the minority *volk* avant-garde and the other that could not. This gives an added significance to the change in the censors' attitudes in the mid-1970s and to the fact that neither of the first Afrikaans titles to be banned was published by a mainstream Afrikaner-owned firm. While the censors undoubtedly inaugurated a new era in the history of the relationship between Afrikaans writers and the apartheid state when they suppressed *Kennis* and *Skryt*, they also brought to an end a process of exclusion that began some years earlier within the *volk* avant-garde itself.

This was as much a process of self-exclusion, as Brink and Breytenbach, among others, sought to dissociate themselves from the established tradition of 'loyal opposition' and to form new alliances within the broader resistance not as Afrikaners but as dissident Afrikaans-speaking South Africans (see Chapter 6). Signalling another important shift, the banning of *Kennis* also persuaded Brink that he had no option but to become a dual-medium writer. Given that he began to translate the novel into English as soon as the ban was announced, it could be argued that the censors' decision to silence him in South Africa launched his international career. Somewhat to Brink's dismay, his British publishers made this a central part of their own marketing campaign for the novel.

Beyond the Volk *Avant-Garde*

Brink's difficulties with the censors and with H & R had a direct impact on the next major development within Afrikaans publishing. In November 1975, when the new censorship bureaucracy was established and the options for interventionist writers seemed to be closing down even further, a group of writers and literary academics affiliated to the new, non-racial Skrywersgilde (Writers' Guild)—Ampie Coetzee, John Miles, and Ernst Lindenberg—decided that the only way to safeguard the future of Afrikaans literature, as they now saw it, was to revive the idea of publication by private subscription with a venture they initially called the Coalition for the Free Book.[30] Based in the Afrikaans Department at the University of Witwatersrand in Johannesburg, all the founding figures had, in fact, been junior colleagues of van Wyk Louw, who was head of the department from 1958 until his death in 1970. Yet, whereas Louw's initiative of the 1930s was intended to protect a nascent *volk* avant-garde, theirs was designed to create an opening for more radically interventionist kinds of writing by sidestepping both the censors and over-compromised publishers like H & R. Taurus, as they eventually called their new imprint, was 'a small, private, non profit-making publishing company', which, as its promotional materials declared, 'gave writers of literature the assurance that it would publish any manuscript of value without any form of pre-censorship being exercised'.[31] Though the need for their new project was made especially urgent when Buren closed down in 1975, it was prompted more immediately by the refusal of H & R, and two other publishers, to take *Oomblik in die Wind* (Instant in the Wind), Brink's historical novel about interracial love. By this stage, though significantly only after *Kennis* had been banned, H & R was beginning to defend its own position in purely financial terms, claiming that it had refused the novel because the printing costs and the risks of censorship were too high.[32]

Though Taurus was later registered as a private limited company—again, like many other small interventionist publishers, largely for legal, rather than financial, reasons—it began as a cross between a clandestine publisher and a mail-order book club, following the strategy Coetzee and his colleagues adopted with the hardback edition of *Oomblik in die Wind*, their first title. After placing an advertisement for the novel in the Afrikaans press inviting interested readers to send cheques for R8.95 to an anonymous postbox address in the Johannesburg area (despite this relatively high price, the entire first print run of 1,000 copies was ordered in five days mainly by writers, academics, and university students), they used the funds to cover the printing, distribution, and royalty costs and then sent the novel out to subscribers by post. To avoid any possible complications with printers they used a local Asian-owned company, whose compositors could not read Afrikaans. This strategy cut their financial risks by ensuring that the entire print run could be distributed before the censors were in a position to act. Even though some more mainstream book-shops continued to refuse to stock their titles, they began to use more conventional modes of distribution during the era of 'repressive tolerance' in the 1980s.

Despite Taurus's careful planning, *Oomblik* was picked up by the censors on two occasions. In February 1976, two months after it was distributed, the chief censor himself submitted a copy, though, after an initial assessment, he decided against putting it before a committee (P76/1/31). Four months later, in response to a complaint from a morally outraged woman reader a committee, including Merwe Scholtz (chair) and Anna Louw, passed it largely on literary grounds. They thought it was a class above *Kennis van die Aand* because it displayed no 'sign of commitment', but they also argued that its setting in the eighteenth century softened the impact of its 'most problematic element: the affair between the white woman and the coloured slave' (P76/10/37). After Brink switched back to H & R with *Gerugte van Reën* (Rumours of Rain, 1978), which, as we have seen, was scrutinized but not banned, he returned to Taurus when the more established firm once again rejected *'n Droë Wit Seisoen* (A Dry White Season, 1979), his next, supposedly more 'committed', novel. Like *Gerugte*, it went through the absurdly involved bureaucratic process set up to protect literature after the *Magersfontein* debacle. Having initially been declared 'undesirable' by the security censors, it was then released on appeal after the chief censor decided to test the new arrangements. Though the Appeal Board's committee of experts, which again included Merwe Scholtz and Anna Louw, was not willing to defend the novel as literature, they argued against banning, in part because they felt this would give it more attention than its 'unorthodox manner' of publication had achieved.[33] The fact that both the English and Afrikaans editions were being considered by the censors at all had, of course, already made the novel a national and international media event.

While it is possible to describe other Afrikaans publishers of the apartheid era as interventionist—Buren, for instance, and the small black Afrikaans poetry firm Prog launched in 1988—Taurus was undoubtedly the most prominent and successful. It developed a substantial list of over eighty titles, including all of

Breytenbach's later works, the little magazine appropriately entitled *STET*, and a number of important political studies. It also worked closely with the new generation of internal English-language publishers, notably Ravan Press with whom it co-published a local edition of Gordimer's *July's People* (1981). By that stage Gordimer was eager to support local publishers who refused to have anything to do with the censors. Its strategy for evading the system was, for the most part, effective. It appears it fell foul of the system only during the particularly repressive and anti-literary Pretorius–Snyman era (1975–80) when eight of Taurus's literary titles were submitted. Unusually for an Afrikaans publisher almost half came from the police. Of these, four—all literary works by younger writers—were banned for various periods: John Miles's political satire *Donderdag of Woensdag* (Thursday or Wednesday, 1978) and his children's story *Stanley Bekker en die Boikot* (Stanley Bekker and the Boycott, 1980), André Le Roux's experimental fiction *Te Hel met Ouma!* (To Hell with Granny, 1980), and Dan Roodt's anti-*volk* satire *Sonneskyn en Chevrolet* (Sunshine and Chevrolet, 1980).

The extent to which Taurus alone safeguarded the future of Afrikaans literature in the late apartheid era was, however, a point of contention, particularly with H & R. In 1985 the two publishers became embroiled in a vitriolic public quarrel about the quality of their respective lists and the integrity of their editorial policies. H & R claimed, disingenuously, that Taurus had produced a 'bunch of rubbish', which other publishers had turned down for 'literary reasons'.[34] They also pointed out that their own firm had incurred considerable costs fighting the *Magersfontein* case in court and securing the eventual release not only of André Le Roux's *Struisbaaiblues*, one of their own titles, in 1980 but of Brink's *Kennis* two years later. Though, as one of Taurus's supporters noted, this strategy gave the 'whole disgusting system' an air of 'respectability' (Taurus itself had a policy of non-cooperation with the censors), the overheated dispute had as much to do with the two publishers' divergent attitudes to censorship as with their very different positions with regard to the *volk* avant-garde.[35]

More than anything else, the *Magersfontein* case confirmed H & R's well-established alliance with the more acceptable, if still always marginal, tradition of 'loyal resistance' and its representative literary censors, particularly Merwe Scholtz and Anna Louw, who argued vigorously against the banning (see Chapter 6). The various repercussions—censors resigning, the legislative amendments, etc.—revealed that this particular episode in the late 1970s was simply a replay of the tensions of the early 1960s between the *volk* avant-garde and the government, rather than a new development. What distinguished Taurus was that, unlike H & R, it opened up space for an anti-*volk* (and anti-apartheid) literary tradition to develop, and, more importantly, for a post-*volk* avant-garde to start finding its voice. Tellingly, in 1989 Antjie Krog, who had until then been a sometimes carefully managed H & R author, moved to Taurus with her eighth volume of poems, *Lady Anne*. By then Krog, who had become increasingly perturbed by H & R's entanglements with the collaborationist Nasionale Pers, had begun to establish closer ties not just with the figures behind Taurus but with the progressive cultural bodies that emerged in the late 1980s, including the ANC-aligned Congress of South African Writers. Part ready-made poetry (it uses quotations from various documents, primarily Lady Anne Barnard's (1750–1825) colonial writings on the Cape), part self-reflexive meditation on the ethics of writing, *Lady Anne* raised unsettling questions about the situation of the privileged white woman writer and the place of European literary traditions in Africa. Emerging as it did out of the cultural debates of the 1980s, which centred as much on matters of literary authority (who writes? on whose behalf?) as on broader problems of cultural dominance (who publishes? for whom?), it cast a new, sceptical light on the more radical Sestiger attempts to open up the whole country for Afrikaans writing. Given the tensions of the mid-1980s, it is worth noting that when Taurus stopped operating in 1992, H & R did a volte-face and took over its list.

English publishing

Out of London

Writers who adopted English as their main literary medium were always in a different position from their peers who chose to write in one or other of South Africa's minority languages, not least because they had access to a global literary marketplace. For W. P. Ker, the manager of the local publishing division of Longmans, Green, then the second-largest multinational in South Africa after Oxford University Press, this was less a fact about the trade in English-language books than a measure of cultural value. 'If a novel is worth publishing at all,' he commented in 1959, 'it is worth publishing in England for the world market.'[36] At one level, this claim, which is as much a statement about the economic legacies of the colonial book trade as it is a testament to the endurance of old networks of cultural patronage and prestige, is borne out by the publishing history of most novels, and many autobiographies, originally written in English by South African-born writers before 1960 and indeed well into the 1970s. Poetry and short stories, which often appeared first in periodicals, circulated in other, sometimes intersecting, channels, a point to which I shall return. At another level, however, Ker's colonialist phrasing belies the complexity of the globalized market for literatures in English in the second half of the twentieth century. This is in part because the writings deemed worthy of publication by British-based cultural arbiters were produced not 'in England for the world market' but chiefly by a limited number of independent London publishers for a UK, (post-)colonial, and Commonwealth market. Oxford University Press was the principal exception to the metropolitan rule.

These more subtly differentiated, if still residually colonial, ties were strengthened, rather than weakened, in the immediate post-war era, despite the rise of New York as rival centre and the growth of the publishing industry in South Africa and across Africa generally. Under the Traditional Markets Agreement, signed in 1947, Britain and the United States divided the increasingly competitive Anglophone 'world market' into a series of protected trading zones, giving British publishers exclusive selling rights in South Africa and throughout the Commonwealth. Though this collapsed in the mid-1970s, the patterns it consolidated remained more or less unchanged throughout the apartheid era. US literary publishers would, of course, continue to have a considerable impact on the fortunes of numerous writers and works from Alan Paton's iconic novel *Cry, the Beloved Country* (1948) to Mark Mathabane's topical autobiography *Kaffir Boy* (1986), but these trading arrangements meant that they remained largely unaffected by the hazards of dealing with the South African censors, who controlled access to the local market. Initially the risks fell mainly on British publishers, who continued to dominate the import trade. In the 1940s and 1950s this meant, above all, the pioneering group of independent literary publishers in London that were founded in the previous two decades, some of whom were, at the time, fighting their own battles against the constraints of English obscenity law. Some, like Victor Gollancz and Secker & Warburg, had close links to the British left, while others, like Jonathan Cape and Faber & Faber, had strong African interests or connections.

Though South Africa was not the largest market in the Commonwealth for British publishers in general (Australia held that prime position), it was the largest in Africa and it was inevitably a vital source of income for these literary publishers. That Gollancz, whose politics were never otherworldly, negotiated to reduce Gordimer's advance on *The Late Bourgeois World* (1966) by almost half—from £500 to £300—if it was banned, indicates just how significant local sales could be commercially.[37] The trouble was, to access this important market, British publishers had to contend with South Africa's draconian and highly politicized customs legislation, the foundations of which were, as we have seen, laid well before the Nationalists came to power in 1948. As the fate of Stuart Cloete's popular and unflattering fictionalization of the Voortrekkers, *Turning Wheels* (1937), revealed, this put some London publishers—the well-established literary imprint Collins in this case—on an antagonistic footing not just with the affronted Afrikaner nationalist press but with the first Board of Censors, which scrutinized imported books from 1934, and, in the end, with the government itself, since under this system the Minister of the Interior had the final say. In the course of the 1950s and early 1960s the Nationalist government began to make extensive use of this older legislation to suppress a series of literary works that reflected on the devastating rise of apartheid.

Yet, even here, elementary bibliographical considerations, which are intimately bound up with questions of readership, complicated the otherwise crudely repressive process. Nadine Gordimer's relatively innocuous story of interracial sociability *A World of Strangers*, for instance, which was passed as an expensive Gollancz hardback in 1958, was banned in the cheaper paperback edition published by Penguin in 1962; whereas Alan Paton's story of miscegenation and its disastrous consequences *Too Late the Phalarope* was approved in its Panther paperback edition in 1958, despite concerns about its 'objectionable' cover. It featured a powerful black woman and hinted at a dark history of 'intermingling' (see Chapter 4). By contrast, Harry Bloom's fictionalized narrative of the early 1950s defiance campaigns *Transvaal Episode* (Collins, 1956; Seven Seas, 1961) was banned in both formats; while Hans Hofmeyer's story of migrancy and race relations on South African mines *The Skin Is Deep* (Secker & Warburg, 1958), Sylvester Stein's political satire *Second-Class Taxi* (Faber, 1958), and Daphne Rooke's sombre tale of miscegenation *The Greyling* (Gollancz, 1962) were all banned in their first hardback editions. Black writers were treated particularly severely, especially those who, as Richard Rive later put it, wrote 'primarily for a White readership to remind it of its moral and political responsibilities'.[38] Four major autobiographies were all banned in their first hardback editions in this period: Peter Abrahams's *Tell Freedom* (Faber, 1954, banned 1957), Alfred Hutchinson's *The Road to Ghana* (Gollancz, 1960), Todd Matshikiza's *Chocolates for my Wife* (Hodder & Stoughton, 1961), and Bloke Modisane's *Blame me on History* (Thames & Hudson, 1963). Though Es'kia Mphahlele's first autobiography, *Down Second Avenue* (Faber, 1959), escaped banning, the first edition of his important critical study *The African Image* (Faber, 1962) did not (see Chapter 5).

When the censors began to see themselves as guardians of the literary, after the new legislation was introduced in 1963, this already highly politicized and opaque process became even more unpredictable, as all the mainstream British literary publishers discovered to their cost. Most of their books inevitably continued to enter the system via customs, though, as Gollancz discovered with Gordimer's *The Late Bourgeois World*, things could sometimes be trickier. When increasingly cautious booksellers refused to order the novel unless it had been passed by the censors, Gollancz, who, as they had previously shown with Rooke's *Mittee* (1951), were willing to put pressure on authors to expurgate works themselves, were put in the awkward position of having to agree to let their local representative submit a proof copy prior to publication.[39] Later, when these ethical dilemmas were further exacerbated by the new review and appeal procedures, other British firms, including Collins, Faber, Heinemann, Oxford University Press, and Penguin, adopted a similarly pragmatic stance. Though often anxious about the implications of trading with South Africa, which had been the focus of an energetic cultural boycott by prominent international writers' and artists' groups since the early 1960s, they worked with the system to try to secure the release of some of their titles. Only Heinemann went so far as the courts, however, and then only once, with Wilbur Smith's first novel, *When the Lion Feeds* (1965).

In the early 1960s, however, it was not only changes in the censorship bureaucracy that affected relations between British publishers and local writers. Developments within the international book trade itself, notably the advent of two innovative paperback series, Seven Seas Books and the Heinemann African Writers Series, and the rise of new African imprints like Mbari in Nigeria and the East African Literature Bureau in Kenya, also had a profound effect on the structure and dynamics of the market, not least because they rapidly attracted a new generation of young black writers. Partly because of this, the key group of independent literary publishers in London came to be associated almost exclusively with white writers after 1960. Bessie Head, who was initially published by Gollancz, Peter Abrahams, who remained with Faber, and Lewis Nkosi, who was published by Longman and Oxford University Press, were the main exceptions. The consequences of this were significant, as we shall see, but it is worth noting that this new division in the market did not entail a return to an earlier colonial era in any simple sense. The close relations publishers like Faber, Cape, Gollancz, and Secker developed with major white writers of the apartheid era, which were usually brokered by literary agents, brought obvious benefits for all parties. In exchange for the prestige and commercial rewards writers of the stature of Breytenbach (Faber), Brink (Allen and Faber), Coetzee (Secker), and Gordimer (Gollancz and Cape) brought to their various imprints, the publishers provided the support of influential literary editors as well as access to a vast transnational market, to potentially lucrative advances, and to UK prizes. They also offered less tangible benefits, not so much because of their metropolitan or formerly colonial status but because of their cultural standing within the British literary world.

For Brink the specific forms of validation these publishers afforded had a particularly powerful significance. In the early 1980s he provoked a costly court case by moving from W. H. Allen, who published *Looking on Darkness* (1974) and all his subsequent novels of the 1970s, to Faber after he became dissatisfied with the increasingly mass-market orientation of Allen's list. 'My whole life as a writer', he explained in a letter to his editor at Allen, 'has been devoted to the use of serious literature as a means of fighting for justice and freedom within my own unjust and unfree society; and this struggle can only achieve the right resonance if it is experienced, not only in its own right but also contextually, as serious literature.'[40] This no doubt goes some way towards explaining the hold H & R continued to have over Brink in South Africa, despite its own more problematic 'resonance'. He later described Allen's first edition of *Looking on Darkness*, which launched his international career, as a 'ghastly publication

FIG. 2.2. The cover of the first edition of André Brink's *Looking on Darkness* (1974), which made his name internationally.

which looked like a billboard for a massage parlour'.[41] The front cover did carry a large, garish red banner saying 'The Novel That Scandalized White South Africa', but, somewhat contradictorily, it also included the following headline quotation from Alan Paton, who was described as the 'author of *Cry, the Beloved Country*': 'This is a novel of stature that explores our cancerous condition more persistently than any novel has done before, and without benefit of anaesthetic.'[42] The inside flap developed this contrast by setting Paton's enlightened views of pornography against those of J. D. Vorster, the Moderator of the General Synod of the NGK, who declared, 'if this is art, then a brothel is a Sunday school'.[43]

Other writers were equally alert to the power the right London publishers had, not just to endorse their own literary projects, but to shape their reputations by promoting and presenting their books in particular ways. Though J. M. Coetzee initially felt a small avant-garde press, like John Calder or Peter Owen, would have provided a more likely venue for his writings, the long association he began with Secker & Warburg in 1977 was successful, in his view, because they 'to a very large extent allowed me to present myself, through their medium, as a novelist pure and simple'. Above all, unlike his local publisher Ravan Press, Secker did not attempt to turn him, a 'novelist of South African birth', into a 'South African novelist', a conventional, and at that time politically questionable, literary role he publicly refused on a number of occasions (see Chapter 8).[44] Yet, as Gordimer discovered, things were rarely so straightforward. On the one hand, given the emphasis she placed on her own interventionist stance as a writer opposed to the racism of apartheid, she did not approve of being championed merely as a feminist in Virago's paperback reprint series in the 1970s.[45] On the other hand, given her increasing commitment to a specifically African identity as a writer, she had to contend with the fact that Gollancz and, from the 1970s, Jonathan Cape preferred, for obvious marketing reasons, to present her novels in more universal terms (see Chapter 4). In the inevitably politicized circumstances of literary publishing in the apartheid era, both in the multilingual 'internal' market and in the larger 'external' Anglophone market, these acts of validation had a peculiarly powerful significance, especially given the way the global market began to change in the 1960s.

African Writers and Seven Seas

The new developments can be seen clearly in Richard Rive's early publishing career. Having earned a reputation in the 1950s as a notable short-story writer in various local magazines (among other things he won a prize competition run by *Drum* in 1956), Rive made his international debut with four books in the early 1960s: two of his own, *Emergency* (London: Faber, 1964) and *African Songs* (East Berlin: Seven Seas, 1963), and two edited collections of short stories, *Quartet: New Voices from South Africa* (New York: Crown, 1963) and *Modern African Prose* (London: Heinemann African Writers Series, 1964). All but the last were banned. The provenance of the last three was especially telling, particularly as they bore witness to a series of emergent networks around which new transnational solidarities were beginning to develop. While the Faber link had already been established by Peter Abrahams, Rive's association with Crown was made possible by Langston Hughes's championship of African writing in the United States. Crown had published Hughes's popular *African Treasury* anthology in 1960, which was dedicated 'To the young writers of Africa' and which included one of Rive's short stories.[46] Rive repaid the compliment by dedicating *African Songs* to Hughes.

Rive's own Crown anthology, which contained short stories by three other writers in his immediate circle (Alex La Guma, James Matthews, and Alf Wannenburgh), looked back to the multiracial ideals of the 1950s (it was dedicated to Es'kia Mphahlele and it had an introduction by Alan Paton), but his contacts with Hughes, and more generally with the American civil rights movement, looked forward to the new Black Consciousness formation that would emerge in South Africa at the end of the decade. Seven Seas and the Heinemann African Writers Series (AWS), which were, unlike Faber and Crown, newcomers to the literary scene, opened up other avenues, particularly for young black writers, some of whom were having difficulties establishing themselves on the London literary scene. While Alex La Guma, who was published first by Mbari in Nigeria, then by Seven Seas and finally by AWS, was rejected by Jonathan Cape and Secker & Warburg in the 1960s, Bessie Head moved from Gollancz to AWS in the 1970s, where she found that her work received more sympathetic consideration.[47] The developing lists for the two new series often overlapped, but, given the distinctive nature of their markets and projects, the way in which they presented their authors was significantly different.

Seven Seas (1958–78), an English-language paperback series published out of East Berlin, was a product of the cultural Cold War. It was founded by Gertrude Gelbin, the American wife of the East German dissident Stefan Heym—both were exiles from McCarthyite America—and, given the inexpensive price of the books, it was most probably heavily subsidized by the Ministry of Culture in the GDR. Intended to promote the cultural and political values of international socialism, it included a range of titles supporting the anti-colonial resistance across Africa, the American civil rights movement, and the anti-apartheid struggle. As its name indicated, it was internationalist in outlook and ambition, though, in practice, its books were often more widely distributed outside the UK and the United States in part because of the protective copyright agreements but also because American customs officials were hostile to books emanating from communist countries. Unlike their South African counterparts, however, who routinely sent Seven Seas books to the censors to be banned, US customs simply insisted that they be stamped forbiddingly 'Produced in Soviet occupied territory'.[48]

In the 1960s the Seven Seas list included a diverse group of interventionist black and white writers: paperback reprints of Jack Cope's *The Fair House* (1960), Harry Bloom's *Transvaal Episode* (1961), and Es'kia Mphahlele's *Down Second Avenue* (1962); first editions not just of Rive's debut short-story volume

African Songs (1963) but of Alex La Guma's novels *And a Threefold Cord* (1964) and *The Stone Country* (1967); as well as edited collections, one by Gelbin herself, *Following the Sun: 17 Tales from Australia, India and South Africa* (1960), and one by Herbert L. Shore, *Come Back, Africa: Fourteen Short Stories from South Africa* (1968). Seven Seas presented all these books as 'protest' literature, though, as Shore, a leading American Africanist, made clear in the introduction to his anthology, the series also had a wider revisionist purpose: to challenge the stereotypically racist portrayal of blacks in white writing (he specifically cites Cloete's *Turning Wheels* and C. M. van den Heever's Afrikaans farm novels *Droogte* (Drought, 1930) and *Somer* (Summer, 1935)) and to open up space for black self-representation.[49] This aspect of the venture appealed most to a writer like Rive, who was uncomfortable with Gelbin's more general aesthetic ideals. Her 'enthusiasm' for 'communist' art and architecture made him 'sink into an aggressive cynicism', and he rejected the idea that literature had to be 'subservient to the common good, which was in turn reflected in State policy'.[50] At that point, as a writer, he still saw himself in exclusively liberal terms as a dedicated individualist. What he appreciated was that, unlike the four other overseas publishers to whom he sent *African Songs*, Gelbin was willing to 'risk publishing relatively unknown writers'.[51] After her death in 1969, the South African element in the series all but disappeared.

The long-running Heinemann African Writers Series (1962–2004) was a less self-consciously political enterprise. It was the most successful attempt by a major colonial educational publisher to reinvent itself as a post-colonial African literary imprint, partly as a public relations exercise, partly to consolidate its share of the market. By working closely with prominent African literary editors (Chinua Achebe, the founding editor, was followed in the early 1970s by Henry Chakava in Nairobi and Aig Higo in Ibadan), and by focusing, at least initially, on the Anglophone African market, it set out to develop a modern literary canon fashioned 'by Africans for Africa'.[52] Though the series early on included Richard Rive's *Modern Prose* anthology, the first edition of Mandela's collection of political essays *No Easy Walk to Freedom* (1965), and reprints of Peter Abrahams's *Mine Boy* (1964) and Rive's collection *Quartet* (1965), its list of South African contributors began to expand rapidly when James Currey took over as managing editor in 1967. Currey, who had previously worked for Oxford University Press in South Africa, had close ties to the liberal journalist Randolph Vigne, who edited the *New African* (1962–8), one of the leading anti-apartheid monthlies of the 1960s, and, as a consequence, AWS published a number of authors from the *New African* stable, including Rive, Bessie Head, Dennis Brutus, Mazisi Kunene, and D. M. Zwelonke. Reflecting his broader commitment to the cultural struggle against apartheid, Currey also published a second, expanded edition of Barry Feinberg's anthology *Poets to the People* (1980), which was first brought out by Allen & Unwin in 1974, and Robert Royston's *Black Poets of South Africa* (1974), which was first published by the South African firm Ad Donker under the title *To Whom It May Concern* in 1973.

Like all the other prominent South African contributors to the series—Steve Biko, Modikwe Dikobe, Alex La Guma, Arthur Nortje, Cosmo Pieterse, Mongane Serote, Sipho Sepamla, and Can Themba—the contributors to these anthologies had particular significance for Currey as AWS authors. Since some were classified as 'Coloured' under apartheid, their presence ensured that the word 'African' in the title had a geographical, rather than racialized, meaning. Currey underscored this feature of the series in the 1970s by persuading his colleagues in Ibadan and Nairobi to reprint Doris Lessing's *The Grass Is Singing* (1973) and to add Nadine Gordimer's specially selected collection of short stories *Some Monday for Sure* (1976). Later he also reprinted Hugh Lewin's banned prison autobiography *Bandiet* (1981). Yet, as Currey's correspondence with Bessie Head over *A Question of Power* (1974) in 1972 suggests, this inclusiveness at times unsettled his own understanding of the unstable term 'African', which was not simply geographical. He found her complex study of the 'terrifying experience' of madness, which Gollancz had rejected, powerful but difficult and worried that it was not 'really African' in a more normative, aesthetic sense, though, he added, the 'whole race thing gets across'.[53] It was, in his view, 'more closely related to the mainstream of Anglo-American internal writing'. While he was willing to go ahead with it 'as an experiment' for the African market, he felt that for its full effect to be appreciated she should also try to place it with Secker & Warburg for the hardback edition and Penguin or Pan for 'the U.K. bookstall market'. As it turned out, the hardback edition was published by the obscure London firm Davis-Poynter. A Penguin edition did eventually appear, though only in 2002. It is difficult not to assume that similar aesthetic anxieties lay behind Currey's decision to turn down J. M. Coetzee's *Dusklands*, which Ravan Press sent to him in the mid-1970s.

Given the nature of their publishing projects, it is not surprising that Seven Seas and AWS books were closely scrutinized by the censors. That they were not routinely banned is more remarkable. Seven Seas suffered the most. Though, as we saw in Chapter 1, Jack Cope's *The Fair House* passed, albeit on strategic grounds, the other three titles scrutinized under the new legislation in the 1960s were banned for political reasons. This was largely because Alex La Guma was 'listed', though, as Murray argued in his report on *The Stone Country*, which made no reference to the novel's literary merits, it was also because of the way he was presented as a Seven Seas author. The novel was, Murray claimed, 'a little rough' about life in jail, but 'not enough to warrant banning'. What 'damned' it was the dedication, the note 'About the Author', and the blurb on the back cover (BCS 1/70). The novel, which was dedicated 'to the daily average of 70,351 prisoners in South African gaols in 1964', included a short biographical sketch on the inside pages that focused on La Guma's own history of banning, imprisonment, and eventual exile, and described his decision, taken while under house arrest, to turn to writing as means of continuing his fight for justice. This was underscored in the blurb, which briefly described the contents of his first three novels and made it clear that, while they revealed a 'gleam of humanity' and a 'touch of hope', their purpose was not merely or chiefly literary, since 'there is no Art for Art's sake in a book based on the truth about apartheid, or for an author who chooses this shameful and vicious oppression of people as his theme'.[54]

Of the nineteen AWS titles that appear to have been scrutinized between 1964 and 1990, just under half were banned, including two collections of political essays by Nelson Mandela and Oliver Tambo. In some cases, as with Zwelonke's quasi-autobiographical *Robben Island* (1973), which described the abuse of political prisoners in detail and praised Poqo, the armed wing of the Pan Africanist Congress, the outcome was predictable. It was banned on moral and political grounds in 1973 and for possession in 1976 and 1985. In other cases, however, the looseness of the system, which relied heavily on the idiosyncrasies of particular censors' judgements, made the final result anything but obvious. That Bessie Head's *A Question of Power* (1974) was let through, despite its 'frequent references to and gibes against the South African system' and its 'occasionally obscene' descriptions of Elizabeth's 'fantasies', was especially unpredictable. It is difficult not to assume that the initial reader's crudely racialized comments affected the Kruger Board's final decision. The reader, J. Klopper, who was neither astute nor self-consciously literary, claimed that the novel was about the 'difference between [Elizabeth, the central consciousness] as coloured and the local black people' in Botswana; and it was 'based on the beliefs—superstitions—of undeveloped black people'. Moreover, he noted, Elizabeth's relations with 'Whites' are 'good' (2049/74).[55] Unlike other part-time members of the Kruger Board, including Cloete, Grové, Nienaber, and Merwe Scholtz, Klopper did not belong to the literary professoriate. He was a retired civil servant then in his sixties who had no university education.

Presentational factors and questions of literariness contributed to the unpredictability of the process in a number of other cases, however. This was particularly evident in the way the censors responded to the AWS editions of Feinberg's anthology *Poets to the People* (1980) and Royston's *Black Poets in South Africa* (1974). Jansen, the key security censor who acted as initial reader and chair in both cases, was concerned about the 'variable quality of the poems' in the Royston anthology, all of which belonged, in his view, to the tradition of 'protest literature' (P79/1/161). He identified a number as especially 'provocative', including Serote's 'What's in this Black "Shit"', Gwala's 'Gumba, Gumba, Gumba', Mtshali's 'Men in Chains', and Sepamla's 'To Whom It May Concern'. Nonetheless, because he felt they were not 'repugnant' (*weersinswekkend*) and because they were 'poems' and 'by black people', he argued that a 'higher pain

There is no Art for Art's sake in a book based upon the truth about apartheid or for an author who chooses this shameful and vicious oppression of people as his theme ... In his first novel **A Walk in the Night,** Alex La Guma depicted the corrosion brought by brutality to a location settlement. In **And a Threefold Cord,** his second novel, published by Seven Seas Books, he gives answer to the great call for the battle against apartheid ... In **The Stone Country,** his third novel, he presents another phase of life in South Africa based on his experience as an oft-time prisoner, jailed for illegal activity, subject to all the indignity and cruelty a South African apartheid jail can devise ... And yet, even in this almost hopeless milieu, the great struggle of his countrymen of colour brings to mankind's lower depths the gleam of humanity and the caressing touch of hope ...

FIG. 2.3. The front and back cover of Alex La Guma's *The Stone Country* (1967), showing the note on the back to which the censors took exception.

threshold' had to be applied. Moreover, given that the earlier local edition had been let through in 1974, he could see no reason for banning the AWS version, which, apart from the title, was the same. He did not comment on Royston's introduction, which drew attention to the 'intensely personal' quality of the poems in characteristically liberal–literary terms. Observing that poetry provided the 'most effective vehicle' for 'psychological self preservation', Royston emphasized that there was 'no bravado' or 'special pleading' in their 'assertiveness' and that 'the tone of their work is terse, confidently defiant, humorous, "cool"'.[56]

By contrast, when Jansen came to consider Feinberg's anthology, which contained a number of the same poems, two years later, in 1981, he focused on the editor's introduction, on the fact that some poems were dedicated to 'communists', notably Bram Fischer and J. B. Marks, and that the anthology as a whole was dedicated 'To South Africa's political prisoners and to the African National Congress and its allies' (P81/8/85).[57] After noting that Feinberg was himself a member of the ANC, he drew specific attention to his comment in the introduction about the 'increasing need for South African poets *to identify themselves with* the aspirations of the majority of their people and therefore with the aims of the national liberation movement, *the ANC*' (Jansen's emphasis).[58] Though he did mention that some of the poems 'glorified leaders (among others Mandela) and members of the ANC' and that many had a 'militant tendency', he did not comment on their literary form or qualities, or, indeed, on their status as 'protest literature', even though the censors had by then accorded this category official legitimacy. As a consequence, the security censors, reconfirming their decision about the earlier Allen & Unwin edition, banned the expanded AWS version of *Poets to the People* on political grounds and for possession.

The opposite happened to Nadine Gordimer's AWS collection *Some Monday for Sure* (1976), which was passed, this time by a literary committee, despite its 'militant' introduction and dedication. As Merwe Scholtz, the initial reader, noted, Gordimer declared her commitment to 'unqualified franchise' in the introduction, carefully distinguishing her own political views from those of her compromised and self-deluding characters. He also observed that the collection was dedicated 'To fellow South African writers now banned and in exile, whose work endures and will be read again at home'.[59] Nonetheless, he took the view that the stories themselves were not 'propagandistic' (P76/9/152). The 'ironized' mode of narration ensured that any 'seditious' tendencies they had were not 'sufficiently direct' to be politically 'effective', he claimed. True, many of Gordimer's characters come from 'liberalistic' circles, but, he added, she 'mercilessly strips away' their 'window-dressing'. He did not consider the larger justifications for this, which centred on Gordimer's preoccupation with liberal complicity.

FIG. 2.4. The front cover of Robert Royston's anthology of Black poets *To Whom It May Concern*, which Ad Donker first published in 1973. The censors passed it, but the title and presentation created some controversy among the younger generation of Black poets.

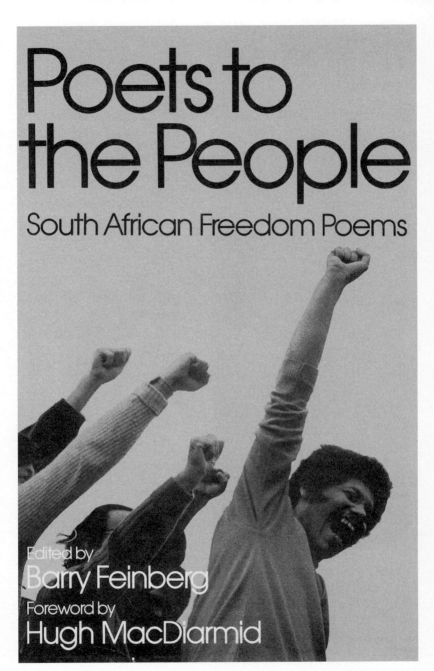

FIG. 2.5. The front cover of Barry Feinberg's anti-apartheid, and specifically ANC-aligned, anthology *Poets to the People*, which was banned for possession. This is from the first edition, published by George Allen & Unwin in 1974.

It is worth mentioning, in this context, that six of the thirteen stories originally appeared in the *New Yorker* in the 1950s and early 1960s, when the magazine had first reading rights on all Gordimer's short stories, but three were rejected, partly because they did not conform to the editor's idea of the literary. They were too political, or, as Roger Angell remarked in a letter to Gordimer dating from 1964, apropos 'Not for Publication', 'you seem less involved with your characters as individuals, and more aware of them as representatives of a group or social class or as figures in some larger contemporary drama'.[60] In her reply Gordimer, who was always sensitive to criticism of this kind, rejected the charge emphatically: 'I had hoped—and hope—to bring to people who could be dismissed as categorical "victims", "oppressors", etc. exactly the same scrupulously personal approach that I have always used for people whose labels are not so easily read—in fact, I have wanted to peel off the labels, as it were.'[61] Despite these tensions over the literariness of her stories, she continued her close association with the magazine well into the 1980s.

Books imported under the imprints of the more mainstream London literary publishers often fared no better or worse than Seven Seas or AWS titles, again largely because of the unpredictability of the censors' literary guardianship. Their belief that mass-market genre fiction was not literature, for instance, which influenced their decisions to ban novels by Wilbur Smith (Heinemann), John Gordon Davis (Michael Joseph), and Stuart Cloete (Collins) on moral grounds, also informed their rulings against anti-apartheid political thrillers like Wessel Ebersohn's *Store up the Anger* (Gollancz, 1980) and Andrew McCoy's *The Insurrectionist* (Secker, 1978). By contrast, their aestheticist assumption that great literature rose above contemporary politics made it possible for them to pass manifestly interventionist novels like Gordimer's *Occasion for Loving* (1963), *A Guest of Honour* (Cape, 1971), and *The Conservationist* (Cape, 1974), as well as J. M. Coetzee's fictions *In the Heart of the Country* (Secker, 1977), *Waiting for the Barbarians* (Secker, 1980), and *Life & Times of Michael K* (Secker, 1983). This assumption could, of course, also work the other way round. Gordimer's *Late Bourgeois World* (Gollancz, 1966), Jack Cope's *The Dawn Comes Twice* (Heinemann, 1969), Brink's *Looking on Darkness* (Allen, 1974), as well as C. J. Driver's two novels about various phases of the resistance *Elegy for a Revolutionary* (Faber, 1969) and *Send War in Our Time, O Lord* (Faber, 1970) were all banned, in part, because they failed the universality test. Most of these decisions were, however, internally contested, and in Driver's case the bans were finally imposed only because Grové persuaded his doubtful colleagues that the novels were, on balance, more propagandistic than literary. While acknowledging that *Elegy*, for instance, 'unmasked' the 'amateurish' group of white saboteurs whose failed endeavours are at the centre of the story, he felt the novel had to be banned because their actions are 'romanticized' and their 'ideals are never criticized' (BCS 632/69).

Periodicals and the Cultural Cold War

In the 1950s and 1960s English-language literary publishing was divided along broadly generic as well as territorial lines. While novelists and autobiographers generally turned to London, poets and short-story writers relied primarily on the opportunities local magazines afforded or, in the case of a select few, leading British and American literary periodicals such as the *New Yorker*, *Encounter*, and *London Magazine*. Despite the short-lived success of Julian Rollnick's African Bookman series (1943–7), which inaugurated the internal intervention-ist publishing tradition, and the advent of new commercial firms like Howard Timmins (1944) and A. A. Balkema (1948), it was only in the early 1970s, when a new generation of publishers emerged, that local book publishers began to transform the literary marketplace. Until then, periodicals of all kinds, ranging from relatively successful mass-market monthlies to precariously underfunded 'little magazines', shaped and reshaped the internal, largely white-controlled literary culture by seeking out and defining new markets, creating space for emergent writers, becoming centres of association and self-promotion, and by defending or contesting particular literary norms and categories. Like all literary cultures, this one was riven by internal disputes of various kinds and hampered by financial constraints. Unlike most, however, it was also acutely alert to the ethical and political challenges of literary publishing in a 'divided society' and constantly imperilled by the government's broader assault on the public sphere.

The most iconic periodical of the 1950s was undoubtedly *Drum*, the long-running mass-market monthly which targeted a newly urbanized black reader-ship. Launched by the eccentric entrepreneur Jim Bailey in 1951, it was, as Lewis Nkosi put it in a 1965 retrospect, 'not so much a magazine' as a 'symbol of the new African cut adrift from the tribal reserve—urbanised, eager, fast-talking and brash'.[62] Hence the alarm it caused the Cronjé Commission in the mid-1950s. In its pages, as Nkosi implied, the ideals of the earlier New African movement entered the age of an Americanized consumer culture. For Njabulo Ndebele, this new kind of new African was typified by Detective Morena, the self-made hero of Arthur Mogale's popular *Drum* stories.[63] Yet the magazine was not simply a mass-market venture. By the mid-1950s, it had become the product of a collaboration between a new generation of interventionist black journalists and aspirant short-story writers, who, together with the magazine's first white editors, Anthony Sampson and his immediate successor, Sylvester Stein, created a format, and welcomed contributions, that blurred distinctions among campaigning journalism, social commentary and fiction, traditional and modern, serious and popular kinds of writing. As Michael Chapman put it, the writings *Drum* published in the 1950s 'show signs of welding older, rural patterns of experience onto a stridently urban environment, tales of intrigue and melodrama involving Americanized Sophiatown gangsters and their molls,

118

and testimonies and opinion pieces which utilize story-telling conventions of atmosphere, dialogue and character presentation in the service of social exposés and factual reportage'.[64] In all this, Es'kia Mphahlele, who was fiction editor from 1954 until he went into exile in 1957, played an especially formative role.

Influential as it was, *Drum* was not the only contemporary periodical to encourage collaboration among journalists and writers or crossover writing of this kind. The largely white-controlled political periodicals, notably the quarterly *Africa South* (1956–61), the monthly *Fighting Talk* (1942–63), and the weekly *New Age* (1954–62), which supported and helped to define the multiracial resistance movement, or Congress Alliance, of the 1950s, also created significant openings. *New Age*, which was just one of the many names of *The Guardian* (1937), the public voice of the underground South African Communist Party (SACP), ran short-story competitions and became one of the principal outlets for Alex La Guma and Alfred Hutchinson. Later, the *African Communist* (1959–), the SACP's longest-running magazine, took over as the main forum for Marxist-Leninist literary opinion, providing a platform for, among others, La Guma, Brian Bunting, and Barry Feinberg, all of whom contributed regular book reviews and essays on cultural issues. By contrast, *Fighting Talk*, which was first edited by Bunting and then by Ruth First from 1955 to 1963, and Ronald Segal's *Africa South* reflected a broad spectrum of contemporary anti-apartheid opinion and attracted contributions from writers as diverse as Guy Butler, Alan Paton, Nadine Gordimer, and Arthur Maimane. Yet all the main political periodicals of the 1950s also championed many of the writers who belonged to the celebrated *Drum* stable. Short stories by La Guma and James Matthews, for instance, appeared not just in *Drum*, but in *Fighting Talk*, *New Age*, and *Africa South*; and while *Drum* published all of Casey Motsisi's fictionalized reportage, all of Can Themba's early writings, and many of Richard Rive and Es'kia Mphahlele's short stories, the latter also appeared in all three political periodicals. Though their editorial policies were eclectic rather than programmatic (despite their Marxist-Leninist orientation even *New Age* and the *African Communist* did not advocate a specific revolutionary aesthetic), they, too, contributed to the inventiveness of the period by publishing writings that disturbed established ideas of the literary.

The only English-language periodical of the 1950s to set itself up more self-consciously as guardian of the literary was the *Purple Renoster* (1956–72), arguably the most typical 'little magazine' of the apartheid era. It began as an inexpensive mimeographed publication; it was always underfunded, relying on occasional individual donations at best; its circulation remained in the hundreds; and, with only twelve issues appearing in sixteen years, it was at most a sporadic annual. Its young editor, Lionel Abrahams (1928–2005), who, like Gordimer, First, and Segal, came from a Jewish immigrant background, shared

119

van Wyk Louw's commitment to the idea of an autonomous 'Republic of Letters' and always remained unapologetic about what he later called 'the error of my individualistic-liberal ways'.[65] Yet his unpretentiously, sometimes self-mockingly unmagisterial project was, in almost every respect, the antithesis of *Standpunte*. For one thing, it was neither nationalist nor avant-garde. If it was inspired by the poet and literary academic Guy Butler's clarion call for English-speaking writers to develop their own national tradition—hence the impossibly ambitious subtitle of its first number, 'A South African Literary Quarterly'—Abrahams never felt burdened by ethnic imperatives that permeated Butler's thinking. As he later explained, the word 'Renoster' (Afrikaans for 'Rhinoceros') in his title was simply meant to convey a loose sense of something 'richly indigenous'.[66] By contrast, Butler, who identified with a British settler tradition Pringle and Fairbairn inaugurated in the 1820s, defined his own ostensibly anti-colonial project in narrower ethno-linguistic terms, which were closer to van Wyk Louw's. Moreover, there was nothing self-consciously avant-garde about Abrahams's colour-coded aestheticism. 'The point about purple is its pointlessness,' he remarked semi-seriously in his inaugural editorial.[67] His new magazine would, he went on, be 'passive about standards in prospect', but it would focus on 'writing done in response to the need for self expression—as distinct from that produced primarily to the requirements of journalism, academicism and crusaderism'. What mattered most, in other words, was 'the sense of individual personality behind the writing'.[68]

What this idea of the literary, which was at once non-instrumental, individualist, expressivist, and anti-political, meant in practice, and how it differed from other less anxiously scholastic ideas in circulation at the time, can be seen in Mphahlele's single, judiciously selected contribution to the *Purple Renoster*. In keeping with his ambitions, Abrahams was eager to ensure that his 'little magazine' did not remain a coterie publication, largely restricted to his immediate circle of Johannesburg Jewish literary friends, and so, early in 1957, at Gordimer's suggestion, he visited the *Drum* offices to ask Mphahlele if he had a suitable story to contribute. What Mphahlele offered was 'The Woman Walks Out', a sequel to 'The Woman', which had appeared in *Standpunte* four years earlier. Partly because of his stature and the diversity of his œuvre, but also perhaps because of his own capaciously humanistic sense of what counted as literature, Mphahlele was undoubtedly the most omnipresent black writer of the 1950s. A short prefatory note to the *Renoster* story explained that 'The Woman' drew 'a detailed portrait of the old woman 'Me 'Madira who ruinously domineers over her children and their spouses'.[69] 'The Woman Walks Out' developed the old matriarch's uncompromising character further and offered another perspective on her testy attitudes to modernity, focusing on her resentment about being obliged to accept Christian ideas of death. No doubt, for Mphahlele, this story, like its predecessor, was safely 'literary' in Abrahams's

FIG. 2.6. The front cover of Lionel Abrahams's the *Purple Renoster* (1971), arguably the most archetypical 'little magazine' of the apartheid era.

particular sense, unlike 'The Master of Doornvlei' or 'The Living and Dead', two of his other stories from the same period. The former, which he placed, appropriately enough, in *Fighting Talk* in 1957, is a story of a battle of wills between an authoritarian Afrikaner farmer and his equally authoritarian black foreman, who provokes a strike among his fellow workers; while the latter, which appeared in *Africa South* a year later, is a study of a minor apartheid official's inner struggle to repress his ordinary sense of fellow feeling towards his black servant.

By the early 1960s, though, tellingly, before the new censorship bureaucracy was established late in 1963, the intimately connected literary and political worlds of the 1950s had been shattered. With the exception of the *African Communist*, which, despite being banned, continued in exile from 1963, all the political periodicals, which had already been subject to constant harassment and repeated bannings, had been closed down, and their editors detained or forced into exile or both. *Drum*, which was kept under constant scrutiny and banned for three years in the late 1960s, had adopted a more cautious editorial policy after Mphahlele's departure ('avoid the highbrow, political kind of story', Bailey advised his new editor).[70] And even the *Purple Renoster* had lost its innocence. Responding to the blanket banning of 102 anti-apartheid activists in 1962, including Segal, who was already in exile, La Guma, Dennis Brutus, and Cosmo Pieterse, Abrahams produced an angry editorial in his fifth issue, denouncing B. J. Vorster, then Minister of Justice. The bans, Abrahams argued, 'infringed' the 'autonomy' of all editors and publishers, making them complicit with the government's 'hysterical superstitious terror'.[71] In defiance, he began the issue with five anonymous love poems, which were in fact by Dennis Brutus. A year later, the security police launched Abrahams into what he called, with some irony, his 'own political career' by seizing some of his papers, questioning him, and submitting a copy of the fifth number to the censors, ostensibly on the grounds that it contained an obscene story ('Dolores' by Barney Simon).[72] Merwe Scholtz, who acted as the initial reader, argued that the story was undesirable primarily on account of its blasphemous and obscene expletives—he made no mention of its literary merits—and that Abrahams's editorial amounted to 'subversive propaganda' (BCS1314/64). The Dekker Board agreed, and so, over a year after it was first published in a print run of 200, this single number of the *Purple Renoster* was banned. Characteristically, given the way the security police tended to operate, there was no mention of the five poems, or of Dennis Brutus, throughout the entire process. Abrahams continued to denounce the government in his editorials in the years ahead, particularly after the further blanket bans imposed on writers in 1966, and to find ways of drawing attention to the new repressive conditions and the questions of complicity they raised. In his tenth issue, which listed all the names of banned and exiled writers, he included the byline: 'Edited by Lionel Abrahams with the

Publications Control Board, The Minister of Justice, The Police Force and The Legal Profession'.[73]

Despite the government clampdown during the emergency period in the early 1960s, a series of new periodicals emerged that attempted to pick up and reshape the cultural remnants of the previous decade. Censorship remained the major threat to their survival, but the most immediate pressures they faced were financial, since, like *Standpunte* and the *Purple Renoster*, but unlike *Drum*, most existed outside the market economy. To remain viable the new periodicals had to rely on patronage and, as many enterprising editors throughout the world discovered in the 1950s and 1960s, the Americans were among the most active and obliging patrons of literature and the arts at the time. Like many notable contemporary literary periodicals, including *Encounter* in Britain, *Black Orpheus* in Nigeria, and *Transition* in Uganda, Jack Cope's *Contrast* (1960–89), Randolph Vigne's *The New African* (1962–8), and Nat Nakasa's *The Classic* (1963–71) were all initially sponsored to varying degrees by the Congress of Cultural Freedom (CCF) or the Fairfield Foundation, which was, along with the Ford Foundation, one of the CCF's principal backers. The CCF had also initially helped to finance Segal's *Africa South*, and in 1975 Sipho Sepamla, one of the most indefatigable champions of the arts in the late apartheid era, would use some of the funds left over from Nakasa's venture to launch his own, revamped *New Classic*.[74] By contrast, reflecting the other side of the cultural Cold War, the *African Communist*, like Seven Seas, received substantial East German backing.

The CCF was itself a product of this global cultural struggle. Established by a leading group of American and European intellectuals in 1950, it set out to create an elite worldwide liberal alliance that would promote Western ideas of culture and act as a bulwark against communism and the broader threat of totalitarianism. Edward Shils, the Chicago-based professor of sociology who, alongside Sartre's adversary Raymond Aaron, was one of the most influential figures within the CCF, set out the kind of thinking that informed its ambitions in Africa in an article first published in 1967. For Shils, the originator of the centre–periphery model of transnational cultural relations, the long-term strategic goal was not just to free African (and Asian) intellectuals from the 'loyalties nurtured by the self-identification of color' but to 'weaken' their 'revolt against Western values' and to enable them 'to emerge from provinciality to centrality'.[75] The CCF was, to this extent, concerned not just about the communist threat but about the Non-Aligned Movement, which was at that point gathering momentum across post-colonial Africa and Asia. As part of its effort to expand its involvement in Africa, where it already had connections with Ulli Beier, the leading German-born Africanist, who founded Mbari in Nigeria, the CCF appointed Mphahlele in 1961, on Beier's recommendation, to act as director

FIG. 2.7. The front cover of Jack Cope's *Contrast* (1969), the principal platform of the liberal-literary elite in the apartheid era.

FIG. 2.8. The front cover of *The Classic* (1968), one of the most important literary magazines of the 1960s. It was initially edited by Nat Nakasa.

of its Africa programme and, among other things, to help identify which periodicals would be worth supporting.

When it was revealed in 1966 that this universalizing project dedicated to promoting ideas like the autonomy of the public sphere was in part funded by the CIA, via the dummy Fairfield Foundation, Mphahlele was, like most African intellectuals, outraged. The 'CIA stinks', he wrote in a letter to *Transition*. Yet on the question of whether or not the revelations undermined all they had done with CCF support, through conferences, scholarships, and broadcasting and publishing initiatives, he was equally emphatic. It would, he argued, be 'dishonest to pretend that the value of what has thus been achieved is morally tainted'. He had undertaken the directorship, he insisted, on the understanding that African intellectuals should not be expected to 'develop with reference to the reflexes of the West' and that the 'elementary realities of culture can best be appreciated within a national context, even when intellectuals in Africa seek to give it a pan-African meaning at one level and a universal one at another'.[76] Though some of Mphahlele's views at the time chimed with CCF policy, particularly his reservations about the 'cult of negritude', as his article in *Encounter* in 1961 put it, his carefully qualified position on the idea of the universal, which informed his developing commitment to a specifically African humanism, stood in marked contrast to the organization's general outlook and, more particularly, to Shils's version of its ambitions (see Chapter 5).[77] These disagreements were reflected in the South African periodicals the CCF sponsored, especially in the markedly different editorial policies and practices of Cope's *Contrast* and Nakasa's *Classic*.

Following its basic principles, the CCF saw itself as having an enabling rather than directive function. It financed periodicals it identified as being broadly sympathetic to its aims, but did not interfere with their editorial policies. On this basis, it refused to back *Fighting Talk* because it was, under Bunting and First's editorships, supposedly too communist, but it helped to fund *Africa South* and the *New African*, both of which published a wide range of anti-apartheid articles, some of which were avowedly Marxist. Of all the South African periodicals it supported in the 1960s, Jack Cope's *Contrast* came closest to embodying Shils's vision of a liberal world order in which 'intellectual performance' would be evaluated 'with little or no reference to nationality, religion, race, political party, or class'. 'An African novelist', Shils confidently declared, 'wants to be judged as a novelist, not as an African.'[78] Like Butler, Cope was among the honourable defenders of a long, specifically South African liberal tradition, which he traced back to 'Thomas Pringle's historic clash with authority when he launched the *South African Journal*'.[79] In theory, his magazine, which took a firm stand against government censorship, set out to defend the ideal of a liberal 'Republic of Letters' and the associated tradition of 'polite literature'. As Cope put it in his inaugural editorial, it aimed 'to keep out of the rough and tumble of parties and groups and yet to cross all borders and to hold a balance between conflicting opinions'.[80] This supposedly disinterested stance, which relied on an oversimplified distinction between politics and culture, was immediately condemned as a piece of liberal bad faith and it remained a point of contention throughout the magazine's long history.

In practice, though *Contrast* published a number of black writers, including Rive, who was also an assistant editor for a period, Nkosi, and Sepamla, it became caught up in a project to 'wean the younger generation' of Afrikaner writers 'away from the compulsive grip of the Nationalist establishment', which, in Cope's view, included van Wyk Louw, even though he was 'sharply critical of some aspects of Nationalism'. Crucially, it undertook this mission 'not on political grounds but towards the literary ideal of thinking and acting as unfettered individuals'.[81] To this end, Cope engaged the liberal anti-nationalist Jan Rabie as Afrikaans editor, who brought in contributions from, among others, Breytenbach, Ingrid Jonker, Etienne Leroux, Adam Small, and Uys Krige, the leading liberal Afrikaner of the older generation. This not only qualified Cope's ideal of crossing 'all borders', it also meant that, despite its best intentions, *Contrast* became entangled in the kind of reflex ethnic thinking that dogged Guy Butler's anti-colonial ambitions and many white-controlled literary prizes, notably the CNA Award, which was founded in 1961, a year after *Contrast* was launched.

As C. J. Driver quickly pointed out in a critical review of the magazine's first year, 'all this talk of the "culture of the English group" is a sort of reaction to Afrikaner and African nationalism', which it was best for 'South African writers in English' to avoid. They should 'try to forget that they are members of an "English group"'. Prefiguring the internal debates about ethnicity among the Sestigers in the late 1960s, he suggested they 'try to see that they are members of a South African nation', which was yet to come, but which was 'growing' and '*will* happen'.[82] Commenting on the achievements of magazines like *Contrast* and the *Purple Renoster* later in the 1970s, J. M. Coetzee was more generous, though no less alert to the questions these publishing ventures raised. They had, he felt, 'performed honourably in terms of their own liberal, non-racial credo'. Yet, by then, the 'acid test' for them had become the 'test of what constitutes literature' and 'there are certain things that cannot be said in the liberal white magazines, not because their editors see themselves as exercising the censor's function', but 'because in terms of their own ethos these quarterly literary journals are not the appropriate forum for overtly "political" and "raw" reportage'. By 1979, he noted, a 'wholly *different* kind of magazine' called *Staffrider*, the emergence of which I discuss below, had begun to reshape the space of the literary in radically new ways—hence Coetzee's wariness about his own terminology.[83]

If *Contrast* reflected the CCF's ideals most clearly, and revealed their limitations in practice, *The Classic*, which, unlike Cope's venture, was founded after

Mphahlele took up his directorship in 1961, embodied his own ambitions most fully. For one thing, as Gordimer, who acted as editorial adviser, remarked, *The Classic* was 'openly dedicated from the first number to the creation of a common literature'; for another, it was launched and initially edited by Nat Nakasa (1937–65), one of the leading young black journalists of the 1950s.[84] Though he had no literary background himself, Nakasa originally proposed the idea of a multiracial 'artistic magazine' to Can Themba in a shebeen (or township bar) behind a laundry called The Classic, hence the title.[85] As a consequence, Nakasa, with Gordimer's support, ensured that it included a significant proportion of black contributors from the outset. Yet, for Mphahlele, multiracialism was not the only issue. Reflecting his own early sympathy for the liberal tradition, he had initially encouraged the CCF to focus on *Contrast* and the *New African*, but he had from the start also been eager to found a new pan-African journal. *The Classic* was the closest he came to achieving that particular goal, though the fact that it pointedly eschewed *Contrast's* liberal neutrality also harmonized well with Mphahlele's own revisionist ideals. As Nakasa put it in his inaugural editorial, the magazine would seek out 'African writing of merit'— hence the inclusion of contributions from across the continent, sometimes in translations from French or Portuguese—and it would welcome the 'work of writers with causes to fight for, committed men and women'. This was not because *The Classic* was going to pursue a particular political line, he insisted. It was just that, if the stories about the 'daily lives' of blacks and whites happened to show that they were 'governed by political decrees', then that would be 'reflected in the material published by *The Classic*'.[86] Unsurprisingly, the first number included contributions by all the leading figures of the 1950s for whom *Drum* was no longer an option: Themba, Nkosi, Rive, Mphahlele, and Motsisi.

As far as the censors, and the security police, were concerned, the only CCF-funded publications to pose a significant threat, after *Africa South*, were Vigne's the *New African* and the newsletter *South Africa: Information and Analysis* (1962–8), which was initially edited by Mphahlele and, after he left the CCF in 1966, by Nkosi. The old Board banned the importation of all issues of the latter early in 1963 and the new Board banned the *New African* initially in single issues in 1964, ostensibly on moral grounds, and then, a year later, in its entirety. By that time, Vigne had, following Segal, gone into exile in London, where he continued to publish his magazine for another three years alongside Nkosi, who joined him as literary editor. Though the banning of the *Purple Renoster* in 1964 set a precedent for the censors' later actions against other equally precarious 'little magazines' in the 1970s and early 1980s, neither *Contrast* nor *The Classic* was banned. The former was scrutinized and passed at least twice in 1964 and 1977, the latter only once in 1966. Significantly, only *The Classic* was submitted by the police. Like the *Purple Renoster*, however, both literary periodicals were deformed by the blanket bans imposed in 1966, which made it a criminal offence for them to publish Kunene, Matshikiza, Modisane, Mphahlele, Nkosi, and Themba, all of whom were by then in exile.

Yet, prior to this, other government actions had already radically altered the fortunes of *The Classic*. When Nakasa was awarded a scholarship to study in the United States in 1965, he was forced to leave on a one-way exit permit and to abandon his editorship after only three issues. His suicide soon after his arrival in the United States was 'an apartheid tragedy, and a tragedy of exile', as Essop Patel later put it.[87] For the next six years, despite Motsisi's continued involvement, a succession of white writers, Barney Simon primarily, took over the main editorial responsibilities, a development which provoked a tense exchange between Nkosi and Gordimer in the banned CCF bulletin in February 1967. For Gordimer, the question was how to hold open a space for the future of black writing in the face of censorship. Though she recognized the dangers of what she would later call 'white proxy', she argued that *The Classic*'s 'raison d'être will be those others, as yet unknown, who have something creative to say, for so long as they are able to say it'.[88] For Nkosi, the more pressing question was how to deal with the problem of white editorial control, which had the 'effect of maintaining White Supremacy'. A year later, when he saw a new generation of young black poets beginning to appear in *The Classic*, he conceded that it might 'after all' still be 'a deserving journal', a point Gordimer underscored in 1969 when she co-edited a number (3/2) featuring Mbuyiseni Mtshali, Njabulo Ndebele, Mongane Serote, and Mafika Gwala.[89] Yet, if this was a vindication of Gordimer and Nakasa's vision for *The Classic*, and the particular kind of multiracial alliance for which it stood, one that rejected the tenets of liberal neutrality and accommodated multiple forms of collective identity (pan-African, national, etc.), it was at best temporary. For the new generation of poets, who shaped and were shaped by the emergent Black Consciousness movement, inclusiveness, even on these terms, was no longer acceptable. In their view, the future depended on a strategic withdrawal from white-dominated literary culture and the creation of autonomous Black cultural spaces.

The late 1960s and early 1970s saw the emergence of a number of new 'little magazines', notably *Ophir* (1967–76), *Izwi* (1971–4), and *Bolt* (1970–5), most of which emanated from university English departments. All continued to play an influential role as guardians of the literary by providing a venue for a new generation of poets and short-story writers from both sides of the racial divide and, in the case of *Izwi*, from across South Africa's diverse linguistic traditions. *Ophir* and *Izwi* also had a strong internationalist orientation. None were deemed to pose a serious threat to the state, however. The exception was *Donga* (1976–8), a multilingual literary broadsheet launched by a group of younger Afrikaans writers, many of whom were closely associated with new anti-*volk* imprint Taurus. In apartheid South Africa's male-dominated, white-controlled, and, at best, bilingual (English–Afrikaans) literary world, *Donga* stood out in a number of ways. For one thing, it was proposed and at first primarily edited by two women writers, Welma Odendaal and Rosa Keet; for another, it had a strong Africanist orientation and a multilingual editorial policy, designed, as the first number announced, 'to accelerate mutual understanding and enrichment and to be a mouthpiece for all young writers'.[90] Its name was derived from the isiXhosa and isiZulu word *udonga*, meaning 'eroded gulley', which had been assimilated into the two official languages and become part of a peculiarly South African lingua franca. In all these ways, *Donga* emphatically rejected the apartheid order. With its interest in emergent writers, and its openness to non-realist literary forms and to Marxist-influenced styles of cultural critique, however, it was also opposed to the established liberal tradition, which it identified above all with Jack Cope, Guy Butler, *Contrast*, and PEN SA. Given all this, Odendaal was surprised that they managed to obtain some initial financial backing from a number of Afrikaans publishers, including Perskor, H & R, and Tafelberg, 'strange allies', as she later commented.[91] Perhaps more surprisingly, given the fiercely polarized climate of the 1970s, their project was also welcomed in Black Consciousness circles. After the young writer and literary academic Mbulelo Mzamane joined the editorial board, *Donga* established close ties with Medupe, the short-lived Black writers' group formed in 1977. This, more than anything else, proved to be its undoing, however.

Though morally offended individual Afrikaner readers complained about the new broadsheet, which led to the fourth number being banned, it was only after the editors announced their association with Medupe in their sixth number that *Donga* attracted the attention of the security police as well. After questioning Odendaal, and raiding her home and the printers she used, the police submitted the seventh number to the censors. This was on 7 October 1977, two weeks before Medupe, along with a range of other Black Consciousness groups, was itself declared illegal. Etienne Malan, the initial reader, successfully persuaded a security committee, which he chaired, to ban the September issue on the grounds that it was obscene, harmful to race relations, and seditious. On the last point, he focused on the fact that it presented 'communists and radicals like Dennis Brutus, Peter Abrahams and Nat Nakasa as innocent victims', and 'spoke in praise of the organization Medupe' (P77/10/66). He was less concerned about the 'contemptuous and vicious' comments Mzamane made about the censors themselves, though he claimed that his references to Black poetry escaping censorship 'because it often goes miles above the minds of our white overlords' suggested that the publishers of *Donga* were prepared 'willingly and knowingly' to violate the Act.[92] In the future, he added ominously, it might be necessary to ban it for possession as well. As it happens, when the next number, which was dedicated to Breyten Breytenbach, then serving a prison sentence on terrorism charges, was submitted, the censors banned it and all

FIG. 2.9. The front cover of *Donga* (July 1977), one of the most innovative literary magazines of the 1970s. It ran for four years and was banned in 1978.

future issues. Though the editors attempted to salvage their project by imme-diately launching a successor entitled *Inspan*, it only survived for two numbers, after which it, too, was shut down. This decision also led to a failed attempt to prosecute its editor, Isabel Hofmeyr, under the Suppression of Communism Act.[8] Though *Donga* and *Inspan* were both short-lived, some of their ideals were, as we shall see, taken forward in new directions by *Staffrider*, the most popular literary magazine of the apartheid era.

Liberal Books

The most significant development of the early 1970s, however, was that peri-odicals ceased to be the focal point of the internal interventionist publishing tradition. With the emergence of three new white-owned imprints—David Philip (1971) in Cape Town, and Ravan Press (1972) and Ad Donker (1973), both in the Johannesburg area—the focus shifted to book publishing. Even though they were all general publishers, who covered a range of fields, including revisionist history, sociology, and politics, they all developed substantial literary lists and their advent transformed the literary marketplace. In the course of the 1970s and 1980s each brought out over seventy literary titles, around a third of their total output. As the writer and academic Stephen Gray commented in 1974, 'a local publishing industry, marked by the nervy rise of independent publishers functioning exclusively within the Southern African market, has unexpectedly made writing (poetry and prose) not only possible, but even profitable'.[93] Their impact was indeed national, regional, and even inter-national. Though they did not start exporting books abroad on a large scale, reversing the well-established trade relations of the colonial era, they did enter into various co-publishing or sub-licensing arrangements with British and US publishers, ranging from small specialist firms like Rex Collings in London and Third World Press in New York to larger-scale Africanist projects like Longman's Drumbeat Series and AWS. Depending on the agreements negotiated, they tended to retain exclusive selling rights in South or Southern Africa. In practice, this meant that from the early 1970s local English-language writers could potentially reach any one or more of five overlapping markets within the increasingly complex global Anglosphere: South Africa, Southern Africa, Anglo-phone Africa, the Commonwealth, or North America.

Like many of the new literary periodicals, all three imprints actively cham-pioned an inclusive, primarily English-language tradition and risked publishing 'Books That Matter for Southern Africa', as David Philip's company motto put it, in spite of censorship. This was not because they adopted particularly confron-tational editorial policies. As Peter Randall, one of Ravan's founders, later recalled, it was 'inevitable' that 'some self-censorship had to be practised for sheer survival'.[94] For Philip it was more a matter of having to 'develop a blanking of the mind' towards the legislation and 'not to be guided by it'.[95] Indeed, this was one of his primary motivations for establishing his own imprint. Having worked for Oxford University Press in South Africa since 1953, he decided to leave when it was 'made clear to me by OUP in Oxford that I would be expected to publish almost exclusively school textbooks'. From the early 1970s, following Longman, OUP went into the 'African school market and concentrated on being distributors of imported books', as a consequence of which they 'ceased to be regarded as oppositional publishers' during the 'years of the dominance of the apartheid state'.[96] Given its own interventionist stance, David Philip, like the other new firms, was kept under close scrutiny by the security police, and, like Ravan, it was subject to more overt forms of intimidation and harassment. Of course, like all the other firms, it also had to contend with the vagaries of the increasingly repressive censorship system.

If Ravan, Donker, and Philip all gave new life to the interventionist publishing tradition, the transformation they effected in the literary marketplace was far from straightforward. This was not just because they were white-owned or because they continued to market their books primarily for a white readership and to depend on the network of generally cautious established booksellers, all of which were located in white areas. It was also because they worked within what Randall later called the 'framework of a dominant white liberal culture' and obliged black authors 'to write and publish within that culture as well'.[97] Alert as he was to the imperatives of the Black Consciousness movement, Randall recognized that to bring about significant change 'black control over at least some of the communications media is vitally important'. In this regard there were, he noted in 1975, 'a number of hopeful signs'.[98] The Black Community Programmes, one of the driving forces behind the new movement, had begun to publish the annual *Black Review* (1972–7); and in 1974 James Matthews launched his own small imprint, BLAC (Black Literature and Arts Congress), which survived entirely outside the established structures of the book trade (see Chapter 7). Sepamla's *New Classic* (1975–8) was an equally promising development. Though it was initially made possible by what was left of the original Fairfield Foundation grant given to Nat Nakasa (to the dismay of some exiles, it was, like *Contrast*, later funded by Anglo-American, South Africa's largest mining company), Sepamla's venture was intended, as he made clear in his first editorial, primarily to create space for the younger generation to 'articulate new definitions' of 'blackness', not simply to continue Nakasa's legacy.[99] These various initiatives formed the foundation of a nascent Black culture, but, as the *Black Review* put it in 1973, the most compelling expression of the 'true Black self' was to be found in 'unpublished revolutionary poetry'. Dissemination in manuscript form, as a 'precious document, circulating in many hands', or through public performances, was, it noted, the best way of bypassing the double peril of censorship, on the one hand, and 'white paternalism', on the other.[100]

FIG. 2.10. The front and back cover of Sipho Sepamla's *New Classic* (1975), including an advertisement for Ravan Press's new list of literary titles.

While Philip, Ravan, and Donker may not have altered the underlying racialized economic structures of the book trade in the early 1970s, they did not enjoy a particularly secure position within the exploitative capitalist order. If Donker, who received some support from Dutch investors abroad, and Philip, who initially relied on his OUP pension for start-up capital, both set out, despite a serious lack of resources, to develop successful publishing businesses, Ravan always existed on the margins of the market economy. Given its origins in the anti-apartheid Christian Institute, established in 1963 by the dissident NGK theologian Beyers Naudé, its founders, Randall, Danie van Zyl, and Naudé—the initial letters of their surnames gave it its name—saw themselves not as politically engaged entrepreneurs but as 'moral crusaders' committed to a gradualist programme of political reform.[101] Though set up, like Donker and Philip, as a private limited company, this was largely a legal fiction designed to afford some minimal protection against government interference. Randall's salary was initially paid by the Institute's publishing programme Spro-Cas (the Study Project on Christianity in Apartheid Society), which he directed and which was funded by a range of progressive European, especially Dutch and German, church organizations. In the years ahead, this network of foreign donors, which included the Swedish government by the late 1980s, would remain crucial to Ravan's precarious survival, and capacity to innovate, in the face of the financial losses incurred as a consequence of censorship, various management crises, and frequent harassment by the security police. In 1979 J. M. Coetzee reported that Ravan lost around R25,000 in its first three years of operation 'as a result of official harassment'.[102]

Despite Randall's own prudently pragmatic approach, which led him on occasion to turn down some more controversial works, Ravan soon earned a reputation as 'a radical, risk-taking publisher'.[103] Even though Randall himself did not have a particularly self-conscious vision as a literary publisher—his own background was in education—his evolving literary list contributed significantly to this image. While Ad Donker, who started out as an Africana imprint, developed a particular interest in the new generation of Black Consciousness writers following the unexpected commercial success of Mbuyiseni Mtshali's *Sounds of a Cowhide Drum* (1971), Philip began by focusing on the relatively secure trade in established white writers, including Cope, Butler, and Paton. By contrast, Ravan's early list, which Randall began to develop while still part of Spro-Cas, included an eclectic range of new, often highly experimental writers. This, too, set Ravan apart from the dominant liberal tradition. As *Donga* pointedly observed, Cope, who was as editor of *Contrast* then identified as the principal guardian of that tradition, was not especially sympathetic to the new literary trends. He took exception to the kind of postmodernism associated with John Barth, for instance, which he considered politically irresponsible, and believed that 'you betray your craft by turning from the realistic depiction of events in the real world'. 'The South African reality is not the reality Cope imagines it to be,' *Donga* replied acerbically.[104]

Though Spro-Cas was primarily a Christian project committed to political reform—among other things, it sponsored the Black Community Programmes, in association with Steve Biko and others, and launched the *Black Review*—its output for 1972 also included *Cry Rage!*, an innovative collection of anti-poems by James Matthews and Gladys Thomas, which became one of the icons of the Black Consciousness movement. Developing this experimentalist line under the Ravan imprint, Randall then brought out Wopko Jensma's *Sing for our Execution* (1973), a self-consciously avant-garde collection of writings and woodcuts, which also formed part of a growing anti-poetic tradition (see Chapter 7). Published in conjunction with the 'little magazine' *Ophir*, this was Ravan's first literary title. In the same year, Randall published *The Black Interpreters* (1973), Nadine Gordimer's important critical evaluation of Black and African writers. This growing list immediately attracted the attention of the police. In the early 1970s they submitted *Sing for our Execution* and *The Black Interpreters*, which the censors passed, as well as *Cry Rage!*, Jensma's second volume, *where white is the colour where black is the number* (1974), and Khayalethu Mqayisa's playscript *Confused Mhlaba* (1974), which they banned. Indeed, in the years ahead, Ravan continued to be the focus of police attention, particularly during the most repressive period in the late 1970s and early 1980s when it adopted a more radical publishing programme. Overall the police submitted almost a quarter of its literary titles (at least twenty-two), just under half of which were banned. By contrast, the literary lists Donker and Philip developed escaped relatively lightly. While Sheila Roberts's *He's My Brother* (Donker, 1977), Breytenbach's *And Death White as Words* (Philip, 1978), and Sepamla's *A Ride on the Whirlwind* (Donker, 1981) and *The Soweto I Love* (Philip, 1977) were banned for various periods, Serote's *Tsetlo* (Donker, 1974), Gwala's *Jol'iinkomo* (Donker, 1977), Royston's anthology of Black poets *To Whom It May Concern* (Donker, 1973), and Paton's *Ah, But Your Land Is Beautiful* (Philip, 1981) were all let through.

Yet, for all his openness to new literary developments, Randall remained, like Donker and Philip, firmly part of the 'dominant white liberal culture' as his own general thinking about literature and the arts revealed. Explaining his decision to move into literary publishing in the early 1970s, he commented: 'Artists are able to interpret our situation and speak to people of all groups in a universal medium and in a way that academics, journalists and clergy cannot because they are so firmly labelled in their ethnic or denominational boxes.'[105] It is worth noting that this kind of liberal thinking presupposed not only that all writers and artists existed as 'unfettered individuals' (to use Cope's phrase), but that all art, including the verbal arts, was as universally accessible as music. At the same time it is clear that for Randall, as for Cope, artists were not quite as unworldly or as unsituated as this would suggest, since they also belonged to a specifically South African tradition of liberal interventionism. For younger writers affiliated to the Black Consciousness movement, which decisively rejected this tradition and its associated cultural assumptions, the costs of being published on these terms were particularly acute. This was, as we shall see, especially evident to Miriam Tlali when she made her debut as a Ravan author in 1975. Yet, as J. M. Coetzee discovered when he emerged on the literary scene under the Ravan imprint the year before, being absorbed into the cultural narrative of South African liberalism raised questions for some younger white writers as well.

After failing to find an agent in New York and London willing to take him on, and, more particularly, after receiving a discouraging response from Cope, to whom he appealed for advice, Coetzee 'gave up' trying to find a publisher for *Dusklands*, his first work of fiction. Then, in 1973, when a friend suggested he try 'a South African publisher, and mentioned the name of Ravan Press', he sent the typescript to Randall, who agreed to publish it, despite being baffled by its strangeness. As Coetzee later commented,

> I knew little about Ravan except that it had been in trouble with the government, which was a good sign, and that it had some kind of Christian background, which was not necessarily a good sign. I was surprised that they took the book: *Dusklands* was quite a 'literary' book, and Ravan was not a 'literary' publisher.[106]

For Randall, just hanging on to Coetzee was the primary difficulty. Though Coetzee remained loyal to Ravan after he moved to Secker & Warburg and Harper & Row with his second fiction, *In the Heart of the Country* (1977)—he personally ensured that Ravan retained the Southern African rights to all his works up to and including *Foe* (1986)—it was, Randall commented later, 'painful to know that as a small publisher we could not compete with international houses to retain authors for whom we had taken the initial risks'.[107] For Coetzee, the difficulty lay not only with the fact that Ravan could not guarantee overseas distribution or pay advances on royalties, but that it presented him, from the start, in terms he found uncongenial. Though *Dusklands* contained two fictions—'The Vietnam Project', which has a contemporary setting in the United States, and 'The Narrative of Jacobus Coetzee', which is set in the Cape during the early colonial period—the cover, which was based on a watercolour by Thomas Baines, the nineteenth-century Africana painter, depicted a colonial-era South African landscape with ox-wagons and distant hills and the blurb called it 'probably the first truly major modern South African novel' (see Chapter 8).[108]

For Miriam Tlali, one of Randall's other key discoveries in the early 1970s, the process by which her own first typescript, which was originally entitled 'I AM . . . NOTHING', became a Ravan book was even more fraught. As the blurb put it,

FIG. 2.11. The front and back cover of J. M. Coetzee's *Dusklands* (1974), which reproduced a characteristic landscape painting by Thomas Baines, a celebrated Africana painter of the nineteenth century.

Muriel at Metropolitan (1975), as it became, represented 'something of a milestone in the publishing of black writing in South Africa'.[109] It was, according to Sarah Nuttall, 'the first novel written by a black woman in South Africa', though it would be more accurate to say *published* in South Africa, given Bessie Head's already considerable œuvre.[110] Yet, as Randall recalled, the typescript he originally received, which Tlali had been trying to get published since 1969, did not resemble a novel in any conventional sense. It was 'a large ring binder crammed with disjointed writings including verses and prayers'.[111] In fact, it was a composite text that Tlali herself saw as a collection of 'essays which have continuity'.[112] It was made up from many documents, including official forms, letters, and quotations from popular Patience Strong songs, and it was not clearly fictional. As Tlali noted in an excised preface, the 'names of persons and places have been changed' for 'obvious reasons'.[113] Randall, who recognized that 'embedded' in this 'mass of material' lay an 'interesting and original narrative', agreed to publish it with significant editorial changes, which he commissioned the writer Sheila Roberts to undertake. In his view, Roberts 'did so brilliantly' and the result was a 'lean and publishable text'.[114] As Nuttall has demonstrated, however, Roberts not only transformed Tlali's 'genre-bending' assemblage into what she thought 'an African woman's novel should be—neither too popular nor too cosmopolitan', she turned a narrative about the 'sheer agony of being black', as Tlali's typescript put it, into a more measured 'autobiographical novel of a black woman in Johannesburg's white-dominated, male-dominated commercial life', as the Ravan publicity had it.[115] Randall reinforced this by using a quotation from Roberts's foreword as part of the blurb, which emphasized that 'Muriel's story is never strident in hatred or resentment.' It displays a 'latent warmth in her attitude towards those "on the other side"' and 'should enlighten, surprise and even delight readers, both black and white'.[116] In effect, Ravan turned Tlali's highly charged and disruptive series of essayistic reflections into a more culturally and legally acceptable exercise in 'polite literature' with feminist overtones.

Whether or not this blurb was designed not just to appeal to a white readership, as Nuttall suggests, but to ward off the censors, or, initially, the police, *Muriel at Metropolitan* successfully avoided being banned for four years. (*Dusklands* escaped the system altogether.) It was only after the less heavily edited second edition, which Tlali considered more authoritative, was published as part of Longman's new Drumbeat Series in 1979 and then submitted by customs that the censors asked the police to pick up a copy of the Ravan edition as well.[117] At that point a security committee banned both versions on political grounds. Admiral Bierman, one of the leading security censors at the time, noted that they did not think the novel especially polite: it 'cannot lay claim to much literary value because [Tlali's] "racism" is so conspicuous that the book is downgraded to "politicking"' (P79/7/2). In a letter to Ravan, the chief censor,

FIG. 2.12. The front and back cover of Miriam Tlali's *Muriel at Metropolitan* (1975), which Ravan Press presented as an exercise in polite literature.

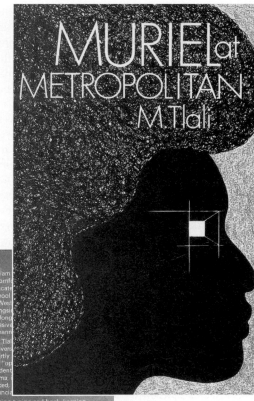

Miriam
Doornf
educate
School
in West
alongsi
no long
massive
Johann

Ms Tlal
Univers
shortly
the "op
student
Roma,
forced,
financie

After returning to Johannesburg and learning typing and book-keeping, Ms Tlali worked as a clerk and typist in the city. It was her experiences during this period that gave rise to this book.

At present, she works from her home in Soweto. She is married, with two children.

MURIEL AT METROPOLITAN is Ms Tlali's first book and it represents something of a milestone in the publishing of black writing in South Africa.

FROM THE FOREWORD BY SHEILA ROBERTS

"Muriel's story is never strident in hatred or resentment against those who have turned her, in Fanon's words, into 'an object in the midst of other objects'. There is even at times a latent warmth in her attitude towards those 'on the other side', a warmth which she knows they will never allow to develop . . . this story should enlighten, surprise, and even delight readers, both black and white . . . ."

ISBN 0 86975 045 3

then J. L. Pretorius, acknowledged that their edition did 'not contain all the parts that were found objectionable in the Longman version'. Nonetheless, it still warranted banning because the 'author refers to Mrs Stein who is Afrikaans speaking as a "lousy Boer" (page 12, bottom); also derogatory remarks about Afrikaners are made on pages 14 and 29'. In fact, the comment about Mrs Stein is made by Donald, one of the characters, who is described as a 'coloured mechanic'; and the other observations are made by Muriel, the first-person narrator.[118] The censors claimed to find over thirty such 'objectionable' passages in the Drumbeat version. Tlali's second work, *Amandla* (Ravan, 1980), a love story set during the Soweto uprisings of 1976, was also banned on political grounds. Significantly, on this occasion, Abraham Coetzee, who had just been appointed chief censor, briefly considered using the new procedures set up after the *Magersfontein* crisis to give the book a second hearing. Partly on the strength of Etienne Malan's reservations, however, he decided against the idea. It was a 'borderline case', Malan admitted. He recognized that Tlali was 'a leading black woman writer' and, now adopting a more nuanced literary analysis, that the 'contentious things actually come from the mouths of her characters—a softening factor', but, he concluded, Tlali 'does not impress me, that is to say, the book cannot be rescued on literary grounds, in my view' (P81/1/108).

Beyond Liberal Guardianship

Randall's enterprising, liberal guardianship of Ravan's literary list came to an abrupt end in October 1977 when he was banned, along with Beyers Naudé, for seven years. This was during the government's general clampdown, in the month following Steve Biko's murder, on the Black Consciousness movement and its affiliates, including the Black Community Programmes, the Christian Institute, and Medupe. It was at this point that Mike Kirkwood, who had already been appointed on a fixed-term basis before the new wave of bans was imposed, stepped in to take over as Ravan's director. Though he had initially been approached by Randall, partly because he had established strong links with Black writers through his editorship of the little magazine *Bolt*, Kirkwood's appointment was finalized by Walter Felgate, the energetic entrepreneur who, having bought out Randall's share of the business, had, in effect, become Ravan's owner and manager in 1977. Felgate, who had connections to the Christian Institute, and, as it turned out, even closer ties to Inkatha, the Zulu ethnic organization Mangosuthu Buthelezi revived in 1975, took over the administrative side of Ravan, leaving Randall to act as general editor and publisher. The plan had been for Kirkwood to become literary editor, but when Randall was banned, he assumed full directorial responsibility, a position he retained until he resigned in 1987.

Kirkwood, a poet and literary academic as well as editor of *Bolt*, was appointed because of his literary background and connections, but he also brought a new political perspective to bear on Ravan. Before joining he had been involved in various worker education projects connected to the emergent black trade union movement, which had, alongside the Black Consciousness student groups, begun to take a leading role in the internal resistance in the early 1970s. He first came to prominence on the literary scene at a poetry festival in 1974 when he gave a provocative paper entitled 'The Colonizer: A Critique of the English South African Culture Theory', which shifted the terms of the debate within white literary circles. Whereas C. J. Driver had, in his critical response to *Contrast* in the early 1960s, focused on the ethnic imperatives fuelling Jack Cope and Guy Butler's anti-colonial ambitions, Kirkwood, who relied on an eclectic amalgam of ideas derived principally from Frantz Fanon, Albert Memmi, and Antonio Gramsci, focused on the residually colonialist assumptions underlying what he called 'Butlerism', an idea of culture which was, in his view, inadequately alert to the structural aspects of white domination.[119] 'This clash', as Attwell comments, was 'seen as marking a serious rift in English-speaking intellectual culture between liberalism and radicalism as the country moved towards what Nadine Gordimer later called its "interregnum" years'. 'Participants at the festival, however, would have been conscious of the potential, at least, for a far more serious clash, one in which the Kirkwood–Butler debate would have been merely a sideshow: a clash between liberalism and Black Consciousness. Indeed, this was the real conflict, though it did not come to a head.'[120] Later Attwell adds, what might have been 'the Serote/Mtshali/Gwala-Kirkwood clash' remains 'a tantalising historical possibility', an 'event that could not take place'.[121] In fact, these various tensions did manifest themselves both openly and behind the scenes in the fraught collaborations between black writers and the new generation of white-owned interventionist publishers. I have already sketched the broad outlines of 'the clash between liberalism and Black Consciousness' which defined the early 1970s; I return to the details in Chapter 7. One of the many tensions of the later 'interregnum' years, however, centred on Kirkwood's energetic, post-liberal directorship of Ravan, and, more particularly, on the questions generated by his two flagship projects: the bimonthly (and then quarterly) literary magazine *Staffrider* (1978–93), and the related low-cost paperback Staffrider Series (1979–86), both of which also tested the censorship bureaucracy at a turning point in its own history.

While giving Ravan a more programmatic literary orientation, Kirkwood also attempted to confront the intractability of his position as a white quasi-commercial publisher committed to promoting black writing. In the first place, he set about reorganizing the way Ravan was run and owned in order to make it a more credible venue within what he saw as a 'transitional culture'.[122] His first move was to make it 'independent' by breaking away from Felgate, whose ties to Inkatha were politically controversial. He also started to look to 'commercial viability for survival in the future', placing most of his hopes in the black 'reading revolution', which he felt was 'on the cards', though, in reality, Ravan remained, throughout his tenure, dependent on substantial foreign donor 'injections'.[123] His second structural move was to create a more cooperative ethos, working closely with the journalist and short-story writer Mothobi Mutloatse and other black editors, notably the poet Jaki Seroke and the dramatist Matsemela Manaka. In 1980 he tried to take this one step further by changing Ravan's status from a privately owned to a 'non-profit company' with the 'controlling membership' vested in the black 'writer's movement' allied to the new branch of PEN SA, which Mutloatse had relaunched in 1978 (see Chapter 3).[124]

When this proved legally and practically unworkable, Kirkwood supported the development of a new black-owned publishing house, the history of which I relate below, and then created the non-racial Ravan Trust. Though set up in part at the request of the Dutch donors who took over as Ravan's principal backers in 1984, the Trust, which held the majority of the shares and had overall responsibility for Ravan's editorial policy, also enabled Kirkwood to create a more devolved management structure. Among the trustees were a number of notable Ravan authors: Achmat Dangor, Ahmed Essop, Njabulo Ndebele, Christopher van Wyk, and Nadine Gordimer, as well as Peter Randall, who was by then unbanned. This ownership structure remained in place for the rest of Ravan's independent existence. At the same time Kirkwood continued to develop a more collectivist approach to its day-to-day operations, though his final efforts eventually led to a crisis, which culminated in his resignation in 1987. The following year the Trust, faced with a disintegrating company and huge debts, 'resolved to constitute a more conventional hierarchy' by appointing Glenn Moss, Kirkwood's successor, as 'manager and publisher'. As Moss later recalled, Kirkwood's last 'experiment', 'regardless of the validity of the ideas behind' it, 'led to the progressive collapse of Ravan's internal structures, administration and staff morale' and threatened to damage the 'pre-eminence' it had 'once enjoyed'.[125]

Yet if Kirkwood's successive attempts to address the problem of white ownership by collectivizing Ravan ended up endangering its reputation, his cooperative editorial approach rapidly made it the most pioneering and, for the police and censors, the most subversive literary publisher of the 'interregnum'. His principal innovation was to devolve the decisions about what constituted publishable literature to writers themselves, or, more particularly, to the numerous Black Consciousness-inspired community arts groups that emerged in the townships in the 1970s. This made it possible for him to minimize, if not wholly abandon, his own position as a guardian of the literary. The primary focus of this publishing experiment was *Staffrider* magazine, which, as its name was intended to suggest, set out to create a new intermediary cultural space and, above all, to reach out to a sizeable reading community in the townships. As Mutloatse explained to Kirkwood, a 'staffrider' was 'somebody who rides "staff" on the fast, dangerous and overcrowded trains that come in from the townships to the city, hanging on to the sides of the coaches, climbing on the roof, harassing the passengers'.[126] Though the association with this 'slightly disreputable' emissary between worlds was intended to signal the new venture's populist ambitions, and to unsettle the literary elite, both black and white, the first editorial, which anticipated a hostile response from the censors, attempted to soften the impact by refiguring the 'staffrider' as a more respectable latter-day Hermes as well.[127]

The magazine's primary objective was to provide a platform for 'the great surge of creative activity which has been one of the more hopeful signs of recent times'. As the first editorial continued, 'the new writing has altered the scope and function of literature in South Africa in ways we have still to discover. The aim of this magazine is not to impose "standards" but to provide a regular meeting place for new writers and their readers, a forum which will help to shape the future of our literature.'[128] Though the influence of the community arts groups lasted for only the first three years, after which *Staffrider* reverted to having a more conventional editorial policy, the aim from the start was to 'encourage and give strength to a new literature based on communities', while also welcoming 'writers who write and publish essentially as "unattached" individuals, yet find the *Staffrider* environment congenial'.[129] This double orientation was reflected in the first issue for March 1978. Alongside a series of poems by young writers from the Creative Youth Association (CYA) of Diepkloof Soweto, including Manaka, the chief figure in the group, appeared 'Soweto Hijack', a short story by Tlali, and 'Hero and Bad Mother in Epic', an experimental, computer-generated poem by J. M. Coetzee. As Kirkwood explained in a letter to Coetzee, the community-centred editorial emphasis also extended to the vexed problem of distribution: 'our distribution is 90% hand-to-hand via an expanding network of contributors and unemployed kids who make you feel that Hermes *is* still alive and well'. The trouble was, he acknowledged, while this network enabled them to bypass the established booksellers and to reach readers in the townships, it did not make much financial sense for any of the parties involved: 'At 25c a copy commission [a sixth of the cover price] no-one can make a living out of selling *Staffrider*, and naturally not all the money comes back.'[130]

Yet if *Staffrider* was never commercially viable, it rapidly established itself at the forefront of contemporary culture in a way that no previous or subsequent little magazine matched. Unlike *Donga*, which at its best achieved a circulation of 700, or the many little magazines that circulated among a small academic elite, the figures for *Staffrider* rose steadily from 2,500 to 7,000 in the first two years (without advertising revenue, which was never significant, the

FIG. 2.13. The cover and contents page of the first issue of *Staffrider* (1/1, March 1978), the most innovative literary magazine of the apartheid era.

About Staffrider

A staffrider is, let's face it, a *skelm* of sorts. Like Hermes or Mercury — the messenger of the gods in classical mythology — he is almost certainly as light-fingered as he is fleet-footed. A skilful entertainer, a bringer of messages, a useful person but . . . slightly disreputable. Our censors may not like him, but they should consider putting up with him. A whole new literature is knocking at the door, and if our society is to change without falling apart it needs all the messages it can get — the bad as well as the good.

Like him or not, he is part of the present phase of our common history, riding 'staff' on the fast and dangerous trains of our late seventies. He is part of the idiom of this time. He appears on page 30 of our first issue thanks to artist William 'Cheeks' Legoale of the Creative Youth Association, Diepkloof.

The magazine which bears his name has been established by RAVAN Press in an attempt to respond, as publishers, to the great surge of creative activity which has been one of the more hopeful signs of recent times.

The new writing has altered the scope and function of literature in South Africa in ways we have still to discover. The aim of this magazine is not to impose 'standards' but to provide a regular meeting place for the new writers and their readers, a forum which will help to shape the future of our literature.

A feature of much of the new writing is its 'direct line' to the community in which the writer lives. This is a two-way line. The writer is attempting to voice the community's experience ('This is how it is') and his immediate audience is the community ('Am I right?') Community drama, 'say' poetry, an oral literature backed and often inspired by music: this is the heart of the new writing, and the signs are that prose forms are re-emerging in a new mould.

It is for this reason that the work appearing in STAFFRIDER flies the flag of its community. We know that there are many groups of writers in Southern Africa whom we haven't been able to reach, and we would welcome their contributions. We hope that the work appearing in the magazine will be selected and edited as far as possible by the groups themselves. The magazine is prepared for publication by RAVAN Press but has no editor or editorial board in the usual sense.

This is our policy: to encourage and give strength to a new literature based on communities, and to establish important lines of communication between these writers, their communities, and the general public. At the same time we welcome writers who write and publish essentially as 'un-attached' individuals, yet find the STAFF-RIDER environment congenial.

FIG. 2.13. (*continued*)

146

'break-even point' was 8,000), and by 1980 Kirkwood estimated that there were 'approximately 500 writers, not to speak of graphic artists, who both help to put the magazine together and, perhaps more important, help to distribute it'.[131] For Njabulo Ndebele, the fact that it created an opportunity for younger writers like Michael Siluma, Joel Matlou, and Bheki Maseko to break with the tradition of 'protest' writing was a key index of its success as a catalyst for a 'new literature'.[132] Writing in 1979, J. M. Coetzee observed that the magazine had 'a unique rationale and unique problems': the 'makeshift financing and distribution of *Staffrider*, the deliberately nebulous editorial control, the precarious existence under the scrutiny of the censors, and above all the anomaly of white money and a black readership—these, taken together, provide no ideal model of how an African literary magazine should be run'. Nonetheless, it was, in his view, 'the most interesting venture on the South African literary scene for years'.[133]

As the inaugural editorial predicted, censorship was the most immediate of the problems *Staffrider* faced. The first number was promptly banned on the grounds of obscenity, harm to race relations, and sedition on 12 April 1978, a week after it was submitted by the police, and a month after it was first published. In his chair's report Etienne Malan noted that it contained some material which was 'of the same undesirable nature as that published in *Donga*' (P78/4/27). Among the writings the censors singled out in *Staffrider*, particularly for undermining the 'authority and image of the police', were Tlali's short story 'Soweto Hijack', 'Stray Bullet', a poem by Hanyane Shikwambane of the CYA, and 'Van', a short story by Peter Wilhelm, who had been one of *Donga*'s guest editors. As the new collectivist Ravan decided not to work with the censorship system, it did not appeal. Instead, Kirkwood held a meeting with J. C. W. van Rooyen, whose reformist approach as prospective chair of the Publications Appeal Board was already being mooted, to defend the project, and Ravan's lawyers wrote to the chief censor to obtain a formal justification for the decision. Following a practice started by *Donga*, Ravan then published the censors' letter alongside its own reply in *Staffrider*'s second number.

Their open letter to the censors began by wryly noting that

> the authority and image of the police are, let's face it, in considerable disrepair as far as blacks are concerned. . . . Nevertheless all the black readers we consulted (did you consult any?) thought that the depiction of the police in the magazine was fair. Moreover, they felt that the depiction, openly published, would relieve tension rather than exacerbate it: a 'safety valve', if you like.[134]

This last statement deliberately echoed van Rooyen's new pragmatic language, which Kirkwood had picked up from his meeting. The letter also noted that 'the narrator in "Soweto Hijack" goes out of her way to look for a "good" policeman and does, in fact, find one'; while the 'policeman in "Van" is in the end a "sympathetic" figure for some readers—perhaps *because* all his weaknesses are shown'. It ended with a plea that *Staffrider* might be 'welcomed pragmatically, not punitively banned' because it had 'brought a measure of hope and trust to our troubled country' and that, in the future, 'black community leaders' and the 'writers themselves', many of whom 'are members of a branch of P.E.N. International recently established in Johannesburg', would be consulted 'before the fate of future issues of the magazine is decided'. As a subsequent report indicates, the more literary censors, including Malan and du P. Erlank, were willing to recognize the force of these arguments. In passing the second issue, they quoted a comment from Ravan's rebuttal, which was in turn extracted from a reader's letter, that '*Staffrider* is great because it inspires one with the desire to resort to the power of the pen compared with the power of the barrel' (P78/6/101).

In the years ahead the police kept the magazine under constant surveillance, and, though two further issues were banned in 1979, it soon became entangled in an internal dispute between the reformist censors, who were beginning to acknowledge that 'protest literature' was 'a recognized literary genre in all languages', as Malan put it in a subsequent report, and the security hardliners, notably Murray and Jansen, who continued to see *Staffrider* as dangerously seditious (P78/9/43). These tensions came to a head in 1980, when the chief censor appealed against a security committee's decision to ban two issues. On both occasions van Rooyen's new Appeal Board overruled the committee's decision, basing its case on the new criteria of likely readership and the legitimacy of 'protest literature'. Using internal evidence alone—the cover price and the magazine's general 'editorial quality'—van Rooyen claimed *Staffrider* could be defended because it did not have a mass readership. Despite its anti-elitist ethos, it was, he claimed, 'written for the literate by the literate'. Tellingly, when he came to define the Board's new attitude to 'protest literature', a tradition from which many black writers had already begun to distance themselves, van Rooyen invoked tried and tested aestheticist formulations, effectively turning 'protest' into a matter of taste. In the first case, which related to the issue for May–June 1980, he argued that 'political criticism is often one-sided and would, in most cases, not fall within the bounds of good taste or be in accord with the opinion of a substantial number of South Africans'. In the second, which related to the issue for September–October, he adopted a loftier, culturally relativistic approach. If 'exaggerated and over-colourful language' felt 'strange on Western ears', he observed, following Etienne Malan's wording in his censor's report, it had to be recognized that 'political invective' is 'almost an art form among Third World nations'. 'Civilized Western man', van Rooyen added reassuringly, is 'often unnecessarily perturbed at these verbal onslaughts which, through their very exaggeration, lose a measure of their effectiveness.' His decision to accommodate *Staffrider* on these terms, which became a feature of the reformist era, set a precedent to which literary censors repeatedly, if inconsistently, referred in the 1980s.[135]

148

Staffrider's editorial policies and ethos were not only a concern for the censors, however. They also became a matter of some internal controversy, reflecting another side of what Coetzee called its 'unique problems'. For one thing, Kirkwood's open policy led two young black writers, Fhazel Johennesse and Christopher van Wyk, to found *Wietie*, a short-lived, more selective little magazine, at the beginning of 1980. As van Wyk later recalled, 'we were not ideologically opposed to *Staffrider* since the Black Consciousness approach was also part of *Wietie*'. The problem lay primarily with the 'system of self-editing', which led to some work appearing which 'did not merit publication'.[136] When *Wietie* was quickly shut down by the censors, van Wyk returned to *Staffrider*, where he took on a more conventional editorial role, after the magazine's policy had changed.[h] For Kirkwood, however, the underlying tensions remained, as a robust exchange he had with Mbulelo Mzamane in early 1980 revealed. As Mzamane made clear, during negotiations over his first collection of short stories *Mzala*, he was, despite his personal admiration for Kirkwood and his earlier involvement with *Donga*, extremely reluctant to have anything to do with white publishers. He was actively seeking publication abroad via his literary agent 'because of the shabby manner in which many of my buddies like Wally [Serote] have been treated before by white publishing houses' and because 'I felt that a strong protest had to be made against all the white *gurus* who control publication.'[137] Kirkwood did all he could to convince him otherwise, in part because he felt especially committed to the collection on literary grounds.

Despite *Staffrider's* open policy, Kirkwood himself had a strong literary vision, derived principally from Walter Benjamin (see Chapter 9). In his view, *Mzala* exemplified the literary possibilities Benjamin outlined in his 1936 essay 'The Storyteller' and, as such, represented an important contribution to the emerging new literature. He felt this made the case for publishing locally all the more compelling. Setting out his offer, he indicated that Ravan would print 5,000 copies in the first instance, keep the price under R3 (around a fifth of the price of an imported hardback), and, as a consequence, 'achieve an immediate in-depth cultural impact' which no overseas publisher could rival.

> International publication usually means delay. The writer becomes a cultural hot property in the international market-place. He is exported back to his country of origin. Usually he is marketed to the educational institutions. The international publisher has no direct line to the cultural struggle in the country of origin. The effect is to create a cultural object which has to a degree been defused.[138]

In the end, after consultation with his agent, who thought the offer was too good to refuse (Ravan's deal included a standard $12\frac{1}{2}$ per cent royalty and left Mzamane with the option to reserve the rights outside Southern Africa), Mzamane finally agreed to go ahead and so *Mzala* appeared as number 5 in the new Staffrider Series in July 1980 (see Chapter 9). A year later it was published as *My*

Cousin Comes to Jo'burg and Other Stories in the Longman Drumbeat Series as well.

Yet, for Mzamane, it was not just Kirkwood's position as the director of a white-owned publishing house that was at issue. Like the editors of *Wietie*, his principal concerns, which revealed the delicacy, if not impossibility, of Kirkwood's position, focused on Ravan's editorial policy, the unhappy consequences of which were, in his view, revealed in the second book in the Staffrider Series: Mtutuzeli Matshoba's short-story collection *Call Me Not a Man* (1979), which was banned as soon as it was published (see Chapter 9). Having been asked to review it for the *Medu Newsletter* (the Medu Art Ensemble was a key exiled arts group based Gaborone, Botswana), he felt he had to point out that it was 'rushed into print in a way that is likely to do [Matshoba] more harm than good as a writer'.[139] The key problem, he felt, was the 'complacency' generated 'by seeing oneself in print' and by 'success', which the censorship system only exacerbated. 'Don't you forget', he reminded Kirkwood, 'that the very act of banning is often used as a measure of success.'

As Mzamane insisted, his own concerns had nothing to do with any anxiety about mixing politics and literature. 'I've no patience myself with critics [he specifically mentioned Jack Cope and Lionel Abrahams] who use smokescreen techniques like "art for art's sake" to distract the writer from carrying out his social obligations, as though content and technique were not inextricably linked in good literature anyhow.' The principal issue, in his view, was one of 'craftsmanship'. He refused 'to use the excuse that Mtutuzeli articulates our fears, hopes and aspirations and should thus be allowed to churn out inferior work'. Since the 'art of writing is re-writing', Kirkwood had a 'duty as editor', which 'has nothing to do with censorship à la Kruger or whoever his successors are', to have 'insisted more on revision' before publication in book form.[140] This would have prevented him from 'evincing just another face of white liberal patronage' and, more importantly, helped to justify *Staffrider*'s more accommodating editorial approach.[141] Aspirant Black writers 'would have had, right before their eyes, the example of Mtutuzeli's work in *Staffrider* (his raw material, as it were), to compare with the finished product in book form'.[142] As Mzamane conceded, his own position, as an educated, middle-class Black intellectual (he was writing from Sheffield, where he was at the time doing a doctorate on Black Consciousness poetry) was itself not unassailable: 'without being uppity about it, I must admit that Mtutuzeli, Ingoapele [Madingoane] *et alia* are more representative of the people, in this downright plebeian sense, than I can ever claim to be'.[143] Nonetheless, he felt his criticisms were valid, not least because some younger black writers were 'growing to be extremely unself-critical'.[144]

In his extended reply to these 'forthright' comments, which he welcomed, Kirkwood produced a manifesto of sorts giving 'the context of our thinking here', which was equally frank. 'We are in for some tussle', he commented.

You speak as one trained literary mind to another: and, yes, you strike home. And yet, you don't. I feel the guilt of a critic who has deserted his 'standards'. And yet, I don't. I feel that special discomfort that comes when someone has said something about one that would have been true yesterday but isn't today.[145]

What really 'put me on the spot', however, was the fact that 'your leverage comes simultaneously from a standpoint that invokes universalist "minimal standards" and from a standpoint *inside* the energy system of a specific revolutionary culture'. By contrast, he felt dislocated: 'neither inside the living body of a language, able to intuit standards whenever English is used, nor inside the revolutionary cultural practice in association with which my working days are spent'.

Yet, as Kirkwood was not 'given to agony', he tried 'to approach this "homelessness" in a practical and useful spirit', hence his decision to take up the position at Ravan and to try to transform it by allowing it to 'embody the work of a writer's movement operating so-to-speak "behind the lines" of the erstwhile (and still formally) "dominant" culture in our country'. This is why he wanted to 'let the standards come from inside the writer's movement', which was the focus of the emergent 'new culture'. As far as Matshoba's collection was concerned, he was unapologetic:

> if ever a book was published in response to popular demand that was it. . . . We printed 5000, and that got the price down to R2 50. On the *Staffrider* network, we parted with nearly all of these before the banning came. With that book we proved that the Staffrider Series was possible. The magazine's momentum was extended to a popular book series.

'Given the background I've sketched as far as my own role is concerned', Kirkwood concluded, 'I think you'll understand why in my view the choice couldn't and shouldn't be mine.' In reply, Mzamane noted:

> of course, I'm in sympathy with your position as an 'outsider'. . . How often have we said to ourselves that we're the only exponents of black experience, in cultural as well as in overall political terms?

Yet, for all this, the underlying economic and political questions remained:

> The moment you create such avenues for self-expression among my people as we have always craved I become uneasy. Why? I think because Ravan is in your hands and not in mine or Mothobi's, for that matter.[146]

As Kirkwood's commitment to the notion of being a transitional publisher and his repeated efforts to restructure Ravan suggest, he continued to feel the force of Mzamane's arguments, and it was for this reason, too, that in 1981 he, along with the writers Jaki Seroke and Christopher van Wyk, entered into negotiations with the newly formed African Writers Association (AWA) to create an independent imprint that would take over the black section of Ravan's list. Given the shifting political and cultural alliances of the early 1980s, however, these eventually broke down. What emerged instead was Skotaville, a wholly separate publishing house established under the auspices of the AWA in 1982, which was the last major literary imprint to be founded during the apartheid era. Dinah Lefakane's black feminist imprint Seriti sa Sechaba, which she founded after leaving Skotaville in 1988 and which also had a strong literary component, was an important, though much smaller, enterprise.

Skotaville was, at one level, the answer to Mzamane's concerns about the economic basis of literary publishing in the context of apartheid. Unlike James Matthews's BLAC imprint, which was always limited by a serious lack of resources, it published just under a hundred titles in the course of the 1980s, mainly in the political, theological, and educational fields, though almost a fifth of its output was specifically literary. As a consequence, it became, for many black writers, a serious alternative, even rival, to Ravan. In keeping with Black Consciousness principles, it was controlled by an exclusively black board under the chairmanship of the unflagging Sipho Sepamla (other founding members included Es'kia Mphahlele and Miriam Tlali), and it was run by two black executive directors: Seroke, who left Ravan to launch the new enterprise in September 1982, and Mutloatse, who joined him six months later. Based in Johannesburg, they started out publishing from the premises of the Federated Union of Black Artists (FUBA), the arts organization Sepamla established in 1978, which was also the home of the AWA. Unlike Ravan, Skotaville was set up from the start as a non-profit venture, which relied on funding from a variety of sources, including local corporate sponsors, the Rockefeller and Ford Foundations, and the South African Council of Churches. The last came about as a result of the close association Skotaville developed with Desmond Tutu.

As the initial AWA announcement declared in 1982, Skotaville's primary objectives were to create space in which the 'needs, aspirations and objectives of Black writers' could be recognized without being 'subject to the criteria, constraints and restrictions' imposed by (white-owned) 'commercial publishing houses'; to offer a 'different perspective on Black South African history, which has hitherto been studied only from a white viewpoint'; and to produce 'alternative' educational books outside the 'framework of Bantu Education'.[147] Yet if Skotaville took the Black Consciousness tradition forward into the 1980s, it also revitalized earlier, specifically pan-Africanist cultural aspirations. As Seroke noted, it was named after Mweli Skota (1893–1976) not just because he was a new African modernizer, a founding figure in the early ANC, and a prominent journalist on the black-owned newspapers of the 1920s and 1930s, but because 'throughout his life he wanted to establish a publishing house, an independent publishing house, that would put a positive image of African people right through the continent'.[148] This aspect of Skotaville's project featured prominently in its first publication, a revived version of *The Classic*, using the old name without Sepamla's additional 'new', which it produced annually and then biannually under Seroke's editorship from 1982 to 1989. 'We took off', Seroke commented, 'from where Nat Nakasa left off.'[149] The ambition to establish continuities across the various African and Black moments in the history of an alternative cultural modernity was also reflected in the efforts Skotaville made to reclaim African-language publishing from the Afrikaner-dominated educational publishers and in the anthology *Umhlaba Wethu: An Historical Indictment* (the title meant 'Our Country or Earth'), which it published in 1987. This was the last volume in Mutloatse's three-part series of anthologies dedicated to archiving black cultural history, the first two volumes of which— *Forced Landing* (1980) and *Reconstruction* (1981)—had been published as part of Ravan's Staffrider Series.

As the initial AWA announcement anticipated, Skotaville's founders recognized that they had to contend with '"anti-white" or "racism-in-reverse" arguments'. On this issue, however, they were unapologetic: their project was 'an inevitable step in the process of Black emancipation', which reflected 'the reality of political life in South Africa'.[150] Despite the inevitably racialized nature of most disputes in the apartheid era, the controversies in which it became embroiled, particularly with Ravan, in the early 1980s were less racial than political. The tensions came to a head in 1984 when, in an interview about Skotaville, Seroke attacked Ravan not just for being 'white-owned', 'Western', and even 'racist', but, revealing his own political sympathies (he was an active member of the banned anti-communist Pan Africanist Congress of Azania, the PAC), for being an essentially Marxist enterprise, which saw the 'South African political situation from the top and with a partisan social democratic view'.[151] In its detailed, characteristically collective response, Ravan rejected these claims, noting, among other things, that 'the strongest "string" at Ravan during [Seroke's] time was its "BC" component'. In answer to Seroke's conspiratorial question 'who was behind Ravan Press?', they replied emphatically: '*we* were and *you* were'. Adding further fuel to the already acrimonious dispute, and picking up on the new political thinking within the resistance, they pointed out that it was Seroke who had 'insisted that the name of the (FOSATU) union [then the key black trade union] be omitted' when they ran 'a worker's story of a factory struggle in *Staffrider*'. 'Since his departure', they commented, alluding to their new Worker Series, 'it has been possible for Ravan to develop much closer contact with worker organisations, who now provide the most significant terrain for cultural activity at a mass level.'[152] Though neither Ravan nor Skotaville followed any rigidly defined political line, the tensions underlying this exchange reflected the fact that Ravan identified with an inclusive political tradition dating back to the 1955 Freedom Charter, which was taken forward by the ANC and the SACP, while Skotaville was more sympathetic to the separatist counter-tradition within the resistance, which can be traced from the PAC, through the Black Consciousness movement, to the socialist Azanian People's

Organization (AZAPO) formed in 1978. Skotaville in fact published a number of key titles by AZAPO leaders in the late 1980s. Demonstrating that the political divisions between the two publishers were by no means clear-cut, it also launched its own more practically oriented Worker Education Series in 1988.

Against the background of these disputes, which reflected the larger political debates within the resistance in the 1980s, the reforms within the censorship bureaucracy appeared increasingly irrelevant. Yet both Ravan and Skotaville continued to be affected by the internal tensions among the censors that marked the new era of 'repressive tolerance', as Seroke called it.[153] Though at least three of Skotaville's key literary titles—Don Mattera's *Azanian Love Song* (1983), Tlali's *Mihloti* (Tears, 1984), and the anthology *Umhlaba Wethu* (1987)— were submitted and passed, largely on the standard reformist grounds, the first number of *The Classic* was banned for sedition in November 1982. Two months later, however, it was released, after Skotaville appealed. While only one further number of *The Classic* was scrutinized—the second, which was passed—the police continued to submit various issues of *Staffrider*, which remained a source of contention among the censors. In 1986, for instance, Jansen, the leading security censor, tabled a separate minority report arguing that one issue should be banned for sedition, partly on the grounds that two poems, 'Aluta Continua' and 'Power to the Workers', encouraged revolution in line with trade union objectives, while notices on the final page, which commemorated the leading graphic artist Thami Mnyele, who had been killed during a military raid on the Medu Art Ensemble in Botswana the previous year, promoted cultural resistance in terms advocated by the ANC and its affiliate Medu. Jansen was, however, overruled by a literary committee and no subsequent issues of *Staffrider* were banned.[154]

Though censorship may no longer have been the major threat facing Ravan, Skotaville, and, indeed, all the key internal interventionist publishers, by the mid-1980s all continued, in varying degrees, to be subjected to more overt kinds of official harassment. At this point the most significant pressures came directly from the security police, who stepped up their campaign of violent intimidation, making regular raids and interfering with the day-to-day operations of their businesses, and from the government, who in 1988 attempted to cut off foreign donor support for the internal democratic movement as a whole. Had this move not been overtaken by events, it would have had a particularly damaging effect on Ravan and Skotaville. For Ravan the police campaign took an extreme turn in 1987 when a further state of emergency was imposed. In March that year its offices were firebombed, a few days after 'thieves' broke into the premises, stealing a significant amount of money and pointedly spray-painting slogans on the walls of the offices, saying 'Raven [*sic*] Communist Pigs' and 'We come back'.[155] Six months later Skotaville was thrown into disarray when Seroke was arrested, for furthering the aims of the PAC, and

Staffrider

Volume 6. No3, 1986 R1.50 (excl. GST)

Days with Poona Poon
memories of a poor white childhood

Temba Makunga
remembers Bonnevilles Softown and Saville Row suits in

The Masquerade Ball

Language, Literature and the **Struggle for Liberation** in **South Africa** by **Daniel Kunene**

Exciting new poetry

freedom and his involvement in South Africa's culture of resistance grew while in exile.

In Botswana he joined the African National Congress, an organisation he always spoke of with fondness and respect. He was also active in Medu, a Botswana-based group of exiled South African cultural workers who hosted the 1982 Conference on Culture and Resistance in Gaborone.

Thami's discipline, hard work and clean living earned him the respect and admiration of hundreds of cultural workers and people from all walks of life.

Like Thami we must fight our huge and brutal enemy so that one day soon our children may wake up from their beds to a peaceful world and not be dragged from underneath them riddled with bullets.

VILLAGE FROM THE PORTION OF MY MIND
Abstract painting by Thami Mnyele

A livid wind sweeps
with monstrous brooms
Leaving 4 huts 4 cows
donkeying skeleton, a shrub
and frail dew-ridden cobwebs.

Moody colours are torpid
while entombed
Grey is more palpable
Cannibal rocks emerge
as the soil is airborne
to Chieftainess Moon.

The sap of beings floats
like a creamcoat
Salty voices crawl
like witch-whispers
Seashells domesticate mixed bones
But the white-hearted sea
sifts 4 fleshy faces
glued to the pale-blue firmament
without shedding a single spark.
Tantalizing mama
evokes and fans fires-in-eyes
Hungering faces cry:
'Mama, nyanya!
'Mama, nyanya!'

But a cloud-chunk drizzles
and blazing hope fizzles.   **Nape Metana**

WE CAN'T MEET HERE, BROTHER
for Thami Mnyele

We can't meet here, brother.
We can't talk here in this cold stone world
where whites buy time on credit cards

I can't hear you brother!
for the noise of the theorists
and the clanging machinery of the liberal Press.

I want to smell the warmth of your friendship, Thami
Not the pollution of gunsmoke and white suicides.

We can't meet here, brother.
Let's go to your home
Where we can stroll in the underbrush of your pain-
tings
Discuss colour
Hone assegais on the edges of serrated tongues..

Chris van Wyk

FIG. 2.14. The front and back cover of *Staffrider* (6/3, 1986), which includes a tribute to Thami Mnyele, the leading graphic artist who was killed in a military raid in June 1985.

FIG. 2.15. A photograph of the Ravan Press offices taken in March 1987 after a raid by the Security Police, who spray-painted various threatening slogans on the walls. This one says 'Commie Pigs'. In the background are posters advertising Nadine Gordimer's *July's People* and other Ravan titles.

detained for four years under the Internal Security Act. Yet, despite this ongoing campaign of harassment and other financial and managerial difficulties, all the major interventionist imprints survived to contribute to the end of apartheid and the beginning of the economic restructuring of the internal publishing industry that followed in the course of the 1990s.[i]

3
WRITERS

In 'Censorship and Polemic', a provocative essay first published in 1990, J. M. Coetzee remarked that it is 'no historical accident' that the origins of the peculiarly intense 'rivalry' between writers and censors can be traced to the 'advent of printing in late fifteenth-century Europe'. For one thing, the technology made possible new ideas of authorship. 'Unlike scribal culture, which is inherently anti-individualist', Coetzee claimed, 'print culture fosters ideas of personal fame by multiplying the author-as-signature indefinitely, projecting him both in space and in time into print-made immortality.' For another, print transformed the notion of the reading community. The 'space opened up by printing in the course of creating a market for its products' brought into being 'for the first time a *public*, a physically dispersed aggregate of people defined by the orientation of their desire toward a common object'. By reshaping the field of culture in these two ways, the new technology set writers on a collision course with the 'early modern state', whose 'characteristic response' to the 'potentialities of print was paranoia'.[1]

So it was again 'no accident' that the rise of the modern author, who could not just 'create and hold a public for himself' but, in less rationalistic terms, command its 'heart', coincided with an 'intensification of censorship'. This only served to promote a new feeling of professional solidarity among writers, however, and, as a consequence, to exacerbate the growing antagonism. 'Just as censorship is an institution developed by the modern state to protect itself against this new force,' Coetzee claimed, 'the closing of ranks among writers on the question of free speech and the formation of a certain orthodoxy of opposition to censorship are measures that writers, as people with a commonality of interests, have taken to constitute themselves as a group and protect themselves against authority, clerical and political.' In his view, this oppositional identity, which underpinned the new ideals associated with the 'Republic of Letters', became more or less institutionalized by the late eighteenth century. By then, he argued, the foundations were laid for the 'dynamic of escalation' that is 'always threatening to overtake controversies over censorship' in which 'the rivals, writer and censor, become less and less distinguishable'.[2] As Coetzee's own self-consciously anti-rationalist language insists ('desire', 'heart', etc.), a cluster of factors, at once psychological and social, cultural and political, all had a part to play in this.

At the time Coetzee had particular methodological and, as we shall see, autobiographical reasons for being especially concerned about the 'megalomaniac' tendencies of his own profession. 'I see the intelligentsia as a class of not inconsiderable power, perhaps preponderant power in the longer run,' he noted, 'and writers of all varieties as a group within the intelligentsia loosely bound by a community of interests and in possession of a great historical advantage: disposition over the last word.' In saying this he was not just putting the conventional wisdom about the relationship between the relatively powerless writer and the omnipotent modern state in question. He was taking a stand in the field of contemporary 'literary scholarship', which was, he argued following Elizabeth Eisenstein's remarks in *The Printing Press as an Agent of Change* (1979), dominated by a 'somewhat unthinking tendency to assimilate [writers] to other classes or factions and regard them as simply their spokesmen'.[3] Though he did not spell this out, this tendency, which had its origins in the Marxist and before that the nationalist traditions, developed in part as a reaction against the countervailing tendency, associated primarily with certain versions of liberal thought, to represent the writer as an 'unfettered individual', an idea about which Coetzee was no less sceptical. In the latter half of the twentieth century the critique of liberalism was, of course, given a new orientation and impetus by the feminist, Black Consciousness, and post-colonial movements. In distancing himself from these mutually opposed traditions, Coetzee was not, it should be said, denying that some writers attach considerable value to the sense they have of themselves as individualists or as spokespersons for some larger collective. Nor was he underplaying the range of socio-political factors, including race, ethnicity, nationality, religion, gender, class, education, and generation, that shape the way they think about their responsibilities or the expectations others have of them. On the contrary, he was attempting to draw attention to the linkage between their broader cultural, social, and political situatedness, on the one hand, and the traditions, identities, and forms of authority they claim, negotiate, or resist *as writers*, on the other.

This methodological reorientation has particular explanatory power in the context of apartheid South Africa, where the overlapping histories of print culture, censorship, and modernity played out in especially fraught and complex ways. Yet before I turn to these I should address a more general question raised by Coetzee's revisionist analysis. While his emphasis on writers' 'community' or 'commonality' of interests, which is inevitable given his preoccupation with their reaction to the threat of censorship, offers a strong justification for the kind of social and institutional history he proposes, it is also potentially limiting. To see writers as a distinct group it is sufficient, I shall argue, simply to recognize that they share specific interests. The advantage of this weaker formulation is that it allows for the possibility that while they might, under certain circumstances, feel compelled to define their *common* interests, they can also share *specific* interests about which they may have little or no agreement. What defines them as a group, in other words, is the broad interests they quarrel over among each other, and often have second or third thoughts about, not just the narrower range they rally around under the threat of censorship.

This distinction has a particular significance in the South African case. At one level, the government's aggressive attempts to frame and fragment the cultural debate, not to mention the reality of life under apartheid, in racialized, ethno-linguistic, and nationalist terms, rejected the very possibility of writers sharing a 'commonality of interests'. One of the goals of apartheid policy was, of course, to prevent a non-racial idea of a 'South African' writer, or, indeed, citizen, from ever emerging. As a consequence, the numerous efforts to establish a united front, particularly on the part of the many voluntary writers' groups constituted during the apartheid era, were inseparable from the wider cultural resistance not just against censorship but against the legacies of colonialism and apartheid itself. In fact, as the controversies surrounding some groups' objectives and memberships revealed, opposing censorship was itself a matter of dispute. In certain cases, particularly for white-led campaign groups, some of whom acted as if censorship of the arts could treated as a distinct threat, opposition itself entailed a form of complicity. By contrast, for many black groups, especially following the rise of Black Consciousness in the 1970s, censorship was just one manifestation of white domination, which had to be circumvented as well as opposed. As such the ideal of 'commonality' was a central point of contention at the level of strategy, not a question settled once and for all in the face of censorship.

At another level, the specific interests writers shared were reflected more in their disagreements among each other than in any consensus they achieved about censorship. These quarrels often centred on questions about how best to define their situation and about the ethics of writing in the context of an overwhelmingly oppressive political reality. What bearing, if any, did their specific interests as writers have on the wider, always various and contested, political demands of the resistance? Were specifically literary modes of intervention relevant or even justifiable? If so, what form could or should they take and to whom should they be addressed? What, in short, did it mean for a piece of writing to be 'literary' or for writers to lay claim to a specifically 'literary' authority given the larger political circumstances? These arguments were further complicated by more basic concerns about terminology, which, given the multiplicity of distinct but also variously intersecting linguistic and cultural traditions in South Africa, sometimes pre-empted discussions about interests. These terminological disputes often centred on the desirability or otherwise of various rubrics or combinations of rubrics—'European', 'Western', 'African', 'Black', 'Third World', 'South African', 'Afrikaner', 'isiZulu', etc.—though, by the 1980s, they extended to the category 'writer' itself.

The Censors and the *Volk* Avant-Garde Revisited

Coetzee's analysis of the 'escalating passions' animating the 'rivalry' between writers and censors, not just in his 1990 essay but in his larger collection *Giving Offense* (1996), ranged widely across various twentieth-century censorship regimes, including the USSR and communist Poland, but it proved especially productive in relation to apartheid South Africa. While his essays on Geoffrey Cronjé and J. C. W. van Rooyen drew attention to the paranoia and self-serving rationalism of the censors, his comments on Brink and Breytenbach, and, indeed, his own autobiographical reflections, testified to the frequency with which white writers recorded 'the feeling of being touched and contaminated by the sickness of the state', even as they made their own overly rationalistic claims about being able to move 'unharmed in the midst of contagion'.[4] That all the censors were, simply as participants in the system, agents of the government's paranoid response to the 'potentiality of print' and that some, like A. H. Murray, were experts in their own forms of rationalistic self-justification also confirms the validity of his analysis. In an internal memorandum from the late 1960s, responding to criticisms of the censorship Board's extra-judicial status, Murray noted: 'My personal belief is that a serious, well-educated scientist, like a professor, is always much more objective about how things stand than a judge, who is usually hidebound by all sorts methodological assumptions.'[5] It is hard not to recall, in passing, that Murray's credibility was famously rubbished by defence lawyers during the Treason Trial in the 1950s, when he appeared as a state expert on communism.

As will by now be obvious, however, Coetzee's universalizing appeal to the notion of 'rivalry', which he derived from René Girard's study of religious and political conflict in *Violence and the Sacred* (1972), conceals more about the perverse complexities of the South African situation than it reveals. In particular, the 'fatal compromise', by which a group of mostly Afrikaner literary professors and some writers came to dominate the system in the 1960s and to play a disproportionately influential role thereafter, makes it difficult to construe the writer–censor relationship in the South African case as straightforwardly rivalrous. For a small faction of Afrikaner writers, the censors were not so much rivals as allies. Given the history of the internal struggles among Afrikaner elites, literary, political, and clerical, that led to the appointment of these literary censors, it is worth recalling that their partisanship did not mean they were committed to protecting the interests of Afrikaner writers in general. As Gerrit Dekker made clear in his inaugural speech as the first chief censor, they saw themselves, above all, as the guardians of N. P. van Wyk Louw's liberal–nationalist idea of the writer as a member of an autonomous, artistic elite, which I have called the *volk* avant-garde. This relatively marginal and informal grouping was, as we have seen, at odds with the more mainstream Afrikaner Writers' Circle,

161

which supported the government's censorship regime. Crucially, Louw's individualistic *volk* elite, who were inevitably hostile to the mass, did not occupy a position of equality alongside other Afrikaner elites. In his social mythology they figured as an embattled, often tragically doomed but still powerful, supra-elite who were caught in an especially intense contest with politicians corrupted by power. This, at least, was the burden of his neoclassical verse drama *Germanicus* (1956) and the focus of his earlier parable 'Tyrant and Humanist' (1947), published in the same year as his first polemic against censorship.

This idea of the writer's centrality to the *volk because* he was a loyal but contestatory individualist and rival to the politician (and cleric) dominated the literary censors' thinking, and, as J. M. Coetzee noted, it also provided younger Afrikaans writers, like Brink, with an initial 'model' on which to base their own 'myth of the writer as hero of resistance' who tells the truth to power.[6] Indeed, in an essay of 1970, Brink explained his own position by paraphrasing Louw's 1947 parable:

> On the eve of his execution, a condemned writer is visited in jail by the head of state. The tyrant promises him a reprieve on the condition that he recant. If not, he will die and every word he has ever written will be destroyed. With quiet assurance the humanist elects to die, bolstered by the conviction that he will win in the end. 'How can that be?' the tyrant asks. 'I have two reasons', replies the condemned man. 'One is that your executioner will see me die. The other is that you have found it necessary to visit me tonight.'[7]

In 1966 Louw himself lived out a less dramatic version of his archetypal scenario when H. F. Verwoerd used a key political speech to attack him for writing an insufficiently patriotic commemorative play about the Boer War. The play begins with a liberal-minded speech about the paradoxes of Afrikaner identity ('a mass, but each with his own name and own being') given by an old woman whose opening line is 'What is a *volk*?'[8] In a later essay of 1982, Brink turned this 'historic clash' into a myth of his own, representing it as the first clear 'symptom of sickness' within the state. It was, he added, 'no accident' that it 'more or less coincided with the introduction of official, codified censorship in South Africa'.[9] What he did not mention, and what, of course, revealed the murky compromises at the heart of apartheid censorship, was that the play was commissioned by a committee, acting on behalf of the Department of Education, Art, and Science, comprising three key literary censors: Dekker, Merwe Scholtz, and du P. Erlank. The antagonism underlying the stand-off with Verwoerd resurfaced in 1968 when Louw publicly denounced a group of Verwoerd's political supporters for setting up a Verwoerd Prize for Fatherland Literature (eventually called the Republic Prize) after his assassination. This 'Stalin-prize' would turn Afrikaner writers, whose true vocation was to discover the 'universal', into crudely patriotic rhapsodizers like their arch-enemy Kipling, Louw declared.[10]

As we have seen, the literary censors' defence of the contestatory role of the Afrikaner writer as Louw defined it, and, more particularly, of the Sestigers as an emergent *volk* avant-garde, entailed a commitment to the associated idea of the literary, which was in their view not a specific idea but a universal norm. This narrowed the terms of their collaborationist guardianship still further. At this point it is possible to identify, in summary form, three of their guiding assumptions:

1. Literature, which is governed by its own rules and unities, constitutes a privileged aesthetic space set apart from more mundane forms of discourse, including pornography, mass-market fiction, journalism, and political writings.
2. Though it belongs, first and foremost, to a *volk*, it is not narrowly local or patriotic. A particular literature achieves greatness only when it takes its place within a series of larger spheres, construed variously as 'European', 'Western', or, ultimately, the 'universal'.
3. Literature does not appeal to a mass readership. It can be appreciated only by a limited and sophisticated public or, in effect, to make the circularity clear, only by literary readers.

A heady amalgam, in other words, in which nineteenth-century aestheticism fused with New Critical formalism, where nationalism collided less predictably with a universalistic idea of Western humanism, and where everything was overlaid with a more familiar set of prejudices against mass culture. As each of the three elements suggests, their thinking was dominated by a precarious logic of distinction at the heart of which lay, paradoxically, a categorical sense of literature's difference from, and superiority to, political discourse. This is paradoxical not simply because van Wyk Louw himself wrote interventionist political plays but because he believed that, left alone to exercise their specifically literary responsibilities, Afrikaner writers would be in a position to fulfil their most important role as individualist spokespersons, which was, in the end, political. By creating a great literature they would, as we saw in Chapter 1, justify the Afrikaners' right to exist as a separate *volk*, which was one of the cornerstones of apartheid.

In the early 1970s the censor–poet T. T. Cloete gave this nationalist form of *Kulturkritik* a new twist when he used it to justify banning the emergent generation of anti-*volk* Afrikaans writers, but the particular use he made of the label 'committed literature' was always implicit in the literary censors' aestheticist thinking. This can be seen from some of their general statements as critics, beginning with Dekker's high-minded response to the black Afrikaans poet, and future censor, S. V. Petersen at the beginning of the censorship era. This is how he assessed Petersen's debut volume, *Die Enkeling* (The Loner, 1944), in his compendious literary history: 'It is not yet true poetry. Petersen had still not achieved the essence of art: giving aesthetic form to emotion. These are raw shrieks of revolt against the "curse of a dark skin" in impotent rhetoric and conventional phrases in formless verses.'[11] In effect, Petersen's frustrations trapped him in an inferior, sub-literary, form of political discourse. As Ampie Coetzee noted, prominent Afrikaner critics continued to use normative arguments of this kind to keep black poets, including Adam Small, out of the canon of *volk* literature well into the 1980s.[12]

At the other end of the censorship era, Anna Louw expressed similar sentiments in an article she published in the British *PN Review* in 1987 on J. M. Coetzee's *In the Heart of the Country*, a work about which she had been intensely preoccupied ever since 1977, when she first read it as a censor (see Chapter 8). In responding to some comments Coetzee made in a 1978 interview, she attempted to co-opt him as an ally on the literature versus politics question: 'Coetzee is not interested in writing or reading politically committed literature which has reached a fever pitch in both English and Afrikaans literary circles in the country, an example perhaps of the general cultural lag to which Coetzee may have been referring when he added that the South African public was living in an historical backwater.'[13] Once again, like Dekker, she invoked a narrative of cultural progress in which the literary is gradually purged of the political and finally achieves its teleological destiny in a purely aesthetic sphere. Her loaded article in fact offers a good illustration of the kind of apartheid thinking that informed the censors' racialized mapping of South African literatures more generally. She took it as axiomatic, for instance, that 'indigenous black writing' was in its 'infancy', and focused her attention on white writing and Coetzee's 'mixed English and Afrikaans' background, praising him as an 'authentic South African voice'. In her view, this background set him above other white English-language writers, like the 'competent Nadine Gordimer with her obsession with the urban African political scene'; and others, like Alan Paton, Jack Cope, and Guy Butler, who 'often sound like the first generation Colonial writing letters home, sometimes over-romanticizing, at other times complaining rather impotently about the other white racial group, the Afrikaners'.[14]

The censors' conception of the writer, and, more particularly, their assumption that the distinctiveness of the literary was achieved at the expense of the political, complicated the ways in which they functioned as guardians of apartheid. In the relatively rare instances when Afrikaner church groups or offended individuals submitted works by leading Afrikaans writers, they defended the regime, though not the cleric's preferred version of it, by protecting the interests of the *volk* avant-garde. As I argue in Chapter 6, these tensions were particularly acute in the case of Etienne Leroux, though they can also be seen in the way the censors defended Wilma Stockenström's powerful farm novel *Uitdraai* (literally, Turn Off, or Evade; Human & Rousseau, 1976), which, like Coetzee's *In the Heart of the Country*, centres on a woman character, frustrated desire, and interracial sex. Merwe Scholtz, the initial reader, noted that this was her debut as a novelist and that she had, as a poet, just won the Hertzog Prize, the ultimate accolade in nationalist literary circles. Summing up his arguments, which the other committee members, Anna Louw, Malan, and du P. Erlank, endorsed, he said: 'This is in my view not damaging for *volk*-relations in RSA—even though the book implicitly contains a serious accusation. But the theme is handled dispassionately without propaganda for any one of the parties' (P77/6/82).

For the most part, however, the censors' aestheticist commitments and entrenched scholasticism served the government's purposes directly by reinforcing, or not unsettling, apartheid policy in more obvious ways. It informed their decisions to pass some works in English by black and white writers, which they recognized were potentially 'undesirable', because their literariness somehow de-emphasized or overwhelmed their political effectiveness. Conversely, though on the same logic, they banned works they judged to belong to the disparaged sub-category of 'committed literature' either because they were too political or because they were in some sense insufficiently literary. It is worth recalling that in 1974 the Supreme Court rejected this particular aspect of the censors' literary case against Brink's *Kennis van die Aand* (Looking on Darkness) and defended his right to political protest on liberal grounds. When van Rooyen took over as chair of the Appeal Board in 1980, he frequently referred back to this decision to justify his new policy towards 'protest literature'.

For most writers, of course, the perverse intricacies of the censors' scholastic judgements remained hidden. Given the secrecy in which the system was shrouded, not to mention the palpable evidence of the censors' attitudes reflected in the ever-expanding list of banned literary works, the censors were just what they seemed to be and, at one level, were: repressive guardians of apartheid law who represented a direct threat to writers and to the freedom of expression more generally. Even a veteran campaigner against the system like Gordimer was, for instance, surprised by van Rooyen's sudden invocation of 'literary standards' in 1980. Though she was not taken in by his reformist agenda, she nonetheless accepted it as 'censorship's new deal'.[15] The trouble was, she commented, echoing the new thinking within the resistance in the early 1980s, van Rooyen was a 'man whose view of culture is elitist, someone in whose mind, whether consciously or not, is posited the idea of an official cultural norm', which was 'still firmly based on a particular myth of power'.[16] As a consequence, his reforms were just 'the pragmatic manifestation of an old, time-dishonoured view of culture, already dead, serving repression instead of the arts, and its belated recognition of literary standards is its chief strategy'.[17]

Gordimer was right on every point, except the basic historical one: namely, that with the exception of the five-year period between 1975 and 1980, when the government, responding to pressures from Afrikaner church groups, attempted to contain though not exclude the literary experts in the system, repression and the arts had been fatally bound together from the start. More disturbingly, for writers who had to endure working under the threat of censorship, versions of their own anxieties, which centred on the inextricably tangled questions of literature, censorship, and the ethics of writing, were built into the system itself, as a consequence of the government's initial compromises with the *volk* avant-garde. This meant that while some apartheid censors, particularly those who dealt primarily with security matters, remained unliterary opponents preoccupied with defending the apartheid order, others emerged as covert literary rivals who had the power not simply to police the space of the literary in secret but to deform the entire literary culture, and the debates about literature and responsibility, by banning some books, and, equally, by granting others unwelcome and unsought official legitimacy.

Individualist Solidarities: Liberal Protest in the 1960s

That Sarah Gertrude Millin founded the first, and most straightforwardly liberal, writers' group to emerge in twentieth-century South Africa was, in part, a testament to the acceptability of certain forms of racialized thinking in the 1920s. The novel that made her name internationally, *God's Step-Children* (1924), a doom-laden story about the consequences of racial mixing, was, as J. M. Coetzee observed, both an obsessive 'tragedy of blood' and 'an adaptation of respectable scientific and historical thought'.[18] The acclaim it received confirmed Millin's reputation as the most accomplished South African novelist of the period. For John Galsworthy, the founding president of PEN, the new international writers' association formed in Britain in 1921, this made her the most obvious person to approach about setting up a local affiliate when he visited South Africa in 1927. With his encouragement, Millin became the first president of the South African PEN Centre (PEN SA), which she launched in Johannesburg in the same year. Millin gave the group some standing and attended the new organization's international gatherings, but she did not do much to promote it locally and for the next two decades it was relatively inactive. It was only after the journalist and minor writer Lewis Sowden and his wife, Dora, decided to revive the Centre in the mid-1940s that it began to attract a more significant membership and to have a more conspicuous impact on the cultural scene. Tellingly, the Sowdens were spurred on in their endeavours by the relative success of the Afrikaans Writers' Circle. Founded in 1934, the Circle was initially chaired by the novelist and Afrikaner cultural historian C. M. van den Heever. By the late 1950s, PEN SA had opened a second branch in Cape Town and, like the Afrikaans group, it had begun to publish a regular yearbook. By that time, it had an overall membership of around eighty.

Following the terms of the international Charter to which it subscribed, PEN SA was committed to a very different set of principles from their more nationalistic Afrikaner counterparts. They were bound not only to oppose 'any form of the suppression of freedom of expression' but to uphold a humanistic, specifically anti-nationalist, and more broadly anti-political idea of the arts. The Charter, which echoed the ideals of the League of Nations, stated that 'literature, national though it be in origin, knows no frontiers, and should remain common currency between nations' and that 'works of art, the patrimony of humanity at large, should be left untouched by national or political passion'. These specifically cultural commitments were, however, predicated on a further belief 'that the necessary advance of the world towards a more highly organized political and economic order renders a free criticism of governments, administrations and institutions imperative'.[19] For all their differences, PEN SA and the Writers' Circle worked closely together on various joint projects to promote works they identified as belonging to the growing canon of South African literature in the 1940s and early 1950s, with PEN SA representing the Afrikaner group at its own international meetings. Indeed, in 1951 it asked van Wyk Louw, then a prominent figure in the Circle, albeit one who was also especially sympathetic to PEN's ideals, to act as its representative at the annual congress held that year in Lausanne.

In theory, PEN SA was, unlike the Writers' Circle, 'open to all qualified writers, editors and translators' who subscribed to the Charter, 'without regard to nationality, race, colour or religion'.[20] In practice, its membership was always overwhelmingly white. Following in the tradition of the South African Literary Society founded in the 1820s, it was also English-speaking and predominantly middle-class. Though Jack Cope and Nadine Gordimer joined in the 1950s, they were, as full-time writers, not typical PEN SA members, many of whom were housewives, journalists, lawyers, and academics who pursued part-time literary careers. Though the group did make various attempts to cross the racial divide, these did little to allay concerns about the seriousness with which it sought to live up to its international obligations. Writing from the perspective of the early 1980s, by which time he had, under the influence of the younger generation of Black Consciousness writers, begun to question his own early liberalism, Richard Rive recalled being invited to become a member in the early 1960s. As he 'suspected', he was 'the first and only Black to be so honoured'. Things did not go well. At his first PEN SA 'luncheon', which was 'held in a White hotel', he seemed to be surrounded by 'middle-aged women with blue-rinsed hair' whose attitude towards him was 'one of affable condescension'. Worse still, none of his fellow diners appeared to see the underlying absurdity of their situation. 'It did not strike them', he noted, 'that the ultimate indignity was for one writer to be prepared to apply for a racial permit to dine with another writer at a public venue.' Unsurprisingly he felt 'singularly ill at ease' and quickly allowed his membership to lapse.[21] If PEN SA was too unselfconscious about its own position for Rive, it had, by that time, also become too mired in controversy for its founding president. Feeling at odds with the group's increasingly firm anti-government stance, Millin resigned her membership in 1960.

For all the controversy, which came to a head in 1955 when the group clashed openly with the Nationalist government, and despite its own engaged and sophisticated anti-censorship campaign in the early 1960s, PEN SA never established itself as a credible proponent of its own principles, or, indeed, as a properly representative body. To some extent this was inevitable. In the South African context it was not only a branch of a cosmopolitan writers' association but a constituent part of the dominant white liberal culture, which prided itself on its principled independence from government. Among the other conspicuous products of this culture were Cope's *Contrast* and the most prestigious bilingual (English–Afrikaans) literary prize the CNA Award, which was founded in 1961. In PEN SA's case, however, this independence was less a cherished ideal than a fate it was obliged to accept when officials cut its government subsidy after taking offence at a number of supposedly anti-Afrikaner statements in its yearbook for 1955.[j] After this, the group had to rely on corporate sponsors, including Anglo-American and the CNA, to fund its various projects. By contrast, the collaborationist Afrikaans Writers' Circle continued, like the Hertzog Prize, to prosper under government patronage.

For all its historical and financial entanglements, PEN SA nevertheless remained committed to the idea that it could, following the terms of its Charter, stand outside or above politics. Presenting itself in orthodox liberal terms as a guardian of polite literature, it encouraged writers to be 'as wary of toeing any official line' as 'of over-reacting to temporary political tempers', as its vice-chair Tony Fleischer put it in 1964. In a more obscure but no less revealing move, he also insisted that the emphasis the group placed on the 'individuality of the writer' had nothing to do with politics because this was supposedly inscribed into the English language itself. 'South Africans who write in English', he observed, 'must in fact be true to principles which belong rather to the sovereignty of their language than to the sovereignty of any particular political or social ideology of the moment.' In this context it is worth recalling that Fleischer, who published under the pseudonym Hans Hofmeyer, was himself not averse to tackling overtly political subjects, as he demonstrated in his debut novel, *The Skin Is Deep* (1958), which was banned. Though PEN SA rejected all narrow nationalisms in keeping with the Charter, it promoted what Fleischer called 'a national English literature', following in the anti-colonial tradition of South African liberalism. Even in its disavowals, then, the organization reinforced its image as a white liberal advocacy group, or, more damningly, a belletristic bourgeois club. That it did not have any immodest avant-garde aspirations only added to this reputation. It was, according to Fleischer, 'not necessarily looking for new literary forms' but 'for new writers whose work is sincere'.[22]

At another level, PEN SA's failure to establish itself as an effective forum for all South African writers was a direct result of the way in which it conducted its anti-censorship campaign. Summing up its general position in 1965, Edgar Bernstein, another member of the executive, commented that PEN SA 'has repeatedly urged' that 'censorship should never be imposed for reasons of prudery or politics, but should be reserved for such works as can be shown in a court of law to offend morals, to commit libel or to promote sedition'.[23] As this indicates, like the official opposition United Party, it firmly rejected the decision to establish a statutory censorship board, while accepting the broad legitimacy of the apartheid state. That it protested vociferously against the suppression of particular literary works, but tended to be less outspoken, and often silent, about the various curbs imposed on writers, only undermined its credibility still further. By the mid-1960s, moreover, it had adopted a more diffidently reformist approach. In 1966 Fleischer, acting on PEN SA's behalf, sent a copy of Ellison Khan's astute legal analysis of the Supreme Court decision relating to Wilbur Smith's *When the Lion Feeds* to the Minister of the Interior in an effort to encourage the government to grant literary works formal exemption. In the article, Khan, a leading academic lawyer and member of the PEN SA executive, focused on the trial and its legal context. Yet in his conclusion he made a few carefully worded remarks about political censorship, which reflected the new thinking within the group. With due professional discretion, he noted that this 'may or may not be the price we pay for internal security', before asking, 'if we find it necessary to go so much further in proscriptions in this sphere than other Western countries, is it also necessary to do so in the sphere of morality?'[24] Like many of his liberal peers, both in South Africa and elsewhere, Kahn assumed that, in the context of apartheid censorship, questions of morality and politics could be neatly disentangled. The Minister duly forwarded his article to the censors, who considered it at length before rejecting all Kahn's proposed reforms.[k]

Unsurprisingly, banned Communist Party intellectuals like Brian Bunting and black writers like Lewis Nkosi and Es'kia Mphahlele took a more emphatic stand against all forms of government repression in the 1960s. Unlike their white liberal counterparts, they recognized that censorship was not just a specific threat to writers, or the freedom of expression, but integral to apartheid itself.[25] Gordimer, who became increasingly disenchanted with PEN SA and the tradition of liberal protest it represented, quickly came round to the same position. Beginning with her essay 'Censored, Banned, Gagged', which first appeared in *Encounter* in June 1963, she consistently spoke out against the government's numerous censorship laws. By the early 1970s, however, she had come to the conclusion that 'we cannot expect to free ourselves of censorship...while apartheid lasts'.[26] One indication of the growing dissatisfaction with PEN SA was that another white-led group, calling itself the Pasquino Society, emerged in 1969. Named after the fifteenth-century Italian satirist who lives on in the literary term 'pasquinade', meaning political lampoon, it was less awkward about political issues and, though it was all but defunct by the mid-1970s, it had a relatively energetic existence. It collected information on censorship, attempted unsuccessfully to have the ban on Jack Cope's *The Dawn Comes Twice* lifted in 1970, and protested vigorously against the proposed reforms of the system early in the new decade.

The ease with which liberal protests against censorship could slide into complicity was perhaps most clearly revealed in the petition 133 writers and fifty-eight artists signed in April 1963. This was the first attempt by a larger group of writers to create a more united front, effectively bringing together many prominent figures within PEN SA and a number of liberal Afrikaners who were dissatisfied with the stance taken by the overtly collaborationist Writers' Circle. Among the more notable signatories were Gordimer, Cope, Paton, and Butler, all of whom belonged to PEN SA; senior figures in the *volk* avant-garde like van Wyk Louw and D. J. Opperman as well as anti-nationalist Afrikaners like Uys Krige; and leading figures among the emergent generation, including Brink, Leroux, Ingrid Jonker, Athol Fugard, and Jan Rabie. Given the timing, their petition was, as we have seen, less a protest against censorship than a plea for the protection of literature. It began by declaring that 'we South African writers feel it a duty on ourselves to make our position clear in relation to this drastic measure', especially given the 'reticence maintained by most official cultural organisations and academic circles'. As it was, indeed, a writers' declaration (the artists simply endorsed their statement), it was neither a libertarian critique of censorship per se—they accepted that 'previous legal controls' could legitimately be used to ban 'obvious pornography'—nor a defence of the freedom of expression as a basic principle of democracy.[27] Instead, it focused on the ways in which the new legislation threatened the arts and their common interests as writers, and, as a consequence, the wider South African community. Working from a set of essentially liberal premises, they presented themselves as a group of individualists whose sense of responsibility extended to society at large, not to a specific section or *volk*. According to Cope, the document was drafted by the liberal Sestiger Jan Rabie, though, at various points, it echoed the formulations favoured by PEN SA and, indeed, van Wyk Louw.[28]

'In our responsibility to our profession and our community', the petition declared in its opening paragraph, 'we have to write as honestly as we can, and cannot allow ourselves to be swayed by political or any other one-sided considerations.' In the interests of 'frank discussion' and 'spiritual growth', and, in keeping with the 'artist's task', which was 'to record faithfully and without prejudice the truth of which he is capable', they had, in addition, to be 'true to their art alone'. As this suggests, they defined their specific interests as writers, and defended the distinctiveness of the literary, in terms that were, at once, anti-political, individualistic, moral, and aestheticist. It followed that their objections to the new Act focused on the fact that it made no provision for the 'nature and intent of a literary work' to be 'considered as a criterion for judgement' and that it was 'in conflict with the most fundamental principle of art—that each work should be judged as a whole'. For the rest, the petition spelt out the emptiness of the concession to the courts—the costs would make publishers 'exceedingly cautious about litigation' and anyway the courts would be 'tied to a strict interpretation of the law'—and highlighted the particular danger the Act represented for 'writers who must publish inside the country'. They 'are liable to be forced either into silence or superficiality— with fatal consequences especially for Afrikaans literature.'[29]

Two writers, Mary Renault, the British-born best-selling historical novelist, then president of PEN SA, and W. A. de Klerk, the popular Afrikaans dramatist and writer, were deputed to deliver the petition to the Minister. It was, according to Renault, an unhappy encounter, particularly for de Klerk, who was subjected to 'endless politicians' crap *in Afrikaans*', none of which she understood.[30] It was also largely ineffective, since the Act was already a fait accompli, though, as I noted in Chapter 1, their intervention had as much to do with the outstanding matter of the new censorship board's membership as with the broader questions of principle. For Es'kia Mphahlele, however, the effectiveness or otherwise of the petition was not the issue. As he reported in a memorandum for the Congress of Cultural Freedom, it lacked credibility because 'only white writers decided to voice a protest unilaterally, in spite of the existence of many African writers who could have been signatories'.[31] The list was, indeed, almost exclusively white (55 per cent English, 42 per cent Afrikaans). The only black writers (3 per cent), all of whom were officially classified as 'Coloured' under apartheid, were James Matthews and Richard Rive, both of whom had by then made a name for themselves as short-story writers in English, and three poets who wrote in Afrikaans, S. V. Petersen, P. J. Philander, and Adam Small.[1]

The fact that the petition wrote African writers out of South African literary history in ways that made it complicit with apartheid was not the only, or even the most tawdry, testament to the compromises some self-declared South African liberals were willing to make to protect their idea of literature. What brought most discredit on that tradition, as we have seen, was the fact that it was not straightforwardly 'outside' the censorship system at all. If the dominant Afrikaner literary censors, allied to the *volk* avant-garde, represented an uneasy hybrid of liberal–nationalism, which was uncomplicatedly pro-apartheid, the more secondary English censors, beginning with C. J. D. Harvey and his successor J. M. Leighton, represented a purer form of literary liberalism, which was not so much complicit as participatory. Unlike Harvey, who felt awkward about his role as a censor, Leighton was willing to justify his own involvement in unabashedly Orwellian terms, while repeatedly appealing to Orwell to clarify his own thinking.[m] In an article first published in 1975, he presented himself as a figure of moderation who, nonetheless, claimed to 'hate and detest all forms of conditioning propaganda' just as much as he hated 'pornography'. The 'enlightened' censor had, he claimed, to 'exert a balanced control, so that no one set of ideas is propagated at the expense of others, so that the democratic rights of one individual or section of the population are not upheld at the expense of others'. Among other things he believed that a clear 'distinction' had to be maintained between 'versified propaganda, aimed at political, social, or moral change without choice, and poetry, with all its checks and balances, that aims at sensitising the reading audience, making them fit persons for the exercise of sensible (in the Jane Austen sense) choice'.[32] No doubt similar forms of casuistical doublethink went on in the minds of his liberal-minded colleagues R. E. Lighton and Etienne Malan.

First Intersection: Mphahlele, Nkosi, and the Space of the Literary

As Mphahlele intimated in his CCF memorandum, many African writers felt as strongly about the new legislation as their white counterparts, and some would at that point have been willing to subscribe to the liberal tenets on which the petition was based. In an essay written in 1962, when he was already in exile, Lewis Nkosi, for instance, denounced the new Act, which was then going through its final stages in Parliament, as a 'severe form of barbarism', which was 'aimed at nothing less than the very spirit of culture and civilisation of which Dr Verwoerd's party so ludicrously asserts to be its manifestation'.[33] Though he was, as he noted, 'speaking here as an African', his arguments were based on the same liberal premisses as the petition, and he shared its literary emphasis. He spoke 'in the name of freedom for which writers and intellectuals have fought, even died, throughout the centuries'; and of the writer's need to be left alone to develop 'his personal vision'; before finally quoting Wordsworth on the poet's capacity to bind 'together... the vast empire of human society, as it is spread over the whole earth, and over all time'. He also stressed that the new legislation would prevent South African writers from developing 'a vocabulary which bears witness to our variousness as a people' and 'our completeness as a nation', though, in this case, Nkosi's idea of the unified nation was more inclusive than the one the petitioners presupposed (122–4).

That Nkosi was attempting to rally support from British writers, who were at the time becoming increasingly involved in the exile-led cultural boycott, only goes some way towards explaining his appeal to liberal principles and his choice of literary references. Though he was robustly critical of this cultural tradition—he insisted, in another essay of the same year, that 'African enthusiasm for Western culture must necessarily be cautious and selective'—much of his early literary criticism presupposed a Western framework and, like the petition, focused on the question of literature's distinctiveness in conventionally moral and individualistic terms (124). What distinguished literature proper from the 'daily newspaper', and, above all, from politically engaged reportage, he noted, following his own scholastic formulations, was the writer's 'moral imagination' and the 'inner tension of creative talent confronting inept matter', especially 'given social facts' (126). On this basis, he argued, Richard Rive's *Emergency* (1964), like many other works by contemporary black South Africans, did not belong to literature, as measured by the canonical standards of Kafka, Joyce, or Dostoevsky. All it did was offer 'a minute glimpse into a literary situation' in which the burdens of political responsibility threatened at every point to overwhelm writers or deflect them from the countervailing demands of literature itself, forcing them to exploit a narrow repertoire of 'ready-made plots of racial violence, social apartheid, and interracial love affairs' (126). 'It may even be wondered', Nkosi added provocatively, 'whether it might not be more prudent', in such 'desperate' circumstances, 'to "renounce literature temporarily," as some have advised, and solve the political problem first' (126). This statement would return to haunt the debates about the ethics of writing throughout the apartheid era.

Yet, as Nkosi's critical review of the first edition of Mphahlele's *African Image* (1962) suggests, it was Mphahlele himself who was at that point most likely to have found the terms of the petition congenial. In this collection of essays, Nkosi argued, Mphahlele emerged as an overly 'joyous' celebrator of the creative 'cultural cross-fertilisation' between 'Africa' and the 'West' that 'has taken place in South Africa', who underplayed the fact that 'the African has had to shed more of his heritage in order to accommodate himself to the ridiculous, and sometimes barbarous, demands of a society controlled by whites for the benefit of whites' (123). This imbalance was also, he felt, reflected in Mphahlele's overly severe criticism of a concept like Négritude, which Nkosi believed had to be defended as a necessary, if sometimes romanticized, 'affirmation and a turning away' from the 'unyieldingly arrogant white world' (124). That Mphahlele went on to endorse the 1963 petition, or what he called the writers' 'Declaration of Principles', in his first extended essay on censorship in 1969 could be taken as a further confirmation of his premature intercultural enthusiasms.[34] Yet, as I argued in Chapter 2, his position was by the early 1960s, particularly with regard to the Congress of Cultural Freedom and its universalizing liberal mission, already more contrary, conflicted, and nuanced than this would suggest, and, by the end of the decade, he had certainly given up on the versions of liberalism prevalent in South Africa. 'Protests within the law', he noted in the essay on censorship, were 'in the true tradition of South African white liberalism, which has always accommodated itself in the safe capsule of

legality; and that means white legality, since the laws are made by whites only'
(200). If he was still willing to describe himself in 1967 as 'an ambivalent
character', he was, he insisted, 'nothing of the oversimplified and sensationalized Hollywood version of a man of two worlds' (121).

Some of these complexities are evident in Mphahlele's essay 'Writers and
Commitment', an extended reflection on questions of Africanness, literature,
and responsibility, which originally appeared in *Black Orpheus* in 1968. Since
his thinking in this essay contrasted with the ways in which white writers
championed their collective interests in the 1960s, and, indeed, with the ways
in which the censors attempted to justify their collaborationist literary guardianship, his arguments, and their underlying tensions, are worth considering in
some detail. In the first place, he refused to subscribe to the assumption that
'political commitment' was inherently 'suspect' (187). 'Politics are a human
activity' and so 'African literature, like the other literatures of the world, is never
going to be totally free of propaganda' (186). This is, in part, why he was always
more sympathetic to a 'self-avowed Marxist' like Alex La Guma than Nkosi, who,
in an essay of 1968, criticized La Guma as a narrowly political writer more
interested in creating 'types' than fully developed 'individuals' (194).[35] Nonetheless, Mphahlele rejected Sartre's particular conception of commitment not
because it violated the purity of the aesthetic, as the censors believed, or the
specifically moral authority of the writer, as liberal-minded white writers
claimed, but because Sartre, in effect, set out to police literature in the name
of democratic freedom. By valuing prose above poetry, and privileging the
'communicative' function, his 'kind of discipline and aims for literature become
inviolable rules for a craft that is always breaking rules, breaking down myths'
(188). For an alternative, less problematically scholastic model, Mphahlele
turned neither to the liberal nor to the Marxist-Leninist traditions, but to
Trotsky's 'incisive and perceptive remarks' in 'The Social Function of Literature
and Art' (1923). Though he remained doubtful about 'how, if we must, we can
make our art "virtually collectivist"', he quoted Trotsky's general case against
artistic prescriptivism approvingly, and highlighted his key statement on the
autonomy of art, which attempted to overcome the impasse between material-
ism and formalism: 'The form of art is, to a certain and a very large degree,
independent, but the artist who creates this form, and the spectator who is
enjoying it, are not empty machines' (195–7).[36]

Sartre had a special relevance to Mphahlele because of the way in which he
had championed Négritude in his introduction to Senghor's *Anthologie de la
nouvelle poésie nègre et malgache de langue française* (1948), and, more particularly, because, after Sartre, 'several people have claimed that African literature is "functional," meaning, I believe, that this writing advocates the black
man's cause and/or instructs his audience' (189). Returning to his earlier preoccupations in *The African Image*, and especially his 'Cult of Negritude' essay,

albeit now from a wider perspective, he questioned both the prescriptivism of this idea of African literature and its wider cultural implications. What concerned him now was, firstly, that 'poetry inspired by negritude is for an elite', not for the 'unassimilated masses' who still formed a vital part of African society; and, secondly, that it threatened to close African literature off from the 'wider circles of humanity' by focusing too narrowly on the need to assert 'black pride' (189, 195). As this phrasing suggests, he traced a direct line from Négritude to the new Black Arts movement that was taking shape across the African Diaspora. By expressing these concerns Mphahlele came into direct conflict with some of the leading advocates of a specifically Black aesthetic, notably the African American critic Addison Gayle, but, as he emphasized, many of his criticisms remained focused on the earlier Francophone African context and did not necessarily apply more widely.[37]

> In the Caribbean and the United States I can see how relevant such poetry is even for the masses. Because, especially in the U.S., the Negro is in a state of siege culturally. He has to locate himself as a Negro with a double commitment: to share in the life of the Americans as a whole, and to assert his cultural importance, so that he is not integrated into the white culture on the white man's terms. (195)

Though Mphahlele continued, like Adam Small and Alex La Guma, to raise questions about the new global movement's cultural consequences, his responsiveness to its local variations also made him more sympathetic to the rise of Black Consciousness in South Africa (see Chapter 5). It is worth noting, in passing, that La Guma framed his own humanistic concerns about the new movement in specifically Marxist terms. In the interests of 'progressive development', he noted in an essay published in the *African Communist* in 1974, it was 'impossible to remain "in the opposing dignity of one's own house", which would be rather like accepting a sort of cultural "Bantustan"'. To fashion a 'modern and progressive world culture', with its 'message of humanism to all mankind', as well as 'our national cultures', it was necessary, he insisted, to 'select and digest all that is best in the cultural heritage of East and West', a view the exiled Medu Arts Ensemble would go on to make a cornerstone of its own cultural programme in the early 1980s.[38]

Mphahlele's defence of an idea of literature which was at once anti-prescriptivist and anti-elitist, African and humanistic, which refused to accept the terms of the oversimplified opposition between 'committed' and 'pure' art, and which characterized African writers as 'pioneers at the frontier, seeking a definition of ourselves and the past from which we have come' (198), was part of his extended argument not only with the Francophone African proponents of Négritude, but with the Western liberal tradition, and with white South African liberals in particular.[39] Yet his resistance to what he would later call the 'ethnic imperative' in literature was also informed at every point by his indebtedness to the modernizing, anti-tribalist New African tradition and by his reaction against apartheid's countervailing *volk* politics.[40] In the 1969 essay on censorship, he criticized the Sestigers, in much the same way as Breytenbach, Brink, and Small were doing at the time, for decrying censorship only on moral grounds as the 'deadweight of Puritanism', and for failing to confront the 'actual racial conflicts that permeate all South African life' because they were 'afraid of the written law and the sanctions of the tribe'.[41] In the 1968 essay, he made more explicit the connection between his anxieties about Négritude and his antipathy to the *volk*, which, for obvious reasons, he did not see as internally conflicted itself: 'I hate to think that one of these days we are going to sink to the degenerate level of Afrikaans writers in South Africa who have always censored themselves and not dared to challenge the government, because it has Calvinist Boer origins, like themselves, because they are all of a tribe.'[42] As I argued in Chapter 2, this accusation could, more fairly, have been levelled at only some Afrikaans writers and at most publishers.

Collective Rifts: Writers' Groups in the 1970s

The first white-led writers' group formed in the 1970s emerged out of the Poetry '74 conference in which, as we have seen, a rift opened up between the established generation of white English-language writers who identified with the tradition of South African liberalism and a younger generation who adopted a more radical position. Reflecting this new kind of thinking, the Artists' and Writers' Guild, which called itself a 'trade union', openly criticized PEN SA for its failings.[43] Commenting in the literary broadsheet *Donga*, Peter Wilhelm, the young writer who chaired the Guild, chastised the more established group for its 'ludicrous categories of membership'—one of their criteria was 'publication of two books by a genuine publisher'—and for the fact that it appeared to be 'unaware of the names of Black writers' who might satisfy its entry qualifications. Addressing his counterpart in the Cape Town branch, he suggested PEN SA had 'outlived any function it might have once had' and recommended 'you officially close down and donate funds to a more representative writers' body'.[44] Though the Guild itself remained, as one of its newsletters put it, 'predominantly white, predominantly bourgeois, predominantly intellectual', it was initially funded by the Programme for Social Change, an offshoot of the anti-apartheid Christian Institute, and it worked closely with the new generation of internal interventionist publishers as well as magazines like *Donga* and *Staffrider*.[45] Like these ventures, all the key members of its founding executive, Peter and Cherry Wilhelm, Mike Kirkwood, Athol Fugard, Jack Cope, Ad Donker, and Sheila Roberts, were in their different ways actively engaged in promoting intercultural and multiracial collaboration. As a consequence, the Guild rapidly attracted a substantial membership of around one hundred mostly white writers and artists. Tlali, Sepamla, Essop Patel, and Ahmed Essop were among its few black members.

The new Guild's manifesto drew attention to its distinctiveness in a number of ways. While it pledged to defend the 'right of every artist and writer to the full expression of his creativity', much like PEN SA, it did not focus only on the particular threat the censors posed. 'Repressive censorship, arbitrary laws and stifling conventions are realities of our society which continually impede and threaten creativity,' the manifesto declared, before adding that 'it is vital for artists and writers to present a common front against all such attempts to restrict their creativity'.[46] In keeping with these principles, the new group rejected any move to reform the censorship system and adopted a more comprehensive programme of resistance. It lobbied the chief censor, organized symposiums on censorship, on one occasion staging a debate between Nadine Gordimer and J. M. Leighton, and, in a more practical spirit, it created a modest fund to assist publishers and writers to fight appeals when the new system was introduced in the mid-1970s. In 1976 it supported Jack Cope's failed attempt to have the ban on *The Dawn Comes Twice* lifted on review and Ravan Press's equally unsuccessful appeal against the banning of Khayalethu Mqayisa's play *Confused Mhlaba*. The Guild also took a leading role in challenging all forms of official harassment by, for instance, organizing public campaigns against the government's refusal to allow various black writers, including James Matthews and Sipho Sepamla, to travel abroad in the mid-1970s. As a consequence of these initiatives it soon earned a reputation for 'political activism', about which it was unapologetic, and attracted the attention of the security police, who kept it under constant surveillance.[47]

As a self-avowed 'trade union', the Guild was, unlike PEN SA, not just committed to upholding the freedom of expression. It pledged itself to defending writers' interests more generally by assisting them to 'work effectively within our society and to free them from the cupidity of agents and middle-men', while also promoting 'contact and interaction among all South African artists and writers'.[48] To these ends they organized regular public readings, advised writers on copyright issues, actively supported little magazines, and liaised with other, like-minded groups. While these projects reflected the Guild's frustration with the relatively passive tradition of liberal protest, which relied on memorandums and letters to the press, its other manifesto commitments revealed its scepticism about the more questionable cultural assumptions underlying PEN SA's anti-political stance. 'A major role of the artist and writer is to respond to the realities of his society,' they insisted, and 'if injustice is a reality of his society he cannot ignore it'.[49] As Peter Wilhelm's public attack on Jack Cope, again in *Donga*, suggests, this did not mean the group accepted that realism provided the only, or even the best, literary model for aspirant interventionist writers. Citing John Barth's critique of the traditional novel in *Lost in the Funhouse* (1968), Wilhelm noted that just as 'it is possible to build sailing boats, but not necessary; so it is possible to write "realism", but not necessary'. 'A sailing boat is a beautiful thing,' he added wryly, 'but best seen quietly drifting away into the sunset.'[50]

By the early 1970s rifts of a different kind were also beginning to open up within Afrikaans literary culture. In this case, however, the generational split was not so much between liberals and radicals as between relatively straight-forward *volk* nationalists and the variously dissenting liberals and Marxists, many of whom had already broken ranks with the Writers' Circle by signing the anti-censorship petition in 1963. By the time Brink's *Kennis van die Aand* was banned in 1974, a more significant rupture was inescapable. What emerged was the Afrikaanse Skrywersgilde (Afrikaans Writers' Guild), which a key group of Sestigers, including the writers and academics behind the anti-*volk* imprint Taurus, formed in July 1975. Unlike the more established and collaborationist Circle, the Gilde was multiracial and independent of government. It was funded exclusively by its own members, who also built up a fund to defend *Kennis* in court. The new group was opposed not just to censorship but, following liberal principles, to any state control over literature. Signalling a clear break not just with the Writers' Circle but with the compromises of the *volk* avant-garde, its constitution declared that 'no person linked to a state body which seeks to control literature can qualify for membership of the Gilde'.[51] This policy in-evitably provoked a confrontation with Anna Louw, who was forced out when she admitted to being a censor. For all this, the Gilde's own approach to dealing with the threat of censorship, particularly its willingness to engage with the system, was the cause of some internal controversy.

At first, in keeping with its constitutional commitment to doing 'everything in its power to combat the detrimental effects' of censorship, it made use of the new review provisions introduced under the 1974 Act in an effort to get various banned books back into circulation.[52] In 1975 and 1976 it submitted titles by Nkosi, Peter Abrahams, La Guma, Mphahlele, and Breytenbach, though it suc-ceeded only in having the first edition of Mphahlele's *The African Image* (1962) unbanned on review. After these initial setbacks, and when the review and appeal procedures, and, indeed, the policy of engagement, became a matter of dispute, it abandoned this idea, though, in 1982, during Brink's tenure as chair, it took advantage of the new reform era and tried again, this time with more success. Both Rive's *Emergency* and Tlali's *Muriel at Metropolitan* were released in the early 1980s on the Gilde's initiative. At that point, however, the publisher David Philip and the South African Library took over as the main proponents of this strategy during the era of 'repressive tolerance'. This is what enabled Philip to launch his major Africasouth reprint series in 1982, which included a number of previously banned titles, beginning with Harry Bloom's *Transvaal Episode*.

More serious internal tensions over the Gilde's own strategy of engagement arose during the *Magersfontein* crisis in 1977. Despite the concerns of some members, Small and Brink most notably, and allies, like the English Guild, it took part in discussions with the government about reforming the system to give more protection to literature, making it once again vulnerable to the charge of complicity. In early 1978 Bartho Smit, who was then chair, and Chris Barnard, his deputy, both of whom belonged to the less radical faction within the Gilde, joined forces with the former censor Merwe Scholtz and the conservative critic F. I. J. van Rensburg to persuade the Minister of the Interior to ensure that the absurd wrangle over *Magersfontein* could not be repeated. As a consequence of this, and a further, separate discussion the Minister had with the Writer's Circle, the government introduced the amendments that laid the foundations for van Rooyen's reforms in the 1980s. In fact, two key changes—the provisions regarding the likely reader and measures introduced to allow controversial books to be released with an age restriction—were initially proposed by the Gilde itself, which began lobbying the government on these issues in early 1976.

As the Gilde's membership encompassed old-style loyal resisters like Bartho Smit, liberal Afrikaners like Jan Rabie, and anti-*volk* radicals like Brink, internal controversies were to be expected. Another key area of contention centred on its pledge to champion 'the interests of Afrikaans literature' only.[53] On this question the group divided into two factions, one led by Rabie, the other by Brink. While the Rabie camp focused on the need to uncouple Afrikaans from the oppressive politics of apartheid and promote it as a 'multi-*volk* (*veelvolkige*) language', the Brink group was more concerned about creating a united front against censorship and apartheid more generally.[54] In 1977 the Brink faction eventually won the argument, as a consequence of which the Gilde began to engage in wider debates, involving writers in all languages, and by the early 1980s, when it had over 150 members, it started to play a more significant role within the broader resistance as well. After calling unsuccessfully for the release of Mandela, it went on to campaign on behalf of the two most famous literary–political prisoners in South Africa, helping to secure the release of Breyten Breytenbach in 1982 and the poet and Communist Party activist Jeremy Cronin two years later. In the late 1980s it extended its role still further by establishing links with the accredited democratic movement within the country and with the ANC in exile. In July 1989 a number of key members, including the chair, Jeanette Ferreria, caused more controversy within Afrikaner nationalist circles by engaging in direct talks with the ANC about South Africa's cultural and political future. Among the other delegates at this landmark conference, which was held in Zimbabwe, were the leading anti-*volk* writers and intellectuals Breytenbach, Brink, Welma Odendaal, Antjie Krog, Ampie Coetzee, and John Miles.[55]

The most momentous cultural rift in the 1970s was, however, created not by the new white-led national Guilds, but by the numerous black-led, generally regional community arts groups that began to emerge in townships across the country in the early part of the decade. The formation of the umbrella body Mdali (Music, Drama, Arts, and Literature Institute, though the word also meant 'Creator') in Soweto in 1972, which brought together a number of already active groups, was followed by what Ndebele called a 'phenomenal mushrooming of writers and cultural groups of all kinds'. He estimated that there were 'at least twenty-five recorded ones'.[56] Among the most notable were the Mihloti (Tears) Black Theatre group, the Creative Youth Association of Soweto, the Guyo Book Club of Sibasa, the Mpumalanga Arts Ensemble, BLAC, and, later in the decade, Medupe (Soft Rain).[57] At one level, their emergence represented the realization of a long-held goal of the resistance. As Ndebele noted, various ideas for a modern, anti-tribalist African academy 'to advance the peculiar and particular needs of African Art' had been discussed both within the ANC and more broadly in the late 1940s, though these were never implemented.[58] There were, however, some vibrant independent groups in the early 1950s, like the Syndicate of African Artists, in which Es'kia Mphahlele played an active part, and BICA, the regional Bantu, Indian, and Coloured Arts group.[59] At another level, the groups that emerged in the early 1970s initiated a wholly new era in the history of the resistance. If they looked back to the Négritude tradition of the 1940s, and the New African tradition before that, they took their main inspiration from the global Black Arts movement of the 1960s and more immediately from the rise of Black Consciousness in South Africa at the end of the decade.

In the South African context, the significance of the self-affirming label 'Black' was, in the first instance, political. It inaugurated a new sense of solidarity among *all* the country's oppressed communities, emphatically rejecting both the divisive racial categories of apartheid—'Coloured', 'Indian', or 'Bantu'—and the racist negation 'non-White'. As the label for a new cultural movement, however, its primary significance lay in the fact that it announced a decisive break with the dominant tradition of liberal, white-led multiracialism. Recognizing that concerns about the threat of censorship only went so far, the proponents of the new movement shifted the terms of the debate from the relatively narrow issues surrounding the freedom of expression to the larger and more urgent question of Black cultural autonomy, or from the specific anxieties about state coercion to the general problem of dependency. As Strinivasa Moodley, who was, along with the poet Mafika Gwala, one of the movement's leading cultural advocates, put it in 1972, the challenge was to wrest control from the 'white liberal magazines' who 'avidly' publish Black writing 'so that the white conscience can be purged' and from 'Alan Paton and the company of whites who capitalise on the Black experience and Black suffering'.[60] Though they maintained contacts with the more progressive elements in white culture (while Mdali, for instance, accepted some modest financial support from the English Guild, Medupe linked up with *Donga*), the new groups focused on

bringing Black artists and audiences together, mainly through theatre performances but also through festivals, workshops, poetry readings, newsletters, and
publishing venues. As we have seen, *Staffrider* became one of their principal
outlets later in the decade.

For Moodley, the imperative to remake the culture along Black lines was
inseparable from the need to escape 'the maze of sophistries and sophistica-
tions of western cultural value' and, more specifically, the dominant liberal
conception of the literature and the arts.[61] If 'all true artists reflect a mood, in
one form or another', he remarked, this was not their 'express property' as
individuals, nor did it mean that they had somehow to 'extract' themselves
from their 'own experience and then talk in objective universal terms'. Rather,
in reflecting this 'mood' the artist was giving voice to his 'own community'.[62]
This did not mean that the Black artist or poet was simply acting as a spokes-
person for the community, however, since the emancipatory cultural project in
which they were engaged was both creative and disruptive. Rejecting the react-
ive passivity implied by the term 'protest', Moodley and the other key theorists
of the new movement set out to develop an affirmative, distinctively Black
aesthetic, while also unsettling established ideas of the literary, and, in some
cases, specifically affronting white liberal assumptions. Hence the strong metapoetic tendency among many Black poets of the 1970s, an issue I discuss in
detail in Chapter 7. If this produced writings that were, as the *Black Review*
put it in 1973, 'charged with fire, exaggerated images of violence, hate and a
counter-balancing love for the Black community', it also avoided the pitfalls
associated with protest poetry, which the reviewer felt were exemplified by
Mbuyiseni Mtshali's *Sounds of a Cowhide Drum* (1971). It did not help that
Mtshali's debut volume was at the time being lauded by white literary critics
both nationally and internationally. 'Like Black Consciousness', the reviewer
insisted, 'the underground Black poetry does not have time to complain': 'it
seeks to find positive alternatives'.[63] The reviewer in this case was most probably Mafika Gwala, who edited the 1973 issue of the *Black Review* and later went
on to form the Mpumalanga Arts Ensemble.

The new Black groups were not only involved in a collective cultural endeavour to escape the perils of white literary guardianship, however. They were also
engaged in a generational struggle with the more established black writers.
As Gwala explained in an open letter to Richard Rive in 1971, in which he
took issue with the older writer's liberalism, their anxieties about cultural
assimilation, which fuelled their doubts about Mtshali's early poetic achievements, also made them question Nat Nakasa's multiracial ideals: 'To those
young blacks (non-whites) with an urge to write, Can Themba was to them
what Nat Nakasa (with his essays) was to the liberals. Both were great hopes.
Can Themba on the side of blackness—Nat Nakasa on the side of whiteness.
(Nat's black face behind a white mask.)'[64] Other younger writers revived

concerns about Mphahlele's critique of Négritude. For Temba Sono, the president of SASO, the leading Black Consciousness student organization, Mphahlele seemed to have conceded too much to the Western idea of a 'common humanity'. Echoing the doubts some of Mphahlele's African American critics raised, he insisted, in an essay of 1971, that the 'Black man ... is Negritude'.[65] One of the most controversial figures in this respect, however, was the black Sestiger Adam Small. Though he ran an important Black theatre group and contributed to the *SASO Newsletter* (one poem, in English, commemorated the SASO leaders, including Moodley and Biko, banned in 1973, and wryly invoked the spirit of 'Walt Witman', i.e Whiteman), Small put his new Black Consciousness credentials on the line when he praised van Wyk Louw's humanistic idea of Afrikaner culture in the essay of 1972 to which I referred in Chapter 1.[66] This, as an anonymous reviewer in the *SASO Newsletter* remarked, amounted to little more than an 'undisguised eulogy of van Wyk Louw's concept on culture', which 'smacks of a sub-conscious desire for an acceptance by the Afrikaner and an assimilation into his culture'.[67] These generational tensions were, as we have seen, felt on both sides. Yet, for all the questions they had about the new movement, Small, Rive, and Mphahlele all recognized the significance of the decisive transformation it effected, established close links with its major advocates, and made its uncompromising vocabulary part of their own lexicon.

Second Intersection: Nadine Gordimer and the Space of the Literary

By the early 1970s, Gordimer, like the founders of the Artists' and Writers' Guild, to which she belonged, had no illusions about PEN SA, and, again like the Guild, she channelled her considerable organizational energies into a more radical anti-censorship campaign and an active programme of multiracial collaboration. One of her key initiatives in the new decade was to found and initially fund the Mofolo–Plomer Prize. Intended in part as an alternative to the CNA Award, which generally went to established white authors, it was specifically designed to encourage young writers, and, as its name suggested, to foster a common literary culture. Thomas Mofolo and William Plomer were both leading literary modernizers in the first half of the twentieth century. In keeping with these ideals, the inaugural adjudicators of the new prize, which was first awarded in 1975, were Small and Paton, and its first joint winners were Peter Wilhelm and Mbulelo Mzamane. The prize, which was later co-sponsored by Ravan, Donker, and David Philip, was not just an implicit comment on the liberal establishment's priorities, however. It was also a response to the rise of Black Consciousness, which Gordimer found acutely unsettling, despite her sensitivity to 'the question of white proxy for black protest'.[68] While the new movement's principled separatism remained her primary concern, she was also anxious about the attitude some younger Black poets seemed to have to the literary demands of their medium. Indeed, for Gordimer, the advent of Black poetry provoked a series of reflections on the question of literature that preoccupied her for the rest of the apartheid era. Since her critical interventions in the 1970s, like Mphahlele's a decade earlier, add a further dimension to the subterranean literary rivalry between writers and censors, it is worth clarifying the grounds for her disquiet.

Given poetry's centrality to the wider Black Arts movement, from Senghor and Césaire to Langston Hughes and LeRoi Jones, and the potential many younger Black South African poets saw in it as a multimedia form in which words, music, and performance could be blended and juxtaposed, it is clear that the shift from prose to poetry in the late 1960s was over-determined. Yet, in Gordimer's view, it was the threat of censorship itself that provided the most obvious explanation for the new trend. As she argued in *The Black Interpreters* (1973), the almost complete suppression of black writing in the 1960s had set the younger generation on a 'subconscious search for a form less vulnerable than those that led a previous generation into bannings and exile'. With other indirect modes of writing in mind—she mentioned Russian *skaz* and Aesopean fables—she suggested that 'black writers have had to look for survival away from the explicit if not to the cryptic then to the implicit; and in their case, they have turned instinctively to poetry'. Quoting Harry Levin, the American critic with whom she developed a close friendship in the 1960s, she observed that the appeal of poetry lay in the fact that it constituted a complex formal 'arrangement of signs and sounds', which was at the same time 'a network of associations and responses'. The trouble was that, in her view, too many younger Black writers saw poetry less as a viable 'hiding place' and more as a 'megaphone', leading her to ask whether or not they qualified to be called 'poets at all'.[69] If they were, as she put it, 're-establishing a black protest literature', were they also 'writing good poetry?'[70]

Having sketched out her initial concerns in 1973, she went on to voice her unease more emphatically in the essay 'A Writer's Freedom', which was first published in Sepamla's *New Classic* two years later. On this occasion she argued that many of the younger Black poets appeared to have given in to the pressures, which were 'more insidious' than censorship, arising from the expectations of those who regarded them as 'their mouth-piece' and who wanted them to embrace the 'jargon of the struggle' in the interests of conforming to 'an orthodoxy of opposition'.[71] This 'is right and adequate for the public platform, the newsletter, the statement from the dock: it is not adequate, it is not deep enough, wide enough, flexible enough, cutting enough, for the vocabulary of the poet, the short story writer or the novelist', she observed.[72] 'Worthwhile writing', she added, switching the terms of her critique, 'always comes from an individual vision, privately pursued,' insisting that the 'integrity' of a 'writer goes the moment he begins to write what he is told to write'. Quoting Sartre, though unwittingly also echoing van Wyk Louw, she observed that a writer 'is someone who is faithful to a political and social body but never stops contesting it'.[73] In *The Black Interpreters*, James Matthews, one of the co-authors of *Cry Rage!* (1972), emerged as the focus of her concern. Calling him the 'paradigm of the black writer', she felt he had not only renounced the title 'poet', but abandoned the language of poetry in favour of 'the clichés of politics, tracts, and popular journalism'.[74] She did not consider the possibility that he was writing in a self-consciously anti-poetic tradition, a point to which I return in Chapter 7.

As this suggests, Gordimer found it easier to distance herself from the terms in which a group like PEN SA conducted its anti-censorship campaign than from the broader cultural legacies of the liberal tradition. From the context it is clear that she thought Sartre could be absorbed into this tradition, albeit as a champion of a more situated form of individualism. Her formulations at times not only echoed the 1963 writers' petition but seemed to be derived from the aestheticist, even specifically New Critical, tradition favoured by the censors and to echo their scholastic habits of thought. That they appeared to share her judgements of the new generation of Black poets only reinforces this impression. While they banned *Cry Rage!*, which they did not consider sufficiently literary, they passed Mongane Serote's debut volume, *Yakhal'inkomo* (The Cry of the Cattle, 1972), which Gordimer praised for its manifest literariness, or, as she put it, its 'craftsmanlike agony', its 'piercing subjectivity', and its refusal of 'generalised definitions of blackness'.[75] Yet, for all these apparent similarities, Gordimer's thinking in the early 1970s, particularly with regard to the questions of literary language, differed from the censors' in important ways, partly as a consequence of Harry Levin's influence. Following his reappraisal of the New Critical tradition in his essay 'Thematics and Criticism' (1968), which she cited in *The Black Interpreters*, she insisted that a poem was not just a self-sufficient 'verbal artifact', as the censors and some New Critics believed. It was, as Levin argued, also a vehicle for 'communicating implicit information and incidentally touching off value judgements'.[76]

This renewed emphasis on the propositional and evaluative dimension of poetry qualified without wholly repudiating New Critical formalism. It also still made the scholastic assumption that the question of poetic (or literary) language could be settled once and for all by determining its essential characteristics. Yet, by starting from these premises, Gordimer adopted a theoretical position that was not just distinct from but diametrically opposed to the kind of linguistic scholasticism that underpinned the censors' judgements. To borrow a cogent distinction Stanley Fish made in 1973, whereas Gordimer, like Levin, defended a 'message-plus' definition of literary language, the censors, like some New Critics, thought in terms of a 'message-minus' formula. 'A message-minus definition', Fish explained, 'is one in which the separation of literature from the normative centre of ordinary language is celebrated; while in a message-plus definition, literature is reunited with the center by declaring it to be a more effective conveyor of the messages ordinary language transmits.'[77] Gordimer's own commitment to a 'message-plus definition' is reflected in her claim that the 'implicit medium of poetry' says '*more than* any tract'. About Mtshali's 'images of dogs "draped in red bandanas of blood" scavenging the body of a baby dumped on a location rubbish heap' in the poem 'An Abandoned Bundle', she commented: 'he says *more* about black infant mortality *than* any newspaper exposé'.[78] For Gordimer, then, the trouble with many of the Black writers who emerged in the early 1970s was not that they appeared to have abandoned the aesthetically purified language of the poet, which, unlike 'popular journalism', say, purportedly made no value claims about the world, but that they seemed to have turned their backs on the specific linguistic resources of their own medium, which would have enabled them to bear witness to the realities of injustice in especially powerful ways.

The appeal Levin's residually scholastic critique of New Criticism had for Gordimer in the late 1960s goes some way towards explaining the interest she began to develop in the later theoretical writings of György Lukács at around the same time. As she commented in a letter to Anthony Sampson, written in 1968, Lukács helped her escape another burdensome critical legacy: it was 'hard to go back to Leavis' after reading *The Meaning of Contemporary Realism* (1963), she wrote, 'all of which leads to the curious (I think) happening that I am growing more left as I grow older'.[79] Whereas Levin guided her thinking about the nature of poetic language, Lukács influenced her ideas about narrative fiction in comparable ways by, in effect, articulating a 'message-plus' theory of the novel. On her reading, his concept of 'critical realism' offered a way out of the impasse between the supposed aestheticism of the 'Western avant-garde', or what she called 'experimental modernism', which appeared to have lost any interest in character and cut itself off from history, and the overly ideological tendencies of 'Socialist realism', which seemed to ignore the 'contradictions in the everyday life of society'.[80] By contrast, like the great 'critical realists' of the past—Gordimer's somewhat idiosyncratic Lukácsian canon included Balzac, Stendhal, Tolstoy, Mann, and Conrad—she argued that 'African English literature's best writers' were producing 'work in which the social changes that characterise our era are *most truly reflected*, character is not sacrificed to artistic pattern and the human condition is understood dynamically, in an historical perspective'.[81] As this suggests, Lukács helped Gordimer not only to theorize her position as a novelist, but to create space for herself as a specifically African writer, which is, in part, what she hoped *The Black Interpreters* would achieve. In her introduction she defined 'African writing' as 'writing done in any language by Africans themselves and by others of whatever skin colour who share with Africans the experience of having been shaped, mentally and spiritually, by Africa rather than anywhere else in the world'.[82] In the context of Black Consciousness, this, too, had a particular strategic significance. Among the key

African 'critical realists' she identified were Peter Abrahams, Richard Rive, Alex La Guma, Chinua Achebe, Wole Soyinka, and Ayi Kwei Armah, all of whom had by then been published as part of the Heinemann African Writers series.

Between them Lukács and Levin provided Gordimer with the theoretical tools she needed in the early 1970s to dispel the anti-political pieties associated with both the liberal and the aestheticist traditions without forgoing her commitment to the distinctiveness of the literary or to her own sense of herself as an interventionist writer. After dismissing Stendhal's lofty claim that 'politics in a work of literature is like a pistol-shot in the middle of a concert', she turned to 'the contemporary American critic, Irving Howe', who, she said, 'put his finger on the legitimate place of political themes in the novel with the statement, "Where freedom is absent, politics is fate" '.[83] In his censor's report on *The Black Interpreters*, Merwe Scholtz, who worried that the book might be used 'for propagandistic ends in schools and universities', drew attention to this quotation and to Gordimer's comments on censorship. However, after consulting the security committee, he agreed that the book could be passed because it 'handled what was inevitably explosive stuff in an expert and relatively balanced way' (P76/9/163).

In the years ahead, Gordimer remained a passionate defender of the specific interests of writers as a group and the distinctiveness of the literary, while also continuing to grapple with the cultural legacies of the liberal tradition. Yet, by the end of the 1970s, her sense of her own authority as a guardian of the literary had changed irrevocably. This was partly because she began to absorb other theoretical influences, notably Roland Barthes and Walter Benjamin, but it was also because, in responding to the challenge of Black Consciousness, she began to think differently about her own situatedness as a white writer whose primary points of reference remained the European high-cultural tradition. Having held up Turgenev as a model of the writer as contestatory individualist in the mid-1970s, she accepted a decade later that there were 'varying concepts, in different societies, of what the essential gesture of the writer as social being is'.[84] At the same time, she developed a deeper structural awareness of the issues at stake, acknowledging that 'it is out of being "more than a writer" that many black men and women in South Africa *begin* to write'.[85] In all this, she once again set herself apart from the censors, who, for all their new tolerance towards 'protest literature' in the 1980s, remained committed not just to an 'old, time-dishonoured view of culture', as Gordimer put it, but to the belief that 'there is a right for a single power group to decide what culture is'.[86]

New Solidarities, New Rifts: Writers' Groups in the late 1970s and the early 1980s

The government's clampdown on the Black Consciousness movement and its affiliates, including the writers' group Medupe, in October 1977 led to the most significant multiracial collaboration among writers of the early interregnum. In July 1978 international PEN, with Gordimer's active encouragement, approved the formation of a reconstituted, black-led version of the more or less moribund Johannesburg branch of PEN SA, which effectively merged Medupe, numerous other township groups, and the Artists' and Writers' Guild. While the large executive included representatives from various community arts groups and the Afrikaans Gilde, Mothobi Mutloatse, the journalist and short-story writer who had been on the Medupe executive, was elected chair, and all the other principal officers—Mike Kirkwood, Peter Wilhelm, and Ahmed Essop—came from the Guild. For the proponents of the new initiative the hope was not just to create a more credible united front and to mount a more robust defence of PEN's ideals—all of which they proceeded to do—but to provide some further protection and support for black writers in particular by working under the auspices of an international body.

This was welcomed, and, indeed, considered long overdue, at the international level, but it did not go down well with the superseded, exclusively white Johannesburg branch and the remaining Cape Town group. The president of the latter, Mary Renault, who was affronted by the sudden new development, which she saw as a woeful example of the politicization of culture, made her objections clear in an extended correspondence with Peter Elstob, the British writer who was then PEN's secretary-general. During the ensuing brouhaha, which dragged on for three years, she narrowly avoided having the Cape Town branch expelled on the grounds of racism by mounting what was, in effect, a liberal case against affirmative action. She took particular exception to the fact that the new group had flouted PEN SA's two-book rule by including among its members journalists and writers who had published one or two poems in *Staffrider*. It fell to a somewhat bewildered Elstob to deal with the fallout as diplomatically as he could. While PEN did not, in the end, expel the Cape Town branch, it made only one small concession to Renault by obliging the new group to call itself PEN (Johannesburg) not South African PEN as it had originally planned.

Like the more active writers' groups of the 1970s, PEN (Jhb) developed a wide range of initiatives, including public readings, conferences, and workshops, the latter often run by Es'kia Mphahlele, another member of the executive, who had amid some controversy recently returned from exile. Unlike the previous white-led groups, however, it avoided any possibility of complicity with the censorship system by deciding to have nothing to do with the review and appeal procedures. Instead, it focused on providing practical and financial assistance, as well as moral support and publicity, to the increasing number of harassed, banned, or imprisoned writers and their families, beginning with the young poet Jaki Seroke, who was convicted for possessing a copy of the banned Freedom Charter in September 1978. It was as a consequence of this policy of

Become A Member of PEN International!

What is P.E.N.? In short it's a world association of writers — 10 000 approximately — and stands for the *ideal of one humanity* living in peace *in one world*. Members pledge themselves to do their utmost to dispel race, class, and national hatreds.

P.E.N. is opposed to any form of suppression of freedom of expression, and opposes arbitrary censorship in time of peace.

Membership is open to all writers, editors, translators who subscribe to these aims, regardless of nationality, race, colour or religion.

Recently a group of writers met to establish a P.E.N. centre which was then accredited at the Annual Congress of P.E.N. in Stockholm. The new centre aims to establish better communication between writers and groups of writers in Southern Africa, and to defend their rights in the spirit of the charter.

At the inaugural meeting on 12 August the following executive was elected: Chairman: Mothobi Mutloatse; Secretary: Mike Kirkwood; Assistant Secretary; Peter Wilhelm; Treasurer: Ahmed Essop. A large executive committee representing writers' groups near and far is envisaged. A full list will be published when elections have been completed. The following executive committee members have already been elected: Miriam Tlali, Nadine Gordimer, Sipho Sepamla, Lionel Abrahams, Ingoapele Madingoane.

More P.E.N. news in future issues of *Staffrider*.

Membership Form /
To be posted to Southern African PEN Centre Johannesburg
P.O. Box 32483, Braamfontein, 2017.

I am a writer and would like to be a member of the Johannesburg P.E.N. International Centre. I enclose the annual membership fee of R3,00.

Name: ....

Address: ....

Telephone: .... Writers' Group (if any): ....

Staffrider Subscriptions

Please send me the following numbers of Staffrider at R1,50 per copy:

☐ Vol 1 No 2 (May/June)   ☐ Vol 2 No 1 (January/February)

☐ Vol 1 No 3 (July/August)   ☐ Vol 2 No 2 (March/April)

☐ Vol 1 No 4 (September/October)   ☐ Vol 2 No 3 (May/June)

☐ Vol 1 No 5 (November/December)   ☐ Vol 2 No 4 (July/August)

I enclose my cheque/postal order to cover the issues of Staffrider at R1,50 per copy that I have ticked in the block(s) provided.

Name ....

Address ....

....

Date .... Signed ....

FIG. 3.1. An appeal from the newly formed, black-led PEN SA, which appeared in *Staffrider* (1/3, July–August 1978).

non-cooperation that Ravan adopted the strategy of writing open letters to the censors in *Staffrider* and that Gordimer published the short exposé *What Happened to 'Burger's Daughter'?* with Taurus in 1980. Though she had herself applied successfully to have *The Late Bourgeois World* released on review in 1976, she followed the new policy and decided not to appeal when her later novel was banned in 1979. Like the *Staffrider* letters, her pamphlet gave the inner workings of the censorship bureaucracy wide publicity for the first time. The new group also strongly opposed van Rooyen's reforms in the early 1980s, noting, in one of its press releases, that 'the only solution is not to liberalise censorship, nor to change chief censors, but to scrap this evil system immediately'.[87]

Though PEN (Jhb) succeeded in maintaining a firm united front against all forms of government repression, it was in almost all other respects a fragile, untimely, and often tense alliance, particularly given the separatist thinking within the Black Consciousness circles. For Gordimer the 'warmth and welcome' of their festive meetings was heartening, but, as she acknowledged in a letter to Anthony Sampson in 1979, they also provided a 'glimpse of the spine-chilling depth of resentment and the anachronistic absurdities of our gathering'. 'It is such a delicate fabric that we have managed to weave crisscross,' she added, 'we are aware that a snagged fingernail could rip it.'[88] Lionel Abrahams, the former editor of the *Purple Renoster*, and self-avowed liberal guardian of the literary, who was, like Gordimer, an elected member of the executive, initially found the cross-cultural 'adventure', as he called it, 'exhilarating'. Yet he soon began to have some 'misgivings', as he put it in a rather pained retrospect about the group published in the early 1980s.[89] Their gatherings were 'mostly concerts of a sort rather than strictly poetry readings, with audiences ranging from a score to hundreds but generally much bigger than we of the submerged Guild were used to'. On these occasions poetry was often performed to the accompaniment of African drums, following a practice Ingoapele Madingoane and his Mihloti group had developed to revive traditions of African orature in the new era of Black pride, a practice Medupe also later adopted.

> But the greatest difference was the sense that these were community events—not exercises in 'culture' conducted by a brave and lonely few, but popular expressions of impulses of the day that ran strongly in the townships. They were, however, not merely entertainments, but didactic episodes of a crusade, consciousness-raising happenings in African idiom (despite the fact that the main medium was English).

In the process, Abrahams noted with dismay, the 'individual poet's individual utterances' were lost.[90] Though many of the events were dominated by a broadly Black Consciousness ethos—as Gordimer commented 'quite a few contemptuous things were said about white writers' particularly by 'young

189

prancing voluble men'—Abrahams also felt that the format opened up additional cleavages between different generations of writers, white and black, and
between Africanists and others.[91] Given the informality of the proceedings,
there was always time to 'accommodate rather different contributions from
whites, coloureds and Indians', he remarked, though the 'incongruity remained
apparent'.[92]

Abrahams was equally perturbed by Mutloatse's 'admonitory introduction' to
the popular anthology *Forced Landing* (1980), which became something of a
PEN (Jhb) manifesto.[93] In his retrospective, he quoted Mutloatse's pointedly
anti-polite call to literary revolution:

> We are involved in and consumed by an exciting experimental art form that I can
> only call, to coin a phrase, 'proemdra': Prose, Poem and Drama all in one!
> We will have to *donder* [bash] conventional literature: old-fashioned critic and
> reader alike. We are going to pee, spit and shit on literary convention before we
> are through: we are going to kick and pull and push and drag literature into the
> form we prefer.[94]

Though Mutloatse did not point this out, it is difficult not to speculate that his
neologism 'proemdra', which featured in *Staffrider* bylines, was, in part at least,
intended not just to confound the clear-cut categories white liberal guardians
like Abrahams cherished, but as a witty gibe at the assumptions encoded in the
name PEN itself. The acronym succinctly restricted its membership to a neatly
compartmentalized list of 'Poets, Playwrights, Editors, Essayists, Novelists'. Yet
Mutloatse did not just want to repudiate liberal scholasticism by disturbing the
boundaries between literature and orature. Touching on another vexed issue for
Abrahams and, indeed, Gordimer, he also insisted, 'we'll write journalistic
pieces in poetry form'.[95] It is worth noting that the censors, who initially banned
Forced Landing on political grounds, eventually passed it on appeal. As the
report produced by the Appeal Board's committee of literary experts revealed,
this did not reflect any significant change in the censors' own cultural assumptions, however. Chaired by Merwe Scholtz, the committee dismissed
Mutloatse's introduction as 'pretentious' and took issue with his conception of
the literary (P80/3/113).[n] This disdainful line of argument set the terms for the
censors' new attitude to 'protest literature' in the 1980s.

Kirkwood, who published *Forced Landing* as the third volume in Ravan's new
Staffrider Series, responded to Abrahams's more nuanced sense of disturbance
in a series of Gramscian annotations printed alongside his retrospective. In his
view, Abrahams's disquiet reflected an unwillingness on his part to question his
own 'hegemonic' cultural assumptions, not least because his selective quotation from Mutloatse's 'deliberate provocation' obscured other 'substantial insights', which were informed by a very different set of Black Consciousness
principles.[96] What Mutloatse had emphasized, Kirkwood noted, quoting

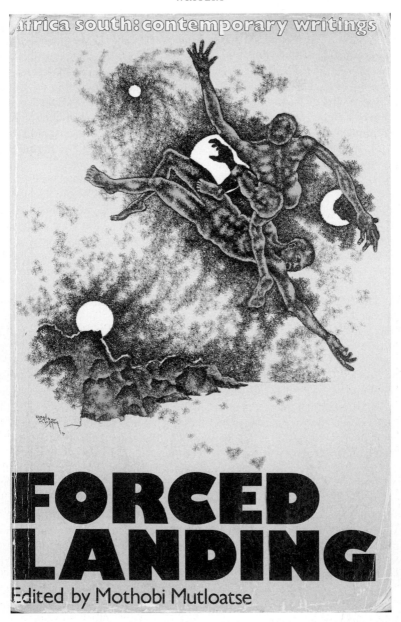

FIG. 3.2. The front cover of Mothobi Mutloatse's anthology of black writing *Forced Landing* (1980), which was banned and then released after the chief censor appealed against his own security committee's decision. See also webnote n.

another section of the introduction, was that 'the black writer should concentrate primarily on his immediate audience'. This was not only because the 'community' formed 'the basis of his writings' but because 'the recognition of his work as authentic by the black community' was the 'vital link in the creative process'.[97] Given the directions in which the cultural debates within the resistance were already beginning to move, it is worth adding that Mutloatse also defined his literary revolution in strongly anti-elitist and anti-aestheticist terms. The 'young black writer cannot afford the "white" luxury of indulging himself in art for art's sake as if it were a game for selfish, self-centred and hermit-like persons, shunning day-to-day contact with the masses at all costs'.[98]

After three years the various tensions within PEN (Jhb) eventually came to a head and, at an executive meeting in January 1981, it was finally decided to disband. Though PEN international saw this as a dismaying development, it did not come as much of a surprise to many local members. Just which 'snagged fingernail' finally unravelled its 'delicate fabric', however, was the cause of some debate. For Kirkwood, the problems were primarily a product of the class-based cultural divisions within the group. 'As a writers' organisation', he commented in April 1981, 'we were evidence that the shape of South African literary culture was radically altering, and would come to be dominated by a much more popular, less highbrow kind of writing', a 'literature that would aim at being of direct assistance in the reconstruction of South African society'. Though the 'overwhelming majority of our members were committed to writing as a cultural weapon in the struggle', a minority failed to accept this largely 'unspoken aim' and it was 'exactly the vagueness of this kind of identification that lay at the root of our failure'.[99] By reading the situation in these terms, he was not asserting the primacy of a Marxist analysis, or, indeed, as he noted, simply echoing Mafika Gwala. He was pointing to the changing political realities on the ground. In much the same way as the government had bought off 'militant white workers in the Twenties by means of racist legislation', he argued, it was now attempting to create a new alliance along class lines with 'so-called "Coloured" and Indian South Africa' while fostering 'class stratification in the African population' in the interests of meeting increasing demands for skills in an industrialized economy. Its goal was to divide 'the exploited and the super-exploited—without benefit of a racial tag'.[100] The task for any future group, he suggested, would be to forge a more 'effective solidarity' across class lines by recognizing that 'different writers' could play 'different roles' while promoting a shared set of 'fundamental cultural values'.[101]

Other members of the group had different views on its demise. For Abrahams, the primary explanation was that, as a liberal–literary association, with 'its individual black and white members, its charter and its international affiliation', PEN (Jhb) 'was not capable of being made over into a simple political instrument'.[102] For many black members, who felt their involvement was undermining their credibility in the townships, the reasons were more obviously political. In the increasingly tense climate of the early 1980s, the kind of alliance PEN (Jhb) represented was not only premature but counter-productive. Even Rive, who continued to defend the idea of the writer as a 'non-conformist' individualist, acknowledged that the 'loyalty' demanded by 'the Group' had to take precedence while 'White-imposed apartheid' remained in place, a view Gordimer shared.[103] As she commented in an interview in March 1981, 'some white PEN writers agreed to the temporary need for a black exclusivist position'.[104] For Sepamla, however, the main point at issue, according to Abrahams's report, was not 'cooperation between the races' but the extent of white involvement in any decision-making, though, in his case, it was the military raids on ANC bases in neighbouring states, which began in earnest in January 1981, which made 'sharing a platform with whites' finally impossible.[105]

Despite having to face various forms of obstruction from local authorities, who refused to let it hold its first meeting in May 1981, the new exclusively black writers' group that emerged after the break-up, which pointedly called itself the African Writers Association (AWA), quickly made its priorities clear. For one thing, unlike the white-led writers' groups of the 1970s, or, indeed, PEN (Jhb), its formation was premised not on the threat of censorship, an issue it ignored altogether, but, recalling the ideals of the Black Consciousness movement, on the more urgent need to promote cultural autonomy. Since the primary obstacle for its members was, in its view, the white-owned publishing industry, it pledged to protect African writers from 'exploitation in their dealings with publishers, literary agents and with the mass media in South Africa and abroad'.[106] Hence the AWA's commitment to developing Skotaville, the first major black-owned publisher to emerge in the apartheid era. For another thing, as its name suggested, the AWA represented one of many new realignments that were beginning to take shape in the early 1980s. Though it was not, as Skotaville's list indicated, opposed to a specifically Black Consciousness ethos, the new group was strongly pro-Africanist, even pan-Africanist. If its first manifesto pledge was 'to establish a bond of fellowship among African writers in South Africa', it also sought to foster 'close and practical links with other African cultural organisations' both 'in South Africa and beyond its boundaries'.[107] In addition, as part of its broader historical endeavour to give a new visibility to specifically African traditions, the AWA dedicated itself to promoting research into 'oral literature in Africa' and inaugurated a series of literary prizes named after key new African modernizers of the early twentieth century, including the H. I. E. and R. R. R. Dhlomo Drama Award, the Sol Plaatje Prose Award, and the S. E. K. Mqhayi Poetry Award.

As these various commitments suggest, Mphahlele, who drafted the manifesto, had a decisive influence on the new group's thinking. He was also a key member of the founding executive, which included Seroke, Sepamla, Tlali, Madingoane, and Mutloatse, who continued as chair. Though the group, which took over the remaining PEN (Jhb) funds and many of its projects, had a core membership of around fifty, it developed an extensive network of associate members who attended the workshops it set up around the country and worked closely with the Federated Union of Black Artists, the arts and educational organization Sepamla founded in the late 1970s. To support these initiatives it co-published a number of Mphahlele's lectures on the art of writing.[108] These ideals were also reflected in the importance the AWA accorded to the need to defend African writers' specific interests *as writers*. Indeed, given the questions that had been raised about Ravan's editorial policies under Kirkwood, the tensions within PEN (Jhb), and the increasingly politicized assumptions among younger black writers, the fact that four out of its eight manifesto pledges stressed the importance of the 'craft of writing' had an especially charged contemporary significance.

Developing a sense of writing as 'craft' was central to its programme of workshops and to its more general pledge 'to instil into all members the desire and will to create a literature that can stand on its own merits without the need to bolster it with loud public slogans'.[109] On this question, the manifesto took a strongly independent and anti-prescriptivist line, again echoing Mphahlele's arguments of the 1960s and 1970s. Its emphasis on the idea of the writer as a 'craftsperson and artist who should learn to master his/her medium' was predicated on a belief that 'we as writers have each to seek and find in ourselves that hairline distinction between on the one hand our role in society as men and women like the rest, and on the other our role as artists who have chosen that way of paying our dues to society as defined by our sense of history'.[110] In the context of the early 1980s the insistence on this 'hairline distinction', which drew attention to writers' specific interests while avoiding established liberal ideas of the writer as contestatory individualist, represented a multiply significant challenge. If it rejected standard liberal ideas, it also took issue with the growing consensus among the post-1976 generation of writers who, as Kirkwood remarked, viewed 'writing as a weapon in the cultural struggle'—one of the key 'public slogans' of the 1980s—and tacitly repudiated the censors' disdainful tolerance of 'protest literature' as a supposedly dominant mode of writing in the 'Third World'.

Third Intersection: Njabulo Ndebele and the Space of the Literary

In the early 1980s Njabulo Ndebele, who was at the time Professor of English Literature at the University of Lesotho, was a figure at the crossroads. Early in the previous decade he had made a name for himself as a young Black poet and a forthright proponent of the modernizing cultural ambitions underlying the Black Consciousness movement. In an important essay of 1972, he argued that

'almost all so-called tribal customs must be destroyed', and insisted that literature and the arts had a vital role to play in the process.[111] 'The blacks must
ignore the frustrated black journalist who says that South African blacks
must win the political kingdom first before they begin to create artistic works
of any meaning and merit,' he observed, no doubt with Lewis Nkosi's arguments of the 1960s in mind. Instead, they needed to recognize that 'it is the
great art works that inspire a bondaged people towards seeking freedom' and 'to
reassert human dignity'.[112] These ambitions made him particularly open to the
AWA's aims and encouraged him to join the group in the early 1980s. Yet, in the
course of the new decade, when he established close ties with Ravan Press and
Staffrider, he also became increasingly sympathetic to the Marxist forms of
analysis that were at that point beginning to dominate the broader thinking
within the resistance. This would eventually affect his relations with the AWA,
which, as we shall see, he eventually left in order to head another group more
closely allied to his own new way of thinking. Yet, in a series of influential
critical reflections on the space of the literary from the early 1980s, he effectively
articulated a nuanced position that took the ambitions of the Black Consciousness movement forward by linking the literary ideals of the AWA to the People's
Culture movement that began to gather strength by the middle of the new
decade.[113] Since his analysis also casts a further light on the submerged cultural
rivalry between censors and writers, especially given the new official attitudes
to 'protest literature', it is, once again, worth considering in some detail.

Ndebele's first major defence of distinctively literary modes of public intervention, a review of Yashar Kemal's *Anatolian Tales* (1983), was originally published as part of a short-lived *Staffrider* initiative in early 1984. In fact, his review
essay, which appeared under the title 'Turkish Tales, and Some Thoughts on S.A.
Fiction', inaugurated a new, Benjamin-inspired *Staffrider* series called 'The
Storytellers', which, as the magazine's headnote explained, comprised 'stories
"from afar" introduced by "home" writers'.[114] *Staffrider* accordingly published
'A Dirty Story' from the *Anatolian* collection alongside Ndebele's review. In the
circumstances, the decision to begin the series with Kemal and Ndebele was
doubly significant. It not only gave a new prominence to questions of narrative,
just as the poetic achievements of Black Consciousness were beginning to seem
outmoded, it also opened up a new way of locating South African writers on the
ever-changing map of world literatures. Kemal's special pertinence lay in the
fact that he was, according to both Ndebele and *Staffrider*, a leading exemplar of
'Third World Writing'. At one level, this was an act of reclamation targeted at the
censors' adoption of the category 'Third World' as a term of opprobrium, which
they used to rationalize their new tolerance of 'protest literature'. At another
level, however, given the AWA's pan-Africanist orientation, not to mention the
censors' ongoing attachment to 'Western' or 'European' traditions, it was a self-
conscious act of cultural remapping. This was underscored and complicated by

FIG. 3.3. The front and back cover of *Staffrider* (6/1, 1984), which contained Njabulo Ndebele's review of Yashar Kemal's *Anatolian Tales*. The back cover includes photographs of the exiled writers Bessie Head, Alex La Guma, and Mongane Serote, and the exiled musicians Eugene Skeef and Mongezi Feza.

the use Ndebele made of Benjamin's 1936 essay 'The Storyteller', which served as a key point of reference and model for his own review. Indeed, thinking about Kemal in 1984 led him back to the contemporary 'South African literary situation, where it seemed something was missing' in much the same way as Benjamin's sceptical appraisal of the dominant bourgeois narrative forms, notably the novel and short story, was provoked by his own reflections on Nikolai Leskov, the nineteenth-century writer who incorporated the conventions of traditional peasant orature into modern Russian literature.[115]

For Ndebele, Kemal's value as a model storyteller was as important as his 'Third World' status. At the most elementary level, this had to do with the range of subjects he wrote about. By being 'fruitful occasions for a serious examination of key social issues affecting some rural and semi-rural communities', his stories exposed the fact that South African writers seemed culpably alienated from the multifarious social realities of their time and 'decidedly preoccupied with urban culture' (11). None of this was helped, of course, by the fact that Afrikaner-owned publishers had given a dubious prestige to stories of rural life in the canon of apartheid writing. More tellingly, Kemal revealed just how much South Africa's urbanized writers had cut themselves off from the rich traditions of orature that continued to flourish as part of a popular urban culture, despite the inroads collaborationist publishers had made into the black mass market. Throughout his analysis, Ndebele distinguished between a 'mass culture', corrupted by capitalism and apartheid, and a genuinely popular 'People's Culture', which included the tradition of oral storytelling.

Compared to the fiction written by the cultural elite, among whom he testily included Mutloatse, Mzamane, Tlali, and Sepamla, which was, he argued, too concerned with a narrow range of 'political' themes, the stories told by the 'countless storytellers on the buses and trains carrying people to and from work in South Africa' covered an extraordinary range of subjects.

> The vast majority of the stories were either tragedies or comedies about lovers, township jealousies, the worries of widows; about the need to consult medicine men for luck at horse racing, or luck at getting a job or at winning a football match; or they were fantastic ghost stories... satires about the assassination of Verwoerd by Tsafendas... about helicopter weddings, about African soldiers seeing ships, the sea and Europe for the first time in WWII. (32)

This was not to say that these popular storytellers were apolitical. It was just that 'if any political concept crept into their stories, it was domesticated by a fundamental interest in the evocation of the general quality of African life in the township' (32).

In Ndebele's view, Kemal gave a new legitimacy to this popular tradition. In addition, his implied authorial position as a storyteller enabled him to establish a particularly democratic contract with his readers. In a deft move, which, following Benjamin, turned the European modernist ideals of impersonality into a primary characteristic of the 'timeless tradition of storytelling', Ndebele remarked that, with Kemal, 'a story is allowed to unfold by itself with a minimum of authorial intervention through which the storyteller might directly suggest how readers or listeners should understand his story' (14). Like the best South African storytellers, among whom Ndebele included Mofolo, Jordan, Mphahlele, and the young *Staffrider* authors Joel Matlou and Bheki Maseko, he gave his readers 'the opportunity to experience themselves as makers of culture' (33). Here it is worth recalling how the *Standard Encyclopaedia of Southern Africa* in the 1970s characterized 'Bantu literature' as essentially didactic (see Chapter 2). Instead of producing an overly moralizing elitist, and, as Ndebele's language implied, consumerist 'art that "sells" ideas to the people', in which the readers figure as 'anonymous buyers', Kemal's stories articulated ideas that could be '*embraced* by the people' as 'equals in the quest for truth'. In all these ways, then, he showed that the storyteller, who was at once open to the intricacies of rural life, wide-ranging in his subjects, and respectful of his readers, 'can only be genuinely committed to politics through a commitment to the demands of his art' (33).

The texture of Kemal's writing itself, or, more accurately, the literary space it opened up, confirmed this and, for Ndebele, spoke powerfully to those South African writers who appeared to have abandoned the specifically literary procedures of storytelling for 'journalism' in the interests of 'imparting social information' and using writing as a 'weapon of moral war' (24). Given Mutloatse's earlier attack on white liberal preoccupations with the sanctity of the literary, not to mention the growing consensus among younger and older black writers, this was an inevitably controversial claim. It did not help that Ndebele sounded as if he was simply rehearsing Nkosi's arguments of the 1960s, to which he explicitly referred. Yet it was precisely at this point that his inventiveness, as a theorist of a 'People's Culture' after Black Consciousness, came to the fore. For all his indebtedness to Nkosi, he was, given the legacies of the 1970s, inevitably more wary of Western literary traditions—hence the appeal of Kemal—and of the 'moralistic ideology of liberalism' (28). Moreover, even though he was an uncompromising defender of the 'autonomy of art', he did not think of this in abstract or overly reverential terms. Like Mphahlele, he recognized that it was itself a hard-won product of specific cultural and institutional histories and that it derived 'its objective validity from and within society' (22).

His most provocative move, however, was to revive the Black Consciousness critique of 'protest literature', while simultaneously revising it along class lines in order to turn it back on the advocates of what he took to be a more journalistic conception of writing. In doing so, he drew on Benjamin's Marxist rejection of the 'information' model of communication, which had, via its principal instrument, the capitalist newspaper press, come to dominate modern European culture in the course of the nineteenth century. Relying as it did on simple notions of plausibility and 'prompt verifiability', this 'new form of communication' had in the process, Benjamin argued, deformed the novel and short story, cutting them off from their origins in traditional storytelling and changing them into vehicles for fictionalized reportage.[116] To this extent, Ndebele's critique of journalistic models of writing was, unlike Nkosi's, not fuelled by aestheticist anxieties. Nor was it based on the kinds of worry Gordimer had about the nature of poetic language. Like Benjamin, he wanted to preserve the autonomous space of the literary to avoid complicity with the capitalist newspaper press, though, for Ndebele, this argument extended to the entire apparatus of white domination.

In his view, the perils of complicity for the journalistic 'writer of indictment' in apartheid South Africa were manifold and not always obvious (24). Like Mzamane, who, as we saw in Chapter 2, made the same point in his correspondence with Kirkwood, he recognized that even the censorship bureaucracy created subtle dangers of its own. About one unnamed writer who 'gleefully told me how honoured he felt' that a book of his had been banned, Ndebele commented:

> What I found disturbing was the ease with which the writer ascribed some kind of heroism to himself, almost glorying in a negation. It did not occur to him, of course, that the censors may have banned his work precisely because they may have seen in it their own 'games', their own tactics, their own quality of propaganda, their own vindictiveness, their own debasement. (26)

The censors' new attitudes to 'protest literature', which simply brought them in line with the dominant outlook of the 'white audience', transformed but did not diminish these dangers, since the 'misnomer', as Ndebele called it in a later essay from 1984, only served to deny that a piece of writing had 'any literary or artistic value'. 'Those who come to the defence of this literature', he added, 'have fallen into the same trap' as the censors and white critics by 'reinforcing the expository intention without establishing its own evaluative literary grounds'.[117] Complicity with the censors and white liberal assumptions was, however, only the most obvious part of the problem for those who fuelled 'creative writing's almost obsessive emulation of journalism' (24). More insidiously, like the 'African political resistance' as a whole, they also ran the 'almost unavoidable' risk of becoming too dependent on 'liberal institutions', including universities, research institutes, and the press, that had come to dominate the 'information giving activity for the general opposition' by 'pouring out masses of information on the iniquities of apartheid' (24).

In advocating a more journalistic kind of writing, then, these writers had, Ndebele claimed, begged an inescapably political question: whose journalism, or, more generally, whose information? Similar questions could, of course, be asked of writers and critics, like Levin and Gordimer, who valued poetry in part because it was a vehicle for communicating 'implicit information' and who defended a 'message-plus' conception of literary language. In this way, Ndebele challengingly absorbed and redirected the ideals of cultural autonomy, which had been central to Black Consciousness thinking, turning them into an equally emphatic defence of the literary as a specific, and politically indispensable, space, which, following the model of Kemal's *Anatolian Tales*, had a particularly urgent appeal in the context of a campaign to build a People's Culture.

New Solidarities, Ongoing Rifts: Writers' Groups in the 1980s

The foundations for a new cultural strategy within the resistance were laid at the landmark Culture and Resistance conference held in Gaborone, Botswana, in July 1982, which was organized by the exiled writers' and artists' group the Medu (Roots) Art Ensemble. A successor to the Pelandaba Cultural Effort, which Mongane Serote formed with the poet Mandla Langa in 1976, this group, which, like the ANC itself, received financial backing from the Dutch, Swedish, and Norwegian governments, effectively served as one of the main cultural structures for the exiled ANC before it formed its own. The conference was, in fact, held in part to celebrate the organization's seventieth anniversary. Though Serote remained a key figure in the new group, which had a variable membership ranging from around fifteen to fifty, he was joined in 1978 by the celebrated graphic artist Thami Mynele, and, later, by the poets Keorapetse and Baleka Kgositsile, all of whom played a central role in shaping Medu's cultural programme. Between 1977 and 1985 it developed a wide range of projects, promoting activities across all media. Its achievements in the graphic arts were particularly distinguished. Medu also created its own publishing imprint, bringing out *The Night Keeps Winking*, a slim volume of Serote's later poems, in 1982, which was promptly banned.

Following the cultural ideals outlined in the 1955 Freedom Charter, which the group reaffirmed, Medu had a strongly internationalist outlook, and, unlike the AWA, or, indeed, the Black Consciousness groups, it insisted that 'an important part of our southern African heritage is the diversity of cultural traditions on which we are able to draw'.[118] This included 'western literature, painting and theatre', the 'cultural experience of the African people', and the 'heritage (both Islamic and Hindu) of our Indian compatriots'.[119] This inclusive ideal formed part of Medu's larger commitment to a modernity which, as Serote later commented, rejected 'racism, tribalism, sexism and other backwardnesses'.[120] Crucially, this kind of thinking also informed the group's effort to embrace the language of non-racialism and to move beyond the multiracialist assumptions underlying previous collaborative projects.

200

FIG. 3.4. The front cover and inside page of *Staffrider* (5/2, 1982), with photographs from the Culture and Resistance conference, Botswana.

FIG. 3.5. The front cover of *Medu Newsletter* (1981), the principal platform of the exiled writers' and artists' group the Medu Art Ensemble, which was based in Gaborone, Botswana.

At the same time, reflecting Medu's adherence to Marxist-Leninist principles, it accepted that the modern 'democratic culture' it was endeavouring to fashion could not ignore history. Following Lenin's 1919 critique of 'old utopian socialism', which dreamt of creating a wholly new world 'from men and women reared in special hothouses and cucumber frames', it recognized that this new culture would have to be 'built, sometimes painfully, upon what has gone before', taking cognizance of 'the scars and blemishes wrought by the past' and, more particularly, the cultural impact of the 'dominant bourgeoisie'.[121] Recognizing that these effects could not be wished away, the group nonetheless set out to undo the assumptions on which the established culture was based and to create space for 'the proletarian culture of the future'.[122] It repudiated the 'bourgeois trap of individualism', the aestheticism of the 'oppressors' who believe 'form is everything, content merely subsidiary', and it sought to 'break down' the elitist 'myth that divides culture from our people'.[123] 'Let us not think that only those who can afford to have books on their shelves and pictures on their walls are practitioners of culture,' their prospectus for the 1982 conference announced. 'Culture embodies the everyday experience of our people' and 'it is the task of the cultural worker' to present this 'in a manner that is both understandable and relevant to the people'.[124] Though the group adopted some specifically Maoist phraseology, as this suggests, it was not blind to the horrors of the Chinese Cultural Revolution.

In keeping with these populist ideals, the Gaborone conference was dedicated to promoting 'unity in action between artists of all kinds and between different art forms'.[125] The programme accordingly covered dance, music, photography, the graphic arts, poetry, novels, and drama. Yet, according to Gordimer, the most prominent white writer among the 600 delegates, a 'whole arsenal of tormented contradictions', particularly about literary and political questions, constantly threatened to 'explode' the proceedings.[126] Reflecting some of these tensions, James Matthews gave a paper defending the ongoing importance of Black poetry, while Gordimer herself returned to her earlier reflections on the distinctiveness of the literary. Though she now acknowledged that 'struggle is the state of the black collective consciousness and art is its weapon', she continued to voice doubts about the 'phony sub-art' of 'agitprop' and to defend the right of the 'black artist' to 'search out his own demotic artistic vocabulary'.[127] Allying herself to the culturally inclusive thinking within Medu, she also defended the 'tools of white culture—most importantly, written literature with all its forms, from blank verse to secular drama and the novel'. These 'tools' had been 'appropriated by blacks', she argued, 'and rightfully, since the evolution of the means of expression belongs to all who have the will to use them'.[128] According to a report on the proceedings published in *Staffrider*, other forums gave rise to heated discussions about the 'dominance of European poetry', the under-representation of women poets, and the relevance of the novel to a future democratic culture given its bourgeois origins.[129] It fell to Keorapetse Kgositsile, who was then a professor of English Literature in Kenya, to reaffirm the call for unity in his keynote address. Quoting Oliver Tambo, the exiled President of the ANC, who had declared 1982 the 'Year of Unity in Action', he called on 'workers, peasants, students, priests, chiefs, traders, teachers, civil servants, poets, writers, men, women and youth, black and white' to 'take our common destiny in our own hands'. Declaring himself to be 'unapologetically partisan', he then set the terms for the nonracial People's Culture campaign that defined the 1980s by encouraging his fellow writers to make 'literature' serve the 'interests of the people', echoing Barry Feinberg's call in the introduction to his anthology *Poets to the People* in 1974.[130]

The campaign of mass mobilization was initially taken forward by the ANC at the international level, especially after Serote established its first cultural desk in London in 1982, and by its principal political affiliates within South Africa: the United Democratic Front (UDF), the internal ANC-aligned umbrella body founded in 1983, and the Congress of South African Trade Unions (COSATU), the ANC-aligned federation of black unions established in 1985. In response, the government launched its own repressive counter-campaign, which included a military attack on various Medu members in June 1985, during which both Mynele and the group's treasurer, Mike Hamlyn, were killed. As a result Medu was forced to disband. In 1987, however, a group of largely black writers sympathetic to its objectives, who had been meeting irregularly for the previous two years as part of an informal Writers' Forum, decided to take the campaign forward by reconstituting themselves as the Congress of South African Writers (COSAW), the last and largest writers' group to emerge in the apartheid era. Reflecting their ties to Medu, the Forum thought of themselves as 'Exiles Within', a title they gave an anthology of poems they published in 1986.[131] At their final meeting the members of the Forum, most of whom were not affiliated to the AWA, decided, as Ndebele later recalled, that they could no longer 'stand aloof from the massive political movements throughout the country' or simply continue to 'talk shop' without adopting 'a clearly defined political position'.[132] Ndebele left the AWA to become COSAW's founding president, while Achmat Dangor, a key figure within the Forum, became its first vice-president. With the full backing of the ANC's new Department of Arts and Culture, which was confirmed at the landmark Culture in Another South Africa festival held in Amsterdam in December 1987, COSAW carried forward the Gaborone ideals through a wide range of cultural initiatives. By the late 1980s the group had over 600 members, and with substantial foreign donor support, principally from the Swedish and Norwegian governments, who directed funds via their own national writers' groups, it had created an extensive countrywide network, linking community arts groups, the cultural groups that had played an important part in the trade union movement since the early 1970s, as well as the UDF, COSATU, and the Afrikaans Writers' Guild.

COSAW's founding constitution brought together, under the overarching strategic objective 'to advance the struggle for the creation of a non-racial, non-exploitative, non-sexist, united and democratic South Africa', a number of principles that had emerged within various writers' groups in the course of the 1970s and early 1980s.[133] In the first place, unlike the AWA, but like the English and Afrikaans Guilds as well as PEN (Jhb), it pledged to 'resist all forms of censorship' and to 'combat state repression in all its forms'. Secondly, following some versions of Black Consciousness and Marxist thinking, which, of course, some hardline nationalists shared, it rejected the liberal idea of the writer as contestatory individualist, and, indeed, the AWA's commitment to defending the 'hairline distinction' between writers' responsibilities as writers and as members of the wider society. Echoing the Gaborone ideals, the second clause of the constitution declared that 'we recognise that writers and cultural workers, generally, are products of and belong to the community' and that 'as such they have a responsibility to serve the community'. Which 'community' was left open, though, as the name COSAW indicated and as the preamble's opening phrasing affirmed—it began 'We, the writers of South Africa'—the assumption throughout was that it referred primarily to the territorially defined national community, or, more accurately, the unitary post-apartheid South Africa that was yet to come. Thirdly, following Medu, the preamble acknowledged the 'central role played by the working-class in a mass democratic movement and in the struggle for liberation', a role that had to be reflected in 'the development of our culture'. Finally, the group recognized both the 'critical role that literature and the other arts must play in the struggle for liberation' and 'the need to promote literature, other arts and culture that are directed to the creation of a new and democratic South Africa'. Significantly, though COSAW, like the AWA, developed an educational programme in both urban and rural areas—it ran workshops, established 'people's libraries', and, like Medu, became a publisher in its own right—it focused not on the 'craft of writing' but on the need to 'teach writers, poets and cultural workers to write critically about the history of our country and to express their aspirations about a new society'.

COSAW's non-racialism and explicitly partisan position clearly set it apart from the AWA, though since it was always a coalition of 'writers' and 'cultural workers'—it did not purge the more traditionalist bourgeois terminology from its official lexicon—its own attitudes to the role of writers were more capacious, and closer to the AWA's, than the imperative language of its constitution sometimes suggested. While it established strong links with COSATU's workers' poetry movement, which, under its leading figures Mi Hlatswayo and Mzwakhe Mbuli, had a strong commitment to the idea of poetry as an immediately serviceable political 'weapon', COSAW itself focused as much on the need to promote writing as a means of building the future nation as it did on its own forms of critical revisionism. These various priorities were reflected in its publishing list, which included workers' poetry as well as gay and women's writing (COSAW also took over *Staffrider* from Ravan in 1991), and in the Alex La Guma/Bessie Head Fiction Award, which it launched in 1988 as a commemorative tribute to the two leading anti-apartheid writers who had recently died. Yet the new group's willingness to accommodate diverse views was perhaps most clearly signalled by the fact that it elected Ndebele as its founding president. Unlike Mphahlele, Mutloatse, and Seroke, who remained sceptical about COSAW's partisan position, Ndebele switched to the new group, which articulated many of the ideals that had informed his own Medu-inspired theoretical reflections on a new People's Culture earlier in the decade. As his inaugural presidential address in July 1987 revealed, however, he was willing to be a challenging, even contrary, figurehead.

In keeping with his general views on the 'mechanisms of modern South African oppression', Ndebele devoted most of his address, entitled 'Against Pamphleteering the Future', to a careful analysis of a pamphlet that been circulating in a local township, which exemplified the government's new strategy of co-optation.[134] Returning to his earlier reflections on journalistic models of writing and the problem of complicity, he remarked that this 'manipulative pamphlet', which purported to come from a residents' 'peace movement', represented the kind of 'writing that is not conscious of the extent to which it may have internalised the textual strategies of the oppressor'.[135] In his conclusion, however, he shifted his attention from the present to the future, in which 'the oppressor, who has deliberately left millions of people outside of all serious human activity, will definitely have to learn to live with the fact that there are going to be drastic revisions to his own texts'.[136] The 'common aim of all writers, at this point in our history', he argued, was to initiate this process of revision.[137] This clearly reinforced COSAW's own goals, although, as Ndebele anticipated, the terms in which he went on to define what form this 'new text' should take was not what all the 150 delegates at the inaugural conference had in mind. Its 'essential characteristics', he suggested, reiterating some of his earlier arguments, would be 'its seriousness, its radical broad-mindedness, its inventiveness, its unbounded respect for the reader, and its understanding that no aspect of the life of the oppressed is irrelevant as a subject for artistic or expository treatment'. 'We need to realise', he concluded, 'that, although this conference has brought together practitioners of a certain kind of writing, there are other kinds of writing that are equally important.'[138] COSAW's own commitment to these 'other kinds of writing' was reflected in the fact that it went on to republish Ndebele's early critical writings in a single volume entitled *Rediscovery of the Ordinary* (1991) as well as collections by the two younger 'storytellers' Ndebele had singled out for particular praise: Joel Matlou's *Life at*

Home and Other Stories (1991) and Bheki Maseko's *Mamlambo and Other Stories* (1991).

Fourth Intersection: J. M. Coetzee and the Space of the Literary

That J. M. Coetzee, who always occupied a risky position as an unaffiliated intellectual, did not join any writers' group during the apartheid era had little to do with any residual commitment he might have had to the idea of the writer as a contestatory individualist. Rather, it reflected the concerns he had about any attempts to require writers to fulfil a prescribed role, including that of individualist, which, as he later put it, 'implies that one is giving oneself to a part that is already written'.[139] These reservations were, in turn, linked to a series of questions he began to raise about the idea that literature could be made to serve a predefined collective enterprise, particularly one understood in national terms. He began to voice these concerns in 1981 after *Waiting for the Barbarians* won him his second CNA Award, a prize he saw as forming part of a dubious, white-led nation-building project (see Chapter 8). Yet if he guarded his testy independence and right to ask awkward questions, he did not remain aloof from the contemporary debates about the politics and ethics of responsibility. In an important statement about his own practice as an interventionist writer, which he first gave as talk during an anti-apartheid cultural festival held in Cape Town in November 1987, he engaged in a sustained, if largely implicit, dialogue about the space of the literary, which echoed, extended, and complicated the debates Ndebele initiated within COSAW and more broadly in the course of the 1980s. Since the terms of his polemic also added a new level of complexity to the rivalry between writers and censors, and brought a different theoretical perspective to bear on the question of literature, they are, once again, worth considering in some detail.

Billed to speak at a session entitled 'The Novel Today', Coetzee used the occasion to defend his own literary practice in unusually forthright terms. Passionate, unapologetic, even combative, he was also characteristically wary. He made a point of noting that, given his remit, he had been obliged to abandon his 'own language'—that is, a specifically literary language—and to 'speak a fragile metalanguage, with very little body, one that is liable, at any moment, to find itself flattened and translated back and down into the discourse of politics'.[140] His position was not made any easier by the fact that the festival had been organized by the *Weekly Mail*, the anti-apartheid newspaper founded in 1985, which was, as he remarked, an 'active and unashamed proponent' of this process of translation (3). His principal concerns were, however, focused on what he took to be the 'powerful ... perhaps even dominant tendency' among literary commentators in South Africa who, like Gordimer, accepted the basic tenets of György Lukács's 'critical realism' (2). It is difficult not to suspect that Gordimer's chary review of *Life & Times of Michael K*, which appeared in the *New York Review of Books* in 1984, was somewhere at the back of Coetzee's mind on this occasion, though, as some of his phrasing suggests, he was also clearly thinking about Stephen Clingman's recent critical study *The Novels of Nadine Gordimer: History from the Inside* (1986), which was no less Lukácsian. As his particular mode of address implied, he assumed that his audience shared these critical precepts.

His main objection to the prevailing view was that it accorded the novel a secondary status by subsuming it, as Clingman's subtitle suggested, under the 'discourse of history' and its 'sub-discourse' politics. 'If the novel aims to provide the reader with a vicarious first-hand experience of living in a certain historical time,' Coetzee observed, 'embodying contending forces in contending characters and filling our experience with a certain density of observation... then its relation to history is self-evidently a secondary relation' (3). As Benjamin and Ndebele had variously argued, this not only begged obvious political questions—in this case, whose version of history?—it also reduced reading to a simple act of verification, 'as a child's schoolwork is checked by a schoolmistress', Coetzee sardonically observed (3). Underlying these objections, however, was a deeper worry about the prescriptivist assumptions on which this idea of the novel rested. It was at this point that Coetzee made his most confrontational move. The Lukácsian critics who, like his implied audience, defined the 'game going on between the covers of the book' according to a narrow set of rules derived chiefly from socio-historical thinking—'the game you call Class Conflict or the game called Male Domination or any of the other games in the games handbook'—made the same kinds of mistakes, he suggested, as the censors (3–4). Why, he asked, had 'censors been so ineffectual, century after century' (3)? Because 'in laying down rules that stories may not transgress, and enforcing these rules, they fail to recognise that the offensiveness of stories lies not in their transgressing particular rules but in their faculty of making and changing their own rules' (3). On this analysis it is not just that such 'stories' possess no 'essential characteristics', to use Ndebele's phrase. By, in effect, creating their own space, they have the potential to evade all attempts to police the boundaries of the literary. In taking this strong anti-prescriptivist position Coetzee echoed some of Mphahlele's arguments of the 1960s. The difference, however, was that whereas Mphahlele had relied primarily on Trotsky's reflections on the autonomy of art, Coetzee, who had a background in linguistics, turned initially to the critique of essentialist theories of literary language that Stanley Fish had proposed in the influential 1973 essay to which I have already referred.

As Fish argued in that essay, the two theories of literary language prevalent at the time, which he called 'message-plus' and 'message-minus', failed to define literature once and for all in purely linguistic terms in part because each rested on specific, and wholly opposed, normative assumptions. This left their proponents in an awkward position of mutually assured contradiction. 'Message-minus theorists are forced to deny literary status to works whose function is in part to convey information or offer propositions about the real world. . . . Message-plus theorists, on the other hand, are committed to downgrading works in which elements of style do not either reflect or support a propositional core.'[141] The peculiar relevance this had to the perversities of the South African situation, and, indeed, to Coetzee in 1987, is not difficult to see. While the censors, who passed his works and others because they were sufficiently literary on their terms, belonged, as we have seen, to the 'message-minus' camp, the supposedly dominant Lukácsian critics, who considered Coetzee's works to be at best irrelevant and at worst inimical to the struggle against apartheid, were on the 'message-plus' side. If this meant that they both misconstrued his practice as a writer, albeit for very different ends, it also meant that they underestimated the endlessly disruptive potential of stories, which not only posed a special challenge to the censors but put the whole idea of literary guardianship in question. Though Coetzee acknowledged that stories could, like cockroaches, be mounted 'in cases, with labels' and 'colonised' for various purposes, he also insisted that 'storytelling can take care of itself' (3–4).

For Fish the impossibility of sustaining either one of the contradictory positions he outlined entailed a major reorientation of the contemporary theoretical debates about the nature of literary language along anti-scholastic lines. For Coetzee, who was, given his remit, 'speaking as a novelist', not as a theorist, Fish's formulations served to justify his own claim that 'stories' constantly unsettle established ideas of the literary by breaking their own rules (2). Adapting Fish's language, and bringing it into the age of the desktop computer, he remarked:

> There is no addition in stories. They are not made up of one thing plus another thing, message plus vehicle, substructure plus superstructure. On the keyboard on which they are written, the plus key does not work. There is always a difference; and the difference is not a part, the part left behind after the subtraction. The minus key does not work either: the difference is everything. (4)

To clarify this guiding principle he then turned from Fish to Walter Benjamin's essay 'The Storyteller', which had as much appeal for him in 1987 as it had for Ndebele three years earlier. Once again, as he had done with Fish, Coetzee simply alluded to Benjamin without explicitly citing him. Unlike Ndebele, who used Benjamin's reflections on the autonomy of stories as the basis for his own defence of a flexible and open-ended People's Culture, Coetzee represented the storyteller as the member of a pre-modern 'tribe threatened with colonisation, a tribe some of whose members have been only too happy—as is their right—to embrace modernity, to relinquish their bows and arrows and their huts in the wilds and move in under the spacious roof of the great historical myths' (3). These colonized subjects were, of course, the novelists and their critical supporters, who saw their medium as a secondary 'supplement' to the 'discourse of history'. By contrast, Coetzee, following Benjamin, defended 'storytelling' as 'another, an other mode of thinking' (4). As this last formulation suggests, Benjamin's affirmation of the lost art of storytelling served, on his analysis, primarily as a means of defending narrative as a cognitive mode in its own right, not just as a guard against complicity with the capitalist newspaper press or, indeed, the *Weekly Mail*. This 'other' kind of writing was, Coetzee argued, 'prepared to work itself out outside the terms of class conflict, race conflict, gender conflict or any other of the oppositions out of which history and the historical disciplines erect themselves' (3).

Understood in these terms, the anarchic and necessarily illimitable space of the literary, for Coetzee, was not amenable to being instrumentalized in any straightforward way, whether as a 'weapon' in the struggle, as a means for building a new People's Culture, or, indeed, as a resource for fashioning one or another idea of the nation as such. Nor could it be revered or dismissed in purely aestheticist terms, which, of course, presupposed that it was, in some sense, possible to distinguish form from content, a distinction which was, as we have seen, central to the censors' defence of the literary. Indeed, as Coetzee's emphasis on the disorienting *linguistic* and *cognitive* otherness of stories suggests, he took particular pains to pre-empt any attempt to read his arguments in familiar aestheticist terms. Parodying 'the position somewhat', he stressed that 'a story is not a message with a covering, a rhetorical or aesthetic covering' (4). To underscore his anti-aestheticist point, he then asked: 'Am I saying these things...in order to distance myself from revolutionary art and ally myself with those people who think there is nothing nicer than cuddling up in bed with a novel and having a good old read, people who, as they will say, see quite enough of reality on the streets, thank you?' 'I hope not,' he replied (4).

Yet the difficulty, which he did not anticipate, lay less with his powerful defence of storytelling as disruptive 'difference' than with his further insistence on it as a 'rival to history' (3). 'In times of intense ideological pressure like the present', he claimed, 'the novel, it seems to me, has only two options: supplementarity or rivalry' (3). This complicated his argument in two ways. Firstly, it threatened to undermine his appeal to the idea of 'difference' by forcing him into the awkward position of simply inverting the terms of the debate. Whereas his Lukácsian opponents tended, he believed, towards a hyperinflation of the historical (and political) at the expense of the literary, his presentation of the literary as a 'rival' risked simply doing the opposite. His own highly charged rhetoric, which did not sit well with his principled anti-prescriptivism, only exacerbated this danger. To characterize literary modernizers as interlopers who had willingly betrayed the customs of the storytelling 'tribe', while at the same time expressing anxiety about being translated 'back and *down* into the discourse of politics', was not to speak from a position of dispassionate neutrality.

Secondly, the slippage in his argument, which used 'autonomy' and 'rivalry' interchangeably, each serving as an antonym of 'supplementarity', had the unhappy effect of implicating him in the troubled European high-cultural tradition of *Kulturkritik*, which, as we have seen, informed van Wyk Louw's thinking about the rivalry between the writer and the politician, and under-pinned the censors' tendency to inflate the literary at the expense of the political. This feature of Coetzee's rhetoric made him vulnerable to the kinds of misreading Anna Louw gave to some of his other general reflections on his own practice as a writer. Based on some comments he made in an interview in 1978, where he had expressed reservations about the models of writing with which some black writers were working and questioned the value of any writer's 'political thinking', she mistook him, as we have seen, for an ally in the aesthe-ticist debates about 'committed literature'.[142] More importantly, however, his appeal to the culturally loaded rhetoric of 'rivalry', in which the literary, accord-ing to a disjunctive logic, figured as a genuine and better alternative to the historical or political, rather than a powerful form of public intervention in its own right, exposed the gulf between his 'fragile metalanguage' and his 'own language' as a storyteller. In his fictions, as we shall see in Chapter 8, he subjected the novel to an equally sustained, and in some ways even more disconcerting, interrogation, which reinforced the idea of the otherness of storytelling without necessarily falling into the trap of rivalry. Perhaps unsur-prisingly, as some of his subsequent reflections indicate, Coetzee later changed his mind about this generalized formulation of the distinctiveness of the literary and his own engagement with the political.

Coda: A Local Affair

On 28 October 1988 Salman Rushdie's *The Satanic Verses* became the last major literary work to be banned by the censors. As a result apartheid South Africa became the only officially Christian and the only non-Islamic country, besides India, to suppress Rushdie's iconic fourth novel. Though this outcome was by no means surprising, given the censors' equivocal attitudes to the literary, everything about the decision-making process was unusual. In the first place, the final decision was taken by a security committee, who, in the greater part of its report, repeated verbatim a protest statement against the novel issued by the Islamic Foundation, which was based in Leicester in the United Kingdom. Citing the report of the Muslim film censor (A. M. Bhorat) who acted as their initial reader, the censors claimed that 'this work, thinly disguised as a piece of literature, not only grossly distorts Islamic history in general, but also portrays in the worst possible colours the very characters of the prophet Ibrahim and the Prophet Muhammad (peace be on them)' (P88/10/144). The film censor himself was simply quoting the statement the Leicester Foundation had faxed to the African Muslim Agency in South Africa on 21 October, a month after the novel was first published, and which had then been forwarded to various Muslim bodies in the country, including the Muslim Judicial Council and the Council of Muslim Theologians. These bodies represented the organized, and more conservative, religious branch of South Africa's sizeable, diverse, and well-established minority Muslim community, which had played an active part in the country's history and public life since the late eighteenth century. The first mosque opened in Cape Town in 1804.

Claiming to speak on behalf of the community as a whole, the leaders of the two Councils wrote to the censors demanding that the book be banned, giving detailed reasons and including annotated passages from the novel which the Leicester Foundation had originally faxed as well. The only comments the censors added themselves focused on the novel's status as literature: 'In reaching its decision, the Committee has taken due consideration of the literary merit of the publication and of the author's previously acclaimed works, literary distinctions, etc.' Following the kind of thinking generally adopted by the security censors, however, they concluded that 'these considerations do not outweigh the obvious offence which his latest work is likely to give to the strongly protesting Muslim community in South Africa who clearly regard the book as offensive to their religious convictions or feelings, and likely to bring them as a section of the inhabitants of the Republic into ridicule or contempt'. In fact the novel was in the end banned only on the grounds of blasphemy.

The other unusual feature of the decision was the speed with which it was taken. The whole process from complaint to banning was completed in a mere four days, which was something of a record, since, as exasperated local booksellers and authors frequently noted, it generally took anything from a month to three months for a book to get through the censorship bureaucracy. On the basis of the archival evidence it is not possible to say if this remarkable efficiency was a direct result of political interference. Yet it is difficult not to infer from the wider circumstances that pressures of some kind were brought to bear. In an article published early in 1989, Gordimer thought that the local 'Muslim extremists', as she called them, who campaigned for the ban were aided by 'a member of the Muslim community with influence in the House of Delegates'. This, as she explained, was 'the segregated "house" of South African Indian collaborators in our apartheid tricameral parliament, which excludes Africans'.[143] In the same article she also claimed that the censors banned the novel without reading it, as she had the only copy in the country at the time— proofs sent to her by Rushdie's American publisher. In fact, they were sent a copy on 26 October, though it is very unlikely that they read it. The chief censor, Abraham Coetzee, refuted both these claims at the time, but the fact that he scribbled a note to his colleagues saying that 'certain things' on the censorship file 'must be removed' suggests that his public version of events was at best partial. There were, after all, particular reasons why certain elements within the government, or, more likely, the security police, would have been eager for the censors to respond promptly to genuine protests by notable Muslim organiza- tions at that specific moment. As the local press reported throughout that week, COSAW had invited Rushdie to speak against censorship alongside J. M. Coet- zee at a high-profile anti-apartheid literary festival in South Africa on 31 Octo- ber. By that stage, the ANC had adopted a more flexible policy towards the cultural boycott in order to support the increasingly robust democratic move- ment within the country. The event was organized jointly by COSAW and the *Weekly Mail*, which was at the time being threatened with a temporary banning order itself.

In fact, the censors' decision to ban the novel three days before Rushdie was due to speak only made a tense situation all the more volatile. The fallout from the 'Rushdie Affair' had already divided the local Muslim community, which did not speak with one voice on the issue, tested anti-apartheid solidarities, and put COSAW in an almost impossible position. At the last minute, after considerable debate, it decided to withdraw Rushdie's invitation on safety grounds. As a consequence, when Coetzee finally took the stage at the festival, he was ac- companied not by Rushdie, but by Gordimer, who, as one of COSAW's key patrons, was there to justify its decision. On this occasion, Coetzee sided with the *Weekly Mail*, which defended Rushdie's right to speak, in part, as one of its regular columnists noted, because the battle against censorship was 'rather low on the agenda of resistance movements'.[144] Coetzee was equally uncomprom- ising. As Attwell later recalled, he argued that it was 'wrong for the organisers to protect a united front at the price of acceding to the demands of fundamental- ists'. They had 'connived in censorship' and, returning the themes of his talk two years earlier, 'violated a key principle of *The Satanic Verses* itself, namely, the protean qualities of writing that could be taken as a model of freedom that the fundamentalists—in their insistence that after the one Book there were to be no more books—would do everything to suppress'.[145]

According to Roberts, who was quoting from a recording of Coetzee's speech, he also 'saw the affair as part of the broader "madness of settler apocalyptics"'. In this Coetzee explicitly grouped the 'Calvinist fundamentalism' of South African apartheid not only with 'Islamic fundamentalism in its activist formu- lation' but also with what he called 'Israeli fundamentalism'. In the wake of COSAW's disinvitation of Rushdie, Coetzee envisaged 'smiles in the mosques;

213

chuckles in the corridors of Pretoria'.[146] Speaking on COSAW's behalf, Gordimer was, as she put it, 'extremely shocked and surprised and distressed' by this unexpected 'public attack upon us'. She acknowledged that the decision was 'a defeat'. 'But', she added, 'we still think the man's life was more important than our principles.'[147] This time, however, the audience was very much on Coetzee's side. 'Unusually', Attwell notes, 'he was saying exactly what [they] wanted to hear: they were on their feet applauding.'[148]

Characteristically Coetzee emerged from what he later called this 'unforeseen and unsettling public disagreement' with no sense of self-satisfaction.[149] Indeed, after the fatwa was pronounced in February 1989 and the full implications of the 'Rushdie Affair' became more apparent, he began to question the validity of his own unyieldingly principled position. 'In retrospect', he observed, 'I think Gordimer, in her prudence, was right, I was wrong.' The incident had, he said, left him with a 'nagging question': 'why was it so hard to think of anything interesting to say about censorship? Did the discussion of censorship simply belong to politics?'[150] It was in an effort to answer these questions and to enquire into the cultural origins of his own uncompromising position that he began to write the series of essays that were eventually collected in *Giving Offense*. As he noted in the preface, the twelve essays that made up the volume, most of which originally appeared between 1988 and 1993, constituted neither a 'history' nor a 'strong theory' of censorship. Rather, they were an attempt, firstly, 'to understand a passion with which I have no intuitive sympathy, the passion that plays itself out in acts of silencing and censoring', and, secondly, 'to understand, historically and sociologically, why it is that I have no sympathy with that passion'.[151] It was, in other words, in part to lay the ghost of his disagreement with Gordimer that he set out to trace the origins of the 'megalomaniac' tendencies of his own profession by looking back to the advent of printing in fifteenth-century Europe.

One of the most important essays from this collection, 'Erasmus: Madness and Rivalry' (1992), also gave him the opportunity to reassess his earlier defence of the space of the literary. Rejecting the more dubious logic underlying the tradition of *Kulturkritik*, he reconsidered his appeal to the rhetoric of rivalry and sought instead to articulate a different 'position for the critic of the scene of political rivalry, a position not simply impartial between the rivals but also, by self-definition, off the stage of rivalry altogether, a *non*position'.[152] In a wide-ranging analysis linking Derrida's critique of Foucault's conception of madness to Erasmus's idea of folly, he now drew attention to the 'weakness' of the literary, emphasizing its fragility as a category, which, paradoxically, constituted the basis of its distinctive cultural value. With an oblique reference to Joyce, he referred to its 'jocoserious abnegation of big-phallus status, its evasive (non) position inside/outside the play' of power.[153] On this still resolutely anti-scholastic analysis, the compelling allure of the literary lay not in its strength as a rival to other modes of public discourse, notably the discourses of politics and history, but in its frailty or, more accurately, in its disarming refusal to enter the public sphere on anything but its own, always vulnerable and polymorphous terms, and its risky impulse to forgo the will to domination.

This formulation, which reaffirmed his anti-scholastic commitment to literature's linguistic and cognitive otherness without invoking the discredited tradition of *Kulturkritik*, recalled his earlier article 'Into the Dark Chamber: The Writer and the South African State', which he first published in the *New York Times* in January 1986. He spent much of this article, which focused on the more subtle ways in which censorship threatened writers' autonomy, reviewing various representations of torture in the works of other writers, including Christopher van Wyk's poem 'In Detention' (1979), Alex La Guma's *In the Fog of the Season's End* (1972), Sipho Sepamla's *A Ride on the Whirlwind* (1981), and Mongane Serote's *To Every Birth its Blood* (1982), but he acknowledged that the questions they raised about the ethics of writing applied as much to himself, given his own interest in the torture chamber in *Waiting for the Barbarians* (1980).

Writers, novelists especially, the world over were, he felt, understandably 'drawn to the torture room'.[154] It was a 'site of extreme human experience' that was, 'like the bedchamber of the pornographer's fantasy', also 'insulated from moral or physical constraint'. In South Africa 'the dark, forbidden chamber' appeared even to be 'the origin of novelistic fantasy per se'.[155] The trouble was, in the South African case, this object, no less than the mystique surrounding it, was an 'obscenity' created by the state and its censorship laws. At the very least, this meant that any attempt to represent it raised questions of taste. 'There is', Coetzee noted, 'something tawdry about *following* the state in this way, making its vile mysteries the occasion of fantasy.' For the writer, however, this only raised a 'deeper problem': how '*not* to allow himself to be impaled on the dilemma proposed by the state, namely, either to ignore its obscenities or else to produce representations of them'. For any writer, then, the 'true challenge', Coetzee insisted, was 'how not to play the game by the rules of the state, how to establish one's own authority, how to imagine torture and death on one's own terms', or, in other words, how to create distinctively literary forms of public intervention which make possible a resolutely 'other mode of thinking'.[156]

In saying this, Coetzee was, as we shall see, not just speaking to his fellow writers or reflecting on the issues in general terms. He was implicitly questioning his own response to the 'dilemma proposed by the state' in *Waiting for the Barbarians* and, indeed, in most of his early works of fiction. In the second part of this book, I develop this line of enquiry by focusing on the ways in which a number of writers negotiated the challenges of writing in a context defined overwhelmingly by apartheid and censorship, while at the same time considering the various, often singular, ways in which their works disrupted the censors' cultural assumptions and sometimes paranoid ways of reading. While this exposes the perversity and injustice of their casuistical position still further, it also raises more general questions about the ineluctable perils of literary guardianship. Each of the six essayistic chapters that follow addresses these more widely pertinent problems from a different perspective and starting point.

PART II

Singular Situations /
Disruptive Moments

4
NADINE GORDIMER AND THE STRENGTH OF THE AFRICAN NOVEL

The censors scrutinized all six of Nadine Gordimer's novels published between 1958 and 1979. While they let through *Occasion for Loving* (1963), *A Guest of Honour* (1970), and *The Conservationist* (1974), they banned the remaining three for varying lengths of time. *A World of Strangers* (1958), her second, was proscribed in paperback only from 1962 to 1973; *The Late Bourgeois World* (1966), her fourth, from 1966 to 1976; and *Burger's Daughter* (1979), her seventh, for three months in 1979. These decisions were, on the face of it, just a further testament to the perversity of their literary guardianship. After all, even if reviewers and critics naturally continued to have different opinions about her works, Gordimer's future as one of the most acclaimed literary figures of the late twentieth century was already looking assured by the early 1960s.

Having begun to establish herself in the previous decade, particularly through her regular contributions to the *New Yorker*, she appeared under some of the Anglophone literary world's most prestigious hardback literary imprints throughout the 1960s—Viking in New York and Gollancz in London—and in 1961 Penguin launched her career as a mass-market paperback author by reprinting *A World of Strangers*. The confidence these metropolitan publishers had in her standing was soon echoed by the judging panels of various national and international prizes. In 1961 *Friday's Footprint and Other Stories* (1960) won the British W. H. Smith Literary Award, her first notable prize, and by the 1970s, after she had added a number of other major awards to her name, including the Booker Prize for *The Conservationist* (co-winner in 1974) and the Grand Aigle d'Or in France (1975), her international reputation was secure. By that time, too, even the white liberal–literary establishment in South Africa, whose attitudes to Gordimer were notoriously prickly, recognized that it could no longer withhold its imprimatur. In 1974 she won the CNA Award for the first time, also for *The Conservationist*. Five years later she repeated the achievement with *Burger's Daughter*, adding a second title, alongside Etienne Leroux's *Magersfontein*,

O' Magersfontein! (1976), to the eccentric sub-canon of prizewinning banned books in South Africa. In Gordimer's case, then, there was no uncertainty about the status of her novels as Literature, in a general honorific sense, although, as we shall see, the censors were not above attempting to defend some of their decisions by calling this in doubt.

That the censors' judgements were perverse is predictable enough. What is puzzling is their selectivity. Why did they consider only some of her novels threatening enough to warrant banning? This question has a special pertinence in Gordimer's case because, despite her constant narrative experimentation and relentless self-questioning, her œuvre displays a remarkable consistency on a number of levels. With the exception of *A Guest of Honour*, which is set in an unspecified post-colonial African country, all the novels from the first three decades of her career have a more or less contemporary South African setting; and all focus on the struggle various white protagonists, from the English expatriate Toby Hood in *A World of Strangers* to the South African Rosa Burger in *Burger's Daughter*, have coming to terms with themselves, their histories, and their responsibilities within the shifting politics of the resistance from the 1950s to the 1970s. All in their different ways also reflect Gordimer's preoccupation with the interpenetration of the public world of apartheid politics and the apparently private spheres of the family, friendships, sexuality, and, indeed, individual thought and feeling. Commenting on her primary interests as a novelist and on the way 'whites among themselves are shaped by their peculiar position', she noted as early as 1965: 'I write about their private selves; often, even in the most private situations, they are what they are because their lives are regulated and their mores formed by the political situation. You see, in South Africa, society is the political situation. To paraphrase one might say (too often), politics is character in SA.'[1] Seen in this way she was an interventionist, perhaps even a 'committed' or 'protest', novelist from the outset.

Yet, as some of her other comments indicate, she was herself always wary of these labels, particularly the last. In a letter to Anthony Sampson, also dating from 1965, in which she was responding to a British reviewer who had used 'the measure of "protest" as a yardstick of literary criticism' to 'beat me over the head', she remarked: 'What do "liberal" Englishmen want of us—yes, of course, manuscripts written in blood and smuggled posthumously out of prison. I'm irritated (what, again?) but not wounded, since the last thing I want is to be labelled a "protest" writer.'[2] These anxieties about her literary standing remained with her. In an interview in 1977, she acknowledged that 'my novels are anti-apartheid', but insisted that this was 'not because of my personal abhorrence of apartheid'. If anything it simply reflected her specifically moral integrity as a witness: 'If you write honestly about life in South Africa, apartheid damns itself.'[3] As I argued in Chapter 3, these concerns also dominated her more general reflections on the ethics of writing and her own struggle to find a viable vocabulary in which to describe, and uphold, the distinctiveness of the literary.

Just what it meant for her novels themselves to be 'literary', in a more specific rather than generally honorific sense, was nonetheless far from self-evident. It was also inevitably a source of some contention. If some British reviewers in the 1960s felt she did not protest enough, the editors of the *New Yorker* had, as we have seen, begun to reject her work by then because it was, according to their criteria, becoming too political. This question also concerned her publishers, who had their own, partly commercial reasons for wanting to insist on the literary status of her novels. In their view, or at least in the view of the publicity departments who produced the blurbs for her books, the crucial distinguishing feature of her writing, which, for one thing, set it apart from mere political reportage, was its universality. Jonathan Cape's description of *Burger's Daughter*, arguably Gordimer's most overtly political novel, is typical of the genre. Having described it as 'an exploration of the self locked in the conflicts of our time', the blurb concluded that it was a 'masterpiece of controlled narrative, surpassing all her previous work, a culmination of her art, transmuting personal and collective experience to a scale that is universal'.[4] Though this did not, according to the standard formulation of the universality principle, which had, of course, been a cornerstone of Western aesthetics at least since Aristotle's *Poetics*, imply that the novel necessarily had significance for all times, it did ensure that its potential appeal was not constrained by its South African setting and concerns. For publishers keen to promote their products across a vast transnational market this particular Western shibboleth had obvious publicity value. Yet it was not only the blurb writers who found it indispensable. As Stephen Clingman, one of Gordimer's most astute early critics, remarked in 1986: 'It is a stock response of critics and reviewers—both inside and outside South Africa—to insist that Gordimer's work is "universal", that it could have been written "anywhere".'[5]

Clingman had his own reasons for rejecting this rhetoric, which had by then become something of a burden for Gordimer as well. By the early 1980s, as we have seen, she had absorbed the lessons of Roland Barthes, György Lukács, and, indeed, of the leading proponents of Black Consciousness, and begun to ask questions of her own about universalist ideas of culture. For Clingman the principal problem was that any appeal to the universality of her work betrayed one of its primary features. 'In the guise of appreciation this is', he commented, 'to deny what Gordimer herself discovers: the radical historicality of South African existence.'[6] Timely as it was, this critique inevitably reopened the question of the specifically literary status of Gordimer's novels. If they were not generally relevant to 'our times', or if they did not disclose the supposedly universal patterns underlying 'personal and collective experience', then what distinguished them from historical writings about contemporary South Africa, or, worse still, well-written fictionalized testimony?

For Gordimer, the answer was at one level relatively straightforward. As she put it in *The Black Interpreters* (1973), 'if you want to read the facts of the retreat from Moscow in 1815 [*sic*], you may read a history book; if you want to know what war is like and how people of a certain time and background dealt with it as their personal situation, you must read *War and Peace*'.[7] According to this account, which drew on a well-worn nineteenth-century defence of realist fiction, novels belong to literature because they give their readers access to 'history from the inside'. Yet, as Clingman noted, and, indeed, as the ambiguity of his subtitle implied, this argument needed to be qualified in one important respect. What Gordimer 'has not considered is that Tolstoy was himself an historical subject', whose view of history was inevitably 'influenced by the needs and assumptions of his time, not to mention any ideological framework or preoccupations that may have modified his vision'.[8] Far from being written anywhere, in other words, novels were written from a determinate situation 'inside' history. In Gordimer's case this was, according to Clingman, defined not simply by her being 'caught up in the midst of the processes she is attempting to depict', nor indeed, on standard Marxist assumptions, simply by her membership of the white middle class, but by her active and always conflicted engagement with the 'whole history of her society', on the one hand, and her own 'marginality' as a white writer, on the other.[9]

Yet since this kind of argument applied to any white writers, not just those working with the medium of the novel, clarifying Gordimer's own historical position in this way still left the question of her novels' specific literariness open. It was at this point that Clingman, following Gordimer, turned to Lukács. For Gordimer, as we have seen, Lukács's appeal lay in the fact that he, or, more accurately, her understanding of his conception of 'critical realism', enabled her to create space for herself as an African writer in the early 1970s and to clarify her commitment to a 'message-plus' conception of literary language. What Clingman took from Lukács was his theory of typicality, which provided a model for thinking about the tension between individuality and representativeness that governed Gordimer's approach to the question of character in fiction, and, as a consequence, a way of understanding the literary operations of her novels. The idea of character as 'type', in Lukács's sense, was, Clingman explained, 'not to be confused with stereotypes, nor with the average, nor the eccentric, but rather should be seen as highly individualised characters who engage in their fullest potential with the social and historical circumstances of their situation'.[10] As we have seen, Gordimer herself insisted, particularly in response to the criticisms levelled at her by the editors of the *New Yorker*, that she never lost sight of the intricate individuality of her characters, though, as Clingman pointed out, she also allowed that 'typicality may be a product of characterization'.[11] This was perhaps most evident in her critical response to Coetzee's early fictions in the *New York Review of Books* in 1984. Having questioned Coetzee's apparent choice of the dubiously universalizing mode of allegory in his first three novels, where, as she put it, 'Man becomes Everyman (that bore)', she praised him for making *Life & Times of Michael K* (1983) a more particularized novel of witness. The trouble was that, by supposedly presenting the hapless, drifting Michael as a representative of the victims of apartheid, he denied, or overlooked, the 'energy of the will to resist evil', an energy that 'exists with indefatigable and undefeatable persistence among the black people of South Africa—Michael K's people'. 'This is a challengingly questionable position for a writer to take up in South Africa, make no mistake about it,' she added.[12]

Clingman, who made no reference to this now canonical review, did not share Gordimer's concerns about the apparent universality of Coetzee's early fictions, nor was he convinced that their practice as interventionist writers was at odds. Indeed, in his view, Magda, the central figure in Coetzee's *In the Heart of the Country* (1977), functioned in much the same way as Mehring in *The Conservationist*. Both characters, as Lukácsian types, represented not a '*universal* crisis of subjectivity' but a crisis for a '*specific segment* of reality', which signified the 'terminal *malaise* of a whole history and culture, and an essential alienation from the land and its people'.[13] Judging Gordimer against Coetzee, or vice versa, was not especially important for Clingman at that point, however. His primary concern was to demonstrate how Lukács's theory of typicality could be used to define and defend the distinctiveness of Gordimer's novelistic practice on its own terms. Her 'types' were 'figures who, in general drawn from Gordimer's observation of life at large, both condense broader social and historical patterns and, in their individuality, engage with them in intense and extreme form'.[14] The anti-universalist thrust of this argument was clear, but it is worth noting that Clingman, like Lukács, narrowed, rather than displaced, the central premiss on which the more orthodox conception of the literary was based. Gordimer's novels, on this analysis, were 'literary' not because they depicted individuals in whom the apparently universal struggles of humanity became manifest, but because they provided an especially powerful way of registering the historicity of their characters' predicament and sense of self.

This feature of Gordimer's practice was evident throughout her œuvre, even in *The Conservationist*, ostensibly her least 'realist' novel. In the figure of Mehring, who, Clingman argued, 'represents primarily a capitalist sector in South Africa that has always been less obviously "ideological" than the state', the 'strength of fiction is revealed, in its capacity to draw together themes of the widest social and historical importance'.[15] Mehring as type, in other words, did not simply reconcile representativeness with individuality, the historical pattern with the details of a particular life. He showed how Gordimer's novels, by using the device of metonymic condensation, provided a special insight into the changing history of white domination. In Mehring, Gordimer had 'condensed the ultimate resources', resources that include 'energy and intelligence', 'realism', and 'ruthlessness', on which the 'ruling class' would draw to 'continue its dominance' as it entered a new 'era of historical contest' in the early 1970s, but which, as Mehring's ultimate fate revealed, the novel predicted would be 'prophetically overthrown'.[16] I shall return, in the chapter on Coetzee, to consider the implications of Clingman's further claim that his point about Mehring's historical representativeness 'is a difficult one to back up empirically', and, more generally, to the questions his critical assumptions raised for Coetzee about the relationship between novels and history.[17] What concerns me most at this point is the bearing this persuasive conception of Gordimer's novelistic practice has on the censor's strangely selective response to her work. If all her novels, even *The Conservationist*, engaged with the historical circumstances of apartheid South Africa in especially powerful and critical ways, then why were they not all deemed equally threatening to the established order?

A World of Strangers and *An Occasion for Loving*

There is no simple, or single, answer to this question, in part because the changes in the censorship bureaucracy from the 1950s to the 1970s meant that the obstacles Gordimer and her publishers faced were never quite the same in each of the first decades of her career. In 1958, for instance, the hardback edition of *A World of Strangers* escaped banning simply for procedural reasons. The Board of Censors, which at that time handled imported publications only, was divided. The liberal-minded English-speaking reader (A. Gordon Bagnall) felt there was nothing 'objectionable' about the novel (BCS 20416). Even though its 'general effect is a picture of an irrationality in racial isolations in Johannesburg', it 'deliberately avoids "protest or propaganda"', he wrote, and 'the reader is never asked to take sides'. An Afrikaner Board member (A. Pienaar), who also read the novel carefully, was less confident. The 'shared lives and intimacy of native and white man [Steven Sitole and Toby Hood] was', in his view, 'alien to our national character (*volksaard*)'; moreover, even if the novel did not 'incite', it amounted to 'a subtle form of anti-government or anti-apartheid propaganda'. Despite this, he was also, on balance, against banning primarily because the novel was not written 'strongly enough to influence people'. Imposing a ban would, he thought, also give it 'unnecessary publicity'. In the end, the chief censor (W. Coetzer), who was at that point required only to make a recommendation to the Minister of the Interior, felt that Pienaar's doubts were too persuasive. He also had concerns of his own about the 'mention of a marriage between a white girl (Anna) and an Indian (Hassein Bhayut [*sic*])'. He referred particularly to a scene in which Anna Louw, the novel's strongest woman character and only communist activist, describes to Toby, the dilettantish, Oxford-educated Englishman whose moral awakening is the focus of the plot, how her marriage to Bhayat is destroyed by apartheid.[18] Taking all this into consideration, and the fact that the 'extremely liberal thoughts of the writer had a strong communistic tendency', Coetzer proposed that the novel should be banned, though the fact that he appended Bagnall's report and warned the Minister that a ban was likely to 'unleash a whole hullabaloo in the press', suggests that even he was not wholly convinced. The Minister, who was unimpressed with this equivocal advice, promptly referred the case back, and there the matter ended, at least until customs submitted the paperback edition four years later.

On this occasion, the English-speaking reader (Mrs M. P. B. Cresswell) was categorically in favour of a ban, primarily because, following her own exclusively racialized typology, the book 'gives a false impression of the African in South Africa—also of the average white people & their way of life' (BCS 26846). Her rudimentary assumptions about the nature of fictional representation, not to mention her indifference to the novel's concern with the complexity of its central characters' *social* identities, speak for themselves. In her view, the 'general policy & theme' of the novel was set out clearly when Toby describes the circumstances behind his family's decision to send him to South Africa as an agent for his great-uncle's publishing firm. In this passage Toby, whose youthful attitudes are rebelliously reactionary, gives a jaundiced account of his family's involvement in international protest politics—his great-uncle Faunce was modelled on Victor Gollancz—and rejects their anti-traditionalist ideal of freedom, which he considers an 'empty international plain where a wind turns over torn newspapers printed in languages you don't understand'. 'Since India had been off their conscience', he notes, 'my family and their set had had an overwhelming supply of victims and their champions from Africa.'[19] Their plan is for him to take up their latest anti-colonial cause, but Toby, who is at this point a Forsterian believer in the primacy of personal relations, has no intention of becoming 'a *voyeur* of the world's ills and social perversions'. 'I want to take care of my own relationships with men and women who come into my life,' he says, 'and let the abstractions of race and politics go hang.'[20] The novel, which, as many critics have noted, can be read as a subtle rewriting of Forster's *A Passage to India*, does not allow him the luxury of this liberal fantasy for long.[21]

This time the Board was in unanimous agreement with the initial reader. In his summary recommendation, the chief censor commented: 'The story of an English journalist who, fresh out of London, fraternizes with the Bantu in Johannesburg and becomes involved in the struggle against the whites. Its predictions are false and biased, while racial mixing, immorality and incidents occur which are designed to cause hatred [literally "angry blood"] among the races.' The principal predication to which he referred was, no doubt, Toby's promise at the end of the novel to be godfather to Sam Mofokenzazi's unborn baby, who becomes an emblem of the longed-for integrated future beyond apartheid. Among the 'incidents' of 'offensive intermingling' the chief censor singled out was a heavily ironized crossover party in a wealthy white suburb, during which the fashionable hostess, who is very pleased with the way the evening is going, breaks off to see 'if our black brothers in the kitchen can't rustle up some tinned soup for us'.[22] He also referred to a heated discussion, which takes place in Toby's flat, about an unhappy example of black–white collaboration in the arts. In this scene, Toby and Steven have just been to see a jazz opera, a prototype of *King Kong* (1959), the most famous example of the genre, which was meant to celebrate 1950s multiracialism. Yet, as Toby comments, it is 'more of a white man's idea of what a black man could write, and a black man's idea of what a white man would expect him to write, than the fusion of a black man's and a white man's worlds of imagination'.[23]

There was some initial confusion about whether or not the censors' new decision, which was announced in January 1962, covered all editions. This was cleared up only after Helen Suzman, for a long time the sole MP representing the more liberal Progressive Party, asked for official clarification. Suzman regularly raised questions about the fate of Gordimer's novels in Parliament. In response, the Minister noted that the Board had intended to ban the less expensive Penguin paperback only. That the censors made no reference to the novel's literariness, or indeed to its subtleties of tone and perspective, at this point is unsurprising. The customs legislation they were required to follow did not differentiate among kinds of imported printed matter and, moreover, the Board did not yet see itself as a guardian of the literary. In the 1950s and early 1960s, the guardians, who, in this case, included individual writers like André Brink and Mary Renault, the local branches of PEN, and the liberal press, all of whom protested vigorously against the ban, were still outside the censorship bureaucracy.

Nonetheless, in April 1963, six months before the new censorship system was introduced, the old Board passed Gordimer's third novel, *Occasion for Loving*, mainly for pragmatic reasons but also on literary grounds. The initial reader (W. A. Joubert) felt the novel should be banned, principally because it dealt more directly and centrally with miscegenation, but the Board was concerned about the bad publicity *A World of Strangers* had brought and about playing into the hands of the 'liberals' (BCS 29087). It also now acknowledged that Gordimer was a 'well-known writer' and argued that the sexual encounters between the white Englishwoman, Ann Davis, and the black artist, Gideon Shibalo, whose love affair drives the plot, were understated. There were 'no real descriptions— more innuendo'. Moreover, following the lukewarm reviews the novel had received in the liberal press, which the censors read, the chief censor decided its impact would be minimal because it was not an especially 'gripping book'. Significantly he made no mention of the fact that the central love affair is, as Clingman rightly observed, 'completely normalised': 'It works within no framework of sin or abnormality, as it does in Millin [*God's Stepchildren* (1924)] or even Paton [*Too Late the Phalarope* (1953)], nor in terms of any "speciality", as it does in Plomer [*Turbott Wolfe* (1925)]. Rather, the novel makes a distinct attempt to see the love affair simply for what it is.'[24]

In this context it is worth noting that the censors recommended banning the Panther paperback edition of Paton's *Too Late the Phalarope* in 1958, only on grounds of its cover and blurb. They took exception to the eroticized image of a strong, seemingly unrepentant black woman on the front cover and to the publisher's description of the novel, which is unquestionably critical of the 'Immorality Act', as 'the tragedy of a man and a woman who defied the barriers of racial prejudice' (BCS 20561). This, according to the initial reader (again W. A. Joubert), was not an accurate reflection of the novel's contents, which, on his eccentric reading, emphasized the 'tragedy which results from violation of the Immorality Act' and served as a useful 'warning of the terrible legal and social consequences' of transgression. This time, however, the Minister decided to let the paperback through, despite its supposedly provocative packaging.

The Late Bourgeois World and The Conservationist

By the time *The Late Bourgeois World* reached the censors in March 1966, the new system was in place and so the censorship Board now approached its task with a sense of mission that should, at least in theory, have made things easier for a writer of Gordimer's stature. Yet, as Gordimer and Gollancz anticipated, her fourth novel, which dealt with the strategic move to an armed struggle within the resistance in the early 1960s, was more likely than any of her earlier works to run into trouble. In the hope of getting it past customs, they published it without a blurb, after deciding it was not really possible to produce a suitably anodyne version. As it happened, this extra safeguard proved unnecessary. After the more cautious local booksellers, notably the CNA, refused to order the book before it had been passed, Gollancz's local representative, with the London firm's reluctant backing, submitted a proof copy to the censors in effect requesting pre-publication approval. Once again, the censors were divided, albeit now along different lines. Merwe Scholtz, the first reader, who was hesitantly against banning, set out the dilemma. On the one hand, the 'book is outspokenly directed against the system of apartheid and its supporters' and it included some equally 'frank' sex scenes, some of which hinted at the 'possibility' of miscegenation. On the other hand, it was 'well written' and, moreover, the 'opinions that are "stated" here can be found in the newspapers every day'. This last point reflected the censors' aestheticist concerns about the extent to which literary works could be said to make claims about the world or contain information. In his summary of their final decision, Dekker was no less equivocal: 'With this novel the Board faces a problem.' Though the 'tendencies of this work give rise to serious misgivings', he noted, 'one can take no pleasure in silencing' an 'artist' like Gordimer who 'is a well-known, meritorious writer' (BCS 272/66).

Harvey, who adopted a broadly liberal position, and Murray, who argued the security case most implacably, represented the extremes on either side of the debate. 'Dislike of apartheid is in itself no reason for banning,' Harvey remarked; moreover, 'there is no incitement to lawlessness or sabotage'. Indeed, given that the novel focuses on the activities of the African Resistance Movement (ARM), a diverse, largely white, group, which was, as Clingman remarked, 'politically committed but badly organised and directed', he felt the 'hopelessness & futility of the underground movements is made very clear'.[25] And though the 'sex passage' in which Elizabeth van den Sandt, the first-person narrator, recalls the pleasure of feeling her lover's 'majestic erection' inside her, was 'forthright', it was, in his view, 'isolated' and not 'obscene or pornographic', an opinion the only woman censor (Rita Theron) shared.[26] Murray disagreed. This passage, as well as other references to 'sexual matters', was problematic. More-over, the 'oblique references to the underground movements' and, more tellingly, the 'presentation of race-relations', particularly in the testily flirtatious exchanges between Elizabeth and Luke Fokase, a Pan Africanist Congress (PAC) activist, made it impossible for him to see how 'the book can be let through'. For Grové, the principal difficulty was not simply that it was a 'serious, well-written book' but that it was a first-person narrative. The 'story is told by a speaker who is anxious and bitter', and so the 'viewpoint we have here is actually that of a specific woman'. This made him uncertain about how to vote and, more particularly, how to judge the 'mixing of white and black'. Nonetheless, the fact that the novel made such 'intrigues' look like the 'most natural thing in the world' meant it was 'not without a seditious effect', and so, for all his doubts, he, too, felt it should be banned.

In the end it fell to Dekker to summarize the majority opinion (five votes against three) in favour of a ban. As far as the politics of the novel were concerned, the title and the epigraph from Maxim Gorky ('The madness of the brave is the wisdom of life') were, he claimed, critical. By determining the novel's 'keynote', which 'is opposition to the established order in South Africa', these framing devices complicated its first-person narrative mode. The phrase 'bourgeois world' in the title referred to 'a middle-class order founded on a glorification of the white skin, white "respectability" and scandalous white capitalist domination' and the word 'late' meant 'doomed to destruction'. On this reading, he argued, the title lent authorial weight to Elizabeth's 'hatred' of her former mother-in-law, Mrs van den Sandt, whom, Dekker noted, she describes as one of the 'bathed and perfumed and depilated white ladies, in whose wombs the sanctity of the white race is entombed!'[27] Similarly, the epigraph from Gorky complicated the reader's response to the 'opponents' of this decaying bourgeois order, even though none of them was ever 'idealised'.

Max, Elizabeth's ex-husband, for instance, is 'everything but a hero'. The disaffected son of a 'patrician Afrikaans family', as Dekker called it, missing out
the nuances of Max's Anglo-Afrikaner parentage, who joins a 'Communist cell'
as a student and goes on to become a saboteur with ARM, ends up betraying
his colleagues and then committing suicide. 'He is a weak figure', Dekker
added, 'who has inherited much of the bourgeois mentality he so detests.'
Moreover, Luke, the 'non-white agitator', is 'vain and unreliable with money'.
The trouble was the epigraph again, which lent authority to Elizabeth's sympathetic description of Max as a 'poor madman' and, more tellingly, to her own
gradual acceptance of the legitimacy of his actions, which, Dekker felt, the
following passage revealed.

> The liberal-minded whites whose protests, petitions and outspokenness have
> achieved nothing remarked the inefficiency of the terrorists and the wasteful
> senselessness of their attempts. You cannot hope to unseat the great alabaster
> backside with a tin-pot bomb. Why risk your life? *The madness of the brave is
> the wisdom of life.* I didn't understand, till then. Madness, God, yes, it was; but
> why should the brave ones among us be forced to be mad?[28]

Like the 'nonchalant acceptance of political and social hobnobbing and solidarity' between 'white and non-white', the 'casual acceptance of subversive
activities and sabotage as normal can', Dekker commented, 'have a dangerously
seditious effect'.

The censors' other major concern was that the 'intimate intercourse crosses
the border of sociability and politics—there are frequent subtle suggestions
(sometimes much more than mere suggestion) of race-mixing in sexual
terms, again treated as wholly normal'. Indeed, Elizabeth, or, as Dekker called
her, 'the white woman', is sometimes 'amused' by the 'subtle sexual element in
her relations with the Bantu Luke', which she describes 'with a certain longing'.
Like Merwe Scholtz, who regarded this particular passage as 'dynamite', Dekker
drew attention to a scene in which the erotic undercurrent in Elizabeth and
Luke's relationship comes to the surface as she is trying establish how far he can
be trusted. 'He's an expert at conveying what one might call sexual regret,' she
observes, 'the compliment of suggesting that he would like to make love to you,
if time and place and the demands of two lives were different.'[29] This is, she
speculates, probably a technique 'he's found goes down very well with the sort
of white women who get to know black men like him; they feel titillated and yet
safe, at the same time'.[30] Yet, throughout this exchange, Elizabeth, who is an
astute observer of others and always more clear-headed than her dreamy ex-
husband, displays a certain self-possessed expertise of her own, withholding
secrets, like the fact that she 'had a black lover, years ago' and keeping her own
desires in check in order to test Luke's probity.[31] It is after this sexually charged
conversation that she decides to become, like Max, more directly involved in the

resistance, principally by using her grandmother's bank account, an icon of her own bourgeois status, as a conduit for channelling overseas funds to the PAC. As the final scenes of the novel reveal, her motives are, at this point, over-determined. If her erotic attraction to Luke plays a part, her decision is also dominated by her reassessment of Max's seemingly failed life, which his suicide had prompted, and by her own new, uncertain and apprehensive sense of political resolve. For the censors, however, these complexities were not import-ant. The depiction of interracial desire alone, taken together with Elizabeth's final reflections, in which she 'expects that Luke will want to have sexual intercourse with her' ('perhaps I want it', she remarks), meant that 'the bound-ary of permissibility had definitely been crossed'.[32] The fact that the novel regarded 'extra-marital sexual relations and promiscuity' as 'perfectly nat-ural'—again Elizabeth's thoughts about erections constituted the most 'openly debauched example'—and that it cast doubt on the 'integrity of the law' were among the censors' other 'serious misgivings', according to Dekker. For these reasons, he concluded, 'the Board decided with regret that it was necessary to forbid the circulation of *The Late Bourgeois World*'.

What is, in the circumstances, most surprising about this outcome is not so much the uncertainty of the final consensus—only two censors voted for banning with any conviction—but the elaborately aestheticist rationaliza-tion the censors gave for their final decision. As most acknowledged, the novel's propositional 'content' was complicated, if not wholly nullified, by its past-tense first-person narrative mode. The novel, as Rita Theron put it, is a multi-layered, temporally complex account of 'one day in the inner-life of a woman'. For at least three of the censors this was in itself a significant mitigating factor. Indeed, when the novel was unbanned, after Gordimer submitted it for review in 1976, this was one of the primary reasons given for the decision. As Merwe Scholtz put it in his later report, any subversive effect the book might have was neutralized—it has 'no punch', he said—because the 'action (the pathetic, melancholy portion of the story which warrants the name action) is so tightly spun into the meditative, sometimes philosophical processes of memory' (P76/2/103). Yet this is what Dekker spent the greater part of his final report attempt-ing to disprove, first by establishing the connections between the framing devices and Elizabeth's narrative and then by insisting that the first-person mode itself had a naturalizing effect. As he remarked, the novel is written in a 'wholly natural and fluent' style, which produces 'a certain enchantment'. What made it finally 'undesirable', in other words, was not so much the fact that it depicted subversive activities or interracial desire, but that it presented them through the eyes of a white woman—Dekker stressed her race and gender throughout—who considered such things as 'wholly normal'. By implication, then, South African readers, and, indeed, the regime, had to be protected from what amounted to a dangerously seditious mode of narration.

Precisely the opposite happened in the case of *The Conservationist*, which the Kruger Board scrutinized in mid-November 1974, two weeks before it was announced that it had been declared co-winner of the Booker Prize and some months before it won the CNA Award. (Though no report on *A Guest of Honour* appears to have survived, it is likely that its setting outside South Africa counted in its favour.) The censors all recognized that *The Conservationist* did not offer a 'reassuring vision for the white man', as Merwe Scholtz put it (1735/74).[33] Nienaber, another Afrikaans literary professor, summed up the general concerns:

> The police are definitely represented as being stupid and unsympathetic. There is clearly no great love to spare for the Afrikaner, the 'Boers' and 'Dutchman' does not sound exactly flattering, and in general the attitude to English-speakers is not positive, especially those from the business world. De Beer [Mehring's bigoted neighbour] is something of a caricatured representative of the Afrikaans farmer and his culture. A cursory reference to the NGK [the main Afrikaans Church] is especially cutting here and there. Her sympathies clearly lie with the blacks.

Moreover, as Grové noted, the novel includes a number of 'sexual scenes', the 'most severe' of which is when Mehring 'fingers a young girl on the aeroplane'.[34] Nonetheless, all the censors, including Murray, who recognized that the problems associated with the 'established' racial order formed a 'background to the whole', agreed that the novel should not be banned. This was in part, as Grové commented, because the 'sexual scenes' were not as 'crude and blatant' as in Brink's *Looking on Darkness*, which they had suppressed earlier in the year, nor did they 'revel in black–white sex' as in *Bourgeois World*. The main point, however, was that *The Conservationist* was not as 'clearly and explicitly written' as the earlier novel. 'Many things remain vaguely suggestive and the transitions are not easy to follow,' Grové remarked. Indeed, given the novel's present-tense free indirect narrative mode, 'the line between fact and fiction, reality and imagination in the central figure is not always easy to draw'. Presumably, on this logic, fantasized sex was somehow less obscene than the fictionalized reality.

For Merwe Scholtz, who agreed that the novel's 'subtle, suggestive texture' saved it, the indeterminacies bred of the narrative mode were decisive because they put the burden of responsibility for any interpretation on the reader. 'One knows farmers like the De Beers, businessmen like Mehring, and Bantus like Mehring's farm workers,' he commented, admiring the novel's realism. Yet 'the book would not let itself be read "just like that"'. It demanded considerable 'labour and diffidence' on the reader's part to 'unravel the symbolism fully', and to 'pass judgement' on it you would have to 'risk an interpretation'. In his view, this was most clearly exemplified by the black body that emerges at various intervals throughout the novel. 'What is one to make', he asked, 'of the murdered Bantu who is stumbled upon on Mehring's farm, who is buried on the spot by the police, again unearthed by the floodwaters and again reburied by the farm-bantu?' The significance of this final act was, in his view, particularly uncertain because the workers 'do not know anything about him', and yet he noted that the 'final paragraph' of the novel claims:

> The one whom the farm received had no name. He had no family but their women wept a little for him. There was no child of his present but their children were there to live after him. They had put him away to rest, at last; he had come back. He took possession of this earth, theirs; one of them.[35]

'Must we infer from this,' he asked, 'as an English reviewer says, that Mehring has bought "what's not for sale",' a claim for which the 'blurb offers some support': 'Only the presence of a dead man, abandoned near the river, asserts that Africa, in the end, is something a white man can't buy.' This is 'certainly possible, and even highly likely', and, as such, it makes 'uncomfortable' reading for the 'white man'. Yet this 'possibility is put in such a way that he need not take offence at it'. It is a 'three-dimensional' work, he claimed, which 'sees history from many points of view and which has a basic feeling of justice which does not turn into fanaticism'. As such it was a book which, 'in terms of our law', must be 'left undisturbed with the good readers it deserves', who will 'probably hesitate over or differ about the symbolism they eventually get out of the story'. Turning the aestheticist arguments used in the *Bourgeois World* decision upside down, it was, in effect, the novel's narrative mode, polyvalent character typologies, and openness to interpretation that saved it.

Burger's Daughter

The fate of *Burger's Daughter*, Gordimer's most sustained literary response to the rise of Black Consciousness, was different again, primarily because it was the only one of her novels scrutinized under the new bureaucratic arrangements introduced in 1975. This had a significant impact on the way it was handled, as did the fact that it entered the system, via customs, in June 1979, that is, after the protracted crisis precipitated by the banning of *Magersfontein, O Magersfontein!*, during which a number of literary censors resigned. Following the new procedures, the chief censor initially sent the novel out to a single reader, M. M. Wiggett, a retired school inspector who had been serving as a censor for five years. Wiggett was no literary expert, though, among the cultural credentials he listed on his application form, he mentioned that he had long been involved in prescribing English literary works for white schools and that he had an interest in amateur dramatics, especially light opera and musical comedy. Unsurprisingly, his report was as crude as it was antipathetic. In

Burger's Daughter, the style of which was 'dull and jejune', he claimed 'the authoress uses Rosa's story as a pad from which to launch a blistering and full-scale attack on the Republic of South Africa' (P79/6/73). Ignoring the novel's complex, self-conscious play on narrative perspective, he argued that Gordimer 'often adopts the literary technique of presenting what are in truth expressions of personal opinion as statements of fact'. What he appeared to mean by this was that she 'uses what is said during (imaginary) court trials and in political group-discussions' to promulgate her own political views. Like all the censors, he did not recognize that some of the dialogue in the 'court trials' was based on actual testimony Bram Fischer gave during his own trial for sedition in the 1960s. Fischer, the celebrated defence lawyer and leading Afrikaner intellectual in the South African Communist Party, who died in 1975, was the model for Rosa's father, Lionel Burger. Wiggett also claimed Gordimer used 'known facts in a one-sided manner to propagate communist opinions'. In short, he recommended that *Burger's Daughter* be banned under all five clauses because it was a 'political novel' centrally preoccupied with 'black consciousness and organizing for the coming black revolution'. It was 'the type of work the London-based anti-Apartheid Committee will welcome and one it might gladly have "commissioned"'.

Under the new system, his report was then passed on to a committee for final adjudication, which, in this case, was made up entirely of security censors. With a few minor clarifications and some more detailed commentary on the novel's politics, it unanimously endorsed Wiggett's recommendation, though Murray added a further minority report arguing that the novel should be banned for possession as well. Among other things, he felt this additional measure was necessary because it 'furthered communism outspokenly', it had no 'saving' literary qualities, and it 'presented a dangerous image of the South African situation for a wide circle' of readers. At this point, however, the chief censor decided to intervene, as he had done a few months earlier in the case of Brink's *Rumours of Rain*, and to make use of the provisions, created after the *Magersfontein* episode, for the decision to be reviewed by the Appeal Board's new committee of literary experts, even though he continued to question the literary merits of the novel himself. In response to various protest letters from, among others, American PEN and the Association of American Publishers, he repeatedly invoked Auberon Waugh's unrepresentatively scathing, not to say obtuse, review in the London *Evening Standard*. 'You will no doubt by this time have discovered that the reviews of the book were by no means uniformly favourable,' he commented in his correspondence, before quoting Waugh's claim that Gordimer was 'lazy, self-indulgent and frequently incomprehensible'. The committee of experts, which was chaired by P. J. H. Titlestad, the one professor of English who also happened to be one of the judges for the CNA Award that year, did not share Waugh's or the censors' low opinion of the novel.

They condemned the report, accusing the censorship committee of 'bias, prejudice and literary incompetence' as well as defamation. They wondered if 'the assertions about Nadine Gordimer's communistic beliefs and psychological state could be made in public, even if true'. *Burger's Daughter* was, they insisted, a 'responsible novel', indeed 'literature of superior quality', which deserved to be passed unconditionally.

By attacking the censorship committee's 'literary incompetence' they were not accusing it of lacking 'any rarefied capacity for the abstruser mysteries of aesthetic appreciation'. They were simply referring to an 'ability which might reasonably be expected of an intelligent and educated layman'. As a consequence, their own report amounted to an elementary lesson in how to read a novel, and, more particularly, how to distinguish the many views staged in *Burger's Daughter* from the implied attitudes of the book as a whole or its author. Indeed, it was, at a number of points, not dissimilar to Gordimer's own defence of the novel, which she published, alongside their report, in the pamphlet *What Happened to 'Burger's Daughter'?* (1980). Yet, as their report revealed, their own more responsible and critically astute reading was not entirely free of prejudice itself even at the rudimentary level of character analysis. Whereas the censors claimed, for instance, that the terms in which Duma Dhladhla, the novel's key representative of Black Consciousness, rejected the older generation's appeal to the martyrdom of the ANC heroes of the 1950s made 'the book' blasphemous—'always the same story', Dhladhla says testily, 'same as Christians telling you Christ died for them'—the experts maintained that this was just the view of 'a very nasty young radical'.[36] In her own defence, Gordimer herself described Dhladhla as 'aggressive and arrogant', noting that his statements are intentionally full of 'black clichés' and 'often contested by other blacks'.[37] Both these judgements are, of course, politically controversial if we read Dhladhla as a Lukácsian type, an interpretation the novel encourages by having him covertly cite Steve Biko.

Judging Dhladhla is, however, complicated by the fact that we only see him from Rosa's first-person perspective. For one thing, while Rosa is certainly unsettled by his fiercely held opinions, which she takes seriously, she is herself not unadmiring. She describes him as an attractive, self-possessed figure with the poise of a 'male dancer'.[38] More importantly, like all the sections of the novel in which she speaks in the first person, her account is further complicated by its dialogic, quasi-epistolary structure. She is always addressing a second-person 'you', a device Gordimer borrowed from Conrad's *Heart of Darkness*, and this, in itself, contributes to her own self-consciousness about the process of communication and, more specifically, about the question of political bias. 'What I say will not be understood,' Rosa comments immediately after her encounter with Dhladhla. 'You will say: she said *he* was this or that.'[39] On this occasion, as it happens, she is addressing Conrad, her first lover, one of the novel's apolitical individualists and representative artistic types. Gordimer's play on Conrad's name here, set alongside her indebtedness to the dialogical structure of *Heart of Darkness*, reflects some of her own ambivalence about the modernist literary tradition Lukács condemned. Unlike Rosa's activist father, but like his literary namesake, Conrad believes that suffering is irremediable and certainly not amenable to political solution, a view Rosa at that point finds attractive. Like Dhladhla, then, Conrad contributes to her growing sense of moral disorientation by fuelling her doubts about her father's legacy. Yet, whereas Conrad does so in broadly existential terms, as we shall see, Dhladhla's critique is directly political. 'Afrikaners, liberals, Communists', he says, 'we don't accept anything from anybody.'[40] The heated political discussions he provokes, in other words, form part of Rosa's ongoing inner debate with Conrad about what it means, for her, to be Burger's daughter and offers further evidence of her disaffection with communism and politics generally. So for Rosa the challenge Dhladhla poses cannot be dismissed lightly or censoriously. Indeed, at this point, he opens up a question that will preoccupy her for the rest of the novel: how to make a future for herself on her own terms given the new political conditions of the 1970s. As she comments to Conrad after the meeting: 'I'm here, the last of my line', 'trying to take hold'.[41]

The fact that *Burger's Daughter* included a verbatim transcript of an actual pamphlet circulated by the Soweto Students' Representative Council (SSRC) posed one of the greatest difficulties for the experts in their attempt to defend the novel in specifically literary terms. Once again, it also tested their own interpretative claims. As the censors noted, the pamphlet had been banned for possession in July 1977 and the SSRC was among the Black Consciousness organizations suppressed that October. In their view, this simply reinforced their case against the novel because it propagated the 'standpoint of an unlawful organization'. While the experts accepted that the 'interpretation of the legal situation must be left to the lawyers', they felt the censors' case was weakened because they failed to 'discuss the function of this pamphlet in the novel'. In their view, it was 'quoted as part of the novelist's presentation of the new situation the Soweto schoolchildren have created' and that 'while her attitude is one of compassion there is no indication that the rather pathetic rhetoric has her total assent'. Indeed, once again reflecting their hostility to the separatist ideals of Black Consciousness and their own willingness to speculate about Gordimer's attitudes, they argued that a sceptical reading of the pamphlet was 'prepared for by an earlier scene, the party at the house of the boxing promoter, Fats Mxenge', at which Rosa meets Dhladhla.

This scene deals with rifts in black opinion, the immediate issue being sports policy. The younger generation of black intellectuals obviously consider Fats a sell-out to the whites, but Fats is not presented unsympathetically. He reappears later, taking refuge in Rosa's flat during the Soweto troubles.

Moreover, the experts claimed the pamphlet is inserted between Rosa's 'devastating quarrel with her childhood friend, Baasie', the black activist her father adopted as a child but who goes on to reject his patronage on Black Consciousness grounds, and her subsequent reflections on the Soweto uprising, in which she asks whether her father 'would have allowed his children to brave the guns of the police in the same way'. Setting up the context in this way reinforced the experts' view that Gordimer distanced herself from the terms of the pamphlet—or so their argument went. In fact, Gordimer, who, as we have seen, initially had her own difficulties coming to terms with the implications of Black Consciousness, remarked in her own defence that 'I reproduced the document as it was, in all its naïveté, leaving spelling mistakes and grammatical errors uncorrected, because I felt it expressed, more eloquently and honestly than any pamphlet I could have invented, the spirit of the young people who wrote it.'[42] She also noted that Rosa herself offers a sympathetic reading of it in the subsequent section of first-person narrative.

Yet to understand its function within the framework of the novel it is not necessary to appeal to Gordimer, or, indeed, to impose a tendentious pattern onto the novel itself. If we consider the pamphlet in its immediate context, it is clear that the implied author of *Burger's Daughter*, who, as an effect of the text, cannot, of course, be identified with Gordimer, views it positively as a vital revolutionary document, which, among other things, helps to explain Rosa's final change of heart. The pamphlet constitutes a free-standing part of the novel's third and final section, which bears the epigraph *'Peace. Land. Bread.'*, the rallying cry of the October revolution. This section focuses, through a number of narrative perspectives, on Rosa's motives for returning to South Africa after she flees briefly to Europe in a state of moral panic, precipitated partly by her encounter with Dhladhla. Her final reason for going is, however, more obscure. After failing to stop an impoverished, drunk, and elderly black man brutally beating a donkey, she feels overwhelmed by the suffering of the world and by the contradictions of her predicament as a 'white woman' in the 1970s. At this point she turns once again to Conrad, the individualist, for reassurance because she thinks he will understand her complex sense of paralysis. 'The real reason why I went is something only you would believe,' she says.[43] Confirming her new appreciation of the alternative he appears to offer to her father's political activism, she adds: 'I no longer know how to live in Lionel's country.'[44] Europe, and the forms of retreat it seems to offer, which include the possibility of an escape into the traditions of high art represented by Madame Bagnelli, Lionel Burger's first wife, soon palls, however, and so Rosa returns to work as a physiotherapist at a major black hospital on the outskirts of Soweto and to take up an active role in the resistance.

It is at this point that the student uprising explodes and that a terrified Mxenge seeks refuge in her flat. In this episode, which is narrated from a third-person perspective, Mxenge describes his fears for himself and his children, caught as they are between the police, who are shooting people in the streets, and the students, who are taking revenge against black collaborators. The pamphlet then follows, after which we switch to Rosa's first-person narrative, now addressed to her dead father. Though she dwells on her own fears about the new circumstances in which she finds herself, she also recognizes that, unlike Mxenge, or, indeed, Conrad, her father would 'know how it is [the children] understand what it is they want'. 'You know how to put it. Rights, no concessions. Their country, not ghettos allotted within it, or tribal "homelands" parcelled out.'[45] Rejecting the views of the liberal whites who condemned her communist father—they 'make you responsible for Stalin and deny you Christ'—Rosa adds that none of them could have 'put it as honestly as that'. Through this structural positioning, then, the novel implies that, for all its limitations, the equally uncompromising pamphlet also knows 'how to put it'. As Rosa comments: 'The kind of education the children've rebelled against is evident enough; they can't spell and they can't formulate their elation and anguish. But they know why they're dying.'[46] Thinking back to Lenin's comments on the way revolutionary practice leads theory, she adds: 'the old phrases crack and meaning shakes out wet and new'. About these reflections the censors, who felt the novel was at this point trying 'to reconcile Black Consciousness with communism', commented: 'Here revolution is stirred up.' It is worth noting in this context that in his critical review of the novel for the *African Communist* Brian Bunting mentioned that it had been banned, which was 'a tribute to be valued higher than the Hertzog or CNA prizes, even though, if, like the authorities, one is searching for revolutionary content one might feel it is underserved'.[47]

The Appeal Board's experts acknowledged that their own reading was inevitably not free of prejudice. The 'interpretation of the law itself is likely to be affected by the outlook of the interpreter', they claimed, 'just as one's reading of the novel is likely to be tinged with subjectivity'. What they did not consider is that it was the cultural assumptions on which their defence was premised, not so much their 'subjectivity' as readers, that were at issue, assumptions which disavowed the specifically literary strengths of Gordimer's novelistic practice. This denial was most clearly evident in the general way in which they defended the novel as 'bona fide literature'. On the one hand, they noted that while *Burger's Daughter* 'is a political novel which brings into its orbit different facets of left-wing politics in South Africa', neither 'communism' nor 'black consciousness' was its central 'theme'. It 'is Rosa Burger's story, and it is her personal dilemma rather than a general political issue which constitutes the thematic interest'. This effectively downplayed the representativeness of any of the novel's characters and privileged Rosa's 'individual destiny' at the expense of her own complex situatedness. On the other hand, they argued, overlooking the novel's historical specificity in more predictable ways, it 'is perhaps even possible to see universal relevance in Rosa's dilemma, for each individual must, whatever the nature of his background, word [*sic*] out the solution to his own personal destiny'. 'It is, in fact, a tragic novel,' they claimed, which not only 'requires sympathy for black suffering' but takes 'all human suffering' for its 'wider theme'.

This apparent even-handedness was most evident, they felt, in the early scene in which a 'white hobo is found dead on a park bench'. Yet this argument once again ignored the complexity of its novelistic presentation. The episode, which is represented twice, first from a third-person perspective, then from Rosa's first-person narrative as addressed to Conrad, serves not only to illustrate Rosa's increasing sense of moral disturbance but to unsettle the idea of the universal. From the third-person perspective, we see her frozen with horror at the sight of the dead man and then, prefiguring her later flight from South Africa, fleeing 'as a thief makes himself indistinguishable from any other passer-by'.[48] Replayed through her own narrative, it becomes a scene of 'mystery', which she uses to rationalize her new doubts about the efficacy of her father's political activism and her growing admiration for Conrad, who is not only an individualist but a universalist who believes that 'sex and death' are the only realities.[49] 'The revolution we lived for in that house would change the lives of blacks,' Rosa comments, but 'the change from life to death—what had all the certainties I had from my father to do with that?'[50] As her final reflections and actions reveal, however, she eventually distances herself from Conrad's apolitical detachment, without wholly repudiating it, and discovers a new respect for her father's revolutionary ambitions, albeit on her own terms. 'I don't know the ideology,' she says: 'it's about suffering' and 'how to end suffering'.[51] At the same time, at the level of narrative rather than story, *Burger's Daughter*, for all its indebtedness to Joseph Conrad, discreetly uncouples itself from his political pessimism, particularly with regard to revolutionaries. Concluding its subtle, multifaceted dialogue with the legacies of European high art, it ends with Madame Bagnelli, who had previously been depicted as being lost in rapt contemplation of the heraldic images on a medieval French tapestry, receiving a letter from Rosa, who is, like her father, by then in a South African jail facing charges for sedition. Tellingly, she is unable to read the one poetic line in the letter describing 'a watermark of light that came into the cell', a coded allusion to something Lionel Burger 'once mentioned', not just because it 'had been deleted by the prison censor', but, the ending implies, because she is blind to the possibilities of ordinary heroism, and, indeed, to the poetry of the everyday, which is all around her.[52]

The Appeal Board, which was then under the acting chairmanship of J. C. W. van Rooyen, in the end agreed to overturn the ban, albeit grudgingly. It accepted the experts' opinion about the merits of the novel and agreed that this counted as an 'extenuating' circumstance. In particular, after taking further advice from an 'expert on security matters', a professor of political science at a leading Afrikaner university, it felt that its status as literature, in the honorific sense, 'outweighed' the 'minimal' possibility that it might prejudice the 'safety of the State' or 'relations between black and white' when read 'as a whole'. It also claimed that 'as a result of its one-sidedness the effect of the book will be counter productive rather than subversive', a perverse argument which not only undermined the literary experts' claims about the multi-voiced form of the novel but contradicted the opinion of the security expert.

> The book is exceptionally well researched [he had claimed in his report] in terms of events. The arguments of communists, liberals and of the supporters of black power are very well represented. (The arguments of 'verligte' [literally 'enlightened'] defenders of evolution as a mode of change are almost all found wanting.) In this respect the book is also of high quality—something that makes its one-sidedness all the more dangerous.

Given its 'level of difficulty', however, he had claimed it would reach only 'literary specialists' and those who have a 'particular interest in subversive movements in South Africa', where it would not do any 'real damage'. 'People who move in these circles' would 'in all likelihood already be familiar with these arguments'. To this extent its literariness was, in the end, seen less as a trumping than as a defusing factor, an argument which, as we have seen, formed a cornerstone of the government's shift towards using the censorship system as a means of containing, rather than repressing, interventionist writers in the 1980s.

Burger's Daughter was the last of Gordimer's novels to enter the censorship system. Though her short-story collection *A Soldier's Embrace* (1980) was scrutinized and passed in 1980, *July's People* (1981), *A Sport of Nature* (1987), and *My Son's Story* (1990) appear not to have been submitted in any of their editions. By that stage customs, who had routinely submitted Gordimer's books in the 1960s and 1970s, had begun to play a less active part in the process, much of the burden falling on publishers or distributors instead. Though *July's People* was also published in a local edition, jointly with Ravan and Taurus, it was not picked up by the police, who had previously sent in *The Black Interpreters* (Ravan, 1973) and *What Happened to 'Burger's Daughter'?* (Taurus, 1980), both of which were passed. The latter did, however, cause some consternation among the security censors, especially for Murray, who argued that passing it would undermine 'public trust' in, and the 'authority' of, the censorship system (P80/8/93). It is worth noting, by way of conclusion, that throughout the apartheid era, the censors received only one complaint against Gordimer from a member of the public. An offended English-speaking reader from Durban wrote to the Dekker Board in 1967 objecting to the fact that *Occasion for*

Loving was freely available in public libraries. He felt the novel was 'really disgusting, especially the part describing love making by the African and a white girl' and that it should be 'banned immediately'. In reply, Dekker noted that the novel had been passed four years earlier and that 'no good purpose would be served by banning it at this stage' (BCS 29087).

5

AFRIKAN VERSUS *VOLKS* HUMANISM: ES'KIA MPHAHLELE'S WORLDLY MUSIC AND THE TRANSCENDENT SPACE OF CULTURE

On 26 June 1955 Es'kia Mphahlele addressed a crowd of almost 3,000 delegates and as many observers attending a political rally in Kliptown, a large vacant space on the outskirts of Soweto. The occasion was the historic Congress of the People, and his purpose was to speak to the idea of culture articulated in the Freedom Charter, which the delegates were about to ratify. The Charter, which became the defining manifesto of the resistance, provoked the notorious Treason Trial that dragged on for five years from 1956 to 1961 before finally ending in acquittal. Mphahlele's speech was, for the most part, a passionate polemic against the tribalist 'nonsense of Bantu culture', as well as the Nationalist government's new policy of 'Bantu education', and an equally robust defence of the Charter's alternative, determinedly modern cultural vision.[1] Towards the end of his speech, however, he shifted into a different mode to reinforce his central message. 'I want to tell you a little tale', he said.

> A snake went up a tree and found the nest of a dove. The dove had its little ones in the nest. The snake swallowed the little ones of the dove, and the dove flew away. The mother dove began to cry, and when she was crying a musician was walking by. The musician realising, hearing the cry of the dove for the loss of its chickens, started to compose a song to the time of the weeping of the dove, and he did this in such a way that his music so moved and stirred all the other animals in the world that they came together and joined forces. They drove the snake out and killed it. (203)

The moral of this 'tiny story' was, he quickly explained, not to ask 'you to kill the snake', which, given the context of the speech as a whole, most probably stood for the anachronistic and self-servingly racialized culture of the 'white man' (203). It was altogether more affirmative. It centred on the musician, whose song represented an emergent new culture that would serve 'the cause of justice' and, as importantly, a non-racial political unity. 'I am looking forward to a day', Mphahlele said, 'when our culture will so much unify us, we shall no more talk of the Congress of the People as an organisation of Coloureds, Indians and Africans and Europeans.' Rather, 'we shall have absolutely no distinction, and we will stand together for a united cause' and, thereby, bring into being 'a culture of the people of South Africa' (203).

As defined in the story, and, indeed, in the rest of Mphahlele's speech, culture constituted, in the first instance, a transcendent humanistic space in which all narrower, specifically racial, identities could be put aside. In taking the platform, Mphahlele emphasized, he spoke not just as one of those 'who have condemned Bantu Education', but 'firstly as a human being with feelings to express like every one of you'. 'Friends, when we are talking of culture', he said, 'we must realise that we are here to talk of human feelings' (202). In this spirit he denounced the apartheid cultural planners, questioned the racialized admissions policy of an Asian-owned theatre in Johannesburg, and encouraged his 'African friends' to 'teach your children to respect the coloured man, to respect the Indian man' (202). Yet if culture opened up a space in which humanity could find its fullest expression, for Mphahlele it also had a special significance locally. This is where the musician's song acquired its particular power as a non-verbal art form, which managed to stir 'all the animals in the world' (203). It embodied Mphahlele's ideals of a unitary national culture conceived in humanistic terms— what he called 'nationalism in a democratic form'—and the all-embracing cultural aspirations of the Charter, which were at once liberal and socialist, national and internationalist. After declaring that the 'government shall discover, develop and encourage national talent for the enhancement of our cultural life', the Charter added that 'all the cultural treasures of mankind shall be open to all, by free exchange of books, ideas and contact with other lands' (207). In addition, it stated that the 'aim of education shall be to teach the youth to love their people and their culture, to honour human brotherhood, liberty and peace'. These were among the specific proposals outlined under the declarative headline: '*THE DOORS OF LEARNING AND CULTURE SHALL BE OPENED!*' (207). The Medu Art Ensemble would reaffirm these ideals at the Culture and Resistance conference in 1982.

At one level, Mphahlele's tale testified to what he would later call the 'euphoria' with which he and other African writers of the 1950s 'assimilated western ways in an industrial context'.[2] It was, he recalled in 1980, only later that 'it occurred to me how we had assimilated the west on its own terms, as a conquered people'.[3] Thirty years earlier embracing such modern, humanistic ideals provided the most immediate means of challenging not only the reactionary governmental proponents of 'Bantu culture', and the Afrikaner-owned publishers who supported them, but liberal anthropologists who were for their own reasons just as eager to fetishize 'African indigenous art'.[4] As Mphahlele noted, the same could be said for the white-owned culture industry in general: 'a gramophone record company which has been recording indigenous music throughout Africa purely as a commercial venture tries to sell its wares by telling us that Duke Ellington, Louis Armstrong, Beethoven, Mozart and so on are foreign and so we should love and stick to our own music'.[5] Yet, at another level, Mphahlele's use of the tale itself as a mode of public persuasion was telling, particularly given the way his own thinking would develop. To invoke a modernity that was yet to come, and which he hoped his audience would make a reality, he drew on the resources of traditional African orature—in this case the animal fable—and, unlike some other speakers at the Congress, he spoke not in his first language (Sesotho) but in English. To encourage his audience to recognize the transcendent possibilities of culture, in other words, he told a story in a particular language and from a specific tradition about a musician who unified the nation (and the world) through song.

At the level of form and language, then, his tale pointed towards the more situated, distinctively Afrikan humanism Mphahlele would repossess and re-fashion in the years ahead, challenging the West's claim to have a monopoly on humanistic values. His non-standard spelling of Afrika was a deliberate anti-colonial gesture. By the early 1970s he had a clear rationale for this project, which, for all its Pan-African ambitions, retained a strong national emphasis. 'We need to develop this humanism for *Africa*,' he insisted, 'for our own edification.' Instead of 'entertaining the white world' or 'shouting about African values we should rid ourselves of white standards in areas of our national life where none but African standards should be paramount'.[6] Reclaiming the word 'African' in this way had, it should be noted, nothing to do with questions of race. As an honorific referring to 'people who are culturally natives of Africa', it signified an 'affiliation', which, he commented, 'whites still have to earn'.[7] This left it open for the former colonizers to accommodate themselves to a new kind of humanism defined on African terms under a democratic dispensation. It is also worth recalling in this context that Mphahlele's later commitment to a specifically African perspective was never insular. For all his indebtedness to the anti-tribalist New African movement of the early twentieth century, and to various anti-colonial intellectuals from Fanon to Mazrui, he also saw himself as carrying forward the legacy of the 'Bengali poet and humanist' Rabindranath Tagore, the figure he regarded as his 'intellectual and spiritual mentor'.[8]

Preparing for the future by fashioning a viable modern culture for a post-colonial era was one thing. Living through the intellectual demands of the complex, fraught, and uncertain process to which he dedicated himself was quite another. In the early 1960s, having left South Africa in 1957 to begin a life of exile, which would take him from Nigeria to the United States, via France and Kenya, Mphahlele initially emerged as an outspoken critic of some anti-colonial conceptions of African culture, notably the Francophone idea of Négritude, which he feared were not only elitist but also potentially as rigid and anachronistic as 'Bantu culture'. Later in the decade, as we saw in Chapter 3, he also questioned some versions of 'Blackness' that were being articulated across the African diaspora. At the same time, his increasingly self-assured Africanist orientation made him a testy and resistant participant in the cultural Cold War. While he developed the African programmes of the Congress of Cultural Freedom, and agreed to appear under the imprint of a publisher like Seven Seas in East Berlin, he became steadily more wary of the universalizing assumptions underlying both liberal and socialist forms of humanism. This scepticism, combined with a clear-sighted recognition of the changing political realities in South Africa, led to his uneasy rapprochement with the kind of separatist thinking associated with the Black Consciousness movement in the 1970s. It also contributed to his new willingness to reclaim traditions of African orature on his own terms and to reassess his earlier doubts about Négritude. When he controversially decided to return to South Africa in 1977, eventually to become the first professor of African literature at the University of Witwatersrand in 1983, he continued to develop his ideas not only in his writings but through his own research into African orature as well as his involvement in organizations like the independent Council for Black Education and Research, which he established in 1980, and the African Writers' Association, of which he was a founding member and a guiding figure. That he did not join the ANC-aligned Congress of South African Writers, the last major writers' group formed in the apartheid era, no doubt had more to do with its partisan orientation than with any concerns about its non-racialism.

Mphahlele did not, of course, have to contend only with the intellectual and political challenges of his revisionist project. He had to deal with the consequences of the Nationalist government's hostility to everything he represented, whether as a champion of a modern, distinctively urban and eclectic 'proletarian culture' in the 1950s or as an Afrikan humanist in the following decades.[9] Though he was not among the 156 people tried for treason after the Congress rally, he was subjected to numerous forms of official harassment. After he condemned the 'Bantu Education' system when it was first promulgated in 1952, he was banned from teaching in any state-controlled school. It was partly as consequence of this that he joined *Drum* as fiction editor before finally deciding to leave the country. In 1966, after nine years in exile, he also became a 'listed communist', according to the absurd official jargon, which technically silenced him for the next twelve years. Until 1978 it was a criminal offence to publish or distribute his writings or any books in which he was quoted. It was partly for this reason that his major works appeared throughout the 1960s and early 1970s under a wide range of imprints from Faber in London and Macmillan in New York to the state-controlled Ministry of Education in Ibadan and the East African Publishing House in Nairobi. It was only after his ban was lifted that he began to be published locally, primarily by Ravan but also by Skotaville.

For the censors, who, as we have seen, occasionally prided themselves on their bureaucratic autonomy, the precise nature and extent of the threat Mphahlele's writings represented was less clear. While they compounded his already total exclusion from the public domain after 1966 by banning his third collection of short stories, *In Corner B and Other Stories* (1967), and the second edition of his major collection of critical essays *The African Image* (1974)—the old Board had already banned the first in 1962—they also passed a number of titles, including his two novels *The Wanderers* (1971) and *Chirundu* (1979), his collection of short stories and poems *The Unbroken Song* (1981), and his first autobiography, *Down Second Avenue* (1959). Such anomalies were not unusual. What gives them a special significance in Mphahlele's case is that they were fuelled in part by the censors' own less reflectively situated version of humanism, which was both broadly Western and narrowly Afrikaner or, more accurately, *volks*.

The Writer as Musician

The figure of the humanistic artist as musician became an integral part of Mphahlele's self-construction as a writer. In the 1950s, when his primary concern was to reject reactionary tribalism, he conspicuously drew attention to the impact Western classical music had on his own literary practice. In a self-reflexive vignette towards the end of *Down Second Avenue*, he described his own compositional practices as a writer, abruptly shifting his retrospective narrative into the present tense.

> Before deciding to write I set on a recording of Vivaldi's *Four Seasons*. As the music floats across to me from the sitting-room, I remember a beautiful winter morning in Nadine Gordimer's big garden in Parktown, Johannesburg. Nadine, Anthony [Sampson], who had come down from London to collect material for a book, and I were listening to Vivaldi in the same fashion.[10]

The seasonal contrast between the hot, Nigerian present and the cold, South African past then becomes entangled with his thoughts about the difference between the 'cool and refreshing experience' of Vivaldi and 'Beethoven's roaring furnaces'. At the same time the coolness of the memory and the music produces an affective cooling 'inside me', which enables him to start coming to terms with the 'prejudices and anger' he has 'brought with' him. 'I'm breathing the new air of freedom,' he remarks.[11] Achieving such inner equanimity was a precondition for becoming the kind of interventionist writer he wanted to be and, as he made clear a few pages earlier, one of his primary motives for going into exile. Arguing with those who tried to encourage him to stay, he commented: 'I'm sick of protest creative writing and our South African situation has become a terrible cliché as literary material.' Clarifying what this meant, he added that in apartheid South Africa he had 'hardly a moment to think of human beings as human beings and not as victims of political circumstance'.[12] By contrast, settling down to write 'in the spacious garden of a Lagos house' with Vivaldi's *Four Seasons* in the air gave him a 'glorious sense of release' and, by implication, access to the equally capacious and transcendent space of culture.[13]

By the 1980s, when he had a secure sense of his own cultural situatedness as a specifically Afrikan humanist, he continued to appeal to the idea of music as the highest form of artistic expression, though now with a different emphasis. While he pointedly entitled the second volume of his autobiography *Afrika My Music* (1984), he used the preface to *The Unbroken Song* to set out his view of the writer's role within a renewed Afrikan humanism. Referring to the rise of Black Consciousness, he commented that 'after our humanism met with an uncompromising cruel rebuff', 'we thought we could withdraw, take cover in our own blackness'.[14] This was politically inevitable 'because we had never been made to forget we are black', but he believed it came at a certain cultural cost: 'We keep talking across the wall, singing our different songs, beating our different drums.'[15] As an Afrikan writer, who sought to occupy a position at the vanguard of a modern sense of community, any such allegiances were, he argued, impossible to sustain in practice: 'The artist, always the spearpoint of a people's sensitivity, cannot but feel and express the paradoxes, the ironies, the stupidities, the follies, the resilience, the fortitude, the fears, the ignorance, the tenderness, the hypocrisies, the yearnings, all these deep-deep down, seeping through between our ghettoes white and black, deep down under the foundation of this wall.'[16] *The Unbroken Song*, which included a selection of his poetry, a reconciliatory letter addressed to Leopold Senghor, the celebrated champion of Négritude, as well as a selection of his own stories dating from the 1950s to the 1960s, was his testament to the continuity of the tradition out of which this artistic ideal emerged. The title alluded to his epigraph, a remark made by the imprisoned Indian nationalist and humanist Acharya Vinoba Bhave to his fellow prisoners in the 1930s, which in turn alluded to the *Bhagavadgītā*: 'Though action rages without, the heart can be tuned to produce unbroken music.'[17] Introducing his own collection, which was published as number 9 in Ravan's innovative Staffrider Series, Mphahlele remarked: 'This, my people, is my unbroken music.' It was, he acknowledged, 'only one kind of music in the orchestration of our time'. Moreover, citing Tagore, he insisted that 'none of its notes is final'. Nonetheless, it formed part of 'the cumulative, continuing poetry of our people' and, again citing Tagore, each note 'reflects the infinite'.[18] As an

Afrikan humanist he was, in other words, both situated and transcendent. Or, to use his own governing trope, while he identified with a particular cultural and linguistic tradition, he also sought to stir the world as if through the more universal medium of music.

In the intensely polarized political circumstances of the 1970s and 1980s Mphahlele's continued commitment to the idea of culture as a transcendent space, and, more particularly, to the literary as distinctively humanistic mode of public discourse, was inevitably controversial. For the censors, however, his willingness to acknowledge the 'paradoxes' of a situation and the 'follies' on both sides made many of his fictional writings acceptable according to their own humanistic assumptions. This was particularly evident in the Appeal Board's arguments in favour of upholding a censorship committee's decision to pass *The Wanderers* in 1983. In his report, J. C. W. van Rooyen, then chair of the Board, defended the novel, which deals in part with the political turmoil of post-colonial Africa, by appealing to the new likely reader test and the legitimacy of 'protest literature'. Yet he also emphasized that it displayed the requisite 'balance' to count as literature. 'However critical he may be of whites,' Mphahlele 'is not uncritical of blacks and the practices in other African states.'[19] To support this reading he pointed, among other things, to a discussion two characters have about corrupt military dictatorships, or, as van Rooyen put it, about the apathy 'among certain African people' that led them to elect a 'dictator' who 'surrounds himself with sycophants and stooges, arranges for his own comfort, and corrupts the state and the government'.[20]

This kind of thinking had also played a part in a security committee's decision to pass *Chirundu* four years earlier. Murray, who acted as chair and initial reader, was concerned about one character's denunciation of 'Bantu Education' and an episode of civil disruption, which takes place in the fictionalized post-colonial African country in which the novel is set—Murray rightly recognized it as Zambia.[21] Nonetheless, he argued against banning because the novel was primarily about the 'psychological currents in a new black state', as reflected in the life of its central character, Chirundu, a political figure who embodies many of the tensions of the post-colonial era. Though the plot runs together a political story of a strike led by Chirundu's nephew and a personal story involving a successful charge of bigamy brought against him by his first wife, Murray drew attention only to the latter in his summary. In his view, which the committee endorsed, the novel was acceptable, in other words, because it contained 'no ideological discussion' and because it privileged the individual inner story of Chirundu's rise and fall (P79/7/33).

Unsurprisingly, however, the censors' humanism had distinct limits. Though Mphahlele's preoccupation with the human complexities of political life, and apartheid in particular, was evident from the first, the Kruger Board decided to ban *In Corner B* in 1974, a collection that included many of his stories from the

1950s. Five years later a security committee upheld this decision when the police resubmitted the volume with a view to having it banned for possession as well. In his chair's report, Jansen noted that while most of the twelve stories were 'absolutely harmless', four were 'problematic' (P79/6/119). He claimed 'The Living and the Dead' (1958), for instance, was seditious. The story centres on Stoffel Visser, a minor apartheid official who experiences a disturbing and brief moment of moral doubt when his servant, Jackson, is unjustly attacked by the police. In a fit of affronted anger Jackson shakes a railway policeman who has picked on him because he is aspiring to better himself through education. He is reading his 'night-school book' on the train.[22] The policeman, together with a group of thuggish colleagues, then exacts his revenge. After being summarily beaten, Jackson is thrown out at the next platform, where he is taken into custody and charged with drunken disorder. Despite all this, Jansen was mainly worried about Jackson's comment after being asked to pay £1 bail: 'I say no and I ask them they must ring you,' he tells Visser; 'they say if I'm cheeky they will hell me up and then they hit and kick again.'[23] According to Jansen, 'A Point of Identity' (1967), a mordant first-person narrative about the absurdity of racial classification, was also seditious. In this case, it was a 'Coloured' character's account of how 'Negro' pass-law offenders are treated, and specifically how they are taken to white farms to 'work like slaves', that seemed most 'problematic'.[24] As in many of Mphahlele's stories, this character speaks in his own unique style of English, though his struggle with large, specifically political abstractions, for which he tends to substitute a nonce-word, 'watchimball', inevitably has a more than mimetic significance given the wider preoccupations of the story.[25]

Though Jansen was also concerned about 'Grieg on a Stolen Piano' (1964), he did not specify why he found it 'undesirable'. He was more forthcoming about 'Mrs Plum', the fourth story on his list. According to the blurb, this 'disturbing short novel', which first appeared in the *Corner B* collection, was 'one of the most damning and bitter indictments of the white "liberals" in South Africa yet printed'.[26] Told in the first person by Karabo, Mrs Plum's domestic servant, the story focuses on the compromised liberalism of the 1960s and, more particularly, on the priorities of a woman like Mrs Plum who, Karabo observes without irony, 'loved dogs and Africans and said that everyone must follow the law even if it hurt'.[27] Much of the power of the story derives from the gulf between Karabo's sensible, increasingly informed, but always limited point of view and the more knowing perspective of the implied author. Jansen had two particular concerns. The first was that the story disturbed the boundary between fiction and history by incorporating an actual person, Lilian Ngoyi (1911–80), into the narrative, albeit in an 'indirect manner'. Ngoyi, who was among those unsuccessfully tried for treason after the Congress of the People, was a leading figure in the resistance and the first president of the ANC Women's League. In the story she offers an alternative political vision to Mrs Plum's paternalistic liberalism which enables Karabo to see through the 'white man's evil game' and, in the end, to redefine the terms of her contract with her employer.[28] Writing in 1979, a year before Ngoyi's death, Jansen noted that she was 'completely inactive at the moment' and, like Mphahlele himself, 'no longer banned'. Nonetheless, the fact that the story in some sense reflected her belief that 'black people must assume power' made it seditious. In his view, the story was also obscene because, as he remarked with some alarm, there is 'an insinuation that "Mrs Plum" *has sexual relations with her dog'*. In this scene, which goes well beyond insinuation, Karabo witnesses her widowed employer having full intercourse with her dog, whose name, Malan, gives her actions a particularly provocative allegorical significance, though one Jansen did not consider. Reflecting on the collection as a whole, he acknowledged that in the adjudication of a book like this (written by a black person) the "pain threshold" must be higher' and so he felt he could not justify banning it for possession. He was, however, in no doubt that the earlier ban on publication and distribution had to be upheld in the interests of state security, race relations, and public morals.

Three years later, when the police submitted *The Unbroken Song*, Jansen was still unsure about 'Mrs Plum', 'The Living and the Dead', and 'Grieg on a Stolen Piano' (P82/6/2). About the latter he now drew the committee's attention to the opening scene, in which the young narrator describes how, as a boy, his uncle is brutally beaten for sport by white farmers. This is part of a retrospective account of the older man's thwarted early ambitions, which goes some way towards explaining why he has turned to a life of opportunistic entrepreneurialism and, indeed, crime. Jansen also singled out a passage in which the uncle stands up to the petty racism of a white post-office clerk. As the half-admiring, half-unnerved narrator observes, his irrepressible, hard-drinking relative has developed his own style of resistance because he does not, as the uncle puts it, 'have the liver to join the Congress Movement'.[29] After his teaching career is destroyed, he ends up trying out various dubious moneymaking schemes and dealing in stolen goods, partly to redistribute wealth and get on in the world, but also, in the case of the piano, to indulge his musical talents by playing his favourite composers, who, tellingly, include Grieg, Chopin, *and* Puluma Mohapeloa. Of the stories collected in *The Unbroken Song*, Jansen also mentioned 'Dinner at Eight' (1961) because it began with an account of police and judicial corruption. This was another early study of the social absurdities bred of white liberalism. Yet on this occasion, partly because of the changes in censorship practice but also, as he noted, because Lilian Ngoyi had died, he recommended that the collection should be passed. *In Corner B* was itself eventually unbanned by a literary committee in 1985, despite ongoing worries about 'Mrs Plum'. The dog scene was 'shocking', Rita Scholtz remarked in her chair's report, but, like the initial reader, she felt it was 'functional', since it reinforced the story's main theme. As the reader (M. G. Scholtz) had put it,

'Mrs Plum' was about the fact that 'the white man has more interest in his dog than in the black man', a reading which, once again, overlooked the bestiality episode's potential as an especially subversive, perhaps even seditious, political allegory of (English) liberalism and (Afrikaner) nationalism (P84/12/23).

The Writer as Public Intellectual

Despite the censors' anxieties about some of Mphahlele's fictional writings, it was his non-fictional works that exposed the limits of their compromised humanism most clearly. This was particularly evident when the police resubmitted *Down Second Avenue* in July 1967, provoking an intense four-month debate within the Dekker Board. Outlining his case against the book, the police commissioner attempted to argue that it 'speaks of a hatred against the whites and shows nowhere that the writer really lays bare his feelings in order to investigate the hate in himself and to admit his own shortcomings' (BCS 522/67). Mphahlele's 'biases' were, he added, continuing his curiously moralistic diatribe, 'wholly attributable to his ignorance and ineptitude but nonetheless he seeks to blame the whites'. After an initial round of deliberations, the censors themselves voted four to two in favour of banning, even though the old Board, which scrutinized imported books only, had let it through in 1959. The distribution of the votes was, however, far from predictable. Mphahlele found himself with two unlikely champions: Murray, the liberal-minded but also hardline security censor, and Endemann, the expert on African languages. The four negative votes were cast by Merwe Scholtz, Cloete, Grové, and Dekker, all of whom saw themselves as dedicated *volks* humanists. As Murray pointed out in a letter to Dekker dated 20 September 1967: 'At the last Board meeting one of our literary members remarked that non-literary members of the Board should give more weight to their views in cases involving sex-descriptions because they have a deeper knowledge of artistic form and artistic expression.' 'In the same spirit', he argued, 'I would like to ask that Board members give due attention to the opinions of those members who have a closer understanding of the three currents of feeling (*meningstrominge*) that exist within the population (Afrikaner, English and Bantu).' The crudity of his social model of South Africa was, of course, integral to apartheid thinking.

For Murray and Endemann, who did not share the police commissioner's intemperate views, the case against banning was straightforward. As Murray, the initial reader, remarked in his first report: 'there is no communism in it'. The book, which traced Mphahlele's life from 'his thirteenth year, through the political changes of the fifties, until the present, when he sits in Nigeria', was written in a 'wholly objective manner' and 'contained not a trace of propaganda'. The 'grievances, justified or not, are dispassionately and objectively described, as are the actions of whites against natives, and police against natives'. His main contention, however, was that it 'contains nothing that is not already known'; moreover, 'the clear presentation of the native's understanding of the historical situation must also be aired in this country', not just abroad. Once he realized he had been outvoted, he stepped up his arguments, insisting, in his correspondence with Dekker, that the decision raised questions of 'principle' and 'policy': 'If we ban this work then it is going to be almost impossible to let through any work by a native who gives an account of the prevailing and unprompted attitudes of the native in this country.'

The literary censors, led by Grové and Merwe Scholtz, who were for banning, focused on Mphahlele's portrayal of the police, the Afrikaner, and history in general. Grové, who was the most emphatic, questioned certain claims—'is it true that natives are not allowed to walk on our pavements?'—and felt Mphahlele was 'bitterly hostile to all that is Afrikaans'. 'What is clear', he added coolly, 'is that we did not manage to "catch" this writer with our university education.' Merwe Scholtz also voted for banning, though with less conviction. He first read the 'strongly felt autobiography' while in Europe in 1959, and on a second reading he still found it 'painful'. He was 'struck', on the one hand, 'by the bitterness and by the inevitably one-sided, distorted vision of the Afrikaner in particular'; and, on the other, 'by the knowledge, which surely no one will deny, that many of these things happened and still happen'. His concerns centred on its likely impact on the 'average native reader', and on the police, who could 'feel differently about their difficult task' after reading it. 'Have we not already decided', he asked, chillingly, that 'it is sometimes not wise to make certain truths available to any and everyone?' After all, 'we have kept out some books about, for example, sexuality because we want to protect an immature and youthful reading public'.

It fell to Dekker to attempt to clarify the issues for a second round of voting. He was in no doubt that *Down Second Avenue* was an 'honourable autobiography of an embittered person who grew up in Pretoria's Marabastad [township], who made it through the degradation and grief of township-life and poverty, uplifted himself through education, was as a consequence of his sharp protest activities forbidden to pursue what he felt was his vocation, that is, teaching, and finally with deep frustration said goodbye to S.A. to teach in Nigeria'. It was also clear that Mphahlele was no 'agitator' but rather 'someone who had no belief in whites, especially the Afrikaner, saw South Africa as a police state and was profoundly disillusioned with the whites' Christian church'. Nevertheless, it 'remained a question' whether or not this 'sombre picture' would have an 'inciting effect on the non-white'. The 'attack on the police' was worrying, but he was equally perturbed by the graphic account of life in the Boer republics at the end of the nineteenth century, which the young Mphahlele hears from his grandmother. In his report he referred particularly to an extended paragraph that begins:

Grandmother never tired of telling us about 'Paul Kruger's day'; of the hard times under Boer rule; of the way they buried Africans alive who were suspected of fighting or spying for the British; of how Boer soldiers cut off Black women's breasts; of the hard-hearted 'Meneer Paulen', the German Lutheran missionary who told his flock that God has sent him to drag them out of the darkness which God's curse had hurled them into.[30]

Yet, in the end, he agreed with Murray that banning it raised a question of 'policy' and that the 'whites had to know what was going on in the mind of the Bantu, to understand his sense of injustice'. After reconsidering the arguments, the Board concurred, and so it was finally approved by a majority of five to one. Only Grové left his vote unchanged, albeit with some hesitation. The police tried to have *Down Second Avenue* suppressed once again in 1974, but on that occasion Kruger, the new chair of the Board, refused to put it through the system for a third time. A security committee did, however, ban a comic-book version produced for black schoolchildren by a non-governmental educational publisher in 1988, only to have its decision overturned on appeal (P88/6/162).

The African Image, the influential collection of Mphahlele's early essays, which Faber first published in 1962, suffered a very different fate. It was suppressed by the old Censor Board as soon as Faber tried to bring it into the country. Though the Board's detailed motivations are unclear—no report seems to have survived—it is very likely that Mphahlele's robust condemnation of apartheid, 'Bantu culture', and 'liberal gradualism' affected the outcome.[31] In December 1976, however, when the dissident Afrikaans Writers' Guild submitted it for review under the new legislation, a predominantly literary committee, chaired by the liberal Etienne Malan, decided to lift the ban. In his report, which the committee endorsed, Malan referred to the changed political circumstances in the 1970s and noted that the government's own attitude to the 'danger' Mphahlele posed appeared to be softening because it had just granted him a visa to visit the country (P76/11/147). Nevertheless his defence of the collection centred on its generic status as a balanced 'academic work' rather than a political polemic. If Mphahlele 'wrote against the Afrikaner, the English—the liberals as much as the conservatives—the Indian and at times the Coloured', he was 'equally critical about aspects of Nigeria, like bribery ("dash"), the ill-treatment of black servants by black employers and the police system'. Moreover, he was 'against Leopold Senghor's negritude, against black nationalism and against the P.A.C.', and, though he felt Mphahlele did not consider 'communism and black nationalism as irreconcilable', he quoted, or rather misquoted, his comment that 'I must see communism in action [in Russia] before I can pass judgement.'[32] Malan omitted the reference to Russia. His principal argument, however, was that Mphahlele was 'wholly realistic'. He cited with approval his remark that in territories like 'Southern Rhodesia' and South Africa, as in Algeria, it would be 'plain madness to tell the whites, the

Indians, Arabs or Coloured people to quit, or even to occupy a status of sufferance'.[33] For Malan, the 'best account of his personal standpoint' was to be found in the essay entitled 'Cheeky Kaffirs, Impertinent Natives'. In the final reflective paragraph, to which Malan referred, Mphahlele insisted on his claim to the 'political rights many other workers in the world enjoy' and predicted that the 'educated black man, frustrations notwithstanding, will emerge tough as tried metal from all this debris of colonial systems the West has thought fit to dump on Africa'. Yet, at the same time, he acknowledged that he had 'seen too much that is good in Western culture—for example, its music, literature and theatre—to want to repudiate it'. The 'big question' that remained was how much the 'African will find of some use in the scrapyard' and 'how much of his past' would survive.[34]

The ban on the first edition of *African Image* was lifted in December 1976, but this outcome was by no means guaranteed. In the same month, another committee, comprising many of the same key members (Malan, Wiggett, Merwe Scholtz), came to a very different conclusion about Lewis Nkosi's first collection of essays, *Home and Exile* (1965), which the Afrikaans Writers' Guild had also sent in for review. Like *Down Second Avenue*, it had originally reached the censors in 1967 via the police, who saw it as 'an attack on our social standards' and as 'propaganda for the legalisation of integration' (BCS 523/67). Once again, like Mphahlele's autobiography, it caused some unexpected contention in the Dekker Board. Murray, the initial reader, claimed that it was not 'scientific'—he felt it was written from a clear 'African nationalist standpoint' and in a 'poetic and emotional' manner—but he still argued it should not be banned. In his view, there was much that was 'impressive in the book' and much with which 'we whites' should 'be familiar'. It reflected an 'existing intellectual outlook', an understanding of which 'will help us find better ways of solving our local problems'. Endemann agreed, albeit more reluctantly this time, but once again they were outvoted. On this occasion Dekker and Grové marshalled the counter-arguments, which ultimately led to the ban. While Dekker recognized the value the collection might have for white readers, he again worried about its impact on the police and 'non-whites'. He was especially anxious about parts of two essays from the book's first section to which Endemann had drawn attention. In the first, 'The Fabulous Decade: The Fifties', Nkosi gave an upbeat, if acerbic and often self-ironizing, account of interracial sociability and sexuality; while in the second, 'Apartheid: A Daily Exercise in the Absurd', he described, with frequent references to Kafka, the 'surrealistic' apartheid legislation that made black lives unendurable. In the conclusion to this essay, which he wrote with a British and American audience in mind, Nkosi also predicted that 'the sixties will see no end to the riot and gunfire', and argued that if the 'Western world' does not wake up to the 'desperation' of 'South African blacks' they 'will look elsewhere for help' (i.e. to the Communist bloc).[35]

In reviewing the Dekker Board's decision nine years later, Merwe Scholtz, the initial reader and chair of the 1976 committee, focused on the collection's first section, entitled 'Home' (the other essays in the volume are grouped under sections called 'Exile' and 'Literary'). He appreciated Nkosi's 'relatively matter of fact' retrospect about the 1950s, noting in particular what he called his 'admission' of Can Themba's 'journalistic excesses' (P76/11/145). At one point, as Nkosi recalled, Themba had, 'in his most melodramatic mood' as a *Drum* journalist, provoked an international outcry, deeply embarrassing to the government, by describing the 'security camps' in which political leaders were being detained as 'South Africa's concentration camps', a description about which Themba was 'unrepentant', as Nkosi noted.[36] Scholtz also commented on Nkosi's 'sophisticated, "informed" concept of the absurd'. Continuing in the same disdainful vein, he added that this 'comic quality' made the collection 'much more effective than an uncontrolled tirade against that which is represented as repression and injustice'. Taking all these factors into consideration, he felt that 'in the current context it was not as "explosive" as it probably had been in the past'. However, he was doubtful enough to suggest that one of the security censors should look at it as well, as a consequence of which Jansen submitted an additional report that persuaded the committee to uphold the ban.

Jansen took particular exception to some of Nkosi's language, noting, among other things, his description of Sharpeville as a 'brutal massacre' and his use of the phrase 'police torture', and he was less appreciative of the collection's satirical tone.[37] He thought the account Nkosi gave of Themba's drunken fantasy about having sex with Prime Minister Strydom's daughter was in 'extreme bad taste'. He also objected to some of his literary opinions, in particular his damning assessment of Alan Paton's *Cry, the Beloved Country* (1948). In the forgiving Reverend Stephen Kumalo, the novel's central figure, Nkosi saw, as Jansen put it, the 'unconsciousness of the whites' and their own fantasy, to use Nkosi's words, that they 'might yet escape the immense penalties they would be required to pay'.[38] Nkosi's critical reading of Paton's Uncle Tom amounted to 'veiled propagandizing for black people to seek retribution against whites', according to Jansen. Tellingly, he made no mention of what any readers might make of Nkosi's interpretation, or, indeed, of his collection of essays as a whole. In his conclusion, Jansen also referred to a contemporary newspaper report about the conviction of nine Black Consciousness leaders, including Strinivasa Moodley, charged under the Terrorism Act. This related to a notorious two-year-long trial involving key figures in the South African Students' Organization and the Black People's Convention. Jansen drew attention to the judge's claim that the convicted men referred to whites as 'rapists, murderers and robbers', used the word 'massacre' to describe Sharpeville, and 'tried to create a Black power bloc which would lead inevitably to violent confrontation'. In his view, which the committee endorsed, the ban on *Home and Exile* had to be upheld because it effectively contributed to the same ends.

Four months later, in April 1977, Jansen persuaded a security committee that the second edition of Mphahlele's *The African Image* (1974), which the censorship directorate itself submitted, represented an even more serious danger. As he reported, 'large parts of the book have been revised' (P77/4/82). He was particularly concerned about the 'omissions, additions and rearrangements' in the first two chapters: the impressionistic meditation 'Blackness on My Mind', which was wholly new, and 'The Nationalist', which was revised. He also worried about Mphahlele's appropriation of the Black Consciousness term 'Boer' as a synonym for 'Afrikaner', although it was often used to refer to all whites. After citing Mphahlele's explanation for his new nomenclature, Jansen remarked, 'he does this with intent because the black people have been named "kaffers", natives and Bantu in a humiliating way by the Afrikaners'.[39] Mphahlele's own tendency to represent 'whites and above all the Afrikaner' as 'contemptible' was particularly evident, Jansen argued, in a passage from 'Blackness on My Mind' in which he imagines returning to South Africa and defiantly tearing up an agreement he is required to sign about keeping 'out of politics'. In this fictionalized scenario, Mphahlele comments, 'I fought your stinking educational policies in the fifties and I'll fight them again.'[40] In an earlier passage, which Jansen also quoted, Mphahlele remarked that, 'come the day when the tables are turned, the white man will have to choose to quit or adopt the majority African culture or be marooned by history'.[41] In addition to his specific attacks on the police and government officials, Mphahlele was now, Jansen emphasized, out to 'encourage revolution'. Pointing to a revised section of the chapter 'The Nationalist', he noted that he endorsed Nkosi's argument, made in an essay of 1971, that 'the black people will only get the kind of attention and assistance they need in any dramatic form when they have decided to fight or to dislocate the machinery of the state'.[42] Jansen did not quote the subsequent comments on the Black Consciousness generation, whom Mphahlele described as 'college-boy theorists'. He was particularly critical of their elitist 'naming antics', calling on them to 'retract the name "Azania" which they arbitrarily gave South Africa, a name some misguided Afro-American militants have also adopted'.[43]

In his chair's report, Jansen remarked that various complicating factors had to be taken into consideration, the most important of which was that Mphahlele had just been given permission to return to South Africa. As such he had 'apparently', Jansen remarked, responded to Prime Minister B. J. Vorster's 'moderate attitude' to those exiles who wished to return having 'changed their ways of thinking'. The security committee nonetheless decided that this was irrelevant, since the 'undesirability of the book had to be decided on the basis of its content alone'. Mphahlele's situation was, it claimed, comparable to that of

Eldridge Cleaver, the 'militant Black power leader', whose works remained banned despite the fact that he had 'recently undergone a change of heart and today seeks to work with whites as a convert and a Christian'. At the same time, contradicting this argument, the committee recognized that Mphahlele was a 'man of stature' whose 'words would as a consequence have a greater influence on people who wish to overthrow the established order with violence'. Its thinking was also influenced by the assessment Adrian Roscoe gave of Mphahlele in his academic study *Uhuru's Fire: African Literature East to South* (1977). Jansen specifically quoted Roscoe's description of Mphahlele as 'a man whose experience in a rough world (badly treated even in independent Africa) has turned a deeply compassionate view of humanity into a conviction that only guns and violence can cure the cancer of apartheid in Vorster's Republic'.[44] This view was particularly 'significant', Jansen argued, because it showed how 'outsiders' saw Mphahlele. For the censors, in other words, the second edition had to be banned under all three political clauses, and, indeed, for possession, because Mphahlele appeared simply to have abandoned his early humanism, which they understood in exclusively Western terms. They made no mention of his efforts to reclaim a specifically African humanistic tradition.

When Macmillan SA, acting on Faber's behalf, applied for a review of this decision five years later, a combined literary and security committee, chaired by Rita Scholtz, decided to uphold the ban, albeit on slightly different grounds and without the additional stipulation regarding possession. In her chair's report, which took cognizance of Jansen's largely unchanged views, she focused on many of the same passages he mentioned in the 1977 decision and, once again appealing to the Western humanistic ideals of political disinterestedness, she emphasized that it was not a 'descriptive scientific work' (P82/5/41). She was especially concerned about Mphahlele's comments on 'John Vorster the Boer', 'Ian Smith the Rhodesian *rooinek* [redneck]', and 'Caetano the Portuguese dictator'. After describing 'this trio' as 'palefaced, worried, frightened, desperate men engineering torture, hangings, banishment, eviction, starvation, extermination, imprisonment', Mphahlele asks pointedly: 'Are they mere monstrous survivals on the fringe of western civilization? No, they are not acting off-stage. They are right there in the centre of the arena of a civilization. Else why would the rest of the white world either actively support them or let them be?'[45]

Scholtz acknowledged the Appeal Board's recent change of policy towards 'protest literature'. She specifically cited a case (43/81) relating to G. D. Killam's critical study *An Introduction to the Writings of Ngugi* (1980), in which van Rooyen had argued that 'South Africans should be informed or inform themselves of what Blacks are thinking and writing not only in the Republic but throughout the continent of which they are a part.' Nevertheless, she felt the ban had to be upheld because the 'probable reader', 'especially black students & intellectuals', would be 'incited to revolutionary action against the Government' and that the book would 'inflame the hatred of a certain section of the community towards the other inhabitants in the R.S.A.'. As a consequence, the second edition of *The African Image*, like Nkosi's *Home and Exile*, which also failed the censors' humanistic test, remained banned throughout the apartheid era.

6
CONNECTED VERSUS INTERNAL CRITICS: BREYTENBACH, LEROUX, AND THE *VOLK* AVANT-GARDE

In August 1968, that auspicious year of revolutions, *Kol* (literally 'Stain' or 'Bulls-eye'), a new Afrikaans literary magazine, initiated a debate among the emergent generation of Afrikaans writers. The main participants were Chris Barnard, Breyten Breytenbach, André Brink, Etienne Leroux, Adam Small, and Bartho Smit, all of whom were identified with the group known collectively as the Sestigers. Derived from the titles they gave their own short-lived little magazines earlier in the decade, first *60* and then *Sestiger* (1963–5), the generational label, which, according to the blurb for Brink's *Looking on Darkness* (1974), meant 'Men of the Sixties', stuck, even though it was in some respects misleading.[1] Despite their overwhelming maleness, and their shared iconoclastic, avant-garde outlook, the Sestigers did not represent a particularly coherent group. For one thing, they were not all of quite the same generation. While Small, Barnard, Brink, and Breytenbach were in their late twenties or early thirties in 1968, Smit and Leroux were by then in their mid-forties. For another, as the debate revealed, their differences were often more significant than their fragile sense of solidarity. The *Kol* debate, as the *Darkness* blurb continued, marked a 'serious rift in the group' between those who 'openly chose an experimental, ivory-tower and essentially apolitical kind of writing' and those who 'insisted on the need for confronting and exposing the South African social and political situation and advocated a more openly committed form of writing, which soon led to their expulsion from the Afrikaner laager, and to various subtle and not-so-subtle forms of persecution'.[2] At issue were questions about the meaning of the Sestiger movement, the responsibilities of the writer, and the future of Afrikaans literature.

Brink, who as the principal editor of *Sestiger* had been one of the group's most energetic representatives in the early 1960s, initiated the exchange with a combative essay entitled 'Between Sixty and Seventy'. While acknowledging that they had successfully enabled Afrikaans fiction to move 'from colonialism to self-governance', he now felt their achievements were starting to look increasingly questionable.[3] 'I begin to be sceptical about the validity', and, indeed, the 'morality', Brink commented, 'of the "aesthetic struggle" which is *even now* being conducted in Afrikaans fiction' (3). As the blurb for *Looking on Darkness* noted, Brink had been one of the chief proponents of this struggle, but it is clear that his critique now focused primarily on Leroux, who had been among the key figures N. P. van Wyk Louw singled out in 1961 for inaugurating a 'renewal of our fiction'. Seven years on, Brink asked in response: 'What is the scope of the renewal of our fiction? A few new forms. A few dodgy words that every good Dopper [member of the extreme Calvinist Reformed Church] and Gatjieponner [member of the less extreme NGK] has long since been using in everyday conversation. A little sleep-with-a-girl. A little satire. A whole lot of symbols' (3). What was missing was 'the consciousness of a social dimension', which had been part of the history of the novel from 'Rabelais and Cervantes' through to 'Joyce and Mann and Kafka' (4). 'In too many Afrikaans novels', Brink claimed, 'the political and social status quo is taken for granted to such an extent that there is not even the slightest evidence of a desire to think further or to entertain the possibility that the status quo might not be just' (4).

For Brink the pressure on Afrikaans writers, the Sestigers especially, to produce what he called 'really contestatory work' was all the greater because none had at that point been banned (4). Unlike 'a Nadine Gordimer, a Raymond Kunene, an Alex La Guma, a Lewis Nkosi', who, as the evidence of the past decade already showed, would be 'summarily forbidden', the 'Afrikaans writer still has just a small chance of being published, ironically because he is part of the power-group' (4). 'If we do not make the most of this opportunity,' he concluded, then 'every "neutral" or "elusive" work that appears in Afrikaans, *irrespective* of its literary merits, tacitly accepts that the status quo is good and just' (5). Breytenbach, who was writing from Paris, where he had lived in voluntary exile since 1962, agreed. His own contribution took the form of a characteristically idiomatic open letter to Chris Barnard, who was, along with Bartho Smit, on *Kol*'s editorial board. In Breytenbach's view, the question facing Barnard and his new magazine was clear:

> What are you as thinker—because you're not just a mouthpiece (would that it would be so easy, hey?)—planning to write, to say and to do in a situation where your people are responsible...for the fact that so many works by our English-speaking countrymen are banned, a situation where so many of your

other-coloured and/or other-thinking countrymen are sitting in jail *as a conse-quence of* their other-thinkingness, a situation where, just north of your borders, some of your fellow citizens have taken up arms against you as a passive or active representative or bearer of your people's policies? (And culture?)[4]

Much, as we shall see, turned on his parenthetical reference to 'culture'. For Breytenbach, this question was made all the more urgent because so many contemporary Afrikaans literary magazines were anodyne, complicit, or directly supportive of the established order. *Standpunte* had, in his view, become an overly academic 'Faculty newsletter'; *Wurm* (Worm), another little maga-zine, reminded him of a 'rebelliously frustrated government official'; and about *Tydskrif vir Letterkunde* (Magazine for Literature), the magazine of the collab-orationist Afrikaans Writer's Circle, he had nothing to say. His only comment was a dismissive shrug: 'Tja' (10).

Brink's tacit claim that Leroux's fantastical, often apocalyptic, always elabor-ately allegorical satires lacked the necessary 'consciousness of a social dimen-sion' was uncharitable. He was evidently less concerned about Leroux's works as such than about the aestheticist terms in which van Wyk Louw and others had championed them. Though it is impossible to extract a simple message from Leroux's oblique, testily ironized, and self-ironizing fictions, there can be no doubt about their underlying social and political 'consciousness'. In a central scene in *Sewe Dae by die Silbersteins* (Seven Days at the Silbersteins, 1962), Leroux's most significant early novel, an 'albino', who finds a dubious new meaning to his life when he is accepted into the novel's surrealistic version of the apartheid order, violently beats back a black gardener when he makes a plea for justice.[5] After this a riot, instigated in part by Julius Jool, the novel's one communist, breaks out in the local township, leading to death and destruc-tion. Reflecting on the causes of the uprising, the central figure, Henry Van Eeden, a typically beleaguered Leroux-style individualist, later comments: 'The fault lies with us Whites.'[6] What complicates Leroux's vision in this novel, and many others, is his tendency to absorb the specifically political ills of apartheid into a larger narrative about the advent of an overly rationalistic and morally bankrupt modernity, a point to which I shall return.

This larger dimension of his work may go some way towards explaining why Leroux accepted the terms of the Brink–Breytenbach critique. In his reply, which appeared in *Kol*'s next issue, he echoed their categorical opposition to what he called the 'disgrace' of censorship.[7] About their call for a greater political self-awareness he was more wary. He worried that they were becoming 'high-minded propagandists', too eager to dispense with their own specifically literary modes of intervention, and too committed, like some 'socialistic writers' groups', to promoting a prescriptive idea of the writer's 'Duty' (4–5). Worse still, their questions sounded, he said, too much like the ones 'conservatives in our country ask—only they expect different answers to you' (5). By contrast, he was 'under the impression' that 'we writers in the West' were free to 'represent the world in our own way following our own rules' without being 'answerable' to 'anyone' (5). If this was not the case, he concluded, he would 'give up writing' because in 'this overly organized age in which we live duties are handed out too freely' (5).

These generalized anxieties about aesthetics and politics were, however, relatively superficial. The real energies of the debate centred on the related, but more specific, issues surrounding the literary identity of the Afrikaans writer, and, more particularly, of the Sestigers as an emergent *volk* avant-garde. Here Breytenbach rather than Brink led the way by addressing a more pointed set of questions to Barnard. As it is impossible to render his complex puns in English, I shall simply note that he was playing on the homophonic linkage in Afrikaans between the words 'own' (*eie*) and 'egg' (*eier*).

> Do you think that work done in the Afrikaans language can offer something to the world? That it should be sensitive and open to questions and problems which are clearly all the more international and intercultural? Or rather, that you must deliver something which is 'own'? (And do you believe as well that that own egg must necessarily be separate and different from any other bloke's own?)[8]

This line of questioning exposed the deepest divisions among the various participants. While Smit made it clear that he would not be willing to write in such a way as to open up South Africa to 'a black majority at the cost of ourselves', Barnard, who admitted he had had no contact with black writers, declared that he 'believed in the task we have appointed for ourselves, and I believe in my people'.[9] Leroux's position was more nuanced. He recognized that 'a great writer is international' and cherished the humanistic ideal of professional solidarity. In an extraordinary premonition, he said to Breytenbach, who was imprisoned on terrorism charges in 1975, 'even if you and Lewis Nkosi and all the forsaken are in jail—we, as writers, are with you'.[10] At the same time, he continued to believe in the *volk*, whom he described as a stubborn 'desert people', and to defend his own style of 'resistance'.[11] Addressing Brink and Breytenbach, he asked: 'Why must you put my resistance on another level as escapism, a shirking behind esoteric symbols?'[12]

The most significant cleavage, then, was between Leroux, the internationalist who continued to believe in the viability of the *volk* avant-garde, as van Wyk Louw had defined it, and Breytenbach, who did not. Or, to refine Michael Walzer's terminology, it was between Breytenbach, the 'connected critic' who was ineluctably linked by history to the Afrikaner community but fundamentally opposed to its governing self-conception, and Leroux, who at that point remained what might more accurately be called an 'internal critic' of the

261

volk.[13] As Breytenbach, who would later describe himself as 'a Whitish Afrikaans-speaking South African African', asked Barnard: 'What have you got to lose except your Afrikanerness?'[14] Small and Brink agreed. Small, the leading black Afrikaans poet who would soon establish ties with the Black Consciousness movement, began his contribution by reflecting on van Wyk Louw's acerbically epigrammatic, self-reflexive poem 'Temporary Death of the Iambic Pentameter', which *Kol*'s editors had conspicuously placed on the first page of their first issue. Its opening lines referred to the 'task' (or 'duty') of the 'Afrikaners', albeit in an ironical, even calculatedly insulting way.

> Breeding boars and -sows (sired and unsired)
> each also has a task—just like Afrikaners.[15]

Small called this a 'valuable', even 'magnificent', piece of 'satire' because it went to the heart of their dispute, which was, he felt, fundamentally about how they ought to construe their situatedness as Afrikaans writers.[16] In his view, the two dominant models, which were not necessarily presented as alternatives, were inadequate. While he rejected Leroux's lofty, universalizing claim about writing for an 'invisible audience' from a 'bird's-eye view', he was equally sceptical about van Wyk Louw's more particularized idea of *lojale verset* and his continued attachment to the term 'Afrikaner'. 'I can understand loyal resistance. But why does V. W. L. want to be so loyal? Even I could write down other names in place of Afrikaners.'[17] This revealed another, more critical side to Small's subtle understanding of Louw's guiding assumptions. Brink, in turn, used his own final contribution to clarify what he meant by his initial call for his fellow Sestigers to 'write-open our country'. Rejecting Smit's fears about a 'black majority', and, indeed, his willingness to think 'in terms of "our little group of whites" as against "that black majority"', he said that 'if I talk of *my people*, then I mean: every person, black, coloured [*bruin*, or mixed-race] and white'. For Brink, in other words, the more inclusive name to substitute for 'Afrikaner' was 'South African'.[18]

The *Kol* debate did not, of course, settle the matters once and for all, particularly for Leroux, who became increasingly sympathetic to Breytenbach's position in the course of the 1970s. Yet the differences articulated in 1968 had a lasting effect on all the key participants' literary careers, not least because they affected their relationship to the institutions of the *volk* avant-garde, notably publishers and prizes. After struggling to make his way in the late 1950s, appearing under various relatively obscure Afrikaans imprints, Leroux finally established a secure association with the new literary publisher Human & Rousseau (H & R) in 1962. Indeed, since he remained on their list for the rest of his career, it could be argued that he became the definitive H & R author, unlike Brink, whose relationship with the leading publisher of the emergent *volk* avant-garde was, as we have seen, always more ambivalent. The same could be said for Breytenbach, whose position in the Afrikaans publishing world was, if anything, even more volatile than Brink's. In the space of five years, after his debut in 1964, he moved from Afrikaanse Pers-Boekhandel (APB) to H & R to the more marginal imprint Buren. With *Skryt* (1972), his sixth and most controversial volume of poems, the title of which plays on the homonymic link among the Afrikaans words for write, shit, and struggle, he abandoned the local publishing scene altogether and turned to his Dutch publisher Meulenhoff. After Buren closed down in 1975, he began a brief, unhappy liaison with APB's successor, the large conglomerate Perskor, before finally establishing a more permanent alliance with Taurus, the leading interventionist and self-consciously anti-*volk* Afrikaans publisher, who remained his primary outlet for the rest of the apartheid era.

The always controversial Hertzog Prize revealed another side to the complexities of the positions all three writers came to occupy in the Afrikaans literary world. Founded in 1915 and named in honour of J. B. M. Hertzog, who formed the National Party a year earlier, this highly politicized, state-sponsored award, which was intended to strengthen the link between Afrikaner nationalism, the language, and its literature, became the most prestigious *volk* accolade of the apartheid era. Van Wyk Louw was awarded it on five occasions. Unlike Brink and Breytenbach, Leroux won, and accepted, it twice: first for *Sewe Dae by die Silbersteins* in 1964 and then for *Magersfontein, O Magersfontein!* in 1979. These quasi-official endorsements were nonetheless always a source of contention, particularly between the literary avant-garde, many of whom served as prize judges for the award, and the more conservative political, cultural, and religious forces within the *volk*. On each occasion that Leroux won the Hertzog, for instance, a predictably vociferous public controversy ensued. It was partly as a consequence of these divisions that some of H. F. Verwoerd's supporters established the abortive Verwoerd Prize for Fatherland Literature (later called the Republic Prize) in 1968. It was apparently awarded only once, to a Professor S. A. Louw for his *Afrikaanse Taalatlas* (Afrikaans Language Atlas) in 1971.

That Breytenbach was repeatedly passed over by the guardians of the Hertzog generated a very different kind of controversy. In 1971, when he was overlooked for a second time, all the major Sestigers, including Brink, Leroux, and the other participants in the *Kol* debate, wrote a letter to the press denouncing the decision as 'laughable' and declaring it an 'attack on the integrity of our literature'.[19] For his own part, Breytenbach, who dismissed the prize as a 'tribal decoration', called on all Afrikaans writers to abandon 'the whole concept of Afrikaner literary awards'.[20] Unsurprisingly, when he finally won the Hertzog in 1984 for *Yk* (To Approve, but also a play on 'Ek', Afrikaans for 'I'), his fifth Taurus book, he refused it. Brink never had the opportunity to make the same gesture because, for all his many national and international accolades—he was shortlisted for the Booker in 1976 and 1978—the Hertzog always eluded him.

Like Breytenbach and Leroux, he did, however, win the Afrikaans CNA Award more than once. Between 1961, when it was launched, and 1990, Breytenbach in fact won the white liberal–literary establishment's most prominent prize four times, Brink three times, and Leroux twice. Unlike J. M. Coetzee, all three writers appeared not to be especially concerned about the politics of this award, which was at least not state-sponsored (see Chapter 8). Yet even in this sector of the local 'economy of prestige', to borrow James English's phrase, Breytenbach provoked controversy.[21] In 1967 the Prime Minister, B. J. Vorster, attempted unsuccessfully to block the award going to *Huis van die Dowe* (House of the Deaf), Breytenbach's second volume of poems, which H & R had published on D. J. Opperman's recommendation. Opperman, the leading poet and senior figure in the *volk* avant-garde, who was then H & R's principal reader, also happened to be one of the key CNA prize judges that year. Demonstrating the tensions characteristic of the Afrikaans literary world at the time, he wrote an apologetic letter to Vorster after the award was announced, explaining that the judges were asked to use '*purely literary*' criteria and not to assess the 'person'.[22] A year later Opperman made his position public by signing an open letter in which H & R distanced themselves from what they called Breytenbach's 'drastic politics'.[23] It was this statement that finally persuaded Breytenbach to sever all connections with the firm. In the years ahead he even refused H & R permission to reprint some of his earlier APB titles.

The fortunes of all three writers in the English-language publishing world were no less revealing of their very different situations. As a 'world author' in English, Brink once again occupied a position that was historically and culturally between Breytenbach and Leroux. After he became concerned about what he saw as W. H. Allen's declining prestige in the 1970s, he moved, as we saw in Chapter 2, to Faber with *A Chain of Voices* in 1982. In effect, he switched allegiance from Leroux's British publisher to the firm that would become Breytenbach's principal English-language outlet in the mid-1980s. Like Brink, Leroux was initially published in English as part of the short-lived Centaur Books series, which the CNA launched in 1964 following the success of *Sewe Dae*. In 1968, however, W. H. Allen, using the same translations, launched his international career with the trilogy of novels comprising *Seven Days* (1968), *The Third Eye* (1969), and *One for the Devil* (1969). This trilogy was subsequently reprinted in one volume, albeit in the wrong order, under the title *To a Dubious Salvation*, as a Penguin Modern Classic in 1972 with a laudatory blurb by Graham Greene, an event that marked the high point and end of Leroux's international acclaim. By contrast, Breytenbach made his name in the Anglophone world in the last decade of the apartheid era. Though his literary reputation began to grow in the late 1970s when David Philip, Rex Collings, John Calder, and Jonathan Cape brought out translations of his poetry, it was finally assured when Faber published his semi-novelistic testimony *Mouroir* (a play on Mirror, and possibly also Murder) and his prison autobiography, *The True Confessions of an Albino Terrorist*, in 1984.

Leroux, the Kerk, and the Censors

Leroux's status as a more acceptable, because internal, critic of the *volk* was clearly manifest in the way the censors responded to his work. Given the comparison with Breytenbach, it is telling that only one of the four novels they scrutinized, *Isis, Isis, Isis* (1969), was submitted by the police. The other three entered the system as a consequence of complaints from morally affronted individual readers who were usually responding to more orchestrated campaigns by Afrikaner church groups. With the exception of *Ysterkoei* (Iron-cow) and *Skryt*, the seven Breytenbach titles submitted came either via customs or via the police.

Though it is not clear precisely how the censors justified their decision to pass Leroux's *Sewe Dae* in early 1965—there are a number of gaps in the record—the general direction of their thinking is clear enough. That the novel reached them three years after it was first published and seven months after it won the Hertzog was itself significant. The accolade not only boosted its sales, which went up from just fewer than 2,000 copies in its first two years to 10,993 in 1964 alone, it provoked a heated public dispute principally between leading Afrikaner literary intellectuals, notably van Wyk Louw, and the NGK, who saw it as a morally subversive work of 'darkness'.[24] As guardians of the *volk* avant-garde, the censors' position within this internal struggle was defined in advance, though it was made all the more delicate because A. P. Grové had been one of the judges who recommended Leroux for the Hertzog. He voted for the novel again as a censor, and had a considerable influence over the outcome, but he tactfully absented himself from the Board meeting at which the final decision was taken.

No doubt deliberately, the novel was first sent to the key non-literary censors, Murray and Endemann, who were not of the same mind about it. Murray, the initial reader, focused exclusively on the 'treatment of sexual passion or the sexual act', noting that the 'theme might be distasteful for the South African—or for the Afrikaner' (BCS 224/65). However, he felt that the 'situation is in no way unnatural and is not described in a cheap manner'. *Sewe Dae* was clearly a work of considerable literary 'quality', which displayed 'not a trace of pornographic treatment'. Endemann disagreed. 'The theme is in my view not only distasteful for the average Afrikaner', he noted, 'but the scenes and musings about sex are overdone' and designed to 'titillate the reader'. Just which parts of the novel he had in mind is not clear—the surviving report does not contain the usual detailed page references—but there is little doubt that he would have been concerned about the orgy that marks the final stage in the central figure's surrealistic seven-day initiation. This occurs in the sixth chapter, called 'Walpurgisnacht', which self-consciously recalls Goethe's *Faust* and, as a consequence, the German version of the pagan festivities where witches commune with their gods. In Leroux's characteristically Jungian lexicon this is the moment in which the innocent van Eeden (the name says it all) comes to terms with what one character calls 'the neglected shadow'.[25] Following the novel's elaborately over-determined allegory, this carnivalesque orgy prepares the young individualist for his own dubiously Faustian pact with the Silberstein estate, a microcosm of the apartheid order and the debased modernity of which it forms a part.

No other reports on the novel seem to have survived, but all four literary censors—Dekker, Grové, Harvey, and Merwe Scholtz—agreed unequivocally with Murray. In the absence of their detailed comments, it is impossible to say what, if anything, they made of the novel's potential political significance, which was very much at the heart of the larger public controversy it caused. While the NGK was concerned that 'subversive books' like *Sewe Dae* were part of a 'liberal and Communist infiltration' designed to undermine 'true Afrikaans cultural values', some of Leroux's supporters, notably Henriette Grové (wife of the censor), defended it not on aesthetic grounds but in terms of its supposedly transparent message.[26] She felt it was about van Eeden's struggle to find his way in a world which is being 'menaced by evil forces' such as 'communism' and 'racial mixing'.[27] For all Leroux's impatience with the political pieties of the left and of the right, this reading is difficult to reconcile with the novel's absurdist parody of apartheid as a sacred, two-tone bull called Brutus, 'raised to the glory of all South Africa', or, indeed, with a figure like Professor Dreyer.[28] A mad scientist, a cuckold, and a buffoon, Dreyer is also the novel's most ardent champion of the 'colour-bar'.[29]

About the literary censors' response to *Die Derde Oog* (The Third Eye, 1966), the final novel in Leroux's trilogy, it is possible to be more precise because Dekker's own seven-page chair's report survived. Like the secretary of the NGK's Commission for Public Morals, the individual complainant who submitted the novel, which she claimed not to have read, saw it as a 'threat to volk mores' (BCS 130/66). Summarizing the censors' response, Dekker relied mainly on the aestheticist defence characteristic of the *volk* avant-garde. 'The evil circumstances and immorality which the author uncovers with Swiftian satire are never represented fully or with delight,' he noted, and the book was, in any case, never 'obscene or pornographic'. Moreover, 'to lift passages out of their context from a misunderstood artwork and to claim they are immoral or blasphemous' was, he insisted, 'a dangerous method that can cause great damage to our literature and to the intellectual life of our *volk*'. In his more detailed remarks, however, Dekker acknowledged that the novel put these criteria under some pressure both morally and politically. 'Almost without exception the main characters live a life of sexual dissipation and drunkenness,' he noted. This included 'the whole D-service, with its homophilic young men and easy compliant girls', which was 'an obvious satire on our Secret Service'. In the novel the head of the Service states that he is charged with protecting 'the community against spiritual crime, against the degeneration of the self, against the subtle onslaught on order'.[30] Dekker went on: 'Even the Captain [the would-be hero, de Goede] cheerfully plays along. His wife, Hope, is an insatiable nymphomaniac who pressurizes her husband into having sex in the presence of the children. Gudenov [the apparently villainous tycoon] is impotent, with perverse tendencies, of which Iole [his mistress] is the victim.' With her 'selfless love for Gudenov', Iole was, Dekker felt, the 'one exception' in this decadent world in which the line between sexual perversion and consumerism is deliberately blurred. He did not mention that she is also the only character directly involved in subversive anti-apartheid activities.

To address these difficulties at the level of content he shifted from a broadly aestheticist defence to a more specific argument from genre. Like the second novel in the trilogy, *Een vir Azazel* (One for the Devil, 1964), *Derde Oog* had all the 'allure of a detective story'. 'The transfer of the detective captain Demosthenes H. de Goede to the D-service, where he is given the assignment to track down the "dog" Gudenov, the secrecy in which this figure is shrouded whose existence everyone feels even though no one actually knows him, Gudenov's decision to destroy his pursuer'—all these and other features meant it might appeal to the 'ordinary sensation-seeking detective story reader'. Yet *Derde Oog* was 'really an extremely complicated idea-novel' in which 'the author gives his vision of humanity and society in our time, the struggle between good and evil in the form of a modern reworking of the Greek Hercules-myth linked to the modern "myths" of the tycoon, the sex-goddess Bee-Bee-Do and the "Shopping Centre"'.

On Dekker's analysis the central problematic of Leroux's 'idea-novel' turned on two versions of the Hercules myth. In one, derived from Sophocles' *Women of Trachis*, he is represented as 'someone who relies on himself and who is half withdrawn from ordinary humanity'; in the other, based on Euripides' *Hercules Furens*, he is 'a man of the *volk*'. Following his Joycean method, Leroux transposed these two faces of Hercules onto his central figures. Whereas Boris Gudenov, a South African-born Jewish business tycoon, is the Sophocles type, de Goede, who is described as the 'South African hero par excellence', plays the Euripidean part.[31] Though Dekker felt that the novel's 'governing conception' was 'not totally clear', he had little doubt about the broader significance of its overall plot. He noted that de Goede's quest to reveal the truth about Gudenov ends in disaster. In a 'fit of madness' he gets into a car chase with the tycoon's Rolls Royce, causing it to crash into a chasm, only to discover that he has 'not killed the hated enemy but his own family'. Moreover, the Brigadier who assigns de Goede his task and who functions as something of an 'oracle' in the novel 'comes to realize that Gudenov has wrongly been seen to be the enemy'. Indeed, according to Dekker, the novel showed that Gudenov and de Goede 'were only each other's opposites' and that 'the good and the evil cannot be separated'. Tellingly, for Dekker, the novel's 'existentialistically coloured wisdom', again evident in the Brigadier's oracular declaration 'God is dead', saved it from being reduced to a simple political satire. Even though the pathologically paranoid D-service 'undoubtedly' had a specific local resonance—he did not consider the possibility that the censors themselves might have been among Leroux's targets—he felt it also 'symbolizes society's powerless struggle against spiritual crimes which in its anesthetized and hypocritical state it tries to locate as a power outside itself until it discovers that they are a product of its own mistaken notions'.

There was less room for any uncertainty about the implied political significance of *Magersfontein, O Magersfontein!* (1976), the fourth Leroux novel the censors scrutinized. (No documents relating to *Isis* appear to have survived.) The quotation Leroux chose to use as an epigraph for *Magersfontein* comes from an inept speech a government minister gives in the epilogue to the novel. Trying to raise the spirits of a dejected local crowd, who have just experienced a devastating flood during which most of the novel's principal characters drown, the Minister strikes a patriotic note, recalling the heroic victory of the Boer forces against the British at the battle of Magersfontein in 1899. 'As in the past, each man shall show his steel', says the Minister. 'I have faith in my *volk*.'[32] For the reader, the absurdity of the Minister's rhetoric, which does not go down well with the crowd, is underscored a few paragraphs later when he comments on the 'international company that has, in collaboration with our own organizations, undertaken a film and television project'.[33] The novel, which has an explicit metafictional quality, centres on this endeavour to represent the famous Boer War battle on a site in the small town of Magersfontein. As the wry narrator comments early on, the project represents an 'attempt, against the background of a tragic-comic event in the past, to reflect on our own time via a modern medium of communication'.[34] Referring to this venture, the Minister confidently remarks: 'I have complete faith that they have given an objective portrayal, and that there has been no sensationalized exploitation of what is dear to us.'[35] Needless to say, as the project is led by a pair of British aristocrats, Lord Sudden, who is partially blind, and Lord Seldom, who is partially deaf, and constantly hampered by a ragbag of equally absurd local assistants, things have not quite turned out the way the Minister believes. Though the novel, which is at its most serious about the meaning of history, does not lose sight of the honourable aspects of the battle, it focuses on the many ways in which its contemporary significance is deformed by contingency, confusion, and misunderstanding, or manipulated, for political and other ends, by blindness, opportunism, and folly.

FIG. 6.1. The front cover of the first edition of Etienne Leroux's *Magersfontein, O Magersfontein!* (1976), which became the focus of public controversy in the late 1970s, contributing to a further reform of the censorship system.

None of this was lost on the literary committee that was convened under the new 1974 legislation to decide the novel's fate. As Merwe Scholtz, the chair, noted at the end of his own report: 'That the satire ends with a pretty dismal piece of symbolism, namely a sort of Deluge followed by the abortively rousing speech by the Minister which is received with "silence and no applause" by the assembled crowd, is a conclusion that is all the more inevitable, given the way things develop in this very important novel' (P 77/1/97). He also recognized that it was a work of 'committed literature', though one not 'committed in the ranting, hysterical manner of pamphlet reading'. Etienne Malan, who, along with Anna Louw, also submitted an individual reader's report, acknowledged that 'high-placed' state officials might 'on a first glance feel bitterly offended at the way they were represented', but, as the novel did not name specific individuals, he did not feel it was seditious. Moreover, he felt there were good cultural reasons for passing a sophisticated literary 'satire' in which 'much use is made of irony, parody, allegory, mockery and simple joking about'. 'One of the distinguishing marks of a *volk*'s maturity', he claimed, 'is that it can tolerate mockery of its highest dignitaries, of its community values and of various holy cows, even if this sometimes brings displeasure.' Anna Louw, who tended to be an exuberant over-reader, was less confident about the novel's political resonances as it was 'difficult to say just what symbolic meaning could be attached to the flood: Black nationalism? Communism? An act of Providence? Or simply Hieronymo gone completely mad this time?' She was, however, in no doubt that it was 'in a certain sense a cry of despair about the current state of Western culture'.

With the memory of the controversy surrounding Leroux in the 1960s still very much alive, however, all three readers focused primarily on the potentially pornographic, blasphemous, or racist aspects of the novel, and all acknowledged that there was much that might be considered 'undesirable' in this regard. Malan believed that Leroux could 'easily have made less use of the word "fuck" and its equivalents', and all remarked on the fact that the novel included some 'shocking' materials: a masturbating Member of Parliament, a traffic policeman who recklessly fires his revolver when he achieves orgasm, a drug-taking young woman whose only often-repeated words are 'Jesus Christ', a 'Coloured' who regularly uses racist slurs and who refers to whites as 'white kaffers'—to name only the most obvious.[36] All nonetheless agreed that these features were acceptable either because they were not described in any explicit detail or because they were in some sense functional. In his individual report Merwe Scholtz took the argument further by drawing attention to the allowances specifically afforded to Leroux as a satirist. In his 'sustained satirical assault' Leroux had 'as it were a permit or passport, like the Greek comedy writers of old, which allowed more freedom of speech'. Developing a point he also made in his final chair's report, he explained that this was 'because everything is set up in advance through a particular perspective, "weaned" of its immediacy by what can be called the "double vision" of the satirist: the satirical representation is simultaneously "schematized" and sharper, more direct'. This made it 'almost impossible for example to consider a satirical treatment of sex as steamy or titillating'. He cited as an illustration the novel's single episode of sexual intercourse, in which the traffic policeman fires his revolver and, as a consequence, unintentionally wounds the film logistics expert who happens to be in the room next door.[37] For all these reasons, the committee concluded the novel could not be banned, a decision the chief censor accepted.

This was in January 1977. Six months later, after it was announced that *Magersfontein* had won the CNA Award, a pressure group linked to the leading Afrikaner churches (Action Moral Standards) initiated a campaign to get the Minister of the Interior to invoke his powers under the Act to have the decision overturned by the new Appeal Board. This was undoubtedly the most vociferous and concerted campaign against a particular book in the history of apartheid censorship. The timing was not fortuitous, since, as Leroux's publisher Koos Human recalled, the National Party was then fighting for re-election.[38] The Minister duly intervened and, as a consequence, the novel was banned on the grounds of obscenity and blasphemy on 21 November 1977, nine days before the Nationalists were once again returned to power by the white electorate. For all its conservative populist appeal, however, this decision, as we saw in Chapter 1, created a damaging rift among the Afrikaner elite. By siding with the moral pressure groups, the Church, and the politicians, the Appeal Board, under the elderly judge J. L. Snyman, alienated a wide spectrum of Afrikaans literary intellectuals from the collaborationist Writers' Circle to the dissident Guild. It also exposed the divisions within the censorship system, which the new anti-elitist and explicitly pro-Christian legislation introduced in 1975 was intended to overcome. In his ruling, Snyman expressly invoked the legal fiction of the 'average man', insisting, not without legal basis, that the 'literary experts were in conflict with the Act'.[39] In saying this he had in mind not only the members of the literary committee who made the initial decision but the additional experts called to advise the Appeal Board and, indeed, A. P. Grové, who, as a member of the Board, submitted a minority report rejecting the decision primarily on aestheticist grounds.

After the ban, key figures within the *volk* avant-garde continued to support Leroux publicly. While Merwe Scholtz and Anna Louw resigned as censors, H & R attempted unsuccessfully and at considerable cost to have the decision overturned by the Supreme Court in 1978. The following year Grové and Merwe Scholtz provoked a further controversy when they led a counter-campaign to recognize the novel's literary status, and to reassert the authority of the *volk* avant-garde, by ensuring that it was belatedly awarded the Hertzog Prize. As a result, *Magersfontein* had the odd distinction of being the only banned prizewinning Afrikaans novel of the apartheid era. Significantly, in his report on the novel as chair of the prize committee, a copy of which he ensured was deposited in the relevant censorship file, Merwe Scholtz not only drew attention to its literary importance and to the generic conventions of satire as set out in Roger Fowler's *Dictionary of Modern Critical Terms* (1973). He downplayed its status as a piece of 'committed literature', focusing instead on the universality of its *moral* vision. He did so by referring in detail to a scene in which the narrator comments caustically on the disrespect shown by Scottish housing developers to the memory of Major-General Andrew Wauchope, 'the darling of Scotland' who was killed at Magersfontein. Recalling that his house and family church were demolished in the 1960s, the narrator observes that 'there is not a single Boer whose house was burnt down seventy-five years ago, who would welcome this revenge'.[40] For Merwe Scholtz, the significance of this was clear. By linking the 'violation of the House of Wauchope' to the 'complete lack of respect the film crew generally shows towards the heroism of Magersfontein', the novel demonstrated that 'the dishonouring of the past is part of the general scheme of things'.

What he left out, of course, was the most pertinent point of the novel's wide-ranging satire: namely, that it was the political leaders of the *volk* in the 1970s who were doing most damage to the honourable aspects of Afrikaner history. This may, however, have been implied in his conclusion, where he remarked that 'satire has always been in the service of right and justice; as such it is a morally healthy literary kind'. When the ban was eventually lifted in March 1980, J. C. W. van Rooyen's more pragmatic Appeal Board made use of the new provisions under the amended censorship legislation by taking advice from a committee of literary experts, which, unsurprisingly, Merwe Scholtz chaired. Among the other key members were W. E. G. Louw, brother of van Wyk Louw, F. C. Fensham, chair of the Writers' Circle, Elize Botha, a member of the Hertzog committee, and Anna Louw. For the opening section of his final chair's report Merwe Scholtz simply reused the text he had written for the Hertzog award, emphasizing the novel's moral value and the universality of its central theme.

Breytenbach, the Broederbond, and the Censors

The censors scrutinized two Breytenbach titles in the 1980s: *The True Confessions of an Albino Terrorist* in its Dutch and British editions (van Gennep and Faber, 1984), and *End Papers*, a collection of miscellaneous writings published by Faber in 1986. All three books were passed by literary committees who simply applied the guidelines relating to protest writing, likely readership, and literary merit that were codified after the *Magersfontein* crisis. Of the three titles examined during the most draconian censorship period in the mid-1970s, however, only *'n Seisoen in die Paradys* (A Season in Paradise,

1976), which Breytenbach published in a self-censored Afrikaans version under the pseudonym B. B. Lazarus, escaped banning. This was, as the blurb announced, emphasizing its generic indeterminacy, his 'report, account, diary, story' of his three-month visit to South Africa in 1973.[41] The more authoritative and complete English edition, first published by Jonathan Cape in 1980, appears never to have been submitted.

In his comments as chair of the committee for *Seisoen*, Merwe Scholtz drew attention to the section called 'A View from Outside', Breytenbach's critique of the Sestigers, which he originally gave as a talk at a literary festival during his visit and which had, Scholtz noted, already been published in the press (P77/1/31). This was, he claimed, both a 'high point' and the most worrying in terms of its 'implications for state security'. About other aspects of the volume he commented that it was

> naturally not pleasant to have to hear that the N. G. Kerk in South Africa has nothing to be proud of (151); or to read about 'game parks for the country's animals | homelands for domesticated people', about 'a native, an inner exile', about the unsettling 'my country my country o bloody anus | and the love like a hard body in my body' (167–8).

Nevertheless, he felt such passages could not be used to justify a ban. Though 'many of the things Breytenbach unsettles' would 'indeed be disturbing to tens of thousands', there were 'many, among them also Afrikaners and Nationalist politicians and other functionaries, who are looking for a way to another dispensation'. 'One does not have to be a dissident', he added, 'to see the "Cape to Rio" [yacht] race starting on the near side of Robben Island as a painful contrast.' After consulting the security censors, the literary committee, which included Malan and Anna Louw, agreed to let *Seisoen* through.

The two exceptions were *Skryt* (1972) and Breytenbach's first collection of poems translated into English, *And Death White as Words* (1978), which included many poems from the earlier volume. Whereas *And Death*, which was co-published by David Philip and Rex Collings, was submitted by the police, *Skryt* was sent in by an offended individual reader. The earlier volume contained various materials, including a series of potentially obscene drawings, but the censors focused almost exclusively on two texts: the major poem entitled 'Letter from Foreign Parts to Butcher', which bore the dedication 'For [or To] Balthazar'; and an untitled poetic memorial, which began with the inscription 'since 1963 the following prisoners had, at the hands of the security police, to give birth to their deaths'.[42] It then listed eighteen names, among them Imam Abdullah Haron and Looksmart Solwandle Ngudle, followed by the phrase 'we shall remember'. In fact, the final decision to ban *Skryt* eventually turned on a narrow series of abstruse, not to say scholastic, questions to do with the referentiality (or otherwise) of poetic language. The key participants in this curiously rarefied debate were Merwe Scholtz, who chaired the original committee; T. T. Cloete, the poet–censor; G. S. Nienaber, another Afrikaans literary professor; two key security censors, Murray and Jansen; and, less predictably, André Brink, who became involved when he tried unsuccessfully to appeal against the ban at Breytenbach's request.

Given the vexed nature of the problems involved, the final outcome was, perhaps unsurprisingly, far from inevitable. When the complaint against *Skryt* was first made in February 1975—that is, seven months before Breytenbach was arrested on terrorism charges—Merwe Scholtz argued firmly against imposing a ban. After having received a complaint from one individual (J. M. van Tonder of Pretoria), it was, he said, not only 'totally pointless' but 'dangerous' to suppress a volume that had been 'seriously in contention for the Hertzog Prize' and that was 'almost unobtainable' in South Africa (P75/4/23). Doing so 'could be reinterpreted as an admission of guilt: which we are certainly not called upon to do'. Moreover, even though some of the 'textual parts', including the 'gravestone' and 'Letter', 'are admittedly not always good poetry, they are poetry'. To see this, he suggested, one had only to compare Breytenbach's descriptions of torture to those in Brink's *Looking on Darkness*: 'Brink's are a weak, even romanticized "paraphrase" of what is communicated here with all the density of poetry.' True, the 'dedication "for Balthazar", makes it a little more difficult: it is clear who the first name is intended to strike'. Yet it would, in his view, be 'oversensitive' to see this as a reason for banning. As he noted, Brink had launched a similarly personalized attack on the Prime Minister, whose full name was Balthazar Johannes Vorster, in his drama *Pavane* (1974), which had not been banned. Nienaber was more concerned about what he called the 'poisonous' postscript by the Dutch critic H. C. van ten Berge and the numerous 'extremely hostile' poems, but in the end he also took a pragmatic line, albeit a more patronizing one. Breytenbach was, he claimed, 'a naughty boy who was looking for attention' and so banning the volume would simply play into his hands.

That T. T. Cloete led the counter-argument was significant. In the early 1970s he had, as I noted in Chapter 2, written a Broederbond paper attacking the new generation of anti-*volk* dissidents. As Galloway comments, this paper, which came to light in the early 1980s, singled out Brink and Breytenbach as writers 'who envisage ending and even violently destroying white minority rule in South Africa; who reject Christian worship and morality and even blaspheme against God, and who champion absolute sexual freedom'.[43] In the same paper, Cloete also mounted an aestheticist critique of 'committed literature', and this, too, informed his response to *Skryt*. In his view, eight of the twenty poems in the volume, most from the first section, ambiguously entitled 'Coloured Verse', 'posed problems' on either political or religious grounds, or both. Though he noted that the line 'we shall remember' in the untitled poetic memorial alluded to a canonical poem by C. Louis Leipoldt, a leading Afrikaner poet of the early twentieth century, he felt the 'poem', as he disdainfully put it, not only amounted to a 'glorification of subversive elements' but 'showed how little the poet cares for poetry when it comes to declaring his political sentiments'. 'Letter' was even more worrying in this regard, not just because it made reference to police torture, but because the 'dedication "for Balthazar" surely refers to the current Prime Minister'. Such a reading was, Cloete suggested, 'evident from the rest of the poem'. The stanza 'I stand on bricks' made 'a clear reference to the case of [Ahmed] Timol', given the wordplay on Timol–*tuimel* in the line 'tuimel uit die tiende verdieping van die hemel' ('tumble out of the tenth storey of heaven'). 'Everything in the poem comes down to the fact that the current Prime Minister is responsible for what happened to Timol, above all because he is called "Butcher"',' Cloete concluded. Later, in a subsequent letter to the chief censor written after he heard that Brink was going to appeal, he confirmed this, citing a Flemish academic article which mentioned that Breytenbach had originally called the poem 'Letter from One Exile to Vorster, the Butcher'.

The security censors did not need much persuasion to follow Cloete's line of argument. Indeed, Jansen, a fellow member of the Broederbond, came to the same conclusion about 'Letter' and the collection as a whole as did Murray. It was only Merwe Scholtz who found the emerging consensus difficult to accept, as his second, more detailed reader's report revealed. He remained committed to the view that Breytenbach was the best Afrikaans poet of his generation and, like Cloete, he recognized that *Skryt* contained 'good poems', albeit ones of 'uneven quality'. Nonetheless, he now agreed with many of Cloete's remarks and accepted that ten Berge's postscript, which described Breytenbach as a proponent of 'engaged art', 'gave a fairly reliable indication of the "climate" of at least a part of the volume'. About 'Letter' he was, after some second thoughts, more circumspect—he added all the qualifications, which I have represented in italics, in pen after typing his report. Though he agreed that it was 'extremely crude', he felt it was only '*fairly* clear' that it referred to the Prime Minister, and he argued that the conclusion carried '*only the implication of* a call to bloody uprising'. In his view, the committee had to make an 'extremely difficult and responsible decision', partly because banning the volume three years after it had been published abroad risked giving it undue 'publicity and thereby defeating the purposes of the Act'. This, of course, is one of the inescapable paradoxes of censorship.

The other 'problem' was that, in a country in which there were inevitably 'fierce differences of opinion', ' "protest poetry" did not come from only one side of the resistance'. To demonstrate this he cited a number of sharply critical poems by N. P. van Wyk Louw and D. J. Opperman. Looking at the issues from a different angle, he then asked, 'is there really, in principle a difference between Breytenbach's "argument" and those we encounter daily in newspapers or magazines or conversations?' 'One difference was', he acknowledged, 'strikingly clear: with Breytenbach we get a dramatized, highly emotional staging of a position, and the issue no longer has two or more sides: the framework is revolutionary and outspokenly anti-white.' Though the literary censors were, as we have seen, generally committed to a 'message-minus' conception of poetic language, this was more consistent with a 'message-plus' definition, according to which literary or poetic language was a more effective vehicle of communication than so-called ordinary language. In the end, after much self-questioning, he concluded 'with hesitation' that the powerful political message of the poems could not be gainsaid, particularly in the 'dangerous year of 1975'. Returning to his 'message-minus' assumptions, he finally conceded that a ban was unavoidable because 'some' of the poems lacked the requisite 'aesthetic distance' and read 'like winged pamphlets', or 'direct statements from a person who often shows himself as his "own I" (no "poetic" I) in his verse'. In his chair's report, however, he noted that the committee gave particular 'consideration' to Cloete's arguments.

In July 1975, soon after the ban was announced, Breytenbach asked Brink to appeal under the new legislation. Throughout the subsequent process, which dragged on for three months, Brink was unaware of the precise reasons for the committee's decision. He was simply told that the volume had been banned under all three political clauses and on the grounds of blasphemy because of the two 'undesirable' poems. His detailed sixteen-page defence focused on a series legal, evidential, and interpretive questions. He gave a carefully argued critique of the contradictions regarding likely readership that were written into the censorship laws, and, unlike the censors, he cited substantial evidence about *Skryt*'s actual readership. Using figures obtained from booksellers and publishers, he established that in three years only 500 copies had been imported into the country—100 by the publisher Buren—confirming that the 'reading public for Breytenbach's work had on the whole always been limited to a small group of highly educated intellectuals, mainly university lecturers and students'. This evidence formed the basis of his larger argument that a 'published work is first activated when it is read', a point that reflected Brink's indebtedness to the basic tenets of 1970s reception theory.

Working from these premises he questioned the committee's appeal to certain self-evident 'facts' about the poems. Concerning 'Letter', for instance, he argued that it 'would be obtuse to interpret the poem simply as a pamphleteering protest-poem against Mr. B. J. Vorster', since Breytenbach's likely readers would see that the reference to 'Balthazar' was also a biblical allusion to the 'tyrannical' Belshazzar in Daniel 5. 'In this sense Breytenbach's poem could also be interpreted as revolt against violence and autocracy in general, a sort of "writing on the wall", before it is too late.' Taking a more broadly contextualist approach, and unintentionally echoing Merwe Scholtz's argument, he insisted that even if the poem was read in 'specifically South

African terms', it could not be considered 'undesirable' because Breytenbach's readers would recognize he formed part of a tradition of writing that had 'become wholly acceptable in our literature'. To support this claim he referred to his own *Pavane*, to various protest poems by younger Afrikaans writers, and to van Wyk Louw's accusatory early poem 'You are the Oppressors'.° '*Skryt* was published in a specific context and it is necessary to keep the relevant reading public constituting that context in mind', he concluded, since 'there was no way they could be shocked or offended by anything in the volume.'

Brink's ambitiously subtle defence was, however, overtaken by events. After being arrested in August 1975, Breytenbach was tried on terrorism charges and given a nine-year prison sentence at the end of November. When Snyman, then chair of the Appeal Board, was informed that the prosecutors were intending to use *Skryt* as evidence to support their case, placing it effectively *sub judice*, he felt he had no choice but to suspend the appeal. In the years ahead, Brink's arguments were not forgotten, however. When a literary committee decided to ban *And Death White as Words* on the same grounds as *Skryt* in January 1979, Etienne Malan referred back to Brink's defence in his chair's report, if only to reject it out of hand. Focusing on 'Letter', which he considered the 'most contentious' of the eight poems singled out by the committee, he remarked that the claim about its general application 'does not impress' (P78/12/30). He felt it was 'interesting to note' that both Brink and Ampie Coetzee, the critic and co-founder of Taurus who wrote an introduction to the English volume, had tried to use this 'excuse'. Clearly taking a little too much pleasure in his own erudition, he remarked that the 'commentator on p. 178 has, deliberately or erroneously, chosen to associate Mr. Vorster's name with that of the cruel tyrant Belshazzar of *Daniel 5:1*, and not that of the prophet Daniel himself, to whom the name Belteshazzar (the difference in spelling will be noted) was given (*Daniel 1:7* and *5:12*)'.

For Malan, the committee, and, indeed, Rita Scholtz, the initial reader, the poem was 'a venomous, vicious and libellous *ad hominem* attack, with none of the grandeur and scope of classical poetic anathema', which 'gives a distorted version of the alleged maltreatment or torture of prisoners for which it blames the "butcher" Balthazar'. While recognizing that the volume 'often contains material of a decided literary value' and that its likely readership was 'limited', factors which Malan noted had recently been given a new importance following the *Magersfontein* case, the committee concluded that *And Death* had to be banned primarily because it was 'calculated to extol and pay homage to the person of Breyten Breytenbach who is at present serving a sentence in jail for one of the most serious statutory crimes in the law'. At no point in his report did Malan mention that during his trial Breytenbach issued a formal apology to Vorster, in which he called 'Letter' 'a crass and insulting poem'.[44] The chief censor considered appealing against the committee's decision, primarily so that the volume could be put before the Appeal Board's new committee of literary experts. After consulting his colleagues, however, he decided against the idea, as a consequence of which *And Death*, like *Skryt*, remained banned for the rest of the apartheid era.

7
BLAC BOOKS, BLACK
(ANTI-)POETICS

Mongane Serote's debut volume *Yakhal'inkomo* (The Cry of the Cattle, 1972) ends with 'Black Bells', a visually arresting, self-consciously disjointed free-verse poem about the anguish of being caught in a double trap. As the poet–speaker acknowledges, the first snare is universal:

> WORDS,
> Like thought are elusive,
> Like life,
> Where everybody is trapped.[1]

The second, however, is peculiar to him (assuming the 'I' is Serote himself) since, in his case, the problem lies not just with the intractability of words as such. The language with which he is struggling is not even his own. It does not take him long to name the agent of his undoing in this second sense: 'Who. and Whitey | Trapped me.'[2] This recognition, which initially leaves him feeling dejected, soon provokes an explosive reaction:

> I know I'm trapped.
> Helpless
> Hopeless
> You've trapped me whitey! Meem wanna ge aot Fuc
> Pschwee e ep booobooodubbooboodu blllll[3]

Just as he threatens to abandon words altogether by resorting to pure sound and ultimately non-sense, he pulls back, hinting at the possibility of a more promising way out: 'Black books, | Flesh blood words shitrrr Haai, | Amen.'[4] As *A Dictionary of South African English* comments, 'Haai', a derivative of the isiXhosa word for 'no' (*hayi*), often functions as a phatic exclamation in South African English 'expressing fellow-feeling in conversation'.[5]

Metapoetic reflections of this kind were by no means unusual among the generation of poets inspired by the Black Consciousness movement in the early 1970s. What distinguishes 'Black Bells' is the inventiveness and urgency with which it articulates the political, cultural, and poetic struggles at the heart of that larger project. At one level the trap 'Whitey' represents is linguistic and literary. As the guardian of the dominant culture, its language, norms, and literary forms, he is the adversary Serote has to overcome by evolving a new, visceral ('Flesh blood') poetic language of his own. Hence the force of the word-sound 'shitrrr' in the penultimate line, which refers back to the earlier poem 'What's in this Black "Shit"'. In that self-avowedly anti-polite poem the poet–speaker affirms his power to curse, a power arising not from any cerebral sense of outrage but from 'the upheaval of the bowels'. Reflecting some of the larger generational issues at stake, this disruptive, unpredictable energy enables him to defy white officials in a way his 'father wouldn't dare do'.[6] At another level, however, as the reference to 'Black books' suggests, the trap 'Whitey' has set is more generally cultural. If the way out is to invent a new Black aesthetic, or, in this case, a distinctively Black poetic, it is also to establish control over the entire process of cultural production. Seen in these terms, *Yakhal'inkomo* was itself a manifestation of the predicament Serote was describing. It was first published by Renoster Books, an offshoot of the little magazine the *Purple Renoster*, a short-lived, seriously undercapitalized literary imprint co-founded by Lionel Abrahams and Robert and Eva Royston in 1971. The problem was not just that *Yakhal'inkomo* was effectively a white book, but that it presented the reader with two very different versions of Serote's poetic persona and poetry, the first contained in the author's prefatory note explaining the significance of the collection's title, the second in the publishers' blurb on the back cover.

For Serote, the title, which referred to 'the cry of cattle at the slaughter house', was a comment on the emergent Black aesthetic. In the first place, as he explained, he got the idea from an anecdote Dumile, the leading Black sculptor, told him about his own bodily reaction to seeing the way cows 'in the country' responded to the sight of one of their own kind being slaughtered. While they 'raged and fought' and 'became a terror to themselves', Dumile reported, he, in turn, 'held the left side of his chest and said that is where the cry of the cattle hit him'. This affective response was a further instance of 'Yakhal'inkomo', Serote remarked. His second illustrative example came from his own experience of watching and hearing the jazz musician Mankunku Ngozi playing the saxophone: 'He grew tall, shrank, coiled into himself, uncoiled and the cry came out of his horn.' Dumile and Ngozi figure once again in 'Hell, Well, Heaven', one of the volume's other key metapoetic poems. Taken together, and, of course, as a preface to Serote's own collection called 'The Cry of the Cattle', these observations constitute a parable of the Black artist. In this story, the sculptor, musician, and poet are figured as second-order witnesses who turn the wider community's instinctive revulsion against bodily suffering into works of art without losing any of the authority of the primary response. Significantly, as Dumile's anecdote insists, the Black artist does not simply recognize the authority of this first-order anguish. He is irresistibly claimed by it. The 'cry' hits Dumile in the heart.[7]

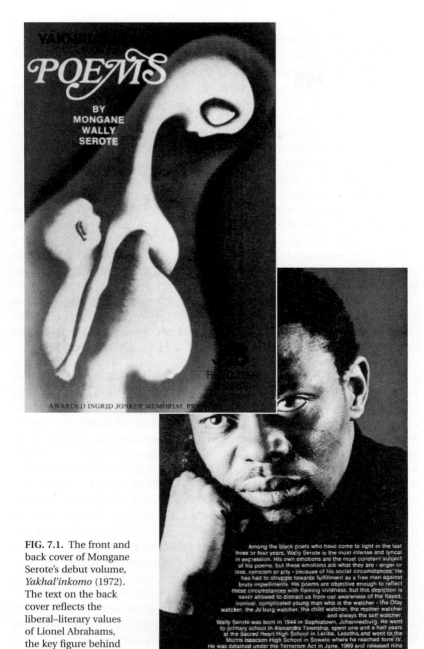

FIG. 7.1. The front and back cover of Mongane Serote's debut volume, *Yakhal'inkomo* (1972). The text on the back cover reflects the liberal–literary values of Lionel Abrahams, the key figure behind Renoster Books.

This double emphasis on the body's pain and responsiveness, on the one hand, and on the relationship between the poet–speaker and the wider community, on the other, runs through the entire volume. In 'Hell, Well, Heaven', for instance, a poem reflecting on the liberated future Black artists like Dumile and Ngozi are painfully but alluringly heralding, the poet–speaker comments that 'my soul aches like a body that has been beaten'; while in 'What's in this Black "Shit"'' he makes it clear that he has learned his own power to curse in part from an 'old woman' who works as a domestic servant and from his father's inarticulate rage.[8] Unlike the son, who defiantly says 'Shit', the still-deferential father vents his frustration and despair at the injustice of his life through violent action. He beats his young daughter for spilling the sugar 'I work so hard for'.[9] The generational energies at work in the collection are also captured in the dedication ('This book is dedicated to my grandmother, my mother and my father') and in the abstract illustration used on the front cover, which shows a young figure looking up enquiringly at a dejected female, suggesting a mother–child relationship.[10] The cover was designed by Thami Mnyele, the celebrated graphic artist who would later go on to play a leading part in the Medu Art Ensemble alongside Serote himself.

All these features of the poetry and the book sit uneasily with the way Serote is presented in the publisher's blurb, which betrays all the hallmarks of the liberal–literary ideals Abrahams and Royston shared. Here Serote is figured, in the text which accompanies a pensive photograph of the author, as a lone individualist who, despite the 'brute impediments' of his background, manages to retain an acceptably literary identity as the 'most intense and lyrical' poet of his generation. Though his 'emotions are what they are—anger or love, cynicism or pity—because of his social circumstances', it is very much 'his own emotions' that are 'the constant subject of his poems'. At the same time, while they are 'objective enough to reflect these circumstances with flaming vividness', 'this depiction is never allowed to distract us from our awareness of the flayed, ironical, complicated young man who is the watcher', the detached *flâneur*–poet who observes his city (Johannesburg), its people, and himself.[11] The blurb then goes on to describe Serote's upbringing in Sophiatown, the multi-ethnic suburb progressively destroyed under the Group Areas Act, 1950, in the course of the 1950s, his truncated school career in Alexandra Township, Lesotho, and Soweto, and his nine-month detention without trial under the Terrorism Act in 1969.

It is worth noting in this context that the poet, painter, film-maker, and anti-apartheid activist Barry Feinberg, writing in the *African Communist*, accepted this liberal version of Serote's poetic persona, criticizing him for being 'too subjective and too acerbic to depersonalise his vision' and comparing him unfavourably to Mbuyiseni Mtshali.[12] Having just put together an anthology of liberation poetry entitled *Poets to the People* (1974), Feinberg was reviewing a number of recent volumes, including *Yakhal'inkomo* and Royston's anthology of Black poetry *To Whom It May Concern* (1973), about which he was equally critical, again because it placed too much emphasis on the merely personal. Like Royston, Feinberg included a number of poems from Serote's debut volume in his own anthology. Though both took 'What's in this Black "Shit"' and 'Hell, Well, Heaven', for instance, only Royston selected 'Black Bells'. As Feinberg commented in his review, he found this poem especially problematic because it displayed 'the estrangement of the individual consciousness' that was 'a well-established phenomenon of capitalist industrial society'.[13] Significantly, though he included a lengthy quotation from the despairing middle section of the poem in his review, he omitted the final lines and did not comment on the reversal they performed. As I noted in Chapter 2, while the censors passed Royston's collection because they considered it sufficiently literary, they banned Feinberg's on political grounds and for possession.

Though *Yakhal'inkomo* went through two impressions under the Renoster Books imprint—they also co-published a third with the small poetry publisher Bateleur Press—it sold less than 600 copies in its first five years and it attracted little national or international attention. It did, however, make Serote the first black recipient of the relatively marginal, white-run Ingrid Jonker poetry prize, which was named after the leading Afrikaans Sestiger poet who committed suicide in 1965. The same cannot be said for Mbuyiseni Mtshali's very different debut volume, *Sounds of a Cowhide Drum* (1971), the only other title to appear under the short-lived Renoster Books imprint. It became something of a global phenomenon and, in the process, raised further questions about the consequences of white liberal patronage. As Feinberg again commented, 'where Mtshali's mildly provocative irony struck a sympathetic chord in the liberal white conscience, Serote's caustic and personally complex vision did not find much empathy'.[14] 'Although this response is not without significance,' he added, 'it is hardly a true measure of the quality of either poet who can only be adequately judged by their impact on their own people, and by the journals which reflect the interests of the masses in South Africa.'[15]

After going through eight impressions as a Renoster Book in its first year and selling over 16,000 copies, partly because of the laudatory reviews it received in mainstream liberal newspapers, *Sounds* earned Mtshali the prestigious Olive Schreiner Prize. This was awarded by the English Academy in South Africa, the well-established national guardian of literary and linguistic standards. The Academy's account of the collection in a press release announcing the award was revealing. Despite its 'naïveté, contrived similes and self-conscious rationalisations', it declared, Mtshali's debut volume was worthy of the award because it was 'the voice of the black majority, caught between the kraal and the city' and 'more importantly, the voice of a sentient individual'.[16] Abrahams's blurb for the Renoster edition reinforced this last point by focusing on the 'very warm and winning spirit behind the poems'.[17]

OSWALD JOSEPH MTSHALI

SOUNDS OF A COWHIDE DRUM
POEMS

FOREWORD BY NADINE GORDIMER

RENOSTER BOOKS

WALD JOSEPH MTSHALI'S is
d to be the first sustained African
h the English poetry of this country
east twenty years. It is emphatically
of our day.

poet was born in 1940 at Vryheid,
where he matriculated. His special
t in poetry began when a teacher
him aware of the living connection
n his classical English set-works and
ff of daily experience.

At 18 he came to Johannesburg where
he had a variety of jobs, published in "The
Star", an article on ritual slaughter as
practised in Soweto and wrote a novel.

In 1967 he began submitting poetry for
publication, and his fresh, ironical work,
vigorously rooted in his life and observations, almost immediately attracted wide
attention. His poems have appeared in
PEN's anthologies of "New South African
Writing", "The Classic", "New Coin",
"Ophir", "Unisa English Studies", "De
Arte", "New Nation", "The Purple Renoster", "Atlas" (U.S.A.) and various local
newspapers, and have been broadcast by
the S.A.B.C. In 1970 he was listed in a
directory of 1,001 important living poets
in English by the St. James Press, London.

In her foreword Nadine Gordimer
praises his "gifts of colloquial irony" and
"almost surgical imagery" and declares that
he triumphs "by forging from bitterness a
steely compassion, by plunging into horror
deep enough to bring forth tenderness". At
the same time the lights of humour and
sensuous vitality reveal a very warm and
winning spirit behind the poems.

Mtshali is married, lives in Soweto and
works as a messenger.

FIG. 7.2. The front and back cover of Mbuyiseni Mtshali's hugely successful debut volume, *Sounds of a Cowhide Drum*, which was first published by Renoster Books in 1971.

284

If this was the currency of cultural prestige within the white liberal tradition, Black cultural brokers saw things differently. Commenting on Mtshali's debut at the Poetry International Festival held in London in 1973, where he appeared alongside W. H. Auden, Stephen Spender, and Allen Ginsburg, the *Black Review* remarked that 'the real critics of Black poetry will not be heard—in the conventional manner'. 'To them', it added, 'poets in the mould of Mtshali are still complaining, are still writing "protest" poetry.'[18] Later that year Njabulo Ndebele developed this critique more fully in his master's thesis on Black poetry, and, as we saw in Chapter 3, he continued to reiterate these concerns in the 1980s in his later arguments against 'protest literature'.[19] In a guardedly favourable review of Mtshali's banned second volume, *Fireflames* (1980), Es'kia Mphahlele, then the leading black critic in South Africa, was more forthright. 'Much of the verse' in *Sounds* 'is mere talkative stuff neatly arranged in verse form,' he remarked. 'For innovation, the deft image, for passion, for intimacy with the subject, for depth' the likes of Serote, Gwala, Sepamla, and Ndebele were all 'superior to Mtshali'.[20]

After its success in South Africa, *Sounds* was taken up by Oxford University Press for its Three Crowns series, a less successful rival to Heinemann's African Writers Series, and by the Third Press in New York, a small imprint with a strong African and African American orientation launched in 1970 by Joseph Okpaku, a young US-educated Nigerian. In all this Nadine Gordimer played a central part as a cultural broker. While her connections with the New York literary world made the US edition possible, she also arranged for *Playboy*, then one of the world's leading literary venues, to publish a selection of poems by Mtshali, Serote, Sepamla, and others in May 1972. More significantly, in a foreword, which was used in all three first editions of *Sounds*, she framed the terms in which she believed the value of Mtshali's debut volume could be recognized. She began by refusing, as a matter of principle, to settle the question of whether or not he had to be read as an 'African poet' in the tradition of, say, Senghor, Kunene, or Soyinka, or as an 'English poet', alongside Blake, Auden, or Plath. She did not at that point entertain the possibility of his being Black. Yet she was in no doubt about his honorific status as a 'poet': 'Many people write poetry, but there are few poets in any generation, in any country. There is a new poet in Africa, and his name is Oswald Mbuyiseni Mtshali.'[21] He warranted this title in part, she argued, because he was dedicated to the 'liberation of the imagination that makes the creative writer freeman of the world'.[22] To support this claim she pointed to what she called the 'manifesto' with which Mtshali ended the poem 'If You Should Know Me':

> Look upon me as a pullet crawling
> from an eggshell
> laid by a Zulu hen,
> ready to fly in spirit
> to all lands on earth.[23]

By reading this as a general statement about the legitimizing universality of his poems, she not only downplayed the emphasis Mtshali placed on his ethnic Zulu origins in this poem and, indeed, throughout the collection. She ignored the complications which his commitment to ethnicity as such engendered within the *volk* politics of apartheid, which were further complicated by the resurgence of Zulu nationalism in the early 1970s, and the anti-tribalist solidarities that underpinned the Black Consciousness movement.

For Gordimer, Mtshali was also worthy of being called a 'poet' because his work 'stands clear in the surety of his verbal magic, at home in his own vocabulary'.[24] In saying this she reiterated one of her guiding assumptions about the distinctiveness of poetic language, which, as we saw in Chapter 3, governed her response to the rise of Black poetry in the 1970s. This normative criterion, which set the poetic against and above the political, was even more evident in the Three Crowns edition. Recalling a peculiarly Yeatsian version of the European tradition of *Kulturkritik*, Jon Stallworthy, the British poet and literary editor who wrote the blurb, claimed that Mtshali's status as 'a poet of rare quality' derived primarily from the fact that he 'wastes no time invoking windy political slogans or the customary abstractions'. His poems gained 'so much of their formidable strength from their lack of rhetorical inflation'. Above all, he 'does not shout about Oppression'. For Stallworthy, as for Gordimer, this did not mean that Mtshali failed to engage with the oppressiveness of life under apartheid. As Stallworthy put it, Mtshali, like Wilfred Owen, wrote 'from the "Front Line" about man's inhumanity to man'.[25] What it meant was that his poetry communicated what Gordimer would later call, following the American critic Harry Levin, 'implicit information' without betraying its saving poeticity or the ideals of liberal politeness.

This was primarily because Mtshali observed the requisite aesthetic unities. The content and form of his poems, or, as Gordimer put it, their 'style' and 'philosophical statement', were 'married successfully', although, as she went on to argue, 'the most striking poems are often those where the verbal magic... contains a sting that finally shrivels the verbal magic away, leaving a question or statement burning in the mind'.[26] This was especially evident in a poem like 'Always a Suspect', she claimed, in which Mtshali, the 'city poet' who 'has forgotten nothing of the black man's rural past', emerged as an 'ironist'.[27] In this poem the first-person speaker, who dresses 'like a gentleman' in a 'white shirt a tie and a suit', reflects bitterly on the fact that every city official treats him with suspicion and every 'madam' fears he is a 'thief'.[28] Here Mtshali adopted what Gordimer considered his pre-eminent role as 'a Villon of Soweto', by which she meant 'the poet of the black Johannesburger' who spoke of, and for, the 'township bully, roadganger, clerk, drunk, chauffeur, nightwatchman' and, indeed, for their 'collective identity in the city as eternal suspect'.[29]

For all its command of an ironic voice, *Sounds of a Cowhide Drum*, which appears, unlike *Yakhal'inkomo*, never to have been submitted to the censors, displayed none of Serote's poetic self-consciousness, formal inventiveness, or, indeed, his commitment to the modernizing project of Black Consciousness. The 'sounds' of its title are the 'ancestral' voices reminding Mtshali of the 'precious heritage' of the Zulu's pre-colonial past that has been 'trampled by the conqueror, | destroyed by the zeal of the missionary'.[30] As such its un-rivalled, sometimes contradictory, critical acclaim—Mtshali was at once an individualist with universalizing ambitions, a spokesperson for the black majority who was pre-eminently a Soweto poet—said more about the condi-tions of literary publishing in the early 1970s than about the relative merits of the emergent generation of Black poets. If various white guardians turned Mtshali, who as the blurbs noted worked as an office messenger, into 'Mtshali', the internationally acclaimed 'poet', they did so exclusively on their terms. As I argued in Chapter 2, the advent of internal interventionist publishers like David Philip, Ad Donker, and Ravan in the early 1970s initially did little to alter this situation. For young Black writers it simply signalled a shift from estab-lished external to newer internal forms of cultural dependency. Though small, black-owned publishers like the Third Press in New York; largely state-spon-sored, post-colonial imprints like the East African Publishing House in Nairobi; and local little magazines like Sepamla's *New Classic*, or the *SASO Newsletter*, were beginning to open up alternative avenues, the only internal outlet that could claim, without qualification, to produce 'Black books' at the time was the BLAC Publishing House, the imprint of the Black Literature and Arts Congress, which James Matthews launched in 1973.

James Matthews, BLAC, and the Censors

BLAC was an extremely marginal, precariously under-resourced, largely one-man enterprise, which operated entirely outside the mainstream book trade. That it was able to exist at all was, for the most part, a consequence of the fact that Matthews was then working as journalist for the *Muslim News*, a local religious (and subsequently anti-apartheid) newspaper, and so had some back-ing, or at least occasional credit, from its proprietors. Though not a Muslim himself, Matthews had close ties to anti-apartheid Muslim groups in the Cape. He dedicated a number of poetic sequences, beginning with 'They Placed him in a prison cell' from *Cry Rage!*, to the leading anti-apartheid Imam Abdullah Haron who died in police custody in 1969. This association also meant he had access to S. S. Printers in Athlone, Cape Town, who produced *Muslim News* and printed all the titles Matthews published during the apartheid era. The books, which were slim, low-cost paperbacks, some looking more like school exercise books, were produced in limited print runs of seldom more than 1,000 copies and distributed informally, especially at literary festivals and other gatherings. Matthews was particularly proud of the fact that he was able to bypass white-owned bookshops like the CNA. The list he developed was modest but telling. Of the eight literary titles he published between 1974 and 1990, four were his own: three collections of what can for now be called poems (*pass me a meatball, Jones*, 1976; *no time for dreams*, 1981; and *Poisoned Wells and Other Delights*, 1990) and one of short stories (*The Park and Other Stories*, 1974). For the rest, his list comprised two debut volumes of poetry by young Black writers (Essop Patel's *They Came at Dawn*, 1980; and Hein Willemse's *Angsland*, 1981, the latter in Afrikaans) and two anthologies of poetry, again mostly by young Black writers (*Black Voices Shout!*, 1974; and *Siren Songs: An Anthology of Poetry Written by Women*, 1989).

The irregular *BLAC Newsletter* (*c.*1973–) also provided a platform for a group of younger writers, among them Mafika Gwala and Mongane Serote, who formed the core of Matthews's immediate circle in the 1970s. Imprisoned, like Serote, without trial for three months in 1976, Matthews himself was kept under constant surveillance by the police, who also harassed his family and routinely submitted his books to the censors. During the most repressive period of literary censorship between 1974 and 1980, all four titles BLAC published were scrutinized, two of which were banned. This put Matthews in the select company of poets the censors believed posed the greatest threat to the established order, which included Dennis Brutus, Breyten Breytenbach, Peter Horn, Madingoane Ingoapele, Wopko Jensma, Mazisi and Daniel P. Kunene. What makes Matthews's campaign for political justice as a writer–publisher especially significant, however, is the specifically cultural terms in which he conducted it. By creating a publishing venue for a generation of young Black writers in the 1970s, he offered a way out of 'Whitey's' cultural trap; and by developing a form of writing that not only repudiated established conceptions of the 'poetic' but put 'Whitey's' fundamental categories—'poet', 'poem', 'politeness', etc.—in question, he opened up an alternative, specifically Black literary space.

By the early 1970s, Matthews already had strong links to the Black Consciousness movement, particularly via the Black Community Programmes, which were being supported by the Christian Institute. It was through these connections that *Cry Rage!* (1972), which he co-authored with Gladys Thomas, came to be published under the Spro-cas imprint. For Matthews, as for other established writers who were classified as 'Coloured' under apartheid, notably Adam Small and Richard Rive, this constituted a new intergenerational as well as political alliance. Whereas most of the poets from the emergent generation were then in their mid-twenties, Matthews, Rive, and Small were relatively senior figures in their forties. Like Rive, Matthews had already earned a national and international reputation as a short-story writer, first in local newspapers and then through the leading magazines of the 1950s and 1960s, including *Drum*, the

New African, Africa South, and *Transition,* and Rive's two anthologies: *Quartet* (1963) and *Modern African Prose* (1964). 'The Park', a tale recounting the anguish of segregation as seen through the bewildered eyes of a young 'Coloured' boy, which became Matthews's most frequently anthologized story, featured in both collections. Matthews also used it as the title story for his own 1974 BLAC collection, which was subsequently reprinted as part of Ravan's Staffrider Series in 1983 and then as a Longman African Classic six years later. The collection had initially been published in Swedish in 1962. Though the police submitted the BLAC edition to the censors twice, once in 1974 and again in 1976, it was passed with some reluctance on both occasions.

Despite or perhaps because of his long friendship with Rive, Matthews tended to accentuate the disparities in their class and educational backgrounds as well as their very different relationship to the white, liberal–literary world. Unlike Rive, who, as he put it himself, 'spoke Coloured middle class' and who went on to obtain a doctorate in English literature from Oxford, Matthews, a former gang member who came from a working-class ghetto, left school at the age of 14.[31] As Matthews later remarked, Rive, who served on the editorial board of the liberal magazine *Contrast,* at times allowed himself to be 'swamped by the crap', whereas he was 'not willing to be co-opted'.[32] In his case, being an anti-establishment outsider was as much a social reality as it was an indispensable persona or cultural ideal. In his autobiographical novel *The Party Is Over* (1963, 1997), which centres on his life in the 1950s and early 1960s, one of the characters observes: 'You're certainly not the first writer to emerge from a slum. Think of Genet. Stop fretting about your past, use it. Put it into writing.'[33] These social energies helped shape his new role as a pioneering Black anti-poet of the 1970s. Equally important for his developing self-understanding as a poet, however, was the South American tradition of revolutionary, often strongly anti-poetic, writing exemplified by Nicanor Parra, Ernesto Calderon, and Ariel Dorfman.[34]

When it first appeared December 1972, *Cry Rage!* had a decisive cultural impact. Despite the ban imposed in March 1973, Spro-cas distributed over 4,000 copies nationally in the first year, and by the end of the year a Dutch edition had been published and extracts had appeared in a French literary magazine. For Serote, however, the importance of this debut volume, which confirmed Matthews's status as a leading figure in the new movement, was revealed earlier in 1972 when he appeared alongside Sepamla, Mtshali, and Serote himself at a Black Consciousness literary festival. In a manifesto–essay entitled 'the black word', which was published in the *BLAC Newsletter,* he recalled how Matthews, whom he called 'the cat', began his reading by declaring 'tonight, is the night of the word according to the way black cats see the word'.[35] He then proceeded to stun his large, responsive black audience—there were only four whites present and they left during Matthews's segment—by reading a shockingly defiant and prosaic series of poem-like statements. This was the moment Matthews opened up a future for 'the word Black', which was 'not made yet' but was 'taking shape', because, Serote remarked, he was 'the only one among us who could say in the right way, "shit"'.[36] His new uncompromisingly assertive, anti-polite tone also signalled a radical break with the past, particularly as embodied in the figure of Nat Nakasa, who, for many poets of the Black Consciousness generation, represented the failure of 1960s multiracialism. 'When I read Nakasa,' Serote commented, 'the mood of his word reminds me of someone mad and frustrated' or 'what we have come to call "non-white"'. More damningly, and, once again, reflecting the generational imperatives at work in the new movement, he was, Serote added, 'my father's son'.[37] In the same essay, Serote observed that he had by then begun to be 'terribly reckless in the way I pick up the white word', in part because he had already 'learnt a bloody lot from the black American word'.[38] Yet, in his view, it was Matthews who 'started to remake the word' that evening by bringing the tradition of protest writing abruptly to an end.[39] As Matthews later put it, the 'militancy in my lines should be understood': 'I am not asking the oppressor to lighten the lash. I am expressing my rage.'[40]

Matthews's affirmation of an anti-poetic 'black word' was in part politically inspired. As the censors noted in their original report, *Cry Rage!* began with a preface that 'immediately gave a person an idea of what you could expect in this book': 'The declarations in this book are by a housewife and myself, a man of no account, who refuse to remain silent at all the injustices done to blacks.... We shall show our contempt for white man's two-faced morality.'[41] The collection then went on to include inspirational sequences like the frequently anthologized 'Freedom's Child', which called on the rising generation to 'fill your lungs and cry rage | step forward and take your rightful place'.[42] Jansen, the author of the report and then a new security censor, considered this a 'key poem' that captured the 'spirit of the book', though the 'most incendiary', in his view, was 'rage sharp as a blade', which amounted to a 'call to violence'. As he noted, it contained the lines 'bring out your guns' and 'only blood can appease | the blood spilled | over three hundred years'.[43] Though Matthews occasionally wrote in the first person, assuming various guises (poet–speaker, torture victim, lover), he also frequently spoke for a first-person collective ('our', 'we', 'us'), figured as an inclusive Black identity and set against a generalized white oppressor ('they', 'the white man'). Jansen was also concerned about two poems that included the phrase 'Black is beautiful'. In his view, this made *Cry Rage!* a uniquely 'vehement attack on the whites', particularly when compared to other Spro-cas books, which were nonetheless all 'very critical'. It was, he concluded, a 'militant book that deserved to be banned', a view the Kruger Board endorsed in 1973. Four years later, when the chief censor himself resubmitted *Cry Rage!* with a view to having it banned for possession—this was after the 1976 Soweto uprising—Jansen upheld the earlier decision without imposing any further restrictions (P77/7/91).

Jansen ended his original report by remarking that as a security censor he could 'naturally not judge its literary value', which was a matter for 'our literary experts'. Though no record of their views appears to have survived, it is clear from the final outcome that they did not feel the book could be defended on these grounds. No doubt Serote's wry summary of the likely white response to Matthews's writing—" 'Militant', 'Bitter', 'Black Consciousness element', 'Is this poetry?' "—was not far off the mark.[44] Writing in *The Black Interpreters* (1973), where, as we have seen, she argued that Matthews simply used poetry as a 'public address system', Gordimer felt the banning of *Cry Rage!* was instructive: 'If there were to be a lesson to be learned in a game where it seems you can't win for long, it would seem to be that only good writing with implicit commitment is equal both to the inner demands of the situation and a chance of surviving publication, whatever the chosen literary form.'[45] Given that other collections, like *Yakhal'inkomo* as well as Serote's second volume, *Tsetlo* (1974), and Mafika Gwala's debut, *Jol'iinkomo* (1977), were passed—the latter because it was deemed to be sufficiently poetic according to the censors' aestheticist assumptions—Gordimer's comments were more astute perhaps than she intended.

Yet to dismiss *Cry Rage!* as bad or failed poetry because it was in some sense too declamatory or too political is to overlook the specifically literary and cultural dimension of Matthews's anti-poetic intervention. Like *Yakhal'inkomo*, his debut volume has a strong metapoetic, or, more accurately, metacultural theme. One sequence, for instance, offers a sardonic portrait of 'missus marshall', a wealthy white patron of the arts, in which the first-person speaker, who is a writer, decides to turn down an invitation to view 'the works of her protégé | another in her collection that numbers a singer, a sculptor | and me'.[46] It opens with a parody of the polite but unthinkingly patronizing register of the formal invitation:

> transport would be arranged
> on the night of the ninth
> you know the trouble with township buses
> the occasion is to honour
> missus marshall's latest discovery.

Tellingly, given her scrupulously bourgeois tastes, she thinks her new acquisition 'paints in the manner | of picasso', that is, before the celebrated modernist started to produce the 'rather strange' works of his later period. Recalling 'my brother in the ghetto', however, the speaker eventually thinks better of giving her another chance to flaunt 'her liberality | in presenting her cultured blacks'. Another sequence satirically parodies ideas of the 'picturesque' by turning the tourists' camera into an emblem of the distancing effect of the aesthetic gaze.

Like a poet's affecting similes, the camera glamorizes poverty, seeing 'the houses old with decay sloping against one another | like old men seated on crumbly stoeps [porches]', or the 'keening of the have-nots', as 'part of the score of a symphony of sorrow'.[47] The broader cultural issue at the heart of the volume, and, of course, Black Consciousness itself, is, however, posed in a short interrogative sequence that begins: 'Can the white man speak for me?'[48]

Yet Matthews did not simply reflect on such questions in *Cry Rage!* He staged them visually and formally by rejecting all the traditional apparatus of poetry (no rhyme, no metre), all the niceties of grammar (no clear syntax, little punctuation), and all the conventional features of the printed poem (no titles, no consistent verse forms). In refusing the label 'poetry' itself—he called his free-verse, prose-poem sequences 'declarations' or 'utterings'—he also set himself against the idea of a distinctively poetic language as such, particularly in so far as it might be thought of as having a trumping or mitigating value. Indeed, as his title indicated, he went further, suggesting that, in the circumstances, even clear, sense-making 'declarations' were inadequate. In the opening sequence that appeared alongside an illustration of a blank-faced, destitute young black boy by Peter Clarke, the leading artist and book illustrator who was Matthews's long-time collaborator, the speaker notes:

> It is said
> that poets write of beauty
> of form, of flowers and of love
> but the words I write
> are of pain and of rage[49]

Having rejected the idea of conventionally 'poetic' subject matter, he goes on to refuse the role of 'minstrel' or 'balladeer', before finally turning his back on language as such: 'I wail of a land | hideous with open graves.' In the concluding sequence to his part of the collection, Matthews returns to these metapoetic reflections and, like Serote, adopts the role of second-order witness to collective suffering:

> To label my utterings poetry
> and myself a poet
> would be as self-deluding
> as the planners of parallel development.
> I record the anguish of the persecuted
> whose words are whimpers of woe[50]

At one level, this was a negative assertion of the primacy of content, whether as bald statement or pre-verbal cry, which put the whole idea of writing poetry within the context of apartheid in question. Given the urgency of the need for justice, the only acceptable option for the Black writer was, by implication, to reverse the aestheticist tradition of *Kulturkritik* by embracing the prosaically political at the expense of the poetic. At another level, however, *Cry Rage!* itself was as much a series of anti-poetic 'utterings' as it was a self-conscious performance of the statement or cry, which presupposed, only to reject, conventional assumptions about the poetic in the interests of creating space for the 'black word' and affirming Black cultural autonomy. It was, to this extent, not just a cry against the manifest injustices of apartheid, but a direct affront to the aesthetic tradition, which rejected the presumptive authority of white liberal guardianship.

The anti-poetics of declaration became a signal feature of all Matthews's BLAC books. Though *Black Voices Shout!*, the collection he edited in 1974, which included contributions from various members of the BLAC group, among them Serote and Gwala, was subtitled 'An Anthology of Poetry', its exclamatory title not only laid claim to a Black solidarity but privileged loudly impolite (Black) speech over the measured restraint of (White) writing. Significantly, however, in a move suggesting that its assertion of Black autonomy was a temporary expedient, it was 'dedicated to a South Africa free of racial taints'.[51] In his preface, Matthews, whose own commitment to Black Consciousness was primarily strategic, emphasized the objective of universal 'citizenship', and all that went with it, including 'freedom of speech and movement' and 'participation in open elections', rather than any narrower politics of identity.[52] In his own collections, however, Matthews continued to adopt a self-consciously anti-poetic stance. He subtitled *pass me a meatball, Jones*, his collection of prison reflections, 'a gathering of feelings', and the blurb on the back cover of *no time for dreams* concluded: 'James Matthews firmly states that he is not a Poet, declaring that his works are expressions of feelings.'[53] Nonetheless, he opened the latter collection with the line 'i wish i could write | a poem', suggesting a new phase in his own development as a writer. This remains only a hypothetical aspiration, however, a necessarily unrealizable desire:

> then i look at people
> maimed, shackled, jailed,
> the knowing is now clear
> i will never be able to write
> a poem about dawn, a bird or a
> bee[54]

In the title sequence, which considers the new cultural developments within the resistance in the early 1980s when 'poems have | become pistols', the present is figured as 'no time for dreams'.[55]

None of this had much impact on the censors, who remained blind to the implications of Matthews's pointed refusal of the poetic. Though Etienne Malan, who wrote the report on *pass me a meatball, Jones*, noted its subtitle,

pass me
a meatball,
Jones

a gathering of feelings
james matthews

FIG. 7.3. The front and back cover of James Matthews's *pass me a meatball, Jones* (1977), which is pointedly subtitled 'a gathering of feelings', reflecting Matthews's refusal of the label 'Poet'. Brought out under his own BLAC imprint, the volume was immediately banned.

he thought of it as a not very accomplished collection of '44 short poems' in an established lyric tradition (P78/4/66). 'Several' were, in his view, 'entirely innocuous', while 'others describe the emotions and frustrations of a person confined in a cell'. 'All these experiences' (he listed, among others, 'boredom', 'fantasies', 'the meaninglessness of time', 'death thoughts') were 'not abnormal to prisoners, and have been better expressed, in some way or other, by works such as Oscar Wilde's "The Ballad of Reading Gaol" (to which reference is made in "patch of blue" on p. 4) and Plato's Phaedo, telling of the last hours of Socrates'. Wilde's own phrase is 'tent of blue', but the fourth sequence begins 'that patch of blue | to which oscar wilde clung | is now my talisman'.[56] Read as universalizing lyric-like expressions of a generic prisoner, the collection could not be considered 'a direct accusation against prison conditions and warders and police in South Africa'. There was, however, one sequence that displayed 'undesirable features' because it dwelt on the sound of victims 'wailing', 'a wind seeking | escape from subterranean | torture chambers'.[57] In this case, and this case only according to Malan, Matthews's short prefatory note insisting that these were not disembodied lyric effusions but intensely personal 'feelings gathered while held in detention in Victor Verster Maximum Security Prison Paarl, Sept.–Dec. 1976' suddenly acquired a new significance.[58] 'Even allowing for poetic language and imagery,' Malan concluded, 'this poem goes too far in undermining the administration of law and prisons in South Africa.' 'It was', he felt, 'the sort of poem that can be readily taken up in underground resistance anthologies together with other poems playing on the alleged torture theme in South African prisons so avidly propagated by the communists and the militant left.' Malan was writing in April 1978, seven months after Steve Biko's widely publicized murder at the hands of the police. This sequence alone made 'the publication as a whole undesirable' and justified his recommendation that it should be banned for sedition, a conclusion the committee endorsed.

Though the 1974 report on *Black Voices Shout!* appears not to have survived, it is likely that it was originally banned on similar grounds. When the South African Library, following its campaign to have numerous bans lifted under the new dispensation in the mid-1980s, submitted it for review in 1985, the initial reader (Mrs R. Stern) argued that one poem in particular—'... and liberty' by a young Black student, Ilva Mackay—could be 'considered fodder for the potential violent revolutionary' (P85/3/22). As she was not familiar with the usual censorship practice, she recommended that this poem and 'two others to a lesser degree'—Matthews's 'Alexandra' and Christine Douts's 'i have seen my people'—be 'removed' so that the collection as a whole could be passed. The committee, which was chaired by a literary censor (J. H. Uys, a retired school-teacher), decided that none of these were, in the end, seditious, even though they did 'seem to advocate & encourage liberation through violent means'.

Matthews's own sequence, which blurred the boundaries between sexual and political violence, describes Alexandra township 'mafias' as

> the fast guns
> young men with violence on their mind
> and in their cock
> cherries hot in the right place
> ready to spark the balls of a brigade[59]

In the concluding lines he focuses on Alexandra as a historical meeting place for two generations of the resistance: the 'remnants of the a.n.c. | warming old bones at the fire of | black power camps'. Mackay's poem, too, addresses the question of generations. The first-person speaker, a young child, sees

> the spade
> my brother holds
> while slaving to the tune of my oppressor
> as a gun.[60]

Equally, the

> bar of soap
> my mother uses
> to wash the filth from the clothes of the oppressor
> is no more than a grenade.

According to Uys's report, the committee argued that the potential for 'incitement to violence' in these lines was neutralized because 'much of the language used is not meant to be factual but rather symbolical (thus on p. 6 the *spade* becomes a *gun* and a *bar of soap* a *grenade*)'. In effect, though the speaker expressly says, in the first stanza, 'a child am I | of guns and grenades', and concludes with a prediction that 'there will be | bangs, blood, bruises, bodies', the figurality of the middle stanzas, the inspirational acts of seeing as, was deemed to be sufficiently poetic to save the poem and the anthology as a whole. 'One could accept much of this under the terms of poetic licence,' Uys concluded. Miraculously, then, despite the chief censor's ongoing concerns (about the decision Abraham Coetzee commented: 'Risky but G.A. [no appeal]'), the once seditious 'declarations' in Matthews's BLAC anthology had become legitimately or at least safely 'poetic' a decade on.

By the 1980s, Matthews was, of course, not only acceptably 'poetic'. As far as the censors were concerned, he now also belonged to the newly legitimized, though for Matthews wholly discredited, tradition of 'protest literature'. Throughout the decade the police continued to submit BLAC books, which the censors generally considered borderline cases, but no new titles were banned, and in 1985 *Cry Rage!*, too, was passed on review. At the same time, and again like many Black writers of the 1970s, including Gwala and

Serote, Matthews's own allegiances began to shift, following the new developments within the resistance and among writers' groups. Though he continued
to publish under the BLAC imprint for the rest of the apartheid era and to
defend the validity of a specifically Black literary tradition (at the Culture and
Resistance conference in 1982 he gave an affirmative answer to his own question in a talk entitled 'Is Black Poetry Valid?'), he had, as his preface to *Black
Voices Shout!* suggests, always thought of Black autonomy as a strategically
necessary phase within a larger emancipatory project, not as an end in itself.

In October 1977, when Gordimer wrote to him about the proposal to form a
multiracial but black-led national writers' group under the auspices of international PEN, he made his own position clear: 'I can only say for myself that it's
because of circumstances that I adopt a black consciousness stance knowing
inwardly that the writer dedicated to truth and exposing society's ills could
never be contained in a pigmented box.' 'If things could work out the way you
propose,' he went on, 'then I would have no hesitation in becoming a member
of a PEN southern Africa branch.'[61] Five years after the revived multiracial PEN
SA disbanded, he joined the short-lived Writers' Forum before becoming one of
the key patrons of the non-racial Congress of South African Writers, alongside
Gordimer and Dennis Brutus. To this extent, though he remained sympathetic
to the Black cultural revival, and continued to write and publish work in the
anti-poetic mode he championed in the early 1970s, he was also alert to the
changing political and cultural imperatives of the last decade of the apartheid
era, during which literature and the arts became a means of mass mobilization
under the auspices of the People's Culture movement.

Wopko Jensma, Ravan Press, and the Censors

It is worth noting, by way of conclusion, that Matthews was not the only
exponent of anti-poetic tradition in South Africa to unsettle the censors' cultural assumptions in the 1970s. The extraordinarily inventive white anti-poet
and graphic artist Wopko Jensma was another challenging case. Unlike Matthews, who rejected the white liberal–literary establishment but went on to
found BLAC and to play a key role in the Black Consciousness movement,
Jensma was always an extreme outsider figure who defied all forms of classification and allegiance both in his life and in his work. After breaking apartheid
laws by marrying across the racial divide, he spent some years living in exile in
Mozambique and Botswana; he suffered debilitating mental health problems
and, after his marriage broke down in 1969, he began to live an itinerant and
finally vagrant life seeking refuge in various welfare institutions; and, with only
three slim books to his name, which never enjoyed a wide circulation, he
remained a marginal presence on the literary landscape. As the critic Michael

Gardiner put it, 'he built no structures, he established no institutions, he created no stable circle of friends and admirers'.[62] He eventually disappeared without trace in 1993, aged 54, presumed dead.

Yet Jensma did attract the support of some prominent cultural brokers in the late 1960s and 1970s, including the editors of the literary magazines *Ophir*, *Wurm*, *Contrast*, and the *Purple Renoster*, the publisher Peter Randall at Ravan, and the critic André Brink, who championed his writings in the Afrikaans press. After making his name in the late 1960s, at least in the small world of little magazines, he published three innovatively composite books with Ravan in the course of the next decade: *Sing for our Execution* (1973), *where white is the colour where black in the number* (1975), which was dedicated to Walter Saunders, who co-edited *Ophir* with the poet Peter Horn, and *i must show you my clippings* (1977). Jensma himself played a key part in designing all three volumes, often in collaboration with various black artists, which experimented with the relationship between text and image, typography and layout. During this creative period, he also earned the respect of a number of young Black poets. As Gwala recalled, 'black readers loved to read the poet–artist Wopko Jensma'. Like 'everybody with whom I discussed poetry of the day', he 'enjoyed Wopko', whose 'observation of the apartheid scenario was brilliant, and very open'.[63] Indeed, for a long time he was convinced Jensma was black. Yet whereas many of the younger Black poets learned from African American writers and the South American revolutionary tradition, Jensma, who wrote in an untranslatable admixture of colloquial English, Afrikaans, and African languages, as well as various dialects and street argots, identified primarily with the European Dadaists of the early twentieth century. His third volume, *i must show you my clippings*, includes the following manifesto-like sequence:

> i state, i recall, recall
> kurt schwitters
> jean arp
> theo van doesburg
> francis picabia
> tristan tzara
> recall, call, fukol, all.[64]

While the police, who submitted both his first volumes to the censors, clearly considered Jensma a serious threat, the censors themselves were less sure. They passed *Sing for our Execution*, despite its politically provocative content, but they banned *where white is the colour*, even though they could make little sense of it. Jansen, the security censor, who was the initial reader for the second volume (no report on the first appears to have survived), found 'the majority of the poems' not 'easy to digest and sometimes incomprehensible' (P75/4/35). Nevertheless, he recommended that the collection be banned, largely because some sequences appeared to 'insult whites' or advocate violent revolution. He also noted that one seemed to refer to the dissident Afrikaner Communist Bram Fischer as the 'bo-baas' ('top boss') and that another called South Africa 'Republic Azania'. His senior colleague Murray agreed, adding that it 'could not be let through, no matter what its literary value might be' because the 'content is consciously grievance-stirring and inciting'. In his chair's report, summarizing the decision to ban the volume under all three political clauses in June 1975, Jansen emphasized that the animus was particularly directed against the 'white Afrikaner', who is 'presented as tyrant, as thief, hypocrite, etc.'.

Yet he acknowledged that it was 'an extremely difficult case', not least because, having consulted two literary censors, Merwe Scholtz and T. T. Cloete, both professors of Afrikaans who were also poets, he recognized that it was 'really "something new" in South African literature'. Though they did not see it as an example of a nascent anti-poetic tradition, it is clear from the literary censors' reports that they did not consider Jensma a bad or failed poet. Merwe Scholtz, who agreed with Jansen's overall assessment, remarked that 'Jensma has a sort of rugged talent and I cannot write him off as of little value from a literary point of view.' 'I can also see', he added, that given its 'difficult and, for me, sometimes impenetrable idiom', the 'collection often obscures its own "message"'. His hesitation about the idea of a poem containing a clear message once again reflected his underlying formalist assumptions about the nature of poetic language.

In an effort to unpack some of these obscurities, Cloete offered an interpretation of two particularly worrying sequences: 'Only the best' and 'Umlilo, So Hell'. Given the referential uncertainties and densely figural nature of the first, he was obliged to speculate about its possible meanings in a way that can only be described as extraordinarily but revealingly paranoid. The sequence begins:

> we walk down streets of love
> brandishing flags of blood
> our eyes ears tongues locked
> in silence
> only the drumbeat of our feet.[65]

About these cryptic lines, which make no explicit reference to any rebels, Cloete commented:

Surely it is ... a clear case predicting revolution ('brandishing flags of blood', 'the drumming of our feet', 'slit throats')—and the rebels are surely the Bantu (the drum gives the decisive clue), and the poem makes out as if they are the hungry

FIG. 7.4. The front and back cover of Wopko Jensma's *where white is the colour where black is the number* (1975). Peter Wilhelm, the critic quoted on the back cover, describes Jensma both as 'a terrifying, new sort of human' and as 'the first South African'.

Hierdie animalisme grief my dieper wese—ook die verbastering van Jensma se taalgebruik (kreolisering van afrikaans en engels)—is skynheilig in die ergste graad. Willens en wetens trek hy die blanke, en ook homself, deur die modder.   —Okker Smit, *Sondagnuus*

At the conference on South African English literature last year, I predicted that Wopko Jensma would, in many ways, point the way for a new eloquence in this country.
                                                                —Ridley Beeton, *S.A.B.C.*

The reader's initial and, indeed, lasting impression is that Jensma is an African—possibly of Sophiatown. His use of words and phrases nevertheless seems, at times, that of an American Negro rather than of a man from the Transvaal.
                                                       —Mary Morison Webster, *Sunday Times*

Jensma is Jensma—he has his own style, an amalgam of languages and song that is his trademark, and his graphic work is familiar enough by now, like a continuing set of variations on a theme that is very much his own.
                                                        —Stephen Gray, *Star Literary Supplement*

This is the clue to Jensma. He stays together, in shape, alchemically combining enormously diverse cultures and experiences. He is a terrifying, new sort of human. He is the first South African.   —Peter Wilhelm, *To the Point*

300

who will rebel to get bread, and bread can here mean: possession of the land. This is again an 'anti-capitalist' poem.

While the first part of the sequence ends with the quasi-messianic lines

> our hands up high as we praise
> the one and only holy dream:
> slit throats for love of bread,

the second more obviously incantatory section focuses on 'our lord's voice in the air'.[66] With its reference to 'the four-colour of yore', it is fairly clear that the 'we' in the whole sequence refers not to the 'Bantu', as Cloete thought, but to the Afrikaner. It is they who recall the four-colour flag of the old Transvaal Republic, known in Afrikaans as the 'Vierkleur' (literally 'Four-colour'), it is they who 'remember our land our greed', and it is, therefore, the Afrikaner who pursues the bloody, sacrificial 'one and only holy dream' no doubt of a racially pure and culturally apart *volk*.[67]

In a similarly paranoid vein, Cloete insisted with some desperation that 'Umlilo', a poem which speculates uncertainly about the mysterious origins of a world riven by racism, played 'the "white collars" off against the non-whites', in part by relying on the 'double meaning' of the word 'boss'. The obscure final lines read:

> and i also know my god is boss
> his son, soul brother jesus
> keeps for me my bottle of red.[68]

On the one hand, Cloete remarked, the word 'boss' refers 'to the Bureau of State Security', the infamous agency founded in 1969 which was known by its acronym, BOSS, but, on the other hand, it 'becomes a new overlord, a new boss, whose son, "soul brother jesus", gives a flask containing something red to the non-whites, and this red cannot be anything other than the red of revolution, and it is not impossible that it is the Communist red'. About another sequence, 'Hide his head', which disturbs all forms of racialized thinking, he remarked: 'the murder victim is surely a white, anyway it is someone with long hair'. In parentheses he added: 'Throughout the collection the "we" and "I" who speak are non-white, and therefore in this case too; the one who murdered the long-haired [or 'arty', if read figuratively] person, is therefore non-white.' Though he felt the sequence entitled 'Trains' was 'for me not clear at all', he also understood this to be a 'freedom song for the non-white.

Yet for all the demands Jensma's self-consciously equivocal, anti-poetic language made on him as a reader, Cloete, like Merwe Scholtz, had no hesitation in recommending that the collection be banned for ridiculing Afrikaners, for harming race relations, and for sedition. In his concluding remarks he observed:

We must not forget that a collection such as this is one of many that are appearing in South Africa today, not an isolated case—think of Breyten's *Skryt*, of the poems of the black poets Matthews, Kunene and Serote, among others. It is becoming a whole thick stream, and should it not be stopped before it is too late?

When the South African Library submitted the collection for review thirteen years later, the situation was reversed. As one of the committee members noted

> The present reader's (Prof. M. G. Scholtz) opinion of this book differs quite significantly from that of the previous three experts who studied this book at the time of its first submission in 1975. They felt that this work had literary merit, but that it should be banned because of its political content. Prof Scholtz calls it out and out rubbish but does not think it is undesirable! (P87/9/96)

Scholtz had remarked that 'there will no doubt be those who would label this poetry, but in my view it is the biggest heap of nonsense I have seen for a long time', which, he added, 'undermined my trust in the publisher's ability to separate the wheat from the chaff before publication'. In the end the committee, which Jansen again chaired, decided to uphold the ban, which the chief censor, Abraham Coetzee, chose not to appeal. When it was eventually lifted in June 1990, the initial reader, who pointed out that the collection would not attract a wide readership, called it 'an example of committed and protest-poetry' (P90/5/44). 'As far as the committee can ascertain, and taking the high praise on the back cover into consideration,' the chair added, 'some of the poetry is possibly even of a high quality.' In one of the reviews Ravan used on the back cover, the young writer Peter Wilhelm observed of Jensma: 'He stays together, in shape, alchemically combining enormously diverse cultures and experiences. He is a terrifying, new sort of human. He is the first South African.'[69] As the chair of the censorship committee also admitted, however, 'many of the poems, if they mean anything, are obscure even for intelligent readers'.

8

J. M. COETZEE: THE PROVINCIAL STORYTELLER

JM. Coetzee won the CNA Award, the white liberal–literary establishment's most prestigious accolade, for *In the Heart of the Country* (1977), which also earned him the more marginal Mofolo–Plomer Prize, for *Waiting for the Barbarians* (1980) and for *Life & Times of Michael K* (1983). It was a unique achievement that testified to the rapidity with which he rose to become one of the most acclaimed writers of the late twentieth century both in South Africa and around the world. While *Waiting for the Barbarians*, which made his name internationally and launched his career as a mass-market Penguin author, also won the Geoffrey Faber and the James Tait Black Memorial prizes in Britain, *Michael K* earned him his first Booker. Welcome as it was, this kind of recognition, and, indeed, the process of recognition generally, always engendered a degree of wariness on Coetzee's part.

Following in what was by then a well-established tradition among his fellow CNA Award-winners, who included Nadine Gordimer and N. P. van Wyk Louw, Coetzee used the occasion of his first obligatory acceptance speech to condemn the censorship system. On the second occasion, however, he turned his attention to the award itself.

> The decisions of these and other awards committees, as well as the thousands of other tiny awards that members of the public make when they decide what to buy or borrow, and the more complex decisions of reviewers and critics as they evaluate books and place them relative to one another, might be seen as part of a larger communal project of defining a South African literary tradition, a South African national literature.[1]

In fact, given that the CNA had been making two awards since the inception of the prize in 1961, it championed 'two South African national literatures'. In this and other ways, it continued the questionable South African liberal–literary tradition Pringle and Fairbairn inaugurated in the 1820s, which, as I argued in the Introduction to this book, rested on its own limited conception of a unified, bilingual nation. The two modern 'national literatures', which the CNA Award championed, one in English, the other now in Afrikaans, inevitably took a very different form, Coetzee remarked, since Afrikaans writers had, unlike their English-speaking counterparts, long been part of a 'national struggle for survival, independence, unity, hegemony or whatever'. Nevertheless, it was, he felt, worth asking in general terms whether this 'communal project' was 'a good idea, a just idea'. Extending the range of his argument further still, while restricting himself to the English-language tradition, he wondered if there could be 'a good motive', besides, that is, the 'political motive of wishing to span in the energies of writers for national ends', for regarding 'any of the bodies of writing in English coming out of Africa' as 'national literatures'.

For Coetzee the answer was clear. Speaking for himself, and he hoped for 'at least some other practising writers', he suggested it was simply a 'misnomer, from the standpoint of literary history, to call South African literature in English, both that which currently exists and that which is likely to come into being in the foreseeable future, a national literature'. In saying this he was not making any grand ideological or even 'metaphysical' claims. He was simply speaking from his own experience as a writer. The challenge of writing, he noted, which involved facing the 'daily problem of wedding subject matter, or content, to form', lay not so much with finding the right 'content'. If 'you have enough passion, imagination, fluency, enough sense of what the world is like and what it could be like, and one or two other qualities, you do not lack for things to say'. The trouble was that 'what you can say, what you can think, what you can feel, are always limited and defined by the forms in which they can be expressed', forms that were 'not easily changed, much less invented'.

It was at this point, when it came to the question of the ways in which literary forms are modified or created, that his argument took a provocative turn. Any 'important adaptations' tended, he claimed, not to take place on the 'periphery' but 'where the overlay of old forms is densest and where the resistance of old form to new expression is felt most oppressively, that is to say in the cultural centres of the civilization, which I will gather under the name of the metropolis'. Bearing in mind the anti-colonial, (white) nation-building aspirations at the heart of the CNA Award, aspirations which, as we have seen, rested on a disavowal of the continuing realities of white domination, this was not what his audience, or the award's sponsors, wanted to hear. His conclusion, which recalled the birth of the imperfectly and dubiously unified Union of South Africa in 1910, was even more discomfiting. 'Despite the flags and anthems and other national paraphernalia', the relationship of the South African writer 'to the metropolis, like that of other African writers in English, is not all that different from what it was seventy years ago'. 'What we are doing', he concluded, 'is not building a new national literature, but instead building on to an established provincial literature.' Later, he would give this earlier tradition the more encompassing name of 'white writing'. Once again resisting efforts to police cultural borders (or temporalities) too insistently, he took this to refer not to any racialized corpus of writing but to work that 'is generated by concerns of people no longer European, not yet African'.[2]

In making his revisionist case he was not, he emphasized, seeking to revive colonial ideas about writers on the 'periphery' having only two options: 'pitying ourselves our provincial lot, or plotting an escape to the metropolis'. What he was proposing was a 'more constructive' alternative both to these atavistic colonialist sentiments and to the cultural nationalizer's politically motivated counter-project. The task, as he saw it, was to challenge the assumption that a 'provincial literature' is 'necessarily minor' and to remove the 'stigma of inferiority' by 'rehabilitating the notion of the provincial so that being a provincial writer becomes a fate one can embrace without ignominy'. This was, he recognized, never going to be 'easy', particularly because 'the humanist–internationalist values that the artist derives from his metropolitan heritage and orientation and affiliations put him in conflict with provincial mores (something we are familiar with in South Africa)'. Nonetheless, it was necessary not least to avoid the pitfalls of cultural nationalism, which, for all its anti-colonial ambitions, too often simply played up to a new set of metropolitan expectations. With a more confident sense of their value as literary 'provincials', writers would, he felt, be able to 'dismiss the cries from metropolitan critics for, let us say, an "authentically South African" art which does not "ape European or American models" but "finds its own roots"'. 'Demands of this kind', he commented, 'come out of a naïve, idle and typically metropolitan yearning for the exotic, a yearning we should recognize as of no importance.' No less objectionable, in his view, was the metropolitan perception of apartheid South Africa as a 'paradise' for the writer because 'at least you have a great subject staring you in the face'. 'South Africa may offer a great subject,' Coetzee countered, 'but great subjects do not make great novels.' Moreover, 'oppression and exploitation on a massive scale, the struggle against oppression and exploitation—these are certainly not a new subject'.

Coetzee's testiness on this occasion was by no means unusual. His doubts about judging literary works primarily or exclusively in terms of their 'content' or 'form', his concerns about seeing literary history in political terms, his scepticism about the kinds of recognition many literary prizes afforded, his desire not to comply with metropolitan or local expectations—all these refusals would, as we have seen, remain central to his self-understanding as a writer. Nor was his testiness motivated by a lofty belief in the writer's inviolable unworldliness. He always acknowledged that he would have to negotiate and, if necessary, sidestep the roles and forms of authority thrust on him by critics, reviewers, prize judges, and publishers, a technique he developed into a fine art as an interviewee. What is more remarkable is that on this occasion he claimed an alternative literary identity for himself. By defending the idea of the 'provincial writer' in these terms, he was not only questioning the assumptions on which the CNA Award was based. He was attempting to position himself on an alternative, necessarily inexact, and specifically literary map and to create space for his own metropolitan 'affiliations'. At a time when his identification with a cosmopolitan modernist literary heritage that extended from Joyce to Beckett, via Kafka and Faulkner, was considered at best contentious, at worst politically irresponsible, his revisionist anti-nationalism had a personal as well as a broader public significance.

These canonical modernist writers belonged, of course, to the literary tradition György Lukács had condemned for 'its subjectivism, its static view of the human condition, its dissolution of character, its obsession with pathological states and its lack of a sense of history', as Gordimer had succinctly put it in *The Black Interpreters*.[3] By claiming this tradition as his own, Coetzee not only set himself against Lukács's countervailing ideals of 'critical realism', which was, on the face of it, a more acceptable mode for an interventionist writer to adopt in the South Africa of the 1970s. He risked cutting himself off from the new generation of African writers, who were, according to Gordimer, developing a form of 'critical realism' that was shaped by their desire to 'look at the world *from Africa*' and not to 'look *upon Africa* from the world'.[4] This danger was underscored when *Dusklands*, his first work of fiction, which, as we have seen, was published by Ravan as an innovative contribution to a 'South African national literature', was turned down for Heinemann's African Writers Series. At the same time, however, Coetzee's identification with the experimentalist legacies of modernism allied him to the younger generation of writers in South Africa, like Peter Wilhelm and others within the Artists' and Writers' Guild, who embraced anti-realist modes of writing, challenging the dominance of more established figures like Jack Cope and, indeed, Gordimer.

Coetzee always recognized the potential hazards of his position. In an early essay on Alex La Guma of 1972, he referred back to Lewis Nkosi's critical writings of the 1960s and then asked pre-emptively:

> If Nkosi allows that a literature based on African traditions and a literature employing Western 'techniques' are equally valid choices for the African writer, are we not entitled to ask...whether there might not be a whole spectrum of valid literatures open to Africa, and to suggest that the writer should not, so to speak, choose his tradition at random, but rather choose it with some sense of the social implications of his choice?[5]

Dusklands itself can be read as his first attempt to provide an affirmative answer to his own question. At one level, like many first books, it is a work of conspicuous indebtedness. If Faulkner's presence is discernible in its structure—like *Wild Palms* (1939) it comprises two disjunctive but interwoven stories—Joyce's

306

in its extended use of parody, and Beckett's in its anti-realist epistemology, the entire tradition of literary modernism lies behind its anti-rationalist emphasis on the waywardness of desire. At another level, however, *Dusklands* reveals how far Coetzee had by that point already absorbed the lessons of modernism and begun to make them part of his own repertoire as a 'provincial writer' who was also in dialogue with the history of 'an established provincial literature'. If he used all the resources of Joycean parody to stage and unmask Eugene Dawn's rationalistic treatise on psychological warfare in 'The Vietnam Project', he also turned them on the self-delusions of Dutch colonial writing and Afrikaner nationalist historiography in 'The Narrative of Jacobus Coetzee'. Similarly, if he questioned the assumptions of the contemporary realist novel in Beckettian terms—he specifically cites Patrick White's *Voss* (1957) and Saul Bellow's *Hertzog* (1964)—he applied the same strictures to the conventions and pretensions of colonial adventure fiction. As significantly, in *Dusklands* as a whole, he turned the modernist's preoccupation with the dissolution of the unified self into a larger, though still specifically literary, argument about the darker, sadistic energies at the heart of Western rationalism. If we read Dawn, the late twentieth-century American propagandist, and Jacobus Coetzee, the eighteenth-century Dutch frontiersman, as supposed historical types, understood in the broadly Lukácsian terms *Dusklands* ostentatiously eschews, then they are incomparable. Read as literary devices, or, more precisely, as self-deceiving first-person narrators in a work of fiction, they share at least one characteristic. Both are pathological rationalists who attempt, without success, to redeem their solipsistic selves through horrifyingly savage acts of violence.

Coetzee's self-consciousness about the 'social implications' of his own choice of tradition is, however, most clearly revealed in the way *Dusklands* plays on his own name. The figure to whom Dawn submits his absurd, and ultimately self-defeating, treatise for official approval is called Coetzee, who specifically comments on its 'avant-garde' style. Tellingly, this Coetzee also observes that Dawn is 'working in a novel and contentious field and must expect contention'.[6] In the second narrative, 'J. M. Coetzee' appears in the pseudo-academic preface as the translator of both Jacobus's original eighteenth-century Dutch journal and of the Afrikaans Afterword by the nationalist historian Dr S. J. Coetzee, who is supposedly the fictional J. M.'s father. This additional story of authorial complicity with the overlapping histories of Western writing *Dusklands* interrogates in its own resolutely literary terms was more explicit in the first Ravan edition. Much to the actual Coetzee's dismay, the biographical note on the inside flap included a quotation from one of his letters to his publisher, Peter Randall, in which he described himself as 'one of the 10 000 Coetzees, and what is there to be said about them except that Jacobus Coetzee begat them all?'[7] Coetzee had himself objected to Randall's suggestions for a more detailed biographical blurb because the facts Randall chose to emphasize made him, he said, 'a player in the English–South African game of social typing' and obliged him to 'settle for a particular identity I should feel most uneasy in'.[8] Yet, by using his name to disturb the fictional frame, Coetzee, in his guise as a modernizing provincial who was at the same time a provincializing modernist, wrote himself and *Dusklands* into the politically overburdened history of 'white writing' he was attempting to undo from within.

One of the 10,000 Coetzees and the Censors

For the purposes of his revisionist argument in his 1981 CNA speech, Coetzee's distinction between the ready availability of 'content' versus the relative intractability of 'form' had an obvious value. Yet, as he observed on other occasions, things were seldom so simple for writers working under the threat (or spur) of censorship. Given what he called censorship's 'deforming side effects', 'content' produced difficulties of its own. 'The very fact that certain topics are forbidden creates an unnatural concentration upon them,' he commented in an interview in 1990, before adding: 'I have no doubt that the concentration on imprisonment, on regimentation, on torture in books of my own like *Waiting for the Barbarians* and *Life & Times of Michael K* was a response—I emphasise, a *pathological* response—to the ban on representing what went on in police cells in this country.'[9] Though he did not specifically mention *In the Heart of the Country*, it is clear from his remarks about the effects of the ban on representations of 'sex between blacks and whites' that it was a no less 'pathological' response to governmental anxieties about representations of interracial intimacy. As we saw in Chapter 3, his exacting self-diagnosis was motivated by his concerns about the way the 'dilemma proposed by the state, namely, either to ignore its obscenities or else to produce representations of them' threatened his own autonomy as a writer.[10]

What makes the once secret history of Coetzee's fate at the hands of the censors so challenging is that the three fictions in which he opted to 'produce representations' of the state's 'obscenities', which also happened to be the ones that won him the approval of the CNA judges, were in fact scrutinized by the censors and passed. *Dusklands, Foe* (1986), and *Age of Iron* (1990), his other fictions of the apartheid era, never entered the system. Reflecting on this puzzling situation, Coetzee characteristically put the burden of responsibility as much on himself as on the censors. 'I regard it as a badge of honour to have had a book banned in South Africa,' he observed. 'This honour I have never achieved nor, to be frank, merited.'[11] And yet, as the censors recognized, the three fictions they examined were not exactly innocuous. So how was it that Coetzee, unlike so many of his contemporaries, was deprived of that particular 'badge of honour'? And what bearing do the terms in which he refused the role of 'South African writer', as defined by the CNA Award or Ravan during its early liberal phase, have on the way the censors responded to his work?

Despite his concerns about the way he was presented as a Ravan author, Coetzee ensured that it retained the Southern African rights to all his fictional works up to and including *Foe* (1986). This was, in part, because he 'liked and admired' Peter Randall and Mike Kirkwood and maintained a keen interest in their project.[12] Nonetheless, *Country*, *Barbarians*, and *Michael K* were all submitted as imported Secker & Warburg books to the censors by customs. These consignments, which were generally small, formed part of the rights agreements Ravan negotiated with Secker. Given the looseness of the bureaucracy introduced under the new censorship legislation in 1975, there were never any guarantees that his books would be scrutinized by literary experts. Yet all three happened to have been sent to a select group of readers for an initial assessment and then passed by literary committees. This had a significant, though never determinative, influence on the final outcome. *Country* was, rather unusually, posted to three readers: Merwe Scholtz, Anna Louw, and F. C. Fensham. Following the more common practice, *Barbarians* and *Michael K* were each sent to one reader: the former went to Reginald Lighton, the latter to Rita Scholtz.

In their variously detailed reports, all the readers acknowledged that at the elementary level of content, which was, of course, their primary concern as censors, the three works of fiction were potentially 'undesirable'. Fensham, for instance, detected what he called 'traces of protest literature' in *Country*, while Lighton noted that in *Barbarians* the scene in which Warrant Officer Mandel reads the charges, ranging from incompetence to treason, against the Magistrate might be construed as seditious (P77/7/103). From the page number, it is most likely that he was concerned about the Magistrate's comments on the Bureau's cynical abuse of due process. 'They will use the law against me as far as it serves them, then they will turn to other methods. That is the Bureau's way. To people who do not operate under statute, legal process is simply one instrument among many.'[13] Lighton may also have been worried about his subsequent analysis of Mandel's character, however. The Magistrate goes on to describe Mandel as one of those 'men who might as easily go into lives of crime as into the service of the Empire (but what better branch of service could they choose than the Bureau!)'.[14] For Rita Scholtz, the main source of concern in *Michael K*, at least in terms of the Act's political clauses, was the description of the police raid on the Jakkalsdrif Relocation Camp outside the small rural town of Prince Albert (123–9).[15] Though this is a labour camp for men, women, and children officially classified as 'vagrants', Oosthuizen, the local police captain, ransacks it in a brutal reprisal for an attack on Prince Albert. His men and their dogs move through it 'like a swarm of locusts', creating havoc, beating and terrorizing the inmates. Yet it soon becomes clear that Oosthuizen has little evidence that they are, in fact, to blame—though he calls them 'Criminals and saboteurs and idlers!' (125)—and that he is driven mainly by feelings of professional *ressentiment* against the army. He sees the Free Corps guards at the camp as loafers and debauchees. Scholtz's remarks about this scene elicited a gnomic comment from Malan when he confirmed that the chief censor would not appeal against the committee's final decision: 'Against the army and the SAP [South African Police], but...' (P83/10/168).

What concerned the readers most, however, was the Act's first clause, which covered what might be deemed 'indecent or obscene or offensive or harmful to public morals'. While they sedulously itemized instances of what Rita Scholtz called 'crude words', they focused primarily on the fictions' preoccupations with the vagaries of desire and, more particularly, on the sexual episodes they occasionally included. Having listed variants of the word 'fuck' in *Michael K*, especially as used by the police, Rita Scholtz drew attention to the 'mention of cunnilingus' (243–4). In this scene towards the end of the narrative, a prostitute fellates K—Mrs Scholtz was endearingly confused about sexual practices—who has, by then, become an object of charity for a gang of drifting carousers. The potentially obscene passages Lighton noted in *Barbarians* generally centred on the Magistrate's various actual or imagined sexualized encounters with the young barbarian girl (30, 40, 44, 55, 63, 66, 149), a town girl (42), and an older woman (151). He was especially perturbed by the scenes describing full intercourse, including one in which the Magistrate voyeuristically witnesses sex between the town girl and a young boy (97). Under the obscenity clause, he also highlighted the scenes of 'brutality', especially Colonel Joll's public flogging of the captured barbarians (103–8) and Warrant Officer Mandel's torturing and mock hanging of the Magistrate (115–16, 119–21). For the rest, he simply counted up the words 'fuck' ('8 times') and 'shit' ('6 times')—again he found the soldier's abusive language on page 138 especially noteworthy (P80/11/205).

Yet, as Coetzee himself anticipated, *Country* was potentially his most problematic fiction from a moralistic point of view. In June 1975, before the manuscript was complete, he wrote to Peter Randall asking what he felt about taking on a work that might 'conceivably be banned on one or both of the grounds that (1) it impairs good race relations, (2) it is obscene etc.'.[16] In reply, Randall assured him that, despite the precariousness of Ravan's financial situation and the rumours about its imminent closure, 'if I believe it has great merit, we shall publish it irrespective of possible banning by the PCB'.[17] Two years later, when the Secker & Warburg edition was under embargo, Coetzee wrote again proposing various strategies for dealing with a possible ban when it came to Ravan's own edition, which included using a suitably anodyne blurb as well as removing or blanking out three of the 266 numbered sections into which the narrative is divided. The first, no. 206, records the moment at which Hendrik, the farm's black foreman, appears to rape Magda, the white landowner's virginal daughter and the first-person narrator; in the second, no. 209, she appears unwillingly to allow herself to be orally stimulated and penetrated by him on a separate occasion; and in the third, no. 221, she briefly records another encounter in which she feels especially 'humiliated' because he 'does it to me from behind like an animal'.[18]

Despite his concerns about these three sections, Coetzee nonetheless thought it unlikely that *Country* would be banned. As he mentioned to Randall, he had, in the course of his correspondence with Secker & Warburg, who were themselves worried about the consequences of a ban, sought out Klaas Steytler's opinion and asked him to read the typescript. Steytler was a writer, journalist, and editor of *Huisgenoot*, who later went on to become a leading publisher, and, like his wife, the eminent novelist Elsa Joubert, to play a key role in the dissident Afrikaans Writer's Guild in the 1980s. Having served as a censor a decade earlier, however, he also had an intimate working knowledge of the system. He did not think *Country* would be banned and reported that 'it is attacks on police torture etc. which are the current no-no', a telling observation given what Coetzee would later say about his own choice of subject matter in *Barbarians* and *Michael K*.[19] As it happens, once the imported edition was released, Ravan went ahead with its own version without any cuts or blanks. In keeping with Coetzee's original intentions, most of the dialogue in the local edition is also in Afrikaans. Following Coetzee's advice, Ravan did, however, use a review from the *Irish Times* as its blurb. Unlike the blurb for the Secker & Warburg edition, which focuses on the theme of miscegenation, especially in relation to Magda's father and his desperate 'bid for private salvation in the arms of a black concubine', the parts of the review Ravan used centred on Magda, her various 'delusions', and the narrative's metafictional indeterminacies.[20]

Coetzee's concerns about the rape scene were not unfounded. It was the only scene all three readers agreed was problematic, though they all had very different interpretations of its overall significance. Knowingly or tellingly, Merwe Scholtz, who emphasized Magda's apparent patricide, all but ignored it: 'Hendrik becomes increasingly uppish, later sleeps with her (the sexual intercourse between the two is, seen from her side, affectingly pathetic, with absolutely no fulfilment).' Fensham was more matter-of-fact and optimistic on the issue: 'Magda is raped by Hendrik, but she later achieves a sexual awakening with him.' And Louw, who identified strongly with Magda, whom she saw as a tragic heroine of the spirit, noted:

> To avenge himself, to humiliate his former mistress as much as possible, Hendrik rapes her, makes her his kept woman. Even out of this ruin Magda tries to rescue a little of the regard she has had to forfeit for so long in her life, as well as spiritual rewards for all three of them [herself, Hendrik, and Klein-Anna, Hendrik's young wife]. To no avail.

About all the other potentially doubtful passages the readers highlighted there was no unanimity at all. The only other section Louw identified was no. 64, where Magda, the modern Electra, thinks about the odd intimacies between her father and herself made inevitable by their shared use of the farm's 'bucket-latrine'. She imagines how their excrement becomes 'looped in each other's coils, the father's red snake and the daughter's black embrace and sleep and dissolve'.[21] This also concerned Scholtz, who detected evidence of an incest theme, but not Fensham. The two male readers, who were either more vigilant or more conservative than Louw, were, however, in broad agreement about most of the narrative's other explicit moments. They both listed Magda's thoughts about her body and her speculations about her sexual destiny (no. 87), her baffled glimpse of Hendrik's erect penis and his sexual advances on Klein-Anna (no. 144), and her less brutal but still forced and disturbing sexual encounters with Hendrik after the rape (nos 217–22 and 228). Fensham alone found the description of the father's seduction of Klein-Anna (no. 75), as well as Hendrik's provocative striptease before Magda (no. 196), potentially problematic. And only Scholtz drew attention to Magda's proleptic fantasy about having sex with Hendrik (no. 167), to the detailed images of the father's putrefying corpse (nos 157 and 182), and to the black comedy of the burial scene (no. 182). The only worrying passages most probably classified under the Act's blasphemy clause were no. 248, mentioned by Scholtz, and no. 259, singled out by Fensham, both of which include comments on God's indifference to, or active part in, human suffering.

In detailing all these potentially 'undesirable' aspects of the fictions, the readers were simply doing what was required of them. The forms on which they generally wrote their reports included a section headed 'Portions that May Possibly be Regarded as *Undesirable*'. When they came to make their own recommendations in the following section, they all argued that, despite these questionable portions, none of the works could be considered 'undesirable' within the meaning of the Act. In the case of *Country* and *Barbarians* this was, in part, because they did not have a contemporary South African setting. With *Barbarians*, Coetzee's most abstract experiment in anti-realism, this was self-evident, though Lighton still felt it raised some questions. Having begun his report with a series of quotations from the confrontational blurb, which emphasized that the Magistrate's situation 'is that of all men living in unbearable complicity with regimes which elevate their own survival above justice and decency', he quickly noted: 'The locality is obscure; some oasis in an arid region north of the equator, where winters are icy.'[22] What he wanted to stress was that 'it is nowhere near Southern Africa, nor is there any white populace' and that 'there are no apparent parallels', though he added, 'some symbols may be found'. In his general summary he singled out the potential that figures like Mandel and Joll had as representatives of 'the arrogant tyranny of State senior ideologists—their blinkered ideological outlook & ruthlessness'. Despite its own blatant disregard for the realist ideals of historical accuracy, *Country* was also saved partly by its various displacements, though just what these were inevitably produced some disagreement. Whereas Merwe Scholtz thought the 'period is apparently the late nineteenth century, the place unspecified except that one knows that the farm is in a colony', Fensham was convinced it was set on 'a sheep farm in the loneliness of a desert (Karroo)', while Louw thought the 'background is South African' and the 'time is an undefined "colonial" epoch, probably about one and a half centuries ago'. In his chair's report, Merwe Scholtz confidently remarked that 'sex across the colour bar occurs, but the characters are historico-geographically so situated that it is perfectly acceptable'. Rita Scholtz, who did not mention that *Michael K* is set in a dystopic future South Africa, assumed that it had a direct, albeit not narrowly local, contemporary relevance.

These temporal and spatial displacements were not only an integral part of Coetzee's anti-realism. They reflected his sustained and always evolving anti-aestheticist commitment to what he would later call 'storytelling as another, an other mode of thinking', an ambition that also went some way towards explaining his deliberate effort to avoid racialized language of any kind, especially in *Barbarians* and *Michael K*.[23] By contrast, for the censors, these anti-realist elements of his writing simply obscured or complicated the relationship between his fictions and the contemporary realities of apartheid South Africa and, as such, contributed to what they regarded as their saving aesthetic qualities. The fact that they based their defence primarily on the idea that Coetzee's fictions were *too literary* to warrant banning of course begs a number of large questions, not least because it meant various things. They were literary firstly in the sense that they had 'no popular appeal', as Lighton put it. After all, *Barbarians* was, in his view, an unsettlingly grim read. He was in no doubt that because 'doom, brutality and suffering suffuse this sombre book unrelieved by any lighter touches', its 'likely readership will be limited largely to the intelligentsia, the discriminating minority'. This quasi-sociological conception of the literary, which set a writer like Coetzee apart from a mass-market author like Wilbur Smith, did not simply mean that the fictions were passable because their impact in South Africa was expected to be slight. It also assumed that undesirability was relative.

No 'content' was inherently or absolutely 'undesirable', since its power to offend or threaten depended on the number and kind of readers it was likely to reach and/or on the way in which those putative readers were likely to respond to it. To this extent, the censors' arguments also depended in part on their aestheticist construction of the 'literary reader'. As Rita Scholtz claimed in her report on *Michael K*, its 'sophisticated & discriminating' readership would 'experience the novel as a work of art'. Significantly, though her judgement was, at that point, informed by the shift towards the relativistic 'likely reader' test introduced in the early 1980s, the literary committee for *Country*, who were supposedly working with the legal fiction of the 'average man', based its decision partly on the same logic. In his chair's report, Merwe Scholtz noted that it was a 'difficult, obscure, multi-dimensional work which will be read only by intellectuals'. This was, of course, not an unreasonable assumption. Though Coetzee's fictions were, after the success of *Barbarians* and *Michael K*, quickly reprinted as Penguin paperbacks, they never had, nor were they intended to have, a mass appeal.

It was when the censors turned from questions of readership to the specific ways in which the fictions qualified for exemption as literature that an unbridgeable gulf opened up between their cultural assumptions and the works they happened to be judging. For Lighton, whose report was suffused with literary references, *Barbarians* seemed, for instance, to fit naturally into an established European novelistic tradition. It was, he said, a 'somewhat Kafkaesque type of narrative, with the narrator an elderly somewhat Quixotic Magistrate', while the 'locale was as obscure as Erewhon'. By contrast, for Merwe Scholtz, whose emphasis was more nationalistic, *Country* was 'an exceptional contribution to our South African prose literature in English'. Louw, who quickly reworked her censor's report into two local newspaper reviews, declaring *Country* to be her book of the year for 1977, went further still. 'This product of our own soil is', she commented, 'one of the few works of stature in the world of South African English letters.' A decade later, as we have seen, she would go on to praise Coetzee in her *PN Review* article as an 'authentic South African voice'.[24]

The censors' nationalist aesthetic was not, of course, incompatible with their belief in the idea that true art was, in the end, universal. Indeed, in keeping with their style of *Kulturkritik*, a work's honorific status as literature within a particular national tradition depended, to a very large extent, on its power to represent abiding truths about the human condition. That this was a key mitigating factor in Coetzee's case was clear from Lighton's report. After he mentioned that, for all its obscurity, *Barbarians* was, at the secondary level of its supposed 'symbolism', partly about the 'arrogant tyranny' of state officials, he immediately added as a corrective afterthought: 'All is of world-wide significance, not particularized.' This kind of thinking dominated Rita Scholtz's report. Though she acknowledged that *Michael K* 'deals with sensitive political issues in South Africa' and 'contains derogatory references to and comments on the attitudes of the state, also to the police and the methods they employ in the carrying out of their duties', she was confident that its 'likely readers' would recognize that 'this rich novel could be read on many levels—as a fable, as a comment on the human condition in South Africa or as a protest novel: in the sense that it protests against the way in which people are caught up in processes

314

beyond their control'. Above all, in experiencing it 'as a work of art', they would 'realise that although the tragic life of Michael K is situated in South Africa his problem today is a universal one not limited to S-Africa'. To justify this final claim, she went on to quote some of the medical officer's words about K: 'He is like a stone, a pebble that, having lain around quietly minding its own business since the dawn of time, is now suddenly picked up and tossed randomly from hand to hand.'[25] Used as evidence of the narrative's legitimizing universality, this quotation harmonized well with her interpretation of the whole. As her synopsis made clear, she saw *Michael K* as a study in 'alienation' and K as a 'puppet...thrown from one situation into another'. Indeed, like a traditional tragic hero, his fate would, she believed, elicit 'pity' from the reader. This was why the 'description of fellatio is not in the least offensive—when Michael submits to this act it is the ultimate stage that he has reached as a object of pity'. 'The probable reader will only feel compassion & sympathy when reading these two pages,' she concluded.

The peculiar admixture of cultural assumptions, which were at once aestheticist, nationalist, and unreflectively humanistic, underpinning the censors' defence of the fictions was perhaps most evident in their reports on *Country*, especially in the way they justified its concern with miscegenation. All the readers agreed that the complex narrative mode, which, as Merwe Scholtz put it in his chair's report, left the reader unsure about the 'boundary between reality and the rich, afflicted imaginary world of the spinster-narrator', meant it would not give offence or threaten the established order. In her own report, however, Louw took the aestheticist argument one step further, linking it directly to the shibboleth of universality. 'Owing to the striking technique employed by the writer,' she claimed, 'the reader is made to see the events taking place as if through a bell-jar so that details and incidents that might, in a different context, be questioned as being undesirable function, by means of the distancing achieved, solely as parts of the mystery of being human.' On this reading, the first-person mode of narration presumably had a neutralizing effect because it was simultaneously aestheticizing and universalizing, or, indeed, because these two conventionally prized powers of the literary were in some sense causally related. The narrative's universal scope was reinforced, she thought, by the title, which suggested that *Country* was 'essentially' about what happens 'in the secret human heart—that seat of emotion and consciousness—and not only to people of a specific time and place'. In an absurd twist, Fensham claimed that the scenes of miscegenation could be justified on more narrowly realist grounds as well. 'The circumstance of the spinster who is cut off from all life's comforts, who sits alone on a farm, can develop into a situation when things across the colour-bar can occur,' he claimed. 'The same goes for Magda's lonely father.'

The Gaze of the Censor and the Question of Reading

'Being subjected to the gaze of the censor is a humiliating and perhaps even enraging experience,' Coetzee remarked in 1990. 'It is not unlike being stripped and searched.'[26] Yet, such are the paradoxes of censorship, it was also 'a sign that one's writing is being taken seriously: seriously, that is, in the stupid way characteristic of the censor, who has only two words in his lexicon: *Yes* and *No*'. Having said this, he added parenthetically: 'But who would desire the censor's *Yes*?'[27] This reading of the situation, of course, presupposed that the bureaucracy was primarily a manifestation of the government's paranoia about the printed word and that the censors were simply unliterary bureaucrats. It did not include the unsettling possibility that, behind closed doors, at least some might take his writing seriously as literature. Yet, as the archives reveal, this is precisely what happened in Coetzee's case, and, indeed, in the case of many other interventionist writers they passed on similar grounds. What is equally clear is that their yes to Coetzee rested on general assumptions about the status, nature, and function of the literary, and of the novel in particular, that were not only inappropriate to his work, but wholly at odds with it. If they passed him as 'A Great South African Writer', in the nationalistic sense Coetzee refused in his CNA speech, they also believed him to be a 'Great Novelist' whose works displayed all the traditional qualities, verities, and canonical authority of the novel and, by extension, of Western art in general. This was perhaps the greatest paradox of their response.

As Derek Attridge, Coetzee's most astute critical champion, has argued, much of the peculiar power of his writing, which once again reflects his indebtedness to the modernist tradition, lies in its disturbing capacity to disrupt the kinds of naturalizing readings to which the censors subjected his works. At the level of 'content', *Dusklands*, say, or *Country* provide, as Attridge notes, 'no new and illuminating details of the painful history of Western domination'.

> All this brutality and exploitation is certainly there in the novels to be felt and condemned, but it is not what makes them singular, and singularly power-ful. It is what they do, how they happen, that matters: how otherness is engaged, staged, distanced, embraced, how it is manifested in the rupturing of narrative discourse, in the lasting uncertainties of reference, in the simultaneous exhibiting and doubting of the novelist's authority.[28]

For Attridge, who is perhaps too confident about Coetzee's commitment to the novel as such, this singularity is especially evident in the way the fictions foreground the 'unknowable otherness' of figures like Hendrik, the Barbarian girl, and K, who resist the dubiously motivated desires on the part of the various first-person narrators—Magda, the Magistrate, and the Medical Officer—to understand and so reach an accommodation with them.[29] The challenge these opaque and always subordinated strangers pose applies equally to the reader, particularly the kind of reader who expects fictional characters to function as representative or allegorical types, whether historical or universal. 'The task Coetzee seems to have set himself', Attridge suggests, 'is to convey the resistance of these figures to the discourses of the ruling culture (the culture, that is, which has conditioned the author, the kind of reader which the novels are likely to find, and the genre of the novel itself) and at the same time to find a means of representing the claims they make upon those who inhabit this culture.'[30]

For the reader, however, these challenges at the level of story (character, action, etc.) are matched, if not surpassed, by the demands Coetzee's fictions make at the level of narration (voice, tense, etc.), which put the authority of the novel and the novelist in question in still more radical ways. This is perhaps no more evident than in Coetzee's scepticism about traditional past-tense narration and his preference for present-tense modes. In the case of *Barbarians* and *Country*, both of which are told from a first-person perspective in the present tense, which is strictly impossible from a realist point of view, this makes Magda and the Magistrate as resistant to what Attridge calls 'allegorical interpretation' as Hendrik or the Barbarian girl.[31] As the story moves through the perpetually flowing now of narration into an uncertain future, the reader is never able to decide, once and for all, if the Magistrate, say, is, as Lighton thought, 'a compassionate, sincere man, a loner who has gone "semi-native"', or just a self-deceiving agent of Empire who, as the original blurb had it, 'unnervingly highlights the thin line dividing the emotions of the torturer and victim from those of lover and object of desire'. The same blurb, which Coetzee himself wrote, also aptly sums up his present-tense narrative as 'a compulsive mixture of irony, eroticism, introspection and horror'.[32] Magda, too, resists easy assimilation into some pre-established allegory, not because she is a complex individual who testifies, as Louw put it, to the 'mystery of being human', but because the present-tense narrative never allows us, as readers, to reach a definitive conclusion about her. Again, the original blurb, for which Coetzee was also largely responsible, is revealing: 'Magda's response to an Africa that will not respond to her is violence and madness; yet in the end we cannot help feeling sympathy for this passionate, obsessed and absurd woman.' Far from being a novel in any conventional sense, *Country* is presented as 'a fable of a consciousness adrift and trying to construct itself out of nothing', and Magda as a simultaneously ludicrous and sympathetic figure who may, or may not, have murdered her apparently transgressive father in an act of 'bloody revenge' after he disturbs the 'uneasy feudal peace'.[33]

Of all the fictions the censors scrutinized, *Michael K* is perhaps most radically disruptive in these terms because it appears to reassert the authority of traditionally novelistic forms of narration. Though Part II is told mainly in the present tense from the Medical Officer's questionable point of view, through a series of journal-like entries and letters, the first and final parts are narrated in the past tense from a complex but seemingly conventional, third-person perspective. As Attridge puts it, Coetzee in these sections 'uses directly represented thought and something that hovers between free indirect discourse and narratorial reporting to engage us with K's mental processes' while at the same time 'registering' their utter 'strangeness'.[34] Against other, more critical readings of this precariously unstable narrative mode, which see it as presumptively 'speaking for' K, Attridge claims that it signals 'the authorial voice's inability or reluctance to speak for the character by means of free indirect discourse'.[35] This is a persuasive argument, except in so far as it misses the parodic energies at work in *Michael K*, which turns its back on the traditional novel and its claims to representational authority. This is evident from its arch title (we only have to think of renaming *Burger's Daughter* as *Life & Times of Rosa B* to get the idea) to its unsettling third-person voice, which is not in any straightforward sense authorial. On this analysis, the radical singularity of *Michael K*, like any inventive piece of writing, lies in its capacity to disrupt scholastic habits of thought. Creating its own space by refusing to align itself with any established generic or other categories, it demands its own kind of reading.

The shocking, perhaps even offensive consequences of this are clarified only in the final paragraph, where the third-person narrator, who has, revealingly, switched into the hypothetical past conditional, describes K imagining meeting a 'little old man' and teaching him how to live.[36] This scene is often taken to represent the moment in which K emerges, at the level of story, as a minimalist (anti-)hero of elemental being or as a figure of ultimate resistance, in effect the kind of figure the Medical Office wants him to be. The narrator reports that 'if' K met this man he 'would' lower a teaspoon down into a well and that 'when he brought it up there would be water in the bowl of the spoon; and, in that way, he would say, one can live'.[37] At the level of narrative, however, this is the moment at which the entire novelistic edifice of *Michael K* finally crumbles. To borrow Coetzee's own comments on Kafka's 'The Burrow'—a story that haunts *Michael K* like no other—it is at this point that 'the construct of narrative time' collapses and we are left only with 'the time of narration, the shifting *now* within which his narrative takes place, leaving behind it a wake (a text) of failure, fantasy, sterile speculation'.[38] The emphasis the final paragraph places on the suspect modalities of traditional forms of narration, and, by implication, on K's radical intractability as a novelistic character, is signalled not only by the use of the conditional but by the self-reflexively ironizing parenthetical observation with which it opens: '(things were gathering pace now)'.[39] It is, then, only with its last words that *Michael K* reveals itself to be neither a great tragic novel, in Rita Scholtz's sense, nor, indeed, a questionably pessimistic or even irresponsible political novel, in Gordimer's sense, but an elaborately staged mock novel. Gordimer, it should be said, was not the only commentator to express disquiet about Coetzee's seemingly disengaged outlook. In his critical review of *Michael K* for the *African Communist*, which focused exclusively on its 'content', Brian Bunting shared her sense of dismay, arguing that the 'novel' offered little instruction to 'those interested in understanding or transforming South African society'. 'Michael K has no resentment, no anger, no ambition and no hope,' he remarked, and, in any case, he 'is a bore'.[40]

Since Coetzee's style of self-reflexive writing risked being seen by some cultural guardians as 'merely literary' in the worst sense, or as a dubiously apolitical gesture of disenchantment, the stakes were inevitably high. Yet, for Coetzee, the wager was unavoidable because it was central to his project as an interventionist writer. At the most abstract, philosophical level, his choice of the present tense, or his parody of traditional past-tense modes, exposed and destabilized what Roland Barthes called the 'unreal time of cosmogonies, myths, History and Novels'.[41] Hence, in part, Coetzee's own scepticism about the modern term 'Novel'—Barthes's capitalization betrays a comparable wariness—and his preference for the more archaic designation 'story'. Instead of offering us a retrospectively novelistic account of 'a world which is constructed, elaborated, self-sufficient, reduced to significant lines', and which might, therefore, function as a supplement to 'History', his stories enact 'an other mode of thinking' by depicting an as yet unexplained world 'which is sent sprawling before us, for us to take or leave'.[42] At an equally important, though more culturally and historically specific level, this self-reflexivity shows that, despite Coetzee's sometimes confrontational choice of subject matter, the 'Novel', as a literary form with a specific history, remained his principal target as an interventionist writer. In *Country, Barbarians*, and *Michael K* his own medium emerges not as a universally valid vehicle for making authoritative statements about the human condition, or, indeed, about specific episodes in the long history of Western aggression, but as the content-saturated artefact of a particular modernity that, like any literary form, limits and defines 'what you can say, what you can think, what you can feel'.[43]

It is perhaps unsurprising that, after completing *Michael K*, Coetzee began a more sustained enquiry into the origins of the 'Novel' in English, beginning with the founding authority of Defoe's *Robinson Crusoe* (in *Foe*) and moving on to Richardson's *Pamela* (in *Age of Iron*), two celebrated products of the emergent bourgeois public sphere in eighteenth-century England. For the censors this was, in the end, the most testing, if unintended, consequence of his antinovelistic interventions as a provincial storyteller. By exposing the limits of the 'Novel' and by provincializing the form itself, while at the same time challenging the universalizing authority of Western art more generally, Coetzee subverted their own project as guardians of the literary, which was, as we have seen, integral to their understanding of their role within the larger political project of defending apartheid. The fact that the censors failed to see this was less a reflection on Coetzee's practice as a writer than an indication of the tenacity with which some readers remain committed to certain preconceived ideas of literature-in-general and to a belief in their own authority as guardians of culture.

9
PROTEST AND BEYOND: THIRD WORLD PEOPLE'S STORIES IN THE STAFFRIDER SERIES

When you open *Forced Landing* (1980), Mothobi Mutloatse's popular anthology of black writing, the first thing you encounter is not the title page but the following announcement, which appears below a stylized map of Africa:

> The *Staffrider Series* aims at bringing new books at popular prices direct to the readers of *Staffrider* magazine. Ingoapele Madingoane's *Africa My Beginning* (*Staffrider Series* No. 1, banned May 1979) and Mtutuzeli Matshoba's *Call Me Not A Man* (*Staffrider Series* No. 2, banned November 1979) showed the way. News of other forthcoming titles will appear regularly in *Staffrider* magazine.[1]

As I noted in Chapter 3, *Forced Landing*, the third title in the new series, was itself banned for five months in 1980. Like the magazine from which it derived its name, and many of its contributors, the Staffrider Series was the flagship of Mike Kirkwood's transformed, post-liberal Ravan Press. The series was designed, as Mutloatse explained in his preface to the anthology, to turn 'the *Staffrider* dictum that black literature is the property of the people loaned to creative writers' into a book-publishing initiative.[2]

By producing low-cost paperbacks that could be sold at 'a drastically cut price not exceeding R3' (under half the usual price for a paperback at the time) and by using the writers themselves as an informal distribution network—an 'unheard-of phenomenon in the literary world, in which the writer also doubles up as a mobile bookshop'—the series set out to 'take our contributions to our rich black heritage back to the people', to establish an 'intimate relationship between writer and audience', and to enable the black writer to fulfil her 'duty as a mass-communicator'.[3] Writing in January 1980, Mutloatse felt that the new initiative had a particular urgency because 'the Press seems to have given up the fight for freedom of thought and expression, so as to survive financially'.[4]

Staffrider Series

The *Staffrider Series* aims at bringing new books at popular prices direct to the readers of *Staffrider* magazine. Ingoapele Madingoane's *Africa My Beginning* (*Staffrider Series* No. 1, banned May 1979) and Mtutuzeli Matshoba's *Call Me Not A Man* (*Staffrider Series* No. 2, banned November 1979) showed the way. News of other forthcoming titles will appear regularly in *Staffrider* magazine.

FIG. 9.1. The first inside page of Mothobi Mutloatse's anthology *Forced Landing*, describing the initial history and ambitions of Ravan's Staffrider Series.

The Staffrider Series was, in other words, conceived as an ambitious publishing experiment intended to bypass the white-controlled book trade, which focused on bookshop sales in the white city and the apartheid education market, by reaching out directly to a mass, black readership in the townships. Since 'the majority of whites are complacent' and 'don't like their dream-world to be interfered with', they were not a factor, Mutloatse commented. Besides, 'the literature being produced by black scribes today is uncompromising and does not appeal to the white man for recognition'.[5]

Yet translating the populist, anti-hegemonic, and broadly Black Consciousness ethos of the magazine into a viable book-publishing project was not straightforward. For one thing, as the announcement made clear, books remained particularly vulnerable to censorship. Launched before the 'repressive tolerance' of the 1980s, the series was badly affected in its first four years. Between 1979 and 1982 the police submitted eleven of the initial fifteen titles—the series comprised twenty-eight in all when it came to an end in 1986—seven of which were banned for various lengths of time.[P] The consequences of this were crippling. After *Call Me Not a Man*, for instance, which was first published in September 1979 in a print run of 5,000 copies, sold out almost immediately, Ravan reprinted a further 5,000 before the ban was imposed in November. This left them with a stock of 4,000 that they were obliged to sell on the adjacent Southern African market. Though the ban was lifted in 1985, it took a costly eight years for the second impression to be exhausted. A third was produced only in 1988.

Much to Matshoba's dismay, the ban effectively closed down the informal distribution system. When it was lifted, the volume's continued success depended primarily on its sales in the education market, especially at the university level. This was true for many of the series' more successful titles, including Mongane Serote's *To Every Birth its Blood* (1981) and Njabulo Ndebele's *Fools and Other Stories* (1983). Though Ravan continued to use its network of informal sellers, it had by the mid-1980s also begun to rethink its marketing strategy by inaugurating what Kirkwood called a 'new kind of "literary launch"', starting with Ndebele's debut volume. As he explained in a letter to Mafika Gwala, they wanted to 'abandon the suburban cocktail party in favour of a fairly disciplined dialogue between the author and the media public'. There would, he hoped, 'be, among the journalists, etc., enough writers, critics and others to supply the vital context in which the work is appearing, and which reviewers often miss'. As importantly, however, 'an attempt would be made to link in key participants "countrywide": e.g. Modikwe [Dikobe] in Settlers, yourself in Mpumalanga, etc.'. To make this possible, the 'book would arrive, with its explanatory letter, in time for you to get back with questions and comments which would be fed into the launch proceedings, with answers and subsequent debate coming back to you'.[6] Ravan pioneered this new approach in January 1984 with *Fools and Other Stories*.

Part carefully managed marketing strategy, part exercise in participatory democracy, and part 'high-focus cultural event', this new initiative was in fact characteristic of the post-liberal Ravan. After all, for all its collectivist and anti-capitalist ideals, which were to some extent made possible by the substantial support it received from foreign donors, all its books, including the Staffrider Series, remained intellectual property in the traditional sense, subject to copyright law and the conventional ideas of authorial ownership it encoded, as well as the vagaries and opportunities of the increasingly complex transnational market. *Call Me Not a Man*, for instance, carried the conventional mark of ownership '© Mtutuzeli Matshoba' on its inside pages. In this context the new Ravan was as much a centre for proto-democratic cultural innovation, heralding the advent of a People's Culture, as it was a de facto agent for many of its authors, dealing with a marketable commodity.

These complexities are, once again, well illustrated by the fortunes of Matshoba's debut volume, which was, in the end, like *Forced Landing*, one of the series' best-sellers. After its initial, if short-lived, local success, Ravan was able to sell translation rights for French, German, and Dutch editions; film rights to the story 'A Glimpse of Slavery'; rights for a taped edition for the blind; as well as foreign book rights to a range of English-language publishers. After Rex Collings, the small London publisher who specialized in African books and frequently co-published with Ravan and David Philip, brought out a limited hardback edition in 1979, Longman included a paperback in its Drumbeat Series two years later, before finally reprinting it as an African Classic in 1987. Though the initial Longman agreement stipulated that Three Continents Press, then one of the principal Africanist publishers in the United States, had the first option on the remaining English-language rights, they did not take them up and no US edition was ever produced. Not all the titles in the series survived the effects of censorship so well. After Miriam Tlali's second novel, *Amandla* (1980), was banned, it took Ravan four years to exhaust the Southern African edition, which was also produced in an initial print run of 5,000, and after Longman turned the novel down in 1980 it was unable to find a buyer for the remaining English-language rights. As Kirkwood noted, Longman felt it was 'too didactic–political'.[7] When the ban was lifted, again in 1985, Ravan itself did not reprint.

The Staffrider Series encompassed a variety of genres—poetry, novels, stories, anthologies—by a wide range of writers, including reprints of work by established figures like James Matthews, Can Themba, and Nat Nakasa, as well as new titles by relative newcomers like Ndebele, Mbulelo Mzamane, and Achmat Dangor. Yet one of its principal innovations from a literary point of view was that it became a vehicle for the revival of a local storytelling tradition. Behind the scenes Kirkwood was an active promoter of this project from the start, but it was, as we saw in Chapter 2, publicly launched as a *Staffrider* initiative in early 1984 to coincide with the publication of *Fools and Other Stories*. As Kirkwood explained in a letter to Gwala, he saw the project as a means of revitalizing 'the "literature and commitment" debate', particularly given that the era of the 'Soweto poem' was 'over'. 'Our weakness—vis à vis the criticism from the "cult of sensibility" side—has always been that we cannot answer the charge that "political" writing "leaves out" important human facts,' he observed, recalling the debates he had had with the likes of Lionel Abrahams and other liberal guardians of the literary. 'Whereas the truth is that by killing off the story western literature killed off the means of satisfying important human needs, giving rise to bastardized commodity forms like the thriller and "true life stories", dividing literature into "high" and popular.' As he pointed out, Benjamin saw this in his 1936 essay 'The Storyteller', but 'without realising that storytelling communities would survive in Africa'.[8]

Reclaiming and reinventing this tradition was especially worthwhile, he felt, because 'the story is a more powerful form—stronger than the novel, remembering that some novels are really long stories, like Kemal's *Memed, my hawk* [1961]—in the Third World than the literary metropolises where publishers turn up their noses at collections of stories'. There were, moreover, 'good historical reasons' for the added significance this tradition had in the South Africa of the 1980s, the most important of which was that 'the story relates directly to the story-teller's own experience or the experience of his community'. As a consequence, unlike the relatively 'alienated form' of the novel, it had 'real counsel to offer'. In saying this he was not, he insisted, seeking to lessen the value of a work like *Life & Times of Michael K*, which he felt was a 'great book'. The only trouble was that 'its transformative power is limited by the tiny elite it reaches, ignoring the suburbanites who read it for fashionable reasons and fashion its meaning to their needs'. By contrast, with its capacity to engage a mass readership, not least by speaking directly from and to their 'experience', the cultural impact of the story was potentially far greater, particularly if it could be published in an appropriate medium like the Staffrider Series.[9]

This kind of thinking lay behind the particular commitment Kirkwood had to publishing *Call Me Not a Man*. In his testy exchange with Mzamane in 1980, which I discussed in Chapter 2, he defended the decision to publish the volume in part because he saw Matshoba as the 'story-teller come to life'. His 'narrator is a participant' who 'carries the function of the story-teller into the midst of the fractured lives of the prisoners of apartheid'.[10] About Mzamane's own debut volume, *Mzala* (1980), which appeared as number 5 in the Staffrider Series, he was even more upbeat. It was, he wrote to Mzamane, 'actually part of the foundation of a whole new culture, if you want a non-technical opinion'.[11] This was, in part, because the collection's central figure, Mzal' uJola, the country cousin of the city narrator, is the 'kind of human being in *stories*—as opposed to "short stories"'.[12] A resilient jack of all trades who refuses to be trapped either by apartheid laws or ordinary social conventions, uJola, he remarked, 'is a folk-figure, a sort of indestructible Proteus sprung from the people'.[13] Mzamane had, he believed, also found an appropriate form in which to narrate uJola's eventful, serio-comic escapades. By adopting a loose, 'episodic style' and a quasi-autobiographical first-person narrative voice, he foregrounded the 'intentions of the story-teller, the particular presence memory and anecdote establishes in each tale', making them an integral part of the performance and thereby establishing a special intimacy between writer and reader.[14]

For Kirkwood, and, indeed, for the Staffrider Series, the storytelling tradition did not just privilege the 'voice of the teller'. It gave a new value to the writer's own situatedness as a member of a particular community. In the early years of the series, Ravan drew attention to this by beginning each collection with an autobiographical note, partly to give a richer sense of the author's social identity and to serve as an inspirational narrative for the many aspirant young writers who read and contributed to *Staffrider*. The main purpose of these short prefaces, however, was to establish the author's authority as a People's story-teller. In Mzamane's case, this required some editorial finessing. For the *Mzala* note, he agreed to let Kirkwood keep the 'parts with most appeal to the Staffrider Series readership', which meant cutting out a lengthy section detailing Mza-mane's experiences at a private church school, where his parents sent him to escape the degrading Bantu education system, and his subsequent career as a scholarship student first at the University of Botswana, Lesotho, and Swaziland and then at the University of Sheffield.[15] The basic facts of his education were, however, included in the blurb on the back cover.

After a brief description of his early schooling, the edited note focused on the circumstances that led to his 'decision to become a writer', his early reading, and his literary influences, among whom Mzamane pointedly included Es'kia Mphahlele, Can Themba, Alex La Guma, Bloke Modisane, Richard Rive, and James Matthews.[16] As he commented to Kirkwood, 'I'm trying to say to the guys back home these are the writers you should try and get hold of, who have been the founders of your literary tradition.'[17] Unlike other writers of his generation, he remarked in the published note, 'I was never undernourished on an unvarying diet of Shakespeare, Wordsworth, Keats, Austen, Dickens and the rest,' though he admitted he did go through a 'brief phase' in which 'I fancied myself another John Keats.'[18] In the final paragraphs, Mzamane turned to the stories themselves, emphasizing that they were principally inspired by his 'own family, relatives and friends': 'Mzala, who is my own cousin and was ignominiously repatriated to the Transkei for the umpteenth time only the other day, is a real person.' After quoting from Kirkwood's letter praising uJola, Mzamane added, recalling the concerns Black Consciousness writers had about the 'protest' tradition, 'he's a living testimony to all that's indestructible in my people: their resilience, resourcefulness, vitality, humour and positive think-ing'. 'In this respect I claim absolutely nothing for myself', he concluded, before adding 'so be it: POWER TO THE PEOPLE! AMANDLA!'[19]

The note Matshoba provided for *Call Me Not a Man* did not require substan-tial editing. As Mzamane himself remarked, he was 'more representative of the people', although Matshoba, too, managed to escape some of the worst effects of ghetto life in Soweto, but not Bantu Education, when one of his teachers advised his parents to send him away to a former mission school at the age of 14.[20] Like Mzamane, Matshoba gave an account of his literary formation, which, given his background and schooling, centred on Shakespeare and 'English poetry', but his note primarily recounted the story of his political awakening. He recalled witnessing the 'menacing saracens' at the time of the Sharpeville atrocities in 1960, seeing his friends being taken off to prison (as he had been at the age of 19), and hearing the leading Black Consciousness figures, including Strinivasa Moodley and Steve Biko, give inspirational talks at Fort Hare University in the early 1970s.[21] Yet it was the student uprising in Soweto in 1976 that finally turned him into a writer. When that event 'exploded in my face', he wrote, 'memories of old were revived' and 'I started scribbling and burning the scraps of paper on which I wrote, torn between writing or heading for the beckoning horizons, my country become my enemy.'[22]

With encouragement from Mutloatse, who accepted his first story for *The Voice* newspaper in 1978, and from Kirkwood at Ravan, Matshoba finally chose to write rather than go into exile, primarily because he wanted 'to reflect through my works life on my side of the fence, the black side'.[23] Again, like Mzamane, he emphasized that many of his stories came directly from his own experience or the experience of those around him. While 'A Pilgrimage to the Isle of Makana' was based on a visit to his brother, who was imprisoned on Robben Island, the title story 'Call Me Not a Man' emerged out of his own encounters with violent and corrupt black police reservists in the townships. For Matshoba the decision to write was in part an act of self-reclamation directed against scare-mongering and dehumanizing government propaganda. He wrote 'so that whatever may happen in the future, I may not be set down as "a bloodthirsty terrorist"'.[24] This, as we shall see, informed the underlying humanistic vision of the stories. Yet he also wrote to set the historical record straight, or, as he put it, 'so that I may say: "These were the events which shaped the Steve Bikos and the Solomon Mahlangus and the many others who came before and after them."'[25] Despite this, and, as we shall see, for good reason, Ravan made a point of declaring on the inside pages under the publication details that the 'characters and occurrences in this collection of stories are fictional'.[26]

Kirkwood saw the promotion of the story form as a literary project in the first instance, but he shared Matshoba's commitment to the idea of the storyteller as

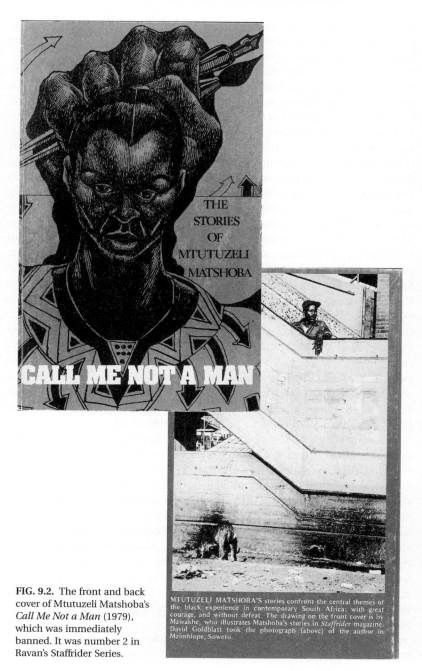

FIG. 9.2. The front and back cover of Mtutuzeli Matshoba's *Call Me Not a Man* (1979), which was immediately banned. It was number 2 in Ravan's Staffrider Series.

MTUTUZELI MATSHOBA'S stories confront the central themes of the black experience in contemporary South Africa: with great courage, and without defeat. The drawing on the front cover is by Mzwakhe, who illustrates Matshoba's stories in *Staffrider* magazine. David Goldblatt took the photograph (above) of the author in Mzimhlope, Soweto.

a People's historian. As he remarked to Gwala, 'just as the storyteller gave back to an isolated rural community the concrete continuity of its life, so another kind of story-telling can give history back to the communities that lost their history at conquest', communities that were 'now thoroughly penetrated and scattered by the capitalist nexus'. Indeed, he conceived the new initiative as the 'popular end' of Ravan's revisionist New History series, which began with Peter Delius's *The Land Belongs to Us: The Pedi Polity, the Boers and the British in the Nineteenth Century Transvaal* (1983).[27] As I noted in Chapter 3, Njabulo Nde- bele, in his role as the leading theorist of the People's Culture movement in the 1980s, emphasized the literary aspects of the project to revive the story form. For him, re-establishing links with the traditions of popular orature, which continued to form a vital part of everyday township life, was principally about reclaiming the space of the literary in the affirmative terms he outlined in a series of critical interventions throughout the decade. Importantly, a number of titles in the Staffrider Series, which, in his view, read more like works of literary reportage than fictionalized popular history, failed in this respect. At best what they offered was an 'aesthetics of recognition', which simply confirmed what their readers already knew about the injustices of apartheid, particularly from the details published in the liberal press.[28] The most worrying consequence of this, for Ndebele, was that these works also reinforced the 'protest' tradition Black Consciousness writers had rejected in the early 1970s. As he recalled in his 1984 *Staffrider* essay, this had formed the basis of the 'dissatisfaction with the early poetry of Oswald Mtshali'.[29] Though, in making this argument, Ndebele was mainly influenced by Black Consciousness thinking, the issues were, as we have seen, given a new urgency by the censor's legitimization of 'protest' in the 1980s and by their declared reasons for banning some titles in the series, which, in their view, amounted to little more than seditious journalism.

About *Call Me Not a Man*, Ndebele remarked: 'Matshoba's depiction of social reality in his stories [is] too overwhelming.' His 'basic technique has been to accumulate fact after fact of oppression and suffering, so that we are in the end almost totally grounded in this reality without being offered, at the same time, an opportunity for aesthetic and critical estrangement'.[30] In his view, Mza- mane's historical novel *The Children of Soweto* (1982), which was published as number 13 in the Staffrider Series, fell into the same trap. (Sadly, he did not comment on *Mzala*.) 'Grounded almost entirely in the events of June 16, 1976', the novel appeared to have 'no independent narrative line that permits any reader involvement beyond the act of recognition'.[31] Serote's *To Every Birth its Blood* (1983) was, he felt, a more impressive, though still flawed, achievement. It 'attempts to deal with the ordinary concerns of people while placing them within the broader political situation of the country', he claimed, but in the end 'the spectacle takes over and the novel throws away the vitality of the tension generated by the dialectic between the personal and the public'.[32]

By contrast, Tlali's *Amandla* was, in his view, 'the best of the novels written on the events of June 16' because in recounting the fortunes of two young lovers during the upheavals she was 'not "just reporting", she was telling a story'.[33] Questions about the specifically literary status of these stories and novels in the Staffrider Series also arose during the censors' deliberations, though their judgements were unsurprisingly less consistent and less nuanced than Ndebele's. They were also, in some cases, just crudely opportunistic.

Passing Stories: *Mzala* and *Fools*

Of the story collections, both *Mzala* and *Call Me Not a Man* were submitted by the police as Staffrider books soon after they were published. *Fools and Other Stories*, however, entered the system via customs as an imported Longman African Classic in 1988, five years after it first appeared locally. Like *Mzala*, it was passed by a literary committee, albeit for different reasons, given the official change in censorship practice after 1982. The initial reader in Mzamane's case, an Afrikaner clergyman (J. A. Victor), who was undecided about whether the volume constituted a collection of 'short stories' or 'sketches', noted that it contained some passages that could be deemed obscene or blasphemous (P81/1/107). He was concerned, among other things, about the way the first-person narrator in one story describes his 'nagging' wife as having him 'by the cock', and by another character's bilingual exclamation '*Here*, God!'[34] In its report the committee claimed this 'vulgar language' was acceptable because it was apparently 'in keeping with their ["the Blackman's"] modes of speech'. Despite these relatively minor concerns, the reader felt the collection as a whole could be passed because its overall 'tendency' was not 'subversive or propagandistic', a point on which the committee concurred. It also agreed with his argument that the 'book had to be evaluated against the background of the thought, life-, and world-view of the Blackman', since it 'would not enjoy a high literary status in terms of Western culture'. Neither the reader nor the committee mentioned that the stories, which had first appeared in various little magazines, earned Mzamane the Mofolo–Plomer Prize (jointly with Peter Wilhelm) in 1976, judged that year by Adam Small and Alan Paton.

The committee that decided the fate of *Fools and Other Stories* was more confident about its status as literature, noting that it was 'a collection of short stories written by South African born, award-winning N. S. Ndebele, professor of English at the University of Lesotho' (P88/2/23). The Longman blurb mentioned that the collection had won the prestigious Noma Award for publishing in Africa in 1984. The committee also felt that the 'possibly undesirable passages marked by the reader'—M. A. Hendricks, one of the sizeable group of 'Coloureds' who joined the system in the late 1980s—were 'acceptable'. All came from the end of the eponymous long story 'Fools', in which, Hendricks noted, the derogatory word 'Boer' occurred on a number of occasions. In this dramatic final episode, the complex generational tensions at the heart of the story, which is set in 1966 at a key transitional moment in the history of the resistance, come to a head. A brutal assault by a 'white man', who the narrator later calls 'the Boer', abruptly shatters the fraught triangular relations among the first-person narrator, Zamani, described by the reader as a 'disgraced black teacher', Zani, a 'confused young student activist', and Lehamo, a collaborationist school principal.

In an effort to prevent Zani, who is perhaps more accurately described as an idealistic and overly theoretical activist, from disrupting a community picnic he has organized to celebrate a festival of colonial domination, Lehamo attempts to drive him away by pelting him with stones. One accidentally hits a passing car driven by 'the Boer', who proceeds to take his revenge with a whip. This pivotal scene acquires a deeper historical resonance if we recall that the Sharpeville atrocities were, according to the police, supposed to have been provoked by a stone-throwing incident. In the mêlée that follows only Zamani emerges with his dignity intact. While both Zani and Lehamo flee, becoming, as Zani regretfully observes, 'fools', or, victims 'feeding on their victimness', Zamani surprises himself by standing up to the assault.[35] Hendricks noted that this episode could 'possibly be regarded as offensive to the white population group', though he felt the term 'Boer' was not in itself problematic because it was 'generally used by black people'. The exclusively white literary committee agreed, noting that the passages 'often describing the humiliation of blacks at the hands of whites' were 'acceptable in context'. 'Granting the acceptability of "protest literature"', its report concluded, the collection contained 'no undesirable elements, no sexually obscene passages, gratuitous violence, no encouragement to violence or revolutionary action'. In short, it offered, according to the norms the censors adopted in the 1980s, a safely literary 'picture of life—the social, political, economic issues—in the '60s in a township'.

Though the committee's defence of the collection as a series of 'short stories' in the 'protest' tradition went against everything Ndebele had set out to achieve, the terms in which it justified its decision, particularly the idea of it as a 'picture of life', tie in with one of the key questions in the critical debate about *Fools and Other Stories*. This debate has focused on the extent to which Ndebele reinforces a 'Western realist' tradition, or embraces other, experimental, specifically 'modernist' possibilities.[36] There is no doubt that for Ndebele the appeal of the *story* in his special sense was, in part, motivated by a desire to 'rediscover the ordinary' in relatively straightforward 'realist' terms. In the case of 'Fools' this is evident in its semi-rural setting, in its preoccupation with the intricate social and sexual dynamics of the African community it describes, and in the moral complexity of its central figure, Zamani, who is not unambiguously heroic. In the narrative past he disgraced himself by raping Zani's sister. Yet these aspects of the narrative had less to do with Ndebele's commitment to realism as such, or, indeed, to any concern he might have had about questions of realism versus modernism, than with his ambition to leave behind the by then doubly discredited tradition of 'protest' writing. As we have seen, the story form, considered as part of a specifically Third World tradition, crossing the boundary between modern literature and traditional orature, played a central part in the way he conceived this project.

That this was his overriding preoccupation, particularly in 'Fools', is especially evident in the way Zamani's encounter with 'the Boer' is described. Tellingly, for all its brutality, this scene does not conform to the conventions of the 'protest' tradition, detailing, as the censors claimed, the 'humiliation of blacks at the hands of whites'. On the contrary, without in any way diminishing 'the Boer's' racist violence, it turns these generic expectations on their head. By impassively taking the blows Zamani reduces his exasperated attacker to tears and finally defeats him. This act of defiance has personal significance for Zamani, who, before he allowed himself to become overwhelmed by cynicism induced primarily by his own sense of moral failure, had been looked on as a potential leader of the local community. As he makes clear, however, his actions also have a wider meaning. 'I had crushed him with the sheer force of my presence. I was there, and would be there to the end of time: a perpetual symbol of his failure to have a world without me.... And the sound of his car when he drove away seemed so irrelevant.'[37] Zamani's reflections also lead him to prophesy that 'the people of the north will come down and settle the land again, as they have done for thousands of years'.[38] Ndebele no doubt had this kind of moment in mind when he contrasted merely journalistic forms of 'recognition' with the specifically literary ideal of 'transformation'.[39] Stories, in this sense, did not offer a 'picture of life'; they constituted a mode of public intervention in their own right, the primary object of which was to change the way their intended (black) readers saw themselves, their world, and the future.

Just what was at stake in all this becomes clearer if we compare the terms Ndebele attributes to Zamani with those he himself used during a dispute over the publication of a Ravan poetry anthology in 1982. In a letter to Kirkwood, which was subsequently published in *Staffrider*, he explained that he refused to give permission for one of his own poems to appear in the anthology, the proposed title of which was *Ask Any Black Man*, because this title 'really represents no conceptual advance on *To Whom it May Concern*'.[40] Here he was referencing Robert Royston's earlier collection of Black poets, which Ad Donker had published in 1973. At that time, Ndebele commented acerbically, 'we were being revealed to White South Africa', the 'liberal publisher was bringing us out to dance', and the 'onus was on us to prove our humanity'.[41] The title for the new volume simply repeated this, since the 'logic points out ... that it's the white man who has to ask any black man'. It could obviously not refer to 'any African' because 'we know and have known for centuries the agony of oppression'.[42] To explain why he considered this a 'very serious matter', he then added:

> None of my poems have been written for people who wanted to hear me complain. They have been written in order to share serious insights, to share perceptions, and to *alter* perceptions in the most profound manner. I have gone *far beyond* begging to be 'heard'. I am not even demanding. It is the pure force of my people's inevitable presence that I want to consolidate. And I want to help to consolidate it to a point where we shall overcome, much more profoundly, with the very fact of our positive existence.[43]

As O'Brien observes, this recalls Zamani's affirmative language of 'sheer force', turning his reflections within the fictional frame of 'Fools' into an allegory not just of an incipient African renaissance but of writing beyond protest.[44] Seen in this light, the final episode of 'Fools' acquires a special literary, indeed, specifically metafictional, significance, the full transformative potential of which was especially pronounced in the context of the Staffrider Series. As a result of Ndebele's intervention, the anthology was retitled *The Return of the Amasi Bird* (1982), an allusion to the poem by Daniel P. Kunene with which it ends. Appropriately enough, this poem 'prophesies the inevitable return of the symbolic amasi bird to its rightful owners and the triumphant dawn of a new era'.[45]

Banning Stories: *Call Me Not a Man*

Call Me Not a Man suffered a very different fate from *Fools* primarily because it fell into the hands of a hardline security committee that, unlike the more literary censors at the time, refused to recognize the legitimacy of 'protest literature' as a category. The first reader (A. H. Murray) thought most of the 'short stories', as he called them, were 'harmless' (P79/10/82). Only 'A Glimpse of Slavery' and 'Son of First Generation' seemed to him problematic. About the former he noted: 'Experiences of a prison-hireling on a farm. A little worrying: second reader please. Too much sjambok [whip].' The latter was, he noted, about the 'lives of young natives in Johannesburg: white youth is in love with black waitress: both drink too much at a party: a baby arrives. Again second reader, but I think harmless.' The second reader (Admiral Bierman) was more categorical. The 'series of short stories or rather sketches', which took the 'lot of the Black man in the RSA as theme', contained a number of pieces like 'My Friend the Outcast' and 'Call Me Not A Man' that were 'very readable and encouraged the readers' sympathy'. 'Unfortunately', however, two stories, 'A Glimpse of Slavery' and 'A Pilgrimage to the Isle of Makana', were 'without doubt written with the goal of undermining whites and the state'. These stories had 'little or no literary value and can be considered seriously contentious'. The committee, which Murray chaired, agreed, and as a consequence the entire collection was banned for sedition, even though, as Murray noted, they had already passed 'A Pilgrimage' when it appeared in an abridged version in *Staffrider* in April 1979.

When Kirkwood wrote requesting an explanation for the ban, these inconsistencies put the censors in an awkward position. In an attempt to avoid any difficulties the chief censor prepared a special version of the committee's final report, referring only to 'A Glimpse'. This new statement, which, following his usual practice, Kirkwood duly published in *Staffrider*, took the censors' capacity for spurious 'literary' rationalizations to a new level.[46] Unlike the other stories in the collection, which the committee felt were 'generally of a high quality', the writing in this one 'comes near to the reporting type and the appeal lies not in the literary creation and composition, but rather in the objectionable nature of the events which are presented'. 'Even if all these situations had occurred, which is improbable,' it went on, 'the presentation of these scenes in a popular medium would be undesirable.' This further claim of course assumed that the story was in fact a piece of reportage. As such, the censors concluded, it 'is calculated to exacerbate race feelings between black and white races reciprocally; it is calculated to promote a sense of grievance without sufficient particular grounds to justify grievance feelings in the minds of African readers; and it offers material for emotional propagandistic action of a violent kind (a type of material used only too often in anti-state underground documents)'. In effect, 'A Glimpse' was seditious because it was insufficiently literary and because it appeared in the Staffrider Series.

This was not the first time that the seemingly high-minded question of the status of 'A Glimpse of Slavery' as a work of literature attracted official attention. In April 1979, six months before the censors read it in book form, the Department of Prisons issued a formal complaint against Ravan after the story had appeared in *Staffrider*. In their view, it gave a 'factually untrue' account of prison life.[47] They were especially concerned that one of the opening scenes takes place at Modderbee, a notorious apartheid prison near Johannesburg. In this scene the hiring out of prisoners to the brutal Afrikaner farmer Koos De Wet is compared, following the story's governing figure, to an auction of slaves. The censors, who appear not to have known about this earlier complaint, made no mention of the prison setting during their own deliberations. Their primary claim, at least in their specially prepared statement, was that the story failed to pass their aestheticist test for literariness. In their view, the apparently journalistic quality of the writing, which privileged 'content' over 'form', betrayed the author's propagandistic desire to incite black readers to violence against the state. Their unpublished comments revealed that they were especially worried about the portrayal of De Wet, who uses his 'sjambok' and his infantilized black foreman, Bobby, to maintain a regime of fear on his farm.

They also drew attention to the political discussions the prisoners and the other farm labourers have among themselves. After hearing the first-person narrator's account of how he ended up in jail for defending an elderly black co-worker from being attacked by a corrupt white manager, for instance, one of the farm labourers observes, 'there is no justice in this country', a comment the committee considered seditious.[48] Taken together with Ndebele's very different concerns about *Call Me Not a Man* as a whole, some of which, as we have seen, Mzamane shared, these official judgements give a particular significance to the questions surrounding the literariness of Matshoba's writing. This is further complicated, and made still more pressing, by the way Longman presented the collection in its African Classics series. Claiming that it belonged to both 'a worldwide tradition of the literature of protest' and to a 'new school of black South African writing that has emerged since the Soweto uprising of 1976', the blurb added that Matshoba's 'writing, uncluttered by literary artifice, bears witness to his profound understanding of the daily realities of township life'.[49]

That Matshoba saw himself, at least in part, as a witness to events, like the abuse of prisoners and farm labourers, is clear from his prefatory note. This is also underscored in 'A Glimpse' itself when the first-person narrator explains his own motives for telling his story: 'These things are never heard of outside the farms because desperation and need keep the victims in silent desolation.'[50] Yet, as Matshoba insisted in a legal statement he was required to produce in response to the complaint from the Department of Prisons, he also saw the story form as a specifically literary medium. In this context he appealed primarily to the principle of fictionality. The main events of the story, he pointed out, take place on a farm called Traanfontein (literally 'Tear-fountain'), which is entirely fictitious, and, though he had also described Modderbee, he said he had chosen it simply because it was well known, suggesting, in other words, that in the context of the story the proper noun functioned metonymically rather than referentially. Having said this, anticipating what he would go on to say in his prefatory note, he also insisted that his writings drew on his own experience. In the case of 'A Glimpse', he noted that he was initially inspired by a report in a local newspaper and the subsequent discussion it generated among his friends, some of whom had witnessed the brutal treatment of prison labourers by farmers at first hand.

Kirkwood, who was also required to make a formal deposition as publisher, developed this line of argument in his own statement, but he began by shifting the focus from the internal evidence of the story's fictionality to various contextual indicators of its literariness. The official complaint was, he argued, based on the false premiss that the story was 'written and presented as a *factual report*, similar to an "exposé" article in a newspaper'.[51] In fact, it had appeared in a 'magazine devoted to literary items such as poems, reviews, novels-in-progress, filmscripts, playscripts, etc.', where it was described as 'a "new story" by the author, who is a regular contributor'. This was not simply his view as publisher, he insisted. Citing the censors' more sympathetic reports on the magazine and the enthusiasm with which *Staffrider* had been greeted by the 'literary-minded public', he pointed out that 'a considerable spectrum of public and official opinion has recognised the value of protest and the need to grant "poetic licence" in regard to this magazine'. Returning to the fictionality argument, he added that the 'use of "real" place names is a commonplace convention of fiction the world over', citing Dickens as an example. Moreover, while recognizing that the Department had a right to take action against the 'publication of false information concerning prisons', he insisted that 'we absolutely contest that we published *information* as such'. Rather, as a work of fiction, and, more particularly, as a story in Benjamin's sense, what 'A Glimpse' depicted was not reality but '*perceptions* of reality', which were 'typical of those held by a great many black South Africans'. It would not, he felt, be difficult to prove this in court or, indeed, to 'show how those perceptions are formed'. Unlike the censors, the Department of Prisons appeared to be convinced by this argument, or at least by the doubts it raised about the juridical sustainability of their own allegations, because it eventually dropped the case.

Kirkwood's argument that the story, as a work of literature, stages 'perceptions of reality' applies especially to its depiction of prison labour as a form of slavery. It is also pertinent to what is arguably Matshoba's most significant literary device: his use of a participant first-person storyteller as a narrator who is not simply an eyewitness to the events but the primary vehicle for his humanistic intervention. As a frustrated artist who was obliged by his parents to take a more mundane job as a clerk, the unnamed narrator not only has a particular character and social identity—he frequently reflects on the awkwardness of his own position as one of the 'educated'—he also has a specific history.[52] In the narrative past he was something of an apolitical dissolute. At one point he wonders if the 'Traanfontein experience' had been 'set aside by Providence to take me out of my aimless life in Soweto and show me by a practical example of how my people were demeaned because they happened to have a dark skin, while I jived around a shebeen table covered with beer bottles'.[53] The religious inflection is characteristic of his language, which is also saturated with references to African proverbs and to canonical English literature, especially Shakespeare. To this extent 'A Glimpse' is not only a work of testimony, seemingly devoid of 'literary artifice', but a *Bildungsroman* describing a process of political awakening which is, in the end, humanistic rather than specifically ideological. 'Some may pass their time thinking that they are better than others,' the narrator comments explaining his general outlook, 'but in death we finally achieve the desired ideal state of equality which we unsuccessfully try to pursue through the hokum we call ideology.'[54] The story ends with him rejecting his past life and facing an uncertain future, albeit with a firmer sense of responsibility.

The narrator's humanistic outlook, which is pointedly not racialized, in fact dominates the story. When he defends himself against the white manager, for instance, he stresses that it was 'not a white man I was belting': it was 'a bully who needed some straightening out'.[55] Moreover, though he regards both De Wet and Bobby as 'a pair of sadists', he also wants to believe that their tendency to violence can, to some extent, be explained in historical or sociological terms.[56] While the other farm labourers simply dismiss Bobby, who was born on the farm, as 'selfish, cruel and as bone-headed as they come', he recognizes that his antipathy to the prisoners is, in part, driven by the 'contempt rural people have for city people'.[57] He also tries, without much success, to probe Bobby's inner life. 'Are you afraid that if you leave the cruel patron who keeps your stomach full of crumbs', he asks, 'to try to stand on your own feet and be counted with the real men of the world who face their suffering without turning judas, you'll be a loser?'[58] When it comes to De Wet's own capacity for violence, the narrator bases his analysis on Bobby's history of the farm.

> This is where *baas* Koos's great-grandfather was killed by Ndebele savages and lies buried. Later, when the Ndebele thieves were conquered his sons claimed this land and called it Traanfontein because their tears flowed here. They vowed never to leave the land and my people came to work for the De Wets before *baas* Koos was even born.[59]

Unlike Bobby, the narrator recognizes this as a thoroughly colonialist version of history. Yet he also acknowledges that it goes some way towards explaining why De Wet prefers 'manual labour', even though he can 'afford to keep pace with modern technology': 'its cheapness, and the vengeance sworn by the family against black people'. By wielding his 'sjambok', he is 'visiting the "sins" of the fathers upon the second and third generations'.[60]

When another security committee decided to lift the ban on *Call Me Not a Man* in 1985, after hardliners like Murray and Bierman had been eased out, it focused not on the legitimacy of 'protest literature' but on what it took to be *Matshoba*'s humanism. Since he wrote 'with bitterness against corruption and barbarity by all races (and not just by whites)', he could not 'in any way be seen to be predicting or promoting violence or rebellion, sedition or revolution' (P85/2/64). The plea for 'mutual respect' by the first-person narrator in 'A Pilgrimage to the Isle of Makana', who also refers to the Robben Island prisoners' 'burning desire to see justice and fairness', lay at the 'heart of the stories' and, citing another passage from the same story, reflected *Matshoba*'s 'hope for a flame of life that will burn away the chains of racial prejudice'.[61] Indeed, the committee argued that the collection ought to be unbanned because it could 'help to open people's eyes to what is wrong so that human relationships can be put on a better footing'. This more dispassionate reading harmonized well with Matshoba's desire to challenge government propaganda by telling stories that repudiated the label 'bloodthirsty terrorist'. Seen in Ndebele's terms, however, it also confirmed his association with the 'protest' tradition. In the end, this was not so much, as Ndebele himself argued, because his stories constituted little more than a form of reportage—they remained specifically literary in a number of key respects—but because Matshoba in writing *against* white racism, or, more specifically, government propaganda, conceded too much by assuming that the 'onus' fell on him to 'prove our humanity'. By contrast, for Ndebele, writing beyond protest, as he set out to demonstrate in 'Fools', meant establishing an autonomous literary space outside the structure of opposition, a space within which 'our humanity' would go without saying and white attitudes (and readers) would become as irrelevant as the sound of 'the Boer's' retreating car.

To Ban or not to Ban: Two Staffrider Novels

Given the anxieties about the journalistic qualities of 'A Glimpse of Slavery', it is worth, by way of conclusion, briefly comparing the censors' response to two more conventionally novelistic titles in the Staffrider Series: Serote's *To Every Birth its Blood* (1981) and Mzamane's *The Children of Soweto* (1982). Both were initially submitted by the police as Staffrider books, read by security censors, and then adjudicated by joint committees. The two decisions were in fact taken a month apart, the former in mid-June 1982, the latter in mid-July, with the same literary censor (Rita Scholtz) acting as chair in both cases. Like Tlali's *Amandla*, both novels focused on the pivotal moment of the 1976 Soweto uprising, and both adopted a formally inventive narrative structure.

To Every Birth is divided into two parts. In the first Tsi Molope, a former journalist and occasional actor, gives a first-person account of his abject, often dissolute and despairing life in the township of Alexandra. The second, which is told from multiple perspectives largely in the third person, focuses on the efforts to unify the various generations within the resistance and to re-energize the armed struggle. In this second part, which Ndebele felt was less successful than the first, Tsi finds a way out of his self-absorption through collective action. Though the novel remains a novel, not a disguised exercise in autobiography, it is possible to read it as a particularly inflected narrative of Serote's own changing self-understanding from his early years as a Black Consciousness poet to his later involvement as a leading cultural activist within the Medu Art Ensemble and the ANC.

The Children of Soweto, which is subtitled 'A Trilogy', also contains multiple narratives. The first and third parts, which describe the background to the uprising, the events of 16 June itself, and their immediate aftermath, are narrated in the first person by Sabelo, one of the student leaders who, like Tsi, ends the novel exiled in Botswana. A short middle section, told in the third person, focuses on a black travelling salesman's efforts to save a terrified white colleague who finds himself caught up in the momentous events of the day. This structure reflected Mzamane's dual conception of his project as both a historical novel and a traditional story. He wanted not only to 'tell more of the truth than the historian's truth', according to the Aristotelian tenets of realist fiction and 'message-plus' conceptions of the literary, but to 'preserve the memory of these events, as in the "tales" of my people I was told as a child'.[62] Unlike Serote, who was more preoccupied with the birth-pangs of a post-revolutionary future, Mzamane saw himself as documenting the inside story of the uprising from a black perspective: 'I try to convey, in a way that several accounts by white reporters do not, what it felt like to be one of those involved' and 'I have hardly bothered to disguise the didactic purpose of my tale.'[63] In another context, however, he also noted that he incorporated newspaper reports into the text 'on principle' because the 'separation between aesthetics and politics, fiction and fact, is one of the fundamental dichotomies the novel seeks to overcome—in the spirit, I might add, of Brecht's epic theatre'.[64]

For Admiral Bierman, the security censor who served as the initial reader in Serote's case, the central preoccupations of *To Every Birth* were unsurprising and self-evident. 'As can be expected', he noted, it 'describes the appalling life-circumstances in the area' of the Alexandra township and the 'black man's frustration about his existence in South Africa' (P82/6/6). It also made his 'feelings' about the established order 'very clear'. One passage from the first part, an extended quotation from a fictionalized township play describing the long history of the violent suppression of black resistance, left him in no doubt about the novel's disposition towards 'whites'; while, in his view, the third-person narrator's comment that 'South African cops' are the 'number one enemy of black people' encapsulated its general attitude to the police.[65] He singled out a number of descriptions of police 'methods of interrogation' which he thought were 'realistically sketched'. In one, Tsi gives a powerfully impressionistic account of being brutally abused by the police, an experience that only exacerbates his self-absorption and sense of hopelessness.[66] In another, from the novel's second section, Tsi's young nephew Oupa, who is an active member of the armed resistance, is tortured to death.[67] In his synopsis of the novel, Bierman also noted that the final section describes a campaign of 'widespread sabotage in which a number of the main characters die or flee the country', suggesting, by implication, that the novel ends on a note of defeat. In fact, in the concluding scene, which reverts to the first person, Tsi, now exiled, like Serote, in a war-torn Gaborone, witnesses the painful and bloody birth of a baby. His figural language—the blood is twice compared to 'the sun's rays'—turns the birth into an indirect expression of utopian hope, not to mention an oblique justification for violent revolution, confirming that 'every birth' does indeed have 'its blood'.[68]

Bierman, who thought the novel 'good and readable', was in no doubt about its status as a work of literature. Yet, in recommending that it should be passed, he appealed once again to the link between literature and journalism, now turning his earlier argument against 'A Glimpse' on its head. In this case, it was not so much that *To Every Birth* warranted banning because it read like a piece of reportage, but that it could be passed because its avowedly 'realistic' descriptions of police torture said 'nothing new'. Referring specifically to Ahmed Timol's death in police custody in 1971 and Neil Aggett's in 1982, he commented that 'incidents' of this kind, which he now demoted to 'allegations', had 'enjoyed wide publicity in the local press' ever 'since Sharpeville'. They had also featured prominently 'in the work of black writers, not to say anything of André Brink', though, as he acknowledged, 'most of these writers had been banned'. Significantly, his arguments, which made no reference to the new likely reader test, centred on the scenes of torture and abuse. He did not mention the political discussions among the characters, which feature prominently throughout the novel and which, as we saw in Chapter 2, played a decisive role in the censors' decision to ban Tlali's *Amandla*. Given this, he felt it was 'appropriate to wonder if the black reader of this publication has not already heard more often than he would care to imagine about the alleged heavy handedness of the police'. In his view, it could be passed not only because it was very unlikely to have an 'undue influence on the black man', who had heard it all before, but because it was 'important that the whites get an insight into the thoughts of the black people, their frustrations, etc.'. The committee agreed, and, though Etienne Malan thought the decision 'doubtful', principally because of the novel's portrayal of the police, no other members of the censorship Directorate questioned it, leaving the chief censor free to confirm that there would be no appeal.

Precisely the opposite rationale was given in the case of *The Children of Soweto*. The initial reader, another prominent security censor (J. P. Jansen), felt it had to be banned because it was 'more than a factual report' (P82/6/128). 'It is a strongly emotional kind of book', which he felt centred on the death of Muntu, one of the students shot by the police. He was also concerned that it detailed the student's interest in the writings of Marx, Guevara, and Mao Zedong, and endorsed Ngugi wa Thiong'o's ideas of collective resistance. In his view, Sabelo's final reflections on the aftermath of the uprising were 'actually the heart of the book': 'We were the children of the new diaspora, we, the children of Soweto, germinating everywhere we went little new seeds of vengeance, hatred, bitterness, wrath, on the fertile soil of our hearts, watering our cherished seeds with our own blood, sweat and tears and that of our people.'[69] Almost all the offending passages Jansen highlighted, many of which centred on police violence, came from the novel's third and last section. Outlining his specific reasons for the ban, he noted that it cast 'the police (the upholders of peace and order), the army and the Bantu Administration boards in a very bad light'; harmed race relations; and contained one blasphemous reference. In addition, the extensive use it made of revolutionary slogans and 'freedom songs' revealed that it had a 'militant aspect'. What made it ultimately 'unacceptable in the current circumstances', however, was that its 'likely reader would be the black youth'.

In her comments as chair, Rita Scholtz confirmed that the primary reason for the ban was that the novel went beyond mere reportage. Echoing Bierman's line of argument, she noted: 'I find this novel contains no inciting material that does not also appear daily in some of our newspapers.' Nevertheless, she agreed with Jansen that this did not save it, since the 'manner in which the Soweto disturbances are handled will encourage the youth to revolt'. It was seditious, in other words, not simply because it represented the uprising in a positive light but because it did so in an especially effective way, using all the literary resources of a particular kind of narrative fiction (documentary realism, first-person narration, etc.) to say more than any actual newspaper report. Like Gordimer's *Late Bourgeois World*, it was, in effect, banned because it was too literary, albeit according to the 'message-plus' criteria the aestheticist censors rejected. In 1985, when the South African Library submitted the novel for review, a security committee upheld the ban. Two years later, however, when the Library tried again, another security committee overturned the decision primarily because it doubted that the novel would make the 'overwhelming majority' of its likely readers 'any more inclined to political violence' than they would otherwise already be (P87/9/13).

Postscript

Two Statements

Literature is, in principle, unpoliceable. Literature is, in fact, always being policed.

The apartheid censors' collaborationist, necessarily erratic, and inevitably unjust literary guardianship amply confirms the truth of these two statements and, more particularly, the force of their juxtaposition. That something similar could be said of the intervention that is often taken to mark the beginning of the end of the long, fractious, and resilient cultural struggle against apartheid is less expected. In 1989, while still in exile, Albie Sachs, the acclaimed human rights lawyer, ANC activist, and victim of a failed assassination attempt by apartheid security agents, had a paper entitled 'Preparing Ourselves for Freedom' delivered on his behalf at an ANC seminar on culture held in Lusaka, Zambia. Picking up on a number of themes he had been addressing throughout the year at various cultural events held under the auspices of the international anti-apartheid movement, and, indeed, on arguments he had long been making in his contributions to the debates within the Medu Art Ensemble, he gave a resolute, even self-consciously provocative, endorsement of the first statement, which he extended to the arts more generally.[q] Yet, as some commentators later claimed, his language and judgements at times confirmed the truth of the second.

In fact, Sachs made two interventions on this occasion, each in a different capacity. In the first, which focused on the need for the ANC to move from thinking of culture as a specially tailored instrument of mass mobilization to seeing it as a more opened-ended space for democratic nation-building, he spoke as a critic and writer who, having written the banned *Jail Diary of Albie Sachs* (1966), would in the years ahead go on to publish three further autobiographical volumes. With characteristic incisiveness and finesse—Sachs has always been, dare I say it, the most 'literary' of lawyers—he began his first intervention by saying, 'we all know where South Africa is, but we do not yet know what it is'.[1] With this astute rhetorical gesture he simultaneously cast off the 'multiple ghettoes of the apartheid imagination', not to mention centuries of colonial domination, and cleared the way for a new kind of thinking about the field of culture in a liberated future (239). To speed this process along he then made this self-avowedly 'controversial' declaration: 'our members should

343

be banned from saying that culture is a weapon of struggle' (239). 'Fully aware of the fact that we are totally against censorship and for free speech', he none-theless suggested that this moratorium should last for 'a period of, say, five years' (239). This drastic measure was necessary, he argued, in order to 'break free from the solemn formulas of commitment' and to open up the space of culture by enlarging the 'range of themes' that could legitimately be addressed—he wanted to allow room for 'all that is funny or curious or genuinely tragic in the world'—by welcoming modes of writing that embraced 'ambiguity and contradiction', and by allowing artists to regain a 'genuine confidence' in their work, knowing that 'it springs from inside the personality and experience of each of them, from popular tradition and the sounds of contemporary life' (239–41). 'If you look at most of our art and literature,' he remarked, 'you would think we were living in the greyest and most sombre of all worlds, completely shut in by apartheid' (239). With the prospect of liberation in sight, what was needed was an idea of culture which was at once more capacious and more autonomous, which 'bypasses, overwhelms, ignores apartheid, establishes its own space' (241).

Given the many political traditions within the ANC, and the compromised history of liberalism in South Africa, his second intervention was no less 'challenging' (242). This time he spoke not as a cultural critic but as a human rights lawyer who was then drawing up the ANC's guidelines for a future democratic constitution and leading a campaign to reclaim the 'bourgeois' language of rights as an 'instrument of liberation'.[2] To guide its thinking and give a 'concrete meaning to the statement [in the 1955 Freedom Charter] that the doors of learning and culture shall be opened' he argued that the organiza-tion should base many of its own key constitutional proposals relating to matters of cultural policy on liberal principles (247). Rejecting the past policies of enforced and self-servingly racialized communitarianism pursued by the apartheid cultural planners, and, looking further back, the kind of coercive assimilation practised by the British colonists who 'tried to force everyone into the mould of the English gentleman', he proposed that the ANC should 'acknowledge and take pride in the cultural variety of our people' without imposing a 'model culture' (244). 'It ill behoves us to set ourselves up', he commented, 'as the new censors of art and literature' (247). 'Subject only to restrictions on racist propaganda and on ethnic exclusiveness such as are to be found in the laws of most countries of the world,' he explained, 'the people in the South Africa envisaged in the Guidelines will be free to set up such organisations as they please, to vote for whom they please, and to say what they want' (246). With these constitutionally guaranteed freedoms in place, he felt it would be possible to create a common civic identity within a unified demo-cratic state and to lay the foundations for a 'multilingual', 'multifaith', and 'multicultural' future that would be properly open-ended and securely rights-based (244). 'We will have Zulu South Africans and Afrikaner South Africans and Indian South Africans and Jewish South Africans and Venda South Africans and Cape Moslem South Africans'—indeed, since the 'terminology' would be determined by the people 'for themselves', a potentially unlimited variety of cultural groupings, mapped along professional, gender, religious, sexual, ethnic, and other non-racial lines, some of which might, of course, be conceived in cosmopolitan or transnational terms (244). The rise of the Internet as a medium for global networking in the 1990s only strengthened the latter possibility.

After receiving a mixed reception from the in-house audience for whom it was first intended—Sachs was later informed 'we were split right down the middle'—a much wider debate followed within South Africa when an edited version of his paper was published in the *Weekly Mail* in February 1990, the month Nelson Mandela was released.[3] This equally frank and vigorous debate, which ran for the next six months and centred primarily on Sachs's comments as a cultural critic, took place in the progressive forums that had emerged in South Africa in the late 1980s, including the columns of the two anti-apartheid newspapers, the *Weekly Mail* itself and its Afrikaans counterpart, *Vrye Weekblad*, and among the membership of the Congress of South African Writers (COSAW) and the many community arts projects affiliated to the Congress of South African Trade Unions (COSATU). Though Sachs's provocations were widely welcomed and seen as a turning point in the cultural debates of the 1980s, they also attracted some strong criticism.

A few commentators refused to accept the moratorium, but others took issue with the fact that Sachs was speaking not only as a leading figure within the ANC but as an exile who had lost touch with the thinking and political diversity among progressive groups in the country. Others, like Frank Meintjies, a former COSATU officer and executive member of COSAW, noted that many of Sachs's remarks, as a cultural critic, had been made before, not only by Nadine Gordimer, Christopher van Wyk, and Njabulo Ndebele but by worker poets like Mzwakhe Mbuli and Mi Hlatshwayo. In a more surprising, though not implausible, move, designed in part as a response to Sachs's own reconciliatory efforts to include the Afrikaner community, Ampie Coetzee, the Afrikaans Marxist critic who was a key figure within Taurus, saw some precedents in the critical writings of N. P. van Wyk Louw. Recognizing that Louw could 'only think in terms of his volk', Sachs's arguments nonetheless reminded Coetzee of the leading Afrikaner poet's ambition to create a more capacious modern Afrikaans literature in the 1930s.[4]

Other commentators questioned the normative assumptions underlying Sachs's apparently anti-prescriptive, even specifically Trotskyite, ideas of art and literature. The literary critic Tony Morphet, for instance, doubted that Sachs had, as some believed, found a way of accommodating the sometimes apparently contradictory imperatives of revolutionary and avant-garde art, claiming that his appeal to outdated conceptions of the 'imagination' was in the end retrogressive.[5] Unsurprisingly, in the euphoria of this utopian moment, no one raised J. M. Coetzee's more astringent doubts about the reliability of literature (on some definitions) as an ally in any nation-building project, or, indeed, any collective cultural enterprise. By far the most robust critique came, however, from leading figures within the community arts movement. While Meintjies called Sachs's 'sweeping value judgements of the nature of past progressive cultural work' both 'rhetorical and unhelpful', a workers' collective belonging to the regional Culture and Working Life Project vigorously defended the 'revolutionary style' adopted by 'younger people' in the 1980s, which 'created meaningful solidarities, co-operative, total commitment to the importance of creativity, self-sacrifice to community betterment, and in the trade unions discipline and innovation'.[6] 'A policy of non-hegemonic leadership which encourages freedom of expression is desirable,' they concluded, 'but it would only encompass at the moment an articulate and already tolerant creative elite primarily drawn from the middle classes.'[7]

Ari Sitas, a poet and member of COSAW with strong trade union links, echoed these sentiments, citing the French sociologist Pierre Bourdieu's sceptical critique of taste as a 'form of violence perpetrated by the strong on the weak' where the 'power to *make* the rules' of art and literature all too quickly 'turns into hegemony'.[8] 'Our history is littered with examples,' Sitas noted, referring to, among other things, 'the way liberal patronage offended the Bikos, Gwalas, and Lekhotas; the way later Ravan Press's and Black Consciousness dominance treated the rest, and so on, down the years'.[9] For obvious reasons, he did not mention the censors themselves, whose collaborationist literary guardianship was all but invisible. On his return to South Africa in 1990, Sachs engaged his critics in various public forums around the country, which, as he later reflected, proved that 'the culture of debate is perhaps more important than the debate of culture'.[10] The experience nonetheless led him to express 'regret that my paper came as a shock to many people working in the field of community arts, who saw it as implying that their work has no value, because it failed to meet high aesthetic standards'.[11] In the end, what he learned from the process of 'fierce discussion' was that 'perhaps we should not even try to define art, just to do it and respond to it and argue about it'.[12]

Towards Another Future

Sachs's final, pointedly anti-scholastic remark serves as a fitting conclusion to a book about the grotesque cultural consequences of turning specific literary guardians, who might ordinarily be powerful brokers within the relatively autonomous field of culture, into officially sanctioned literature police who possess the power to ban. Yet it also raises the question of the state's future role within the wider culture of public debate about literature and the arts. As the British government commission to which I referred in my Introduction concluded in 1979, the only plausible way of putting decisions about what counts as literature beyond the law, thereby leaving them to the voluntary groups, institutions, and media who constitute the modern literary world, is to lift all legal curbs on the 'printed word'.[13] Though the Williams Report addressed these issues specifically in relation to obscenity legislation, its arguments could, in principle, be applied to laws against blasphemy and sedition, and no doubt extended to the digital word as well. Adopting a policy of total disengagement in this area of the law would have a number of clear advantages. It would fulfil the long-held liberal dream embodied in the classic conception of the 'Republic of Letters', and, seen in more instrumental terms, it would safeguard authors and publishers from the threat of prosecution while also effectively absolving the state from the 'scholastic' problems associated with literary expertise, which remain intractable.[14] Yet, since few legal systems have, despite the changed media environment, entirely left behind the deeply entrenched anxieties about the medium of print, and none treat the freedom of expression as an unconditional absolute, this is unlikely to be realizable in practice. It is also at least debatable whether or not, in a just society, it is desirable in principle. Indeed, when modern democracies recognize literature as a public good, or afford it explicit legal protection, as South Africa does today, it could be argued that the question of the state's juridical relationship to the field of culture has to be asked anew.

Since 1996 literature's destiny in South Africa has been tied not just to a properly autonomous and still significantly transnational book trade, but to the chance of a multilingual constitutional democracy, of a unitary state with a strong internationalist orientation, of a reclaimed liberalism, and of a rights-based multi- or interculturalism.[15] At two key levels of legislation, however, it has also been linked to the inevitably uncertain guardianship of state-appointed literary experts. The Constitution of the Republic of South Africa, 1996, the supreme guarantor of its young democracy, includes a Bill of Rights that embodies many of Sachs's revisionist ideals, though its provisions covering the freedom of expression are, in certain respects, both more positive and more exacting than those he envisaged in 1989. The relevant section (16) reads as follows:

1. Everyone has the right to freedom of expression, which includes—
   (a) freedom of the press and other media;
   (b) freedom to receive or impart information or ideas;
   (c) freedom of artistic creativity; and
   (d) academic freedom and freedom of scientific research.

2. The right in subsection (1) does not extend to—
   (a) propaganda for war;
   (b) incitement of imminent violence; or
   (c) advocacy of hatred that is based on race, ethnicity, gender or religion, and that constitutes incitement to cause harm.[16]

Given the history of apartheid censorship, it is worth noting that clause 2 makes no reference to obscenity or blasphemy, or directly to sedition. Like all the rights in the founding Bill, those identified in section 16 are also subject to a general limitation clause (section 36), which allows for them to be restricted, under certain specified conditions, 'to the extent that the limitation is reasonable and justifiable in an open and democratic society based on human dignity, equality and freedom'.[17] This further provision, taken together with the specific inclusion of the 'freedom of creative activity', effectively ensures that the state functions not just as relatively disengaged guarantor of the rights underlying the 'culture of debate' but as a potential participant in the 'debate of culture'. It opens up a future role for literary (and other) experts within state structures, not, of course, as shadowy censors, but as witnesses who can be called on to testify on behalf of particular works in open court or other tribunals.

This possibility was strengthened under the Publications Act, 1996, another key legal instrument reflecting the importance officially accorded to literature and the arts in today's South Africa. In August 1994 Nelson Mandela's Minister of Home Affairs, Mangosuthu Buthelezi, appointed a task group to draft new legislation in accordance with the Bill of Rights, which would replace the repressive Publications Act, 1974, and its associated 'homeland' versions. In keeping with the reconciliatory spirit of the Mandela presidency, the group included among its members J. C. W. van Rooyen, the ousted former chair of the Appeal Board, who headed up the new group, and Abraham Coetzee, who was then still chief censor. The new Act radically modernized the legislation. It followed the Bill of Rights by criminalizing the distribution of any publication which 'judged in context' fell under any one or more of the three exclusions stipulated under section 16 (2).[18] Yet, in a more surprising move, which effectively privileged the constitutional guarantees covering the 'freedom of creative activity', it explicitly exempted, among other things, what it called 'bona fide' literary publications.[19] It also applied this extra safeguard to its own provisions regarding publications given an XX classification, which criminalizes distribution, or an X18 rating, which restricts its sale to adults. These classifications are directed principally at the 'visual presentation, simulated or real' of child sex, bestiality, violent sexual conduct, or 'extreme violence which constitutes an incitement to cause harm', but they also cover publications in which such acts are *described* 'predominantly and explicitly'.[20] In legal terms, then, the new Act represents an emphatic break with the past. Reflecting internationally agreed norms, and the guarantees enshrined in the Bill of

Rights, it rejects censorship in favour of classification, focuses on relatively measurable questions of harm, avoiding any reference to value-laden ideas of blasphemy or moral repugnance (i.e. obscenity), and affords literature explicit statutory protection.

When it came to the question of how the new Act might be implemented, the task group decided against a system 'based solely on criminal law' via the courts and against the option of self-regulation by the relevant media industries along the model of the film classification boards in the UK, the United States, and Germany.[21] Instead, it successfully argued for an 'administrative structure funded by the State, but which functions independently of Government, and which draws on available expertise'.[22] As a consequence, South Africa now has a national statutory Film and Publication Board (FPB) as well as a Review Board, comparable to the Offices of Film and Literature Classification in Australia and New Zealand, which is empowered to appoint literary experts to assist in its deliberations. According to van Rooyen, the task group 'came to the conclusion that if the preponderance of expert opinion classifies a film or publication as bona fide art or literature, any measure taken by the state to limit its distribution or display to adults would be disproportionate to the slight, if any, possibility of harm'.[23]

For all the similarities to the bureaucracy introduced under the 1974 Act, the new structure, which came into operation in 1998, is different in a number of crucial respects. For one thing, the panel set up to advise the President on the appointment of FPB members is obliged to invite nominations from the general public. Whereas the old system had been dominated by a group of government appointees, all male Afrikaners, the first chair of the new Board, Dr Nana Makaula, was one of South Africa's leading black woman academics with a background in psychology and education. The more robustly independent FPB also appoints its own 'classification committees' and, at *their* request, its own experts. Finally, when it comes to publications, the FPB, unlike the apartheid censorship bureaucracy, which was for the most part a conduit for submissions from the police and customs, responds only to complaints from the general public. Film distributors, by contrast, are required to apply for classification in advance.

In the absence of a substantial archive of decisions relating to publications— since 1998 the FPB has dealt primarily with films, DVDs, and issues of child pornography on the Internet—it is not possible to say what long-term cultural consequences this new democratic form of guardianship will have for literature. Yet if the one key case considered in the first decade of the new system is anything to go by, it is clear that the future will be neither wholly predictable nor uncontroversial. In February 2002, when the 14-year-old ban on Salman Rushdie's *The Satanic Verses* (1988) was technically lifted under the terms of the new Act, many of the same local Muslim organizations who had campaigned against the novel in the apartheid era wrote to the FPB requesting that a ban be reimposed, some casting their objections in especially threatening terms. As the chair is required to refer a complaint to a committee for examination and possible classification, a group, which included a number of literary experts, was duly appointed to consider the case. Following the new spirit of openness and debate, representatives from among the complainants were invited to the meeting (though none turned up). The committee acknowledged that it faced a difficult problem not just because in its judgement the option of outright banning had to be ruled out in this case, but because 'it might be argued that in a secular state, questions of religious propriety have no place in governmental decision-making'.[24] Under the Bill of Rights, it was, of course, also bound to uphold Rushdie's 'freedom of artistic creativity' as well as his and his publishers' property rights. Fully aware of its legal obligations, and despite its own objections to the aggressive tone in which the complaints had been made, the committee nonetheless felt 'sympathetic to the charge of blasphemy and of severe hurt to the religious sensibilities of the Muslim community' and an acute 'sense of responsibility to the complainants, and to the public at large, to take these issues seriously'.

Unlike the committee of security censors who originally banned *The Satanic Verses* on grounds of blasphemy in 1988, the new committee considered both the text of the novel and the history of the furore it provoked in detail. Like the apartheid censors, however, it accepted the complainants' status as representatives and, as a consequence, the authority of their claim that the novel is 'considered profoundly blasphemous and injurious by the Muslim community'. Yet it firmly rejected their view that *The Satanic Verses* still constituted a word crime. Referring to section 16 (2) of the Bill of Rights, it argued that the novel 'does not in fact advocate hatred against Islam or indeed against any other religion or faith system' and that it 'certainly does not argue, in its pages, any incitement to cause harm or civil violence'.

> The material which is found to be injurious is a parodic literary deconstruction of ancient Islamic lore and belief, which is an unpacking of tenets of faith by an author, who, in the novel, questions the basis of his own belief. Salman Rushdie's Rabelaisian scepticism may well be profoundly shocking and hurtful to many of the Islamic faith but it does not invite hatred towards Islam.

Moreover, bearing in mind the terms of the Publications Act, it noted that '*The Satanic Verses* is without argument a *bona fide* literary work by a leading international literary figure.' For these reasons the committee concluded it was not 'legally possible' to consider giving the novel an XX classification, which would, in effect, have banned it by 'restricting all public access or possession'. In fact, as an unillustrated book, this would have criminalized its distribution only, which was prohibitive enough.

Strictly speaking, the committee had, at that point, fulfilled its obligations under the law. Yet, going against the precise terms of the Act, it decided to give the novel an X18 classification and, more controversially, to recommend that it 'should not be for sale *in public* in South African commercial booksellers or any other commercial outlet, nor should it be available for borrowing from any municipal or public library' (this did not include legal deposit or university libraries). Tellingly, these last restrictions, which the FPB accepted, were imposed not under the Publications Act but in accordance with the general limitation clause in section 36 of the Bill of Rights. Though it is arguable whether or not this mainly affects Rushdie and his publisher's property rights, there is little doubt that many would see the decision to make the public display of the novel illegal and to inhibit its availability as an unwarranted infringement of Rushdie's freedom as an author and, more strongly still, as a worrying example of excessive state intervention. As Ronald Dworkin, the foremost American legal theorist, argued during the Danish cartoon crisis in 2006, 'freedom of speech' is 'a condition of legitimate government', not 'just a special and distinctive emblem of Western culture that might be generously abridged or qualified for other cultures that reject it'.[25] Seen in these terms the FPB's decision looks like a generous or perhaps even indulgent concession designed to assuage Muslim feeling, which further damages the reputation some official South African bodies earned as defenders of the freedom of expression in the first decade of democracy. As Victoria Bronstein, the South African academic lawyer, observed in 2007, the higher courts in the country have 'spoken of freedom of expression in expansive terms'—in one notable case Justice Sachs described 'subversive humour' as 'an elixir of constitutional health'—but some lower courts and tribunals had been less enthusiastic.[26] In early 2006, to cite just one pertinent example, a lower-court judge issued an injunction preventing a prominent newspaper from reprinting the satirical Danish cartoons on the grounds that protecting the human dignity of Muslims and a fragile national unity had to be given priority over the freedom of expression. In Judge Jajbahy's view, the cartoons 'advocated hatred and stereotyping of Muslims', though, as Bronstein comments, he avoided the issue of whether or not they also amounted to 'an incitement to cause harm'.[27]

Yet the comparison with the Jajbahy ruling clearly does not bear much scrutiny, nor is it possible to see the FPB decision as a simple concession in which, say, human dignity is allowed to trump the freedom of expression. On the contrary, by arguing that the limitation it imposed on the public display and availability of the novel was 'reasonable and justifiable in an open and democratic society based on human dignity, equality and freedom', the committee believed it could 'satisfy the theological and religious concerns of the South African Muslim community while also allowing for the crucial principle of right of access and freedom of expression'. As it noted, the restriction on display did not prevent a book-buyer from asking a local bookseller to order a copy for her, or, 'given the transnational nature of the contemporary book trade', from buying one for herself over the Internet. It did not consider the consequences of the curb on borrowing from public libraries, however, which effectively means only university students, or those who can afford to buy books, have relatively unhindered access to *The Satanic Verses* in South Africa today. Despite this worrying omission, the ruling, which was accepted by the complainants and not contested by any other parties, was clearly more judicious than Jajbahy's. In response to secularist, liberal, or literary arguments against censorship, the committee upheld the right of some adult readers to make their own judgements about the novel and Rushdie's commitment to literature as a space in which, as he put it in an interview in September 1988, 'there are no subjects which are off limits'.[28] In response to Muslim calls for an apartheid era ban to be reimposed, it offered not censorship (nor a reinstatement of blasphemy law) but recognition, at the level of the state, of the genuine offence many law-abiding South African Muslims feel the novel has caused them and their faith. In making this double move the FPB also implicitly acknowledged that literature, understood in Rushdie's terms, has the power to produce shattering real-world effects.

That this adjudication, which relies on a particular interpretation of the flexibility introduced under section 36 of the Bill of Rights, unsettles the positions around which the highly charged public debates about the freedom of expression tend to polarize is indisputable. Whether or not it is defensible, or, indeed, just is another matter. No doubt Dworkin, who takes as his point of departure the First Amendment tradition in the United States, would consider the limited curbs excessive and, in a certain sense, anti-democratic. As he put it in the *New York Review of Books* article to which I have already referred, 'in a democracy no one, however, powerful or impotent, can have a right not to be insulted or offended' and, he added, this 'principle is of particular importance in a nation that strives for racial and ethnic fairness'.[29] On this analysis, the FPB ought, as a guardian of democratic values, to have stopped once the committee established that *The Satanic Verses* no longer constitutes a word crime, and the complainants ought to have accepted that being offended is a price everyone pays for enjoying the advantages of living in a secular democracy.

Yet if we agree that the restrictions imposed on the public display and availability of the novel are consistent with the general limitation clause, then the FPB's decision acquires a different meaning and import. While it defended Rushdie's right to give offence and upheld the guarantees that underpin the South African state *de jure*, it also went one step further by publicly acknowledging that secular democracies, which are *de facto* intercultural and multi-faith, include within their midst minorities whose conception of the sacred is not written into the constitution. Moreover, by invoking the general limitation clause, it made this hospitable accommodation at minimal cost to the hard-won culture of rights. Seen in this way, it could be argued that the ruling constitutes a just and creative accommodation, not a dubiously generous concession, which raises important questions about the future of literature and the ethics of literary judgement in our globalized, intercultural, and multi-media age. In my view, this conclusion is easier to defend in relation to the decision to prevent the novel from being displayed in bookshops; less so, given the veiled issues of class or elitism, when it comes to the curb on its availability in public libraries.

Having said this, we cannot ignore the fact that in at least one important respect *The Satanic Verses* does not constitute a good test case for the new legislative framework in South Africa. Somewhat like D. H. Lawrence's *Lady Chatterley's Lover* in the landmark British and US trials of the late 1950s and early 1960s, its status as a '*bona fide* literary work' was, like Rushdie's reputation, too securely established by 2002 (though it is, of course, still contested in some quarters). It is possible to imagine other kinds of writing, say, a parody of vicious racist thinking or of pornographic violence against children published by a previously unknown author on the Internet, about which it might, in principle, be impossible for any classification committee or group of literary experts to reach a consensus. Internet publication is especially testing in this context because it need not necessarily bring with it all the extrinsic markers of literary prestige (imprint, book format, paper quality, etc.) associated with the traditional medium of print. In the face of these difficulties, which will no doubt become more acute in the future, it is clear that van Rooyen's continued faith in the authority of literary experts looks wishful. In his report as chair of the 1996 task group, he insisted that decisions about what counted as 'bona fide' litera-ture 'must not be understood to be based on the purpose of the writer from his or her point of view'.[30] Rather, the 'objective appraisal by experts should be the test and the publication or film itself should be the object of appraisal'.[31] Given the lessons of the past, his unwaveringly scholastic faith is to say the least perturbing. For all the reasons detailed in this book, there can be no guarantees that South Africa's democratic literary guardians will always succeed where their repressive predecessors repeatedly failed. Nevertheless, the fact that the FPB's ruling on *The Satanic Verses* went beyond anything the task group was able to envisage in 1996, not least by taking advantage of the essentially ethical space built into the Bill of Rights, suggests that there are good grounds for being confident about the future of literature in a democratic South Africa. Yet, since it is impossible to predict who the literary will strike next, or where its historic association with the 'daring experiment' of free speech will lead, it will always pay to remain, following the now familiar adjuration, 'eternally vigilant' as well.[32]

Chronology

Date	Politics	Censorship	Publishing	Culture	Selected decisions
1910	Union of South Africa created out of the nineteenth-century Boer republics (Orange Free State and Transvaal) and British territories (Cape and Natal)			Official languages are Dutch and English	
1912	South African Native National Congress (precursor to the African National Congress) formed			New African movement gains momentum	
1913		Customs Management Act			
1914	National Party formed				
1915			Nasionale Pers founded	Hertzog Prize founded	
1916			*Die Huisgenoot* founded		
1918	Afrikaner Broederbond formed				
1921	South African Communist Party formed			International PEN founded in Britain	
1922	Inkatha founded				
1925				Afrikaans replaces Dutch as second official language in the Union	
1927				SA PEN founded	
1930				Négritude movement launched in Paris	

355

(*Continued*)

Date	Politics	Censorship	Publishing	Culture	Selected decisions
1931		Entertainments (Censorship) Act establishes the first Board of Censors			
1932			Afrikaanse Pers founded (later APB)		
1934	United Party and Purified National Party formed	Censorship Board's powers extended to imported books		Afrikaans Writers' Circle founded	
1935			Bantu Treasury Series launched	Afrikaans Coalition for the Free Book launched	
1937					Cloete's *Turning Wheels* banned
1939				Van Wyk Louw coins the phrase *lojale verset* ('loyal resistance')	
1942			*Fighting Talk* founded		
1943			African Bookman Series launched		
1945			*Standpunte* launched; mission presses still dominate African-language publishing	Afrikaner historians affirm their own cultural history in narrowly nationalist terms	
1947			Traditional Markets Agreement ensures that British publishers continue to dominate English-language publishing in South Africa until the 1970s		

1948	D. F. Malan's National Party comes to power on a platform of apartheid				
1949	Prohibition of Mixed Marriages Act				
1950	Suppression of Communism Act, Population Registration Act, Group Areas Act, Immorality Amendment Act; SACP banned	Press Enquiry launched			
1951			*Drum* founded; *Tydskrif vir Letterkunde*, journal of the Afrikaans Writers' Circle, launched		
1952	ANC-led nationwide Defiance Campaign				
1953	Non-Racial Liberal Party and Congress of Democrats formed; Bantu Education Act; SACP reconstituted underground				
1954		Cronjé inquiry into 'Undesirable Publications' launched	*New Age* founded		
1955	Congress of the People adopts the Freedom Charter	A new Customs Act consolidates previous measures to control imported books			
1956	Treason Trial begins		*Africa South* founded; *Purple Renoster* launched	Butler calls on English-language writers to affirm their own national tradition	Bloom's *Transvaal Episode* banned

(Continued)

Date	Politics	Censorship	Publishing	Culture	Selected decisions
1957		Cronjé Report published			Abrahams's *Tell Freedom* banned
1958	H. F. Verwoerd becomes Prime Minister		Seven Seas founded in East Berlin		Gordimer's *World of Strangers* (hardback) and Paton's *Too Late the Phalarope* (paperback) passed; Hofmeyer's *The Skin Is Deep* and Stein's *Second-Class Taxi* banned
1959	Pan Africanist Congress (PAC) formed after a split within the ANC, partly over SACP links		Human & Rousseau founded; *African Communist* launched		Mphahlele's *Down Second Avenue* passed
1960	Sharpeville atrocities; ANC and PAC banned; Alex La Guma and Brian Bunting detained		*Contrast* founded		Hutchinson's *Road to Ghana* banned
1961	South Africa becomes a Republic; Treason Trial ends in acquittal; ANC adopts armed struggle			Central News Agency Award founded; Mphahlele becomes head of the Congress of Cultural Freedom's Africa programme; exile-led international cultural boycott gains momentum in Britain	Matshikiza's *Chocolates for my Wife* banned
1962	General Law Amendment Act (Sabotage Act); Bunting and La Guma under house arrest	Blanket bans affect individual writers, including La Guma, Pieterse, and Brutus	Heinemann African Writers Series founded; *New African* launched; *South Africa: Information and Analysis* started		Mphahlele's *African Image*, Gordimer's *World of Strangers* (paperback), Rooke's *Greyling*, and La Guma's *Walk in the Night* banned
1963	Rivonia Trial (the well-known trial of Mandela) begins; foundation of the Christian	New Publications and Entertainments Act covers imported and	*Classic* founded; *Sestiger* launched	Sestiger group emerges	Modisane's *Blame me on History* and Rive's *African Songs* banned

	Institute; First, Brutus, and La Guma detained	locally produced books; Dekker Board formed			Rive's *Emergency* and Smith's *Lion Feeds* banned; one issue of *Purple Renoster* banned; Brink's *Lobola* and Mutwa's *Indaba* passed
1964	Eight Rivonia accused, including Mandela, imprisoned for life; Hugh Lewin, a member of the African Resistance Movement, and Brutus imprisoned				
1965		Trial of Smith's *When the Lion Feeds*			La Guma's *Threefold Cord* and Abrahams's *Wreath for Udomo* banned; Leroux's *Sewe Dae* passed
1966	Verwoerd assassinated; B. J. Vorster becomes Prime Minister; Bram Fischer sentenced to life imprisonment	Blanket bans affect individual writers, including Kunene, Matshikiza, Modisane, Mphahlele, and Nkosi, all by then in exile			Gordimer's *Late Bourgeois World* banned; Leroux's *Derde Oog* passed
1967					Nkosi's *Home and Exile* and *Jail Diary of Albie Sachs* banned
1968	Liberal Party dissolved; South African Students' Organization (SASO) formed	Kruger Board formed	*Kol* launched; Buren founded	Rise of Black Consciousness; Sestigers divided over *lojale verset*; UN General Assembly endorses the cultural boycott	Brink's *Miskien Nooit* passed
1969	Bureau of State Security created; Serote imprisoned				Cope's *Dawn Comes Twice* banned
1970	UN General Assembly declares apartheid 'a crime against the conscience and dignity of mankind'				La Guma's *Stone Country* banned

(Continued)

Date	Politics	Censorship	Publishing	Culture	Selected decisions
1971	Ahmed Timol murdered in prison		David Philip founded; Renoster Books launched		
1972	Black People's Convention (BPC) formed		Ravan Press founded; *Black Review* launched	Music, Drama, Arts, and Literature Institute founded	
1973	Widespread strikes by black workers; rise of independent trade unions	Kruger Commission launched; Biko, Strinivasa Moodley, and other members of SASO banned	Ad Donker founded	Black Literature and Arts Congress founded	Serote's *Yakhal'inkomo* passed; La Guma's *Fog of the Season's End* and Matthews's *Cry Rage!* banned
1974		New Publications Act passed; trial of Brink's *Kennis van die Aand*		Non-racial English Artists' and Writers' Guild founded; Kirkwood condemns 'Butlerism'; Mphahlele affirms a specifically African humanism	Brink's *Kennis/Looking on Darkness*, Lewin's *Bandiet*, Matthews's *Black Voices Shout*, and Mphahlele's *In Corner B* banned; Royston's *To Whom It May Concern*, Gordimer's *Conservationist*, and Head's *Question of Power* passed
1975	Breytenbach imprisoned; Inkatha revived	Three-tier censorship bureaucracy created, which includes a Publications Appeal Board (PAB); beginning of the Pretorius–Snyman era	Taurus founded; *New Classic* launched	Non-racial Afrikaans Writers' Guild founded; Mofolo–Plomer Prize inaugurated	Breytenbach's *Skryt*, Feinberg's *Poets to the People*, and Jensma's *where white is the colour* banned
1976	Soweto student uprising, partly against the imposition of Afrikaans as a primary medium of instruction; Transkei declared the first 'independent' homeland; Jeremy Cronin,		*Donga* founded		Brink's *Instant/Oomblik* passed

Year					
1977	James Matthews, and Strinivasa Moodley imprisoned; Steve Biko murdered; SASO, BPC, and Christian Institute banned; United Party disintegrates, Progressive Federal Party becomes official opposition		Peter Randall banned	Medupe founded and banned; Medu Arts Ensemble formed in Gaborone	Coetzee's *Heart of the Country*; Gwala's *Jol'iinkomo* and Stockenström's *Uitdraai* passed; Leroux's *Magersfontein* and Sepamla's *Soweto I Love* banned
1978	P. W. Botha becomes Prime Minister; Azanian People's Organization founded; Don Mattera detained	Trial of Leroux's *Magersfontein*; amendments to the 1974 Act create a special committee of literary experts to advise the PAB	*Staffrider* launched; *Inspan* founded	PEN (Johannesburg) formed; Federated Union of Black Artists founded	Breytenbach's *Death White as Words* and first issue of *Staffrider* banned; *Donga* and *Inspan* banned
1979	Federation of South African Trade Unions formed; Jaki Seroke imprisoned		Staffrider Series founded; Longman Drumbeat Series launched		Madingoane's *Africa*, Matshoba's *Call Me Not a Man*, and Tlali's *Muriel* banned; bans on Brink's *Dry White Season* and Gordimer's *Burger's Daughter* lifted on appeal
1980		Van Rooyen becomes chair of the PAB	*Wietie* founded		La Guma's *Butcherbird* and *Wietie* banned; Coetzee's *Barbarians* passed; ban on Mutloatse's *Forced Landing* lifted on appeal
1981		Abraham Coetzee becomes chief censor; beginning of the Coetzee–van Rooyen era		PEN (Johannesburg) disbanded; African Writers Association (AWA) founded; international cultural boycott re-energized with UN backing	Mzamane's *Mzala* passed; Sepamla's *Ride on the Whirlwind* and Tlali's *Amandla* banned

(*Continued*)

Date	Politics	Censorship	Publishing	Culture	Selected decisions
1982	Internal Security Act; ANC opens its first cultural desk in London		Skotaville founded; David Philip's Africasouth Series launched, reprints many previously banned titles; *The Classic* revived	AWA founds the H. I. E. and R. R. R. Dhlomo Drama Award, the Sol Plaatje Prose Award, and the S. E. K. Mqhayi Poetry Award; Culture and Resistance conference held in Gaborone	Serote's *To Every Birth* passed; Mzamane's *Children of Soweto* banned; ban on the first issue of *The Classic* lifted on appeal
1983	United Democratic Front (UDF) formed, establishes its own cultural desk			Launch of the People's Culture movement	Serote's *Night Keeps Winking* banned; Coetzee's *Life & Times* passed
1984	New tricameral Parliament created, giving limited rights to 'Coloureds' and 'Indians'; P. W. Botha becomes first executive State President				Freedom Charter unbanned
1985	Congress of South African Trade Unions (COSATU) formed, establishes its own cultural desk; first in a series of States of Emergency declared			Military raid on Gaborone kills members of Medu and the group disbands; Writers' Forum founded	
1987	Serote detained; COSATU headquarters bombed; Mbuli heads up the Transvaal Interim Cultural Desk, aligned to the UDF; Congress of South African Writers, and COSATU; right-wing Conservative Party becomes official opposition		Ravan firebombed	COSAW founded; Culture in Another South Africa Festival in Amsterdam	

1988	UDF premises destroyed; UDF and COSATU restricted along with other organizations; Mbuli detained; government attempts to cut off foreign donor support		COSAW founds the Alex La Guma/Bessie Head Fiction Award
1989	F. W. de Klerk becomes State President		Progressive writers hold discussions about cultural matters with the ANC in Zimbabwe
1990	Nelson Mandela released; ANC, PAC, SACP unbanned	Van Rooyen not reappointed as chair of the PAB	Sachs's paper 'Preparing Ourselves for Freedom' provokes extensive debate
1994	First democratic elections held; Nelson Mandela becomes President		
1995	Constitutional Court inaugurated; Truth and Reconciliation Commission established		
1996	Democratic constitution signed into law	New Publications Act passed, abolishing the censorship system	New South Africa has eleven official languages

Notes

Introduction

1. Thomas Pringle and John Fairbairn, Prospectus, in Pringle and Fairbairn (eds), *The South African Journal*, 2 vols (1824), South African Library Reprint Series (Cape Town: South African Library, 1974), p. ix; all subsequent references to the Prospectus are to the 1974 edn and are given in parentheses in the main text.
2. Unsigned [Pringle and Fairbairn], 'Conditions', *South African Journal*, 1/1 (Jan.–Feb. 1824), in Pringle and Fairbairn (eds), *The South African Journal* (1974), p. x; all subsequent references to the *South African Journal* are to the 1974 edn.
3. Unsigned [Pringle and Fairbairn], 'To Correspondents', *South African Journal*, 1/2 (Mar.–Apr. 1824), 86.
4. Ibid.
5. Prospectus, p. viii.
6. The other publishers were T. and G. Underwood and Longman & Co. in London; and A. Constable & Co. and D. Brown in Edinburgh.
7. Thomas Pringle et al., *Papers of the South African Literary Society* (Cape Town: W. Bridekirk, 1825), 3 (repr. Cape Town: Africana Connoisseurs Press, 1963); page references are to the 1825 edn.
8. Ibid. 6.
9. Ibid. 3.
10. Prospectus, p. viii.
11. Pringle et al., *Papers of the South African Literary Society*, 3.
12. N, 'On the Writings of Wordsworth', *South African Journal*, 1/1, 13; 1/2, 117.
13. Unsigned [John Fairbairn], 'On Literary and Scientific Societies', *South African Journal*, 1/2, 89–90.
14. Leroy Vail and Landeg White, *Power and the Praise Poem* (London: James Currey, 1991), 5, 18.
15. Marshall McLuhan, *The Gutenberg Galaxy* (Toronto: Toronto University Press, 1962), 18; cited in Vail and White, *Power and the Praise Poem*, 19.
16. Vail and White, *Power and the Praise Poem*, 71.
17. Ibid. 74.
18. I am grateful to Russell Kaschula for clarifying this distinction and for his advice on translation.
19. Unsigned [John Fairbairn], 'On Literary and Scientific Societies', *South African Journal*, 1/1: 50.
20. Cited in Saul Dubow, *A Commonwealth of Knowledge* (Oxford: Oxford University Press, 2006), 32.
21. [Fairbairn], 'On Literary and Scientific Societies', *South African Journal*, 1/2: 90.
22. Ibid. 1/1: 50.
23. Jürgen Habermas, *The Structural Transformation of the Public Sphere* (1962; Cambridge: Polity Press, 1989), 111.
24. [Fairbairn], 'On Literary and Scientific Societies', *South African Journal*, 1/2: 87.
25. Ibid. 1/1: 55.
26. Ibid.

27. Prospectus, p. viii.
28. Dubow, *A Commonwealth of Knowledge*, 33; A. M. Lewin Robinson, Introduction, in Pringle and Fairbairn (eds), *The South African Journal*, p. iii.
29. Pringle et al., *Papers of the South African Literary Society*, 10.
30. Ibid. 3.
31. Ibid.
32. Ibid. 8.
33. Unsigned, 'On the Present State and Prospects of the English Emigrants in South Africa', *South African Journal*, 1/2: 159.
34. Pringle et al., *Papers of the South African Literary Society*, 17.
35. Ibid. 18.
36. Ibid. 23.
37. Dubow, *A Commonwealth of Knowledge*, 27.
38. This is the first book based on the detailed evidence contained in the archives of the censorship bureaucracy. Christopher Merrett and Margreet de Lange, the two scholars who have made the most significant single contributions to the history of apartheid censorship to date, did not have access to the archives, which were opened only in 1997. Merrett's *A Culture of Censorship* (Cape Town: David Philip, 1994) offers an indispensable survey of all aspects of apartheid censorship legislation. De Lange's *The Muzzled Muse* (Amsterdam: John Benjamins, 1997) focuses mainly on the issues of literary censorship.
39. For this brief comparative analysis, I am indebted to Arlen Blyum's *A Self-Administered Poison: The System and Functions of Soviet Censorship* (Oxford: Legenda, 2003), and to David Balmuth's *Censorship in Russia 1865–1905* (Washington: University Press of America, 1979).
40. In 1978 a further bureaucracy Goskomizdat, the State Committee for Publishing Houses, Printing Plants, and the Book Trade, became the focus for the ideological control of literary production. It grew out of Brezhnev's State Committee for the Press. Working in conjunction with the Writers' Union, it played a 'much more decisive role in Soviet literary life than Glavlit', according to John and Carol Garrard. See *Inside the Soviet Writers' Union* (London: I. B. Tauris, 1990), 173.
41. For details on the GDR, see Ian Wallace, 'German Democratic Republic (East Germany), 1949–1989', in David Jones (ed.), *Censorship: A World Encyclopedia*, ii (London: Fitzroy Dearborn, 2001), 934–6; and Robert Darnton, 'Censorship, A Comparative View: France 1789–East Germany 1989', in Olwen Hufton (ed.), *Historical Change and Human Rights* (New York: Basic Books, 1995).
42. J. M. Coetzee, 'Censorship and Polemic: The Solzhenitsyn Affair', *Pretexts*, 2/2 (Summer 1990), 13.
43. Obscene Publications Act 1959 (c. 66), <http://www.statutelaw.gov.uk/content.aspx?activeTextDocId=1128038>, accessed 12 Feb. 2008.
44. Bernard Williams et al., *Report of the Committee on Obscenity and Film Censorship* (London: Her Majesty's Stationery Office, 1979), 110.
45. Ibid.
46. Ibid. 110, 126, 160.
47. Maurice Blanchot, *The Space of Literature*, trans. Ann Smock (Lincoln: University of Nebraska Press, 1982), 211. The first French edition appeared in 1955.
48. Sartre's manifesto itself had a complex, even ambiguous, impact. If his own categorical definitions of literature, which privileged prose above poetry, the communicative above the poetic function, reinforced traditions of essentialist thought, his insistence on literature's complex situatedness as the product of particular writers writing for determinate readerships in a specific place and time contributed to the historical turn within

literary theory. Recognizing that there is 'no guarantee that literature is immortal', he famously linked its future specifically and concretely to the 'chance of Europe, of socialism, of democracy, and of peace'. Given the developments across Africa, of which Sartre was well aware, this was itself a revealingly contentious claim to make on the threshold of the 1950s. See Jean-Paul Sartre, *What Is Literature?*, trans. Bernard Frechtman (London: Routledge, 1993), 229.

49. See Peter D. Mcdonald, 'Ideas of the Book and Histories of Literature: After Theory?', *PMLA* 121/1 (Jan. 2006), 214–28.

50. Tzvetan Todorov, 'The Notion of Literature', *New Literary History*, 5/1 (Autumn 1973), 5.

51. Ibid.

52. See Es'kia Mphahlele, 'Landmarks of Literary History in South Africa: A Black Perspective' (1980), in Mphahlele, *Es'kia* (Cape Town: Kwela Books, 2002), 295–311; and also David Attwell, *Rewriting Modernity: Studies in Black South African Literary History* (Scottsville: KZN Press, 2005); Isabel Hofmeyr *The Portable Bunyan* (Johannesburg: Wits University Press, 2004); Leon de Kock, *Civilizing Barbarians: Missionary Narrative and African Textual Response in Nineteenth-Century South Africa* (Alice: Lovedale Press; Johannesburg: Wits University Press, 1996); and Mcebisi Ndletyana et al., *African Intellectuals in 19th and early 20th Century South Africa* (Cape Town: HSRC Press, 2008).

53. See Dipesh Chakrabarty, *Provincializing Europe* (Princeton: University of Princeton Press, 2000), esp. pt 1.

54. Mafika Gwala, 'Writing as a Cultural Weapon', in M. J. Daymond et al. (eds), *Momentum: On Recent South African Writing* (Pietermaritzburg: University of Natal Press, 1984), 47.

Chapter 1

1. Ellison Kahn, *'When the Lion Feeds*—and the Censor Pounces: A Disquisition on the Banning of Immoral Publications in South Africa', *South African Law Journal*, 83/3 (Aug. 1966), 280–3.

2. *Union Gazette Extraordinary*, 28 (5 June 1931), p. xxviii.

3. Students' BBFC web site, <http://www.sbbfc.co.uk/student_guide_history1912.asp>, accessed 12 Aug. 2006.

4. For a contemporary account of these initiatives, see Brian Bunting, *The Rise of the South African Reich* (Harmondsworth: Penguin, 1964), esp. ch. 12.

5. Hermann Giliomee, *The Afrikaners: Biography of a People* (Cape Town: Tafelberg, 2003), 471. Though Giliomee downplays Cronjé's influence, claiming that he had 'no standing in D. F. Malan's inner circle', and emphasizes his links to the 'extra-parliamentary pro-Nazi Ossewa Brandwag', the fact that he was appointed to chair the Commission suggests that he was not wholly cut off from mainstream Nationalist politics in the 1950s.

6. J. M. Coetzee, *Giving Offense: Essays on Censorship* (Chicago: University of Chicago Press, 1996), 183.

7. Cronjé's writings offer a particularly disturbing case study to support Martha Nussbaum's liberal critique of the legal sanctioning of disgust. See Martha C. Nussbaum, *Hiding from Humanity: Disgust, Shame, and the Law* (Princeton: Princeton University Press, 2004), particularly ch. 2.

8. Geoffrey Cronjé et al., *Report of the Commission of Enquiry in Regard to Undesirable Publications* (Pretoria: Government Printer, 1957), p. ii; all subsequent references are in the text.

9. See Kahn, *'When the Lion Feeds'*, 287–9.

10. For a deft analysis of this aspect of the Report, see Mark Sanders, 'Undesirable Publications: J. M. Coetzee on Censorship and Apartheid', *Law and Literature*, 18/1 (Spring 2006), 101–14.

11. Geoffrey Cronjé, 'Keer die Verspreiding van Aanstootlike Leestof', *Die Huisgenoot*, 7 Oct. 1957, 6–7.
12. Kahn, '*When the Lion Feeds*', 280.
13. The best account of van Wyk Louw's thinking currently available in English is Mark Sanders, *Complicities: The Intellectual and Apartheid* (Durham, NC: Duke University Press, 2002), 57–92. See also, Giliomee, *The Afrikaners*, 472–4.
14. For the best perspective on Louw's early politics, see J. C. Kannemeyer (ed.), *Ek ken jou goed genoeg ... Die briefwisseling tussen N. P. van Wyk Louw en W. E. G. Louw 1936–1939* (Pretoria: Protea Boekhuis, 2004).
15. N. P. van Wyk Louw, *Versamelde Prosa 1* (Cape Town: Tafelberg, 1986), 502.
16. Ibid. 457. Here I have used Sanders's translation; see *Complicities*, 75.
17. Giliomee, *The Afrikaners*, 474.
18. J. C. Steyn, *Van Wyk Louw: 'n Lewensverhaal* (Cape Town: Tafelberg, 1998), 1113.
19. Sanders, *Complicities*, 61.
20. Adam Small, 'Towards Cultural Understanding', in Hendrik W. van der Merwe and David Walsh (eds), *Student Perspectives on South Africa* (Cape Town: David Philip, 1972), 217; all subsequent references are in the text.
21. C. M. van den Heever et al., *Kultuurgeskiedenis van die Afrikaner*, i (Cape Town: Nasionale Pers, 1945), p. i.
22. Francis Mulhern, *Culture/Metaculture* (London: Routledge, 2000), 86.
23. N. P. van Wyk Louw, 'Sensuur of Pornographie?' (Censorship or Pornography?) (Oct. 1947), in Louw, *Versamelde Prosa 1*, 406–7; all subsequent references to this essay are in the text.
24. 'Skrywers Sien Gevaar in die Cronjé-verslag', *Die Huisgenoot*, 21 Oct. 1957, 14–15. Among the strongest critics were Gerrit Dekker, one of Louw's key allies, and W. A. de Klerk.
25. Steyn, *Van Wyk Louw*, 832. Louw's articles appeared on 19 and 26 Feb. 1958.
26. South African PEN Centre, Memorandum, n.d. [*c*.1960], South African Library, Cape Town, 2; all subsequent references are in the text.
27. Christopher Merrett, *A Culture of Censorship* (Cape Town: David Philip, 1994), 51.
28. For a contemporary English account of this history, see W. H. B. Dean, 'Judging the Obscene', *Acta Juridica* (1972), 61–150. For an Afrikaans account, see Pieter B. Geldenhuys, *Pornografie, Sensuur en Reg* (Johannesburg: Lex Patria, 1977). It is also worth noting here that very few charges were brought under the Act at this time: forty-one leading to twenty-seven convictions. See Merrett, *A Culture of Censorship*, 62.
29. Publications and Entertainments Act, *Statutes of the Republic of South Africa 1963*, 26 (Pretoria: Government Printer, 1963), 276–300. Section 5 (2) also included a sixth clause covering disclosures relating to judicial proceedings.
30. Publications Act, No. 42, 1974, *Government Gazette*, 112/4426 (Pretoria: Government Printer, 1974), 7.
31. Appeal Board Case 144/76. The text of the decision is included in the file relating to the review of Cope's *The Dawn Comes Twice* in 1975 (see Western Cape Provincial Archives and Records, Cape Town (WCPA), P75/12/80). All Snyman's comments come from pp. 29–35 of the Board's Report.
32. Publications and Entertainments Act, 1963, 284–6.
33. For a critique of this, see Ian McDonald, 'Defending Censorship Legislation in Terms of a Society's Right to Protect Public Morals', in Theo Coggin (ed.), *Censorship* (Johannesburg: SA Institute of Race Relations, 1983).
34. Sir Patrick Devlin, *The Enforcement of Morals* (London: British Academy, 1959), 15–17; and see also Nussbaum, *Hiding from Humanity*, 75–9.
35. Steyn, *Van Wyk Louw*, 955. His letter was dated 18 Mar. 1963.
36. N. P. van Wyk Louw, *Versamelde Prosa 2* (Cape Town: Human & Rousseau, 1986), 329.

37. Abel Coetzee, 'Die skrywer en die gemeenskap teenoor mekaar' (The Writer and the Community against Each Other), *Tydskrif vir Letterkunde*, 1/3 (Aug. 1963), 6–14. For the details of Coetzee's views, see web note c.

38. WCPA, BCS vol. 22, ref. M2.

39. Publications and Entertainments Act, 1963, 278.

40. Ampie Coetzee, 'Literature and Crisis: One Hundred Years of Afrikaans Literature and Afrikaner Nationalism', in Martin Trump (ed.), *Rendering Things Visible* (Johannesburg: Ravan, 1990), 345.

41. N. P. van Wyk Louw, *Versamelde Prosa 2*, 553.

42. Steyn, *Van Wyk Louw*, 966.

43. For more details about the censors' biographies, see the web site attached to this volume.

44. Gerrit Dekker, Inaugural Address, Nov. 1963, WCPA, BCS vol. 17, ref. B1, 2; all subsequent references are in the text.

45. As the Board was not at this stage required to make its reasons public, this survey is based on the bibliographical details (author, title, and publisher) that were included in the lists of banned publications published every month in the *Government Gazette* for 1965.

46. 'Controlling Undesirable Publications', n.d. [*c.*1966], WCPA, BCS vol. 17, ref. B1, 2.

47. H. van der Merwe Scholtz, personal interview, 22 Aug. 2001.

48. André P. Brink, *Looking on Darkness* (London: W. H. Allen, 1974), inside flap.

49. André P. Brink, *Miskien Nooit* (Cape Town: Human & Rousseau, 1967), inside flap.

50. See WCPA, BCS 764/66 and 73/66.

51. Des Troye, *An Act of Immorality* (Johannesburg: Trans-world Publishers, 1963), front cover.

52. Richard Rive, *Emergency* (London: Faber & Faber, 1964), p. ii.

53. 'Rumpff on Why "Lion" Should Not Be Banned', *Sunday Times*, 5 Sept. 1965, 7–8.

54. See W. D. Beukes, *Boekewêreld: Die Nasionale Pers in die Uitgewersbedryf tot 1990* (Cape Town: Nasionale Boekhandel, 1992), 49.

55. *Report by the Commission of Inquiry into the Publications and Entertainments Bill (A. B. 61-'73)* (Pretoria: Government Printer, 1974), 10.

56. Small, 'Towards Cultural Understanding', 202–3.

57. Francis Galloway, *Breyten Breytenbach as Openbare Figuur* (Pretoria: Haum-Literêr, 1990), 88–9.

58. In a series of five historical fictions, published over twenty years, Rabie traced the mixed origins of the Afrikaner *volk* from the first encounters between Europeans and Khoikhoi in the 17th century to the racial conflicts of the 20th century. It was called the *Bolandia* series because most of the fictions explored this history as it worked itself out in the Boland, a region in the Western Cape. The five fictions were: *Eiland voor Afrika* (Island before Africa, 1964), *Die groot anders-maak* (The Great Other Making, 1964, 1968), *Waar jy sterwe* (Where You Die, 1966), *Ark* (1977), and *En Oseaan* (And Ocean, 1985). Rabie translated *Waar jy sterwe* into English. It was published as *A Man Apart* by Collins in 1969.

59. André P. Brink, *Kennis van die Aand* (Cape Town: Buren, 1973), p. v.

60. Brink, *Looking on Darkness*, p. iii.

61. Geldenhuys, *Pornografie, Sensuur en Reg*, 93.

62. Ibid. 95.

63. 'Hofsake', Supreme Court transcript, WCPA, DP 3/7, vol. 1, 25.

64. Ibid. 26.

65. Geldenhuys, *Pornografie, Sensuur en Reg*, 96–7.

66. Ibid. 88–90. The letter originally appeared in the Afrikaans weekly *Rapport*, 27 Jan. 1974.

67. Geldenhuys, *Pornografie, Sensuur en Reg*, 80.

68. Though initially against universal franchise, the Liberal Party accepted this fundamental principle in 1960. It dissolved in 1968 when the government declared all multiracial parties illegal.

69. *Report by the Commission of Inquiry into the Publications and Entertainments Bill (A. B. 61-'73)*, 4; all subsequent references are in the text.

70. Publications Act, 1974, 51.

71. Ibid. 53.

72. Appeal Board Case 144/76, 16. The text of the decision is included in the file relating to the review of Cope's *The Dawn Comes Twice* in 1975 (see WCPA, P75/12/80).

73. Appeal Board Case 144/76, 22.

74. Ibid. 9.

75. The 'independent homelands' of Bophuthatswana and Venda adopted similar legislation in 1979 and 1983 respectively.

76. This analysis is based on the figures published in *Report by the Commission of Inquiry into the Publications and Entertainments Bill (A. B. 61-'73)*, 10; and in the reports of the Directorate of Publications for the period 1975–80. These were first published in the government Blue Books and then, from 1978, in the Annual Reports of the Department of the Interior.

77. For a detailed analysis of this change, see André du Toit, 'The Rationale of Controlling Political Publications', in Coggin (ed.), *Censorship*.

78. The figures for 1975 and 1984 are based on my own analysis of the records in the Western Cape Provincial Archives. See WCPA, IDP files, vols 1–5. The figures for 1992 come from a list used by the censors at the time, a copy of which René Dinkelman kindly gave me in 2001. Ms Dinkelman was at the time the Director's personal secretary.

79. J. M. Coetzee, personal correspondence with the author, 7 Oct. 2003.

80. Under Pretorius, the key security censors were Murray, Jansen, Admiral Bierman, a retired navy admiral, and Tony Hickman, a United Party politician; while the literary censors included Merwe Scholtz, Cloete, Malan, Anna Louw, and Lighton, as well as M. G. Scholtz, then a professor of Afrikaans at the University of Port Elizabeth, and F. C. Fensham, a professor of Semitic languages at the University of Stellenbosch who would go on to be the chair of the Afrikaans Writers' Circle. For further details on the censors' biographies, see the web site attached to this volume.

81. I have discussed this in detail elsewhere; see Peter D. McDonald, 'The Politics of Obscenity: *Lady Chatterley's Lover* and the Apartheid State', *English Studies in Africa*, 47/1 (2004), 31–46.

82. Mafika Gwala, *Jol'iiknomo* (Johannesburg: Ad Donker, 1977), p. v.

83. Appeal Board decision AP 67/78 and 68/68, 26. The text of this decision is included in the WCPA file P78/9/93.

84. Louise Silver (ed.), *Publications Appeal Board: Digest of Decisions*, 4 vols (Johannesburg: Centre for Applied Legal Studies, 1979–86), Case 70/78, 3.

85. Charles Malan and Martjie Bosman, *Sensuur, literatuur en die leser: 'Donderdag of Woensdag' as totesgeval* (Censorship, Literature and the Reader: *Thursday or Wednesday* as Test Case; Pretoria: Sensal, 1983), 77.

86. J. C. W. van Rooyen, *Publikasiebeheer in Suid-Afrika* (Cape Town: Juta, 1978).

87. Appeal Board Cases 81/79 and 82/79, 11. The text of the decision is included in the files relating to *Dry White Season* (WCPA, P79/8/61 for the English version, P79/9/19 for the Afrikaans).

88. Coetzee, *Giving Offense*, 192.

89. J. C. W. van Rooyen, *Censorship in South Africa* (Cape Town: Juta, 1987), 115.

90. Appeal Board Cases 81/79 and 82/79, 2, in Silver (ed.), *Publications Appeal Board*. The experts' report is in the same censorship file.

91. H. van der Merwe Scholtz, personal interview, 22 Aug. 2001.

92. Jaki Seroke, 'The Voice of the Voiceless', *African Book Publishing Record*, 10/4 (1984), 203.
93. Silver (ed.), *Publications Appeal Board*, annexure to Case 43/82, 39; all subsequent references are in the text.
94. Appeal Board Case 114/81; see WCPA, P81/6/152.
95. Silver (ed.), *Publications Appeal Board*, Case 101/81.
96. Abraham Coetzee, personal interview, 28 Aug. 2001.
97. WCPA, P81/1/28, included a copy of Mphahlele's review, which originally appeared under the title 'Mtshali's Strident Voice of Self-Assertion', *Rand Daily Mail*, 19 Dec. 1980, 16.
98. Appeal Board Case 2/81, the full text of which is in WCPA, P81/1/28.
99. Abraham Coetzee, personal interview, 28 Aug. 2001.

Chapter 2

1. David Philip, 'Oppositional Publishing in South Africa from 1945 to 2000', *Logos*, 2/1 (2000), 41–2.
2. Cited in Jeffrey Peires, 'Lovedale Press: Literature for the Bantu Revisited', *English in Africa*, 7/1 (Mar. 1980), 71. For more on the missionary control of publishing, see Peter Midgley, 'Author, Ideology, Publisher: A Symbiotic Relationship' (MA thesis, Rhodes University, 1993).
3. Ntongela Masilela, 'South African Literature in African Languages', in Simon Gikandi (ed.), *Encyclopaedia of African Literature* (London: Routledge, 2003), 509. See also Mcebisi Ndletyana et al., *African Intellectuals in 19th and early 20th Century South Africa* (Cape Town: HSRC Press, 2008).
4. David Attwell, *Rewriting Modernity: Studies in Black South African Literary History* (Scottsville: KZN Press, 2005), 55.
5. For a detailed analysis of this debate, see ibid. 77–110.
6. Sol T. Plaatje, *Mhudi* (Lovedale: Lovedale Press, 1930), p. v.
7. D. Ziervogel, 'Bantu Literature', in *Standard Encyclopaedia of Southern Africa*, 12 vols (Cape Town: Nasou, 1970–6), ii. 114.
8. Ibid. 115–16.
9. Es'kia Mphahlele, *The African Image* (London: Faber, 1962), 37.
10. For an analysis of the state of the educational publishing field in the 1980s, see Susan Joubert, 'Publishing in Another South Africa', *African Publishing Record*, 17/1 (1991), 9–15.
11. *Report of the Select Committee on the Publications and Entertainments Amendment Bill* (Pretoria: Government Printers, 1973), 8.
12. Though this disparity could sometimes be attributed to the scale of the trade in publications imported from the United States and above all Britain, it is worth noting that in 1979, to keep to my sample year, marginally more submissions came from the police than from customs (903 as against 822). For the figures, see Department of the Interior, *Annual Report for the Calendar Year 1979* (Pretoria: Government Printer, 1980).
13. J. C. Kannemeyer, *Die Afrikaanse Literatuur, 1652–2004* (Cape Town: Human & Rousseau, 2005), 122.
14. N. P. van Wyk Louw, 'Toeriste-Kuns', *Standpunte*, 2/2 (Apr. 1947), 67–9.
15. G. Dekker, *Afrikaanse Literatuurgeskiedenis* (Cape Town: Nasionale Boekhandel, 1961), 176.
16. For Louw's *Vernuwing in die Prosa* (1961), see N. P. van Wyk Louw, *Versamelde Prosa 2* (Cape Town: Human & Rousseau, 1986).
17. W. D. Beukes (ed.), *Boekewêreld: Die Nasionale Pers in die Uitgewersbedryf tot 1990* (Cape Town: Nasionale Pers, 1992), 427.
18. André P. Brink, 'Antwoord aan Smit', *Kol*, 1/3 (Oct.–Nov. 1968), 5–6.
19. André P. Brink, 'Ons sal oorwin', *Standpunte*, 21/5 (June 1968), 22.

20. Beukes (ed.), *Boekewêreld*, 431.
21. Ibid. 435.
22. Koos Human, *'n Lewe met Boeke* (Cape Town: Human & Rousseau, 2006), 58.
23. Beukes (ed.), *Boekewêreld*, 205. For further details about APB's fraught relations with the Sestigers, see Jack Cope, *The Adversary Within* (Cape Town: David Philip, 1982), esp. 86–8.
24. Beukes (ed.), *Boekewêreld*, 226.
25. Ibid. 232, 426.
26. Ibid. 229.
27. Ibid. 230.
28. Antjie Krog, 'My Beautiful Land', *Sechaba*, 5/1 (Jan. 1971), 16. Krog's debut volume, *Die Dogter van Jefta* (1970), was published the year before on Opperman's recommendation.
29. Breyten Breytenbach, *End Papers* (London: Faber, 1986), 57–8. The essay 'Vulture Culture' first appeared in the banned anthology *Apartheid* (1971), edited by Alex La Guma.
30. For a detailed history of Taurus, see Rudi Venter, 'Inventing an Alternative through Oppositional Publishing: Afrikaans Alternative Book Publishing in Apartheid South Africa—the Publishing House Taurus (1975–1991) as Case Study', *Innovation*, 35 (Dec. 2007), 86–114. For a contemporary account, see Ampie Coetzee, 'Taurus Publishers', *Index on Censorship*, 13/5 (Oct. 1984), 32.
31. Nadine Gordimer et al., *What Happened to 'Burger's Daughter'?* (Emmarentia: Taurus, 1980), back cover.
32. Unsigned, 'Brink Roman Tog Uitgegee', *Rapport*, 16 Nov. 1975, 18; cited in Venter, 'Inventing an Alternative through Oppositional Publishing', 108.
33. For the full text for the Appeal Board Cases 81/79 and 82/79, see WCPA, P79/8/61.
34. Beukes (ed.), *Boekewêreld*, 376.
35. Ibid. 377.
36. Cited in David Philip, 'South Africa', in Philip G. Altbach and Edith S. Hoshino (eds), *International Book Publishing: An Encyclopaedia* (New York: Garland, 1995), 417.
37. Ronald Suresh Roberts, *No Cold Kitchen* (Johannesburg: STE Publishers, 2005), 241.
38. Richard Rive, *Writing Black* (Cape Town: David Philip, 1981), 110.
39. According to Ian Glenn, Gollancz 'pushed Rooke to omit an important inter-racial rape in the novel, for fear of censorship or controversy in the UK'. See Ian Glenn, 'Daphne Rooke', *Times Literary Supplement*, 1 Sept. 2006, 15.
40. André Brink to Bob Tanner, 20 Jan. 1983, National English Literary Museum, Grahamstown, South Africa, file 2001.34.4.1.
41. André P. Brink, 'Kennis van Sensuur 2004', <http://www.litnet.co.za/cgibin/giga.cgi?cmd=cause_dir_news_item&news_id=17763&cause_id=1270>, accessed 7 Aug. 2007.
42. André P. Brink, *Looking on Darkness* (London: W. H. Allen, 1974), front cover.
43. Ibid., inside flap.
44. J. M. Coetzee, personal interview, 27 July 1999. For a further discussion of this, see Ch. 8.
45. For Gordimer's response to Virago, see Roberts, *No Cold Kitchen*, 389.
46. Langston Hughes (ed.), *An African Treasury* (New York: Crown, 1960), i. The anthology included Rive's 'The Bench'.
47. For a detailed discussion of this, see Andrew van der Vlies, *South African Textual Cultures* (Manchester: University of Manchester Press, 2007), 106–27.
48. Andrew van der Vlies, 'Constructing South African Literatures in Britain, 1880–1980', D. Phil. thesis (Oxford University, 2004), 251.
49. Herbert L. Shore, *Come Back, Africa: Fourteen Short Stories from South Africa* (East Berlin: Seven Seas, 1968), 25–6.
50. Rive, *Writing Black*, 90.
51. Ibid. 18.

52. James Currey, 'The African Writers Series at 30', *Southern African Review of Books* (Mar.–Apr. 1993), 4.
53. James Currey to Bessie Head, 24 Aug. 1972, University of Reading Library, Heinemann African Writers Series Archive, file 13/3. By permission of Pearson Education.
54. Alex La Guma, *The Stone Country* (East Berlin: Seven Seas, 1967), pp. viii, 172, and back cover.
55. Censors' Report (2049/74), National Archives and Records of South Africa, Pretoria, Censorship Board, files PR2/142 and 1/74 part 8. This is one of the rare reports to survive from the Kruger era.
56. Robert Royston (ed.), *Black Poets in South Africa* (London: Heinemann, 1974), 7.
57. Barry Feinberg (ed.), *Poets to the People* (London: Heinemann, 1981), p. v.
58. Ibid., p. xii.
59. Nadine Gordimer, *Some Monday for Sure* (London: Heinemann, 1976), p. i.
60. Roberts, *No Cold Kitchen*, 272.
61. Ibid. 273.
62. Lewis Nkosi, *Home and Exile* (London: Longmans, Green, 1965), 10.
63. Njabulo Ndebele, *Rediscovery of the Ordinary* (Johannesburg: COSAW, 1991), 39.
64. Michael Chapman (ed.), *The Drum Decade* (Pietermaritzburg: University of Natal Press, 1989), p. viii.
65. Lionel Abrahams, 'My Face in My Place', in M. J. Daymond et al. (eds), *Momentum: On Recent South African Writing* (Pietermaritzburg: University of Natal Press, 1984), 4.
66. Lionel Abrahams, '*The Purple Renoster*: An Adolescence', *English in Africa*, 7/2 (Sept. 1980), 34.
67. Lionel Abrahams, Editorial, *The Purple Renoster*, 1 (Sept. 1956), 3.
68. Ibid.
69. Ezekiel Mphehlele [*sic*], 'The Woman Walks Out', *The Purple Renoster*, 2 (Spring 1957), 4.
70. Cited in Walter Ehmeir, 'Publishing South African Literature in the 1960s', *Research in African Literatures*, 26/1 (Spring 1995), 123.
71. Lionel Abrahams, Editorial, *The Purple Renoster*, 5 (Summer 1963), 5.
72. Abrahams, '*The Purple Renoster*', 40.
73. Front cover, *The Purple Renoster*, 10 (Summer 1970–1), 1.
74. For Sepamla's account of the challenges he faced as a magazine editor, see Sipho Sepamla, 'A Note on *New Classic* and *S'ketsh*', *English in Africa*, 7/2 (Sept. 1980), 81–5. For more on Sepamla's activities, see Stephen Gray (ed.), *Free-lancers and Literary Biography in South Africa* (Amsterdam: Rodopi, 1999), 135–56.
75. Edward Shils, *The Intellectuals and the Powers* (Chicago: Chicago University Press, 1972), 480.
76. Ezekiel Mphahlele, 'Mphahlele on the CIA', *Transition*, 7/3 (Dec.–Jan. 1967–8), 5.
77. Ezekiel Mphahlele, 'The Cult of Negritude', *Encounter*, 16/3 (1961), 50–2.
78. Shils, *The Intellectuals and the Powers*, 476.
79. Jack Cope, 'The World of *Contrast*', *English in Africa*, 7/2 (Sept 1980), 1.
80. Ibid. 5.
81. Ibid. 8.
82. C. J. Driver, 'No Politics Is Politics', *New African*, 1/4 (Apr. 1962), 13.
83. J. M. Coetzee, '*Staffrider*', *African Book Publishing Record*, 5/4 (Oct. 1979), 236.
84. Cited in Ehmeir, 'Publishing South African Literature in the 1960s', 120.
85. Can Themba, 'The Boy with the Tennis Racket', in Nat Nakasa, *The World of Nat Nakasa*, ed. Essop Patel (Randburg: Ravan, 1975), pp. xviii–xix.
86. Nat Nakasa, Comment, *The Classic*, 1/1 (1963), 4.
87. Patel, (ed.), *The World of Nat Nakasa*, p. xii.
88. Cited in Ehmeir, 'Publishing South African Literature in the 1960s', 124; and Nadine Gordimer, 'South Africa: Towards a Desk Drawer Literature', *The Classic*, 2/4 (1968), 69.

89. Ehmeir, 'Publishing South African Literature in the 1960s', 124.
90. Editorial, *Donga*, 1 (July 1976), 1.
91. Welma Odendaal, *'Donga*: One Angry Voice', *English in Africa*, 7/2 (Sept. 1980), 70.
92. Mbulelo Vizikhungo Mzamane, 'The Short Story Tradition in Black South Africa', *Donga*, 7 (Sept. 1977), 1.
93. Stephen Gray, Introduction, in Gray (ed.), *On the Edge of the World* (Johannesburg: Ad Donker, 1974), 10.
94. Peter Randall, 'The Beginnings of Ravan Press: A Memoir', in G. E. de Villiers (ed.), *Ravan: Twenty Five Years* (Randburg: Ravan, 1997), 11.
95. Philip, 'Oppositional Publishing in South Africa from 1945 to 2000', 43.
96. Ibid.
97. Peter Randall, 'Introductory Remarks', in Susan Gardner (ed.), *Publisher/Writer/Reader: Sociology of Southern African Literature* (Johannesburg: University of Witwatersrand Press, 1986), 14.
98. Peter Randall, ' "Minority" Publishing in South Africa', *African Book Publishing Record*, 1/3 (July 1975), 221.
99. Sipho Sepamla, Editorial, *New Classic*, 1 (1975), 2.
100. Unsigned [Mafika Gwala?], 'Arts and Entertainment', in Mafika Gwala (ed.), *Black Review* (1973), 111.
101. Peter Randall, personal interview, 17 Aug. 1998.
102. J. M. Coetzee, *'Staffrider'*, 235.
103. De Villiers (ed.), *Ravan*, 11. Randall specifically regretted the 'decision to exclude a Peter-Dirk Uys play from *Contemporary South African Plays*', a volume Ravan published in 1976. Uys was a noted political satirist.
104. Editorial, *Donga*, 6 (July 1977), 1.
105. Peter Randall, *A Taste for Power* (Johannesburg: SPRO-CAS, 1973), 81.
106. J. M. Coetzee, personal interview, 8 May 1999.
107. De Villiers (ed.), *Ravan*, 9.
108. J. M. Coetzee, *Dusklands* (Johannesburg: Ravan, 1974), inside flap.
109. Miriam Tlali, *Muriel at Metropolitan* (Johannesburg: Ravan, 1975), back cover.
110. Sarah Nuttall, 'Literature and the Archive: The Biography of Texts', in Carolyn Hamilton et al. (eds), *Refiguring the Archive* (Cape Town: David Philip, 2002), 283.
111. De Villiers (ed.), *Ravan*, 9.
112. Nuttall, 'Literature and the Archive', 289.
113. Ibid. 282.
114. De Villiers (ed.), *Ravan*, 9.
115. Nuttall, 'Literature and the Archive', 287; Ravan publicity, *New Classic*, 1 (1975), back cover.
116. Tlali, *Muriel at Metropolitan*, back cover.
117. For Tlali's own views on *Muriel*'s complex publishing history, see the introduction to the subsequent edition entitled *Between Two Worlds*, which was published under the innovative Canadian imprint Broadview Press in 2004.
118. Tlali, *Muriel at Metropolitan*, 14.
119. See Peter Wilhelm and J. A. Polley (eds), *Poetry South Africa: Selected Papers from Poetry '74* (Johannesburg: Ad Donker, 1976), 102–33.
120. Attwell, *Rewriting Modernity*, 138–9.
121. Ibid. 140.
122. Mike Kirkwood, *'Staffrider*: An Informal Discussion', *English in Africa*, 7/2 (Sept. 1980), 31.
123. Mike Kirkwood to J. M. Coetzee, 18 Oct. 1978, Macmillan SA, Johannesburg, Ravan Press Archives (RPA).

124. Mike Kirkwood to Mbulelo Mzamane, 17 Mar. 1980, RPA, *Mzala* title file. For a discussion of this correspondence, see also Mbulelo Mzamane, 'Black Consciousness Poets in South Africa 1967–1980', Ph.D. thesis (Sheffield University, 1984).

125. De Villiers (ed.), *Ravan*, 19.

126. Kirkwood, '*Staffrider*', 23.

127. Unsigned, 'About *Staffrider*', *Staffrider*, 1/1 (Mar. 1978), 1.

128. Ibid.

129. Ibid.

130. Kirkwood to Coetzee, 18 Oct. 1978, RPA.

131. Ibid.; and Kirkwood, '*Staffrider*', 24.

132. Ndebele, *Rediscovery of the Ordinary*, 46–8.

133. J. M. Coetzee, '*Staffrider*', 235. Coetzee based his analysis on his own reading of the magazine and the correspondence he had about it with Kirkwood.

134. The publishers, 'An Open Letter', *Staffrider*, 1/2 (May–June 1978), 3.

135. The two Appeal Board decisions (AP 122/80 and AP 140/80) are included in the censorship files for *Staffrider*: WCPA, P80/7/31 and P80/10/146.

136. Christopher van Wyk, '*Staffrider* and the Politics of Culture', *Staffrider*, 7/3–4 (1988), 165–6.

137. Mzamane to Kirkwood, 6 May 1980, RPA, *Mzala* title file.

138. Kirkwood to Mzamane, 17 Mar. 1980, RPA, *Mzala* title file.

139. Mzamane to Kirkwood, 25 Feb. 1980, RPA, *Mzala* title file.

140. Ibid.; and Mzamane to Kirkwood, 6 May 1980, RPA, *Mzala* title file.

141. Mzamane to Kirkwood, 25 Feb. 1980, RPA, *Mzala* title file.

142. Mzamane to Kirkwood, 6 May 1980, RPA, *Mzala* title file.

143. Ibid.

144. Ibid.

145. Kirkwood to Mzamane, 17 Mar. 1980, RPA, *Mzala* title file.

146. Mzamane to Kirkwood, 6 May 1980, RPA, *Mzala* title file.

147. Cited in 'Skotaville', *Index on Censorship*, 5/84 (Oct. 1984), 35.

148. Jaki Seroke, 'The Voice of the Voiceless', *African Book Publishing Record*, 10/4 (1984), 201.

149. Ibid.

150. Cited in 'Skotaville', 35.

151. Seroke, 'The Voice of the Voiceless', 202.

152. Mike Kirkwood, Christopher van Wyk, et al., 'A Reply from Ravan Press', *African Book Publishing Record*, 10/4 (1984), 205–6.

153. Seroke, 'The Voice of the Voiceless', 203.

154. Case P86/07/64 related to *Staffrider*, 6/3 (1986).

155. Dan Side, 'Three Armed Men Firebomb Offices of Liberal Press', *The Star*, 19 Mar. 1987, 26. Slogans taken from photographs in RPA.

Chapter 3

1. J. M. Coetzee, 'Censorship and Polemic: The Solzhenitsyn Affair', *Pretexts*, 2/2 (Summer 1990), 4–5. Though this essay is primarily a sceptical appraisal of Solzhenitsyn's authorial self-construction as a dissident, Coetzee also used it to sketch out some of his general thinking about censorship, which eventually formed the basis of his collection *Giving Offense* (1996).

2. Coetzee, 'Censorship and Polemic', 4–5.

3. Ibid. 4.

4. J. M. Coetzee, *Giving Offense: Essays on Censorship* (Chicago: University of Chicago Press, 1996), 35, 209.

5. A. H. Murray, 'Commentary on Professor Kahn', WCPA, BCS vol. 22, ref. M1.

6. Coetzee, *Giving Offense*, 205, 208.
7. Andre P. Brink, 'Mahatma Gandhi Today' (1970), in Brink, *Mapmakers* (London: Faber, 1983), 56.
8. N. P. van Wyk Louw, *Die Pluimsaad Waai Ver of Bitter Begin* (Cape Town: Human & Rousseau, 1972), 9.
9. Brink, *Mapmakers*, 234.
10. J. C. Steyn, *Van Wyk Louw: 'n Lewensverhaal* (Cape Town: Tafelberg, 1998), 1087–8.
11. Dekker, *Afrikaanse Literatuurgeskiedenis*, 266–7. I have based my translation in part on Hein Willemse's version in his essay 'Emergent Black Afrikaans Poets', in Martin Trump (ed.), *Rendering Things Visible* (Johannesburg: Ravan, 1990), 387.
12. Ampie Coetzee, 'Literature and Crisis: One Hundred Years of Afrikaans Literature and Afrikaner Nationalism', in Trump (ed.), *Rendering Things Visible*, 346.
13. Anna M. Louw, '*In the Heart of the Country*: A Calvinist Allegory?', *PN Review*, 14/2 (1987), 50.
14. Ibid.
15. Nadine Gordimer, *The Essential Gesture* (London: Jonathan Cape, 1988), 260.
16. Ibid. 256.
17. Ibid. 260.
18. J. M. Coetzee, *White Writing* (Johannesburg: Radix, 1988), 138–40.
19. 'PEN Charter', *South African PEN Yearbook* (Johannesburg: CNA, 1954), 96.
20. Ibid.
21. Richard Rive, *Writing Black* (Cape Town: David Philip, 1981), 110–11.
22. Tony Fleischer, Editorial, in Fleischer (ed.), *New South African Writing*, 2 vols (Johannesburg: Purnell, 1964–5), vol. i, pp. v–vi.
23. Edgar Bernstein, 'The Cat in the Censorship Bag', in Fleischer (ed.), *New South African Writing*, ii. 188.
24. Ellison Kahn, '*When the Lion Feeds*—and the Censor Pounces: A Disquisition on the Banning of Immoral Publications in South Africa', *South African Law Journal*, 83/3 (Aug. 1966), 333. For similar liberal views on the question of banning pornography, albeit from a more international perspective, see Unesco, *Apartheid: Its Effects on Education, Science, Culture and Information* (Paris: Unesco, 1967).
25. For Bunting's comprehensive analysis, see *The Rise of the South African Reich* (Harmondsworth: Penguin, 1964), esp. ch. 9.
26. Nadine Gordimer, 'Apartheid and Censorship', in J. S. Paton (ed.), *The Grey Ones* (Johannesburg: Ravan, 1974), 6.
27. WCPA, BCS vol. 22, ref. M2. The petition was also published in the national and international press.
28. Jack Cope, *The Adversary Within* (Cape Town: David Philip, 1982), 85.
29. WCPA, BCS vol. 22, ref. M2.
30. David Sweetman, *Mary Renault* (London: Chatto & Windus, 1993), 235.
31. Es'kia Mphahlele to Armand Gaspard, 31 Oct. 1963, University of Chicago Library, Congress for Cultural Freedom Papers, Special Collections Research Center, ser. 2, box 22, folder 2.
32. J. M. Leighton, 'Censorship: One or Two Points in Favour and Some Against', *Index on Censorship*, 5/1 (Spring 1976), 41–5. The article was first published in the *Newsletter*, 4 (July 1975), produced by the Artists' and Writers' Guild, a new group formed in the early 1970s.
33. Lewis Nkosi, *Home and Exile* (London: Longmans, Green, 1965), 120–1; all subsequent references are in the text.
34. Ezekiel Mphahlele, *Voices in the Whirlwind* (London: Macmillan, 1973), 203; all subsequent references are in the text.

35. For Nkosi's views on La Guma, see 'Alex La Guma: The Man and his Work', *South Africa: Information and Analysis*, 59 (Jan. 1968), 1–8; repr. in Lindy Stiebel and Liz Gunner (eds), *Still Beating the Drum: Critical Perspectives on Lewis Nkosi* (Amsterdam: Rodopi, 2005).

36. Mphahlele was citing Leon Trotsky, *Literature and Revolution* (Ann Arbor: University of Michigan Press, 1960), 170–1.

37. For Mphahlele's response to Gayle's critical review of *Voices in the Whirlwind*, see 'My Destiny Is Tied to Africa' (1973), in Mphahlele, *Es'kia* (Cape Town: Kwela Books, 2002).

38. Gala [Alex La Guma], 'Against Literary Apartheid', *African Communist*, 58 (1974), 102.

39. Mphahlele, *Voices in the Whirlwind*, 198.

40. Ezekiel Mphahlele, 'The Function of Literature at the Present Time: The Ethnic Imperative', *Transition*, 9/2 (1974), 47–54.

41. Ibid. 215.

42. Ibid. 196.

43. Peter Wilhelm, 'The State of the Union', *Artists' and Writers' Guild Newsletter*, 6 (1976), 1.

44. [Peter Wilhelm], 'Pen Letters', *Donga*, 6 (July 1977), 1. Though this was unsigned, it was printed as an editorial in an issue edited by Wilhelm. He was responding to a letter, which he quoted in full, from Frank Bradlow of PEN SA in the Cape.

45. Wilhelm, 'The State of the Union', 1.

46. Ibid.

47. Ibid.

48. Ibid.

49. Ibid.

50. [Wilhelm], 'Pen Letters', 1.

51. Bartho Smit, 'Tien jaar Afrikaanse Skrywersgilde', in Smit, *Skrywer en Gemeenskap* (Pretoria: Haum Literêr, 1985), 8.

52. Ibid.

53. Ibid.

54. Ibid.

55. See Ampie Coetzee and James Polley (eds), *Crossing Borders: Writers Meet the ANC* (Bramley: Taurus, 1990).

56. Njabulo Ndebele, *Rediscovery of the Ordinary* (Johannesburg: COSAW, 1991), 146.

57. For a history of the theatre groups in particular, see Robert Kavanagh, *Theatre and Cultural Struggle in South Africa* (London: Zed Books, 1985).

58. Ndebele, *Rediscovery of the Ordinary*, 145.

59. See Es'kia Mphahlele, *Bury Me at the Marketplace: Selected Letters of Es'kia Mphahlele, 1943–1980*, ed. N. Chabani Manganyi (Johannesburg: Skotaville, 1984), 23, 33.

60. Strinivasa Moodley, 'Black Consciousness, the Black Artist and the Emerging Black Culture', *SASO Newsletter*, 2/3 (May–June 1972), 19. It is worth recalling that Alan Paton was not simply well known as the author of *Cry, the Beloved Country* (1948). He was also leader of the short-lived Liberal Party; see Ch. 1 n. 68.

61. Ibid. 20.

62. Ibid. 19–20.

63. [Mafika Gwala?], 'Arts and Entertainment', *Black Review* (1973), 111–12.

64. Mafika Gwala, 'Letter to Richard Rive', *South African Outlook*, 101/1207 (Dec. 1971), 178.

65. Temba Sono, 'Some Concepts of Negritude and Black Identity', *SASO Newsletter*, 1/2 (June 1971), 18.

66. Adam Small, 'A Poem after the Bannings', *SASO Newsletter*, 5/2 (Mar.–Apr. 1973), 8.

67. Unsigned, review of *Student Perspectives on South Africa*, *SASO Newsletter*, 2/2 (Mar.–Apr. 1972), 12.

68. Nadine Gordimer, *The Black Interpreters* (Johannesburg: Ravan, 1973), 67.

69. Ibid. 52.

70. Ibid. 53.

71. Gordimer, *The Essential Gesture*, 106.
72. Ibid. 107.
73. Ibid.
74. Gordimer, *The Black Interpreters*, 68–9.
75. Ibid. 62.
76. Harry Levin, 'Thematics and Criticism', in Levin, *Grounds for Comparison* (Cambridge, Mass.: Harvard University Press, 1972), 92. Gordimer omitted the final claim about value in her own quotation.
77. Stanley Fish, 'How Ordinary Is Ordinary Language?', in Fish, *Is There a Text in This Class?* (Cambridge, Mass.: Harvard University Press, 1980), 103.
78. Gordimer, *The Black Interpreters*, 107, emphasis added. 'An Abandoned Bundle' appears in *Sounds of a Cowhide Drum* (Johannesburg: Renoster Books, 1971; Oxford: Oxford University Press, 1972).
79. Ronald Suresh Roberts, *No Cold Kitchen* (Johannesburg: STE Publishers, 2005), 300.
80. Gordimer, *The Black Interpreters*, 31–2.
81. Ibid. 32, emphasis added.
82. Ibid. 5.
83. Ibid. 33.
84. Gordimer, *The Essential Gesture*, 286. This is from the title essay, 'The Essential Gesture' (1984).
85. Ibid. 290.
86. Ibid. 256, 260.
87. Rose Powell, 'Writing Is Part of the Struggle', *Index on Censorship*, 9/6 (Dec. 1980), 9–10.
88. Roberts, *No Cold Kitchen*, 354–5.
89. Lionel Abrahams, 'From Shakespeare House to the Laager: The Story of PEN (Johannesburg)', *Sesame*, 3 (Summer 1983–4), 8.
90. Ibid.
91. Roberts, *No Cold Kitchen*, 355.
92. Abrahams, 'From Shakespeare House to the Laager', 8.
93. Ibid. 12.
94. Mothobi Mutloatse (ed.), *Forced Landing* (Johannesburg: Ravan, 1980), 5.
95. Ibid.
96. Abrahams, 'From Shakespeare House to the Laager', 12.
97. Mutloatse (ed.), *Forced Landing*, 2.
98. Ibid. 3.
99. Mike Kirkwood, 'Reflections on PEN', *Sesame*, 3 (Summer 1983–4), 24. Kirkwood originally gave this as a talk to the Afrikaans Skrywersgilde in April 1981.
100. Ibid. 25.
101. Ibid.
102. Abrahams, 'From Shakespeare House to the Laager', 19.
103. Cited in Francis Galloway (ed.), *SA Literature 1981* (Johannesburg: Ad Donker, 1983), 94. Rive originally made his comments in an article entitled 'Non-Racialism and Art', which appeared in *Contrast* in June 1981.
104. Galloway (ed.), *SA Literature 1981*, 95.
105. Abrahams, 'From Shakespeare House to the Laager', 18.
106. Cited in Galloway (ed.), *SA Literature 1981*, 124. The manifesto was first published in the *AWA Newsletter*, 1/1 (Sept.–Oct. 1981).
107. Galloway (ed.), *SA Literature 1981*, 124.
108. See, for instance, Es'kia Mphahlele, *Let's Talk Writing: Prose* (Johannesburg: AWA and the Council for Black Education and Research, 1985).
109. Galloway (ed.), *SA Literature 1981*, 125.
110. Ibid.

111. Njabulo Ndebele, 'Black Development', in B. S. Biko (ed.), *Black Viewpoint* (Johannesburg: Spro-cas, 1972), 26.
112. Ibid. 27.
113. For an overview of Ndebele's theoretical interventions, see Anthony O'Brien, 'Literature in Another South Africa: Njabulo Ndebele's Theory of Emergent Culture', *Diacritics*, 22/1 (1992), 66–85.
114. Yashar Kemal, 'A Dirty Story', *Staffrider*, 6/1 (1984), 7.
115. Ndebele, *Rediscovery of the Ordinary*, 11; all subsequent references to this essay are in the text.
116. Walter Benjamin, 'The Storyteller', in Benjamin, *Illuminations*, trans. Harry Zohn (London: Fontana Press, 1992), 88.
117. Ndebele, 'The Rediscovery of the Ordinary', in Ndebele, *The Rediscovery of the Ordinary*, 46.
118. Medu Publications and Research Unit, 'Opening the Doors of Culture', *Medu Newsletter*, 4/1 (1982), 10.
119. Ibid.
120. Mongane Serote, 'Naledi Writers Workshop', *Medu Newsletter*, 6/1 (1984), 22.
121. Medu, 'Opening the Doors of Culture', 10–11. The group was quoting Lenin's 'A Little Picture in Illustration of Big Problems', which appeared in his collection *On Literature and Art* (Moscow: Progress Publishers, 1970).
122. Medu, 'Opening the Doors of Culture', 14.
123. Ibid. 13–14.
124. Ibid. 13.
125. Ibid. 10, 13.
126. Gordimer, 'Living in the Interregnum' (1982), in Gordimer, *The Essential Gesture*, 279.
127. Gordimer, 'Relevance and Commitment', in Gordimer, *The Essential Gesture*, 137. According to Clingman, Gordimer used this paper, which she first wrote in 1979, for her keynote address on literature at the conference.
128. Gordimer, 'Relevance and Commitment', 141–2.
129. Cynthia Kross, 'Culture and Resistance', *Staffrider*, 5/2 (1982), 11–12.
130. Keorapetse Kgositsile, 'Culture and Resistance in South Africa', *Medu Newsletter*, 5/1 (1983), 24–5.
131. Achmat Dangor et al., *Exiles Within: An Anthology of Poetry* (Johannesburg: The Writers' Forum, 1986). The contributors included Farouk Asvat, Achmat Dangor, Don Mattera, James Matthews, Essop Patel, and Gladys Thomas.
132. Ndebele, 'The Writers' Movement in South Africa', in Ndebele, *Rediscovery of the Ordinary*, 150.
133. I am grateful to Peter Horn, COSAW's former National Secretary, for letting me cite his copy of the constitution.
134. Ndebele, 'Against Pamphleteering the Future', in Ndebele, *Rediscovery of the Ordinary*, 135–6.
135. Ibid. 142.
136. Ibid.
137. Ibid. 142–3.
138. Ibid. 143.
139. 'J. M. Coetzee in Conversation with Jane Poyner', in Jane Poyner (ed.), *J. M. Coetzee and the Idea of the Public Intellectual* (Athens: Ohio University Press, 2006), 23.
140. J. M. Coetzee, 'The Novel Today', *Upstream*, 6/1 (1988), 3; all subsequent references to this essay are in the text.
141. Fish, *Is There a Text in This Class?*, 103.

142. A. M. Louw, '*In the Heart of the Country*', 50. Louw was interpreting circumspect comments Coetzee had made in an interview with Stephen Watson in the literary magazine *Speak*. She probably had in mind his remark that he doubted 'that the political thinking of writers is of any more interest or value than anyone else's', and his subsequent comments about some black writers 'working with models which I regard as very dubious'. See 'Speaking: J. M. Coetzee', *Speak*, 1 (May–June 1978), 22–4.

143. Gordimer's article 'Surely a Novel Can't Shake Islam', a copy of which was included in the censorship file, originally appeared in the *New York Times*, 22 Feb. 1989.

144. Cited in Roberts, *No Cold Kitchen*, 494.

145. David Attwell, 'The Life and Times of Elizabeth Costello: J. M. Coetzee and the Public Sphere', in Poyner (ed.), *J. M. Coetzee and the Idea of the Public Intellectual*, 27.

146. Roberts, *No Cold Kitchen*, 494.

147. Ibid. 494–5.

148. Attwell, 'The Life and Times of Elizabeth Costello', 27.

149. J. M. Coetzee, *Doubling the Point* (Cambridge, Mass.: Harvard University Press, 1992), 298.

150. Ibid.

151. J. M. Coetzee, *Giving Offense*, p. vii.

152. Ibid. 84.

153. Ibid. 103.

154. J. M. Coetzee, *Doubling the Point*, 364.

155. Ibid. 363–4.

156. Ibid. 364.

Chapter 4

1. Cited in Stephen Clingman, *The Novels of Nadine Gordimer* (London: Allen & Unwin, 1986), 10.

2. Ronald Suresh Roberts, *No Cold Kitchen* (Johannesburg: STE Publishers, 2005), 251.

3. Clingman, *The Novels of Nadine Gordimer*, 12.

4. Nadine Gordimer, *Burger's Daughter* (London: Jonathan Cape, 1979), inside flap.

5. Clingman, *The Novels of Nadine Gordimer*, 18.

6. Ibid.

7. Gordimer, *The Black Interpreters* (Johannesburg: Ravan, 1973), 7.

8. Clingman, *The Novels of Nadine Gordimer*, 17.

9. Ibid. 17, 224.

10. Ibid. 9.

11. Ibid.

12. Nadine Gordimer, 'The Idea of Gardening', *New York Review of Books*, 2 Feb. 1984, 3, 6.

13. Clingman, *The Novels of Nadine Gordimer*, 155.

14. Ibid. 9.

15. Ibid. 143.

16. Ibid. 144.

17. Ibid. 143.

18. See Nadine Gordimer, *A World of Strangers* (London: Gollancz, 1958), 166–7.

19. Nadine Gordimer, *A World of Strangers* (Harmondsworth: Penguin, 1961), 34.

20. Ibid. 36.

21. See Dominic Head, *Nadine Gordimer* (Cambridge: Cambridge University Press, 1994), 54.

22. Gordimer, *A World of Strangers* (1961), 172.

23. Ibid. 212.

24. Clingman, *The Novels of Nadine Gordimer*, 80.

25. Ibid. 92. One of the key figures of ARM, Hugh Lewin, who was imprisoned along with others in 1964, recorded his experiences in *Bandiet*. It was banned in 1974.
26. Nadine Gordimer, *The Late Bourgeois World* (London: Gollancz, 1966), 61.
27. Ibid. 38.
28. Ibid. 92.
29. Ibid. 138.
30. Ibid.
31. Ibid.
32. Ibid. 160.
33. National Archives and Records of South Africa, Pretoria, file PR 2/141, 1/74.
34. Nadine Gordimer, *The Conservationist* (London: Jonathan Cape, 1974), 122–5.
35. Ibid. 252.
36. Gordimer, *Burger's Daughter*, 153.
37. Nadine Gordimer et al., *What Happened to 'Burger's Daughter'?* (Emmarentia: Taurus, 1980), 23.
38. Gordimer, *Burger's Daughter*, 154.
39. Ibid. 171.
40. Ibid. 157.
41. Ibid. 170.
42. Gordimer et al., *What Happened to 'Burger's Daughter'?*, 30.
43. Gordimer, *Burger's Daughter*, 196.
44. Ibid. 210.
45. Ibid. 349.
46. Ibid.
47. Z.N. [Brian Bunting], 'The Politics of Commitment', *African Communist*, 80 (1980), 101.
48. Gordimer, *Burger's Daughter*, 76.
49. Ibid. 47.
50. Ibid. 80.
51. Ibid. 332.
52. Ibid. 361.

Chapter 5

1. Thomas Karis and Gail M. Gehart (eds), *From Protest to Challenge: A Documentary History of African Politics in South Africa, 1882–1964*, 3 vols (Stanford, Calif.: Hoover Institution Press, 1972–7), iii. 202; all subsequent references to vol. iii are in the text.
2. Es'kia Mphahlele, 'Opening Address: Education and the Search for Self', *Teachers' Journal*, 23/5 (1980), 2; cited in Catherine Woeber, 'Educating the Educator: Es'kia Mphahlele's Schooling at St Peter's', in Sam Raditlhalo and Taban Lo Liyong (eds), *Es'kia* (Johannesburg: Stainbank and Associates, 2006), 123.
3. Ibid.
4. Ezekiel Mphahlele, *The African Image* (London: Faber, 1962), 35.
5. Ibid. 34.
6. Ezekiel Mphahlele, *The African Image* (London: Faber, 1974), 36.
7. Ibid. 14.
8. Es'kia Mphahlele, *Es'kia Continued* (Johannesburg: Stainbank and Associates, 2005), 185.
9. Mphahlele, *The African Image* (1962), 34.
10. Ezekiel Mphahlele, *Down Second Avenue* (London: Faber, 1959), 220.
11. Ibid.
12. Ibid. 210.
13. Ibid. 220.
14. Es'kia Mphahlele, *The Unbroken Song* (Johannesburg: Ravan, 1981), p. x.
15. Ibid.

16. Es'kia Mphahlele, *The Unbroken Song* (Johannesburg: Ravan, 1981), p. x.
17. Ibid., p. viii.
18. Ibid., p. ix.
19. Louise Silver (ed.), *Publications Appeal Board: Digest of Decisions* (Johannesburg: Centre for Applied Legal Studies, 1979–86), Case 103/83.
20. Es'kia Mphahlele, *The Wanderers* (Johannesburg: Ravan, 1983), 168.
21. See Es'kia Mphahlele, *Chirundu* (Johannesburg: Ravan, 1979), 145, 153.
22. Ezekiel Mphahlele, *In Corner B* (Nairobi: East Africa Publishing House, 1967), 93.
23. Ibid. 94.
24. Ibid. 68.
25. Ibid. 67 and *passim*.
26. Ibid., back cover.
27. Ibid. 164.
28. Ibid. 201.
29. Mphahlele, *The Unbroken Song*, 195.
30. Mphahlele, *Down Second Avenue*, 106.
31. Mphahlele, *The African Image* (1962), 67.
32. Ibid. 85.
33. Ibid. 20.
34. Ibid. 66.
35. Lewis Nkosi, *Home and Exile* (London: Longmans, Green, 1965), 41.
36. Ibid. 13.
37. Ibid. 8, 11.
38. Ibid. 5.
39. See Mphahlele, *The African Image* (1974), 14.
40. Ibid. 42–3.
41. Ibid. 35.
42. Ibid. 58.
43. Ibid.
44. Adrian Roscoe, *Uhuru's Fire: African Literature East to South* (Cambridge: Cambridge University Press, 1977), 228.
45. Mphahlele, *The African Image* (1974), 23.

Chapter 6

1. André P. Brink, *Looking on Darkness* (London: W. H. Allen, 1974), inside flap.
2. Ibid.
3. André P. Brink, 'Tussen Sestig en Sewentig', *Kol*, 1/1 (Aug. 1968), 2; all subsequent references are in the text.
4. Breyten Breytenbach, 'Klad, Teiken of Skimmelvlek?, *Kol*, 1/1 (Aug. 1968), 11; all subsequent references are in the text.
5. Etienne Leroux, *To a Dubious Salvation* (Harmondsworth: Penguin, 1972), 97; all the quotations are keyed to this edition, which is the most accessible.
6. Ibid. 117.
7. Etienne Leroux, 'Daardie brief was ook aan my gerig', *Kol*, 1/2 (Sept.–Oct. 1968), 3; all subsequent references are in the text.
8. Breytenbach, 'Klad, Teiken of Skimmelvlek?', 11.
9. Bartho Smit, 'André Brink tussen sestig and sewentig', *Kol*, 1/1 (Aug. 1968), 8; Chris Barnard, 'Brief aan Breyten', *Kol*, 1/1 (Aug. 1968), 17.
10. Leroux, 'Daardie brief was ook aan my gerig', 3–4.
11. Ibid. 2.
12. Ibid. 4.

13. See Michael Walzer, *The Company of Critics* (New York: Basic Books, 2002), esp. 210–24, which focuses on Breytenbach.
14. Breytenbach, 'Klad, Teiken of Skimmelvlek?', 13; id., *End Papers* (London: Faber, 1986), 34.
15. N. P. van Wyk Louw, 'Voorlopige dood van die jambiese vyfvoeter', *Kol*, 1/1 (Aug. 1968), 1. I am grateful to John Gouws for his advice on this translation.
16. Adam Small, 'Kol-kol oor vier se gesprek 'n vyfde', *Kol*, 1/2 (Sept. 1968), 9.
17. Ibid. 9, 13.
18. André P. Brink, 'Antwoord aan Smit', *Kol*, 1/3 (Oct.–Nov. 1968), 5–6.
19. Francis Galloway, *Breyten Breytenbach as Openbare Figuur* (Pretoria: HAUM-Literêr, 1990), 111–12.
20. Ibid. 112–13.
21. James F. English, *The Economy of Prestige* (Cambridge, Mass.: Harvard University Press, 2005).
22. Galloway, *Breyten Breytenbach as Openbare Figuur* 82.
23. Ibid. 85.
24. W. D. Beukes (ed.), *Boekewêreld: Die Nasionale Pers in die Uitgewersbedryf tot 1990* (Cape Town: Nasionale Boekhandel, 1992), 245, 243.
25. Leroux, *To a Dubious Salvation*, 136.
26. Galloway, *Breyten Breytenbach as Openbare Figuur*, 103.
27. Beukes (ed.), *Boekewêreld*, 245.
28. Leroux, *To a Dubious Salvation*, 69.
29. Ibid. 107.
30. Ibid. 178.
31. Ibid.
32. Etienne Leroux, *Magersfontein, O Magersfontein!* (Cape Town: Human & Rousseau, 1976), pp. v, 190.
33. Ibid. 191.
34. Ibid. 16.
35. Ibid. 191.
36. Ibid. 17, 183.
37. Ibid. 89.
38. Koos Human, *'n Lewe met Boeke* (Cape Town: Human & Rousseau, 2006), 49.
39. Appeal Board Case 77/77. The full text is in the censorship file P77/1/97 (WCPA).
40. Leroux, *Magersfontein, O Magersfontein!*, 91.
41. [Breyten Breytenbach], *'n Seisoen in die Paradys* (Johannesburg: Perskor, 1976), inside flap.
42. Breyten Bretyenbach, *Skryt: Om 'n sinkende skip blou te verf* (Amsterdam: Meulenhoff, 1972), 26–7, 29.
43. Galloway, *Breyten Breytenbach as Openbare Figuur*, 86–7.
44. For a detailed discussion of this, see J. M. Coetzee, *Giving Offense: Essays on Censorship* (Chicago: University of Chicago Press, 1996), 215–23.

Chapter 7

1. Mongane Wally Serote, *Yakhal'inkomo* (Johannesburg: Renoster Books, 1972), 52.
2. Ibid.
3. Ibid.
4. Ibid.
5. Penny Silva (ed.), *A Dictionary of South African English* (Oxford: Oxford University Press, 1996), 272.
6. Serote, *Yakhal'inkomo*, 8.
7. Ibid., p. iii.

8. Serote, *Yakhal'inkomo*, 16, 8.
9. Ibid. 8.
10. Ibid., p. iv.
11. Ibid., back cover.
12. Scarlet Whitman [Barry Feinberg], 'Poetry and Liberation', *African Communist*, 59 (1974), 113.
13. Ibid. 114.
14. Ibid. 112.
15. Ibid.
16. Unsigned, '*Cowhide Drum* Wins Schreiner Prize', English Academy Press Release, 9 Sept. 1974, National English Literary Museum, Grahamstown, South Africa.
17. Oswald Joseph Mtshali, *Sounds of a Cowhide Drum* (Johannesburg: Renoster Books, 1971), back cover.
18. Unsigned, 'Arts and Entertainment', *Black Review* (1973), 112–13. This was probably by Mafika Gwala.
19. For a discussion of this, see Anthony O'Brien, *Against Normalization* (Durham, NC: Duke University Press, 2001), 44–6.
20. Es'kia Mphahlele, 'Mtshali's Strident Voice of Self-Assertion', *Rand Daily Mail*, 19 Dec. 1980, 16.
21. Mtshali, *Sounds of a Cowhide Drum*, p. ix.
22. Ibid., p. vi.
23. Ibid. 39.
24. Ibid., p. vi.
25. Oswald Mbuyiseni Mtshali, *Sounds of a Cowhide Drum* (Oxford: Oxford University Press, 1972), back cover.
26. Mtshali, *Sounds of a Cowhide Drum* (1971), p. vi.
27. Ibid., p. vii.
28. Ibid. 29.
29. Ibid., p. vii.
30. Ibid. 68.
31. Richard Rive, *Writing Black* (Cape Town: David Philip, 1981), 11.
32. Hein Willemse (ed.), *More than Brothers: Peter Clarke and James Matthews at 70* (Cape Town: Kwela Books, 2000), 45.
33. James Matthews, *The Party Is Over* (Cape Town: Kwela Books, 1997), 48.
34. James Matthews, personal interview, 5 Apr. 2002. For an account of some key aspects of this lineage, see also Michael Chapman, *South African English Poetry: A Modern Perspective* (Johannesburg: Ad Donker, 1984), and Louise Bethlehem, ' "A Primary Need as Strong as Hunger": The Rhetoric of Urgency in South African Literary Culture under Apartheid', *Poetics Today*, 22/2 (Summer 2001), 365–89.
35. Mongane Wally Serote, 'the black word', *BLAC Newsletter*, 1/2 [c.1975], 4.
36. Ibid. 5.
37. Ibid.
38. Ibid. 4.
39. Ibid. 5.
40. M. J. Daymond et al. (eds), *Momentum: On Recent South African Writing* (Pietermaritzburg: University of Natal Press, 1984), 74.
41. James Matthews and Gladys Thomas, *Cry Rage!* (Johannesburg: Spro-cas, 1972), p. iv. The original censors' report, dating from 1973, is included in the later file P77/7/91 (WCPA).
42. Matthews and Thomas, *Cry Rage!*, 68.
43. Ibid. 65.
44. Serote, 'the black word', 5.

45. Nadine Gordimer, *The Black Interpreters* (Johannesburg: Ravan, 1973), 70.
46. Matthews and Thomas, *Cry Rage!*, 50.
47. Ibid. 20.
48. Ibid. 9.
49. Ibid. 1.
50. Ibid. 70.
51. James Matthews (ed.), *Black Voices Shout!* (Cape Town: BLAC, 1974), p. iii.
52. Ibid., p. iv.
53. James Matthews, *pass me a meatball, Jones: a gathering of feelings* (Cape Town: BLAC, 1977); id., *no time for dreams* (Cape Town: BLAC, 1981), back cover.
54. Matthews, *no time for dreams*, 1.
55. Ibid. 53.
56. Matthews, *pass me a meatball, Jones*, 4.
57. Ibid. 10.
58. Ibid., p. i.
59. Matthews (ed.), *Black Voices Shout!*, 51.
60. Ibid. 6.
61. James Matthews to Nadine Gordimer, 12 Oct. 1977, Lilly Library, Indiana University, Nadine Gordimer Papers, Correspondence Oct.–Dec. 1977.
62. Michael Gardiner, 'Looking for Wopko Jensma', *ZA@Play*, 13 Mar. 2000, http://www.chico.mweb.co.za/art/the_rest/0003/000313-jensma.html, accessed 14 May 2006 but no longer available.
63. Mafika Gwala, 'Writing as a Cultural Weapon', in Daymond et al. (eds), *Momentum*, 41.
64. Wopko Jensma, *i must show you my clippings* (Johannesburg: Ravan, 1977), 55.
65. Wopko Jensma, *where white is the colour where black is the number* (Johannesburg: Ravan, 1974), 21.
66. Ibid. 21–2.
67. Ibid.
68. Ibid. 27.
69. Ibid., back cover.

Chapter 8

1. J. M. Coetzee, 'SA Authors Must Learn Modesty', *Die Vaderland*, 1 May 1981, 16; all subsequent references to this speech are in the text.
2. J. M. Coetzee, *White Writing* (Johannesburg: Radix, 1988), 11.
3. Nadine Gordimer, *The Black Interpreters* (Johannesburg: Ravan, 1973), 32.
4. Ibid. 5.
5. J. M. Coetzee, 'Alex La Guma and the Responsibilities of the South African Writer', *Journal of New African Literature and the Arts*, 9/10 (1972), 6.
6. J. M. Coetzee, *Dusklands* (Johannesburg: Ravan, 1974), 2.
7. Ibid.
8. J. M. Coetzee to Peter Randall, 14 Jan. 1974, National English Literary Museum, Grahamstown, South Africa (NELM).
9. J. M. Coetzee, *Doubling the Point* (Cambridge, Mass.: Harvard University Press, 1992), 300.
10. Ibid. 364.
11. Ibid. 298.
12. J. M. Coetzee, personal interview, 8 May 1999.
13. J. M. Coetzee, *Waiting for the Barbarians* (London: Secker & Warburg, 1980), 84; all subsequent references are in the text.
14. Ibid.

15. J. M. Coetzee, *Life & Times of Michael K* (London: Secker & Warburg, 1983); all subsequent references are in the text.
16. J. M. Coetzee to Peter Randall, 27 June 1975, NELM.
17. Peter Randall to J. M. Coetzee, 21 July 1975, NELM.
18. J. M. Coetzee, *In the Heart of the Country* (Johannesburg: Ravan, 1978), 111.
19. J. M. Coetzee to Peter Randall, 19 July 1977, NELM.
20. J. M. Coetzee, *In the Heart of the Country* (London: Secker & Warburg, 1977), inside front flap; Coetzee, *In the Heart of the Country* (1978), back cover.
21. Coetzee, *In the Heart of the Country* (1977), 32.
22. Coetzee, *Waiting for the Barbarians*, inside front flap.
23. J. M. Coetzee, 'The Novel Today', *Upstream*, 6/1 (1988), 4.
24. Anna M. Louw, '*In the Heart of the Country*: A Calvinist Allegory?', *PN Review*, 14/2 (1987), 50.
25. Coetzee, *Life & Times of Michael K*, 185.
26. Coetzee, *Doubling the Point*, 299.
27. Ibid.
28. Derek Attridge, *J. M. Coetzee and the Ethics of Reading* (Chicago: University of Chicago Press, 2004), 30–1.
29. Ibid. 29.
30. Ibid. 13.
31. Ibid. 14.
32. Coetzee, *Waiting for the Barbarians*, inside front flap.
33. Coetzee, *In the Heart of the Country* (1977), inside front flap.
34. Attridge, *J. M. Coetzee and the Ethics of Reading*, 53.
35. Ibid. 50.
36. Coetzee, *Life & Times of Michael K*, 250.
37. Ibid.
38. Coetzee, *Doubling the Point*, 232.
39. Coetzee, *Life & Times of Michael K*, 250.
40. Z.N. [Brian Bunting], 'Much Ado About Nothing', *African Communist*, 97 (1984), 102–3.
41. Roland Barthes, *Writing Degree Zero*, trans. Annette Lavers and Colin Smith (New York: Hill and Wang, 2001), 30.
42. Ibid.; Coetzee, 'The Novel Today', 4.
43. Coetzee, 'SA Authors Must Learn Modesty', 16.

Chapter 9

1. Mothobi Mutloatse (ed.), *Forced Landing* (Johannesburg: Ravan, 1980), p. i.
2. Ibid. 6.
3. Ibid.
4. Ibid. 4.
5. Ibid. 3–4.
6. Mike Kirkwood to Mafika Gwala, 18 Jan. 1984, Macmillan SA, Johannesburg, Ravan Press Archives (RPA), *No More Lullabies* title file.
7. Mike Kirkwood to Mbulelo Mzamane, 3 June 1980, RPA, *Mzala* title file.
8. Mike Kirkwood to Mafika Gwala, 18 Jan. 1984, RPA, *No More Lullabies* title file.
9. Ibid.
10. Mike Kirkwood to Mbulelo Mzamane, 17 Mar. 1980, RPA, *Mzala* title file.
11. Kirkwood to Mzamane, 8 July 1980, RPA, *Mzala* title file.
12. Kirkwood to Mzamane, 3 June 1980, RPA, *Mzala* title file.
13. Ibid.
14. Kirkwood to Mzamane, 22 Aug. 1980, RPA, *Mzala* title file.
15. Kirkwood to Mzamane, 6 Dec. 1980, RPA, *Mzala* title file.

16. Mbulelo Mzamane, *Mzala* (Johannesburg: Ravan, 1980), p. viii.
17. Mzamane to Kirkwood, 28 July 1980, RPA, *Mzala* title file.
18. Mzamane, *Mzala*, p. x.
19. Ibid., p. xii.
20. Mzamane to Kirkwood, 6 May 1980, RPA, *Mzala* title file.
21. Mtutuzeli Matshoba, *Call Me Not a Man* (Johannesburg: Ravan, 1979), p. viii.
22. Ibid., p. x.
23. Ibid.
24. Ibid.
25. Ibid.
26. Ibid., p. vi.
27. Kirkwood to Gwala, 18 Jan. 1984, RPA, *No More Lullabies* title file.
28. Njabulo Ndebele, *Rediscovery of the Ordinary* (Johannesburg: COSAW, 1991), 27.
29. Ibid.
30. Ibid.
31. Ibid.
32. Ibid. 55.
33. Ibid. 32.
34. Mzamane, *Mzala*, 88, 110.
35. Njabulo Ndebele, *Fools and Other Stories* (Johannesburg: Ravan, 1983), 278.
36. For a discussion of this debate, see David Attwell, *Rewriting Modernity: Studies in Black South African Literary History* (Scottsville: KZN Press, 2005), 179–92.
37. Ndebele, *Fools and Other Stories*, 276.
38. Ibid.
39. Ndebele, *Rediscovery of the Ordinary*, 27.
40. Njabulo Ndebele to Mike Kirkwood, *Staffrider*, 5/3 (1983), 44.
41. Ibid. 45.
42. Ibid.
43. Ibid.
44. Anthony O'Brien, *Against Normalization* (Durham, NC: Duke University Press, 2001), 47–8.
45. Francis Galloway (ed.), *SA Literature 1983*, iv (Pretoria: Haum-Literêr, 1987), 75.
46. For the published version of the letter, see *Staffrider* (Feb. 1980), 47.
47. Mike Kirkwood, 'A Glimpse of Slavery Prosecution', RPA, *Call Me Not a Man* title file.
48. Matshoba, *Call Me Not a Man* (1979), 54.
49. Mtutuzeli Matshoba, *Call Me Not a Man* (London: Longman, 1987), back cover.
50. Matshoba, *Call Me Not a Man* (1979), 55.
51. Kirkwood, 'A Glimpse of Slavery Prosecution'.
52. Matshoba, *Call Me Not a Man* (1979), 49.
53. Ibid. 53.
54. Ibid. 46.
55. Ibid. 30.
56. Ibid. 36.
57. Ibid. 35.
58. Ibid. 40.
59. Ibid. 38.
60. Ibid.
61. Ibid. 122.
62. Mbulelo Mzamane, 'The Uses of Traditional Oral Forms in Black South African Literature', in Landeg White and Tim Couzens (eds), *Literature and Society in South Africa* (Cape Town: Maskew Miller Longman, 1984), 158–9.
63. Ibid.

64. Mzamane to Kelwyn Sole, personal correspondence, 28 July 1986, cited in Kelwyn Sole, 'Authorship, Authenticity and the Black Community: The Novels of Soweto 1976', in Stephen Clingman (ed.), *Regions and Repertoires: Topics in South African Politics and Culture* (Johannesburg: Ravan, 1991), 202.
65. See Mongane Serote, *To Every Birth its Blood* (Johannesburg: Ravan, 1981), 172–3, 269.
66. Ibid. 87–9.
67. Ibid., 309–13.
68. Ibid. 367–8.
69. Mbulelo Mzamane, *The Children of Soweto* (Johannesburg: Ravan, 1982), 244.

Postscript

1. Albie Sachs, 'Preparing Ourselves for Freedom', in Derek Attridge and Rosemary Jolly (eds), *Writing South Africa* (Cambridge: Cambridge University Press, 1998), 239; all subsequent references are in the text. The paper also appeared in Albie Sachs, *Protecting Human Rights in a New South Africa* (Cape Town: Oxford University Press, 1990).
2. Albie Sachs, *Advancing Human Rights in South Africa* (Cape Town: Oxford University Press, 1992), 100. For a detailed discussion of Sachs's initiative within the larger constitutional debates, see also Alfred Cockrell, 'The South African Bill of Rights and the "Duck/Rabbit" ', *Modern Law Review*, 60/4 (July 1997), 531–7.
3. Albie Sachs, 'Afterword: The Taste of an Avocado Pear', in Ingrid de Kok and K. Press (eds), *Spring Is Rebellious* (Cape Town: Buchu Books, 1990), 147. This volume also includes Sachs's original paper.
4. Ampie Coetzee, 'Sachs, kultuur en die struggle', in de Kok and Press (eds), *Spring Is Rebellious*, 40.
5. Tony Morphet, 'Cultural Imagination and Cultural Settlement: Albie Sachs and Njabulo Ndebele', in de Kok and Press (eds), *Spring Is Rebellious*.
6. Frank Meintjies, 'New Thinking—the Broader Political Context', in de Kok and Press (eds), *Spring Is Rebellious*, 119; Nise Malange et al., 'Albie Sachs Must Not Worry: Culture and Working Life Project's Response', ibid. 102.
7. Ibid. 103.
8. Ari Sitas, 'The Sachs Debate: A Philistine's Response', in de Kok and Press (eds), *Spring Is Rebellious*, 94.
9. Ibid.
10. Sachs, 'Afterword', 148.
11. Ibid.
12. Ibid.
13. Bernard Williams et al., *Report of the Committee on Obscenity and Film Censorship* (London: Her Majesty's Stationery Office, 1979), 126, 160.
14. Ibid. 110.
15. My discussion here is indebted to Jacques Derrida's articulation of the linkage between the ideas of literature and of democracy in the essay 'Passions' (1993), and, behind that, to the earlier connection Sartre made in 1948. I would argue that Derrida's formulation acquires particular force when seen in terms of Sartre's more concrete historical analysis, focusing on particular ideas of literature and specific versions of democracy. See Jacques Derrida, *On the Name*, ed. Thomas Dutoit (Stanford, Calif.: Stanford University Press, 1995), esp. 28–9; see also n. 48 in the Introduction to this book.
16. *The Constitution of the Republic of South Africa* (1996), <http://www.info.gov.za/documents/constitution/1996>, accessed 4 June 2006.
17. Ibid.
18. Films and Publications Act, 1996, *Government Gazette*, 377/17560 (Pretoria: Government Printer, 1996), 24.
19. Ibid.

20. Ibid. 30.
21. Kobus van Rooyen, 'Drafting a New Film and Publication Bill for South Africa', in Jane Duncan (ed.), *Between Speech and Hate: Hate Speech, Pornography and the New South Africa* (Johannesburg: Idasa, 1996), 181.
22. Ibid.
23. Ibid. 189.
24. I am grateful to Iyavar Chetty, Senior Executive Officer of the FPB, for giving me a copy of the Committee's report, which is currently lodged with the FPB in Johannesburg. Though the Report itself is in the public domain, the membership of the Committee cannot be disclosed until 2022.
25. Ronald Dworkin, 'The Right to Ridicule', *New York Review of Books*, 23 Mar. 2006, 44.
26. Victoria Bronstein, 'What You Can and Can't Say in South Africa' (draft), <http://www.da.org.za/da/Site/Eng/campaigns/DOCS/Censorship-VictoriaBronstein.doc>, accessed 22 May 2007, 1, 12.
27. Ibid. 14.
28. Shrabani Basu, 'Of Satan, Archangels and Prophets', in Lisa Appignanesi and Sara Maitland (eds), *The Rushdie File* (London: Fourth Estate, 1989), 41.
29. Dworkin, 'The Right to Ridicule', 44.
30. Van Rooyen, 'Drafting a New Film and Publication Bill for South Africa', 189.
31. Ibid.
32. See Lee C. Bollinger and G. R. Stone (eds), *Eternally Vigilant: Free Speech in the Modern Era* (Chicago: University of Chicago Press, 2002), pp. ix–x. As Bollinger and Stone point out, Justice Oliver Wendell Holmes first used the phrase, which they adopted for their own title, in 1919 in *Abrams* v. *United States*.

Select Bibliography

Archival Sources
Lilly Library, Indiana University
Nadine Gordimer Papers

Macmillan SA, Johannesburg
Ravan Press Archives (RPA)

National Afrikaans Literature and Research Centre, Bloemfontein (NALN)
Author and Publisher Papers

National Archives and Records of South Africa, Pretoria
Censorship Board

National English Literary Museum, Grahamstown, South Africa (NELM)
Author and Publisher Papers

New York Public Library, Rare Books Division
Nadine Gordimer Papers
New Yorker Archive

St Hugh's College, Oxford
Mary Renault Papers

South African Library, Cape Town
South African PEN Centre, Memorandum, n.d. [*c*.1960]

University of Chicago Library
Congress for Cultural Freedom Papers

University of Reading Library
Heinemann African Writers Series Archives
Jonathan Cape Archives
Secker & Warburg Archives

Western Cape Provincial Archives and Records, Cape Town (WCPA)
Censorship Board

Digital Sources
Beacon for Freedom of Expression
<http://www.beaconforfreedom.org>, accessed 27 June 2008.

Brink, André P., 'Kennis van Sensuur 2004'
<http://www.litnet.co.za/cgibin/giga.cgi?cmd=cause_dir_news_item&news_id=17763& cause_id=1270>, accessed 7 Aug. 2007.

Bronstein, V., 'What You Can and Can't Say in South Africa' (draft)
<http://www.da.org.za/da/Site/Eng/campaigns/DOCS/Censorship-VictoriaBronstein. doc>, accessed 22 May 2007.

The Constitution of the Republic of South Africa (1996)
<http://www.info.gov.za/documents/constitution/1996>, accessed 4 June 2006.

Digital Innovation South Africa, Freedom Struggles, 1950–94
<http://disa.ukzn.ac.za/>, accessed 25 Apr. 2006.

Gardiner, M., 'Looking for Wopko Jensma', *ZA@Play*, 13 Mar. 2000
<http://www.chico.mweb.co.za/art/the_rest/0003/000313-jensma.html>, accessed 14 May 2006 but no longer available.

Students' British Board of Film Classification
<http://www.sbbfc.co.uk>, accessed 12 Aug. 2006.

Oral Sources
Coetzee, A., personal interview, 28 Aug. 2001.
Coetzee, J. M., personal interviews, 8 May, 27 July 1999.
Kirkwood, M., personal interview, 21 Oct. 2006.
Matthews, J., personal interview, 5 Apr. 2002.
Randall, P., personal interview, 17 Aug. 1998.
Scholtz, H. van der M., personal interview, 22 Aug. 2001.
Scholtz, R., personal interview, 22 Aug. 2001.

Published Sources
Government Documents
Cronjé, G., et al., *Report of the Commission of Enquiry in Regard to Undesirable Publications* (Pretoria: Government Printer, 1957).
Department of the Interior, Annual Reports (Pretoria: Government Printer, 1975–92).
Entertainments (Censorship) Act, No. 28, 1931, *Union Gazette Extraordinary*, 5 June 1931 (Pretoria: Government Printer, 1931).
Films and Publications Act, 1996, *Government Gazette*, 377/17560 (Pretoria: Government Printer, 1996).
Publications Act, No. 42, 1974, *Government Gazette*, 112/4426 (Pretoria: Government Printer, 1974).
Publications and Entertainments Act, No. 26, 1963, *Statutes of the Republic of South Africa 1963* (Pretoria: Government Printer, 1963).
Report by the Commission of Inquiry into the Publications and Entertainments Bill (A. B. 61-'73) (Pretoria: Government Printer, 1974).
Report of the Select Committee on the Publications and Entertainments Amendment Bill (Pretoria: Government Printer, 1973).
Silver, Louise (ed.), *Publications Appeal Board: Digest of Decisions*, 4 vols (Johannesburg: Centre for Applied Legal Studies, 1979–86).
Williams, B., et al., *Report of the Committee on Obscenity and Film Censorship* (London: Her Majesty's Stationery Office, 1979).

Other
Abrahams, L., 'From Shakespeare House to the Laager: The Story of PEN (Johannesburg)', *Sesame*, 3 (Summer 1983–4), 5–19.
—— 'The Purple Renoster: An Adolescence', *English in Africa*, 7/2 (Sept. 1980), 32–49.
Appignanesi, L., and S. Maitland (eds), *The Rushdie File* (London: Fourth Estate, 1989).
Attridge, D., *J. M. Coetzee and the Ethics of Reading* (Chicago: University of Chicago Press, 2004).
—— and R. Jolly (eds), *Writing South Africa* (Cambridge: Cambridge University Press, 1998).
Attwell, D., 'The Life and Times of Elizabeth Costello: J. M. Coetzee and the Public Sphere', in J. Poyner (ed.), *J. M. Coetzee and the Idea of the Public Intellectual* (Athens: Ohio University Press, 2006).
—— *Rewriting Modernity: Studies in Black South African Literary History* (Scottsville: KZN Press, 2005).
Barnard, C., 'Brief aan Breyten', *Kol*, 1/1 (Aug. 1968), 14–18.

Barthes, R., *Writing Degree Zero*, trans. Annette Lavers and Colin Smith (New York: Hill and Wang, 2001).

Basu, S., 'Of Satan, Archangels and Prophets', in L. Appignanesi and S. Maitland (eds), *The Rushdie File* (London: Fourth Estate, 1989).

Benjamin, W., *Illuminations*, trans. Harry Zohn (London: Fontana Press, 1992).

Bernstein, Edgar, 'The Cat in the Censorship Bag', in Tony Fleischer (ed.), *New South African Writing*, 2 vols (Johannesburg: Purnell, 1964–5).

Bethlehem, L., ' "A Primary Need as Strong as Hunger": The Rhetoric of Urgency in South African Literary Culture under Apartheid', *Poetics Today*, 22/2 (Summer 2001), 365–89.

Beukes, W. D. (ed.), *Boekewêreld: Die Nasionale Pers in die Uitgewersbedryf tot 1990* (Cape Town: Nasionale Boekhandel, 1992).

Blanchot, M., *The Space of Literature*, trans. Ann Smock (Lincoln: University of Nebraska Press, 1982).

Bollinger, L. C., and G. R. Stone (eds), *Eternally Vigilant: Free Speech in the Modern Era* (Chicago: University of Chicago Press, 2002).

Breytenbach, B., *End Papers* (London: Faber, 1986).

—— 'Klad, Teiken of Skimmelvlek?', *Kol*, 1/1 (Aug. 1968), 8–13.

—— *'n Seisoen in die Paradys* (Johannesburg: Perskor, 1976).

—— *Skryt: Om 'n sinkende skip blou te verf* (Amsterdam: Meulenhoff, 1972).

Brink, A. P., 'Antwoord aan Smit', *Kol*, 1/3 (Oct.–Nov. 1968), 5–6.

—— *Kennis van die Aand* (Cape Town: Buren, 1973).

—— *Looking on Darkness* (London: W. H. Allen, 1974).

—— *Mapmakers* (London: Faber, 1983).

—— *Miskien Nooit* (Cape Town: Human & Rousseau, 1967).

—— 'Ons sal oorwin', *Standpunte*, 21/5 (June 1968), 22.

—— 'Tussen Sestig en Sewentig', *Kol*, 1/1 (Aug. 1968), 2–5.

Bunting, B., *The Rise of the South African Reich* (Harmondsworth: Penguin, 1964). *See also* Z.N.

Campschreur, W., and J. Divendal (eds), *Culture in Another South Africa* (London: Zed Books, 1989).

Chakrabarty, D., *Provincializing Europe* (Princeton: University of Princeton Press, 2000).

Chapman, M. (ed.), *The Drum Decade* (Pietermaritzburg: University of Natal Press, 1989).

—— *South African English Poetry: A Modern Perspective* (Johannesburg: Ad Donker, 1984).

—— *Southern African Literatures* (London: Longman, 1996).

Clingman, S., *The Novels of Nadine Gordimer* (London: Allen & Unwin, 1986).

—— (ed.), *Regions and Repertoires: Topics in South African Politics and Culture* (Johannesburg: Ravan, 1991).

Cockrell, A., 'The South African Bill of Rights and the "Duck/Rabbit" ', *Modern Law Review*, 60/4 (July 1997), 531–7.

Coetzee, A., 'Die skrywer en die gemeenskap teenoor mekaar' (The Writer and the Community against Each Other), *Tydskrif vir Letterkunde*, 1/3 (Aug. 1963), 6–14.

Coetzee, A. J., 'Literature and Crisis: One Hundred Years of Afrikaans Literature and Afrikaner Nationalism', in M. Trump (ed.), *Rendering Things Visible* (Johannesburg: Ravan, 1990).

—— 'Sachs, kultuur en die struggle', in I. de Kok and K. Press (eds), *Spring Is Rebellious* (Cape Town: Buchu Books, 1990).

—— 'Taurus Publishers', *Index on Censorship*, 13/5 (Oct. 1984), 32.

—— and J. Polley (eds), *Crossing Borders: Writers Meet the ANC* (Bramley: Taurus, 1990).

Coetzee, J. M., 'Alex La Guma and the Responsibilities of the South African Writer', *Journal of New African Literature and the Arts*, 9/10 (1972), 5–11.

—— 'Censorship and Polemic: The Solzhenitsyn Affair', *Pretexts*, 2/2 (Summer 1990), 3–36.

—— *Doubling the Point* (Cambridge, Mass.: Harvard University Press, 1992).

—— *Dusklands* (Johannesburg: Ravan, 1974).

—— *Giving Offense: Essays on Censorship* (Chicago: University of Chicago Press, 1996).

—— *In the Heart of the Country* (London: Secker & Warburg, 1977; Johannesburg: Ravan, 1978).

Coetzee, J. M., *Life & Times of Michael K* (London: Secker & Warburg, 1983).
—— 'The Novel Today', *Upstream*, 6/1 (1988), 2–5.
—— 'SA Authors Must Learn Modesty', *Die Vaderland*, 1 May 1981, 16.
—— '*Staffrider*', *African Book Publishing Record*, 5/4 (Oct. 1979), 235–6.
—— *Waiting for the Barbarians* (London: Secker & Warburg, 1980).
—— *White Writing* (Johannesburg: Radix, 1988).
Coggin, T. (ed.), *Censorship* (Johannesburg: SA Institute of Race Relations, 1983).
Cope, J., *The Adversary Within* (Cape Town: David Philip, 1982).
—— 'The World of *Contrast*', *English in Africa*, 7/2 (Sept. 1980), 1–21.
Cronjé, G., 'Keer die Verspreiding van Aanstootlike Leestof', *Die Huisgenoot*, 7 Oct. 1957, 6–7.
Currey, J., 'The African Writers Series at 30', *Southern African Review of Books* (Mar.–Apr. 1993), 4.
Dangor, A., et al., *Exiles Within: An Anthology of Poetry* (Johannesburg: Writers' Forum, 1986).
Daymond, M. J., et al. (eds), *Momentum: On Recent South African Writing* (Pietermaritzburg: University of Natal Press, 1984).
Dean, W. H. B., 'Judging the Obscene', *Acta Juridica* (1972), 61–150.
Dekker, G., *Afrikaanse Literatuurgeskiedenis* (Cape Town: Nasionale Boekhandel, 1961).
de Kock, L., *Civilizing Barbarians: Missionary Narrative and African Textual Response in Nineteenth-Century South Africa* (Alice: Lovedale Press; Johannesburg: Wits University Press, 1996).
de Kok, I., and K. Press (eds), *Spring Is Rebellious* (Cape Town: Buchu Books, 1990).
De Lange, M., *The Muzzled Muse* (Amsterdam: John Benjamins, 1997).
Derrida, J., *On the Name*, ed. Thomas Dutoit (Stanford, Calif.: Stanford University Press, 1995).
de Villiers, G. E. (ed.), *Ravan: Twenty Five Years* (Randburg: Ravan, 1997).
Devlin, P., *The Enforcement of Morals* (London: British Academy, 1959).
Driver, C. J., 'No Politics Is Politics', *New African*, 1/4 (Apr. 1962), 13–15.
Dubow, S., *A Commonwealth of Knowledge* (Oxford: Oxford University Press, 2006).
Duncan, J. (ed.), *Between Speech and Hate: Hate Speech, Pornography and the New South Africa* (Johannesburg: Idasa, 1996).
Dworkin, R., 'The Right to Ridicule', *New York Review of Books*, 23 Mar. 2006, 44.
Ehmeir, W., 'Publishing South African Literature in the 1960s', *Research in African Literatures*, 26/1 (Spring 1995), 110–31.
English, J. F., *The Economy of Prestige* (Cambridge, Mass.: Harvard University Press, 2005).
Evans, N., and M. Seeber (eds), *The Politics of Publishing in South Africa* (Scottsville: University of Natal Press, 2000).
Feinberg, B. (ed.), *Poets to the People* (London: Heinemann, 1981). *See also* Whitman, Scarlet.
Fish, S., *Is There a Text in This Class? The Authority of Interpretive Communities* (Cambridge, Mass.: Harvard University Press, 1980).
Fleischer, T. (ed.), *New South African Writing*, 2 vols (Johannesburg: Purnell, 1964, 1965).
Gala [A. La Guma], 'Against Literary Apartheid', *African Communist*, 58 (1974), 99–106. *See also* La Guma, A.
Galloway, F., *Breyten Breytenbach as Openbare Figuur* (Pretoria: Haum-Literêr, 1990).
—— (ed.), *SA Literature 1981* (Johannesburg: Ad Donker, 1983).
—— (ed.), *SA Literature 1983* (Pretoria: Haum-Literêr, 1987).
Gardiner, M., *South African Literary Magazines 1956–1978* (Johannesburg: Warren Siebrits Modern and Contemporary Art, 2004).
Gardner, S. (ed.), *Publisher/Writer/Reader: Sociology of Southern African Literature* (Johannesburg: University of Witwatersrand Press, 1986).
Garrard, J. and C., *Inside the Soviet Writers' Union* (London: I. B. Tauris, 1990).
Geldenhuys, P. B., *Pornografie, Sensuur en Reg* (Johannesburg: Lex Patria, 1977).
Giliomee, H., *The Afrikaners: Biography of a People* (Cape Town: Tafelberg, 2003).

Gordimer, N., 'Apartheid and Censorship', in J. S. Paton (ed.), *The Grey Ones* (Johannesburg: Ravan, 1974).
—— *The Black Interpreters* (Johannesburg: Ravan, 1973).
—— *Burger's Daughter* (London: Jonathan Cape, 1979).
—— *The Conservationist* (London: Jonathan Cape, 1974).
—— *The Essential Gesture* (London: Jonathan Cape, 1988).
—— 'The Idea of Gardening', *New York Review of Books* (2 Feb. 1984), 3–6.
—— *The Late Bourgeois World* (London: Gollancz, 1966).
—— *Some Monday for Sure* (London: Heinemann, 1976).
—— 'South Africa: Towards a Desk Drawer Literature', *The Classic*, 2/4 (1968), 64–74.
—— *A World of Strangers* (London: Gollancz, 1958; Harmondsworth: Penguin, 1961).
—— et al., *What Happened to 'Burger's Daughter'?* (Emmarentia: Taurus, 1980).
Gray, S. (ed.), *Free-lancers and Literary Biography in South Africa* (Amsterdam: Rodopi, 1999).
—— (ed.), *On the Edge of the World* (Johannesburg: Ad Donker, 1974).
Green, B., ' "This Beacon in Our Murky Lives": The CNA Literary Award, 1961–81', *English Academy Review*, 12 (1995), 11–32.
[Gwala, M.], 'Arts and Entertainment', *Black Review* (1973), 111–12.
—— *Jol'iiknomo* (Johannesburg: Ad Donker, 1977).
—— 'Letter to Richard Rive', *South African Outlook,* 101/1207 (Dec. 1971), 178–9.
—— (ed.), *Black Review* (1973).

Habermas, J., *The Structural Transformation of the Public Sphere* (1962; Cambridge: Polity Press, 1989).
Head, D., *Nadine Gordimer* (Cambridge: Cambridge University Press, 1994).
Hofmeyr, I., *The Portable Bunyan* (Johannesburg: Wits University Press, 2004).
Hughes, L. (ed.), *An African Treasury* (New York: Crown, 1960).
Human, K., *'n Lewe met Boeke* (Cape Town: Human & Rousseau, 2006).

Jensma, W., *i must show you my clippings* (Johannesburg: Ravan, 1977).
—— *where white is the colour where black is the number* (Johannesburg: Ravan, 1974).
Jones, D. (ed.), *Censorship: A World Encyclopedia*, 4 vols (London: Fitzroy Dearborn, 2001).
Joubert, S., 'Publishing in Another South Africa', *African Publishing Record*, 17/1 (1991), 9–15.

Kahn, E., '*When the Lion Feeds*—and the Censor Pounces: A Disquisition on the Banning of Immoral Publications in South Africa', *South African Law Journal*, 83/3 (Aug. 1966), 278–336.
Kannemeyer, J. C., *Die Afrikaanse Literatuur, 1652–2004* (Cape Town: Human & Rousseau, 2005).
Karis, T., and G. M. Gehart (eds), *From Protest to Challenge: A Documentary History of African Politics in South Africa, 1882–1964*, 3 vols (Stanford, Calif.: Hoover Institution Press, 1972–7).
Kavanagh, R., *Theatre and Cultural Struggle in South Africa* (London: Zed Books, 1985).
Kemal, Y., 'A Dirty Story', *Staffrider*, 6/1 (1984), 7–14.
Kgositsile, K., 'Culture and Resistance in South Africa', *Medu Newsletter*, 5/1 (1983), 23–30.
Kirkwood, M., 'Reflections on PEN', *Sesame*, 3 (Summer 1983–4), 22–6.
—— '*Staffrider*: An Informal Discussion', *English in Africa*, 7/2 (Sept. 1980), 22–31.
—— Christopher van Wyk, et al., 'A Reply from Ravan Press', *African Book Publishing Record*, 10/4 (1984), 205–6.
Krog, A., 'My Beautiful Land', *Sechaba*, 5/1 (Jan. 1971), 16.
Kross, C., 'Culture and Resistance', *Staffrider*, 5/2 (1982), 11–12.

La Guma, A., *The Stone Country* (Berlin: Seven Seas, 1967). *See also* Gala.
Leighton, J. M., 'Censorship: One or Two Points in Favour and Some Against', *Index on Censorship*, 5/1 (Spring 1976), 41–5.
Leroux, E., 'Daardie brief was ook aan my gerig', *Kol*, 1/2 (Sept.–Oct. 1968), 2–6.
—— *Magersfontein, O Magersfontein!* (Cape Town: Human & Rousseau, 1976).
—— *To a Dubious Salvation* (Harmondsworth: Penguin, 1972).

Levin, H., 'Thematics and Criticism', in Levin, *Grounds for Comparison* (Cambridge, Mass.: Harvard University Press, 1972).

Louw, A. M., '*In the Heart of the Country*: A Calvinist Allegory?', *PN Review*, 14/2 (1987), 50–1.

Louw, N. P. van Wyk, *Die Pluimsaad Waai Ver of Bitter Begin* (Cape Town: Human & Rousseau, 1972).

—— 'Toeriste-Kuns', *Standpunte*, 2/2 (Apr. 1947), 67–9.

—— *Versamelde Prosa 1* (Cape Town: Tafelberg, 1986).

—— *Versamelde Prosa 2* (Cape Town: Human & Rousseau, 1986).

—— 'Voorlopige dood van die jambiese vyfvoeter', *Kol*, 1/1 (Aug. 1968), 1.

McDonald, Peter D., 'Ideas of the Book and Histories of Literature: After Theory?', *PMLA* 121/1 (Jan. 2006), 214–28.

—— 'The Politics of Obscenity: *Lady Chatterley's Lover* and the Apartheid State', *English Studies in Africa*, 47/1 (2004), 31–46.

Malan, C., and M. Bosman, *Sensuur, literatuur en die leser: 'Donderdag of Woensdag' as totesgeval* (Pretoria: Sensal, 1983).

Masilela, N., 'South African Literature in African Languages', in S. Gikandi (ed.), *Encyclopaedia of African Literature* (London: Routledge, 2003).

Matshoba, M., *Call Me Not a Man* (Johannesburg: Ravan, 1979; London: Longman, 1987).

Matthews, J., *no time for dreams* (Cape Town: BLAC, 1981).

—— *The Party Is Over* (Cape Town: Kwela Books, 1997).

—— *pass me a meatball, Jones* (Cape Town: BLAC, 1977).

—— (ed.), *Black Voices Shout!* (Cape Town: BLAC, 1974).

—— and G. Thomas, *Cry Rage!* (Johannesburg: Spro-cas, 1972).

Medu Publications and Research Unit, 'Opening the Doors of Culture', *Medu Newsletter*, 4/1 (1982), 10–15.

Meintjies, F., 'New Thinking—the Broader Political Context', in I. de Kok and K. Press (eds), *Spring Is Rebellious* (Cape Town: Buchu Books, 1990).

Merrett, C., *A Culture of Censorship* (Cape Town: David Philip, 1994).

Moodley, S., 'Black Consciousness, the Black Artist and the Emerging Black Culture', *SASO Newsletter*, 2/3 (May–June 1972), 19–20.

Morphet, T., 'Cultural Imagination and Cultural Settlement: Albie Sachs and Njabulo Ndebele', in I. de Kok and K. Press (eds), *Spring Is Rebellious* (Cape Town: Buchu Books, 1990).

Mphahlele, E., *The African Image* (London: Faber, 1962; new, rev. edn, 1974).

—— *Bury Me at the Marketplace: Selected Letters of Es'kia Mphahlele, 1943–1980*, ed. N. C. Manganyi (Johannesburg: Skotaville, 1984).

—— *Chirundu* (Johannesburg: Ravan, 1979).

—— 'The Cult of Negritude', *Encounter*, 16/3 (1961), 50–2.

—— *Down Second Avenue* (London: Faber, 1959).

—— *Es'kia* (Cape Town: Kwela Books, 2002).

—— *Es'kia Continued* (Johannesburg: Stainbank and Associates, 2005).

—— 'The Function of Literature at the Present Time: The Ethnic Imperative', *Transition*, 9/2 (1974), 47–54.

—— *In Corner B* (Nairobi: East Africa Publishing House, 1967).

—— *Let's Talk Writing: Prose* (Johannesburg: AWA and the Council for Black Education and Research, 1985).

—— 'Mphahlele on the CIA', *Transition*, 7/3 (Dec.–Jan. 1967–8), 5.

—— *The Unbroken Song* (Johannesburg: Ravan, 1981).

—— *Voices in the Whirlwind* (London: Macmillan, 1973).

—— *The Wanderers* (Johannesburg: Ravan, 1983).

—— 'The Woman Walks Out', *The Purple Renoster*, 2 (Spring 1957), 4–6.

Mtshali, O., *Sounds of a Cowhide Drum* (Johannesburg: Renoster Books, 1971; Oxford: Oxford University Press, 1972).

Mulhern, F., *Culture/Metaculture* (London: Routledge, 2000).

Mutloatse, M., 'Indigenous Publishing in South Africa: The Case of Skotaville Publishers', in P. G. Altbach (ed.), *Publishing and Development in the Third World* (London: Hans Zell, 1992).

—— (ed.), *Forced Landing* (Johannesburg: Ravan, 1980).

Mzamane, M. V., *The Children of Soweto* (Johannesburg: Ravan, 1982).

—— *Mzala* (Johannesburg: Ravan, 1980).

—— 'The Short Story Tradition in Black South Africa', *Donga*, 7 (Sept. 1977), 1.

—— 'The Uses of Traditional Oral Forms in Black South African Literature', in L. White and T. Couzens (eds), *Literature and Society in South Africa* (Cape Town: Maskew Miller Longman, 1984).

Ndebele, N., 'Black Development', in B. S. Biko (ed.), *Black Viewpoint* (Johannesburg: Spro-cas, 1972).

—— *Fools and Other Stories* (Johannesburg: Ravan, 1983).

—— *Rediscovery of the Ordinary* (Johannesburg: COSAW, 1991).

Ndletyana, M et al., *African Intellectuals in 19th and early 20th Century South Africa* (Cape Town: HSRC Press, 2008).

Nkasa, N., Comment, *The Classic*, 1/1 (1963), 4.

—— *The World of Nat Nakasa*, ed. E. Patel (Randburg: Ravan, 1975).

Nkosi, L., 'Alex La Guma: The Man and his Work', *South Africa: Information and Analysis*, 59 (Jan. 1968), 1–8.

—— *Home and Exile* (London: Longmans, Green, 1965).

Nussbaum, M. C., *Hiding from Humanity: Disgust, Shame, and the Law* (Princeton: Princeton University Press, 2004).

Nuttall, S., 'Literature and the Archive: The Biography of Texts', in C. Hamilton et al. (eds), *Refiguring the Archive* (Cape Town: David Philip, 2002).

O'Brien, A., *Against Normalization* (Durham, NC: Duke University Press, 2001).

—— 'Literature in Another South Africa: Njabulo Ndebele's Theory of Emergent Culture', *Diacritics*, 22/1 (1992), 66–85.

Odendaal, W., '*Donga*: One Angry Voice', *English in Africa*, 7/2 (Sept. 1980), 67–74.

Paton, J. S. (ed.), *The Grey Ones* (Johannesburg: Ravan, 1974).

Peires, J., 'Lovedale Press: Literature for the Bantu Revisited', *English in Africa*, 7/1 (Mar. 1980), 71–85.

'PEN Charter', *South African PEN Yearbook* (Johannesburg: CNA, 1954).

Petersen, S. V. et al., 'Binnelandse Sensuur' (Domestic Censorship), *Standpunte*, 30 (Dec. 1953), 1–32.

Philip, D., 'Oppositional Publishing in South Africa from 1945 to 2000', *Logos*, 2/1 (2000), 41–8.

—— 'South Africa', in P. G. Altbach and E. S. Hoshino (eds), *International Book Publishing: An Encyclopaedia* (New York: Garland, 1995).

Plaatje, S. T., *Mhudi* (Lovedale: Lovedale Press, 1930).

Powell, Rose, 'Writing Is Part of the Struggle', *Index on Censorship*, 9/6 (Dec. 1980), 8–12.

Poyner, J. (ed.), *J. M. Coetzee and the Idea of the Public Intellectual* (Athens: Ohio University Press, 2006).

Pringle, T., and J. Fairbairn (eds), *The South African Journal*, 2 vols [1824], South African Library Reprint Series (Cape Town: South African Library, 1974).

—— et al., *Papers of the South African Literary Society* (Cape Town: W. Bridekirk, 1825; repr. Cape Town: Africana Connoisseurs Press, 1963).

Raditlhalo, S., and T. L. Liyong (eds), *Es'kia* (Johannesburg: Stainbank and Associates, 2006).

Randall, P., 'The Beginnings of Ravan Press: A Memoir', in G. E. de Villiers (ed.), *Ravan: Twenty Five Years* (Randburg: Ravan, 1997).

—— ' "Minority" Publishing in South Africa', *African Book Publishing Record*, 1/3 (July 1975), 219–22.

—— *A Taste for Power* (Johannesburg: SPRO-CAS, 1973).

Rive, R., *Emergency* (London: Faber & Faber, 1964).
—— *Writing Black* (Cape Town: David Philip, 1981).
Roberts, R. S., *No Cold Kitchen* (Johannesburg: STE Publishers, 2005).
Roscoe, A., *Uhuru's Fire: African Literature East to South* (Cambridge: Cambridge University Press, 1977).
Royston, R. (ed.), *Black Poets in South Africa* (London: Heinemann, 1974).
Sachs, A., *Advancing Human Rights in South Africa* (Cape Town: Oxford University Press, 1992).
—— 'Afterword: The Taste of an Avocado Pear', in I. de Kok and K. Press (eds), *Spring Is Rebellious* (Cape Town: Buchu Books, 1990).
—— 'Preparing Ourselves for Freedom', in D. Attridge and R. Jolly (eds), *Writing South Africa* (Cambridge: Cambridge University Press, 1998).
—— *Protecting Human Rights in a New South Africa* (Cape Town: Oxford University Press, 1990).
Sanders, M., *Complicities: The Intellectual and Apartheid* (Durham, NC: Duke University Press, 2002).
Sartre, J.-P., *What Is Literature?*, trans. B. Frechtman (London: Routledge, 1993).
Sepamla, S., 'A Note on *New Classic* and *S'ketsh*', *English in Africa*, 7/2 (Sept. 1980), 81–5.
Seroke, J., 'The Voice of the Voiceless', *African Book Publishing Record*, 10/4 (1984), 201–6.
Serote, M. W., 'the black word', *BLAC Newsletter*, 1/2 [c.1975], 4–5.
—— 'Naledi Writers Workshop', *Medu Newsletter*, 6/1 (1984), 21–2.
—— *To Every Birth its Blood* (Johannesburg: Ravan, 1981).
—— *Yakhal'inkomo* (Johannesburg: Renoster Books, 1972).
Shils, E., *The Intellectuals and the Powers* (Chicago: Chicago University Press, 1972).
Shore, H. L. (ed.), *Come Back, Africa: Fourteen Short Stories from South Africa* (East Berlin: Seven Seas, 1968).
Sitas, A., 'The Sachs Debate: A Philistine's Resonse', in I. de Kok and K. Press (eds), *Spring Is Rebellious* (Cape Town: Buchu Books, 1990).
Small, A., 'Kol-kol oor vier se gesprek 'n vyfde', *Kol*, 1/2 (Sept. 1968), 9–13.
—— 'A Poem after the Bannings', *SASO Newsletter*, 5/2 (Mar.–Apr. 1973), 8.
—— 'Towards Cultural Understanding', in H. W. van der Merwe and D. Walsh (eds), *Student Perspectives on South Africa* (Cape Town: David Philip, 1972).
Smit, B. (ed.), *Skrywer en Gemeenskap* (Pretoria: Haum Literêr, 1985).
—— 'André Brink tussen sestig and sewentig', *Kol*, 1/1 (Aug. 1968), 5–8.
Sole, K., 'Authorship, Authenticity and the Black Community: The Novels of Soweto 1976', in S. Clingman (ed.), *Regions and Repertoires: Topics in South African Politics and Culture* (Johannesburg: Ravan, 1991).
Sono, T., 'Some Concepts of Negritude and Black Identity', *SASO Newsletter*, 1/2 (June 1971), 18.
Sowden, L., et al. (eds), *South African PEN Yearbook* (Johannesburg: CNA, 1954–6).
Stiebel, L., and L. Gunner (eds), *Still Beating the Drum: Critical Perspectives on Lewis Nkosi* (Amsterdam: Rodopi, 2005).
Sweetman, D., *Mary Renault* (London: Chatto & Windus, 1993).
Tlali, M., *Muriel at Metropolitan* (Johannesburg: Ravan, 1975).
Todorov, T., 'The Notion of Literature', *New Literary History*, 5/1 (Autumn 1973), 5–16.
Troye, D., *An Act of Immorality* (Johannesburg: Trans-world Publishers, 1963).
Trump, M. (ed.), *Rendering Things Visible* (Johannesburg: Ravan, 1990).
Unesco, *Apartheid: Its Effects on Education, Science, Culture and Information* (Paris: Unesco, 1967).
Vail, L., and L. White, *Power and the Praise Poem* (London: James Currey, 1991).
Van den Heever, C. M., et al., *Kultuurgeskiedenis van die Afrikaner*, i (Cape Town: Nasionale Pers, 1945).

van der Vlies, A., *South African Textual Cultures* (Manchester: University of Manchester Press, 2007).

van Rooyen, J. C. W., *Censorship in South Africa* (Cape Town: Juta, 1987).

—— 'Drafting a New Film and Publication Bill for South Africa', in J. Duncan (ed.), *Between Speech and Hate: Hate Speech, Pornography and the New South Africa* (Johannesburg: Idasa, 1996).

—— *Publikasiebeheer in Suid-Afrika* (Cape Town: Juta, 1978).

van Wyk, C. '*Staffrider* and the Politics of Culture', *Staffrider*, 7/3–4 (1988), 165–70.

Venter, R., 'Inventing an Alternative through Oppositional Publishing: Afrikaans Alternative Book Publishing in Apartheid South Africa—the Publishing House Taurus (1975–1991) as Case Study', *Innovation*, 35 (Dec. 2007), 86–114.

Walzer, M., *The Company of Critics* (New York: Basic Books, 2002).

White, L., and T. Couzens (eds), *Literature and Society in South Africa* (Cape Town: Maskew Miller Longman, 1984).

Whitman, S. [B. Feinberg], 'Poetry and Liberation', *African Communist*, 59 (1974), 110–18.

[Wilhelm, P.], 'Pen Letters', *Donga*, 6 (July 1977), 1.

—— 'The State of the Union', *Artists' and Writers' Guild Newsletter*, 6 (1976), 1.

—— and J. A. Polley (eds), *Poetry South Africa: Selected Papers from Poetry '74* (Johannesburg: Ad Donker, 1976).

Willemse, H. (ed.), *More than Brothers: Peter Clarke and James Matthews at 70* (Cape Town: Kwela Books, 2000).

Woeber, C., 'Educating the Educator: Es'kia Mphahlele's Schooling at St Peter's', in S. Raditlhalo and Taban Lo Liyong (eds), *Es'kia* (Johannesburg: Stainbank and Associates, 2006).

Ziervogel, D., 'Bantu Literature', in *Standard Encyclopaedia of Southern Africa*, 12 vols (Cape Town: Nasou, 1970–6).

Z.N. [B. Bunting], 'Much Ado About Nothing', *African Communist*, 97 (1984), 101–3.

—— 'The Politics of Commitment', *African Communist*, 80 (1980), 100–1.

Theses

Midgley, P., 'Author, Ideology, Publisher: A Symbiotic Relationship', MA thesis (Rhodes University, 1993).

Mzamane, M., 'Black Consciousness Poets in South Africa 1967–1980', Ph.D. thesis (Sheffield University, 1984).

van der Vlies, A., 'Constructing South African Literatures in Britain, 1880–1980', D.Phil. thesis (Oxford University, 2004).

Acknowledgements

It would not have been possible for me to research, let alone write, this book without the support of various institutions and the generosity of an extraordinary number of people. Though I remain solely responsible for its contents, and all its errors, they helped to make *The Literature Police* happen and to make it a better book than it might otherwise have been.

I am especially grateful to the Arts and Humanities Research Council, St Hugh's College, Oxford, and the Oxford University English Faculty for the financial support that bought me precious time and enabled me and my co-researchers to investigate a wide range of archives scattered across the globe. Though Faith Binckes, the most exemplary of assistants, led the research side of the project—and to my relief and delight rose miraculously from the dead to bring it to completion—others, including Zabeth Botha, Andrew van der Vlies, and Hedley Twidle, made significant contributions during the feverish, early stages of the archival trawl. Special thanks to Paul Burns and Jillian Mustard for managing all the practicalities with such tact and attentiveness, and to Nicholas Perkins for dealing with the local fallout so charitably.

To the keepers of the archives in the UK, the United States, and South Africa, who represent the heroic front line for all of us with a passion for the past, I owe a special debt of gratitude. I would like, in particular, to thank Malcolm Hacksley, Ann Torlesse, and Andrew Martin at the National English Literary Museum, Grahamstown, South Africa; Erika Terblanche, formerly of the National Afrikaans Literature and Research Centre, Bloemfontein; Mike Bott and Verity Andrews of the University of Reading; Jolanda Hogg and her colleagues at the Western Cape Provincial Archives, Cape Town; Terence Ball, formerly of Macmillan SA; Esther van Driel of the University of Western Cape Mayibuye Archives; the proprietors of the CAFDA second-hand bookshop in Cape Town; Sue Usher at the English Faculty Library, Oxford University; Debbie Quare, Librarian at St Hugh's; as well as all the staff at Rhodes House and the Bodleian in Oxford and the South African Library in Cape Town. All gave of their time and expertise in ways that went far beyond the call of duty. I would also like to record my thanks here to Nana Makaula and Iyavar Chetty of the Film and Publication Board in South Africa, who gave me access to the censorship materials that remained in their possession in the period 2000 to 2005, and to René Dinkelman, Pattie Myburgh, and all the other employees of the former censorship bureaucracy then still in post who regaled me with their own tales of its mysterious inner workings and helped me to start making sense of the labyrinthine archival records.

For giving me permission to quote from previously unpublished sources, and for sharing their knowledge about and perspectives on the tangled subject of apartheid censorship and its cultural consequences, I would like to thank André Brink, Iyavar

Chetty, Abraham Coetzee, J. M. Coetzee, Peter Horn, Mike Kirkwood, James Matthews, Es'kia Mphahlele (via Mike Stainbank), Mbulelo Mzamane, Peter Randall, H. van der Merwe Scholtz, and Rita Scholtz. Thanks, too, to Heinemann (via Pearson Education) for permission to quote materials from their archives in Reading; to the Jensma family, Jane Abrahams, HarperCollins, Random House, Jonathan Ball Publishers, and Macmillan SA for allowing me to include a number of illustrations in this book; and to Michael Gardiner for his advice on various copyright and other issues.

I also owe an enormous debt to all those who have willingly allowed me to pester them with various queries via all possible media over the years. They have supplied countless vital details, offered many astute comments, and much more besides. I can thank only a few here: Derek Attridge, David Attwell, Victoria Bronstein, Amit Chaudhuri, James Currey, Robert Darnton, Tim Davies, Francis Galloway, Joshua Getzler, John Gouws, Patrick Hayes, Kinch Hoekstra, Mike Holland, Tim Huisamen, Russell Kaschula, Antjie Krog, David Medalie, Jon Mee, Cheryl-Ann Michael, Glenn Moss, Mothobi Mutloatse, David Philip, Rajeswari Sunder Rajan, Tore Rem, David Robertson, Mark Sanders, Christopher Saunders, Jaki Seroke, Mongane Serote (via Lindiwe Baloyi), Michael Suarez, Kobus van Rooyen, Christopher van Wyk, Malvern van Wyk Smith, Danie van Zyl, and Rudi Venter.

For their enthusiastic endorsement of this project and careful handling of the publishing process, I am most grateful to Jacqueline Baker, Laurien Berkeley, Sophie Goldsworthy, Andrew McNiellie, and Fiona Vlemmiks at Oxford University Press; and for his expert help with the supplementary web site, my thanks go to Andrew Kirkpatrick.

While working on this project, I have been privileged to enjoy the company of an outstanding group of students from all corners of the globe, whose energetic engagement with the questions of literature, and what it might mean to ask them anew on the threshold of the twenty-first century, has been a constant source of inspiration. I also owe much to audiences in Norway, South Africa, the UK, and the United States, who commented probingly on talks I gave during the formative stages of this book, and to the editors of Book History, English Studies in Africa, PMLA, Stilet, and the Times Literary Supplement, who published articles in which I attempted to sketch out some of my preliminary findings and ideas.

My other particular debts can only be hinted at here. To Anne, Zoe, Ben, Simone, Debbie, Mike, Judie, and the rest of the family, I owe much more than thanks for their patience and encouragement, not to mention their frequent, and always welcome, reminders that writing books is not everything. This particular book is for Seamus, who asked the right question in 1987, and for Glen, who once recommended Es'kia Mphahlele's Down Second Avenue and George Orwell's Down and Out in Paris and London to a disaffected and despairing teenager in the hope that they would help. They did.

Index